KANSAS CITY ROYALS
A ROYAL TRADITION

ROYALS

EDITED BY BILL NOWLIN

ASSOCIATE EDITORS: BILL CARLE, LEN LEVIN,
CURT NELSON, AND CARL RIECHERS

FOREWORD BY RYAN LEFEBVRE

SABR

Society for American Baseball Research
Phoenix Arizona

Kansas City Royals, A Royal Tradition
Edited by Steve Bill Nowlin
Associate Editors: Bill Carle, Len Levin, Curt Nelson, and Carl Riechers

All photographs courtesy of the Kansas City Royals

ISBN **978-1-970159-03-5**
(Ebook ISBN **978-1-970159-02-8**)

Book design: Wrenn Simms
Society for American Baseball Research
Cronkite School at ASU
555 N. Central Ave. #416
Phoenix, AZ 85004
Phone: (602) 496-1460
Web: www.sabr.org
Facebook: Society for American Baseball Research
Twitter: @SABR

TABLE OF CONTENTS

INTRODUCTION

"Admittedly life would have gone on in Kansas City without baseball... But who would want to live in a city without a soul?" – Joe McGuff, Kansas City Star sports editor; National Baseball Hall of Fame J.G. Taylor Spink Award Winner

There is a proverb that claims absence makes the heart grow fonder. We can all think of instances where that sentiment has played out in our own lives. If a city can experience that same emotion then Kansas City had such an adventure with the game of baseball – and it helps explain the strong and enduring bond between the Royals and our hometown.

The Kansas City Royals played their first game on April 8, 1969 in a hometown that had not had a professional baseball home game for an entire 559 days. Now at first glance that doesn't sound like a long stretch of time, but it was the longest such absence since the Kansas City "Unions" of the Union Association first took the field in 1884. In fact, at that time this outpost on the Missouri River had been known as the Town of Kansas, City of Kansas, or Westport – not officially taking the name Kansas City until 1889. Yes indeed, Kansas City had baseball before it even had its name.

And in all those decades Kansas City didn't just have baseball, baseball had a hold on Kansas City. Fans got to enjoy the thrill of championship seasons, watch many of the greatest players the game has ever produced, and where entertained by – or at times subjected to – some of the most colorful characters baseball has ever known.

Hall of Famer Sliding Billy Hamilton, whose 192 runs scored in 1894 (some claim 198) with the Philadelphia Phillies remains the MLB single-season record, began his major league career with the 1888 Kansas City Cowboys of the American Association. Another Hall of Famer, Charles "Kid" Nichols, who holds the major-league pitching record for most career 30-win seasons with seven, retired to lead the 1902 Kansas City Blue Stockings to a Western League title before eventually returning to the big leagues. Charles Dillon Stengel was born in Kansas City and that resulted in him being given the nickname "Casey" by his teammates once he began his professional baseball playing career – in fact he played part of his first professional baseball season with the 1910 Kansas City Blues. He took his hometown's name with him to Cooperstown as well.

Through his skill, courage, and the content of his character, Jackie Robinson earned an enormous place not only in baseball history, but in the history of the United States. And it was as a member of the 1945 Kansas City Monarchs that Jackie began his professional baseball career. Of course Jackie was only one of the Kansas City Monarchs that left an indelible mark on the game of baseball from Satchel Paige to Buck O'Neil and many more. Baseball's M&M boys from the historic season of 1961 also had links to Kansas City. Mickey Mantle played for the 1951 Kansas City Blues after he had made his major-league debut wearing #6, before he returned to the Yankees later that season wearing his immortal #7. Roger Maris debuted with Cleveland, but first became an All-Star with the 1959 Kansas City Athletics.

All of that serves as just a small excerpt of Kansas City baseball history dating from the Unions of 1884 through the Athletics of 1967, before it all stopped for 559 days – including every day of 1968, the only year without a professional baseball team in the history of Kansas City. Then the story resumed, and the love affair between a city and the game of baseball returned with many more chapters written by the Kansas City Royals beginning in 1969.

Now half a century later, those Royals chapters have only added more richness and depth to the Kansas City baseball story. Fifty years of highs and lows, thrilling moments, and memories to last a lifetime for those that lived them. More great players and colorful characters – and yes, more championships as well. This book is meant as a marker in time on this golden anniversary of Kansas City Royals Baseball to celebrate all that that has taken place in 50 years and those whose work and skill made it all happen. Best of all for a city that once went without baseball, brief as that time was, there is no end in sight, the story continues...

Those of us that call Kansas City home like to think of our hometown as the heartland of America, and geographically speaking the claim has merit. As a matter of fact the geographical center of the contiguous 48 states of the United States is two miles outside of Lebanon, Kansas — not all that far from Kansas City (about 250 miles to the west). But we think the claim has merit beyond mere geography and though I'm hopelessly biased in the matter, the centrality of baseball to our cultural fabric and history is part of the reason why.

Kansas City is fertile ground for baseball, and the Royals have flourished here — they have also been a worthy heir to the historic legacy that preceded them. Kansas City is the heart of America in my view, and I believe baseball is certainly a significant part of the Kansas City's soul.

Curt Nelson
Director - Royals Hall of Fame

FOREWORD

BY RYAN LEFEBVRE

KC Strip $12.99. As soon as I walked into the Coral Reef Restaurant in Rochester, Wisconsin, I immediately noticed the small, glass marquee with yellow neon marker telling patrons the evening's special. It was December 23, 1998 and I'm positive that I was the only one who felt more satisfied by seeing those words than actually eating the steak. One hour before, I had hung up the phone with Dave St. Peter, future president of the Minnesota Twins, telling him I was leaving to broadcast for the Royals. My brain had calculated the pros and cons and all arrows pointed south on I-35. My heart was saying, "What have you just done?" I was visiting my grandparents for Christmas.

As the Royals celebrated 50 years of baseball in 2018, I was celebrating 20 years in Kansas City. The team lost 104 games but I was grateful. The Royals have lost 90 or more games 16 times in their 50-year history; I was there for 12. The Royals have lost 100 of more games in their history; I was there for all of them. The Royals have been to the World Series four times, I have been along for the ride for two. I had the privilege of calling the final out for the 2014 Wild Card win over Oakland, the eighth inning in Houston at the 2015 ALDS, and the final out of the 2015 World Series. I stood before 800,000 people at the World Series parade and led everyone in a "Let's Go Royals" chant. There are many third-world dictators who have never spoken to that many people. I broadcast my 5,000th major-league game in 2017 at Kauffman Stadium. All of the time, people ask me about my most memorable moment.

On a personal note, I met my wife, Sarah, in Kansas City in 2003. I lost a brother in Kansas City in 2013. All four of my children were born in Kansas City. I had a public battle with depression in 2005 and was comforted and rescued in Kansas City by Kansas Citians.

It wasn't supposed to be that way for many reasons. After the 1998 season, the Royals announced that longtime and popular radio announcer Fred White was not going to return the following season. This was not Fred's decision. For 25 years, Royals Radio was Denny and Fred or Fred and Denny. Meanwhile, I was wrapping up my fourth season broadcasting radio and TV for the Minnesota Twins. I was only 27 years old and planned to be there another 40 years, at least. I had left one comfort zone, Los Angeles, in the fall of 1989 to begin a college baseball career (and academics) in Minnesota. I did not plan to attend the University of Minnesota but I accepted their invitation to visit and that changed everything. After college and a brief minor-league career, I returned to pursue my broadcasting career.

Truth be told, I didn't plan to work for the Royals but, like my fateful trip to Minneapolis nine years prior, I accepted their invitation to visit and that changed everything. (Full disclosure: I interviewed with the Royals for leverage with the Twins. I never used that leverage, I just took the job in Kansas City.) I figured I would stay two or three years and return triumphantly to Minneapolis. I never left.

I have met almost every former player you'll read about in the following pages. Mike Sweeney became one of the most important people in my life. Joe Randa helped me move into my house. I've broadcast games with Paul Splittorff, Frank White, Kevin Seitzer, Jeff Montgomery, and even a few spring training games with Darrell Porter. 2018 was my 20th year working with Hall of Fame broadcaster Denny Matthews. I've learned more about broadcasting from Denny than any other announcer in the business. Depending on what I've needed at various points in my career, Denny has been a mentor, friend, father figure, and a great broadcast partner.

The most memorable moment? It had nothing to do with a play on the field or my words into a microphone. After the Royals won the 2014 American League Wild Card game, I left the radio booth and walked to a television set in right field for postgame duty. In order to get there, I had to walk through the Loge concourse. I had never seen anything like the unbridled and euphoric enthusiasm shared by the fans who were leaving their seats and headed to the parking lot. In a good way, they were out of control. Complete strangers were high-fiving and hugging each other. I began to realize how much Royals baseball meant to Kansas Citians and what a relief it was for them to go from laughingstock to playoffs. I had always selfishly dreamed of broadcasting an iconic moment so that my call would play over and over, year after year, as if it was all about me and my career. Well, just a few minutes after my iconic moment I realized how big this moment was and how little I felt. And it was a good feeling. It wasn't about me and my career, at all. It was about Kansas Citians and I was proud to be one of them.

So you see I had no idea what was ahead of me when I left my other comfort zone, Minneapolis, after that 1998 season. I turned to my grandparents and told them, "I think I just did the right thing but I'm not sure. Let's go out to eat." KC Strip $12.99. I felt reassured. And I think about how blessed I have been every time I see that iconic Kansas City steak on a menu, whether I'm in Rochester or wherever the Royals schedule takes me.

KEVIN APPIER

BY CLAYTON TRUTOR

Right-handed pitcher Kevin Appier, who played 16 major-league seasons (1989-2004), was one of the best starters of his generation. He was the rare hard-throwing pitcher who developed an array of elite secondary pitches to complement his fastball. Appier's slider and forkball were notoriously devastating, enabling him to remain a top-notch starter even after a series of injuries took away his high-octane fastball.

Appier won 169 games in his career against 137 losses with a 3.74 ERA, a notably strong mark for a pitcher who spent the latter half of his career competing in the "Steroids Era." "Ape," as he was nicknamed, pitched for four major-league clubs. He spent the vast majority of his career with the Kansas City Royals (1989-1999, 2003-2004). As of 2018 he was the franchise's career leader in strikeouts (1,458) and fourth in wins for the Royals (115). Appier spent his other major-league stints with the Oakland Athletics (1999-2000), New York Mets (2001), and Anaheim Angels (2002-2003) before returning to the Royals to wind up his career. He was selected for the 1995 All-Star Game, finished third in AL Rookie of the Year voting in 1990, and third in AL Cy Young Award voting in 1993. In 2002 Appier earned a World Series ring as a member of the Anaheim Angels. In 2011, he was inducted into the Kansas City Royals Hall of Fame.[1]

Robert Kevin Appier was born on December 6, 1967, in Lancaster, California, in Los Angeles County. He was one of three siblings and was raised by his mother, Betty Appier, who worked as an accountant.[2] Appier starred for the Antelope Valley High School baseball team, a perennial LA County baseball power that had previously produced 1966 number-one draft pick Steve Chilcott and former Brewers, Tigers, and Angels pitcher Jim Slaton (1971-1986). By the end of his high-school career, Appier had grown into the 6-foot-2, 180-pound frame that he carried for the rest of his career.[3] He accepted a scholarship to play at collegiate power Fresno State but left the Bulldog program after just three appearances in 1986 and spent the 1987 baseball season with the Antelope Valley College Marauders. "He's a once-in-a-lifetime coach's dream," Antelope Valley College coach Ted Henkel told the Los Angeles Times. Henkel worked closely with Appier, helping him beef up his fastball into the 90s. After Appier posted an 11-6 record with a 2.65 ERA for the Marauders, Kansas City selected him in the first round of the 1987 draft and he signed with the Royals shortly thereafter.[4]

Appier progressed quickly through the Royals organization. In 1987, he posted a 3.04 ERA for the Eugene Emeralds of the Single-A Northwest League. He split 1988 between the Class-A Baseball City Royals of the Florida State League and Double-A Memphis Chicks of the Southern League. Appier won a combined 12 games against 9 losses and posted a 2.64 ERA. He spent most of 1989 with the Omaha Royals of the Triple-A American Association, where he went 8-8 with a 3.95 ERA. Appier had a brief stint with the Royals in June and July 1989 but struggled to a 1-4 record with an ERA of 9.14 in six appearances.[5]

After a brief stay in Omaha in 1990, the Royals called Appier up and eased the 22-year-old back into major-league action. In late April and May, Appier worked primarily as a reliever. By early June, Appier had moved into the Royals' highly talented starting rotation which included two-time Cy Young Award winner Bret Saberhagen, Mark Gubicza, Tom Gordon, and Storm Davis. Appier proved to be a bright spot in an otherwise disappointing 1990 season for the Royals, who finished sixth in the AL West after being the runners-up to Oakland the previous season. The rookie right-hander ended up having the standout season among Kansas City's rotation, posting a 12-8 mark and a staff-best 2.76 ERA. He finished third in Rookie of the Year voting behind Yankees slugger Kevin Maas and Indians catcher Sandy Alomar Jr., the unanimous selection of the Baseball Writers Association of America. The Sporting News named Appier its 1990 Rookie Pitcher of the Year.

Appier avoided a sophomore slump, posting a 13-10 record with a 3.42 ERA with three shutouts in 1991. While the Hal McRae-managed Royals faded into oblivion in 1992, finishing tied for fifth and winning just 72 games, the third-year pitcher asserted himself as the ace of the mound staff. With the departure of Bret Saberhagen in a trade to the New York Mets, Appier took the lead in Kansas City's suddenly-slim starting pitching staff. He made the first of his six consecutive Opening Day starts for the Royals. For the season he went 15-8 and posted a 2.46 ERA, second best in the AL behind Boston's Roger Clemens. In July Appier earned the AL Pitcher of the Month Award, finishing the month 4-0 with a 1.55 ERA in six starts. Despite the strong pitching performance, Appier was once again left off the AL All-Star team roster, a victim of his team's poor performance.

In 1993 Appier asserted his claim to recognition as one of the AL's best pitchers. Pitching a career-high 238⅔ innings, he posted a career best 18-8 record and an AL leading 2.56 ERA. He finished a career-best third in AL Cy Young Award voting behind winner Jack McDowell and distant runner-up Randy Johnson.

Appier fell from the heights of 1993 during the strike-shortened 1994 season, struggling to stay above .500 as his ERA jumped more than a run to 3.83. As a franchise, the Royals had returned to form, boasting a 64-51 mark, good for third place in the new, highly competitive AL Central Division. David Cone, who went 16-5 with a 2.94 ERA, was the ace of Hal McRae's rotation in 1994 but was traded to Toronto for three prospects by the cash-strapped Royals before the start of the 1995 season.

Appier bounced back in 1995, retaking his position as Kansas City's ace. He won 11 of his first 13 decisions. The 27-year-old earned his only All-Star Game selection that season and pitched two perfect innings in relief of Randy Johnson. After his fantastic start to the season, Appier faded in the second half. His record fell to 15-10 and his ERA ballooned to 3.89.[6]

As offense ballooned during the latter half of the 1990s, Appier remained a strong, if somewhat less spectacular starter, on Bob Boone's noncontending Royals teams of 1996 and 1997. The right-hander's ERA hovered in the mid-3's both seasons (3.62 in 1996 and 3.40 in 1997), though his won-lost records differed considerably (14-11 in 1996 and 9-13 in 1997). Appier put significant mileage on his arm both seasons, throwing a combined 447 innings. Before the 1996 season, Appier entered salary arbitration with the Royals, winning a salary increase to just over $5 million per season, a jump of more than $663,000 from the season before.[7]

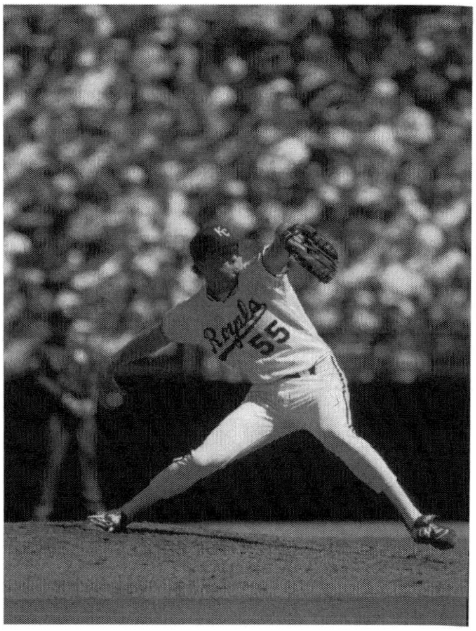

In 1998 Appier faced his first significant injury as a pitcher, suffering a torn labrum in spring training that cost him virtually the entire season. He made just three September appearances. He also battled through a difficult first half of the 1999 season, compiling a 9-9 record with a then career-worst 4.87 ERA through the end of July. At the trading deadline, the rebuilding Royals shipped their longtime ace to the suddenly contending Oakland A's for pitchers Jeff D'Amico, Blake Stein, and Brad Rigby. Appier continued to win games but his ERA ballooned further against steroids-era hitting. He finished the year 16-14 with an ERA of 5.17. The A's finished the season eight games behind the AL West Champion Texas Rangers and seven games behind the Red Sox for the wild card.

In 2000, Appier, 32, played a prominent role in the "Moneyball" A's ascent to the franchise's first division title since 1992. He went 15-11 while posting an ERA of 4.52. He provided veteran leadership on a young staff that included Tim Hudson, who had his breakout season in 2000, and Barry Zito, who was on the cusp of greatness. Appier made his first-ever playoff appearances in the Division Series against the New York Yankees. He pitched in two games in the hard-fought series that was won by New York, three games to two. In Game Two, Appier surrendered three runs in 6⅓ innings in a 4-0 home loss. Appier gave up one run in four innings of relief in the deciding fifth game.

On December 11, 2000, the Mets signed Appier to a four-year, $42 million contract, bringing the veteran right-hander onto the staff of the defending NL champions. Appier posted an 11-10 record in 2001 with a 3.57 ERA in 206⅔ innings pitched. The addition of Appier did not prove to be the final piece in the Mets' World Series-winning puzzle. The club struggled to an 82-80 mark in 2001, finishing third in the NL East. After the season, the Mets traded Appier to the Anaheim Angels for former AL MVP Mo Vaughn.[8]

Appier proved a stalwart on the Angels' young staff, posting a 14-12 mark and a 3.92 ERA for the 99-win wild-card-winning club. Though Appier struggled during the 2002 postseason, surrendering 15 earned runs in 21⅔ innings of work, the Angels upset the Yankees, Twins, and Giants en route to the franchise's first World Series victory.

In 2003 Appier struggled along with the Angels in their World Series hangover season. A series of nagging injuries, most notably a torn flexor tendon in his right elbow, hampered him throughout the season. He went 7-7 with an ERA of 5.63 for the 77-win Anaheim team, and was released on July 30. A week later Appier returned to the Royals. He made just four starts for Kansas City before having season-ending surgery. He missed most of 2004 recovering from elbow surgery, making just two starts that season. Appier struggled for the next two years (2005-2006) to make a major-league comeback, first with the Royals and then with the Seattle Mariners. In 2006 he retired as a Royal, more than two years after his final major-league appearance.[9]

Appier was a right-handed hitter who rarely batted. In a career spent primarily in the AL, Appier had 90 career plate appearances, 67 of which came during his season with the New York Mets. He posted a .096 career batting average.

In retirement, Appier moved full time to his soybean farm in Paola, Kansas, about 45 miles south of Kansas City. He and his wife, Laurie, have three children: Garrett, Britney, and Evelyn. Garrett Appier is a three-time Division II national champion in the shot-put for Pittsburg State University in Kansas.[10]

Notes

1 Dick Kaegel, "Appier to Take Place Among Royals Greats," Royals.com, June 24, 2011. Accessed on July 2, 2018: wap.mlb.com/kc/news/article/2011062420940432/?locale=en_US; "NY is Appier of Eye," *New York Daily News*, December 12, 2000. Accessed on July 2, 2018: nydailynews.com/archives/sports/n-y-appier-eye-article-1.885307.

2 Gene Morris, "Appier Inducted into Royals Hall of Fame," *Miami County* (Kansas) *Republic,* June 30, 2011. Accessed on July 2, 2018: republic-online.com/news/appier-inducted-into-royals-hall-of-fame/article_78a46445-9d5b-5ede-a39b-4f9ee9e50495.html; "Kevin Appier," *Biographical Dictionary of American Sports,* 2000. Accessed on July 2, 2018: books.google.com/books?id=AUFUw01sIWYC&pg=PA34&lpg=PA34&dq=betty+appier&source=bl&ots=fASRBhFomy&sig=mrtEkP4e-HOuu-

UNkeKSLJj1lT7c&hl=en&sa=X&ved=0ahUKEwiso4iN8YXcAhXGrVkKHdMyD9kQ6AEIMzAC#v=onepage&q=betty%20 appier&f=false.

3 "Antelope Valley High," *The Baseball Cube*, 2013. Accessed on July 2, 2018: thebaseballcube.com/hs/profile.asp?ID=1070.

4 Theresa Munoz, "Ape's World: Kansas City Pitcher's Unorthodox Formula for Success Results in Winning Equation," *Los Angeles Times*, July 16, 1992. Accessed on July 2, 2018: articles.latimes.com/1992-07-16/sports/sp-3738_1_kansas-city-royals/2.

5 Ibid.

6 Tim Kurkjian, "A Royal Start," Sports Illustrated, May 15, 1995: 81; Mike DiGiovanna, "NL Wins Battle of Homeric Proportions," *Los Angeles Times*, July 12, 1995. Accessed on July 2, 2018: articles.latimes.com/1995-07-12/sports/sp-31290_1_homer-in-all-star-game.

7 "Royals' Appier Tops $5 Million," *New York Times*, February 3, 1996: 33.

8 Ben Walker, "Kevin Appier Signs with the Mets," ABC News, December 11, 2000. Accessed on July 2, 2018: abcnews.go.com/Sports/story?id=100096&page=1.

9 Gregg Bell, "After Two Year Absence, Appier Looking for Way Back," Lawrence (Kansas) Journal-World, April 21, 2006. Accessed on July 2, 2018: 2.ljworld.com/news/2006/apr/21/after_twoyear_absence_appier_looking_way_back/.

10 Dick Kaegel, "Appier to Take Place Among Royals Greats."; Adam Burns, "Appier Returns from Injury After Contemplating Retirement," Joplin (Missouri) Globe, January 24, 2018. Accessed on July 2, 2018: joplinglobe.com/sports/local_sports/appier-returns-from-injury-after-contemplating-retirement/article_d46acf4d-605c-5b07-8083-6c0b19f36f81.html.

GEORGE BRETT

BY RUSSELL BERGTOLD

Few players have been as synonymous with a team as George Brett and the Kansas City Royals. Yet the amiable, self-deprecating, and sometimes volatile Brett never viewed himself as being greater than the team he loved. A throwback to an earlier time, Brett favored pine tar over batting gloves, chewing tobacco over bubble gum, and cold beer over weightlifting. As the Royals reached the half-century mark, Brett remained the only player to represent the team in baseball's Hall of Fame.

George is the youngest of four brothers. All four boys wound up playing baseball professionally. John, the oldest, got as far as Class-A ball in 1968, playing for the Waterloo (Iowa) Hawks in the Midwest League. Bobby, the second youngest, played one season of minor-league ball in 1972 before moving on to have a lucrative career in real-estate development.[1] The brother who was the most promising was Ken Brett, the second oldest, who was affectionately known as "Kemer" throughout the Brett household.

Ken Brett pitched in 14 major-league seasons with 10 different teams. He made his major-league debut in Fenway Park with the Boston Red Sox on September 27, 1967, pitching the last two innings in a 6-0 loss to the Cleveland Indians. Two weeks later, at 19 years old, he replaced Sparky Lyle on the postseason roster to become the youngest pitcher in World Series competition when he threw 1⅓ scoreless innings in his two relief appearances. Sitting in the stands cheering him on, was 14-year-old George as Ken was allowed to invite his parents, siblings, and high-school coach John Stevenson to witness the fall classic.[2]

In 1973, while pitching for the Phillies, Ken surrendered Hank Aaron's 700th home run. A year later, as the lone representative of the Pittsburgh Pirates, he was the winning pitcher in the 1974 All-Star Game. Although Ken's pitching career was plagued by arm problems, he was also an excellent hitter. In 1973 he set a record for the most consecutive games by a pitcher (four) with a home run. On October 3, 1981, his "little" brother George had come full circle: from watching his older brother pitch in the World Series to playing alongside him in his final major-league appearance. Kemer pitched two innings, allowing one run, as the Royals lost 8-4 to the Oakland A's in Kansas City. George homered in the sixth off Rick Langford.

The Brett boys grew up in El Segundo, California. John, Ken, and Bobby were born in Brooklyn, New York. George was born on May 15, 1953, in Glen Dale, West Virginia, before the family moved out west when he was 2 years old.

Their father, Jack Brett, was a Brooklynite who cheered for the New York Yankees. Although he came from a good household (his father worked on Wall Street), he dropped out of high school to work in a factory. By the age of 18, he enlisted in the US Army and fought in World War II. His tour of duty ended when he was shot in the leg in France. Upon returning home, he enrolled at Pace College in New York, where he earned a degree in business administration. He worked as an accountant for Mattel Toys. In 1945 he married Ethel Hansen.

Ethel, who worked as a bookkeeper for a furniture company, was a loving, nurturing mother. Jack was the disciplinarian in the household, whose wrath was felt mostly by George. While the older siblings seemed to apply themselves both athletically and academically, George was seen as somewhat lazy and lacking motivation. He preferred bumming around Redondo Beach to playing baseball. George later admitted that if it were not for his baseball skills, he more than likely would have wound up as a bartender or a construction worker.

Like his brothers before him, 7-year-old George began playing Little League baseball at Recreation Park in El Segundo. As a child his favorite players were Mickey Mantle, Carl Yastrzemski, and Brooks Robinson. By the ninth grade, George was only 5-feet-1 and 105 pounds when he tried out for the El Segundo High School baseball team. Initially Dave Reed, a junior-varsity coach, wanted to cut George from the squad for his lack of size, but he was overruled by varsity coach John Stevenson, who coached George's three older brothers. As it turned out, the ambidextrous George broke his wrist and had to sit out his freshman year anyway.[3]

Over the next two years George grew and filled out. His first love was football, and George was the starting quarterback for his high school team. Because of his propensity for throwing interceptions, he was converted to a wide receiver in his senior year. As a high-school baseball player, he could never measure up to his older brother Ken, who was already pitching for the Red Sox. He was also overshadowed by high-school teammate Scott McGregor, who went on to have a 13-year major-league career pitching for the Baltimore Orioles.

Initially Brett was a third baseman, but he moved to shortstop in his junior year. Throwing right-handed but batting left-handed, he imitated a Yaz-like stance at the plate. He established such a flair for the dramatics in crucial situations that his teammates nicknamed him "Mr. Drama."

By Brett's senior year the 1971 El Segundo Eagles were one of the finest high-school baseball teams ever assembled in the California Interscholastic Federation (CIF). They posted a 33-2 record and won the CIF championship. Six players, including Brett, were drafted by major-league teams, yet George was never offered a college scholarship for his baseball prowess.[4]

Because Brett still had some baby fat around his midsection, many scouts passed on him. Even some of the scouts for the expansion Kansas City Royals were skeptical. However, scouts Tom Ferrick and Rosey Gilhousen saw Brett as a diamond in the rough. Gilhousen pushed the hardest for the Royals to draft Brett, basing his assessment on the intangibles of desire, instincts, and aggressiveness. He persuaded the Royals vice president for player personnel, Lou Gorman, to see Brett in action during a high-school game. The fact that Coach Stevenson and Gorman were in the Navy together may have helped sway the Royals into taking Brett with the fifth pick in the second round of the June 1971 amateur draft.)

Brett began his professional career in the rookie-level Pioneer League. On June 15, 1971, shortly after his high-school graduation, he arrived in Billings, Montana, to play for the Mustangs. Garbed in beach-bum attire when he met his new manager, Gary Blaylock, Brett was politely told to wear some shoes and a shirt the next time they met.[5] It was there that Brett was converted from a shortstop to a third baseman.[6] For the season Brett batted .291 with 5 home runs and 44 RBIs.

He was sent to the Winter Instructional League in Sarasota, Florida, between seasons and was promoted to San Jose of the Class-A California League for 1972. In June his brother Bobby became a teammate when he signed with the Royals. He played 19 games with the Bees before calling it a career. George finished the season with a .274 batting average, 10 home runs, and a team-leading 68 RBIs.

In 1973 Brett was invited to the Royals spring-training site in Fort Myers, Florida. On the flight to Fort Myers he met another Royals prospect, Jamie Quirk.[7] The two would form a lifelong friendship, but for now they were competing for a spot on the Royals Opening Day roster.

It didn't take long before Brett was back on a plane heading to Omaha after he was one of the first cuts in spring training. Playing for the Omaha Royals in the American Association, Brett made the Triple-A all-star team and finished with a batting average of .284, 8 home runs, and 64 RBIs before being called up to the Royals. Filling in for the injured Paul Schaal, Brett made his big-league debut on August 2, 1973, at Comiskey Park in Chicago. Batting eighth, Brett lined out to the pitcher, Stan Bahnsen, in his first plate appearance. The second time up he recorded his first major-league hit – a broken-bat bloop single to left field. Brett finished the season with a .125 batting average in limited action as Kansas City improved to 88-74, six games behind the league-leading Oakland A's.

It is worth noting that Brett wasn't the only player making his Royals debut that year. The Royals had acquired outfielder Hal McRae in an offseason trade with the Cincinnati Reds. McRae's vehement passion for the game was a major influence on Brett as the culture of the Royals clubhouse gradually changed in the coming years.[8]

Heading into 1974, it was no secret that Royals manager Jack McKeon was not overly thrilled with having Brett on his team.[9] Despite the fact that incumbent third baseman Paul Schaal led the majors with 30 errors in 1973, Brett found himself back in Omaha to start the new season. In fairness to Schaal, the newly constructed Royals Stadium featured artificial turf which may have contributed to his defensive struggles.[10]

On April 30, 1974, Schaal was traded to the California Angels for outfielder Richie Scheinblum. Frank White filled in at third base for a few games before the Royals recalled Brett from Omaha. When Brett took over for White in early May, he struggled defensively and offensively. Nearing the All-Star break, Brett was barely hitting above .200 when hitting coach Charley Lau approached him. For the rest of the season, Lau worked with Brett daily on revamping his swing. One day, after Brett didn't show up for practice, Lau called him a "mullet head" for his complacency.[11] (It was later shortened to "Mullet.") Suffice it to say that Brett never missed a session with Lau again.

Under Lau's tutelage, Brett's batting average soared to .292 with three games left in the season when Jack McKeon unexpectedly fired Lau.[12] A devastated Brett collected one hit in those last three games and finished with a .282 average.[13]

The 1975 season was one of transformation for Brett and the Royals. It began with Brett changing his jersey number from 25 to his more familiar number 5. He did this to pay homage to one of his favorite players (who also played third base), Brooks Robinson.[14] After 96 games into the season, the Royals replaced manager McKeon with Whitey Herzog. One of the first things Herzog did was to rehire Charley Lau as their hitting coach. Brett went on to lead the league in hits (195) and triples (13). He also finished with a .300 batting average (.308 to be exact) for the first time in his professional career. The Royals posted their best record so far, finishing 20 games above .500, but were still spectators for the postseason. Kansas City fans were growing weary of seeing the Oakland A's win another divisional title, their fifth in a row.

When Charlie O. Finley moved the team to Oakland before the 1968 season, many fans in Kansas City were ambivalent about their departure. The Athletics never finished above .500 in the 13 years they played in Kansas City, yet it was demoralizing to see the A's finish above .500 in their inaugural season in Oakland. Like a bitter divorce, the animosity only got worse as the A's continued to get better, culminating in three straight World Series titles (1972-1974).[15] The Royals finally seized their opportunity to wrest the division crown away from the A's in 1976, after Finley began to dismantle his dynasty in an effort to save money.

The '76 season began with Brett making headlines almost immediately. From May 8 to 13, he collected three hits in six consecutive games to tie a major-league record.[16] The Royals claimed first place by a half-game on May 19 and never relinquished their lead. By August 6 they had built it into a 12-game lead over the second-place A's. During an extra-inning game against the Cleveland Indians on August 17 at Royals Stadium, Brett pulled off one of the rarest feats in baseball by stealing home for the walk-off win.[17] From that point on, the Royals sputtered with an 18-27 record, but were able to stave off a late-season surge by the A's to capture their first division title by 2½ games.

Even though the Royals were headed to the postseason in 1976, the last game of the regular season was marred in controversy when Brett edged out McRae for the AL batting title. With the Royals trailing the Minnesota Twins 5-2 in the bottom of the ninth, Brett came up to bat with one out and nobody on base. He lofted a routine fly ball to left field, which many felt could have been caught by Twins outfielder Steve Brye. Instead, Brye played it into an inside-the-park home run, thereby giving Brett the title. McRae, an African-American, was outraged by Brye's lackadaisical attempt and accused him of being a racist. Brett felt terrible about the whole situation, and said that if he could split the award in half he would gladly do it. In spite of his disappointment, McRae held no ill will toward his friend and teammate as they embarked on their first American League Championship Series against the New York Yankees.[18]

Brett had an inauspicious beginning to his postseason career when his two errors led to two runs in the first inning of Game One at Royals Stadium. The Royals lost, 4-1, but they managed to push the series to the decisive Game Five. During that game, at Yankee Stadium, the national audience got their first glimpse at Brett's penchant for delivering in crucial moments as he belted a three-run homer to tie the game, 6-6, in the top of the eighth inning. That home run is often forgotten as Chris Chambliss led off the bottom of the ninth with a solo homer that put the Yankees in the World Series for the first time in 12 years.

Although the Royals came up short in the ALCS, they would continue to dominate the American League West by appearing in six of the next nine postseasons. It is not a coincidence that 1976 was also the first of Brett's 13 consecutive All-Star selections. When the season ended, he was the runner-up to Thurman Munson for the American League Most Valuable Player.

The 1977 ALCS was a rematch of 1976. In the deciding Game Five at Royals Stadium, Brett hit an RBI triple off Ron Guidry in the first inning. When Brett slid in hard at third, Yankees third baseman Graig Nettles took exception and kicked him in the face. Brett jumped up with a haymaker to ignite a bench-clearing brawl. After order was restored, both players were allowed to stay in the game. Losing 3-2 in the top of the ninth, New York scored three unanswered runs to snatch the pennant away from Kansas City once again. For the second year in a row, the Royals lost the pennant to the Yankees in the final inning of the final game.

With their rivalry now firmly solidified, the 1978 postseason marked the third straight year the Royals faced the Yankees in the ALCS. This time the Royals won only one game. Brett provided some highlights in the third game by becoming the fourth player to hit three home runs in a postseason game.[19] All three homers were served up by Catfish Hunter. To Brett it was small consolation as the Royals lost, 6-5. They would lose more than the series as dissension was festering among the ranks. During the regular season Whitey Herzog was losing his patience with the results of his hitting guru, Charley Lau.[20] Shortly after the ALCS, the Royals announced that Lau would not return in 1979. Seizing the opportunity, the Yankees quickly hired Lau as their hitting coach.

Brett began 1979 by breaking his right thumb in an offseason charity basketball game.[21] Because of the injury, plus the absence of Charley Lau, Brett got off to a slow start but he finished the season with a league-leading 212 hits and 20 triples. His .329 batting average was second in the league to Fred Lynn's .333. Despite Brett's production, the Royals missed the playoffs for the first time in four years. Whitey Herzog and all his coaches were fired. The future looked bleak.[22]

The Royals had won three division titles under Herzog, but never got past the Yankees in the Championship Series. Entering the 1980 season, they were now playing for rookie manager Jim Frey. Frey, hired just days after his Baltimore Orioles lost the 1979 World Series to the Pittsburgh Pirates, had been a coach under Earl Weaver for 10 years.

On May 15, 1980, Brett's 27th birthday, the Royals were 16-14 while enjoying an offday. In lieu of a ballgame it was the nationally televised Miss USA Beauty Pageant that had fans in Kansas City cheering. The contest's "Miss New York," Debra Sue Maurice, informed host Bob Barker that she was dating George Brett. Brett, who tried to downplay his long reputation of being a lady's man, was caught off-guard by her statement. He acknowledged having had a few dates with Miss Maurice but nothing more serious than that.[23]

Whatever distraction it may have caused was insignificant as the bigger story of the 1980 season was Brett's unlikely pursuit of a .400 batting average. During a June 10 game in Cleveland, he tore a ligament in his right foot while trying to steal second base.[24] Unable to play again until July 10, Brett was batting .337 at the time he was hurt. No one could have predicted that he would be soaring around .400 by season's end. Beginning on July 18, Brett started a 30-game hitting streak that would help catapult him over the vaunted mark. He topped .400 on Sunday, August 17, when he went 4-for-4 against the Toronto Blue Jays in Kansas City. His fourth hit, a bases-clearing double in the eighth inning off Mike Barlow, put him over the top. As he stood on second base, acknowledging the hometown crowd, the scoreboard flashed ".401."[25]

A week earlier, on August 11, the Royals had signed George's older brother, left-hander Ken Brett, to help out in their bullpen. Released by the Dodgers in the spring because of a sore left elbow, Ken was playing for the semipro Orange County A's when the Royals came calling.[26] He made five appearances with the Omaha Royals before making his Kansas City debut on September 1 against the Brewers. With the Royals down 4-1 to Milwaukee, Ken relieved Rich Gale in the top of the fourth to get the final out. He remained in the game to pitch four more shutout innings. Whether it was coincidence or a backhanded tribute, Ken wore the number 25, the same number his "little" brother wore when he first came up to the Royals in 1973. Regardless of the motive, playing alongside his older brother at the major-league level is one of George's most cherished moments in baseball.[27]

With his brother by his side, George's average hovered around .400 for over a month. It wasn't until September 20, when he went 0-for-4 against Oakland, that his average dipped below.395. Plagued by nagging injuries which caused him to miss 45 games during the season, the media attention also took its toll. To avoid the press, the Brett brothers would often drive together in George's Mercedes and park in a tunnel behind the Royals bullpen for an easy escape after games.[28] Eventually his average dropped to .390 to close out the campaign. As of 2018, it was the closest any player has gotten to .400 since Ted Williams batted .406 in 1941.[29] Additionally, Brett led the league in on-base percentage (.454) and slugging percentage (.664). It is worth noting that he also belted 24 home runs yet only struck out 22 times in 515 plate appearances.

The Royals clinched their division by 14 games over the second-place A's. For the fourth time in five years, they would face the Yankees in the American League Championship Series. The Royals won the first two games, leaving them one win away from their first World Series appearance. Game Three featured one of the most memorable moments in playoff history. The Royals were trailing 2-1 in the top of the seventh. Yankees pitcher Tommy John got the first two outs before Willie Wilson doubled. Reliever Goose Gossage gave up a single to U L Washington and Wilson went to third. With two out and two on, Brett stepped in to face the imposing Gossage and hammered the first pitch to him for a three-run homer to put the Royals ahead. That held up to give the Royals a 4-2 victory and their first trip to the World Series.

The Royals faced the Philadelphia Phillies, who were also vying for their first World Series title. The first two games were won by the Phillies in Veterans Stadium. In the second game Brett began to feel severe pain. After collecting a walk and two singles, he asked to be taken out of the game. On the way back to Royals Stadium for Game Three, Brett went to St. Luke's Hospital in Kansas City for minor surgery to have hemorrhoids removed. It was national news by the time Game Three got underway as Brett found the grit to suit up. In his first at-bat, just hours after the surgery, Brett drove a Dick Ruthven pitch into the right-field stands for a home run that gave the Royals a 1-0 lead. The Royals held on to win the game, but lost the Series in six games.

On an individual basis, 1980 would prove to be Brett's most defining year as a major leaguer. He won the American League Most Valuable Player Award, but individual accomplishments didn't matter much to Brett. He was disappointed that he fell short of hitting

.400, but admitted that it would have eased his pain if the Royals could have won the World Series.[30]

With his pursuit of .400, his tryst with a beauty pageant contestant, his first World Series appearance, and his hemorrhoids, Brett's stature was now on a national level. His waning days of casually hanging out in Kansas City with teammates Jamie Quirk and Clint Hurdle for burgers and beers in the bars of Westport and the Country Club Plaza were now over.[31]

A players strike in 1981 divided the season into two halves. Manager Jim Frey was fired after the team went 10-10 to start the second half, and was replaced by former Yankees skipper Dick Howser. Under Howser the Royals went 20-13 to finish with a second-half record of 30-23, earning them a playoff berth; they were swept by the Oakland A's in the American League Division Series.

The Royals missed the playoffs altogether in 1982 and 1983. Brett continued to put up decent numbers in those two seasons, although he missed a combined 57 games during that span. However, one of his games stood out: It was played on July 24, 1983, at Yankee Stadium and is referred to in baseball lore as "The Pine Tar Game."

Heading into the game, the Yankees and Royals were two games back in their respective divisions. The Yankees were winning 4-3 entering the top of the ninth inning. Yankees pitcher Dale Murray retired the first two Royals hitters before surrendering a single to U L Washington. Yankees manager Billy Martin replaced Murray with Goose Gossage to face Brett. Brett fouled off the first pitch. The next pitch was up and in, but Brett was able to get the barrel of the bat on the ball and tomahawked it over the right-field wall to give the Royals a 5-4 lead. As Brett circled the bases, Martin was out of the Yankees dugout to have the umpires inspect Brett's bat for excessive pine tar, insisting that Brett had violated Rule 1.10(c), which stated that "a bat may not be covered by such a substance more than 18 inches from the tip of the handle."[32] After some debate among the umpiring crew, rookie umpire Tim McClelland measured the bat against the 17-inch width of home plate and determined that the bat did indeed violate the rule. He pointed with the bat toward Brett in the dugout and called him out. Brett went ballistic, charging out of the dugout toward the 6-foot-6, 250-pound McClelland. Brett had to be restrained by crew chief Joe Brinkman, who held him in a headlock. Umpires Drew Coble and Nick Bremigan, along with Brett's teammates Leon Roberts and Joe Simpson, joined in to prevent Brett from getting to McClelland. Meanwhile Royals pitcher Gaylord Perry unsuccessfully attempted to confiscate the bat by handing it off to teammate Steve Renko, who was later stopped by two of the umpires and stadium security guards.

When order was restored, the two teams made their way back to their dugouts. With the home run stripped away and Brett called out, the game was over. The Yankees won, 4-3. However, this ruling did not sit well with the Royals. Their vice president of player personnel, John Schuerholz, filed a letter of protest with American League President Lee MacPhail, who overturned the ruling on the field. The game was resumed on August 18, much to the chagrin of the Yankees, who felt it was unnecessary. Out of defiance for using a day off to complete the game, Billy Martin made a mockery of the ruling by inserting pitcher Ron Guidry in center field and moving left-handed first baseman Don Mattingly to second base to finish the top of the ninth. Goose Gossage was replaced by George Frazier on the mound. Out of spite, Martin ordered Frazier to appeal every base, so he stepped off the rubber and did as he was told. Martin knew that the new umpiring crew would be unable to verify the appeals. However, when they did, Martin came out of the Yankees dugout for an explanation. He was greeted by crew chief Dave Phillips, who produced an affidavit signed by the four original umpires confirming that Brett and Washington had indeed touched all the bases. A flabbergasted Martin stormed through the dugout and went straight to the clubhouse. Frazier promptly struck out Hal McRae for the third out. In the bottom of the ninth, reliever Dan Quisenberry retired the side in order to give the Royals a 5-4 victory. As for George Brett, he was ejected from the game for charging McClelland and was replaced by Greg Pryor at third base. Brett spent the afternoon watching the game on TV in a restaurant near the airport.[33]

During the offseason, the Royals' Willie Mays Aikens, Jerry Martin, and Willie Wilson, and former Royals pitcher Vida Blue pled guilty to charges of cocaine possession. All but Wilson were released by the team. On the business side, Ewing Kauffman sold 49 percent of the team to real-estate developer Avron Fogelman.

Despite the offseason turmoil with team personnel, the Royals managed to win their division in 1984 with an 84-78 record. They were swept in the ALCS by the Detroit Tigers. Brett played in only 104 regular-season games. After the ALCS Fogelman told him, "You've spent 43 days on the disabled list and I'm paying you more money than anybody else on the team. What I want you to do next year is go get yourself in the best shape you possibly can, and you come to spring training and go help us win a World Series."[34]

Brett followed Fogelman's advice. He showed up for spring training considerably thinner and went on to have one of his finest seasons, finishing second to the Yankees' Mattingly for the MVP. He set a career high with 30 home runs and won his only Gold Glove Award.

However, the 1985 Royals did not run away with the division. They were only two games above the .500 mark at the All-Star break, 7½ games behind the division-leading California Angels. Gradually they closed the gap and on September 6 they caught up to the Angels. For the remainder of the season the teams went back and forth until the Royals clinched the division on October 5 with a walk-off victory over Oakland. In the final week of the season, played in front of his hometown fans, Brett went 9-for-20 with 5 home runs and 11 RBIs as the team finished with a 91-71 record. Next up were the Toronto Blue Jays in the American League Championship Series.

The LCS changed in 1985 from a best-of-five to a best-of-seven format.. The Blue Jays won the first two games in Toronto's Exhibition Stadium. On October 11, nearly five years to the day after he hit his game-winning homer off Goose Gossage in Game Three of the 1980 ALCS, Brett put on another Game Three ALCS postseason clinic. With the series now in Kansas City, he homered off Doyle Alexander in the bottom of the first inning to give the Royals a 1-0 lead. With one out in Toronto's third, second baseman Damaso Garcia doubled and went to third on an error by left fielder Lonnie Smith. The left-handed Lloyd Moseby slashed a one-hopper down the third-base line that Brett speared. With his momentum carrying him into foul territory, Brett whirled and fired an off-balance strike to catcher Jim Sundberg to nail Garcia at the plate. Pitcher Bret Saberhagen then picked off Moseby at first and the inning was over.

In the bottom of the fourth inning, Brett doubled and eventually scored to give the Royals a 2-0 advantage. Then the Blue Jays erupted in the top of the fifth to take a 5-2 lead. Sundberg answered with a solo homer to make it a 5-3 game. In the bottom of the sixth Willie Wilson led off with a single. With Doyle Alexander still on the mound, Brett launched a two-run homer to tie it, 5-5.

In the bottom of the eighth, with the score still 5-5, Brett led off with a single. Hal McRae bunted him to second and Frank White's grounder to short moved Brett to third. Pat Sheridan was intentionally walked to bring up Steve Balboni, who singled up the middle to score Brett with the eventual winning run as the Royals won, 6-5.

The Royals lost Game Four, 3-1, and were down three games to one. Danny Jackson tossed a shutout in Game Five to keep the Royals alive as they headed to Toronto for Games Six and Seven. The Royals knotted the series with a 5-3 victory in the sixth game, with Brett reaching base three times and scoring twice. The decisive Game Seven was played on October 16; the Royals led the whole way with a final score of 6-2 and won their second pennant. Brett was named the MVP of the series. Earlier in the day the St. Louis Cardinals had beaten the Dodgers in Los Angeles for the National League pennant.

Since the Royals and Cardinals played their home games at the opposite ends of Missouri, the 1985 World Series was unofficially dubbed the "I-70 Series" when play began in Kansas City. The heavily favored Cardinals were managed by former Royals manager Whitey Herzog. Herzog often regarded Brett as the best player he ever managed and instructed his pitchers not to let Brett beat them.[35] His staff followed orders as Brett's influence was reduced to one extra-base hit and only one RBI. He still managed an on-base percentage of .452 while hitting .370 for the Series. A talented young Royals rotation held the Cardinals to a .185 batting average. Their OBP was a meager .248, and for all their speed, the Cardinals swiped only two bases in five attempts. The Royals also benefited from a blown call in Game Six along with an uncharacteristic fielding miscue from a St. Louis team that led the National League with a .983 fielding percentage.

In Game One, the Royals jumped out to a 1-0 lead in the second inning, only to lose 3-1. In the second game, with a 2-0 lead and two outs in the ninth inning, it appeared that the Royals would tie the Series. However, the Cardinals rallied for four runs to snatch a 4-2 victory in front of a shocked crowd in Royals Stadium. The Royals now found themselves down two games as they headed across the state for Game Three in St. Louis.

Thanks to a complete game by pitcher Bret Saberhagen, the Royals took Game Three, 6-1. Brett reached base all five times with two singles and three walks. John Tudor of the Cardinals returned the favor in Game Four with a 3-0 shutout. Just as in the series against Toronto, the Royals found themselves down three games to one.

Danny Jackson followed the recipe for success by hurling a complete game to give the Royals a 6-1 win in Game Five. The game that is talked about most often is Game Six, in Kansas City. The Royals were trailing 1-0 in the bottom of the ninth. Herzog brought in Cardinals closer Todd Worrell to relieve Ken Dayley. Leadoff hitter Jorge Orta hit a slow grounder to first baseman Jack Clark, who tossed it to Worrell covering the bag. Orta was called safe by first-base umpire Don Denkinger. Replays confirmed that Denkinger had missed the call. With Orta on first base, Steve Balboni hit a pop foul that Clark misplayed. Balboni then stroked a single into left field and was replaced by pinch-runner Onix Concepcion at first, with Orta on second. Royals catcher Jim Sundberg bunted but the Cardinals were able to get the force out at third for the first out. Concepcion moved to second, with Sundberg on first. Hal McRae pinch-hit for shortstop Buddy Biancalana. A passed ball allowed both runners to move up, so McRae was intentionally walked and replaced by pinch-runner John Wathan. With the bases loaded, former Cardinals utilityman Dane Iorg pinch-hit for reliever Dan Quisenberry. Iorg singled to right field to knock in Concepcion and Sundberg as the Royals forced a Game Seven.

The Royals won Game Seven with an 11-0 trouncing of the dispirited Cardinals. Saberhagen threw the shutout and was named the Series MVP. It was the first time a team had come back from two 3-1 postseason deficits to win a championship.

The 1985 championship season was the pinnacle of Brett's tenure with the club. Brett's Royals never reached the postseason again. However, Brett still had a few good years left in him and a few personal milestones to reach.

At the All-Star break in 1990, the 37-year-old Brett was hitting .267 with two home runs in 302 plate appearances and appeared to be a mere shadow of his former self. In 305 plate appearances after the All-Star break, Brett added 12 home runs and hit at a .388 clip. He wound up winning the American League batting title with a .329 average, and is the only player to win a batting title in three different decades.

By now the former All-Star third baseman was used primarily as a first baseman and designated hitter. As he entered the twilight of his career, he also had a change in his marital status. Before the 1992 season, Brett – who had been a confirmed bachelor throughout his playing days – married Leslie Davenport. They raised three sons, Jackson, Dylan, and Robin.

That 1992 season was Hal McRae's first full year as the Royals skipper, after he replaced John Wathan halfway through the year before. The Royals lost 16 of their first 17 games under McRae and never reached .500. After Labor Day they were simply playing out the string as the season wound down. When they arrived in Anaheim for a series beginning September 28, the focus shifted to Brett's quest for his 3,000th hit. Just four hits away from the coveted milestone, Brett missed the first two games of the series with shoulder inflammation but suited up for the game on Wednesday, September 30. In typical fashion, he doubled in the first, singled in the third, and singled in the fifth. In the seventh inning, Brett smashed a one-hopper over the glove of second baseman Ken Oberkfell for hit number 3,000. The crowd of 17,000 gave him a standing ovation. His brother Ken was in the Angels broadcast booth calling the game. His newlywed wife and family were in the stands as Brett was mobbed by his teammates. When the hoopla subsided, play resumed. Gregg Jefferies flied out to right for the second out. With Mike Macfarlane up to bat, an embarrassed Brett was picked off first to end the inning. The first-base umpire who called him out was Tim McClelland - the same umpire who called him out in the Pine Tar Game.

A year later, on September 25, 1993, with his wife, Leslie, by his side at a press conference in Kauffman Stadium, Brett announced that he would retire at the end of the season to become a vice president within the organization.[36] Although the 40-year-old Brett was no longer the player he was in his 20s and 30s, he still posted respectable numbers. The fact that the Royals offered him a substantial amount of money to play one more year can attest to that. But Brett had had enough, "I've always said I'd never play the game for money. ... That wouldn't be fair to the Royals, to the people of Kansas City. The game deserves better than that."[37]

Over the course of his career, Brett missed about 300 games due to injuries. Those who played with him were amazed that he played as often as he did.

Brett retired with 3,154 hits, 317 home runs, and a .305 batting average. As of 2018 he led the Royals in several offensive categories. His ability to hit in the clutch was evidenced repeatedly in postseason competition.

The Royals retired Brett's number less than a year after his final game. In 1999, his first year of eligibility, Brett was inducted into Baseball's Hall of Fame.

After retiring as a player, Brett served in various capacities in the Royals organization, from vice president to hitting coach. He and his brother Bobby formed an investment group that tried unsuccessfully to purchase the Royals in 1998. They later purchased several minor-league teams. To better acclimate himself to his new role as an entrepreneur/executive, Brett took a few courses at a junior college.[38] In memory of a friend, Keith Worthington, who died in 1984 of Lou Gehrig's disease Brett began raising money to find a cure for the disease.

Sources

In addition to the sources cited in the Notes, the author also consulted Baseball-Reference.com, and *George Brett: A Royal Hero* (New York: Sports Publishing, 1999), published by the Kansas City Star.

Notes

1 John Garrity, *The George Brett Story* (New York: Coward, McCann and Geoghegan, 1981), 89.

2 Gib Twyman, *Born to Hit, The George Brett Story* (New York: Random House, 1982), 18. Most details regarding the Brett family come from either Twyman's book or Garrity's.

3 "Becoming George Brett: From the Beach to Billings and Beyond," interview by the Kansas City Star: youtube.com/watch?v=gXq2qtrL-p8.

4 Ibid.

5 Twyman, 27-28.

6 Twyman, 29.

7 Twyman, 31-32.

8 Twyman, 50-52.

9 Twyman, 37-39.

10 Twyman, 37.

11 George Brett with Steve Cameron, *George Brett: From Here to Cooperstown* (Lenexa, Kansas: Addax Publishing, 1999), 45.

12 Garrity, 18.

13 Twyman, 48.

14 Garrity, 65.

15 Denny Matthews with Matt Fulks, *Tales from the Kansas City Royals Dugout* (New York: Sports Publishing, 2015), 35-42.

16 According to *Baseball Almanac*, Brett tied Sam Thompson for the major-league record: baseball-almanac.com/recbooks/rb_bstrk.shtml.

17 According to *Baseball Almanac*, a game-winning steal of home has happened only 35 times: baseball-almanac.com/feats/Game_Ending_Steals_of_Home.shtml.

18 Garrity, 126-133.

19 It has been accomplished six more times since Brett did it in 1978: usatoday.com/story/sports/mlb/2017/10/20/mlb-three-home-runs-playoff-game-enrique-hernandez/783026001/

20 Garrity, 164.

21 Garrity, 172.

22 Garrity, 187.

23 Garrity, 213-215.

24 Del Black, "Royals' Leonard Sports Sharp New Style," *The Sporting News*, July 5, 1980: 13.

25 Garrity, 17.

26 Jonathon Arnold, "Ken Brett," Society for American Baseball Research, BioProject: sabr.org/bioproj/person/5e904106, retrieved October 6, 2018.

27 Steve Cameron, *George Brett: Last of a Breed* (Dallas: Taylor Publishing, 1993), 79.

28 Dave Kaegel, "Brett Everybody's Pet," *The Sporting News,* September 20, 1980: 4.

29 In the strike-shortened 1994 season, Tony Gwynn hit .394 for that year's batting title.

30 Matthews with Fulks, 30.

31 Garrity, 211, 212.

32 The 2018 Major League Baseball rule book now cites that as Rule 3.02(c).

33 Filip Bondy, *The Pine Tar Game* (New York: Scribner, 2015), 186-187.

34 Bondy, 204.

35 Cameron, 52.

36 On July 2, 1993, Royals Stadium was renamed Kauffman Stadium in a ceremony to honor Royals owner and founder Ewing M. Kauffman. kansascity.royals.mlb.com/kc/history/ballparks.jsp, retrieved on October 7, 2018.

37 Cameron, 163.

38 Cameron, 184.

STEVE BUSBY

BY JOHN DIFONZO

On June 18, 1974, Paul Splittorff threw a two-hit shutout against the Brewers in Milwaukee. After the game Splittorff and his roommate, Steve Busby, were talking about no-hitters. Splittorff did not consider himself to be a no-hit-type pitcher. But he had a list of pitchers who he considered could throw a no-hitter every time out – which included Nolan Ryan and Busby. Busby, who had pitched a no-hitter the previous season, said, "I got all over him for saying this because I really don't consider myself to be a no-hit pitcher. I think I've been more fortunate than a lot of other pitchers because obviously it takes a lot of luck to pitch one."[1] The next day Busby threw his second no-hitter. Busby would be forever associated with the no-hitter and rotator cuff surgery, but there is much more to his story.

Steven Lee "Buzz" Busby was born on September 29, 1949, in Burbank, California, to Marvin and Betty Busby, who were of English and German descent. Marvin played football at USC and professionally for the Los Angeles Dons of the All-American Football Conference.[2] This had an influence on his son, Steve, who grew up preferring football to baseball. When Marvin's football days were over, he worked as a petroleum and chemical engineer. Betty taught American history at the University of California at Berkeley before leaving to raise their children. Busby said he was raised to believe that the team was more important than the individual and that individual accomplishments didn't mean much if they didn't contribute toward the team winning.[3]

Busby grew up in Fullerton, California, and was a three-sport star at Union High, excelling in basketball, baseball, and football. (Hall of Famers Arky Vaughan and Walter Johnson also attended the school.) While in high school, Busby threw two no-hitters. He cited his baseball coach there as one of his early influences. "Jim Bass is the best teacher of fundamentals ... catching, throwing, pitching mechanics," Busby said. "I learned pitching mechanics from him, learning to win from him."[4]

Playing football during his senior year, Busby suffered a knee injury that required an operation. In 1967 the San Francisco Giants selected Busby in the fourth round of the June draft. When Busby's knee gave out during a workout, the Giants discovered that there were still lingering effects from the injury and cut their bonus offer in half. Busby decided to accept a scholarship to the University of Southern California and to play for the legendary coach Rod Dedeaux.

In 1968 Busby went 8-3 and batted .422 and was named the team's most valuable player for the USC freshman team.[5] In 1969, his sophomore year, Busby required surgery to relocate the ulnar nerve in his right arm. His arm strength was gone and he realized that he had to start developing other pitches. Before the surgery he threw 80 percent fastballs; after, he developed a slider and made the transition from thrower to pitcher. Busby's arm strength eventually returned and he became a more complete pitcher.

In 1971 Busby compiled an 11-2 record for the Trojans with a 1.92 ERA in 21 games and made the All-American team. Busby was the team's leading pitcher, and though he lost an early-round game to Southern Illinois University in the College World Series, he redeemed himself in the deciding game. Busby struck out Southern Illinois' Bob Blakely with the bases loaded to seal the 7-2 victory for the Trojans. Busby's major at USC was business administration He also studied computer technology because he enjoyed the mathematical analysis. While at USC, Busby took a creative writing class taught by the creator of *The Twilight Zone,* Rod Serling,[6] and was inspired to write science-fiction novels. Busby thrived on challenges, and he wanted to see if he could "make all the pieces fit together."[7] His novels were described as not the "stars and galaxy kind, but the Rod Serling type ... the psychological experience ... and some occult."[8]

Busby was selected by the Kansas City Royals in the second round of the secondary phase (June) of the amateur draft in 1971. Despite being one semester short of graduating and having a year of college eligibility left, Busby signed with the Royals for a $37,500 bonus. He was described in *The Sporting News* as "not merely being early maturity, rather a happy blend of intelligence, perspective and competitive intensity, tempered with self control. He seemed already to know how to pitch. If he didn't pitch well, he knew why not and he knew how to accept victory or defeat."[9] Busby credited Dedeaux, saying, "I attribute a lot of my attitude to Coach Dedeaux. He always emphasized that you should do the best you can and not blame anyone else for failure. Don't downgrade anyone else."[10] He added, "I didn't appreciate the things Rod Dedeaux taught us until I got into pro ball. He taught me how to win including the psychological part of the game, how to recognize the small things: whether the outfielder was left-handed or right-handed, watching people in the infield, and looking at every possible way to beat you, whether it was good fielding, a good pickoff move, by intimidation or being lucky."[11]

Pitching for the Royals' San Jose farm team (California League), Busby compiled a 4-1 record with an 0.68 ERA, giving up only three earned runs in 40 innings and striking out 50. In the Florida Instructional League he continued to impress, with a 5-2 record, 1.50 ERA, and a league-leading 67 strikeouts in 60 innings.

It was felt that Busby had a shot to make the major-league roster out of spring training in 1972; he was the talk of the newcomers and had the poise of a veteran. He started the season at Triple-A Omaha. On May 4 Busby struck out eight consecutive Tulsa batters and broke up the opposing pitcher's no-hitter in the fifth inning en route to a 7-1 victory. In another game against Tulsa he struck out 16 in a pitching duel he won over Jim Bibby. Busby twice came close to pitching no-hitters during the season. The first time his bid was broken up with one out in the ninth, the second in the seventh. His manager, Jack McKeon prophetically counseled Busby "not to worry, that I'd pitch a couple of no-hitters and it'll be in the big leagues."[12] Busby led the league in strikeouts (221), innings pitched (217), and complete games with 17. He compiled a 12-14 record with a 3.19 ERA, for a team that the Royals felt victimized its pitchers with its poor defense. Busby said he benefited from McKeon's counsel, particularly on pitch selection.[13]

Busby got a surprise call-up after Omaha's season after Dick Drago's jaw was broken by a line drive on September 1. He made his major-league debut on September 8, 1972, started against the Minnesota Twins at Kansas City's Municipal Stadium. Cesar Tovar and Rod Carew greeted Busby with singles and the Twins took an early 1-0 lead. Busby settled down and pitched a complete-game 3-2 victory, striking out seven and allowing only five hits.

In Busby's third start, against the California Angels in Anaheim, just a 15-minute drive from his childhood home in Fullerton (and the first time his parents saw him pitch in the majors), he lost a grand slam after smacking pitcher Lloyd Allen's offering over the left-field fence. First-base umpire John Rice had called time before the pitch to eject Jerry May for suggesting that Rice speak to his tailor about "adding an extra panel in his suit." Royals manager Bob Lemon and Dick Drago also were ejected. When play resumed, Busby singled to center for his first major-league hit and collected two RBIs. Busby got two other hits, and the three were his only major-league base hits, because the American League adopted the designated hitter the next season. (A good all-around athlete, Busby was against the DH.) Busby started five games for the Royals in '72 and was 3-1 with a 1.58 ERA.

In 1976 Busby found out what happened on that night when he was convalescing in the hospital. Busby's roommate and best friend on the team, Paul Splittorff, came to see him. Busby recalls years later with a chuckle, "My arm is strapped to my chest and I'm still kind of woozy from all the medication they were giving me... He said hey I got to fess up to you and he told me the story about what he had said and he hid behind somebody as he was yelling it. He was the one who suggested to Rice about the tailor. He said you know I feel terrible about it. I was completely out of it. 'I said yah, whatever.' It was a month later, I finally came to and realized what he had told me. I had to corner him about it. He said, 'I figured you're not going to come back and pitch anymore anyways so I might as well get it out of the way and I'm not going to have to worry about rooming together.' That was kind of my impetus to get back to pitch the major league level and room with him again so I can give him a hard time."[14]

At the start of the 1973 season expectations were high for Busby. He was slated to be in the starting rotation and there was speculation from McKeon, the Royals new manager, that Busby had the makeup to win 20 games. "There isn't a hitter that can intimidate Busby," McKeon said.[15] Busby and Doug Bird combined to no-hit the Detroit Tigers in an exhibition game, Busby pitching the first six innings. He followed with seven hitless innings against the Cardinals. Busby was the Opening Day starter, but struggled, losing to California. In his first four starts he was 1-2 with an 8.04 ERA. He lasted only one inning and gave up five runs in a 16-2 defeat by the Chicago White Sox. Busby had some stiffness in his shoulder and was held back a few days before his next start. He recalled McKeon telling him that if he didn't show improvement in his next start, he would be sent down to work it out in Omaha.[16]

Did he ever show improvement! On April 27, a cold evening that Busby described as perfect for pitching, he threw the Royals' first no-hitter, beating the Detroit Tigers, 3-0. Busby became the 14th rookie to throw a no-hitter. He was wild, walking six. He had trouble locating his breaking pitches and threw mostly fastballs. At the time Busby downplayed the individual achievement, noting that first baseman John Mayberry bailed him out with a line-drive double play in the ninth. "It was blind luck. It had nothing to do with skill," Busby said of his feat.[17] More recently he said, "It was less than 40 degrees, I was wilder than a March hare, the Tigers were a veteran ballclub that didn't feel like swinging the bats." [18] (The umpire whose time-out call cost Busby his grand slam, John Rice, was the home-plate umpire for the no-hitter.)

Busby pitched well in his next game but then slumped and his record was 4-9 on July 2. But from then until the end of the season he was 12-6, helping the Royals to finish in second place in the American League West. Against Milwaukee on July 10 Busby struck out 13, tying the Royals team record at the time. He finished the season with a 16-15 record and a 4.23 ERA. It was the most wins by an American League rookie since 1968 and Busby was named *The Sporting News* American League Rookie Pitcher of the Year.

Despite high expectations for 1974, the Royals struggled early in the season and were two games under .500 and 4½ games behind Oakland on June 11. Owner Ewing Kaufman fired general manager Cedric Tallis, whose trades were credited with making the Royals the most successful expansion team in baseball history at the time. The timing was disruptive and the team was also grumbling about manager Jack McKeon and his handling of the pitching staff.

Busby got off to a better start in 1974, 8-6 with a 3.66 ERA going into his June 19 start in Milwaukee. Busby threw a gem. He walked only George Scott to lead off the second inning and retired the final 24 batters to record his second no-hitter, defeating the Brewers 2-0. Busby became the first and as of 2016 the only pitcher to throw no-hitters in his first two major-league seasons. Modestly, he said, "There were some outstanding plays behind me. I had good stuff but it could have been a four- or five-hitter."[19] Busby recalled that both no-hitters were low-scoring games and he had to focus on keeping the opposition off the boards rather than thinking about the no-hitter.[20]

Busby started his next game by retiring the first nine batters he faced. He broke the American League record by retiring 33 consecutive batters. (The record was tied in 1977 and broken in 1998.[21]) In both of Busby's starts after his no-hitters he pitched 5⅓ no-hit innings.

Busby started the season 13-9 with a 3.31 ERA to earn his first All-Star Game selection, but did not pitch. The Royals were a streaky team and won 16 of 22 games in late August to pull to within four games of the division-leading A's. But on a long homestand they lost 10 of their next 11 games to fall out of contention.

On September 17, Busby became the Royals second 20-game winner, but it was bittersweet as he hadn't won a game in three weeks as the Royals slid from contention. "It has no value because we didn't accomplish what I consider valuable, a championship," he said.[22]

Controversy struck the club again when McKeon fired hitting coach Charlie Lau before the last home game of the season. The move was sharply criticized by the players. Busby, the team's player representative, was very critical of the move. "We'll never win a pennant with this type of thinking," he said. "... If this organization is not interested in winning, then I don't want to be part of it. ... You can't win a championship without horses ... and they have taken away one of the very best horses they've had available."[23] It was rumored that McKeon was jealous of Lau and that the players went to Lau for help rather than McKeon.

Busby finished the season at 22-14 with a 3.39 ERA and a club record 292⅓ innings pitched. Busby was in the top 10 in almost every pitching category including WAR (seventh) and strikeouts per nine innings (fourth). The innings pitched may seem high by today's standards but Busby was only ninth in the league in innings pitched.

Controversy followed the Royals into the 1975 campaign. Busby resigned as player representative in May. Rumors were swirling that he threatened to leave the team in New York on May 18, because he had been at odds with McKeon and he wanted Buck Martinez and not Fran Healy, who caught both his no-hitters, to catch him. Busby dispelled any rumors of quitting after his meeting with McKeon and general manager Joe Burke.[24]

Busby was having his best season and started out 10-5 with a 2.57 ERA. He began to experience pain in the front of his shoulder, tendinitis, but a new pain in the rear of his shoulder began to appear. He compensated by altering his pitching motion, a step that caused mechanical issues. In a *Sports Illustrated* article in August 1978, Busby detailed what happened next: "On the 25th of June I threw 12 innings in Anaheim and won 6-2, but I struggled for the last seven. It was really a chore to throw. The next time I pitched was July 1 against Texas. Normally I recuperate fast between starts, but this day I just couldn't throw well. I was having strength problems: I couldn't grip the ball well and I had a lessened ability to snap my wrist. I couldn't even make a tight fist. ... I pitched on through the middle of September with very little success."[25]

Busby was named to his second All-Star Game and pitched two innings in relief. After two months of speculation, Jack McKeon was fired as manager of the Royals on July 24 and was replaced by Whitey Herzog. GM Burke cited McKeon's poor relationship with his players and the media as the main reason. The club was a disappointing 50-46, 11 games behind the A's. Herzog brought back hitting coach Charlie Lau.

The Royals finished seven games behind Oakland. Busby was held out the last week of the season because of shoulder soreness. He recalled, "By that time, I had no sensation of strength when I threw the ball."[26] He finished with an 18-12 record and a 3.08 ERA 260⅓ innings.

After the season Busby saw Dr. Frank Jobe, who prescribed different therapies. Busby thought his problems had been caused by bad mechanics and began an offseason training program. Busby was counted on to be a key contributor to the Royals' hopes to win the American League West crown in 1976. Dr. Jobe recommended that Busby pitch until he could no longer be effective. He started the season on the disabled list, joined the team in early April and pitched his first game on April 18. The Royals lost, 6-0; Busby gave up two runs in six innings but walked seven. After the game he was optimistic: "There is no doubt in my mind I'm healthy. My arm is fine."[27] Herzog added, "Busby threw freely and had no pain. He threw better than he did all last September."[28] Busby pitched an impressive game against the Yankees on May 1 and "removed any doubts about the condition of his arm."[29] But the relief over Busby's arm was short-lived. He left his May 12 start in the fifth inning as a precaution. At the time the seriousness of his arm condition was not known. Busby said, "It's not really serious. It's a muscle problem, an injury most pitchers suffer during spring training."[30] At the time it was reported that Busby was recovering from an elbow problem that he suffered late in the 1974 season.

Busby was held out of his next start and then was put on a pitch count. He pitched 15 innings in his next three starts restricted to 100 pitches and gave up only one run. (Though Busby has been said to be the first pitcher held to a pitch count, this was common practice at the time for a pitcher recovering from an injury.) Through June 2 Busby pitched in only seven games, but the Royals were off to a great start and were leading the American League West.

By June 15 Busby's season was described "an on again off again comeback" in *The Sporting News*.[31] Herzog summed up the situation: "We can't go on like this not knowing what his status is. If he needs complete rest, than let's go that route."[32] On June 22 Busby gave up nine runs to the White Sox; he said, "The arm feels good, but the results aren't."[33] On July 6 Busby gave up four runs in seven innings to the Yankees. One of the Yankees said, "He had nothing, no fastball, no curveball."[34] Both Busby and Herzog knew this, too, and decided to find out what was wrong.

Busby recalled, "[Dr. Robert] Kerlan [Dr. Jobe's partner] ordered me to have a shoulder arthrogram. Dye is injected into the joint, and if it leaks out into the surrounding tissue, there is a problem — and it showed that I had a tear in the rotator cuff. Rest wouldn't help an injury that serious. If I were to pitch again, I would have to have surgery."[35] Busby was done for the season; he finished with only 13 starts, a 3-3 record with a 4.40 ERA in 71⅔ innings. The tear in his rotator cuff was caused by the upper bone in the arm rubbing up against the top bone in the shoulder. Surgery lasting 3½ hours was required to cut the shoulder open, sew up the hole, cut three-quarters of an inch off the shoulder bone and shave off the back of the upper arm bone to reduce the friction.[36] This was the first time this procedure was performed on an active pitcher. Dr. Jobe performed the groundbreaking surgery on July 19, 1976. Jobe had previously done the surgery on tennis players and it was expected that Busby would regain full use of his arm, but his future effectiveness as a pitcher was unknown. A torn rotator cuff had ended many pitchers' careers including that of Don Drysdale. Dr. Jobe recommended that Busby seek other employment, but Busby wasn't ready to give up.

Meanwhile, the Royals went on to win their first American League West Division title and Busby found solace in the team's accomplishment. Busby said, "It was such a great feeling."[37] The Royals lost the ALCS to the Yankees on Chris Chambliss's walk-off home run. Busby worked on a rehab program overseen by Dr. Jobe. Given the nature and severity of the injury the Royals were not counting on him. They took a gamble and left Busby exposed to the 1977 expansion draft. Busby was not selected at least for two rounds (24 players selected) by the Toronto Blue Jays and Seattle Mariners.

There was no timetable for Busby's return; there was no one to whom one could compare his situation. He was confident he would return and could be effective with reduced velocity if he could control his breaking pitches. Busby appeared in one minor-league game and fared poorly. He reinjured his left knee while altering his pitching delivery and strengthening his shoulder. Dr. Jobe operated on the knee.

Baseball had taken a toll on Busby's personal life. He had placed baseball as his first priority, which led to a separation from his wife. During the summer of 1977 he got back together with his wife and two daughters and placed family as his first priority.

Although the Royals were not counting on Busby for the 1978 season, he showed up in camp after more rehabilitation to his arm and knee and made the staff out of spring training. He started out well with a shutout, then was hit hard in his next three starts and was sent to the minors. Busby was called up in September and appeared in three games.

During spring training 1979 the 29-year-old Busby was competing for the fifth starter/long reliever role for Kansas City. He made the squad and posted a 6-6 record and 3.63 ERA, appearing in 22 games and starting 12.

During the offseason, Busby had arthroscopic surgery on his oft-injured right knee. In 1980 he competed again for the fifth starter/long reliever role. He made the staff and appeared in relief until he was sent to the minors in April. While in the minors, Busby was impressive with Omaha, posting a 2.48 ERA and throwing a one-hitter. He was recalled by the Royals and started six games. Busby posted a 1-3 record with a 6.17 ERA. The Royals wanted to use left-handed reliever Ken Brett in the playoffs and released the 30-year-old Busby on August 29, just two days before he would have been playoff eligible. Busby expressed his frustration. "It was disappointing watching the playoffs, not being able to pitch every year through 1980. I wanted to pitch so bad, I could taste it."[38] It is one of the great what-ifs: If Busby had been healthy from 1976 to 1980, would the fortunes of the Royals had been different? They lost the ALCS to the Yankees three times and lost the 1980 World Series to the Phillies.

In 1981 Busby was reviewing his business options, including broadcasting, a car dealership, and a beverage distributorship, when Herzog invited him to spring training with the St. Louis Cardinals as a nonroster player. Busby did not make the team and he retired. In 1984, at age 34, Busby was considering a comeback. "It's been nagging at me for three years," he said.[39] But he decided against pitching winter ball and his pitching days were over. In 1986 Busby and Amos Otis were inducted as the inaugural members of the Royals Hall of Fame.

While Busby was rehabilitating, former Royals play-by-play announcer Buddy Blattner recommended that he get into broadcasting. In 1981 Busby worked as a weekend sports anchor with the local Kansas City NBC affiliate. In 1982 he had two job offers, from the Boston Red Sox and Texas Rangers. He chose the Rangers because they were closer to home, and in Boston he would be filling the big shoes of the legendary Ken "Hawk" Harrelson.[40] Busby became one of the rare ex-athletes to become a play-by-play announcer. He described how this came to be: "When I first started out, I was very fortunate to have one of the all-time greats in broadcasting, Merle Harmon, that I was paired with down here in Texas, and Merle made it a point to get me to learn how to do play-by-play and help him out during ballgames. He didn't have to do it for nine innings of play-by-play. So the first spring training that we worked together, he and I went out to games that we weren't broadcasting and took a tape recorder and Merle made me do five, six, seven innings of play-by-play. Then we would go back to the hotel after the game and listen to it. He would critique me and give me pointers and really got me going. If it hadn't been for someone like that taking the time and making the effort to help me get settled in to being a broadcaster, I never would have done it. Merle was one of the nicest people in the world. You don't find many people in this business or for that matter in most competitive businesses who are willing to take the time to train somebody else and help them advance themselves."[41]

In 1996 Busby worked as the play-by-play announcer for the Royals alongside his close friend, Paul Splittorff. Busby struggled with his retirement from baseball for many years even though he had made a career as a broadcaster. "I always said that it doesn't bother me and that it was part of the game, and that was a bunch of garbage," he said. "It bothered me. It hurt. That injury and the subsequent injuries stripped me of my identity."[42] Busby had what he would describe as a "rebirth" in late 1997. "I finally got OK with me being me. Just saying, 'OK this is who you are, this where you are, and what do we do from here on out?'"[43] Busby spent more time with his children. He took a year off from broadcasting and began working with high-school pitchers, teaching them the finer points of pitching.

As of 2016, Busby was the play-by-play announcer for the Rangers. He said being a former player gave him the advantage of having a very comfortable conversation with his partner, Tom Grieve.[44] Their broadcasts have been described as "watching baseball, telling stories, eating cookies and pastries, and most of all, having fun."[45]

Notes

1 Gib Twyman, "No-Hit Hurler? 'Not Me! Says Busby," *The Sporting News*, July 6, 1974: 13.

2 Wil A. Linkugel and Edward J. Pappas, They Tasted Glory: Among the Missing at the Baseball Hall of Fame (Jefferson, North Carolina: McFarland, 1998), 128.

3 Author's interview with Steve Busby on April 20, 2016 (hereafter Busby interview).

4 Randy Covitz, "Busby's heart lasted longer than his arm," *Kansas City Star* June 5, 1986: 3B.

5 Busby player file at the National Baseball Hall of Fame library.

6 Busby interview.

7 Rosemarie Ross, "Busby: Can He Win 20 in His First Full Season?" *The Sporting News*, April 21, 1973: 20.

8 William Barry Furlong, "0-Hit Kid Steve No Stereotype," unidentified newspaper clipping from Busby player file.

9 Twyman.

10 Ibid.

11 Covitz.

12 Sid Bordman, "'Steve Buzz's Bomb Act Captures Tigers Again," *The Sporting News*, May 12, 1973: 12.

13 Ross.

14 April 2014 interview with Steve Busby, www.clubhouseconversation.com/2014/05/steve-busby/.

15 Ross.

16 Busby interview.

17 Covitz.

18 Busby interview.

19 Covitz.

20 Busby interview.

21 Seattle Mariners relief pitcher John Montague tied the mark in 1977, and David Wells of the New York Yankees broke the record and set a new mark of 38 innings on May 24, 1998. Busby's USC teammate, Jim Barr, held the National league record of 41 set in 1972 and this wasn't broken until 2009 by Mark Buehrle. Yusmeirio Petit of the San Francisco Giants set a new record of 46 in 2014.

22 Joe McGuff, "20-Win Champagne Has Flat Taste for Busby," *The Sporting News*, October 5, 1974: 22.

23 McGuff, "Player Yelps Following the Bouncing of Lau," *The Sporting News*, October 19, 1975: 30.

24 Bordman, "Healy Gets Healthy and So Does Royals Catching," The Sporting News, June 14, 1975: 14.

25 Ron Fimrite, "Stress, Strain and Pain," Sports Illustrated, August 14, 1978.

26 Bill Reiter, "Finding Steve Busby," *Kansas City Star*, April 1, 2007.

27 McGuff, "Busby, Little Spruce Up Royals' Hill Staff," *The Sporting News*, May 8, 1976: 18.

28 Ibid.

29 McGuff, "Swift Wolhford's Magic Glove Wows Royals," *The Sporting News*, May 22, 1976: 19.

30 "Busby Hurt Again," *The Sporting News*, May 29, 1976: 30.

31 "Busby Still a Puzzle," *The Sporting News*, July 3, 1976: 24.

32 Ibid.

33 "Royals," *The Sporting News*, July 10, 1976: 30.

34 McGuff, "Pitching Shy Royals Storm Heights with Bats," *The Sporting News*, July 24, 1976: 13.

35 Fimrite.

36 "Busby Rebuilding Family Life, Career," *Chicago Tribune*, April 21, 1978.

37 Covitz.

38 Ibid.

39 Jim Reeves, "Rangers Roundup," *The Sporting News*, July 20, 1984: 49.

40 Busby interview.

41 April 2014 interview with Steve Busby, clubhouseconversation.com/2014/05/steve-busby/.

42 Bill Reiter, "Finding Steve Busby," *Kansas City Star*, April 1, 2007.

43 Ibid.

44 Busby interview.

45 Jim Reagan, "Steve Busby: Locked Into the Job He Loves," *Durant* (Oklahoma) *Democrat*, March 19, 2016.

JOHNNY DAMON

BY MARK S. STERNMAN

A run-scoring-machine leadoff hitter with great speed (408 career steals) and good power (235 homers), Johnny Damon had "good range defensively but ... one of the worst outfield arms in the big leagues."[1] Offensively, Damon had his best years with Kansas City in 2000 and Boston in 2004, and won World Series titles with both the Red Sox in 2004 and the Yankees in 2009. Damon's legacy largely stems from his starring role in leading the Red Sox to the franchise's first championship in 86 years, notoriety that says as much about the outsized role of baseball in the Boston landscape and Damon's media-friendly personality as it does about Damon's on-field accomplishments.

Johnny Damon owes his life to the Vietnam War. His parents, Jimmy and Yome, met in his mother's native Thailand, where his father served as a US Army sergeant. Yome's father practiced holistic medicine, and his mother farmed. Yome gave birth to James Damon in Bangkok in 1971 and to Johnny in Kansas two years later. The family moved first to Illinois before settling in Florida, where Jimmy worked as a security guard and Yome as an office cleaner. "Johnny was like Yome, all nervous energy," an observer wrote. "Once, when he was 14, he took his mother's car to Daytona. ... Stopped by a police officer, Johnny said he'd forgotten his license. When asked his name, he gave the name of his big brother. The ruse worked ... when the officer didn't show up for the court date."[2]

Leading up to the 1992 draft, *The Sporting News* called Damon, then a senior, "probably ... the best high school player available this year. 'He has great speed, is extremely strong, and his throwing has improved,' [Damon's] high school coach Danny Allie says. 'He's also got great power ... and 3.8-second speed to first base. A lot of guys have compared him to Ken Griffey Jr.'"[3]

Kansas City drafted Damon with the 35th pick in the first round of the 1992 draft. "A straight-A student in high school, he walked away from a baseball scholarship at the University of Florida to sign with the Royals for $300,000"[4] Aside from his future teammate Derek Jeter, Damon would have the best career of his fellow first-round draftees.

Displaying the same skills that he would show in the majors, Damon hit for average, stole scores of bases, and flashed occasional power in the minors. He won the J.G. Taylor Spink Award as the National Association Minor League Player of the Year for his performance in Wichita in 1995 even though he did not play a full season in Double A that year.

Called up from Wichita, Damon made his major-league debut against Seattle on August 12, 1995, leading off and playing center field. Facing Tim Belcher, Damon popped out to short in his first AL plate appearance. After flying out in his second at-bat, he tripled and scored in the fifth inning against Belcher, had an RBI single in the sixth off Salomon Torres, and singled against Torres again in the eighth as the Royals won, 7-2.

On August 31, Kansas City trailed Milwaukee 6-5 going into the bottom of the ninth. Damon hit his first homer in the majors to tie the game off Mike Fetters, and the Royals won in unusual walk-off fashion thanks to a bases-loaded throwing error on a pickoff attempt by Fetters. Damon's teammates had quickly taken to the talented rookie. "He's our sparkplug right now," first baseman Wally Joyner said.[5] "He's going to do just about everything you could want...," Royals manager Bob Boone said. "I'm pleased he's this good. But I'm not surprised."[6]

On August 10, 1996, Damon set a career high with seven RBIs in an 18-3 win over the Angels. But "he slumped near season's end ... as his confidence fell."[7]

After beginning 1997 as Kansas City's fourth outfielder, Damon rebounded somewhat although he had a career-worst 61.5 percent stolen-base rate, perhaps due to knee soreness that worsened in July and would necessitate offseason surgery.[8] Retrospectively, Damon credited Tony Muser, who replaced Boone for the second half of the season, with his resurgence. Damon recalled, "My first couple years, I didn't play every day. I would sit against left-handers sometimes. And then when Muser started managing ... he said, 'Guess what? You're going to be batting leadoff for me every day, and the only times you're not going to play is if you break something.'"[9]

Damon scored 100 runs for the first of 10 times in his career in 1998. In 1999, he hit over .300 for the first of five times for a Kansas City team that went 64-97 in spite of a strong outfield with Damon in left, Carlos Beltran in center, and Jermaine Dye in right.

Damon's improved play ironically shortened his time with the Royals, as the small-market Kansas City franchise risked losing him for nothing as he approached free agency after the 2001 season. *The Sporting News* reported rumors of Damon going to the Yankees for Alfonso Soriano,[10] to the Mariners for Griffey Jr.,[11] or to the Dodgers for Eric Gagne.[12]

"There are clubs with higher payrolls in bigger markets that would give anything to have Johnny, because he's the one piece that a club thinks can cement the playoffs or World Series," said Royals general manager Herk Robinson.[13]

Because of or despite the rumors, Damon had his best year in a Kansas City uniform in 2000 with career highs in plate appearances (741), at-bats (655), runs (136), hits (214), doubles (42), steals (46), batting average (.327), on-base percentage (.382), slugging percentage (.495), OPS (.877), and total bases (324). He led the AL in both runs and steals.

In June, the Royals reportedly offered Damon a three-year contract for $15 million. "But Damon is adamant about a five-year deal," *The Sporting News* reported, adding, "He also labeled the average yearly salary Boston gave Jose Offerman, $6.5 million, as his 'starting point.'"[14]

Damon batted .436 in July 2000, .382 in August, and .322 in September. Kansas City had tapped Allard Baird as GM to replace Robinson. Baird, the scout who had signed Damon for the Royals, upped the KC contract offer to $32 million over five years, which agent Scott Boras rejected on Damon's behalf.[15]

Recognizing that Kansas City could not keep Damon, Baird shipped him to Oakland as part of a three-way deal that also involved Tampa Bay. "I was in Kansas City for five years," Damon said. "I had a home there. I had my family there. I had everything. It was great for me there, except for losing."[16]

Damon also liked hitting in Kansas City. "It plays fair. The waterfalls are cool. When I came up in the league, that was one of the toughest places to hit and to hit home runs. But as I developed, and as the years have gone by, it has become one of the easiest for me."[17]

Damon left the losing behind with the Royals. The A's had gone 91-70 in 2000 before falling to the Yankees in five games in the ALDS. Damon thought that he could help make Oakland take the next step. "Looking at this team on paper, I think we're the team to beat out there," Damon said. ... "This is a great situation to be in."[18]

With Damon, Oakland improved to 102-60, but Seattle, which had also won 91 games in 2000, captured 116 in 2001. Damon did not enjoy his first trip as a visiting player to Kansas City, where "a radio station sponsored a 'Boo Johnny Damon Day' ... including a sweepstakes for a free big-screen TV if he committed an error."[19]

The A's returned to the playoffs via the wild card but did so with only modest contributions from Damon, who failed to hit 10 homers for the only time from 1998 to 2009. Damon blamed it "partly (on) the A's strategy that calls for hitters to work the count to tire opposing pitchers. As a result, he said, he was less aggressive and found himself facing more two-strike counts."[20] Oakland would again face New York in the ALDS.

The series began in the Bronx. In his first career playoff game, Damon went 4-for-4 with a walk and two steals as the A's won 5-3. In Game Two, Damon doubled off Andy Pettitte and tripled off Mariano Rivera. Damon scored an insurance run after the triple as the A's triumphed 2-0 and needed just one win to advance to the ALCS. "It's hard to believe he was being called one of baseball's biggest disappointments at midseason and was being followed by rumors that he would be traded ... because his contract was up at season's end. 'I know that he was very hard on himself for a time,' A's manager Art Howe said. 'Sometimes it just takes a person time to get adjusted to his surroundings.'"[21]

Neither Damon nor Oakland could keep up the good start. Damon went 3-for-13 as the Yankees won the last three games, eliminating the A's again and ending Damon's brief sojourn in Oakland as he signed with Boston as a free agent. "Damon wanted to play closer to his Florida home, where he and his wife, Angie, are raising twins who [turned] 3 in [2002]. 'Oakland did everything in their power to sign me,' Damon said. 'The biggest thing was the moving back to the Eastern time zone. It boiled down to my family.'"[22]

Boston won 82 games in 2001, but 93 games with Damon in 2002. "I had a feeling about this team when I signed in the offseason because of the attitude I bring," said Damon ... "[W]ith guys like Rickey Henderson, Carlos Baerga, and Tony Clark ... I feel we can do something special here."[23]

Damon brought both swagger and swat to Boston. "Damon has ... been ... the heart of the team," said [Sox teammate Pedro] Martinez. "He has done everything. He gets on base. He puts pressure on the other teams — on the catcher and the pitcher."[24] Damon led the American League with 11 triples, made his first All-Star team, and "benefited from the tutelage of hitting instructor Dwight Evans. Early in spring training, Evans noticed that Damon was releasing his top hand too soon, and he got Damon to keep both hands on the bat."[25]

In 2001, Damon started poorly but finished strongly. He did the reverse in 2002 when he "went through a difficult divorce from his high-school sweetheart, which may have affected him even more deeply than his active role in labor negotiations and the knee injury that slowed him but did not require postseason surgery."[26] Boston failed to make the playoffs in 2002, but reached the postseason in the remaining three years of Damon's Hub tenure.

Damon must have had flashbacks entering the 2003 ALDS. In his second playoffs, he faced Oakland, the team that had first taken him to the postseason. As in 2001, the A's won the first two games and needed just one more win to advance to the ALCS. Oakland lost the third game, 3-1, and the fourth game, 5-4, thanks in part to Damon hitting a two-run homer (the first of his 10 career playoff bombs) and throwing out Jose Guillen attempting to go first-to-third on a single.

Facing Barry Zito, Boston trailed 1-0 going into the top of the sixth of the deciding game. Jason Varitek homered to tie the game, and Damon followed with a walk. With two outs and two on, Manny Ramirez homered to give Boston a 4-1 edge. Behind Martinez, the Red Sox led 4-2 in the bottom of the seventh with two outs "when Jermaine Dye lifted a pop fly into shallow center. [Second baseman Damian] Jackson ... sprinted into the outfield ... while Damon came charging in, calling for the ball. The ball ... landed in Jackson's ... glove when ... the right side of Jackson's head squarely struck Damon's head, also on the right side."[27]

Damon left the game in the next inning for a pinch-hitter, and the Red Sox held on to win in spite of Damon's departure due to a concussion. Later that week, Damon admitted, "I had no idea what was going on for the next four or five hours. ... I was in really bad shape."[28]

Boston faced New York in an epic ALCS. Damon missed the first two games before returning to go 3-for-4 in Game Three. But he went just 1-for-16 in the final four games. Damon missed a key chance to blow the deciding contest wide open when Boston led 4-0 in the top of the fourth with runners on first and third and none out as Mike Mussina replaced Roger Clemens. Mussina fanned Varitek and induced a double play from Damon to keep the margin at four runs. The

Yankees rallied to win the game and the pennant, 6-5, on Aaron Boone's 11th-inning walk-off homer.

Damon and Boston got their revenge in 2004. Damon set career highs with 94 RBIs and 76 walks. After not getting his hair cut in the offseason, Damon became "a cult figure virtually overnight."[29] As the longtime *Boston Globe* columnist Bob Ryan opined, "Johnny Damon is, and has always been, a good player, beard or no beard, hair down to his tushie or hair neatly cropped. He is a leadoff man whose job is to get on base and ignite an offense, and if you measure his value by looking at runs you'd have to say he's been pretty good."[30]

A master marketer, Damon rebranded the supposedly cursed Red Sox as carefree idiots, commenting, "Maybe it's not the greatest thing to say, but for the most part, we are. We just play the game. ... We're not too bright of [*sic*] guys. In essence, we're idiots. We go out there and swing the bat as hard as we can. We make fun. ... We've got the long hair, the ponytails."[31]

Boston swept Anaheim in the ALDS to set up an ALCS rematch against New York. The Red Sox dropped the first two games in the Bronx as Damon struggled. "It starts with me," said Damon, who fanned four times in four at-bats in the Game One loss, and followed with an 0-for-4, including one more strikeout, in Game Two. "I take full responsibility for these two games. ... I'm very disappointed with myself."[32]

Boston returned to Fenway Park only to get shellacked 19-8. After the rout, Damon faced the media and confessed, "We're very upset. And we're definitely stunned. We thought we had the better team coming in and right now it doesn't look that way."[33]

The prospects of the Red Sox brightened after Boston won the next three games to force an elimination contest. Damon led off with a single and stole second, but a relay from Hideki Matsui to Jeter to Jorge Posada cut him down trying to score on a Ramirez single. The Red Sox led 2-0 in the second inning when Damon came up to bat against Javier Vazquez, who had just relieved Kevin Brown. On Vazquez's first pitch, Damon hit a grand slam that gave Boston an insurmountable lead. Damon later hit a two-run homer against Vazquez as well en route to a 10-3 win. "To do this against the Yankees in their ballpark is definitely a very special feeling," Damon said after the win that gave the Red Sox the AL pennant.[34]

Damon's postseason power continued as Boston sought to end its 86 years of baseball misery. He "ignited the Red Sox ... with his left-field double in the first inning off Woody Williams that put the team on its way to an 11-9 win over the St. Louis Cardinals in Game 1 of the World Series. ... 'This is the World Series, so you want to make an impact out there,' Damon said."[35]

Damon started the championship clincher with "a rope into the Cardinals' bullpen on the game's fourth pitch from Jason Marquis."[36] He later tripled as Boston swept St. Louis to win the 2004 World Series.

Helping bring the title back to a rabid baseball-championship-starved fan base transformed Damon from a baseball cult figure to a boldfaced name with broader celebrity appeal in Boston,[37] partially fulfilling a prediction Damon made at his post-signing press conference in Boston: "When we win a World Series," he said, "we're going to be put on a pedestal and be immortalized forever."[38] In Damon's case, the adulation lasted only a year, but the bitterness that began in 2006 lasted several seasons.[39]

In December 2004, he married for the second time, to Michelle Mangan, an event deemed worthy of a photo and extensive coverage on the society page of the *Boston Globe*.[40] But the Red Sox front office declined to engage with Damon as his contract approached its conclusion at the end of the 2005 season. "I'd like to finish my career here and get locked up for a long time," Damon said. "I know it's always been Red Sox policy to wait until after the season, but that can get hairy. ... I'm in a good spot ... but the Red Sox know that this is the best spot for me personally."[41]

For the second and last time in his career, Damon made the All-Star team in 2005, this time as a starter. He also had a 29-game hitting streak that ended in a loss to Tampa Bay. "I definitely felt like if I could have gotten past today, I could have taken it further," said Damon. "The funny thing is, the swing really hasn't felt great during this streak, and I'm amazed that it got up to 29."[42]

Boston's quick dismissal from the playoffs after an ALDS sweep by Chicago made Damon's regular-season accomplishments less meaningful. With the Red Sox trailing by a run in the sixth inning of the final game with two outs and the bases loaded, Damon worked the count full against Orlando Hernandez. In his autobiography, published after the 2004 World Series, Damon had mockingly touched on the unique stylings of Hernandez, writing, "He's one of those 50-year-old Cuban pitchers with all the funky motions and all the funny pitches and different speeds, but he knows what to do. ... If he doesn't have his good stuff, he starts innovating."[43]

Hernandez did indeed know what to do. "After a foul, El Duque fooled Damon with a wicked breaking ball that wound up in the dirt. Damon committed with his swing and was rung up to end the inning. 'The right pitch at the right time,' conceded Damon."[44] In his final plate appearance in a Boston uniform, Damon struck out swinging again for the second out of the ninth inning in a game the Red Sox lost, 5-3.

A month later, Boras began advocating for his free-agent client with a paper that "confidently predicts that Damon will join the 3,000 hit club in 2012, and ... dares to place Damon in the company of Hall of Famers if he produces through 2015 the way he has [from 2002-2005]."[45]

The Red Sox offered Damon $42 million over four years,[46] but he signed with the Yankees for $52 million over four years instead. The *Boston Globe* editorialized on Damon's departure. In a particularly poor piece of Christmas Eve prognostication, Boston's paper of record wrote, "Marvelous as the beloved Idiot was in that championship season of '04, Red Sox fans needs to cast a cold eye on the future value of a weak-armed 32-year-old center fielder stationed in 2009 in the great expanse of Yankee Stadium."[47]

In 2006, Damon hit a career-high 24 homers in his first season in the Bronx, a figure he matched in 2009, where he brought great value to the Yankees outfield. In August 2006, a Boston writer conceded that Damon "has been worth every bit of the extra $12 million George Steinbrenner ponied up to take him away from the Red Sox. The Yankees got a very good player while taking one away from their biggest competition."[48]

While New York won the division with 97 wins in 2006, Damon could not deliver in the playoffs against Detroit, which knocked out New York in four ALDS games. Michelle gave birth to her first child and Johnny's third after the 2006 season. (They had a second child together after the 2008 season.) The Yanks slipped to 94 wins in 2007, which secured a wild card. In the ALDS, New York dropped the first two games at Cleveland and trailed 3-1 in Game Three going into the bottom of the fifth in the Bronx. Melky Cabrera hit an RBI single to cut the deficit to a single run, and Damon then hit a three-run homer as the Yanks rallied to an 8-4 win. But the Indians won the fourth game, meaning that Damon and New York had in consecutive years lost the ALDS in four games.

Under new manager Joe Girardi, the Yankees regressed and missed the playoffs in 2008. For the first time since 1999, Damon made most of his outfield starts in left rather than center field. His lighter defensive responsibilities may have led to his improved offensive performance. On June 7, Damon went 6-for-6 against Kansas City to tie a team record for hits in a game. His two-run single in the eighth tied the game at 10-10. After a David DeJesus homer in the ninth put the Royals back up 11-10, Posada tied the game with a homer in the bottom of the ninth before Damon hit a walk-off RBI single to give New York a wild 12-11 win.

In 2009, Damon relinquished his leadoff role to Jeter[49] and his center-field spot to Cabrera. The Yankees won 103 games for the first time since 2002 and got past the ALDS for the first time since 2004.

Damon made his most memorable contribution in pinstripes in Game Four of the World Series at Philadelphia. With the game tied, 4-4, two outs, and none on in the top of the ninth, Damon faced Brad Lidge and won a "nine-pitch battle ... that sparked the winning rally. After going down, 0-2, he fouled off a number of pitches before lining a single into short left field. ... Girardi called it 'an incredible at-bat.'"[50]

With Mark Teixeira up, the Phillies shifted to the right side of the infield with the switch-hitter batting lefty against the righty Lidge. Damon took off for second on the first pitch. After third baseman Pedro Feliz fielded the short-hop throw, Damon, after a brief hesitation, popped out of his slide and took off for the uncovered third base with Feliz in futile pursuit.[51] Damon received credit for two stolen bases on the play and, from one longtime Philadelphia baseball writer, credit for making the transformative play of the whole World Series.[52] "I'm just glad that when I started running, I still had some of my young legs behind me," Damon quipped.[53]

Lidge, possibly unnerved by his failure to cover third, then hit Teixeira. Alex Rodriguez doubled in Damon for a 5-4 lead, and Posada singled in two more runners to put New York up 7-4. Rivera preserved the win, putting New York up three games to one in the Series that the Yankees took in six games.

Seemingly picking a good time to go back into free agency, Damon and his agent Boras played a good hand weakly. The Yankees offered Damon a two-year contract for $14 million; Boras countered with $20 million over two years. New York turned down Boras, and Damon signed with Detroit for $8 million for the 2010 season.[54] Leaving the Tigers after a year, Damon joined Tampa Bay for 2011 and played in 150 games for the first time since 2004. The Rays made the playoffs, and Damon, batting fifth as the DH, got Tampa on the board with a two-run homer in Game One off C.J. Wilson in the only contest the Rays won as Texas took the ALDS.

Playing for his fourth team in four years, Damon signed with Cleveland after the 2012 season had already begun. Damon lasted less than four months with the Indians before the team released him. In November 2012, Damon joined Thailand as it attempted to qualify for the 2013 World Baseball Classic. "I'm enjoying the experience of playing for my mom's country," Damon wrote in a text message to a reporter.[55]

In spite of his desire to keep playing, Damon's career ended with Thailand. As a famous former athlete, Damon appeared on reality TV shows such as *Celebrity Apprentice* in 2015 and *Dancing with the Stars* in 2018.

Baseball analyst Jay Jaffe aptly summed up Damon's career: "He was a very good and very popular player for a long time, but not quite enough for Cooperstown."[56] Underappreciated in the smaller media markets of Kansas City and Oakland, Damon thrived in a leadership role in Boston and continued to excel as a member of a strong supporting cast in the Bronx before becoming a baseball vagabond for the remainder of his impressive career as a professional hitter.

Notes

1 Steve Rock, "Kansas City," *The Sporting News*, May 1, 2000: 36. Damon had a good glove to go along with his weak arm. His "major league-best streak of 249 games without an error ended … on August 31[, 2002] when he could not cleanly come up with a ground ball that turned out to be a game-winning hit. Damon had not committed an error in 592 chances dating back to August 27, 2000." Michael Silverman, "Boston Red Sox," *The Sporting News*, September 16, 2002: 63.

2 Gordon Edes, "Fortune of Soldier," *Boston Globe*, February 10, 2002.

3 Mike Eisenbath, "Martinez Follows in the Big Man's Footsteps," *The Sporting News*, May 11, 1992: 34.

4 Bob Hohler, "Johnny on the Spot," *Boston Globe*, March 29, 2002.

5 Dick Kaegel, "Kansas City Royals," *The Sporting News*, September 11, 1995: 28.

6 Alan Schwarz, "The Meaning of Johnny Damon," *Baseball America*, February 19-March 3, 1996: 12. This article and several others referenced below come from the National Baseball Hall of Fame and Museum's file on Damon. Thanks to Reference Librarian Cassidy Lent for scanning the Damon file.

7 La Velle E. Neal III, "Kansas City Royals," *The Sporting News*, November 25, 1996: 31.

8 Dick Kaegel, "Kansas City Royals," *The Sporting News*, September 1, 1997: 35.

9 "When It Clicked: Johnny Damon, Yankees," *Washington Post*, September 6, 2009.

10 Luciana Chavez, "Kansas City," *The Sporting News*, December 13, 1999: 65.

11 Jon Heyman, "Inside Dish," *The Sporting News*, January 10, 2000: 61.

12 Jason Reid, "Los Angeles," *The Sporting News*, July 17, 2000: 56.

13 Jeff Pearlman, "Force Three: The Hard-Hitting Young Kansas City Outfield Storms to the Top," *Sports Illustrated*, April 17, 2000.

14 Steve Rock, "Kansas City," *The Sporting News*, June 19, 2000: 29.

15 Gordon Edes, "He Can't Give Sox Royal Treatment," *Boston Globe*, November 12, 2000.

16 Chris Snow, "Damon Finds a Home Again," *Boston Globe*, June 8, 2002.

17 Steve DiMeglio, "Five Minutes with … Johnny Damon," *USA Today Sports Weekly*, May 19-25, 2004: 24.

18 Thomas Hill, "With A's, He's Johnny Dangerously," *New York Daily News*, February 28, 2001.

19 Bob Hohler, "Damon Loyal, but Not a Royal," *Boston Globe*, April 21, 2002.

20 Bob Hohler, "Leadoff Man Damon Sets a Positive Tone," *Boston Globe*, February 20, 2002.

21 Roger Rubin, "Damon Center of Revival," *New York Daily News*, October 13, 2001.

22 Bob Hohler and Gordon Edes, "Damon Touches Down," *Boston Globe*, December 21, 2001.

23 Gordon Edes, "No Waiting Damon," *Boston Globe*, April 23, 2002.

24 Michael Vega, "Starring Role for Damon," *Boston Globe*, June 27, 2002.

25 Nick Cafardo, "Damon Touches Bases," *Boston Globe*, May 1, 2002.

26 Gordon Edes, "Damon Not Buying A's Owner's Story," *Boston Globe*, March 17, 2003.

27 Gordon Edes, "Damon Hospitalized after Collision," *Boston Globe*, October 7, 2003. Damon and Jackson "couldn't hear one another in the loud playoff din, which is not uncommon." Roger Rubin, "Head Clear, Damon Takes Center Stage," *New York Daily News*, October 11, 2003.

28 Peter Botte, "Damon Likely Out Till Game 3," *New York Daily News*, October 9, 2003.

29 Jackie MacMullan, "Johnny on the Spot," *Boston Globe*, October 15, 2004.

30 Bob Ryan, "Damon Has Been Johnny on the Spot in This Heat Wave," *Boston Globe*, July 10, 2004.

31 Nick Cafardo, "Damon Is Having a Recurrence of Migraines," *Boston Globe*, October 8, 2004.

32 Kevin Paul Dupont, "A Low Point from the Top of the Order," *Boston Globe*, October 14, 2004. Damon credited Mussina for his sparkling performance in the opener. "He was pretty awesome. For him to make me look silly like that all day, that doesn't happen too often," said Damon, who was also fanned by Tom Gordon for the first out in the eighth. Peter Botte, "Damon Still in Swing," *New York Daily News*, October 14, 2004.

33 Roger Rubin, "Bosox Tipping Caps to Yanks but Damon Still Has Faith," *New York Daily News*, October 17, 2004.

34 Julian Garcia, "Damon's Suddenly Mane Man," *New York Daily News*, October 21, 2004.

35 Nick Cafardo, "Damon Takes the Lead," *Boston Globe*, October 24, 2004.

36 Jim McCabe, "Again, the Winners Were Happy Followers of Damon," *Boston Globe*, October 28, 2004.

37 "Damon was listed in the *Boston Herald* gossip column 64 times in 2004, or roughly once every five days." Tom Verducci, "The Yankee Clipper," *Sports Illustrated*, February 13, 2006: 64.

38 Bob Hohler, "Johnny Damon, Superstar," *Boston Globe*, July 11, 2005.

39 "I get booed. They absolutely despise me. I just have to say, 'You're welcome for '04. You're welcome for making it fun again over there.'" Peter Abraham, "Damon's Got Ear to Ground," *Boston Globe*, April 11, 2011.

40 Carol Beggy and Mark Shanahan, "Damon's Wedding Is a Rocking Hit for All," *Boston Globe*, December 31, 2004. Mangan also briefly became a minor media celebrity in Boston. A profile of her revealed that "Mangan and Damon both like Boston. 'It's a lot prettier than New York,' she says though there has been talk that he will head to the Yankees should the call come. 'I can't see him in a Yankees uniform,' Mangan says." Bella English, "Batting Around with Michelle Mangan," *Boston Globe*, October 1, 2005. Damon signed with the Yankees three months and two days after this article appeared.

41 Nick Cafardo, "Damon Enjoying Star Turn," *Boston Globe*, March 10, 2005.

42 Mike Petraglia, "Damon's Hit Streak Snapped at 29 games," MLB.com, July 19, 2005.

43 Johnny Damon with Peter Golenbock, *Idiot* (New York: Crown Publishers, 2005), 201. In a masterstroke of snarky brevity, columnist Dan Shaughnessy called the book "a work often compared with Tolstoy's 'Anna Karenina' and Dostoyevsky's 'Notes From the Underground.'" Dan Shaughnessy, "He Must Have His Reasons, but What Are They?" *Boston Globe*, August 25, 2010.

44 Dan Shaughnessy, "Curses, Again," *Boston Globe*, October 8, 2005.

45 Gordon Edes, "What to Read into All This? Some Odd Chapters on Epstein, Damon," *Boston Globe*, November 23, 2005. In fact, Damon got his last hit, number 2,769, in 2012. He received a paltry 1.9 percent share of the 2018 Hall of Fame balloting. As Shaughnessy wrote, "I just got through checking out Scott Boras's dossier on Johnny, and until now I had no idea Johnny was

better than both Willie Mays and Joe DiMaggio. What a crock." Dan Shaughnessy, "Is Johnny Damon Worth $10M a Year?" *Boston Globe,* November 27, 2005.

46 Gordon Edes and Chris Snow, "Damon Jumps to Yankees," *Boston Globe*, December 21, 2005.

47 "Steinbrenner's Folly," *Boston Globe*, December 24, 2005.

48 Nick Cafardo, "Damon Is Long Gone But Not Hard to Find," *Boston Globe*, August 19, 2006.

49 "When Girardi made the move, he stated a number of times that 'Johnny is really good at moving the runners over.' Clearly, the move was made to keep Jeter from hitting into so many double plays, as well.... Damon also pointed out that the move allowed him to really go for the long ball every once in a while." Kevin Kernan, *Girardi: Passion in Pinstripes* (Chicago: Triumph Books, 2012), 174.

50 Nick Cafardo, "Damon Smarter Than Most Idiots," *Boston Globe*, November 2, 2009.

51 youtube.com/watch?v=cCfmj6mnN0I (accessed May 21, 2018).

52 Jayson Stark, "Damon Steals the Show in Game 4," ESPN, November 1, 2009.

53 Nick Cafardo, "Damon, Yankees on the Verge," *Boston Globe*, November 2, 2009.

54 Bob Klapsich, "Johnny Damon, Scott Boras Really Blew This One," NorthJersey.com, February 23, 2010.

55 Benjamin Hoffman, "Unsigned for 2013, Damon Takes an International Step to a Possible Last Hurrah," *New York Times*, November 14, 2012.

56 Jay Jaffe, "One-and-Dones Pt. 3: Johnny Damon, Hideki Matsui Were Popular, but not Hall of Famers," *Sports Illustrated*, December 28, 2017.

MARK GUBICZA

BY STEPHEN KATSOULIS

(On arriving at Kauffman Stadium for the first time)
"As we drive up we see the Crown. There was a little mist and I'm thinking 'this is an unbelievable sight.' The lights are on. It doesn't get any better than that. Then all of a sudden we pull in, we go into the clubhouse, and I said, 'This is bigger than my house at home in Philly, and it has more than one shower.'... I said, 'I love this place.' Then later that night to cap it off, I call my parents. I'm trying to explain to them about how beautiful the field was, the locker room, the big crown. I said, 'Guess where I'm calling from?' They go, where? I said, 'I'm calling from George Brett's house. I'm living with George Brett. ... He let us live in his house.' I said, 'Dad, this is a dream.' He goes, 'Son, never wake up.' And I haven't woke up."
-- Mark Gubicza's Royals Hall of Fame induction speech, March 27, 2012

For Mark Gubicza, it was a dream realized for both a father and his son. Mark's father, Tony, pitched in the White Sox organization before a shoulder injury cut short his career. Post-baseball, Tony became a mail carrier and full-time coach and catcher for his son.

"He caught me all the time. There were a lot of times he'd catch me with his bare hands."[1]

Mark was born on August 14, 1962 in Philadelphia. Athletic success did not fall just on his father's side of the family. His uncle Robert Ames, the brother of his mother, Patricia, played on the 1954 NCAA champion LaSalle Explorers basketball team. So it was no surprise that baseball and basketball ran through Mark's blood and would lead to a constant debate in his mind throughout his formative years.

Besides starring on the court and on the diamond, Mark played football and hockey, and even boxed. However, "[H]e wasn't really good inside the ring, so that didn't last long."[2] In Little League, Mark pitched and played shortstop. He recalled a stretch where he had 57 hits in just 17 games. Whether at the plate or on the mound, there was no doubt Mark knew what he wanted to be when he grew up.

"Most kids wanted to be a fireman or police officer where I grew up. I only wanted to play in 'The Show.'"

Mark continued to grow on the field dominating the junior and senior leagues of his neighborhood, while at the same time growing his passion of the game watching his beloved Phillies. Despite having attended dozens of games at Veterans Stadium, he had never been to a game with his father until the chilly evening of October 21, 1980. It was Game Six of the World Series. Mike Schmidt and the Phillies trying to win their first World Series, taking on, of all teams, the Royals, led by George Brett. It was that night, Gubicza called "the best day of his life," he and his father watching as Tug McGraw struck out Willie Wilson, delivering the city its first World Series championship.

At the time, Gubicza was a high-school star. Under his father's tutelage, he had adapted a drop-and-drive pitching mechanic, emulating Tom Seaver. He was able to generate velocity on his fastball, hitting 92 mph on the radar gun. Being 6-foot-5 did not hurt, either. His curveball was topping out at 81-82 mph and he was quickly becoming a star at William Penn Charter School. Besides Seaver, he took a little from his idol, Hall of Famer Jim Palmer.

"I like the way he gets the job done, there's no wasted energy in his pitching motion and he's so darn consistent."[3]

Because of city rules, Gubicza was unable to play varsity baseball as a freshman. But once he was eligible, he was a three-year starter. He also started at forward his junior and senior seasons for the Quaker basketball team. He had decisions to make. Basketball or baseball? Shortstop or pitcher? Gubicza was getting some college hoop offers and he knew he could be a successful hitter in the big leagues, but his arm was the way to go. He knew it, the colleges knew it ... and baseball scouts knew it. Gubicza was named to the all-city league as a sophomore, junior and senior. His numbers his final season with Penn Charter were off the charts. 8-1, 0.48 ERA, 83 strikeouts, and just 27 hits allowed in 58⅔ innings. His team won the Inter-AC title.[4] Gubicza was named the *Philadelphia Daily News'* All-City Pitcher of the Year, picked by coaches, who declared, "Gubicza earned the award as far back as late April, the first time we saw him pitch."[5]

Just as impressive as his stats were the number of college coaches and major-league scouts who were taking notice. Pro scout Brad Kohler described some of Gubicza's attributes:

"Live arm. Will have above avg. fastball. Gets ball over with ability to get ahead of hitters. Many college offers. Loves BB (baseball). Definite ML prospect."[6]

"It was very odd and somewhat uncomfortable when I looked up and saw scouts with radar guns at all of my games," Gubicza said.

"My dad gave me the best advice: Just focus on what you can do and the rest will work its way out."

Colleges were also calling. Gubicza made the rounds. "Visiting colleges during my recruitment process was pricey," he said. "I met coach (Bear) Bryant at Alabama, Coach K (Mike Krzyzewski) at Duke, met Herschel (Walker) and Dominique (Wilkins) at Georgia. Visited 'The Ohio State' and realized how big that campus was. And had one last visit to choose from (USC [University of Southern California], the other USC [University of South Carolina], OSU [Oklahoma State] and U of Miami)."

Despite settling on Duke, it was the prospect of being drafted that was first and foremost for Gubicza. He was sure to be selected in the June 1981 draft, but how high would he go and who would take him? Royals scout Tom Ferrick had been keeping an eye on him. He was sending reports to the Royals director of scouting and player development, John Schuerholz, who remembered Ferrick talking about not only Gubicza's physical attributes, but also his makeup both on and off the field. Gubicza recalled his conversations with Ferrick as "open and honest throughout the entire process."

June 8 was draft day. Gubicza had heard rumors about the Braves and Yankees and that the Phillies were interested. "My ultimate dream in life was to put on the Phillies uniform," he said.

It didn't happen. Gubicza was selected in the second round by the Kansas City Royals, the club his beloved Phillies had just beaten in the World Series. Gubicza was picked ahead of future Hall of Famer Tony Gwynn as well as another future Hall of Famer, the last pick of the second round: John Elway.

"I was extremely excited to get drafted by an organization that won every year," Gubicza said in 2018. He remembered playing stickball that day with his friends when he got the word from his father: "My dad drove up and shouted, 'You got drafted,' and all my boys from the schoolyard went nuts. They were so happy one of us got the chance of a lifetime. My dad and brothers were super pumped, but my mom was sad. She wanted me to go to Duke in the worst way. She loved the campus."

The Duke scholarship was still on the table as negotiations began. Schuerholz had come from Kansas City and met the Gubiczas for the first time. "Here I was sitting at their dining room table with the entire family negotiating a contract," he recalled.

"I still remember John telling me years down the road that, and I quote, 'I better get this done or else your whole family may put cement shoes on me and throw me in the river by your house,'" Gubicza said. "I laughed forever with that. A Hall of Famer who loved me and my family."

No cement was needed and the deal was done. But leaving the comforts of home for the unknown of minor-league baseball wasn't easy. He would write to his family and friends daily. Gubicza was assigned to the Royals Gold, one of the club's two entries in the Gulf Coast Rookie League. He immediately found success. When he took the hill for the first time, he was amazed "because his landing foot didn't land in a huge hole." The field was well groomed. As were his stats. He finished his first season in the organization going 8-1 with a 2.25 ERA, 40 strikeouts, and just 38 hits allowed in 56 innings pitched.

"It's hard to believe. I wanted to do well, but I never dreamed of stats like that. When I got there, I was thinking that the adjustment period – to the hitters, to the incredible heat, to being away from home – would take lots of time. But I felt comfortable almost from the start and that made it much easier to pitch. The coaches treated me nice and so did my teammates. There were only four high-school kids. The rest were coming out of their junior and senior years of college. But we (the young kids) were never looked down upon."[7]

That fall Gubicza was assigned to the Royals Instructional League program, which was designed to accelerate the progress of top-notch prospects. The program was headed by Gary Blaylock, to whom he credits much of his success, saying, "Gary was stern, but very good at getting his point across."

It was there that Gubicza began the transition from a straight fastball/curveball pitcher to adding a sinker and slider to his repertoire. He also became friends with a pair of future teammates, David Cone and Tony Ferreira, and they quickly became known as the Three Musketeers throughout the organization. They would go to each other for tips as well as support. Not to mention rooming together to save money.

In 1982 all three were assigned to the Fort Myers Royals of the Class-A Florida State League. While Cone and Ferreira found success, Gubicza was working on honing his new pitches, which was not always easy. He finished the season just 2-5 with a 4.13 ERA and 25 walks in 48 innings. Despite the numbers, Schuerholz was receiving glowing reports.

"The praise Mark received continued to escalate throughout the organization," Schuerholz said. "It was clear he had not only the talent package, but a bulldog mentality which would be a key to his future success."

Once again Gubicza was assigned to the Fall Instructional League, where he worked with a couple of other top pitching prospects. Gubicza, left-hander Danny Jackson, and right-hander Bret Saberhagen were the three who really stood out to Schuerholz and the organization.

"Gary (Blaylock) kept telling me he was certain Mark, DJ, and Bret could pitch in the big leagues," Schuerholz said. "I kept asking him about their makeup. Was it strong enough to withstand temporary failure? The answer continued to be that their makeup was great."

In 1983 Gubicza attended his first big-league spring training, in Fort Myers. "I loved my first big-league spring training because I got to pick the brains of people like Vida Blue, Dennis Leonard, Steve Renko, Gaylord Perry, etc.," he said. Out of camp, he was assigned to Jacksonville of the Double-A Southern League.

"Toward the end of my year at Double A, Gene Lamont, my manager, said don't worry about Triple A next year because you might not even need to see that level next year. I said 'Hmmm, maybe?'"

Around the same time, the Royals were dealing with major off-field issues. After the 1983 season, four players were sentenced to federal prison for involvement with cocaine. At this point, Schuerholz and the organization decided to go in a different direction. "Due to the positive reports on DJ, Bret, and Mark, I was confident they could handle any potential temporary failures," he said. "We made the decision to clean the slate and we were going to go with the young pitchers."

Before that could happen, Gubicza needed a strong spring training to impress the front office. And he delivered right from the start. In his first outing, he beat the defending American League West champion White Sox, including striking out future Hall of Famer Carlton Fisk as well as Greg Luzinski, whom he had watched playing for the Phillies World Series championship team. The 21-year-old pitched well and was tabbed to go north with the Royals. "I came to spring training trying to make a good impression," Gubicza said. "I was being realistic. I didn't think I had a shot. I was just hoping to be assigned to Omaha. I would have been happy with that. But here I make the team and am going to pitch in the starting rotation. I almost have to pinch myself."[8]

He was named the team's fourth starter, joining a rotation that featured four southpaws. "They needed someone who was right-handed and hopefully could throw hard, and I fit," Gubicza said.[9] His teammates knew the benefit of having a righty in the mix. Said Frank White, "If you can fit him in the middle of those left-handers, it might break the timing of the other teams. Sometimes a guy who throws hard and has good stuff can mess things up and help the guys who don't throw as hard."[10]

Before taking the mound he and Saberhagen, who had made the team as a long reliever, needed a place to stay. Enter a legend. "George Brett asked me and (Saberhagen) if we had a place to stay and we said no. So he said, 'You do now, you are staying with me.'"

Days later he was in his first big-league clubhouse. "It was a total honor and privilege to put on that Royal uniform for the first time," Gubicza said. "I watched them in the World Series against the Phillies and knew they were real good."

He took the Royals Stadium mound for the first time as a big leaguer on April 6, 1984, against the Indians. "Before my first game, my teammates and dad said the same thing: Have fun and remember this is a special day." But it was not a memorable start to his big-league career. The first batter he faced was Indians center fielder Brett Butler. "I walked him on four pitches. After that I settled down."

Actually the box score shows the speedy Butler reached on an infield single, stole second, advanced to third on Tony Bernazard's single, and scored on a groundout by Julio Franco. Just like that, he was down 1-0. But he did settle down, and despite taking the 2-0 loss, it was a quality start in his big-league debut. Six innings pitched, five hits allowed, one run, one walk, four strikeouts. "Hall of Fame pitcher Bert Blyleven pitches for them that night. My mom and dad were at my first MLB start. They were so excited."

Gubicza finished his first season going 10-14 with a 4.05 ERA. He walked 75 while striking out 111 in 189 innings. He threw four complete games, including two shutouts. He finished seventh in the Rookie of the Year balloting, one spot below Roger Clemens. He was also introduced to his first big-league nickname: "I was known as Goob or Little Goob all my life. But once I got to the Bigs, it became Goobie!"

As Goobie would often mention, it was a nickname that would come in handy following a rough home outing.

"I always told myself they (the fans) weren't saying boooo. ... They were saying Gooob."

Despite the offseason turmoil and Brett's torn meniscus, costing him the first six weeks, the 1984 Royals hung around the top of the AL West. Gubicza picked up one of his most important wins of the season on September 4. He gave up one run in 8⅔ innings, helping the Royals catch the Minnesota Twins atop the division. KC finished the month 17-11. When the Twins suffered back-to-back walk-off losses, the Royals clinched the division. They finished with just 84 wins and a playoff date with the wire-to-wire AL East champion Detroit Tigers. Goobie did not pitch in that series as the Royals were swept in three straight by the team that eventually won the World Series. A bitter ending, but the foundation had been laid for future success.

"The energy was great on our team in '84," Gubicza said. "We had veteran players and a bunch of young talented rookie pitchers."

Schuerholz said at the time, "We have a brighter future than anticipated. We'll be better next year and better than that the year after."[11]

Gubicza's future also looked brighter off the field when he attended his best friend's wedding.

He recalled, "I met (Lisa) at Bret Saberhagen's wedding. It sounds cliché, but I knew at that moment I was going to marry her."

Gubicza got off to a tough start in 1985, winning just one of his first seven starts with an ERA hovering around 5. His season turned around on June 8 in a game in Anaheim against the Angels. He had a shutout working into the ninth before Ruppert Jones hit an RBI single, knocking him from the game. Dan Quisenberry got Reggie Jackson to hit into a double play, giving the Royals a 4-1 win. Gubicza then went 12-3 over his next 18 starts. In his final start of the season, he defeated the Oakland A's, pitching 6⅓ innings of one-run ball. Quisenberry closed it out. That win, coupled with an Angels loss, meant the Royals clinched at least a tie for the division crown. The next night Willie Wilson singled in the 10th, driving home Pat Sheridan, and the Royals walked off with the AL West title. Armed with Saberhagen (20 wins, Cy Young Award), Charlie Leibrandt (17 wins), Jackson and Gubicza (14 wins each), and Bud Black (10 wins), the Royals faced Toronto in the ALCS.

Gubicza's first postseason appearance came in relief during Game One. With the Royals trailing 6-0, he entered in the fifth and pitched three hitless and scoreless innings in a game the Royals lost, 6-1. That performance led to his first playoff start. With the Royals trailing the best-of-seven series three games to two and on the brink of elimination, manager Dick Howser handsed the ball to Gubicza for a win-or-go-home Game Six at Exhibition Stadium.

"I remember just before Game Six George Brett came up to me and joked, either we play Game Seven or we play golf the next day," Gubicza said. "It helped me relax."

The Royals were staked to a 1-0 lead in the first inning , but in the Blue Jays' first, a leadoff double by Damaso Garcia and a single by Lloyd Moseby put runners on the corners with nobody out. Gubicza got Rance Mulliniks to bounce back to the mound for a 1-6-3 double play. Garcia scored, tying the game. The Royals again took the lead in the third, but Gubicza ran into more trouble in the bottom of the inning. With one out, Tony Fernandez doubled down the left-field line, went to third on a wild pitch, and scored on a groundout, tying the score again. In the fifth, Brett hit a then record ninth LCS home run, giving the Royals the lead for good. There was a tense moment in the sixth when Mulliniks nearly took Gubicza deep for a two-run shot, but Willie Wilson was able to track it down. Gubicza left the game a batter later with a 5-2 lead. Black and Quisenberry finished the job and the Royals evened the series, 3-3.

After the game Howser was asked about the decision to start Gubicza in the crucial Game Six. He replied, "Gubicza was a starter for me all year, I had no qualms about starting him. That gave me the luxury of having a guy like Bud Black in the bullpen."[12]

The Royals took Game Seven in Toronto, earning a trip to the World Series. It was the "I-70 Showdown Series" or the "Show-Me Series" against their interstate rival, the St. Louis Cardinals. With the Royals going to a four-man rotation, Gubicza did not pitch in the Series. It was a thrilling series highlighted by one of the most controversial calls in World Series history. In Game Six, with the Cardinals leading the Series three games to two and the game 1-0, Jorge Orta led off the bottom of the ninth with a grounder between first and second. Cardinals first baseman Jack Clark threw to pitcher Todd Worrell covering first. Umpire Don Denkinger called Orta safe on a bang-bang play. Replays showed Orta should have been called out.

"I was in the bullpen at the time," Gubicza said. "I thought from my angle that Worrell missed the base and that's why Don called him safe."

With no instant replay available in 1985, the call stood, and eventually pinch-hitter Dane Iorg blooped a single to right, driving in the winning runs. The Series was tied.

As exciting as Game Six was, Game Seven was anticlimactic. Saberhagen threw a shutout and the Royals pounded the Cardinals, 11-0, winning Kansas City's first World Series title.

"After we won the World Series, all I could think of was I was there for the Phillies clincher in 1980 with my dad and now I get to experience what the Phillies players must have felt," Gubicza said.

Success did not carry over to the 1986 season. Gubicza got off to a terrible start, going 0-4 with an ERA of nearly 7.50. He finally broke into the win column on May 14 with a three-hit shutout of the Indians.

On June 5 Gubicza suffered one of his worst starts in the big leagues, lasting just 1⅔ innings, giving up two runs on a hit and four walks. At one point he missed the strike zone on 13 straight pitches. And in his next start, two days later, he was struck on the head by a thrown ball during batting practice. Gubicza was placed on the disabled list with a fractured outer plate of the right orbital sinus. Returning in July, he worked out of the bullpen. He returned to the rotation in August and had a great finish to the season, winning eight of his final nine decisions and lowering his ERA nearly a run a game. Gubicza ended the season 12-6 with a 3.64 ERA. The Royals finished third in the AL West.

That was the season Bo Jackson made his debut. "Playing with Bo was beyond cool," said Gubicza. "Besides playing with George Brett, no one came close to their talents. They made you stop and watch every second."

That year Gubicza also picked up another win off the field. On November 7 he and Lisa were married.

Gubicza got off to another slow start in 1987, winning just three of his first 13 starts. Nevertheless, he was showing the type of mound mentality GM Schuerholz knew his tall right-hander had, as Gubicza completed nine of his final 22 starts, including two shutouts.

"Mark was a bulldog," said Schuerholz. "He was tough-minded and wanted the ball. Every time he took the mound, he wanted to beat every opponent. He had the aptitude and attitude to just keep fighting and never wanted to come out."

Despite a 13-18 record, Gubicza made 35 starts, threw 241⅔ innings and had 10 complete games. The Royals again missed the playoffs, finishing two games behind the eventual World Series champion Twins.

Gubicza got off to a better start in 1988, winning three of his first four starts. However, three straight losses to start May left him with a 3-4 mark. Looking to right the ship, Mark looked for help. "I had a long conversation with our new pitching coach, Frank Funk," he said. "We talked about 'trying easy.' It was the turning point for my career."

By backing off what Schuerholz called a "forced delivery," Gubicza started to see great results. He hit the All-Star break winning nine of 10 and earning the June American League Pitcher of the Month Award. His final start before the break was a four-hit shutout of the Yankees. The dominant stretch earned him his first All-Star Game selection.

Gubicza entered the game, at Cincinnati's Riverfront Stadium, in the fourth inning, giving up a single to leadoff hitter Vince Coleman. The speedster stole second and went to third on a bad throw by catcher Terry Steinbach. After Gubicza struck out Ryne Sandberg, Coleman scored on a wild pitch. Back-to-back singles by Andre Dawson and Darryl Strawberry (neither ball leaving the infield), put Gubicza on the ropes, but he got Bobby Bonilla to line out and Will Clark to ground out.

Gubicza then pitched a scoreless fifth as the American League won, 2-1. For Gubicza, "The coolest thing ... was meeting Willie Mays, Lou Brock, and Vice President George Bush!"

Gubicza was just as dominant in the second half of the season. On August 27 he beat the Twins, allowing just one run and striking out 14. He ran his record to 16-7. On September 26 he shut out Seattle for his first 20-win season. He finished 20-8 with a 2.70 ERA, in 269⅔ innings pitched. He was a serious contender for the Cy Young Award, and finished third in the balloting. "Frank Viola [the winner] was amazing for the Twins in 1988, but I felt good about my numbers as well," Gubicza said.

Gubicza was once again a workhorse in 1989. He led the league with 36 starts. He stayed around the .500 mark most of the season, but did have a hot stretch in June. For the second season in a row, he was named the June American League Pitcher of the Month. He was also named to his second consecutive All-Star Game, and pitched a 1-2-3 fourth inning as the American League won, 5-3.

He was hot again after the break, winning five straight in late August/early September. By season's end he was 15-11 with a 3.04 ERA in 255 innings for the second-place Royals. However, internally something was not right. "My shoulder started hurting toward the end of '89. An average of 250-plus innings took a toll."

The 1990 season did not start well for Gubicza. He was just 2-4 with an ERA over 8 after his first start in

May. After a June 29 start against the Tigers, he was 4-7 with an ERA of 4.50. It was his last start of the season. On July 10 he was placed on the 21-day disabled list with inflammation in his right shoulder. The hope was that he would be able to begin throwing in a week or two. "Being injured and not being able to compete with my teammates was very difficult," Gubicza said.

On July 27 it was announced that he would undergo arthroscopic surgery on a partially torn rotator cuff in his throwing shoulder and would miss the rest of the season.

"Talking to my dad is what got me through the tough times. But he passed away shortly after my major surgery," Gubicza said.

After missing just over a month at the start of the 1991 season, Gubicza was back on the hill on May 14 against the Blue Jays. He took a loss, but struck out eight in five innings. Since he was still recovering from the surgery, he was not expected to be the workhorse of years past. He was limited to just 133 innings, finishing 9-12 with a 5.68 ERA.

Gubicza seemed to be back to full strength in 1992. Heading into July, he had already thrown 105⅓ innings. He was 7-6 with an ERA just under 4. But on July 5 he left his start against Milwaukee with stiffness in that right shoulder. Five days later, he came out after just an inning. On July 15 he was placed on the disabled list again with inflammation in the shoulder. On August 14, the day he turned 30, Gubicza experienced more pain while warming up for a simulated start. On August 24 he was examined in Los Angeles by Dr. Lewis Yocum, who determined that the pain was most likely caused by weakness in the rotator cuff. Gubicza was shut down for the remainder of the season.

After signing a one-year deal in the offseason, Gubicza was ready to go in the spring of 1993. He was back in the rotation, but struggled out of the gate. He gave up seven runs in just 1⅔ innings in his first outing. After a loss on May 20, his record stood at 0-5 with an ERA close to 7. The next day he was pulled out of the rotation and put into the bullpen.

"It'll be a new experience, trying to be ready every two days or so," Gubicza said at the time. "But if it helps the team, that's great. I just hope it turns out to be a meaningful role."[13]

Gubicza flourished out of the pen. In 43 appearances, he won five games and recorded the first two saves of his career. He struck out 61 in 72⅓ innings.

"Goobie is very tough mentally. He's a fighter, a battler," said pitching coach Guy Hansen. "That's the type of mentality you want for that job. And I think he's done a terrific job."[14]

But at the same time, Gubicza was left pondering the future. As a free agent after the season, and now working out of the bullpen, would the team keep him in the fold?

"Mark has been a loyal part of this organization," said GM Herk Robinson. "He could have left after last year, but he chose to come back. If it can be worked out, we'd love to have him back."[15]

Still, Gubicza filed for free agency after the season. He fielded offers from Kansas City and other clubs, and in December he decided to return to the Royals for an 11th season. "It was a little tempting with the Phillies," he said, "but I'm not sure I wanted to go prove myself again with another team."[16]

Gubicza agreed to a one-year deal. Near the end of spring training, he learned he was back as a part of the Royals rotation. He hovered around the .500 mark most of the season, but on the positive side, he was again throwing six to seven innings a start. By the end of July, he had thrown nearly 130 innings. On August 1 he beat the Yankees as the Royals won their 10th straight game. The streak reached 14 and ended on Gubicza's final start of the season, on August 6. Four days later the players went on strike. The walkout lasted the rest of the season and into spring training of 1995.

Gubicza was now playing a role off the field instead of on it. "I was the alternate player rep so I was constantly on the phone and tried also to keep the fans in KC, whenever I ran into them, hopeful that the season wouldn't be lost," he said.

It would be. There was no World Series. On April 2, 1995, the strike ended. After a spring full of replacement players, the big leaguers were coming back. "It's a fresh start right now," Gubicza said. "I think the players are excited to get it going."[17]

Gubicza was slotted into the Royals rotation as the number-three starter. The only remaining member of the 1985 World Series champions, now he was the veteran pitcher surrounded by a bunch of hungry kids.

Nearly five years after his rotator-cuff surgery, he was no longer the power pitcher he had been. By using more of his slider and concentrating on ball placement, he was pitching pain-free. Despite finishing 12-14, he was back to being the innings-eater of his prime. He led the league with 33 starts, throwing 213⅓ innings.

After the season Gubicza was back on the free-agent market. He had talks with other teams, but again decided to stay in Kansas City, signing a two-year deal.

Things did not go as planned in 1996. Gubicza struggled out of the gate and never really caught fire. He lost all five starts in June, leaving him with a 4-12 record. His season was cut short on July 5 against the Twins. With two outs in the bottom of the first, Paul Molitor hit a line drive off his left knee. He was diagnosed with a fractured tibia, costing him the rest of the season. The pitch that Molitor smashed was Gubicza's last in a Royals uniform. In October the Royals traded their longest-tenured player to California for designated hitter Chili Davis. Gubicza had a chance to veto the trade, but agreed to go to California, where he and his family now lived.

"I thought I would be a Royal for life because I had survived many a trade rumor," Gubicza said. "But when I was traded to California it was a blessing in many ways because my daughter was just starting school and being close to home allowed me to be there every day."

Gubicza's Angels career was short-lived. Starting in spring training, he began experiencing pain in his shoulder. He had hoped to pitch through it. However, after being unable to hold a 7-1 lead in his first start and getting shelled in his second start, he knew something had to be done.

"I thought I could battle through this, make some pitches, get some outs. But there were times I didn't have anything on the ball," he said. "I'm obviously not doing the club any good going out there and not giving them a chance to win."[18]

Gubicza initially received good news as an MRI was normal. The hope was that a trip to the 15-day disabled list would be all he needed. He was further encouraged on May 12 when he was able to throw off the mound for 10 minutes without pain. However, after he threw a simulated game in June, the pain returned. He was shut down until at least July 1. On August 5, with a rehab stint in sight, the club determined that, if healthy, Gubicza would not return to the rotation. As it turned out, he would not return at all. Despite his attempts to make it back, he could not shake the pain in his shoulder and his season was over.

Entering the winter of 1997, Gubicza was again a free agent. He had hoped to return to Anaheim, but was unable to work out a deal. "The most difficult and disappointing time in my professional career was not being able to pitch well for the Angels," Gubicza said. "It still hurts because I felt I owed them so much and I didn't produce on the field for them."

Gubicza eventually signed a minor-league deal with the Los Angeles Dodgers. However, just days before heading to Vero Beach for 1998 spring training, he decided to retire. "I'm disappointed I'm not able to go down to Florida and compete for a job with the Dodgers, but I just didn't think I could pitch the way my shoulder has been feeling," he said.[19]

After the 1998 season, Gubicza contemplated a comeback. He declined the Royals' offer of a job as a roving minor-league pitching instructor. "The Red Sox called me to try out for them. I did, which was another dream come true. But I didn't sign with them and stayed retired," Gubicza said. After nearly two decades in baseball, at age 36, his playing days were over.

"When I retired, all I thought of was spending time with my family," he said. Mark and Lisa, whom he called "my hero since the day I met her," along with their three children, settled into retirement in Southern California.

"I got a chance to coach a travel team with Bret Barberie shortly after my retirement and I knew that I wanted to do that," Gubicza said. "It led to being the head coach at Chaminade High School in the West Hills area of Los Angeles."

Among the players he coached at Chaminade were Blue Jays outfielder Kevin Pillar, veteran pitcher Dan Runzler, and Yankees 2016 first-round pick Blake Rutherford.

"I always told my players to work hard, have a ton of fun always believe someone is looking at you. So run out everything and run to your positions every inning," Gubicza said.

One day he received a phone call from Fox Sports Net. They were interested in having him audition for a role on a new show, *Baseball Today*.

It was something Gubicza had been indirectly training for throughout his big-league career. One way he would pass the time between starts was coming up with nicknames for players. Not exactly Chris Berman's "Bermanisms" (i.e., Bert "be home" Blyleven, Wally "Absorbine" Joyner), nevertheless he was proud of a few.

"I gave Jeff Montgomery the nickname "Snake Bliskin" for the character in *Escape from New York*. Because he would sneak under home plate like a snake and place the baseball anywhere he wanted for a strikeout."

John Schuerholz knew Gubicza would be a good fit in television, saying he had "the ability to match movie-star looks with tenacity to get people out."

Joining other ex-big leaguers like Steve Sax, Ron Darling, and Kevin Kennedy, Gubicza began his broadcasting career as an analyst. Talking about something he loved was not a hard transition.

"TV certainly wasn't anything I thought much about after retirement. But it feels great to be back in the game, expressing opinions," he said. "It's like I'm back in the clubhouse again – and I get to go home afterward."[20]

Gubicza eventually became an analyst on Angels pre- and postgame shows for Fox Sports West, then took on his current role (as of 2018) as the Angels color commentator on FSW. He was happy to emulate a couple of his childhood heroes, "Harry Kalas and Richie Ashburn. "(They) were my favorites," he said. "I loved how they entertained me and educated me at the same time."

Sixteen years after pitching at Kauffman Stadium for the final time, Gubicza returned to the mound again in 2012, this time as a newly inducted member of the Royals Hall of Fame. As of 2018 he was third on the Royals career list for wins (132), second in innings pitched (2,218⅔), and second in strikeouts (1,366).

Gubicza called his induction a "tremendous honor," the perfect ending for a little boy who grew up to realize his big-league dreams.

A few fun facts from Mark himself and Baseball-Reference.com:

Toughest hitter faced: Don Mattingly (.413, 4 HR, 17 RBIs in 80 at-bats).

Surprise success against: Kirby Puckett (.238 in 84 at-bats), Rickey Henderson (.229 in 70 at-bats), Dave Winfield (.245 in 49 at-bats).

1,000th strikeout: Dan Gladden (September 10, 1991).

Author's note:

I would like to thank my friend Mark (Goobie!) for his time, energy, and enthusiasm in talking with me and answering more than a few questions.

I would also like to thank John Schuerholz (and his wife, Karen, for taking the wheel) for answering my questions while driving through the mountains of Georgia.

Sources

In addition to the sources cited in the Notes, the author consulted Baseball-Reference.com.

Notes

1 Joseph Turkos, "Far from Phila., Not Far from Home," mongomerynews.com, August 21, 2009.

2 All otherwise unattributed quotations come from interviews conducted with Mark Gubicza on August 21 and October 11, 2018 as well as a telephone interview with John Schuerholz conducted on August 16, 2018.

3 Ted Silary, "Big Leagues Eye Gubicza," *Philadelphia Daily News*, April 17, 1981: 65.

4 Inter-AC is the Inter-Academic League, a high school athletic conference consisting of private schools in the Philadelphia area and the surrounding suburbs.

5 Ted Silary, "Gubicza Easy Selection as Best Pitcher," *Philadelphia Daily News*, June 24, 1981: 50.

6 National Baseball Hall of Fame Scouting Reports Collection: collection.baseballhall.org/PASTIME/mark-gubicza-scouting-report-1981-march-31-1#page/1/mode/1up.

7 Ted Silary, "Gubicza Has Major Success in Minors," *Philadelphia Daily News*, September 9, 1981: 59.

8 Warren Mayes, "A Storybook Beginning," *Springfield* (Missouri) *Leader and Press*, April 6, 1984: 6D.

9 Ibid.

10 Ibid.

11 Max Rieper, "A Look Back at the 1984 Royals," royalsreview.com, September 13, 2017.

12 John Sonderegger, "Royals Force a Seventh Game," *St. Louis Post-Dispatch*, October 16, 1985: 1D.

13 Associated Press, "Gubicza Loses His Position in Royals' Pitching Rotation," *Des Moines Register*, May 21, 1993: 1S.

14 "Gubicza's Career as Royal Is Nearing an Intersection," *St. Louis Post-Dispatch*, August 22, 1993: 3F.

15 Ibid.

16 Associated Press, "Gubicza Signs with Royals," Manhattan (Kansas) *Mercury*, December 8, 1993: B2.

17 Associated Press, "KC's Boone Ready for Second Spring Season," *Manhattan* (Kansas) *Mercury*, April 3, 1995: B2.

18 Mike Digiovanna, "Indians Put Angels in Deep Freeze," *Los Angeles Times*, April 12, 1997: C7.

19 Associated Press, "Trachsel Stays With Cubs, Gets Nearly $3 Million," *Arizona Republic*, February 14, 1998: C7.

20 Tom Hoffarth, "Full-Service Olbermann," *Los Angeles Daily News*, July 21, 2000.

LARRY GURA

BY RICHARD BOGOVICH

Health activities embraced by Larry Gura in 1976 were so unusual for a pro pitcher that veteran *Sports Illustrated* writer Bill Nack devoted a long newspaper article to them. "An idea fixed in conventional baseball wisdom is that a pitcher, of all people, should not involve himself in weightlifting, should not strain over weighted pulleys or barbells," Nack wrote, yet that consumed Gura's offseason. "Gura also has engaged in an elaborate series of muscle-flexibility exercises — squats, bends, rotations and jumping jacks — and indulged in a high protein, low carbohydrate diet that includes an exotic mixture for breakfast ... of three raw eggs, two tablespoons of strained honey, three tablespoons of protein powder and 14 ounces of whole milk in a blender."[1] In hindsight, Gura proved to be much more an innovator than an oddity. "He was a pioneer in baseball, a fanatic about nutrition and weight training, years before it became commonplace for all ballplayers to pay attention to such matters," said longtime Royals broadcaster Steve Stewart in 2008.[2]

Nothing in Gura's formative years suggested this particular niche for him in baseball history. Lawrence Cyril Gura was born on November 26, 1947, to Charles J. Gura Jr. and Gretchen L. (Barnett) Gura in Joliet, Illinois,[3] about 40 miles southwest of downtown Chicago. Joliet's population was about 50,000 at the time.[4]

Charles Gura, of Slovak descent, was a lifelong resident of the area and for over 40 years was a baker for the American Baking Company, maker of Rainbo Bread. He belonged to the local Loyal Order of Moose lodge. Gretchen was a widow when she married Charles. She had children from her first marriage, and Larry grew up with two brothers and two sisters. Gretchen became a teacher's aide at Joliet East High School, which opened in 1964. Larry was a senior there during the school's first year. His mother also served as a president of the Air Force Mothers Club locally and was quite involved in the Belmont and Ingalls Park Athletic Clubs on Joliet's east side. Larry played Little League baseball at Belmont Park and Pony League ball at Ingalls.[5]

According to a niece of Larry's, the family was very athletic. His brother Chuck played football in high school, but several other relatives mainly played on the diamond. Their father pitched and played third base for the Moose team, and their mother played softball during her youth. Charles Gura's brother Emery also played for the Moose, and because Emery was left-handed, like Larry, it was that uncle who taught Larry how to pitch during Little League.[6]

Joliet has long had a "reputation as a great baseball community," according to a longtime journalist there.[7] During the last decade of Gura's pro career, a Chicago Tribune sportswriter even called Joliet "baseball-crazy."[8] Baseball in Joliet made the news nationwide when Larry was a baby, and another of Larry's uncles was on the periphery. In 1948 the Joliet area's new semipro baseball league was called the Will County Athletic Association (WCAA), and the Joliet Moose had one of the circuit's eight teams. Starring for them that year was 5-foot-9, 18-year-old Francis "Fuzzy" Gura, who the local daily said was "undoubtedly the most effective hurler in the league."[9] Also in the WCAA was St. Joseph's American Legion team. In an exhibition game for that team on July 20, pitcher Bernice Metesh became the only female semipro baseball player in the United States at the time. She and Frank Gura didn't pitch against each other because she was added to the roster too late to be eligible for regular WCAA games.[10] Instead, she pitched in more exhibition games across northern Illinois for which she received newspaper and radio coverage coast to coast.[11]

Frank Gura may have been overshadowed as he compiled a record of nine wins and three losses for the Moose team, to go with a .421 batting average, but he didn't go unnoticed. In January of 1949 he was signed to a professional contract by White Sox scout Doug Minor. The White Sox' announcement of his signing noted that in 1947 he had a pitching record of 6-1 for Joliet Catholic High School, and that three of those victories were one-hitters, after which he went 15-1 for a Junior American Legion squad, while batting .687 with a streak of 12 consecutive hits. The White Sox assigned him to Madisonville (Kentucky) Miners of the Class-D Kentucky-Illinois-Tennessee (Kitty) League.[12] Gura won 14 games and lost 8 for the Miners. In 1950 he was promoted to the Superior (Wisconsin) Blues of the Class-C Northern League. He won four games and lost four, but in midseason he was sent down to the Wisconsin Rapids White Sox in the Class-D Wisconsin State League and that was the conclusion of his professional career.

About three years later, his nephew Larry started playing baseball in earnest. "As a little kid, I always wanted to play for the Yankees," he recalled in 1976. "Whitey Ford was my idol and he helped me when he was the Yankees' pitching coach."

Gura added, "I remember when I was pitching in the Little League on a team called the Caterpillars, my dad promised me a new fishing rod if I shut out the other team, and I shut them out. At the time that was real pressure." He also took pride in accomplishments while playing American Legion ball in Joliet: "I pitched back-to-back no-hitters with 23 strikeouts in each game."[13]

"Growing up, I didn't try to throw the ball that hard," Gura recalled on a later occasion. "I concentrated on control. It took me six months to learn a changeup." In addition to location, he said, the other key to his success was patience.[14]

According to Charles Gura's entries in city directories, Larry grew up at 9 North West Circle Drive, just a stone's throw from Ingalls Park, where he played his Pony League ball. During the summer of 1962, Gura earned some national exposure as the Joliet Pony League All-Stars were advancing to the final four of the Pony League World Series double-elimination tournament in Washington, Pennsylvania. Facing a team from Northbrook, Illinois, in Davenport, Iowa, on August 21, he replaced Joliet's starting pitcher with two out in the second inning. Over 5⅓ innings he struck out 13 batters. His opponents could manage only one walk, four hits, and a run as Gura and Joliet triumphed, 10-5.[15]

During the spring of 1964 Gura was a junior at Joliet Township High School (now Joliet Central) and didn't pitch an inning. "I don't think that's real surprising, though," he said a few years later, "because the two top pitchers on that club were Bill Sudakis and Dale Spier." Sudakis had an eight-year major-league career (albeit never as a pitcher) and Spier pitched in the minors, peaking at Triple A from 1970 through 1972. But Gura had a 5-1 pitching record for his Colt League team that summer, and earned a spot on the city's team in national Colt League World Series tournament.[16] They reached the final game in Shawnee, Oklahoma, against a team from Houston, thanks in large part to Gura amassing a tournament record of 11-0. He got his team into the final game by beating a team from Riverside, California, on August 21 for the second time in 48 hours. "Gura's control was perfect as he spun a five-hitter and struck out seven in lowering his earned run average to 1.65 over 58 innings of work," his hometown daily reported. Gura didn't play the next day when it took an extra eighth inning for Houston to beat Joliet, 2-1, and claim the crown.[17]

By switching to Joliet's brand new East High School for his senior year, Gura was able to pitch for the varsity baseball team. He was also a competitive swimmer and runner for the school.[18] "I guess I started thinking about playing pro ball in my senior year of high school," Gura said a few years later. At Joliet East he was coached by Elmer Bell, who played minor-league ball briefly for the Philadelphia Phillies around the time of the Korean War. Bell was once a teammate of Bobby Winkles, the baseball coach at Arizona State University. As a result, Gura accepted a scholarship to enter ASU in the fall of 1965.[19]

Gura's college years were very eventful, both with the Sun Devils and with other teams during his summer breaks. Jon Cole, an All-American for ASU in the discus and shot put, and a future Olympic weightlifter, later directed Gura through the trailblazing regime documented in the 1976 article by Bill Nack.[20] Gura was a sophomore on the ASU team that won the 1967 College World Series tournament, and he delivered a key victory on June 14 against top-ranked Stanford with a scoreless, three-hit relief stint.[21] That summer he had a 7-1 record for the semipro Cowboys of Halstead, Kansas, for whom he played in the 1967 National Baseball Congress tournament. Then, as a junior back at ASU during the spring of 1968 his mediocre 4-4 record was offset by an earned-run average of 1.90 in 90 innings and an average of more than 11 strikeouts per game. By that point he had reached his adult height of 6-feet and weighed 180 pounds.[22]

During that summer Gura compiled a record of 12-1 for the Collegians of Boulder, Colorado, and starred for them in the 1968 National Baseball Congress tournament. He hurled no-hitters three days apart on the way to being named to the all-tourney team.[23] Then in November Gura and fellow Joliet resident John Lucenta were on the US team in a four-country round-robin tournament tacked onto the Olympics in Mexico City. The US squad hurdled teams from Puerto Rico and Mexico and received gold medals, defeating Cuba 2-1 in the final contest.[24]

The spring of 1969 was monumental for Gura. One harbinger was a game between ASU and the expansion Seattle Pilots on March 15. Gura and freshman Craig Swan combined to beat the major leaguers, 5-4.[25] Toward the tail end of his record-setting season for the Sun Devils, he became a second-round draft pick of the Chicago Cubs, on June 5, 1969. He also received a bachelor's degree in physical education.[26] But he still had work to do for ASU in the College World Series. On June 13 he lost the opening game but on June 20 he beat Tulsa in the finale to give ASU another championship.[27]

Gura became the winningest pitcher in collegiate baseball history by virtue of a 19-2 record that included two wins and a save in the College World Series. In the process, he established ASU career records with 325 strikeouts and an ERA of 1.73, and his 1969 ERA of 1.01 was the best for a single season by a Sun Devil.[28] He and University of Texas pitcher Burt Hooton were named to the 1969 American Baseball Coaches Association/Rawlings NCAA Division I All-America First Team.[29]

On June 25 Gura and the Cubs agreed on a contract, with a $30,000 signing bonus that was called "a surprisingly high figure" in at least one Arizona newspaper.

The Cubs assigned Gura to their top minor-league team, Tacoma in the Triple-A Pacific Coast League. To start his pro career, Gura lost to Hawaii on July 6 but shut out Tucson on July 11.[30] All told, his half-season with Tacoma wasn't particularly satisfying, with a 4-8 record and an ERA of 3.17. Before the end of the season, Gura celebrated a milestone of a very different kind. At 11:00 A.M. on August 21, he married his ASU girlfriend, Cindy Davenport, back in Arizona. Gura credited her with making a difference in his collegiate career. "On the days I was to pitch at ASU, she really took great care of me," he said. "She saw that I ate properly, got in early and had plenty of rest." The couple had planned the wedding two months earlier and couldn't have anticipated that he'd be expected to pitch in a minor-league game that same night. "All the fellows tell me I'll be scared stiff for the wedding," Gura told a reporter the evening before. "But it doesn't bother me at all. I'm more worried about pitching tomorrow night." His record was 3-6 at the time. "I wanted the wedding to take place on the mound," Gura added, tongue in cheek, "but she wouldn't go along with that." He lost that night's start.[31]

When Tacoma's season concluded, Gura was shifted to the Arizona Instructional League, the only time he ever pitched minor-league ball below the Triple-A level. He also pitched in the minors for parts of 1970 through 1974, and again during his last year as a pro. He did well in his 11 games in the Instructional League, posting a 5-2 record, 3 saves, and an ERA of 2.25. In 52 innings he stuck out 46 batters and walked eight.

In 1970 Gura had a 2-1 record with the major leaguers in spring training but started the regular season back in the Pacific Coast League. He wasn't there long. On April 22, the Cubs purchased his contract from Tacoma.[32] He made his major-league debut on April 30. He shared his recollections many years later:

> *We were playing the Braves in Atlanta. I was in the bullpen and I had just gotten up to throw a few, just to loosen up. All of a sudden I'm in the ballgame facing Rico Carty, Orlando Cepeda and Henry Aaron, two future Hall of Famers and a batting champion, all right-handed hitters. I said to myself, "Oh, great, this is a good way to start your career." I got Aaron and Cepeda but I contributed to Carty's 31-game hitting streak.*
>
> *I got my first win in Montreal. I actually got a start and we got some runs early. Joe Becker, our pitching coach, came out to the mound in the third or fourth inning and I said, "Don't you dare take me out of this this game." In those days, the infielders could all come in to the mound so Santo, Kessinger, Beckert, and Jim Hickman all heard me, and, to tell you the truth, I think they were kind of impressed with my aggressiveness. At any rate, I stayed in the game and I think we won, 11-3.*[33]

Gura's memory about his debut was pretty good, though he focused on the second of the two innings he pitched. He entered a lopsided game in the seventh inning with the bases loaded and two outs. He yielded a single to George Stone that added two more runs, then issued a walk, but next Tony Gonzalez became the first batter he retired, on a fly to center. Aaron, Carty, and Cepeda were indeed the first three batters he faced in the eighth inning; he retired Felix Millan to end the frame. He was spot-on about his first victory, which occurred on August 5.

Gura appeared in 20 games for the Cubs in 1970, six in 1971, and 7 in 1972, and then 21 in 1973. All were relief outings except for three starts in 1970 and seven in 1973. He found the overall experience frustrating, summed up by one observation: "One year, I was with the Cubs for three months and had six innings of work."[34] Nevertheless, he retained some fond memories with that team:

> *I remember sitting in the bullpen and watching Ernie Banks hit his 500th home run. It brought tears to your eyes, it really did. And playing with guys like Banks and Jenkins and Billy Williams. And Fergie Jenkins winning 20 games all those years in that ballpark. How'd he do that? It was great. I enjoyed those years.*[35]

On November 14, 1973, the Cubs sent Gura to the Texas Rangers as the player to be named later when they acquired Mike Paul on August 31. Gura didn't actually play a regular-season game for the Rangers because on May 7, 1974, they traded him to the New York Yankees, with some cash, for Duke Sims. Still, Gura was with Texas just long enough in 1974 to have his first annoying experience with Billy Martin. "I pitched one inning in spring training and he sent me out [to the minors]. He told me I needed to work on my control," recalled Gura. "My control? That was always my strong point. And he had a pitching staff [that] couldn't hit the broad side of a barn. But he sent me to Spokane."[36]

Yankees manager Bill Virdon summoned Gura to the majors for September and gave him eight starts. Gura excelled. His record was 5-1, with four complete games, two shutouts, and an ERA of 2.41. For the rest of his time in the American League, he was done with the minors. In 1975 he pitched in 26 games for the Yankees, 20 of which were starts. He went 7-8 with an ERA of 3.51. Tragically, from Gura's perspective, Virdon was fired in August and replaced with none other than Billy Martin.

During the 1976 playoffs, Gura commented bitterly about the first half of that year under Martin:

The first thing in spring training, he told me he was going to start me every fourth day but he didn't start me at all in the exhibition games. When the season began, I thought he'd at least use me in long relief, but every time the situation came up, he used Tippy Martinez instead. He didn't use me at all. Finally, after four weeks, he told me on a Friday he was going to start me the following Wednesday, and that Friday night Catfish Hunter got knocked out in the second inning. I thought for sure he'd use me in long relief then, to get me ready for the start. When he used Martinez instead, I asked him why and he said Tippy needed the work, he hadn't pitched in two weeks. I told him I needed the work, too, I hadn't pitched in four weeks. Two days later I was traded.[37]

On May 16, 1976, the Yankees dealt Gura to the Royals for Fran Healy. Since then, much has been written about the animosity between Gura and Martin. Martin's disdain for Gura reportedly stemmed from the pitcher's interest in playing tennis for relaxation, which Martin considered beneath a real man's dignity.[38]

Despite the fresh start in Kansas City, by September of 1976 Gura was on a pace to have his lowest innings-pitched total since 1972 with the Cubs. He started only one game for manager Whitey Herzog before that month. Bill James, the statistics guru and a diehard Royals fan, summed up Gura's significant September succinctly: "He had cut his ERA from 3.57 on September 1 down to 2.79 on September 28, had not given up a run in September, when Whitey Herzog decided to start him at Oakland on September 29. Huge, huge game," James wrote, and of course offered a statistic quantifying just how huge. "Oakland had won the division five straight years, three world championships. Kansas City had lost four games in a row, blowing more than half of a six-game lead. They were clinging to a 2½-game lead with four games left. ... Gura threw a 4-hit shutout, effectively ending the pennant race." In due time, Herzog trusted Gura in similar situations, and James said Gura "became Herzog's Big Game guy." James identified 30 contests that he considered "a high percentage," and in them Gura went 14-10 with an ERA of 3.04.[39]

The magic didn't linger into the playoffs. Gura started two games in the American League Championship Series versus the Yankees, taking one loss with a so-so ERA of 4.22. He didn't think pressure on him was a factor. "I've been playing baseball 23 years and I've been on 12 championship teams, that's a lot of big games," he said at the time.[40] The Royals lost in the ALCS to the Yankees in 1976, 1977, and 1978.

In 1977 Gura pitched much more, and pitched well, but had only six starts. He went 8-5 with 10 saves and a 3.13 ERA. In the ALCS he started one game but the Yankees pounded him, and he was charged with the loss.

In 1978 Gura joined the Royals' starting rotation, and was a fixture for seven seasons. That season only Ron Guidry and Nolan Ryan yielded fewer hits per nine innings than Gura.[41] He achieved his highest winning percentage as a starter, .800, going 16-4 with an ERA of 2.72. He ranked seventh in postseason voting for the Cy Young Award and 23rd for the Most Valuable Player. He started the second game of the ALCS against the Yankees, pitched six scoreless innings, and won, 10-4. As gratifying as it may have been for Gura, it was his team's only victory.

In 1979 Gura and the team as a whole had an off year. He was an average starter (13-12, 4.47) and the Royals didn't make the playoffs. He turned that around quickly in 1980, when at the end of April he had what he considers the best performance of his career, a one-hitter against the Toronto Blue Jays. The only hit off him came at the beginning of the sixth inning when Damaso Garcia legged out a double on a softly hit ball toward left field. "All four pitches were working today, which is the main reason the game went the way it did," Gura said after the game. "When all of my pitches are working, there are nine different places a batter has to look for." Catcher John Wathan said, "He changes speeds better than anyone in the league."[42]

That game was no fluke, because about two months later Orioles manager Earl Weaver named him an American League All-Star, the only time Gura received that honor. He didn't play in the All-Star Game but that didn't affect his performance, because he was named AL Pitcher of the Month for July, and he finished the season with a career-high 18 wins (10 losses) and a 2.95 ERA. He was sixth in voting for the Cy Young Award. Gura pitched exceptionally well in the postseason, and played in his only World Series. His start in the ALCS was a complete-game, 7-2 victory over the Yankees.[43] Though he didn't win either of his starts in the World Series, which the Royals lost to the Phillies in six games, his ERA in 12⅓ innings was 2.19.

In the strike-shortened 1981 season, Gura lowered his ERA to 2.72, had the third lowest walks per innings pitched in the league, and was named AL Pitcher of the Month for September. He was ninth in voting for the Cy Young Award. He had one last playoff game, losing a start against Oakland in the Division Series.

In 1982 Gura matched his career high with 18 wins (12 losses) but in 1983 his 18 losses were the most in the league. He had a much better record in 1984, 12-9, but his ERA was his worst in a full season, at 5.18. In 1985 he pitched in just three games for the Royals, and was released on May 18. Ten days later the Cubs signed him, but he pitched in only five games for them. His final game in the majors was on July 27, 1985. Thus, he wasn't on the Royals' roster when they won the World Series that year.

In his 10 seasons as a Royal, Gura had a record of 111-78, and posted the franchise's second best winning percentage, .587. He was named Royals Pitcher of the Year twice, in 1978 and 1981, and was inducted into the team's Hall of Fame in 1992.[44] Including his time with the Cubs and Yankees, he was 126-97 with an ERA of 3.76. As of 2018, only 70 pitchers in major-league history had a better fielding percentage than Gura's .986.[45]

In retirement, golf became one of Gura's primary activities, and it was common to see him play in charitable tournaments, or even organize them himself after he purchased the Bent Oak Golf Course in Oak Grove, Missouri, east of Kansas City.[46] In the mid-1990s he played in the Pro Athletes Golf League.[47] Beyond that, he and Cindy were busy raising their daughters Kristina and Natalie. They also took over operation of the Dale Creek Equestrian Village, near Litchfield Park, Arizona, a farm that has been in her family for decades.[48]

The Royals' official website credits Gura for "guile and guts" in his team Hall of Fame entry. The alliteration may just be a coincidence, but it's easy to find testimonials in support of their overarching thesis about him: "Steady and unflappable, Gura was the textbook example of a crafty southpaw."[49]

Sources

The primary source for statistics herein was baseball-reference.com.

Notes

1 Bill Nack, "Yankees' Gura Anxious to Begin Playing Game," *Poughkeepsie* (New York) *Journal*, March 13, 1976: 11. His teammates were aware of his penchant for health food during his first month with them. See Parton Keese, "Yanks Win, 10□2, Lead by 2; Cubs Rally in 9th to Beat Mets," *New York Times*, September 16, 1974: 45.

2 Steve Stewart, "Images from the K," stevestewart.mlblogs.com/images-from-the-k-7ffb8bc6eb97, August 15, 2008.

3 See his parents' obituaries, at hosting-24990.tributes.com/obituary/show/Charles-Joseph-Gura-92677336 and findagrave.com/memorial/8068513/gretchen-l.-gura.

4 Daniel J. Elazar and Joseph Zikmund II, *The Closing of the Metropolitan Frontier: Cities of the Prairie Revisited* (New Brunswick, New Jersey: Transaction Publishers, 2002), 235, 244.

5 hosting-24990.tributes.com/obituary/show/Charles-Joseph-Gura-92677336 and findagrave.com/memorial/8068513/gretchen-l.-gura; Don Hazen, "Larry Gura Signs Contract with Chicago Cubs," *Herald-News* (Joliet, Illinois), June 26, 1969: 28.

6 Email message to the author from Celine Matthiessen, goddaughter of Larry Gura, July 10, 2018.

7 Don Hazen, "Convicts Served 1890-92 Sentence in Two-Eyed League," *Joliet Herald-News*, May 19, 2002: Joliet Jackhammers Preview Section, 9. A Joliet team played in the earliest documented (as of 2018) baseball game in the Chicago area, in 1851

against a nine at nearby Lockport, according to Mark Rucker and John Freyer, *19th Century Baseball in Chicago* (Charleston, South Carolina: Arcadia Publishing, 2003), 13.

8 Jerry Shnay, "Providence Star Throws Coach Curve," *Chicago Tribune*, April 25, 1988: 3, 10.

9 "NRC Meets Joliet Moose in Crucial WCAA Tilt Today," *Joliet Herald-News*, August 1, 1948: 31. See also "Gura Hurls Moose to Win over Irvings," *Joliet Herald-News*, July 24, 1948: 2 for additional details about the WCAA.

10 "Gal Pitcher Shows Plenty of Ability but Loses Game," *Joliet Herald-News*, July 21, 1948: 16. Metesh's catcher was her brother Bob. She reportedly stood 5-feet-5 and weighed 110 pounds. According to the box score, she had a hit in three times at bat and scored a run.

11 "Girl Pitcher Wins Radio, Movie Acclaim," *Joliet Herald-News*, August 8, 1948: 3. Metesh was also slated to appear "in the newsreels during the near future." Because she was often called "Bea" for short, the local paper typically called her Beatrice rather than Bernice (and her surname was often misspelled Metesch in other sources). See also aagpbl.org/profiles/bernice-metesh-bernie/173.

12 "Chicago Whitesox Sign Sandlot Star," *Oil City* (Pennsylvania) *Blizzard*, January 28, 1949: 4. Oil City had a Class-C minor-league affiliate of the White Sox at the time. The article reported Gura's weight as 170 pounds and his height as "an even six feet," three inches taller than Joliet's daily reported.

13 Dave Anderson, "The Larry Gura-Billy Martin Feud," *New York Times*, October 9, 1976: 13.

14 Grant Hall, "Mudcat Learned About Williams Early," *Northwest Arkansas Times* (Fayetteville), June 26, 1989: B1.

15 "Ponies Win 1st Division Clash, 10-5," *Joliet Herald News*, August 22, 1962: 30. The paper spelled his surname "Gora." Joliet was eliminated a week later: "It's All Over – National City Beats Joliet Pony Stars 5-2," *Joliet Herald News*, August 29, 1962: 28.

16 Don Hazen, "Larry Gura Signs Contract with Chicago Cubs," *Joliet Herald-News*, June 26, 1969: 25, 28.

17 Don Hazen, "Colt All-Stars Win 4-1," *Joliet Herald News*, August 22, 1964: 7; Hazen, "Houston Defeats Joliet, Wins Colt World Series," *Joliet Herald News*, August 23, 1964: B-13.

18 Bob Lueder, "Trojans Drop Pair; Next Foes Thornridge, Thornton," *Chicago Heights Star*, May 2, 1965: 24. Gura pitched an eight-inning complete game over Bloom High School, winning 4-3, and in the fourth inning he drove in two runs to change a 2-1 deficit into a 3-2 lead. In Joliet East's yearbook published around then, The Crown, he was pictured on page 121 with the varsity baseball team, on page 108 with runners, and on page 123 with swimmers (sharing a team with Joliet Central).

19 "Arizona State Unbeaten," *Long Island Star-Journal* (Long Island City, New York), June 15, 1967: 21; baseball-reference.com/bullpen/Elmer_Bell; Denise M. Baran-Unland, "An Extraordinary Life: Shorewood Coach Taught More than Baseball," *Joliet Herald News*, July 26, 2015, theherald-news.com/2015/07/20/an-extraordinary-life-shorewood-coach-taught-more-than-baseball/a6bbwfy/.

20 Nack: 11.

21 "Arizona State Unbeaten."

22 "Arizona State Unbeaten"; *Boulder Collegians 1968 Yearbook:* 9.

23 "Arizona State Unbeaten"; David L. Porter, ed., *Biographical Dictionary of American Sports: Baseball, G-P* (Westport, Connecticut: Greenwood Press, 2000), 605. No-hitters were common in the tournament due to a wide range in the quality of teams; Gura had a no-hitter shortened to five innings by rain, according to Morris Fraser, "Rain Dominates Semi-Pro Meet; Hot Blue Sox Battle ACs Today," *Colorado Springs Gazette-Telegraph*, August 4, 1968: 41.

24 "Name Jolietans to U.S. Squad," *Morris* (Illinois) *Daily Herald*, October 15, 1968: 5; alumni.lewisu.edu/2015/featured-alumni/john-lucenta.

25 Associated Press, "Arizona St. Baseballers Stun Seattle Pilots, 5-4," *Albuquerque Journal*, March 16, 1969: 19. .

26 Porter, 605.

27 baseball-reference.com/bullpen/1969_College_World_Series.

28 "ASU's Gura Inks Chicago Cub Pact Worth $30,000," *Arizona Republic* (Phoenix), June 26, 1969: 65.

29 abca.org/ABCA/Awards/All-Americans/NCAA_Division_I/1969.aspx for the full First Team and Second Team rosters for Division I.

30 "Islanders Triumph, 8-2, then Lose Nightcap, 12-4," *Honolulu Advertiser*, July 7, 1969: 23; "Rookie Gura Hurls Cubs Past Toros," *Arizona Daily Star* (Tucson), July 12, 1969: 18.

31 Verne Boatner, "Horsehide Honeymoon," *Arizona Republic*, August 22, 1969: 53. A box score is on the same page.

32 "Gura to Report to Chicago Cubs," *Tucson Daily Citizen*, April 23, 1970: 34.

33 John C. Skipper, *Take Me Out to the Cubs Game: 35 Former Ballplayers Speak of Losing at Wrigley* (Jefferson, North Carolina: McFarland & Company, Inc., 2000), 165.

34 Skipper, 164.

35 Skipper, 168.

36 Skipper, 166.

37 Anderson, 13.

38 Two examples of the tennis explanation: Maury Allen, *All Roads Lead to October: Boss Steinbrenner's 25-Year Reign over the New York Yankees* (New York: St. Martin's Press, 2000), 44. Christopher Devine, *Thurman Munson: A Baseball Biography* (Jefferson, North Carolina: McFarland & Company, Inc., 2001), 114. See also Tim Sheehy, "Billy Martin and Kansas City Pitcher Larry Gura Say...," UPI Archives, October 9, 1980; upi.com/Archives/1980/10/09/Billy-Martin-and-Kansas-City-pitcher-Larry-Gura-say/8937339912000/.

39 Bill James, "Big Game Pitchers, Part V," January 24, 2014; billjamesonline.com/big_game_pitchers_part_v/.

40 Anderson, 13.

41 Porter, 606.

42 Skipper, 167; "Gura's One-Hitter Lifts KC," *Crescent-News* (Defiance, Ohio), May 1, 1980: 24. Those four pitches were a curve, fastball, changeup, and slider, according to Parton Keese, "Yanks Win, 10□2, Lead by 2; Cubs Rally in 9th to Beat Mets," *New York Times*, September 16, 1974: 45.

43 In fact, by then he had consistent success against his previous team. See Fred McMane, "Yankee-Killer Larry Gura Survived a Second-Inning Home Run Blitz," UPI Archives, October 8, 1980; upi.com/Archives/1980/10/08/Yankee-killer-Larry-Gura-survived-a-second-inning-home-run-blitz/9068263398053/.

44 kansascity.royals.mlb.com/kc/hall_of_fame/member.jsp?name=Gura.

45 baseball-reference.com/leaders/fielding_perc_p_career.shtml. Gura made no errors in 1980, 1981, 1983, and 1984.

46 Hall, "Mudcat Learned About Williams Early"; "Golf Tourney Set," *The Examiner* (Independence, Missouri), April 20, 1991: 4B.

47 Juan C. Rodriguez, "Brodie, Dewveall Win PAGL Open," *Minneapolis Star Tribune*, July 18, 1994: 5C.

48 baseballbytheletters.com/2011/04/20/pitcher-larry-gura-signs-to-save-family-farm-2/.

49 kansascity.royals.mlb.com/kc/hall_of_fame/member.jsp?name=Gura.

BO JACKSON

BY NORM KING

They were ubiquitous. They were funny. And for a while during the late 1980s and early 1990s, the Nike commercials that showed Bo Jackson playing everything from baseball to cricket to hockey – wearing the uniform of the storied Montreal Canadiens no less – brought the phrase "Bo Knows" into popular culture.

These commercials played on Jackson's astounding athletic abilities. His abundant speed, power, agility, and quickness allowed him to play in the NFL and baseball's major leagues. Although he wasn't the first athlete to play two sports professionally – Jim Thorpe holds that distinction – he was the first to become an All-Star in the two leagues in which he played and the first to rise to prominence in the media-driven sports world of the late twentieth century.[1]

Bo Jackson was born on November 30, 1962, in Bessemer, Alabama, the eighth of Florence Jackson Bond's 10 children born. A fan of the television show Ben Casey, Florence, who worked as a housekeeper, named her son Vincent Edward Jackson, after the show's star, Vince Edwards.[2] Young Vincent could never be confused with the program's caring namesake; he was such a difficult youngster, that his family began referring to him as a boar hog. That eventually was shortened to Bo, and the nickname stuck.

Jackson inherited two traits from his absentee father, A.D. Adams, size and a terrible stutter. The size made him big, tough, and athletic, while the stutter made him a target of ridicule among other children. What he did not get from his father was discipline.

"We never had enough food," Jackson wrote in his autobiography. "But at least I could beat on other kids and steal their lunch money and buy myself something to eat. But I couldn't steal a father. I couldn't steal a father's hug when I needed one. I couldn't steal a father's whipping when I needed one."[3]

While not a very good student at McAdory High School in McCalla, Alabama, he found an outlet for his anger and energy in sports. He won two state high-school decathlon titles, but it was his prowess on the football field and baseball diamond as a senior that attracted the scouts. He averaged 10.9 yards per carry as a running back, and smacked 20 home runs in a 25-game baseball season. The New York Yankees drafted him in the second round of the 1982 draft, but Jackson accepted a football scholarship to Auburn University instead.

Jackson had a legendary football career at Auburn. He rushed for 4,303 yards (still a school record as of 2016) with 43 touchdowns during his four years as a Tiger. His 1,786 rushing yards as a senior won him the Heisman Trophy as college football's most outstanding player in 1985.

Yet, as good as he was at football, his goal was to play professional baseball. "My first love is baseball," he said, "and it has always been a dream of mine to be a major league player."[4]

Baseball scouts thought Jackson could make that dream come true. After watching him play on April 13 and 14, 1985, one scout wrote: "A complete type player with outstanding tools; can simply do it all and didn't even play baseball last year. A gifted athlete; the best pure athlete in America today."[5]

As highly regarded as he was, Jackson's baseball career was almost derailed by an NCAA rules violation, a violation he felt was caused deliberately by the Tampa Bay Buccaneers, who planned to draft him number 1 in the NFL draft. Prior to the draft, they flew Jackson to Tampa in owner Hugh Culverhouse's private jet for a physical examination. Even though Buccaneer officials told Jackson that it was within NCAA rules to accept the flight, it was nonetheless a violation. Jackson was suspended for the second half of his senior baseball season.

"I think it was all a plot now, just to get me ineligible from baseball because they saw the season I was having (after hitting .401 in 1985, Jackson was batting .246, with 7 home runs and 14 RBIs in 21 games in 1986) and they thought they were going to lose me to baseball," he said in an ESPN documentary on his life. "(Like) if we declare him ineligible, then we've got him."[6]

If it was a plot, it failed; the Bucs selected Jackson first overall in the 1986 NFL draft, but he declined their offer of a four-year deal worth between \$5 million and \$7 million, opting to play baseball instead. The Kansas City Royals chose Jackson in the fourth round of the 1986 major-league draft. (The California Angels had drafted him in 1985, but he didn't sign with them, either.) While his contract with the Royals was not as lucrative as what the Buccaneers offered, Jackson still inked a solid deal, three years for \$1 million.

The Royals sent Jackson to the Memphis Chicks, their affiliate in the Double-A Southern League, where he performed poorly at the plate early on – he had a .105 average after 10 games – but Chicks manager Tommy Jones wasn't concerned. "Prior to (Jackson's) first game, I said it would take three weeks for him to get comfortable and to adjust to life in baseball," Jones said. "After three weeks, I felt we could make some evaluations. Until then, I don't think it would be fair."[7]

That approach proved wise, as Jackson improved steadily. After 53 games, his batting average had risen to .277, with 7 homers and 25 RBIs. These numbers prompted the Royals, having an offyear after winning the World Series in 1985 (they finished with a 76-86 record), to call him up on September 1, when major-league teams could expand their rosters. He made his debut on September 2, playing right field against the Chicago White Sox, and getting his first major-league hit off 41-year-old Steve Carlton. His first home run came 12 days later when he hit a solo blast in the fourth inning off Seattle's Mike Moore. Jackson remained with Kansas City for all of September, and hit .207 with two home runs and nine RBIs in 25 games.

Jackson left no doubt about his work ethic by how hard he trained for the 1987 season, his first full year with the Royals. He worked with Hal Baird, his Auburn baseball coach, in January, and even Baird noticed a difference in Jackson's intensity. "He was far more diligent in his work habits," Baird said. "I saw more dedication, more willingness to work, than I had ever seen before."[8]

That preparation paid early dividends, as Jackson made the team after very nearly starting the season at Triple A. A few days before the season started, general manager John Schuerholz had decided to send Jackson to the minors for more experience, but then changed his mind after doing something he had never done before. "I talked to several of our veterans – George Brett, Hal McRae, Frank White," Schuerholz said. "I had never done that before, but they told me they thought he could help us."[9]

Jackson made Schuerholz look like a pretty smart guy in the season's first few days. He went 4-for-5 with three RBIs in a 13-1 pasting of the Yankees on April 10. He followed that performance up with a game for the ages on April 14 against the Tigers. He went 4-for-4, with two home runs – including a grand slam – and seven RBIs in a 10-1 laugher over the Tigers. Two weeks later, Jackson got some interesting news when the Los Angeles Raiders chose him in the seventh round of the NFL draft.[10] Naturally this sparked great media interest, so Jackson put a sign over his locker that read: Don't be stupid and ask football questions. OK!"

Regardless of the intelligence of the fourth estate, newspapers reported in July that Jackson was going to sign with the Raiders. Jackson responded to the speculation at a news conference when the Royals were in Toronto on July 11. "Any way you look at it, I have to do my job with the Kansas City Royals before I can do anything else," he said. "Whatever comes after baseball season is a hobby for Bo Jackson."[11]

Jackson's teammates were not happy when he announced that he had reached terms with the Raiders on July 14 during the All-Star break. Even before he signed with the Raiders, some players felt he was only with the team because of his drawing power. There was also the sense that the front office treated Jackson differently than the other players. Most major-league contracts at the time included clauses prohibiting players from participating in off-field activities that could jeopardize their baseball careers, yet Jackson was allowed to play a violent contact sport. One anonymous Royal expressed his unhappiness by changing the sign above Jackson's locker to read: "Don't be stupid and ask any baseball questions."

Fans weren't happy, either, in part because the enmity between the Raiders and the hometown Kansas City Chiefs was palpable. When he took the field in the team's first game after the season resumed, fans booed him lustily. Some even threw toy footballs that were printed with the words: "It's a hobby." Of course, fans being fans, they cheered him just as lustily when he made a spectacular tumbling catch in the fifth inning.

Coincidentally or not, Jackson's play suffered in the second half of the season. He was benched for extensive periods because he was striking out at a prodigious rate – 27 strikeouts in 64 at-bats between July 16 and August 7. After hitting .254 with 18 home runs, 45 RBIs, and 115 strikeouts before the All-Star break, Jackson played in only 35 games in the second half, with four home runs, eight RBIs and another 43 strikeouts. He would have struck out 221 times if he had played in all 162 games.

While Jackson's decision to play two sports was controversial, it also had its lighter moments. In a New Year's Day 1987 column of tongue-in-cheek predictions, *Kansas City Times* writer Bill Tammeus wrote that Jackson would sign a contract to play with the National Hockey League's Buffalo Sabres, then join the Ice Capades as a hobby. Jackson did receive – and this is true – an offer to play basketball with the Orange County Crush of the fledgling International Basketball Association, a league whose players could be no taller than 6-feet-4. The offer, which Jackson turned down, was a publicity stunt.[12]

After playing seven games with Los Angeles and scoring four touchdowns (including one on a 91-yard run against Seattle, the longest run from scrimmage in the NFL that season), Jackson returned to the Royals for 1988, but not before working with Auburn coach Baird again in the offseason. Baird was not impressed with what he saw.

"There's a real need for some concentrated instruction," Baird said. "I can't believe he didn't go to [Triple-A] Omaha last year. I think (the Royals) made concessions and misjudged him a little."[13]

The media reported that Jackson faced competition for the left fielder's spot from rookie Gary Thurman. It wasn't really much of a contest, as Jackson batted .298, with 5 home runs and 12 RBIs in Florida, while Thurman hit .185 and struck out 16 times in 65 at-bats.[14] Jackson went north as the Royals' starting left fielder. He got off to a good start, too; after going 3-for-4 with a two-run homer and a stolen base in a 7-6 Royals win over Texas on May 16, teammate George Brett said: "Bo Jackson proves he belongs here. He still has a lot to learn, but he learns every time he goes out there.[15]

By the end of May Jackson was hitting .309, with 9 home runs and 30 RBIs. But then fate chose to intervene on June 1 when he tore a hamstring muscle running out a groundball. He missed 28 games, and his batting average began falling on his return. By season's end it was down to .246. He hit 25 home runs, one behind team leader Danny Tartabull, and had 68 RBIs. His 146 strikeouts – including nine consecutive whiffs between September 16 and September 19 – were the fourth highest in the American League. He led junior-circuit left fielders in assists, with 12.

If Jackson has a favorite Beatles song, it may be "Come Together," because that's what happened for him in 1989. He started off hot again, so hot that by the All-Star break he had 21 home runs, just four shy of his 1988 total. Even his strikeouts created a sensation; he got his teammates' attention when he broke a bat in two over his knee after striking out against the Twins on May 9. "Some jaws dropped and some eyes got real big in the dugout after that one," said Royals coach John Mayberry.[16]

Jackson's own jaw may have dropped when he saw the results of fan balloting for the 1989 American League All-Star team, as he led the American League, with 1,748,696 votes. He took full advantage of his moment in the sun, batting leadoff for the AL squad and going 2-for-4, including a 448-foot home run to center field and a stolen base as the American League defeated the National League 5-3. He garnered All-Star Game MVP honors, and the admiration of NL manager Tommy Lasorda.

"Bo Jackson was exciting, really" Lasorda said. When he hit (his home run), I thought it sounded like he hit a golf ball. He's awesome and exciting."[17]

But injuries disrupted Jackson's season yet again when the regular season resumed. He missed 15 games between July 23 and August 8 with sore thigh muscles, an injury he had prior to the All-Star break. Unlike previous years, however, his numbers didn't fall off a cliff, and he finished with 32 home runs, 105 RBIs (both career highs), 26 stolen bases, and a .256 batting average. He did lead the league in one category, with 172 strikeouts.

After his third season with the Raiders, in which he played in a career-high 11 games – he also had the longest run from scrimmage for the season, a 92-yard scamper against Cincinnati – Jackson started 1990 by fulfilling a promise to his mother. He had vowed to her that he would earn his college degree, and in January of that year he began taking classes at Auburn toward that end. He received a bachelor's degree in family and child development in 1995. Sadly, his mother died in 1992 and never saw him graduate.

"I will be the first in my family to get a degree from a major college," Jackson said. Hopefully, that will influence my younger relatives in the family as far as nieces and nephews to go on to college to try to be something or someone."[18]

Jackson's propensity for striking out went beyond the diamond and into the arbitration hearing room in February. He was seeking $1,900,001, but the arbitrator ruled in the Royals' favor. Still, he earned a $1 million salary for the season, which, of course, followed the usual route of great start followed by serious setback. On July 17 he was on pace to hit .270 for the season with 39 home runs and 117 RBIs (albeit with 206 strikeouts) when he hurt his shoulder diving for a fly ball hit by fellow two-sport athlete Deion Sanders. He missed 38 games, but continued to hit well on his return, finishing with a .272 average, 28 home runs, and 78 RBIs in 111 games.

Jackson should have known from his arbitration experience that Bo didn't know gambling, because in 1990 he bet once too often that the punishment he received playing football would not affect his baseball career. Jackson could have made sports history when he was selected to play in the NFL Pro Bowl after the season, which would have made him the first athlete to play in all-star games in two different sports. That was not to be, however, as he suffered a hip injury in a Raiders 20-10 playoff win over the Cincinnati Bengals on January 13, 1991, when he was tackled after a 34-yard run. He didn't play in the AFC Championship Game against the Buffalo Bills – which was probably just as well because the Raiders lost 51-3. He never played football again.

Jackson and the Royals managed to avoid an arbitration hearing when he signed a one-year, $2.4 million deal with the team for the 1991 season. The contract didn't really matter, because his hip injury wasn't getting any better. He had developed a condition called avascular necrosis, which meant that his hip cartilage and bone were deteriorating. When spring training came around, he was still walking around on crutches and clearly unable to play. The Royals placed him on waivers on March 18.

Jackson wasn't out of work long enough to apply for unemployment benefits. On April 3 he signed a three-year, $8.15 million contract with the Chicago White Sox, although "only" $700,000 was guaranteed. White Sox owner Jerry Reinsdorf likened the signing to buying an insurance policy. "It's like life insurance," he said. "You pay the premium, the premium is gone. But if it turns out you die, your family is very happy you had the insurance. If he comes back, we'll be thrilled."[19]

Jackson carried out his rehabilitation under the supervision of the White Sox medical staff. They gave him permission in mid-June to walk without the crutches he had been using since suffering the injury. A month later he started taking some batting practice and did some soft throwing. His workouts continued through August, then on August 25 he began a six-game minor-league rehabilitation assignment. Finally, on September 2, Jackson played his first game of the season against, ironically, the Royals. He went hitless in three at-bats as the DH, but drove in a run with a sacrifice fly. He played in 23 games, hit three home runs and had 14 RBIs, all at the DH spot.

Jackson was very happy to have returned to the field but the following offseason was full of bad news for him. On October 10 his football career effectively ended when he failed a physical given by the Los Angeles Raiders doctors. He made it official one month later when he announced his retirement from football. He joined the White Sox for spring training, but it was evident early on that he was not ready to play. The bat was there, but he wasn't going to be much good on the basepaths. "I have to say if my running was like my hitting I'd be satisfied," Jackson said. "But I'm not. I'm very down on myself for the way I'm running."[20]

Jackson had his damaged hip replaced with a prosthetic ball and socket in Chicago on April 4, 1992. The prognosis was that he would be able to run after he recovered from the operation, but not at the level of a professional athlete. Jackson didn't listen to the prognosis. "Medical and athletic experts figured Jackson would not be heard from again," wrote Ron Flatter. "Apparently there were no Bo Jackson experts to be heard."[21]

Jackson let nothing stand in his way from getting back on the ballfield, even his mother's passing on April 27. His rehab was carried out under the watchful eye of White Sox trainer Herm Schneider, and although progress was slow, it was steady. Even with several hours a day of exercise and training, he walked with a limp until July, and didn't begin his running program until January. Amazingly, he was ready to go for spring training, and on March 4 played his first baseball game in more than a year, going 1-for-3 in an 11-10 loss to Pittsburgh. His status with the White Sox wasn't confirmed until the team finally decided to keep Jackson on March 24.

One might wonder why Jackson would put himself through all that work and discomfort – after all, he didn't need the money. The answer lies in a promise he made to his mother. Before she died, she asked if he was attempting a comeback. He said that if he did, his first hit would be for her. On April 9, 1993, he faced a pitcher in a regular-season game as a pinch-hitter in the bottom of the sixth inning. Facing the Yankees' Neal Heaton, he took the first pitch for a strike, then deposited the next pitch over the right-field wall for a home run.

"Lucky for me and unfortunately for the pitcher, I hit a home run," Jackson recalled. "But that hit meant more to me than anything, because I kept my word, my promise, to my mom. I could have retired that night."[22]

Jackson didn't retire that night, but went on to play in 85 games that year, both in the outfield and at DH. He smacked 16 home runs, batted in 45 runs and hit .232. He also made his only career appearance in the postseason, going 0-for-10 with six strikeouts as the White Sox lost the ALCS in six games to the Toronto Blue Jays.

Jackson's offseason was busy. His remarkable comeback from the hip-replacement surgery, and the intense effort he put in to attain that achievement, was honored when he won both the Tony Conigliaro Award and *The Sporting News* American League Comeback Player of the Year Award. (Andres Galarraga won in the National League.) On the playing side, Jackson rejected an offer of salary arbitration by the White Sox, choosing instead to take the free-agent route. He signed with the California Angels, the team that first drafted him in 1985.

Jackson had a good season in a part-time role for California, playing left and right field and at DH. He appeared in 75 games and batted a career-high .279, with 13 home runs and 43 RBIs in 201 at-bats. One of his season highlights was a five-RBI day at Detroit on May 26. But even before his season was cut short by the players' strike, he began to talk about retiring. "When I left college, my lifelong goal was to be retired from professional sports when I was 34 years old (he was 31 at the time)," he said. "Because I don't think I'll start living until after that."[23]

Jackson ended up retiring even sooner than that. The strike delayed the opening of spring training in 1995, and once it resumed, Jackson, who was a free agent, received calls from a few teams, but decided enough was enough. "I got to know my family [during the strike]," he said in explaining why he retired. "That looks better to me than any $10 million contract."[24]

After retiring from sports, Jackson began working in numerous business and charitable activities. As of 2016, he ran a training complex for athletes in Lockport, Illinois. Among his charitable endeavours is the *Bo Bikes 'Bama* campaign. Tornadoes can cause devastating damage in Alabama, so every year he, his celebrity friends, and other participants cycle across his home state to raise money for the construction of community storm shelters.

Jackson and his wife, Linda, as of 2016 lived in Chicago and have two sons Garrett and Nicholas and a daughter Morgan.

Sources

In addition to the sources cited in the Notes, the author used the following:

Auburntigers.com.

ESPN.com.

Footballdb.com.

Observer-Reporter (Washington, Pennsylvania).

Pro-football-reference.com.

Sports Illustrated.

Stutteringhelp.org.

Swaine, Rick. *Baseball's Comeback Players: Forty Major Leaguers Who Fell and Rose Again* (Jefferson, North Carolina: McFarland & Company. 2014).

Notes

1 Thorpe played six seasons in the majors and eight years in the NFL.

2 *Ben Casey* was a medical drama televised on ABC from 1961 to 1966.

3 Ron Flatter, "Bo Knows Stardom and Disappointment," espn.go.com.

4 Ibid.

5 Matt Snyder, "Bo Jackson's 1985 Scouting Report (Hint: He was good at baseball)," cbssports.com, May 7, 2013.

6 Greg Auman, "When Bucs Blew It By Drafting Bo Jackson," *Tampa Bay Times*, April 24, 2015. The incident left Jackson with a bad taste in his mouth, and he warned the Buccaneers that drafting him would be a waste of a pick. The Buccaneers nevertheless chose him number 1 overall in the NFL draft, but he never signed with them.

7 "Bo's Slow Start Doesn't Concern His Manager," *The Tennessean* (Nashville), July 10, 1986: 7-E.

8 "Jackson Leaves Almost All in Awe," St. Louis Post-Dispatch, April 19, 1987: 4F.

9 John Sonderegger, "Heirs Apparent: Jackson Gets Into Swing With Royals, Big Leagues," *St. Louis Post-Dispatch,* May 10, 1987: 11F.

10 Jackson was eligible for the 1987 draft because he did not sign with the Buccaneers in 1986.

11 ESPN Sportscenter, July 11, 1987. Jackson was often criticized as being arrogant for referring to himself in the third person. In fact, he was using a speech therapy technique he learned to prevent stuttering.

12 According to the Association for Professional Basketball Research (apbr.org), the International Basketball Association existed from 1988 to 1892 as the World Basketball League.

13 Rick Hummel, "Classy Horton Not Bitter Over Being Traded," *St. Louis Post-Dispatch,* February 14, 1988: 3G.

14 Thurman ended up playing in 424 major-league games over nine seasons.

15 "Jackson Continues Hot Pace," *Constitution-Tribune* (Chillicothe, Missouri), May 17, 1988: 6.

16 Bill Coats, "Eye Openers," *St. Louis Post-Dispatch*, May 13, 1989: 2C.

17 "Royals' Bo Jackson Is MVP in American League Victory," *Macon* (Missouri) *Chronicle Herald*, July 12, 1989: 2.

18 Marsha Sanguinette, "Eye Openers," *St. Louis Post-Dispatch* January 20, 1990: 6C.

19 Murray Chass, "White Sox Decide to Gamble on Bo Jackson," *New York Times*, April 4, 1991. Note that baseball-reference.com lists his 1991 salary at $1,010,000.

20 Bill Madden, "Bo Jackson's Baseball Career Appears Over," *Southern Illinoisan* (Carbondale, Illinois), March 7, 1992: 4B.

21 Ron Flatter, "Bo Knows Stardom and Disappointment," espn.com.

22 Lindsay Berra, "#TBT: Bo Jackson Misses a Full Season, Homers in First At-Bat," mlb.com, April 9, 2015. Jackson later had the ball bronzed and placed it on his mother's grave.

23 Mike Terry, "Bo Knows Life After Baseball," *San Bernardino County* (California) *Sun*, July 10, 1994: C1.

24 "Well What Do You Know?," Bo Retiring from Baseball," *The Tennessean*, April 4, 1995: 6C.

DENNIS LEONARD

BY GREGORY H. WOLF

Name the winningest right-hander of the mid-1970s to early '80s and most might guess Tom Seaver, Jim Palmer, Nolan Ryan, or Phil Niekro, but they'd be wrong. Over a seven-year stretch, from 1975 through the strike-shortened 1981 season, the Kansas City Royals' Dennis Leonard led all right-handers with 120 victories, a figure that only southpaw Steve Carlton (129) surpassed. A durable workhorse, Leonard was the only big-league hurler to surpass 200 innings pitched in each of those seven seasons, won at least 20 games three times, and helped lead the club to the postseason five times. His greatest accomplishment, however, might be one that doesn't show up in the box score: his grit and determination. In May 1983 he suffered a torn patellar tendon in his left knee, a potentially career-ending injury. Four operations, numerous setbacks, and an agonizing rehabilitation process followed, but Leonard made an astonishing comeback almost three years later and pitched the entire 1986 season before retiring.

Dennis Patrick Leonard was born on May 18, 1951, in Brooklyn, but grew up on Long Island, one of three sons of William and Catherine (Kawara) Leonard. His parents, both born in New York City, married in 1938 and were involved in law enforcement, his father as a longtime NYC police officer (1942-1965) and his mother as a crossing guard for the Nassau County police department. A Baby Boomer growing up in the 1960s, Dennis dabbled in all sports, but began to concentrate on baseball when he fell under the tutelage of Oceanside High School coach Andrew Scerbo, who suggested that he concentrate on one position: pitching. The husky 6-foot-1 right-hander flashed a mean heater, but when he graduated in 1969, it seemed as though his baseball career might be over.

On Scerbo's suggestion, Leonard enrolled at Iona College, a small Catholic institution located 20 miles north of Manhattan in New Rochelle, and earned a spot on the baseball team as a walk-on.[1] Skipper Gene Roberti's Gaels squad won a school record 17 straight games in his sophomore year, but Leonard came down with arm problems in 1971 that scared off any potential scouts. An examination revealed no bone chips; however, a physician suggested that he stop pitching.[2] Leonard rejected that advice and kept hurling. That summer he raised his stock with an excellent performance in the competitive Atlantic Collegiate Baseball League, helping the Brooklyn-Queens Dodgers to the league title.[3]

Leonard's junior year at Iona was life-changing. On December 17, 1971, he married Audrey Pahopin, his high-school sweetheart. Awarded a baseball scholarship, Leonard tossed a no-hitter and beat CCNY, 7-1, on April 18, fanning 19.[4] Kansas City Royals scout Al Diez tracked his progress in May, as did Tom Ferrick, and both highly recommended the hurler to Royals director of scouting Lou Gorman, who initially seemed apprehensive.[5] Despite his misgivings, Gorman selected Leonard in the second round (Jamie Quirk was their top pick), with the 42nd overall pick in the June amateur draft. Leonard received a reported $16,000 signing bonus.[6]

Leonard's professional career started off with a bang. After four starts in Kingsport (Tennessee) of the Rookie-level Appalachian League, Leonard was assigned to the Class-A Midwest League, where he tossed a seven-inning no-hitter and belted a home run in his first start for Waterloo (Iowa) in the second game of a doubleheader against Quincy on July 15.[7]

A full season in Class A in 1973 raised Leonard's stock to the best pitching prospect in the Royals' organization. He went 15-9 with a 2.58 ERA while fanning more than a batter an inning (212 in 206) for the San Jose Bees and was selected to the California League and the Class-A All-Star team.[8] On April 26 he tossed his third no-hitter in two seasons, walking the first Visalia batter he faced, then retiring 27 consecutive, and even belted a home run.[9]

On a fast track to the big leagues, Leonard had no down time. After hurling for San Jose in the Puerto Rican winter league in 1973-74, he was invited to the Royals camp that spring. An expansion team in 1969, skipper Jack McKeon's club was coming off a surprise second-place finish in the AL West (88-74) despite a weak staff that finished 10th among the 12 AL teams in ERA. The inexperienced Leonard was not yet the answer to the team's hurling woes. He was bumped up two levels to Omaha in the Triple-A American Association, where he earned all-star honors (12-13, 18 complete games, 223 innings) despite playing for the circuit's worst team.

A September call-up to the Royals, Leonard joined a team in a dramatic free-fall, loser of 26 of its last 35 games of the season, and he himself was out of gas. "Jack [McKeon] knew I was tired because I had pitched a lot of innings," said Leonard about his struggles. "I didn't feel tired, but I was dropping down from three-quarters to almost side-arm."[10] After tossing two scoreless innings of relief in his big-league debut, on September 4 against the Chicago White Sox at Royals Stadium, it was all downhill. He lost four consecutive starts, yielding 41 baserunners and 13 earned runs in 20 innings.

Leonard was the last pitcher cut in spring 1975, but it was just a matter of time before the 24-year-old found a permanent home on the Royals' staff. That came sooner than expected when 39-year-old reliever Lindy McDaniel landed on the DL with prostate problems and struggling, former 20-game winner Paul Splittorff was shunted to the bullpen in early May.[11] In his fourth appearance of the season, Leonard picked up his maiden victory, tossing a complete-game five-hitter to beat the Boston Red Sox, 5-2, at Fenway Park on May 16. Essentially a fastball/curveball hurler at this time, Leonard was far from impressive. By the end of June, he was 3-4 with a 4.26 ERA, leading to a widespread belief in the organization that he had been rushed to the majors. And then he suddenly turned around his season, indeed his career. From July 4 through the rest of the season, Leonard went 12-3, including seven straight winning decisions, and challenged 25-year-old established star Steve Busby as the ace of the staff. That stretch was punctuated by three consecutive starts to end August when he defeated some of the biggest names in the sport: the Red Sox' Luis Tiant (18-14), the Baltimore Orioles' Jim Palmer (23-11), and the New York Yankees' Catfish Hunter (23-14), and was named the AL Player of the Week for the last week of the month. The Royals finished with a franchise-record 91 wins, but were 7 games behind the Oakland A's; however, a radical sea change in the AL West was on the horizon as the advent of free agency would alter the baseball landscape and end the A's five-year grip on the divisional crown. Leonard (15-7) was runner-up to the Cleveland Indians' Dennis Eckersley as *The Sporting News* AL Rookie Pitcher of the Year, while the Kansas City chapter of the Baseball Writers Association of America named him the Royals pitcher of the year, an award he eventually won three times.

The Royals spring training in 1976 was filled with "soaring optimism," gushed beat reporter Joe McGuff.[12] Skipper Whitey Herzog, who had taken over from McKeon the previous season and led the club to the best record in baseball (41-25) over the last 66 games, had a young club with limitless potential. The Royals assumed the top spot in the AL West on May 18 and never relinquished it, while Leonard got off to a hot start unlike the previous season. On June 4 he went 10 innings for the third time in his last eight starts, tossing a 10-inning complete game to beat the Milwaukee Brewers, 4-3, on Hal McRae's game-winning double. "He threw 121 pitches, but not too many for him," quipped Herzog.[13] An old-school workhorse, Leonard had tossed 177 pitches in 10⅔ innings five days earlier despite a sore back from a cross-country flight to California, and all he had to show for it was a no-decision. In his last start before the All-Star break, Leonard threw a four-hit shutout to beat Mark Fidrych, the Detroit Tigers' entertaining rookie hurler, who had captured the nation's attention with his mound antics, in front of more than 51,000 screaming fans in the Motor City.

Leonard credited his consistency and success to pitching coach Galen Cisco, with whom he had worked tirelessly since spring training to improve his mechanics and delivery. "[Cisco] told me I was dipping down too much and anything I was throwing was flattening out," said the hurler.[14] Leonard's fifth straight win, on August 14, his eighth in nine decisions, pushed his record to 15-4. It appeared as though he'd win 20 and the Royals, holding a 12-game cushion in first place on August 6, would cruise to the AL West crown; neither panned out in that manner. Leonard collapsed, going 2-6 with an ERA approaching 5.00 for the remainder of the season. The Royals lost 25 of their last 40 games, including nine of their last 11, but became the first expansion team to win a division title, holding off the A's by 2½ games. The Royals met the Yankees, playing in their first postseason since 1964, in a classic ALCS. In Game Two, Leonard was staked to a 2-0 first-inning lead, but was pummeled for six hits and three runs and failed to make it through three frames. Splittorff, who had made just one start since the end of July because of an injured finger, tossed 5⅔ scoreless innings of relief as the Royals came back to win, 7-3, and tie the series, one game each. Starting the deciding Game Five in New York, Leonard did not record an out, yielding three straight hits, and was charged with two runs. George Brett's dramatic three-run home run in the eighth tied the game, 6-6, yielding to heartache in the next inning when Chris Chambliss parked Mark Littell's first pitch in the grandstand to give the Yankees the pennant.

Leonard was rewarded with a new five-year, $1 million contract, but his struggles in spring training in 1977 bled into the regular season. A loss on June 20 dropped his record to 4-8 while the Royals' prolonged funk also continued, falling below .500 (31-32), raising tensions in the clubhouse. Leonard's "unexpected ineffectiveness" led to widespread charges of complacency[15] and baffled Herzog, who quipped "[He] has good stuff inside, but not outside."[16] Leonard was struggling with his curveball, mechanics, and delivery, but kept working with Cisco. On June 24 Leonard tossed his second three-hit shutout in his last four starts, beating the A's, 3-0, and fanning 11. Around this time, Leonard unveiled a new pitch. "When he started throwing the slider, it was turning point in the season for him," said Herzog. "It gave him better command of his curveball."[17]

Armed with a pitch that made his heater even that much better, Leonard went on a roll and emerged as the biggest strikeout artist not named Nolan Ryan. He fanned 10 or more six times, and tied the franchise record of 13 twice. "I don't go much for strikeouts except that I might give it something a little extra with two strikes on the batter," said Leonard. "I really prefer to throw few pitches. ... It saves a lot of wear on the arm."[18] He concluded the season on a 16-4 tear (2.35 ERA) and became the franchise's third pitcher to win 20 games, joining Busby and Splittorff, by shutting out the Angels on six hits in the last game of the season. Like their star hurler, the Royals made a dramatic turnaround, winning 38 of their last 49 games to post the best record in baseball (102-60) and capture their second division crown.

Leonard tied Palmer and the Minnesota Twins' Dave Goltz for the AL lead in victories, logged 292□ innings and set team records with 21 complete games and 244 strikeouts. Herzog championed his ace for the Cy Young Award, but lamented that he wouldn't win it because "you just never get any recognition in Kansas City."[19] Favored to win the pennant, the Royals faced their nemesis the Yankees in what proved to be another heartbreaking ALCS. After the teams split the first two games in New York, Leonard spun a four-hit complete-game gem in Game Three, winning 4-2. In Game Five the Royals held a 3-1 lead heading into the eighth inning in Kansas City. After Reggie Jackson's RBI-single cut the lead to one run, Herzog summoned Leonard to start the ninth, just three outs from the World Series, but the Royals never recorded them. Paul Blair led off with a bloop single and Roy White walked, forcing Leonard out of the game, and the flood gates were open. The Yankees scored three runs, Leonard was charged with the loss, and the Yankees captured another pennant.

The Royals seized their third straight West crown in 1978, but it was far from easy. Struggling to play .500 ball through the first half of the season, the club was carried by its starting quartet [Leonard, Splittorff (19-13), Larry Gura (16-4), and rookie Rich Gale (14-8)], which combined to start 134 games. A streaky hurler, Leonard floundered for two months and bottomed out in May (0-5 and 8.13 ERA), before turning his season around, beginning with a six-hit shutout against the Seattle Mariners, 6-0, on June 1 to put the team into a tie for first place, at least temporarily. "If I warm up and my fastball is going good, really moving, my confidence shoots sky-high," declared Leonard. "If not, I think, 'God, I have to start to get tricky, fool them with the other stuff.'"[20]

Leonard didn't need to fool anybody. In July, he strung together five straight complete-game victories, the last of which was an exclamation point 5-2 win over the Yankees on July 24 to give the Royals their 10th straight win and a three-game cushion in the standings. Just hours before that game, a teary-eyed Billy Martin was forced to resign as Yankees skipper for his slur about Reggie Jackson and club owner George Steinbrenner ("They deserve each other. One's a born liar and the other's convicted").[21] The Royals, however, couldn't pull away from the pesky Angels, and briefly fell out of the top spot in late August before a September charge.

On September 25 Leonard beat the Mariners, 7-2, for his 20th victory and 20th complete game to give the Royals at least a tie for the crown, which they eventually won by five games. Leonard (21-17) led the AL in starts for first of three times in the next four seasons, and logged a career-best 294⅔ innings, but was also a tough-luck loser. In 12 of his setbacks, the Royals scored just 17 total runs.

For the third straight season, the Royals faced the Yankees in the ALCS. Under Martin's replacement, Bob Lemon, they emerged as the hottest team in baseball and beat the Red Sox in a dramatic one-game tiebreaker to capture the East crown. The Royals were in their best possible shape: Game One was scheduled for Royals Stadium, where starter Leonard was a staggering 16-5. The Yankees had used their ace Ron Guidry (25-3) the day before and countered with rookie Jim Beattie (6-9). In a crushing defeat, the Royals managed just two hits and lost, 7-1. Leonard was clubbed for nine hits and three runs in four innings, after which Herzog commented, "I don't think I've ever seen him hit so hard."[22] In Game Four, Leonard went the distance, yielding just four hits, but two of them were solo home runs by Roy White and Graig Nettles, while Guidry stymied Royals bats for a 2-1 win and gave the Yankees a third straight berth in the fall classic.

The Royals slipped to second place (85-77) in 1979, doomed by a pitching staff that sank to 10th (out of 14 AL teams) in team ERA (4.45) after finishing second, first, and third in the previous three seasons. For the first time in his big-league career, Leonard was hobbled by an injury, severe tendinitis in his right elbow, and was sidelined for a month in late May and June. After winning just one game in each of May, June, and July, he finally hit his stride on August 25 with a four-hit shutout to beat the Red Sox, 1-0, in Kansas City and pull the Royals to within 3½ games of the lead. Leonard tossed three more shutouts in his next seven starts, but the Royals played just .500 ball in September and finished three games behind the Angels, who captured their first division crown.

Wildly popular in Kansas City, Leonard came across like an average Joe to whom fans could relate, a sentiment that grew exponentially during his comeback. Blessed with down-home personality, Leonard didn't necessarily cut the impression of a big-league pitcher. Standing 6-feet-1 and weighing 190 pounds, he had bushy blond hair and a trademark handlebar mustache, kept a can of Skoal in the back pocket of his baseball pants, and enjoyed a few beers after a game. He was known for signing autographs for kids, joking with the press and teammates, and maintaining an even-keeled personality even after tough losses and postseason meltdowns.

The Royals got a scare in the offseason when Leonard was involved in a boating accident on Christmas Eve, cut three tendons in his hand and required 25 stitches.[23] Fortunately for him and the Royals, it was his left hand and the gritty 29-year-old hurler was ready for 1981 spring training and new manager Jim Frey.

Off to a plodding start, the Royals moved into first place on May 23 when Leonard threw seven innings of mediocre ball, yielding five runs, keeping the burly New Yorker's ERA well above 6.00. In early June Leonard tossed consecutive two- and three-hit shutouts on the road in Texas and Cleveland to emerge as one of the league's hottest pitchers over the last four months of the season. "When I was struggling," said Leonard, "I was trying to strike too many people out instead of keeping the ball down, moving in and out, and just having them hit the ball."[24]

In August he won all five of his decisions and by the end of the month the Royals held an insurmountable 20-game lead. Constantly evolving and working on his mechanics, Leonard attributed his turnaround to his comfort and control of a new pitch: a changeup. "I don't know if I am a different type of pitcher, I'm basically a fastball pitcher," he said, "but getting the changeup over certainly helps."[25] It also helped that the Royals had the game's best closer, Dan Quisenberry. Leonard was still a workhorse, logging 280⅓ innings in a league-high 38 starts, but completed just nine games, as the submariner Quis paced the league in appearances and saves (tied with Goose Gossage). On September 17 Leonard blanked the Angels on three hits in the first game of a doubleheader at home to clinch the West crown.

A 20-game winner for the third time in four seasons, Leonard exorcised his demons in Game Two of the ALCS against the Yankees, hurling seven-hit ball over eight innings and fanning eight in a 3-2 win, which Quisenberry secured. "This is the best I've pitched in the postseason," gushed Leonard, who profited from an excellent throw by left fielder Willie Wilson to nail Willie Randolph at home with what would have been a game-tying run in the eighth inning. "I threw as hard as I could, especially my curve, and I feel that the breaks turned our way."[26]

After sweeping the Yankees, the Royals were favorites against the Philadelphia Phillies in the World Series. Leonard's postseason miseries returned in Game One, when he failed to make it through the fourth inning, yielding six runs in a 7-6 loss on October 14. The mood in the KC dugout changed dramatically four days later in Game Four when Leonard hurled three-run ball (two earned) in seven innings, supported by two home runs by Willie Aikens, to win 5-3, and tie the Series, two games each. Aided by a ninth-inning comeback and a command performance by Steve Carlton in the clincher, the Phillies took the next two games to capture their first title in franchise history.

Described by Kansas City sportswriter Mike DeArmond as "one Royal the club could not afford to lose" to either impending free agency or injury, Leonard once again anchored the staff in the strike-shortened 1981 season.[27] When play stopped on June 12, the Royals (20-30) were mired in fifth place. In response to the strike, cancellation of approximately one-third of the regular-season games, and lost revenue, the owners split the season into two halves, with the divisional winners of each half meeting in a divisional series. The Royals profited from the inequitable plan and unbalanced schedule by winning the second half by percentage points over the Oakland A's (.566 to .551) and Leonard was a major reason. Beginning on September 8, shortly after Dick Howser replaced Frey as skipper, Leonard made seven starts in 26 days, going 6-1 with a 1.36 ERA in 59⅔ innings, and tossed two shutouts. He finished the abbreviated season by leading the majors in starts (26) and innings (201⅔), while posting career-low 2.99 ERA to go along with his 13-11 slate.

The first team in big-league history to advance to the playoff with a losing record (50-53), the Royals faced Billy Martin's upstart A's in the ALDS, where they were swept in three games.[28] Leonard cruised in Game One until a crushing error by third baseman George Brett on what would have been an inning-ending out in the fourth gave the A's an extra chance. The next batter, Wayne Gross, whacked a three-run home run. The Royals had no answer to Mike Norris who blanked them on four hits, 4-0.

Leonard was sidelined for more than 2½ months in 1982 when a ball off the bat of the Texas Rangers' Buddy Bell broke two fingers on his right hand on May 21. He returned on August 8, his middle finger still noticeably swollen and misshapen, won four straight decisions that month, but never found his groove, finishing with a 10-6 slate and a 5.10 ERA for the runner-up Royals.

At the age of 32, Leonard began his 10th season with the Royals with questions about his injured digits and rumors that his fastball had lost a few ticks. After victories in three consecutive starts pushed his record to 6-3, Leonard suffered a vicious injury on May 28 at Royals Stadium against the Orioles. "When I came down on my left knee, it sounded like the Velcro strap I'd been wearing for support just ripped loose," said Leonard about his second pitch to Cal Ripken Jr. with one out on the fourth. "But it was my tendon! My body went left, but I remember feeling like somebody had put me in reverse. I rolled over and over. The pain lasted a minute and a half. It shot up my leg. It hit me in the brain. My kneecap was off to the side, and my leg was straight. I thought I was hit by a line drive. But I remember the umpire yelling, 'Strike!' So I knew that just wasn't right."[29]

Leonard had torn the patellar tendon in his left knee. It was a devastating injury, from which few athletes in any sport ever return successfully. He underwent an operation on May 29, the first of an eventual four surgeries during a string of unimaginable setbacks and heartbreaks. It was almost 2½ years before Leonard took the mound in a big-league game again, and almost three years before he made his next start. On September 29 he underwent a second operation to graft tendons that had deteriorated. After a grueling rehabilitation process, he began throwing off the mound in June 1984 and suffered another setback. His surgeon, Dr. Frank R. Noyes, discovered fluid in his knee that affected the grafts, leading to yet another patellar-tendon graft surgery on July 31. A fourth operation took place several months later. Leonard refused to give up, and began the rehabilitation process again with no guarantees that he'd ever be able to pitch again. "There are a lot of people who doubt I'll be back," he admitted. "[A]t times I wonder, 'Is my career over?' You have those days when physically you're fine, but mentally you're down and you wonder, 'Is this ever going to end?'"[30]

With the ever-present support and guidance of Royals trainer Mickey Cobb, Leonard defied the odds and began throwing off the mound on July 1, 1985. After a stint in the minors, he made an emotional return to the Royals on September 6, tossing an inning of scoreless relief, yielding a hit in the second game of a doubleheader against the Brewers. He tossed another scoreless frame 12 days later in his only other appearance that season as his teammates held off the Angels to win the West for the second straight year under skipper Dick Howser. Leonard was not on the club's postseason roster as the Royals defeated the Toronto Blue Jays in the ALCS and came back from a three-games-to-one deficit against the St. Louis Cardinals and won the World Series.

In the last year of his contract, Leonard returned to the Royals in 1986, determined to battle for a spot in the rotation. "I'm going to spring training like a rookie looking for his first shot in the big leagues," he said.[31] On April 12 Leonard defied expectations by making a start against the Blue Jays in a nationally televised game. "Leonard's return seemed more like a Hollywood concoction than a regularly scheduled American league game," gushed sportswriter Joe Gergen.[32] The 36-year-old spun a three-hit shutout and didn't walk a batter. By June 4 he was 6-4 with a 2.22 ERA and was hailed for one of the inspirational comebacks in baseball history. "I wanted to try to prove I could make it back," said the pitcher. "I owed it to the Royals. They've been good to me."[33] The effects of four surgeries eventually took their toll. Leonard went 2-9 with an ERA north of 6.00 thereafter as the Royals suffered their first losing season (79-83) since 1981.

Released by the Royals in the offseason, Leonard decided not to test the free-agent market and announced his retirement in February 1987. As of 2018 he still ranked among the top three in many career statistical categories for the Royals, including wins (144), starts (302), and innings (2,187), and ranked first with 103 complete games and 23 shutouts. His accomplishments on the diamond have resulted in his induction into the Royals Hall of Fame (1989), the Missouri Sports Hall of Fame (2003), the New York State Baseball Hall of Fame (2015), and the Oceanside High School Hall of Fame (2003).

A constant in Leonard's journey through the minors and his tenure with the Royals was his wife, Audrey. Together they had two children, Dennis Jr. and Ryan. During the offseasons, Leonard operated a baseball academy in Florida and the family raised their children in the Kansas City area, where Audrey opened a successful Hallmark store in 1985 (which closed in 2010).[34]

Leonard remained close to the only big-league club he ever knew. He has served as a longtime guest pitching instructor at spring training and has been an active participant on the Royals caravan and fan festivals. As of 2018 he still resided with Audrey in the Kansas City area.

Sources

In addition to the sources cited in the Notes, the author accessed the *Encyclopedia of Minor League Baseball*, Retrosheet.org, Baseball-Reference.com, *The Sporting News* archive via Paper of Record, and SABR.org.

The author also thanks SABR member Bill Mortell for assistance with the player's genealogy.

Notes

1 Sid Bordman, "'I Plan to Win 20,' Says Royals' Ace Leonard," *The Sporting News*, July 31, 1976: 13.

2 Dick Kaegel, "Leonard, with Slider, Cuts Down Yankees, 6-2," *St. Louis Post-Dispatch*, October 8, 1977: 5A.

3 Atlantic Coast Baseball League. acbl-online.com.

4 "Iona's Leonard 0-Hits CCNY, 7-1," Daily News (New York), April 18, 1972: 103.

5 Lou Gorman, *High and Inside: My Life in the Front Offices of Baseball* (Jefferson, North Carolina: McFarland, 2007), 124.

6 Mike McKenzie, "Leonard Wins and Royals Pay," *The Sporting News*, April 11, 1981: 11.

7 "No-Hit Effort for Waterloo," *Des Moines Register*, July 16, 1972: 36.

8 "Kingston's Whitefield Tops Class A Stars," *The Sporting News*, November 24, 1973: 46.

9 "No-Hitter in State League," *The Times* (San Mateo, California), April 27, 1973: 25.

10 Sid Bordman, "Soph Jinx Just a Joke to Royals Ace Leonard," *The Sporting News*, August 7, 1976: 3.

11 Associated Press, "Royals Assigned McDaniel to Disabled List," *Daily Capital News* (Jefferson City, Missouri), May 3, 1975: 8.

12 Joe McGuff, "Wave of Optimism Is Stirring Up Royals Fans," *The Sporting News*, February 7, 1976: 46.

13 Del Black, "McRae Doubles Home Mayberry to Give Royals 4-3 Victory in 10," *Kansas City Times*, June 5, 1976: 51.

14 Sid Bordman, "'I Plan to Win 20,' Says Royals' Ace Leonard."

15 AP, "Trade Aids Royals," *Chillicothe* (Missouri) *Constitution-Tribune*, April 30, 1977: 12.

16 AP, "Relievers Boost K.C to 5-4 Win," Sedalia (Missouri) Democrat, March 31, 1977: 22.

17 AP, "Leonard's Slider Helps Stop Royals' Slide," *Sedalia* (Missouri) *Democrat*, August 19, 1977: 8.

18 John Hickey, "A's Make Leonard Look Like Ryan," *The Argus* (Fremont, California), June 15, 1977: 11.

19 AP, "Leonard 'Not Worried' about winning Cy Young Award," *Daily Standard* (Sikeston, Missouri), Oct 3, 1977: 5.

20 AP, "Royals Back Atop Heap; Leonard Back in Win Form," *Garden City* (Kansas) *Telegram*, June 2, 1978: 10.

21 AP, "Martin's Slurring Remarks Prompt Ouster as Manager," *Asbury Park* (New Jersey) *Press*, July 25, 1978: 29.

22 Dick Kaegel, "Champ-Like Yankees Flatten Royals," *St. Louis Post-Dispatch*, October 4, 1978: 2D.

23 Sid Bordman, "Left Was Right for Leonard," T*he Sporting News*, February 2, 1980: 41.

24 Del Black, "Royals' Leonard Sports Sharp New Style," *The Sporting News*, July 5, 1980: 13.

25 Ibid.

26 United Press Internaional, "Royals Win, 3-2; Lead Series, 2-0," *Lincoln* (Nebraska) *Star*, October 10, 1980: 19.

27 Mike DeArmond, "Leonard, K.C. – Big Silence," *The Sporting News*, January 31, 1981: 52.

28 The Royals had the fourth best combined record in the West; the Rangers (57-48) and White Sox (54-52) were the big losers of the plan and were shut out of the playoffs. The Yankees (59-48) had the fourth best record in the East; the second-place Orioles (59-46) and Tigers (60-49) were likewise losers in the split-season playoff.

29 Jill Lieber, "A Fight Against Pain and Doubt," Sports Illustrated, July 29, 1985.

30 Leonard Is Facing 3rd Knee Operation," *The Sporting News*, June 25, 1984: 24.

31 Mike Fish, "Squeeze or Swan Song for Leonard," *The Sporting News*, January 20, 1986: 47.

32 Joe Gergen, "Leonard's Is Most Inspiring of Many Comebacks," *The Sporting News*, May 5, 1986: 6.

33 Gergen.

34 Jeff Martin, "Audrey's Hallmark Shop Closes Its Doors After 25 Years," *The Examiner* (East Jackson County, Missouri), May 28, 2010. examiner.net/article/20100528/NEWS/305289739.

MIKE MacFARLANE

BY BOB LEMOINE

"I'm average. I've always been that," Mike Macfarlane humbly said of himself as his career was winding down. "But I've got 12 years of major-league experience and I work hard."[1] Most of us would gladly have taken such an "average" career like his: 13 years as one of the most respected players in the game, a catcher who guided pitchers, provided power when needed, mentored young catchers, and was both an inspiring presence in the locker room and a role model for the fans. His .992 fielding percentage ranked him 57th all-time among catchers as of 2018. "A quiet and dependable leader," was how Jeffrey Flanagan of the Kansas City Star described Macfarlane. "A player who knew the game and how to play it correctly. He didn't complain. He didn't point fingers, and he didn't hesitate to help others. He went out of his way to sign autographs. He helped numerous charities. He never got in trouble with the law, and he not once referred to himself in the third person."[2]

Not a flashy player by any stretch, Macfarlane was a hard worker who overcame obstacles and made it to the major leagues, but never forgot to be grateful for every opportunity. "The Mike Macfarlanes of this world do not play in All-Star Games," wrote Bob Ryan of the *Boston Globe*. "They do not spend hours agonizing over exactly what to say when they're inducted into the Hall of Fame. They are guys who are just good enough to play and who are thankful for the opportunity. They constitute the backbone of sport. A successful team needs its share of All-Stars, and it also needs its happy and willing next-door-neighbor types. Mike Macfarlane is the guy who lends you his ladder."[3] His attitude represented all that is good about the game and endeared him to the fans. "I like playing on grass. I like getting dirty. I like playing hard for three hours each night, knowing I've given my all. I even like waking up in the morning, stiff as a board, my knee not functioning, knowing I'm going to go back out there that night and do it all over again."[4]

Michael Andrew Macfarlane was born to John and Marlene (Boggiano) Macfarlane on April 12, 1964, in Stockton, California. John was a US Navy veteran who coached (football, baseball) and taught at Lincoln High School from 1961 to 1975, and coached Babe Ruth, American Legion, and Little League baseball squads. Mike was a standout baseball catcher at Lincoln. He was named to the All San Joaquin Athletic Association and co-MVP of the league his senior year, in which he batted .422 and threw out 14 of 16 attempted basestealers. He was quoted in his high-school yearbook: "We had a lot of players returning from last years [*sic*] team and we had many quality players come up from the sophomore squad of a year ago. This was one of the factors that made us successful."[5] Macfarlane was also selected to the California State High School All-Star Team along with Randy Johnson and Barry Bonds. His brother Pat played football and baseball at Lincoln, Delta College, and the University of the Pacific.

Mike received a scholarship to Santa Clara University, where he was the starting catcher for three years. As of 2018, he ranked fifth in total home runs (28) and 10th in doubles (47) and total bases (323), and held several single-season records.

Macfarlane was drafted by the Kansas City Royals in the fourth round of the June 1985 amateur draft. He was assigned to Memphis, Kansas City's affiliate in the Double-A Southern League. He batted .269 with 8 home runs and 39 RBIs in 65 games. After the season he caught 30 games in the Florida Instructional League. What neither Macfarlane nor his coaches took into consideration was that including the fall and spring seasons at Santa Clara, Macfarlane had already caught over 100 games. Being young, he didn't consider the toll this was taking on his right shoulder. "I liked to show off because I had a good arm," he said. "I was the type of player who liked to gun every throw," he said, which included not just basestealers but even throwing the ball during warm-ups.[6]

The overwork caught up to Macfarlane during the Instructional League. He blew out his arm and had to been seen by Dr. Frank Jobe, the orthopedic surgeon, in February of 1986. "Everything is disfigured in there," Jobe said. "It's one of the worst I've seen."[7] Macfarlane's rotator cuff was literally sawed in half by a fragmented ligament. His shoulder socket was twice the normal size, and he was told he had to stay out of baseball for at least a year and not catch for two. But using a three-pound weight to strengthen the socket and tossing a roll of tape for 15 minutes every other day, just to do some type of throwing, he kept his arm in shape. "I was just feeling like I was half a player at that point," he said. "I'd always prided myself on being a good defensive catcher, and then my arm is taken away."[8]

His shoulder improved more quickly than anticipated, and Macfarlane was back in Memphis in June, playing exclusively as a DH. "I told myself I'd worked too hard my whole life to shut it down."[9] In 40 games he batted .241 with an astounding 12 home runs, given all the obstacles he had gone through. The Royals also tweaked his throwing motion from a short-arm throw to a full motion, to alleviate the stress on his shoulder.

In March of 1987, Mike married Kathleen Rosenthal, who had also attended Santa Clara. "Part of our honeymoon was driving to Florida for spring training and playing catch with her," Macfarlane remembered. "She was a girlie-girl and we'd go to a high-school field in Texas or Louisiana, driving across those states. Our first marital spat was how bad her soft toss was," he joked.[10] Macfarlane was soon sent to the minor-league camp. He was promoted to Triple-A Omaha, where he gradually worked himself back into being a regular catcher. He caught 76 games and his offensive numbers (.262/13/50) with a .324 OBP put him on the radar for Kansas City. He celebrated a memorable 23rd birthday with a six-RBI game including a grand slam in a victory over Nashville.[11]

Kansas City needed help in late July when Jamie Quirk went on the disabled list. Macfarlane served as the backup to Larry Owen. He made his major-league debut on July 23 as a late-inning defensive replacement in a 2-1 loss to Baltimore. He started the next day and went 0-for-4 against Baltimore, then got his first major-league hit off Dave Schmidt the following day. Macfarlane finished batting .211 in eight games.

Macfarlane was impressive during the spring of 1988 and won a catching job on the Kansas City roster, splitting time with Quirk. He was the Royals' Opening Day catcher on April 4 in a 5-3 loss to Toronto. He went 2-for-4 with two doubles, and continued his hot hitting in April, batting .378 by the end of the month. He hit his first major-league home run on May 21 against Cleveland's Scott Bailes. His batting numbers came back to earth, and he batted in the .260s to .270s for June and July. Macfarlane was surprised when manager John Wathan decided to make a change, calling up Owen from Omaha and demoting Macfarlane. The reason was defense. Owen had thrown out 24 of 53 basestealers (45.3 percent) while Macfarlane had thrown out only 14 of 45 (24 percent).[12] Macfarlane didn't think the numbers justified a demotion. "The arm is in great shape," he said. "I was very happy with the way I was throwing the ball. The reasons they gave me for sending me down are not valid in my mind, but what can I do about it?"[13] But the demotion gave Macfarlane time to refocus. "It really woke me up to the business of baseball," he said. "I don't know who was behind it or what the reasoning was, but that really refocused my attention on catching."[14] He played in 21 games at Omaha, batting .237. Owen threw out 35 percent of basestealers in his 37 games in Kansas

City, and then retired. Quirk's success (27 percent) was still lower than the league average (31 percent). The Royals finished third (84-77). In mid-August Macfarlane suffered ligament damage in his right hand making a tag and was lost for the remainder of the season.[15]

On the surface, it seemed Macfarlane had another huge obstacle to overcome for the 1989 season. The Royals were still hesitant to hand him the starting catcher's job and instead they signed 41-year-old Bob Boone, who would spend the final two seasons of his 19-year career in Kansas City. But instead of this being a setback, since it limited Macfarlane's playing time, it was a chance for the young catcher to pick the brain of a catching legend who as of 2018 was third all-time in games caught (2,225). Macfarlane would often be seen after games chatting with Boone, whom he dubbed "Yoda," with Mike asking questions about game situations. "I've been keeping a notebook on everything he has told me," Macfarlane said. "I'm having a ball with Mike," Boone said. "He wants to learn it all. I get such a kick out of seeing him improve from last year." Macfarlane learned valuable lessons from Boone, such as the main task of a catcher being to set up batters to fail. "It's knowing your own pitching staff, calling the right pitches, setting up hitters and watching them fail," Macfarlane said. "(Boone) was amazing in the way he could manage a game behind the plate. He knew what he needed from the pitcher and how he wanted to work the hitters, but at the same time, he also was in the opposing manager's head and everybody else's, too."[16]

Macfarlane batted .223 in 69 games in 1989, 59 of them backing up Boone behind the plate. He made the most of his opportunities, throwing out 41 percent of would-be basestealers, 10 percentage points higher than the league average. The Royals had a strong 92-70 season but still finished a distant second behind Oakland.

In 1990 the Royals had their worst record (75-86) since 1970 (discounting the 1981 strike-shortened season), but it was a breakthrough year for Macfarlane. Boone was injured and played in only 40 games. Macfarlane finally became the Royals' starting catcher. He batted .255 with 6 home runs and 58 RBIs in 124 games. His range factor per game, a calculation of assists and putouts divided by games played (6.10), ranked fifth in the league for catchers. He would finish fourth or fifth in that category three more times from 1991 to 1994. However, he allowed 68 stolen bases and threw out only 17 percent of would-be basestealers. He had more work to do in spring training 1991, but now the starting job was his as Boone had retired.

Macfarlane was having his best season in 1991, batting .273 with 13 home runs and 39 RBIs and had thrown out 17 of 38 trying to steal by July 15 when an injury sidelined him for two months. It happened on a play at the plate when he locked legs with Toronto's Joe Carter and tore a ligament in his left knee.[17] "Finally I'm hitting my stride and now this," a discouraged Macfarlane said. "It was a freaky play. I'm angry in the sense that he didn't slide, where a slide can avoid the whole situation. I'm angry in that regard. I'm angry that it happened to me, I'm angry that it had to happen, period. It felt like someone jabbed me with a hot poker in there [knee]." He did not return until mid-September, and batted .357 the rest of the season.[18] His caught-stealing percentage was 44.7 percent, third in the AL.

Macfarlane spent the winter strengthening his knee, but still struggled defensively early in 1992. He allowed four passed balls and made three errors by early May, and had thrown out just 27 percent of basestealers. "I certainly don't feel as comfortable as I did last year," Macfarlane admitted as he saw the Royals depending on a catching platoon of Brent Mayne and Bob Melvin.[19] He batted around .200 for much of the season, but hit .271 from August on with 11 home runs, giving him 17 for the year with a .234 batting average. The Royals were 72-90. Macfarlane was also one to "take one for the team," as he led the league in being hit by a pitch, a feat he would repeat in 1994 and finished near the top three other times. He avoided arbitration in the offseason and signed a one-year contract with the Royals for $1.175 million for 1993.[20]

Macfarlane began the 1993 season platooning with Mayne, batting mostly against left-handers, but those plans of manager Hal McRae changed when

Macfarlane batted .338 with six home runs in May. His hitting pace kept up for much of the season; he had the best offensive season of his career (.273/20/67) and threw out 53 would-be basestealers, or 43 percent, fourth in the AL. Runners still tested his arm, however, and he was third in stolen bases allowed (70). He also helped a rejuvenated Royals team (84-78) to a third-place finish. Macfarlane avoided arbitration in the offseason and signed a one-year deal with the Royals for $2.6 million.

Macfarlane started well in 1994, batting .276 with seven home runs through the end of May before he fell into a terrible June slump in which he batted a meager .192. He broke out in a big way as July began, hitting .533 in a four-game series against Toronto, and provided his own fireworks on the Fourth with two home runs. Macfarlane swatted his 14th home run on August 9 in a 5-3 extra-inning win at Anaheim and the Royals were contenders for the AL Central Division title. But the players strike began two days later, and the rest of the season and the World Series were canceled. Macfarlane, who was now a popular Royal with fans and a clubhouse leader of his teammates, was an unrestricted free agent and the Royals chose not to re-sign him.

The Boston Red Sox, looking for a reliable catcher, signed Macfarlane to a one-year contract for $1.5 million with a club option for 1996. "This was my first choice, coming here," Macfarlane said. "I've always enjoyed Boston and I love (Fenway Park) and everything about the organization."[21] In May he hit seven home runs, including a walkoff against the Yankees on Mother's Day, May 14, with his wife, Kristine, son, Austin, and daughter, Megan, looking on. The family saw some scary moments earlier in the day as they watched him get drilled with a pitch, get hit in the jaw with a bat, and throw the ball into center field trying to throw out a runner. "Yeah, I guess I was right in the thick of everything, but that's why you're a catcher," he said. "All the action is back there."[22] Macfarlane batted .225 overall – .300 against lefties with eight home runs. Against right-handers he hit seven home runs but had a much poorer .201 average. He led the league with 26 passed balls, although 13 of them were due to trying to zig and zag in catching Tim Wakefield's knuckleballs. He threw out 35 percent of runners trying to steal and had a .993 fielding percentage. Boston ran away with the American League East Division title, clinching on September 20 when Rick Aguilera struck out Milwaukee's Dave Nilsson, the ball disappearing in MacFarlane's mitt as the team celebrated.

The Red Sox were swept in three games by Cleveland in the Division Series. Macfarlane started all three, going 3-for-9. His lone season in Boston quickly came to an end as the club decided to buy out his contract for $150,000 instead of picking up the $2.3 million option. "I figured they wouldn't pick up the option because of the money," Macfarlane said. "The kind of year I had certainly didn't warrant that type of payoff, but if we can work something out where I can come back for less money, I'm willing to do that. Boston is where I want to be. I can't really explain my troubles at the plate. I never really got going and I don't know the reasons why. I do know I have to spend the winter working hard on my hitting."[23]

Macfarlane returned to the Royals for 1996, signing a two-year contract for $1.6 million. He was happy to be back "home"; the family lived in nearby Overland Park, Kansas. "I'm back home," Macfarlane said. "I know what the situation is here and I know Sal [Fasano] is the future, but hopefully I can give them some production before that happens. I'm anxious to be back working for [manager] Bob (Boone)."[24] The season saw Macfarlane appear in 112 games, 99 of them behind the plate as he competed not only against Fasano but also youngster Mike Sweeney, who would eventually represent the Royals in five All-Star Games. Macfarlane had a steady year at the plate, batting .274 with 19 home runs, quietly reaching six straight seasons with double-digit home runs. His 38.7 percent caught-stealing percentage ranked him fourth in the AL. A year removed from the postseason, Macfarlane's Royals were in the basement of the AL Central (75-86).

Macfarlane's 1997 season began slowly as he dealt with a strained muscle in his left side. Instead of giving himself time to heal in spring training, he kept playing through the pain, managing it with hot packs. Eventually the pain was too much and he started the season on the disabled list. He returned to the field on April 13, but a few days later he landed on his right shoulder diving for a bunt. "I jarred (the shoulder) and didn't think much of it," Macfarlane said, "but obviously something happened in there because a week and a half later it was full of fluid."[25] He returned to the disabled list, and returned to action at the end of May. He was batting a woeful .132 as the calendar flipped to June and he had played in only 22 games. He turned his season around batting .356 (.424 OBP) from July 31 on, and finished the season with eight home runs and 35 RBIs. He played in only 82 games, and the Royals catcher of the future was clearly Sweeney. Macfarlane's caught-stealing percentage dipped to 30 percent. The Royals were again a disappointing basement dweller in the AL Central, finishing 67-94.

Accepting his role as a backup, Macfarlane signed a one-year contract for $700,000 to return to the Royals in 1998, taking a $150,000 pay cut. "I don't look at making the kind of money I'm making as a cut," he said. "I'm playing a game. Where else can I make this kind of money in the real world?"[26] But Macfarlane's tenure with the Royals came to a close just as the season was getting underway. The Royals traded him to the Oakland A's for outfielder Shane Mack and a player to be named later (Greg Hansell). The A's coveted Macfarlane's experience to back up their young catcher, A.J. Hinch. "He's going to bring some leadership behind the plate," said his new manager, Art Howe. "He knows the league inside and out."[27] Macfarlane got into 78 games, batting .251 with seven home runs. He threw out only 28 percent of would-be basestealers in Oakland, his lowest percentage in four years. His highlight of the year was batting .636 as a pinch-hitter (7-for-11). Oakland finished in last in the AL West (74-88). The A's brought him back in 1999 on a one-year contract for $600,000. It would be Macfarlane's final season in the game.

A decade before, it was a young Macfarlane absorbing like a sponge insights from Bob Boone. Now Hinch was playing that role to the seasoned veteran. "It's like a big brother/stepfather situation," Hinch said. "We have lunch about once a city (on the road). We've taken a lot of cabs together. I feel like I'm right behind him everywhere I go. My father is gone, so I kind of use Mac as an older male role model."[28] Hinch would later be a mentor himself, managing the Houston Astros to success, including a World Series title in 2017.

At the end of Macfarlane's 1999 season, reality started to set in that it was time to call it a career. With four young children (Megan, Austin, Allie, and Ryan) between the ages of 2 and 8, he realized there were bigger priorities now in his life. "My dad was around every day of my life, and I'd like to do the same," he said. "I love baseball, but the family side is taking precedence over the professional side. There are things a father does for his children that I have to do."[29] In 81 games, Macfarlane batted .243 with four home runs, but showed he still could throw runners out when he needed to. His 41 percent caught-stealing rate was fifth in the league. "I don't have an Ivan Rodriguez arm, but I throw out my share of runners," Macfarlane said. "I don't move as well as I used to, but I can still block a ball or two. And I still enjoy the game."[30]

Macfarlane's last game was at home against Seattle on October 3, the season finale. The much-improved A's won, 3-1, finishing with 87 wins, their best record in seven years. The A's would be a playoff-caliber team for the next several years. But this was the end of the road for Macfarlane. He came out to crouch behind the plate in the fifth inning, but did not receive another pitch. Howe sent in rookie Ramon Hernandez to replace him, allowing Macfarlane to exit to the dugout under a standing ovation. He responded with a curtain call. "That was something unexpected," Macfarlane confessed. "Never in my wildest dreams did I imagine that; that's the first curtain call I've ever gotten."[31]

Macfarlane caught more games than any other catcher (890) in Royals history going into 2018, although Salvador Perez was likely to pass him by. Perez had already broken two of Macfarlane's records, blasting his 21st home run of the season in 2015 (one more than Macfarlane's season high) and surpassing him in career home runs by a Royals catcher in 2018. Macfarlane had great things to say about the youngster in 2013. "I like everything about him, just love him. I would've loved to have played with him. I would've loved to have caught behind him. You look at what Salvador has done at such a young age, how he's still humble, still respects the game and still plays it the right way. He's got a lot of old school in him."[32]

To keep Macfarlane's career in historical perspective, Bill James, sabermetrics guru, gave an interesting story on Macfarlane, whom he ranked 84th out of 100 of the best catchers all-time. A discussion on Macfarlane led him to compile such a "best 100" at each position.

I was at a game with a friend, Royals game, and I asked my friend whether he thought Mike Macfarlane would be one of the top 100 catchers of all time. He hooted and sneered as if it was ridiculous to suggest such a thing, so my contrarian instincts came out, and I began to argue that he had to be one of the top 50. My friend said he could name 200 better catchers before the game was over. 'Go,' I said. He got to about 30, and then he started naming guys who maybe were better than Macfarlane, and maybe weren't. It then struck me how few really good players there have been in major league history; there are 20, 30 perennial All-Stars at each position, and then it flatted out so that the difference between #40 and #70, at most positions, is just subtle things – ten good years against seven, 15 homers a year against 12.[33]

James also notes how Macfarlane's knack for getting on base via a hit by pitch added to his value.

Indeed, he had the best HBP to GIDP ratio [97 times hit by a pitch, 79 times hit into a double play] *of any catcher in baseball history. Sure, it's a stupid list, but it helps explain why he ranks where he ranks.*[34]

Macfarlane spent the first few years of his retirement working part time as a baseball analyst for ESPN and later contributed to Royals pre- and postgame broadcasts. He was inducted into the Missouri Sports Hall of Fame in 2014.

Most of his time, however, was spent at the Mac-N-Seitz Baseball and Softball Academy, which he founded with teammate Kevin Seitzer in 1996. By 2016, the academy was popular with local youth who were often being trained in how to throw a knuckle-curve. "For years Mac-N-Seitz has been Kansas City's leading baseball and softball development program," says its website. "Thousands of young men and women have come through these doors only to leave equipped with a better understanding of the game and the skills to match. We've had many of our students compete at the collegiate level and many end up going professional. Persistence, hard work, accountability, struggle, success ... all adjectives that describe our way of life."

Those adjectives also describe its co-founder, Mike Macfarlane.

Sources

Special thanks to Mike Macfarlane for previewing this biography before publication, and to Cassidy Lent, reference librarian at the Giamatti Research Center at the Baseball Hall of Fame, for providing a copy of Macfarlane's file. Other sources include:

Baseball Record Book. Santa Clara University. santaclarabroncos.com/sports/m-basebl/record_book. Retrieved April 15, 2018.

Flanagan, Jeffrey. "Former Royal Macfarlane Enjoys Working College Game for ESPN," *Kansas City Star,* June 15, 2004: C2.

Godi, Mark. "Pat Macfarlane Is Tokay Tigers Third Baseball Coach in 38 Years," *Lodi* (California) *News Sentinel*, December 18, 2013.

John Macfarlane Family. Stockton Athletic Hall of Fame. stocktonhalloffame.com/john-macfarlane-family/ Retrieved April 15, 2018.

Kaegel, Dick. "Royals Sign Three; Appier Gets $3.8 Million. Macfarlane and Jose Also Agree to One-Year Deals," *Kansas City Star*, February 5, 1994: D1.

Manderfeld, Luke. "Former Royals Catcher Mike Macfarlane Teaches Unique Pitch to Young Baseball Players," *Kansas City Star,* July 28, 2016.

Missouri Sports Hall of Fame. mosportshalloffame.com/inductees/mike-macfarlane/ Retrieved April 16, 2018.

Notes

1 Susan Slusser, "Macfarlane Catches Praise from the A's," *San Francisco Chronicle*, May 18, 1999: B3.

2 Jeffrey Flanagan, "Macfarlane Leaves Baseball with Little Pomp, Fond Memories," *Kansas City Star*, October 7, 1999: D2.

3 Bob Ryan, "He Doesn't Mask Love for Game," *Boston Globe*, August 23, 1995: 77.

4 Ibid.

5 Off the Wall (Lincoln High School yearbook, 1982).

6 Knight-Ridder News Service, "Macfarlane Overcomes Injury for Which He Shoulders Blame," *San Jose Mercury News*, May 29, 1988: 5D.

7 Ibid.

8 Gordon Wittenmyer, "Macfarlane's Arm Must Answer the 127-Foot, 3-Inch Question," *Fort Lauderdale Sun Sentinel*, March 21, 1988: 9C.

9 "Macfarlane Overcomes Injury."

10 Dick Kaegel, "Macfarlane to Enter Missouri Sports Hall of Fame," mlb.com/news/former-royals-catcher-mike-macfarlane-to-enter-missouri-sports-hall-of-fame/c-64236018. Published November 26, 2013. Retrieved April 20, 2018.

11 Steve Pivovar, "Six-RBI Day Macfarlane Gift to Self, Royals," *Omaha World-Herald*, April 13, 1987.

12 Steve Pivovar, "Macfarlane: Demotion Surprise, Ready to Give Omaha His Best," *Omaha World-Herald*, July 27, 1988: 45.

13 Ibid.

14 Dick Kaegel, "Macfarlane Enters Season Certain of Uncertainties; Royals Catcher Knows How Promise Can Turn to Problems," Kansas City Star, February 21, 1994: C6.

15 "Macfarlane Lost for Year; Omaha's Lead at 3 Games," Omaha World-Herald, August 17, 1988: 37.

16 Joan Ryan, "An Artist at Work – Catching Still Serious Business for Boone," *Tulsa World*, July 17, 1989: 3C; Steve Cameron, "Macfarlane Learning Art of Catching; Making Hitters Fail Is One Part of the Position That He Gleaned from Watching, Listening to Boone," Kansas City Star, June 6, 1991: D4; Mel Antonen, "Macfarlane Catches On After Adopting Boone's Philosophy," *USA Today*, March 27, 1991: 12C.

17 Jack Etkin, "Macfarlane Injures Knee; Torn Ligament Puts Catcher Out 6 to 8 Weeks After Play at Home Plate," *Kansas City Star*, July 16, 1991: C1.

18 Dick Kaegel, "To Macfarlane, DL is 'Doomed to Limbo'; Injured Left Knee Forces Royals Catcher to Sit, Watch His Team Win 17 of 21 Games," *Kansas City Star*, August 9, 1991: D1.

19 Rick Plumlee, "Macfarlane Isn't Playing … But He's Not benched," *Wichita Eagle*, May 9, 1992: 4B.

20 Dick Kaegel, "Mafarlane to Get $1.175 Million; Royals and Catcher Don't Go to Arbitration, Kansas City Star, February 3, 1993: D8.

21 Sean McAdam, "Macfarlane Ecstatic About Joining Sox; Veteran Catcher Signs Contract with Team of Choice," *Providence Journal*, April 9, 1995: C-08.

22 George Kimball, "Crazy Day. Macfarlane's Where Action Is," *Boston Herald*, May 15, 1995.

23 Nick Cafardo, "Sox Opt Out on Macfarlane," *Boston Globe*, October 31, 1995: 71.

24 Jeffrey Flanagan, "Macfarlane Returns to Old Job with Royals – Two-Year, $1.6 Million Deal Brings Back Catcher. Mayne to be Traded or Cut," *Kansas City Star*, December 17, 1995: C1.

25 "Macfarlane Says Experience Is Key Behind Plate," *Kansas City Star*, June 5, 1997: D7.

26 Dick Kaegel, "Longtime Royal Macfarlane Will Be One a Year Longer," *Kansas City Star*, November 26, 1997: D1.

27 Steve Kettmann, "A's Trade Mack for Macfarlane," *San Francisco Chronicle*, April 9, 1998: B4.

28 Jeff Fletcher, "Hinch All Ears as Macfarlane Passes Advice," *Santa Rosa* (California) *Press Democrat*, March 20, 1999: C1.

29 Howard Bryant, "Macfarlane Heads Home; Last Season for A's Catcher," *San Jose Mercury News*, October 2, 1999: 5D.

30 Slusser, "Macfarlane Catches Praise,"

31 Susan Slusser, "With 87th Win, A's Are League's Most Improved; Macfarlane Gets Curtain Call in Finale," *San Francisco Chronicle,* October 4, 1999: C3.

32 Kaegel, "Macfarlane to Enter Missouri Sports Hall of Fame,"

33 Bill James, The New Bill James Historical Baseball Abstract (New York: Simon & Schuster, 2011), 422.

34 Ibid.

JOHN MAYBERRY

BY KEVIN LARKIN

Baseball is a great family sport and father/son duos have been in the game since baseball's early days, from George Sisler and sons Dave Sisler and Dick Sisler, to Yogi Berra and his son Dale Berra right up through the times of Ken Griffey Sr. and Ken Griffey Jr., as well as Cal Ripken Sr. and Cal Ripken Jr. and his brother Bill Ripken. Another set of names that can be added to this list is John Mayberry Sr. and his son John Mayberry Jr. The younger Mayberry followed in his father's footsteps and played in the major leagues from May of 2009 until July of 2015.

Mayberry the elder was born on February 18, 1949, in Detroit, where he traced his roots as a youth. As a youngster he played baseball on the city's sandlots and frequently attended Tigers games at Tiger Stadium.[1] He became close with Willie Horton, who became his idol. Horton gave the youngster batting tips and gave him some bats, good ones that had not been broken.[2]

Mayberry and Horton also had a common bond: They both went to Northwestern High School. While at Northwestern, Mayberry starred in baseball, basketball, and football for four years. The skills he had at basketball were almost as good as his skills on the baseball diamond. Twice during his high-school basketball career he earned a place on the *Detroit News* all-state basketball team. But it was baseball that he enjoyed most.[3]

When it came to choosing a college, Mayberry went to the University of Michigan, starred for the Wolverines as a hitter and as a pitcher,[4] and was drafted in the first round by the Houston Astros (sixth overall behind Ron Blomberg, Terry Hughes, Mike Garman, Jon Matlack, and Johnny Jones). He was also drafted ahead of future major-league players Ted Simmons and Bobby Grich. He had attracted the attention of teams like the Baltimore Orioles, Chicago Cubs, New York Mets, and the Tigers.[5]

Mayberry's professional career began in 1967 with the Covington Astros of the Appalachian League in rookie ball. In 50 games for Covington, he had a .252 batting average. The 1968 season at the beginning saw Mayberry split time between the Greensboro Patriots of the Carolina League, the Cocoa Astros in the Florida State League, and then the Oklahoma City 89ers of the Pacific Coast League. He moved from Single-A ball with Greensboro to Triple-A ball with Oklahoma City before being called up by the Astros. He made his major-league debut for Houston on September 10 in a game against the Cincinnati Reds. Mayberry went 0-for-4 in the game, including a strikeout. He had nine at-bats in 1968 with the Astros and did not record a hit.

Mayberry began 1969 with the Astros in the Florida Instructional league before being recalled by Houston in September. He had four at-bats with Houston in 1969 but still had not gotten his first major-league hit.

April of 1970 began with Mayberry on the Astros. Finally, on April 9 in a game against the San Francisco Giants he got his first major-league hit, a single in the fifth inning off Frank Reberger. Mayberry's first multi-hit game in the major leagues came on April 15, again versus the Giants, at the Houston Astrodome. In the third inning he hit a solo home run off Gaylord Perry that put the Giants ahead 2-1. In the eighth inning Mayberry came to bat with Denis Menke on first and Joe Pepitone on second, both having hit singles. Mayberry got his second hit of the day and second career home run off Perry and this tied the score, 6-6. Houston ended up winning the game on Jim Beauchamp's single that scored Mayberry, who had been hit by a pitch to lead off the bottom of the 10th. After a stint with Oklahoma City, he returned to the Astros in August and ended up playing in 50 games for Houston and batting .216.

In 1971 Mayberry batted .182 in 46 games for the Astros, and spent part of the year with Oklahoma City, where he hit .324 in 64 games.

In December of 1971 Mayberry and minor leaguer David Grangaard were traded to the Kansas City Royals for Lance Clemons and Jim York.

For the next six years Mayberry remained with the Royals, hitting 25 home runs and driving in 100 runs in 1972; 26 home runs and 100 RBIs in 1973; 22 home runs and 69 RBIs in 1974; and 34 home runs and 106 RBIs in 1975. He averaged .261 with 24 home runs, and 92 RBIs in his six years with Kansas City, and made the Royals a respectable club.[6] Sportswriter Peter Gammons argued that Mayberry had done more than anyone else to carry the team. He may have been overtaken by the likes of Reggie Jackson (Athletics), Dick Allen (White Sox), and Sparky Lyle and Bobby Murcer of the Yankees for second-half performances, but halfway through the 1973 season, Mayberry seemed most deserving of the MVP Award.

The 34 home runs and 106 RBIs in 1975 were career highs and Mayberry also led the American League in walks in 1973 (122) and 1975 (119). In 1973 he led the league in on-base percentage at .417. He made his only two All-Star teams in 1973 and 1974. In 1975 he finished second in the American League MVP voting to Boston's Fred Lynn.

On May 24, 1974, Mayberry hit a home run, and then was ejected after he slugged Chicago pitcher Stan Bahnsen in a free-for-all during a 4-2 Kansas City win over the Chicago White Sox.[7] Mayberry's ninth home run of the season came with no one on base in the second inning. Then in the third inning Bahnsen hit Mayberry below the knee with his first pitch. The big slugger dropped his bat and charged the mound, swinging at Bahnsen with both hands.

July 1, 1975, saw the Royals facing the Texas Rangers. Starting for Kansas City was Steve Busby and for Texas it was future Hall of Famer Ferguson Jenkins. Texas had a 2-0 lead after the third inning when Mayberry came to bat with one out in the fourth. Jenkins had struck Mayberry out to end the first inning but then things got a lot better for the big first baseman as he hit an 0-and-2 pitch from Jenkins to right-center field to make the score 2-1 Texas.

Mayberry led off the seventh inning with Texas ahead 5-1 and Jenkins still on the mound. He hit Jenkins' first pitch for his second home run of the game. Mayberry came to bat for the fourth time in the game with one out in the ninth inning. On a 1-and-0 pitch Mayberry went deep for the third time- another solo home run, making the score 5-3. Kansas City sent Harmon Killebrew to bat next and he too hit a 1-and-0 pitch off Jenkins for a home run to make the score 5-4 Texas.

Despite the champagne performance, there was a vinegary aftertaste for Mayberry.[8] The first baseman for the Kansas City Royals had had the finest hour of his major-league career, unloading three home runs off one of baseball's top pitchers. His awesome performance was a bit tainted, however, as his error allowed Texas to score what proved to be the winning run in the 5-4 Rangers victory.

Mayberry's three dingers brought his season total to 12 and he finished the season with a career-high 34 home runs. It was a good year for Mayberry as he also hit .291 in 156 games.

Although a slugger, Mayberry was a good fielder. In his first full year with the Royals, 1972, he made just seven errors at first base for a .995 fielding percentage. In 1973 Mayberry fielded at a .994 clip, making nine errors. He led the league in putouts for a first baseman in 1972, 1973, and 1976. He twice led the league's first basemen in double plays turned (141 in 1972 and 156 in 1973). The big first baseman also led the league in fielding percentage in three seasons: 1972, 1977, and 1979, all with .995 marks. He finished his career with a .994 fielding percentage ranking him ahead of players like Jim Thome, Chris Chambliss, and Gil Hodges.

After a 6-3 win over the Detroit Tigers on June 9, 1976, Royals manager Whitey Herzog smiled and Ralph Houk, the Tigers skipper, shrugged it off. The subject was Mayberry's two-run home run, which helped Kansas City to the win. "I don't know what I am doing, I'm just swinging," said Mayberry, who hit only his fourth and fifth home runs of the year.[9] "I hit a couple of breaking pitches. I went out there looking for them. They've been giving me trouble and I really haven't hit them all year." Slow starts were not new for Mayberry: During the first three months of 1975, he had just nine home runs and 35 RBIs, before exploding for 12 home runs and 32 RBIs in July.

Mayberry's batting average dipped to .232 in 1976 while his home-run total plunged from 34 to 13. He played in a league-leading 161 games as the Royals finished in first place in the American League West and earned a shot at the American League pennant. However, the Royals lost to the New York Yankees three games to two on Chris Chambliss's home run in the ninth inning off Mark Littell.

This was a time of prosperity for the Royals as they began a string of solid finishes in the American League West highlighted by a World Series trophy in 1985. During his career Mayberry played in nine postseason games for the Royals getting just six hits in 30 at-bats for a .200 batting average.

The 1977 season was gratifying for both the Royals and Mayberry; the Royals again won the West Division and Mayberry's home runs rose from 13 in 1976 to 23 in '77, although his batting average dropped a couple points from .232 to .230. On August 8, 1977, Mayberry and his girlfriend, Janice, were married in Jackson, Michigan.[10] (Future major leaguer John C. Mayberry Jr. was born on December 21, 1983, in Kansas City.)

On June 1, 1977, Mayberry had another three-home run game, with five runs batted in during an 11-3 rout of the Blue Jays at Toronto's Exhibition Stadium. Two months later, on August 5, Mayberry became the second Royals player to hit for the cycle. (Freddie Patek was the first.) Facing White Sox right-hander Chris Knapp, at Royals Stadium, Mayberry singled to left field in the second inning. He led off the third inning with a home run off reliever Bart Johnson as the Royals built up an 8-1 lead.

Mayberry was no speed demon on the basepaths, with just 20 stolen bases and 19 triples in his career, but in the fourth inning he tripled to right field off Johnson. He grounded out in the sixth. The Royals led 11-2 when Mayberry stepped into the batter's box in the eighth inning. Al Cowens had hit a one-out single off the third White Sox pitcher, Don Kirkwood. Mayberry doubled to score Cowens with the 12th Kansas City run, and this completed the cycle for the Royals first baseman. Kansas City won the game, 12-2.

After the All-Star Game the Royals went 51-22 to win their second straight American League West title. They lost to the Yankees in the ALCS, three games to two.

In April of 1978 Mayberry's contract was sold to the Toronto Blue Jays in a cash deal. Toronto was still in the growing phase, having entered the American League in 1977 and in Mayberry's four-plus years with the Blue Jays he averaged 18 home runs and 54 runs batted in.

Royals general manager Joe Burke said Mayberry, who was in a slump, had fallen out of grace during the 1977 American League playoffs (he went 2-for-12, .167).[11] In Game Four against the Yankees, the usually slick-fielding Mayberry dropped a pop foul and fumbled a throw at the bag. Before being benched for John Wathan in the top of the fifth, he struck out twice, leading off the second inning, then in the third inning with runners on first and third.

Mayberry's best day in a Blue Jays uniform came on Opening Day in 1980, against the Seattle Mariners at the Kingdome in Seattle. Though the Mariners won, 8-6, Mayberry was 4-for-5 with two home runs and three RBIs.

Mayberry was traded by the Blue Jays to the Yankees on May 5, 1982, for minor-leaguer Jeff Reynolds and Tom Dodd and Dave Revering. His best game as a Yankee occurred on May 8, 1982, in the Kingdome in a 9-4 Yankees win. Mayberry went 2-for-3 with a home run and three runs scored.

Mayberry retired after the 1982 season and for a while was a minor-league coach for the Blue Jays. He also spent a couple of years as a coach with the Royals and worked in the club's community affairs office. In 1996 he was elected to the Royals Hall of Fame.

The Mayberry family was not done with baseball. John Jr. debuted in the major leagues with the Philadelphia Phillies on May 23, 2009. He spent 2009 through the 2013 with Philadelphia and then ended up splitting the 2014 season with the Phillies and the Blue Jays. He ended his major-league career with the New York Mets, playing his last game in the major leagues on July 24, 2015.

Sources

In addition to the sources cited in the Notes, the author consulted Baseball-Reference.com and Retrosheet.org.

Notes

1 Bruce Markusen, "Big John Mayberry Went from Detroit Sandlots to Major League All-Star," detroitathletic.com/blog/2016/10/14/big-john-mayberry-went-detroit-sandlots-major-league-star/.

2 Ibid.

3 Ibid.

4 Ibid.

5 Ibid.

6 Peter Gammons, "The Baseball Beat," *Boston Globe*, July 15, 1973: 89.

7 "Uproar in Kansas City," Calgary Herald, May 25, 1974: 29.

8 Fred McMane (United Press International), "Mayberry Has Big Night," *Lowell* (Massachusetts) *Sun*, July 2, 1975: 30.

9 "And Mayberry: About Time," *Garden City* (Kansas) Telegram, June 10, 1976: 6.

10 Personal data obtained from fellow SABR member Bill Mortell.

11 "Mayberry Sent to Jays," Manhattan (Kansas) *Mercury*, April 5, 1978: 9.

HAL McRAE

BY THOMAS J. BROWN JR.

In many situations, an injury or a trade can end up being a setback to a player's career. Hal McRae turned both of them into an opportunity. After being traded to the Kansas City Royals when an injury reduced his defensive skills, he became one of the best designated hitters of all time.

Harold Abraham "Hal" McRae was one of the standout players in the Royals' first decade of existence. He played an important role in helping Kansas City become the powerhouse team that it became in the late 1970s and early 1980s. Later McRae became the first African-American manager of the Royals and the fifth black manager in baseball history when the team hired him in 1991.

The right-handed McRae was born in Avon Park, Florida, on July 10, 1945. His parents were Willie James and Virginia Lily Foster McRae, who was known as "Sister" by her family. McRae's father was a day laborer who also did yard work to supplement his income. His mother did not work much outside the home beyond some occasional housekeeping jobs since she was kept busy raising the couple's 10 children. McRae grew up with five brothers and four sisters. He was the only one to pursue baseball.

Growing up in such a large household was a challenge. Harold moved in with his maternal grandparents, Lott and Clara Foster, when he was 5 years old. He said the competition of living with all those siblings was too much for him so he stayed with his grandparents. His grandmother had lost her only son to an accident years earlier and welcomed him with open arms. Harold lived with his grandparents until he went off to college.[1]

McRae learned the game of baseball from his father, Willie James, who had been a player and then manager of the Avon Park Black Tigers in the all-black leagues of central Florida. But he truly developed his love of the game playing on the sandlots in his neighborhood. His uncle Moses lived next door with his 11 children. McRae and his brothers and cousins played together. Sometimes they played other teams like the Bradenton Nine Devils. If they had no other team to play, they would choose sides among themselves.[2] Hal would tag along with his father to the Sunday games when he was young. When he got older, he was able to play with the team but only after he attended Sunday church services.[3]

"I think you learn a lot more about the game and about yourself on the sandlot," McRae told sportswriter Leigh Montville about his early exposure to baseball. "You get a lot more swings of the bat. You make your own rules. You solve your arguments. You find out who your leaders are. You don't need parents around. You do everything by yourself."[4]

McRae attended the segregated E.O. Douglas High School in Sebring, Florida. He was a multisport athlete. At the time, football was his first love, and he earned a football scholarship to Florida A&M University. After playing at Florida A&M for a year, he realized that he was not big enough to succeed in football and switched to baseball, playing second base for A&M.[5] He grew to become 5-feet-11 tall and weigh 180 pounds.

McRae had two productive years with the Florida A&M Rattlers before he was drafted by the

Cincinnati Reds in 1965. The Rattlers went 16-4 during his second season. McRae had 78 RBIs that season, a school record that still stood as of 2018. The team won its conference and made the NAIA district tournament. When McRae finally made the majors, he became the first player from the university to do so.

McRae married Johncyna "Jo" Williams, a fellow student, on April 21, 1966. A mutual friend set them up on a blind date. The couple had three children, Brian, Cullen, and Leah. Brian McRae followed in his father's footsteps and played major-league baseball. Cullen also played baseball at Florida A&M.[6]

The Reds chose McRae in the sixth round of the June 1965 amateur draft. They signed him as a shortstop although he spent most of his time in the Reds' minor-league system playing second base. The 19-year-old's first team was the Tampa Tarpons of the Class-A Florida State League. McRae struggled in the 22 games that he played for the Tarpons, batting .154 with just 10 hits in 65 at-bats.

Sent to the Peninsula Grays (Hampton, Virginia, Class-A Carolina League) for the 1966 season, McRae dramatically improved at the plate, batting.287 with 11 home runs and 56 RBIs. McRae lived with a black family during his season with the Grays. He said he didn't experience much racial discrimination beyond some comments in the ballpark.[7] He played with future Reds Johnny Bench and Bernie Carbo, the only players on the team who had better numbers than he did.

McRae started the 1967 season with the Knoxville Smokies of the Double-A Southern League. His production (.290, 10 doubles, 6 home runs, 25 RBIs) was good enough for the Reds to promote him to the Triple-A Buffalo Bisons (International League) for the second half of the season. He continued to hit the ball there although his batting average dropped against the stiffer competition.

After playing winter ball, McRae spent most of the 1968 season with the Triple-A Indianapolis Indians (Pacific Coast League). He continued to demonstrate the ability to hit the ball with power, hitting 16 home runs before the Reds called him up in July.

McRae's major-league debut came on July 11, 1968, against the San Francisco Giants. He started at second base and had two hits in a 7-1 Reds loss. McRae got singles in his first two at-bats against Gaylord Perry, who pitched a complete-game win for the Giants. McRae struggled after his arrival in the majors, batting .196 with just 2 RBIs in 17 games.

After the season McRae played winter ball again, in Puerto Rico. During a game he suffered a multiple leg fracture. The injury cost him much of his quickness and "slowed [my] progress of getting to the big leagues. It hampered my ability to run like I had."[8] When he was able to play, McRae returned to Indianapolis, which was now in the American Association, and played in 17 games in 1969.

When McRae returned to the Reds, they tried using him in the outfield. His injury had taken away much of his mobility and they were hoping that playing in the outfield would make the difference. McRae never quite adjusted to the change although he continued to produce at the plate.

McRae was with the Reds all of the 1970 season. He played second, third, and the outfield in 70 games. His batting average slumped to .248 as he struggled to find his place in Reds lineup. McRae also made his first postseason appearance that year. He started in left field in the second game of the Reds' sweep of the Pirates in the National League Championship Series. McRae also started three games in the World Series against Baltimore. He batted a team-best .455 for the Series. McRae's two-run double in Game Five gave the Reds an early lead although the Orioles came back to defeat them, 9-3, and win the Series.

McRae had his best season with the Reds in 1971. He hit .264 with 24 doubles and 9 home runs. In 1972, primarily coming off the bench, he played in 61 games and batted .278.

When the Reds returned to the World Series in 1972, McRae had several key hits. In the first two games, he pinch-hit in the ninth and smacked singles both times. In the second game, his single scored Tony Perez for the Reds' only run of the game. McRae also came off the bench in the seventh game and his sacrifice fly scored Perez to tie the game, one that the Reds would eventually lose to Oakland.

The Reds continued to feel that McRae had no place in their regular lineup because the 1969 injury had made him a defensive liability.[9] After the 1972 season, they traded McRae and injured pitcher Wayne Simpson to the Kansas City Royals for reserve outfielder Richie Scheinblum and another injured pitcher, Roger Nelson. McRae wanted to play every day and felt he would have more opportunity to do that with the expansion Royals. The trade breathed new life into McRae's career; he developed into one of the most reliable designated hitters in the American League.

The Royals originally planned to use McRae as their primary right fielder. He struggled in the early season and Royals manager Jack McKeon benched him for several games in mid-April. When he returned to the lineup, it was as the designated hitter. In his first game as DH, McRae hit a home run and reached base four times, scoring three runs in a Royals victory. Although he continued to struggle in his first season in Kansas City, he became their most frequently used designated hitter.

When American League started using the DH in 1973, McKeon had said, "I intend to keep juggling the designated hitter (assignment) in order to keep the morale high. We set out in spring training to find 25 guys who were unselfish and willing to do the little things required to win." He changed his philosophy in 1974 and McRae became the primary designated hitter when he was penciled in the lineup in that role 90 times.

"When I was told I was going to be the DH, I hated it," McRae said years later. "You were considered a one-way player and baseball has always been a two-way sport. You were supposed to be good on offense and good on defense to be considered a good player.[10] But he settled into his new role and saw his batting average jump 76 points to .310 in 1974. He hit 15 home runs and had 88 RBIs.

But McRae was not quite ready to give up on being a two-way player. He played left field in 114 games and was the designated hitter in only 12 games in 1975. Although he remained a liability in the outfield due to his lack of range, he continued to produce at the plate, and the Royals used him more and more frequently as their designated hitter after that season.

McRae was chosen for his first All-Star Game in 1975. He pinch-hit for the American League in the bottom of the ninth inning and grounded out to pitcher Randy Jones in a 6-3 loss to the National League. McRae finished the season as one of the Royals' batting leaders with a .306 batting average, 38 doubles, and 71 RBIs.

McRae became the Royals' primary designated hitter in 1976. He played left field in just 31 games but was in the Royals lineup as the DH for 117 games. Although McRae was reluctant to become a full-time DH at first, he later saw it as his "opportunity to get 500 at-bats" and be in the lineup every day.[11] He had a .407 on-base percentage and an .868 OPS that season, both the highest in the league. McRae was chosen for the All-Star Game for a second time and again grounded out as a pinch-hitter.

He also battled his teammate George Brett for the batting title that year. On the final day of the season, McRae led Brett, .33078 to .33073. Rod Carew of the Minnesota Twins was also in contention with a batting average of .32945. The Twins were playing the Royals that day. Carew went 2-for-4 and finished at .331. McRae and Brett both had two hits in three at-bats through eight innings. McRae led Brett, .3326 to .3322. In the bottom of the ninth, Brett hit a fly to left field. Twins outfielder Steve Brye was playing deep and broke in the wrong direction. The ball dropped about 15 feet in front of him and bounced over his head for an inside-the-park home run. McRae greeted Brett at home with a high five and then stepped up to the plate knowing that now he would need a hit to win the batting title. He grounded out against Jim Hughes. Brett was the batting champion at.333 while McRae with .332 was second.

When McRae walked back to the dugout he tipped his batting helmet to a standing ovation by the Royals fans. Then McRae turned and gave the Twins dugout the finger. Twins manager Gene Mauch immediately charged the field and both benches emptied. It took several minutes for the umpires to restore order.

Later McRae accused Brye of misplaying the ball in order to give Brett the title. "This is America, and not that much has changed. Too bad in 1976 things are still like that," he said, citing racism as the reason why he came in second. Mauch denied the charge, saying: "This thing hurts me more than anything that has ever happened in my 35 years in baseball."[12]

McRae developed a reputation as an aggressive baserunner at this time. He explained his baserunning philosophy this way: "I feel that playing like that can put pressure on the defense and sometimes intimidate people. If you can intimidate people, it makes your job easier."[13] Carew once stood in his way at first base so McRae ran into him. In another instance, Mike Cubbage caught the ball and when he went to tag out McRae, McRae kicked the glove off Cubbage's hand and was safe.

McRae made his third trip to the postseason that year. He batted .125 (2-for-16) as the Royals lost to the Yankees in the ALCS. He finished fourth in the voting for the AL MVP that year, but earned his first Outstanding Designated Hitter Award.

McRae continued to produce at the plate in 1977. He played all 162 games and batted .298 with a league-leading 54 doubles as the Royals won the AL West championship again. Although McRae did not get chosen for the All-Star Games that year, he did garner several votes for the AL MVP. In the ALCS, McRae batted .444 as the Royals lost in five games to the Yankees for the second year in a row. His two-run homer in the first game gave the Royals the lead on the way to a win. McRae scored six runs and had several clutch hits in the series but it was not enough to get the Royals to their first World Series.

McRae continued to make news for his aggressive baserunning in the ALCS. He slid into second to break up a double play and took out Yankee second baseman Willie Randolph. McRae barely touched the second base on the slide and took Randolph with him as he slid to the end of the infield dirt.

Roger Angell wrote that McRae's "body block seemed legal but ill-advised."[14] Although he broke up the double play, it fired up the Yankees, who scored three runs in the bottom of the inning on their way to a win.

McRae explained his aggressiveness in this way: "Any opportunity you had to avoid allowing the opponent to turn a double play, you have to take advantage of it. A double play could take you out of an inning. The middle infielder expected you to come in hard."[15]

Even though McRae's slides were legal at the time, they did lead to a change after that season that was eventually called the "Hal McRae Rule." It stated that a baserunner who is not within reach of the base and who takes out an infielder is out and the ball is dead. Other baserunners cannot advance. McRae said that his goal was not to hurt a player but "eliminate the throw. A lot of players would try a leg whip on the infielder. I went in with a cross-body style. My purpose was to not take any chances."[16]

McRae played 153 games as the Royals' designated hitter in 1978 and just three games in left field. His bat helped the Royals to their third consecutive AL West title as he hit 39 doubles and 16 home runs.

Once again the Royals had to get past the Yankees in the Championship Series. McRae's bat was not as potent in this series. He batted .214 and had just three singles as the Yankees won the ALCS in four games.

Both the Royals and McRae slumped in 1979. The Royals finished the season in second place and missed the postseason. McRae played in just 101 games, his fewest since the trade from Cincinnati. He still managed to hit 32 doubles and 10 home runs, with 74 RBIs.

The Royals bounced back in 1980 to win 97 games and reclaim the AL West title. McRae played in 110 games as their designated hitter, taking left field just nine times. He hit .297 and knocked in 83 runs while batting primarily in the cleanup spot in the order. McRae was so important to the Royals' success that he was awarded his second Outstanding Designated Hitter Award that year.

When the postseason arrived, the Royals had to face the Yankees yet again. After losing to the Yankees three times in the 1970s, they swept them in the 1980 ACLS to play in the World Series for the first time. The Philadelphia Phillies won the Series in six games. McRae batted .375 with nine hits that included three doubles.

McRae reshaped the role of the designated hitter. He talked about how he had made the role his own:

"The DH was designed for a clunker: a guy with a name who could stay around a little longer and hit a few more home runs. I think I've given [the role] a new dimension. The DH is now a guy who won't clog up the bases; someone who'll break up the double play, go from first to third on a single, take an extra base on hits and even steal a base or two."[17]

Although McRae had another solid year in 1981, his best was yet to come. He hit .308 in 1982, an improvement of 36 points from 1981. He led the American League in doubles (46) and runs batted in (133), the first time a DH led the league in RBIs. McRae was chosen for the All-Star Game again, his third appearance in the midsummer classic. In his only plate appearance, he walked in the eighth as the American League lost, 4-1. At the end of the year, McRae finished fourth in the MVP balloting and earned a Silver Slugger award. He also won his third Outstanding Designated Hitter award.

Now in his late 30s, McRae started 155 games in 1983 and batted .311, but he started only 81 games in 1984 and 82 in 1985. Yet he maintained a .281 batting average and a slugging percentage of .424 during the latter two years. The Royals returned to the playoffs in 1984 but were swept by the Tigers in three games. McRae pinch-hit twice and had two hits.

By 1983 McRae had stopped playing in the field. He platooned at DH with Jorge Orta. When Orta went 0-for-4 in the first game of the 1985 American League Championship Series against the Toronto Blue Jays, McRae started the rest of the series. He had six hits, including two doubles, and three RBIs as the Royals beat the Blue Jays in seven games to return to the World Series.

McRae saw limited action in the 1985 World Series due to a thigh injury. He pinch-hit in three games and had no hits. McRae earned his first World Series ring as the Royals overcame a three-games-to-one deficit for the second time in the postseason to beat the St. Louis Cardinals. "It was a relief to finally win it. We were in it seven out of 10 years," said McRae in 2014.[18]

Brian McRae, Hal's oldest son, was the Royals' first-round pick in the June 1985 draft. Brian played with his father in a spring-training game before the 1986 season. Brian was just 18 years old at the time while his father was 39. Before the game, Brian said he wasn't nervous about playing with his father "though I'll probably get butterflies when the game starts. Advice from Pop? He said, 'Let it loose.' You know, swing the bat. Be aggressive." Both father and son contributed to a five-run first inning with Brian hitting a single as his father watched from the on-deck circle.[19]

The 1986 season found McRae at the tail end of his career. He continued to platoon as designated hitter, appearing in 58 games. His productivity declined and he had only 70 hits and 37 RBIs. He played in just six games in 1987 before the Royals released him on July 21. His final appearance came as a pinch-hitter in a 3-1 Royals loss four days earlier.

McRae stayed in the Royals organization as a hitting instructor for the remainder of the season. He joined the Pittsburgh Pirates in the same role in 1988. When the Royals fired manager Billy Gardner near the end of the 1988 season, they offered McRae the job. He turned it down because the club would not sign him to a contract beyond the season. "I don't think any situation is a great opportunity if you can't have fun at what you're doing and can't concentrate on the things you should be concentrating on as opposed to concentrating on saving your job with every decision," he said in explaining his decision.[20]

McRae stayed with Pirates in 1989 before becoming the hitting coach of Montreal Expos in 1990. When the Royals fired John Wathan as their manager early in the 1991 season, they again sought out McRae as their manager. This time he agreed to a two-year contract and became the major leagues' fifth black manager. "It'll be like going back home," his wife, Johncyna, said at the time.[21]

McRae had no managerial experience and admitted that developing a managerial style by working in the minor leagues "is probably the best way to do it." But he also noted, "It didn't happened that way and you have to play the cards you're dealt." He also said that pitching decisions were the most difficult ones although "I don't dwell on 'em. It's the human element of the game."[22] The Royals finished the season with a 66-58 record after McRae took the helm.

When McRae became the Royals manager, his son Brian had arrived in the majors to become the Royals' center fielder. As a result, McRae joined a small group of managers including Connie Mack, Yogi Berra, and Cal Ripken Sr. who had managed their own son. When he started his new job, McRae said he "didn't think for one minute about the joys of managing my son. I thought about all the pitfalls. I thought about him being uncomfortable. I thought about me not doing the right thing sometimes because of my son. It was a worry."[23]

His son was also concerned about playing for his father. "It's kind of like having your mother as your teacher in school. I can't worry about my father. I have to play for myself. That's how this game is," Brian said. McRae talked with his son about the challenge and then decided that he would just treat him like any other ballplayer.[24]

After the Royals made several trades in the offseason, McRae found himself managing a very different team in 1992. The team got off to the worst start in its history, losing 16 of its first 17 games. The team finished with a 72-90 record. Despite the disappointing sixth-place finish, McRae was given a second two-year contract by the Royals.

The team once again got off to a slow start in 1993, winning just two of its first 11 games. After the team lost on April 26 to drop its record to 7-12, McRae held his usual postgame conference with reporters in his clubhouse office. The conference took an ugly turn when a sportswriter asked McRae why he didn't pinch-hit Brett with the bases loaded in the seventh inning.

McRae snapped. He had heard enough and a tirade started. "Don`t ask me such stupid (expletive) questions. That's it," McRae shouted. At this point, he started throwing everything off his desk and flinging the items everywhere. One of the reporters was even cut by something that was thrown. After everyone backed out of the office, McRae came into the clubhouse and began shouting at his players. When he finished, he said, "Now, put that in your (expletive) pipe and smoke it."[25]

McRae survived the tirade and eventually apologized to the reporter who was cut. The Royals finished the season with an 84-78 record to improve to third place in the American League West. McRae's Royals were in third place with a 64-51 record when the 1994 season ended after the players struck. When McRae was asked years later what was the hardest part of managing, he said, "Losing. We lost quite a few games. That was the hardest part."[26]

With the strike still on, the Royals decided that they needed a change and fired McRae on September 16, 1994. "I think Hal has done everything possible with the club he had. He's done a good job. But as we move forward we feel we can find a manager who can better lead us into the next several years with the younger players," said general manager Herk Robinson. McRae was diplomatic about the news, saying: "I'm a better person because I've managed. I believe I improved as a manager."[27]

McRae became the Cincinnati Reds hitting coach in 1995. After two years in that role, he moved to the Philadelphia Phillies in the same role. McRae stayed in Philadelphia for three years before joining the Tampa Bay Rays as their bench coach for the 2001 season.

After firing Larry Rothschild on April 18, 2001, the Rays asked McRae to take over. When asked if he managed differently in his second stint as the dugout leader, he said that one learns from experience so that when he became the Rays manager, he "did things a little differently. You learn from your mistakes. You learn to deal with situations a lot easier than you did the first time around."[28] Although they finished with a 58-90 record, McRae remained their manager for the following season. The team did not improve and when they finished with a 55-106 record, McRae was fired.

McRae's record was 399-473 as manager of the Royals and Rays. He remained as an assistant to the Rays general manager until he joined the St. Louis Cardinals as their hitting coach in 2005. Manager Tony La Russa added McRae to his staff to improve the offense. McRae stressed the importance of line drives and making good contact. "The plan [is] to be aggressive. [I don't] care how they swing or how they look. [I] care about results."[29] He remained with the Cardinals until 2009 when he was replaced by Mark McGwire.

McRae retired from baseball after leaving the Cardinals in 2009. As of 2018, he lived in East Bradenton, Florida, with his wife, Johncyna, a retired educator and community volunteer. McRae enjoyed playing golf until he became ill in 2015 and had to limit his activity. He also spends time with his six grandchildren. In addition to his son Brian, who played in the major leagues for 10 years, his other son, Cullen, worked for the Marlins for 17 years and became their first video coordinator in 2014.

Castle Street, the street that McRae grew up on, was renamed in McRae's honor in 1986 after the Royals won the 1985 World Series. It is presently known as Hal McRae Boulevard where it crosses Florida Highway 27 in Avon Park, Florida.[30] McRae was inducted into the Florida A&M Hall of Fame in 1974. He has also been inducted into the Florida Sports Hall of Fame, the Royals Hall of Fame, and the Missouri Sports Hall of Fame in 2004. The Tampa Bay Rays placed a plaque honoring him in their "Walk of Fame" outside the stadium.

McRae will be remembered as one of the pioneers in the role of the designated hitter. He took a position that many thought was added to major-league rosters in order to provide some longevity to aging players and turned it into an essential part of American League lineups. McRae said the DH "gave a little more excitement" to the game and that he had his share of exciting moments in that role.[31] He said his greatest accomplishment was the 1982 season, when he drove in 133 runs and had 27 homers as the Royals DH.[32] He was an aggressive player who always tried to keep the defense off guard when he was on base. McRae maintained that philosophy when he turned to coaching and managing after his playing days.

Sources

In addition to the sources cited in the Notes, the author also used the Baseball-Reference.com, Baseball-Almanac.com, and Retrosheet.org websites for player, team, and season pages, and other pertinent material.

The author is also grateful to Johynca McRae who helped to fill in some of the gaps in Hal McRae's personal life.

Notes

1 Johncyna McRae, email correspondence with author, April 14, 2018.

2 Leigh Montville, "Every Day Is Father's Day," *Sports Illustrated*, June 17, 1991.

3 Johncyna McRae, email correspondence with author, April 20, 2018

4 Montville.

5 Johncyna McRae, email correspondence with author, April 14, 2018.

6 Ibid.

7 Hal McRae, personal interview, April 27, 2018 (McRae interview).

8 Ibid.

9 Steve Price, "This Day in Reds History: Reds Trade Hal McRae and Wayne Simpson," *Red Leg Nation.com*, December 10, 2010. redlegnation.com/2010/12/01/this-day-in-reds-history-reds-trade-mcrae-and-simpson.

10 Robert Falkoff, "McRae One of the All-Time Dominant Designated Hitters," MLB.com, September 10, 2012.

11 McRae interview.

12 Roger Launius, "The Great George Brett/Hal McRae Batting Title Race of 1976," Roger Launius's Blog, May 21, 2012. launiusr.wordpress.com/2012/05/21/the-great-george-bretthal-mcrae-batting-title-race-of-1976.

13 Murray Chass, "McRae of Royals Is a Good 'Hitter' on Basepaths, Too," *New York Times*, October 8, 1976.

14 David Schoenfield," History's Most Notorious Takeout Slides," ESPN.com, June 26, 2015.

15 Tracy Ringolsby, "McRae Discusses Replay, Plays at Second," MLB.com, February 13, 2016.

16 Ibid.

17 Rick Gosselin, "McRae Reshaped Style for DH's," UPI.com, May 23, 1981. upi.com/Archives/1981/05/23/McRae-Reshaped-Style-for-DHs/4912359438400

18 John Lembo, "Kansas City Royals' Run Thrills Bradenton's Hal McRae," *Bradenton Herald*, October 23, 2014.

19 Ira Berkow, "Historic Day for McRae and His Son," *New York Times*, March 14, 1986.

20 "McRae at Home With Decision," *Washington Post*, June 14, 1988.

21 "Robinson Is Fired; Royals Hire McRae," *Los Angeles Times*, May 24, 1991.

22 Robyn Norwood, "Royals Making It Hard for McRae to Look Good," *Los Angeles Times*, July 3, 1991.

23 Montville.

24 Ibid.

25 Chris Jaffe, "20th Anniversary: Hal McRae Loses His Mind," FanGraphs.com, April 26, 2013.

26 McRae interview.

27 "Royals Fire Hal McRae as Manager," *Washington Post*, September 16, 1994.

28 McRae interview.

29 "Hal McRae a Hit with Cardinals," *St. Louis American*, September 15, 2005.

30 Johcyna McRae, email correspondence with author, April 14, 2018.

31 McRae interview.

32 Johncyna McRae, email correspondence with author, April 20, 2018.

JEFF MONTGOMERY

BY MICHAEL ENGEL

When Jeff Montgomery took the mound for the Cincinnati Reds on August 1, 1987, he was living out the storybook baseball tale. A three-sport athlete from small Wellston, Ohio, Montgomery grew up a couple of hours down the road from Riverfront Stadium in the era of the Big Red Machine. His idol, Reds manager Pete Rose, handed him the ball on that day, and Montgomery threw two innings in his major-league debut.

Six months later, he was traded.

Montgomery's path to the big leagues was lined with obstacles and opportunities. When the dust settled, he was a member of the Kansas City Royals Hall of Fame, and the second major leaguer to reach 300 saves with only one team.[1]

Montgomery was born in Wellston on January 7, 1962, to Tom and Mary Montgomery. Tom worked in the coal industry and later started a construction company. He coached Jeff's football team in junior high, and his American Legion teams during high-school summers. Mary was an office manager at Wellston's Pillsbury plant. At Wellston High, Montgomery lettered four years each in baseball and football, starting at quarterback and safety and later making the All-Ohio football team on defense. He also worked as Wellston's placekicker. He lettered in basketball three years, averaging 12.7 points per game. When he graduated in 1980, he held or shared 18 school records.[2]

Montgomery's achievements in high school earned him a spot in Wellston's Athletic Hall of Fame, the 1980 inaugural Willard Fitzpatrick Award as selected by the Southeastern Ohio League Sports Writers and Broadcasters Association, and, later, his own street in Wellston - Jeff Montgomery Way. The Reds were Montgomery's team, as would be expected, and he grew up a fan of Reds pitchers Gary Nolan and Don Gullett while also idolizing Rose.

Montgomery's high-school coach, Pat Hendershot, made sure his team had ample opportunity to play. That enabled Montgomery to play on the high-school team, summer Pony League teams, the American Legion team, and even on men's semipro teams as early as age 15. As a shortstop and right-handed pitcher, he led Wellston's Rockets, drawing interest from Ohio University, Ohio State University, and Miami of Ohio. While Ohio State was Montgomery's first choice, a Reds scout had tipped off Marshall University coach Jack Cook and the university offered Montgomery a baseball scholarship. When the other schools didn't match it, Montgomery went to Marshall.

As a freshman at a smaller school, he was able to "hit the ground running,"[3] and his college career got off to a hot start. Montgomery threw a one-hit shutout in his first start as a freshman, finishing with four complete games in his first season. After striking out 57 in 56 innings with a 3.27 ERA in 12 starts, Montgomery earned the Southern Conference Freshman of the Year award.[4] He struggled in his junior year, but a few chance appearances in front of scouts paved his way to the big leagues.

"I pitched a game against the University of Kentucky and there were scouts at the game to watch some players on Kentucky's team. I believe I threw a shutout against them in that game, so the next game

I pitched was against Ohio University and that game they came to see me pitch."[5] This led to a tryout with the Reds two weeks before the 1983 draft. On draft day, Montgomery was golfing with his father when his mother and sister began waving their arms. They had a telegram informing Jeff that he'd been selected with the Reds' ninth-round pick.

The Reds initially offered Montgomery $1,000 to sign and start his pro career, but with a year left on his scholarship, he was able to leverage another year of college eligibility into a $9,000 signing bonus, the estimated value of one year of a scholarship.[6] This was not be the first time Montgomery's pursuit of a degree would pay off for his baseball career.

Montgomery joined the rookie-league Billings Mustangs in 1983 (he'd finish a computer-science degree at Marshall during the offseason after the 1983 and 1984 seasons) and made a great first impression. Mustangs manager Marc Bombard approached Montgomery about a shift to the bullpen in a post-draft minicamp. A starter all through high school and college, Montgomery was initially reluctant to move to the bullpen, unsure of how his arm would hold up. But he took to the change quickly and credited it as one of the best things that could have happened to him.[7] Bombard himself noted that a shift to the bullpen allowed him to use Montgomery to impact more games, and could put him on the fast track to the majors.[8] In 44⅔ innings, Montgomery struck out 90 batters. His strong pro debut placed him ninth on Baseball America's ranking of Reds prospects.

Montgomery opened the 1984 season with Class-A Tampa and pitched well enough to make the Florida State League All-Star Game, which he won after two innings pitched in relief. Two days later, he was called up to Double-A Vermont, still coming out of the bullpen. Between both levels that year, he threw 69⅔ innings and finished with a 2.33 ERA. He moved up in Baseball America's rankings that year, now the seventh-best prospect in the Reds' system. After repeating 1985 in Vermont, Montgomery advanced to Triple-A Denver.

He started in the bullpen again in 1986, but eventually shifted from a role as a long reliever to a starter after a series of doubleheaders and rainouts put him into the rotation.[9] The notorious Denver thin air and altitude affected his performance, and after a 4.39 ERA (the first time it rose above 3.00), Montgomery was invited by Frank Funk, the Royals pitching coach, to play winter ball in Puerto Rico.

At the time, Montgomery had been in the Reds organization for a few years but didn't feel close to the majors. He and his wife, Tina, were parents now and he needed assurance that a shot would be coming, or his Triple-A salary needed to increase. Chief Bender, head of the Reds' scouting department, told him there would be a new contract once he returned from winter ball. After returning from Puerto Rico with the contract unchanged, Montgomery started to look for a career outside of baseball, and in early 1987 had even interviewed to be a systems analyst with Hershey Chocolate.[10]

Montgomery's college degree again gave him some leverage and he got an invitation to big-league spring training as a nonroster player. Montgomery had finished the 1986 season strong with Denver and put up a 2.72 ERA in winter ball,[11] but ended up assigned to Triple-A Nashville (after 1986, the Reds moved their Triple-A affiliate out of Denver) for the 1987 season.

Avoiding Denver for a second season improved Montgomery's numbers, and he was one of the best starters in the American Association. In July he returned to the bullpen, with speculation being that the Reds wanted to see him in a relief role at a high minor-league level. In late July, Montgomery led the American Association in strikeouts and ERA which led to his contract being purchased on July 29, 1987. He made his major-league debut on August 1.

That led to Pete Rose, childhood idol, handing him the ball.

Later in August, Montgomery was tapped to make a start for the Reds, giving up five runs in five innings in a loss for Cincinnati. It was his only major-league start. For the remainder of the year, Montgomery pitched out of the bullpen, rounding out his first major-league action with 19⅓ innings and a 6.52 ERA.

Despite his passable performance in Triple A and in a big-league bullpen, the Reds didn't see a spot for Montgomery in their future pitching staff. Reds general manager Murray Cook told him that Rose handed the front office a list of players who he didn't think could play for him, a list that included Montgomery.[12] The rumor — told with tongue mostly in cheek — was that Rose had bet on Montgomery's big-league start and it put him in the "doghouse."

The Reds came to a deal in February 1988 to send Montgomery to the Kansas City Royals in exchange for Triple-A outfielder Van Snider. Montgomery had drawn the attention of then-Omaha-now-Kansas City manager John Wathan in 1987 during a Nashville-Omaha matchup, and pitching coach Frank Funk had already seen Montgomery and his mix of pitches in Puerto Rico. At the same time, Snider had impressive performances for Omaha against Nashville, piquing the Reds' interest.

The trade made Montgomery "the happiest player in baseball."[13] Just as he reported to spring training, general manager John Schuerholz told him the Royals planned to send him to Omaha to work out of the bullpen. After two months of dominating for Omaha, Montgomery was called up for good. Joining a bullpen led by former All-Star Dan Quisenberry, Montgomery had a strong showing and was named as part of Baseball Digest's All-Rookie team after 62□ innings and a 3.45 ERA.[14]

The strong Royals rookie season led to Montgomery's earning an important spot in Kansas City's bullpen in 1989, helping set up for Steve Farr, who had inherited the closer's job after Quisenberry was released in the middle of 1988. Montgomery started closing games regularly in June and held the role while Farr recovered from knee surgery later in the year. At 5-feet-11, Montgomery's short stature and low-90s fastball didn't portray the image of the dominant, fireballing closer, and his presence in Kansas City led to a relative anonymity that he joked may have helped him out during the successful season. After 18 saves and a 1.37 ERA, manager Wathan stated that Montgomery had the inside track to the closer's job.[15]

However, after the Royals fell short of the playoffs (despite the second-best record in the American League) GM Schuerholz, recalling the dominance of the Royals with Quisenberry at the back of the bullpen in the early 1980s, pursued and ultimately signed 1989's National League Cy Young Award winner Mark Davis.[16] After getting 44 saves for the San Diego Padres, Davis earned the highest one-year salary in baseball ($2,125,000), joining Bret Saberhagen, the American League's winner, on the Royals. The Davis signing made the Royals the first team to have both reigning Cy Young Award winners on their roster. Multiple publications had the Royals picked for a pennant or championship for the 1990 season.

While the team had improved on paper, the acquisition was frustrating for Montgomery, who voiced displeasure about losing a role he'd barely held. "I'm on the best pitching staff in baseball and wanting to leave it," he told one reporter.[17]

Montgomery continued to work on being the best setup reliever in baseball, and by May of 1990 he had regained the closer's job after Davis faltered. Shoddy command and slight injuries made Davis ineffective, and by July the Royals were already experimenting with Davis in the rotation.[18] Montgomery saved 24 games.

With two-plus years of success, Montgomery started 1991 as the closer, but during spring training Wathan wouldn't commit full-time to him. A Montgomery/Davis platoon tandem was floated as well. Still, Montgomery started with the job and his performance gave no reason to make a change. While the Royals started the year 15-22, Montgomery had saved nine of the wins. But the slow start cost Wathan his job and he was replaced by former Royals DH Hal McRae.

It was with McRae at the helm that Montgomery finally cemented his closer status, though it wasn't without its speed bumps early on. In McRae's first week, in a May 28, 1991, game against Seattle, Montgomery entered in the eighth inning to protect a 6-4 lead. In the ninth he recorded the first two outs easily, but an 0-and-2 pitch to Edgar Martinez found the bat and dropped softly into right field for a single. With Ken Griffey Jr. coming up, McRae walked out. When McRae asked for the ball, stating "[Davis] is making too much money down there not to be in this ballgame," Montgomery replied that it would take a bulldozer to get him out of the game.[19] Reluctantly, Montgomery handed the ball over.

When Davis came in, he walked Griffey on four pitches, then gave up a single to make it 6-5 and put the tying run on second. He managed to get a strikeout to preserve the lead, but within the clubhouse, Montgomery's frustrations boiled over. Equipment was thrown, words were yelled, and Montgomery "was not happy at all."[20]

After the game, McRae talked to Montgomery in his office and told Montgomery he was the team's closer. He finished the year with 33 saves.

Buoyed by the trust of his manager and ballclub, Montgomery entered 1992 officially in his coveted role. After 21 saves and a 1.60 ERA, Montgomery made his first All-Star team, traveling with McRae (selected as a coach) to San Diego. On July 24 Montgomery recorded his 100th career save against Cleveland.[21]

In February of 1993, Montgomery signed a three-year, $11 million contract that kept him a Royal through 1995. The Royals also held an option for the 1996 season. Montgomery expressed contentment at the commitment the team had made, and Barry Meister, his agent, noted that it was the second largest relief-pitcher contract to that point.[22] He again made the All-Star team in 1993, recording 25 saves in the first half of the season, which put him on pace to eclipse Quisenberry's team-record 45 saves set in 1983. From May 25 through August 9, Montgomery converted 24 straight save opportunities and finished the year with 45 saves, tying Quisenberry and leading the American League. Montgomery was also named the 1993 Rolaids Relief Man of the Year and finished 13th in AL MVP voting.

The Royals' 84-78 record in 1993 was reason for optimism, but the team was headed for a period of transition. On August 1, 1993, founder and owner Ewing Kauffman died after a brief battle with cancer, a loss felt deeply in the Kansas City community and by the Royals. Kauffman had long covered the team's losses from his personal wealth, allowing the team to pursue the right free agents when the time called for it. Kauffman's death meant that the team would be under the watch of a board of directors, but an official owner wouldn't be found until 2000.

Along with Kauffman, the Royals would be without their franchise's greatest player: George Brett retired at the end of the 1993 season after 21 years with the team. The Royals found themselves without their franchise player and their owner, and, in 1994, staring at the possibility of a strike.

Spring training started normally in 1994, but toward the end of March, Montgomery began experiencing back tightness. In April he developed shoulder soreness. At first, it was attributed to the cold of the early season, but he had also slightly adjusted his mechanics to compensate for the back pain. He would fight shoulder issues all year, with concerns over his velocity popping up in May. He received a cortisone shot for bursitis in June.[23]

After treatment, however, Montgomery's "zip" returned and he converted a string of saves in July. By the end of July, he'd closed out 13 straight chances and, when the Royals went on a 14-game winning streak, Montgomery had saves in eight of the wins.

However, the business of baseball interrupted the Royals' surge. As the team's player representative, Montgomery mentioned numerous times through the year that a strike was a possibility, and in late July, an August 12 strike date was set. When no agreement was found between the owners and the players union, the players went on strike. Despite initial optimism that games might resume, the season was canceled along with the playoffs on September 15. The next day, the Royals fired manager McRae.

Replacing McRae was Bob Boone, whom Montgomery had played with early in his Royals career. But before Boone could lead his team, the labor strife had doomed the Royals. After losing revenue because of the loss of the last six weeks of the 1994 season and playoff revenue shared through the league, the Royals found themselves in financial trouble. With no Ewing Kauffman to cover the team's financial losses, and with the need to remain attractive to a new owner, the team entered 1995 looking to shed payroll.

After the players returned in April, the Royals dealt away two veterans in the span of 24 hours, trading off Brian McRae to the Cubs and David Cone – 1994's Cy Young Award winner – to Toronto. After the delayed start to the season, the post-strike Royals looked much different, and any optimism left from the pre-strike surge was gone. The team seemed to be in a fog to open the year, though it hovered around .500 most of the season. During that 1995 season, Montgomery still anchored the bullpen, notching his 200th career save on June 21.

Late in the 1995 season, the Royals again shook up the roster, dumping Vince Coleman, Chris James, and Pat Borders while calling up Johnny Damon and Michael Tucker. At the time the Royals were in the wild-card hunt, but the sudden moves toward a youth movement led to skepticism from some veterans, including Montgomery.[24]

In November 1995 Montgomery filed for free agency. Earlier in the year, he had stated a preference for staying in Kansas City and had even offered to take a pay cut in exchange for a reworked deal that would offer more long-term security.[25] But he also noted that he didn't anticipate playing in the big leagues much longer. With no postseason experience, he wanted to monitor what other Royals veterans did, as well as how the market unfolded for other closers. After evaluating other offers, he returned to Kansas City, agreeing to a $4.75 million deal for 1996 and 1997 over a $6 million offer for two years from Toronto.[26]

On one hand, Montgomery turned down more money, but as he described it, the difference in money was secondary to staying in a place where he'd built a home and started a family.

As the 1996 season opened, Montgomery was in range of Dan Quisenberry's team record for career saves. But the Royals started slowly and the bullpen "bridge" to Montgomery was shaky, limiting his opportunities. He was also his own worst enemy early in the season, blowing saves while his velocity dipped. In late June, he was still four saves behind Quisenberry and his slump continued into July. Manager Bob Boone tried to rest Montgomery, they tried to vary his pitch patterns, Montgomery did extra work on his mechanics. Anything to find the missing element.

Despite the struggles, Montgomery was selected for the American League All-Star team, his third selection. He had 18 saves in the first half of 1996 and on July 17 tied Quisenberry's 238 saves, closing out a 3-2 win against Cleveland. On July 20 he secured his 239th save as a Royal, a new team record. The save was a typical Montgomery save: a mix of four pitches, a baserunner, but eventually the Royals shaking hands at the end. The record was particularly special for Montgomery since Quisenberry had been helpful as a teammate when Montgomery joined the Royals in 1988 and the two lived in the same community and went on a golfing trip every year.[27]

The rest of the 1996 season was fraught with difficulty. In August Montgomery pitched in eight games and gave up four home runs. The shoulder bursitis that had emerged in 1994 had been a recurring problem and he tried another cortisone shot in August 1996. His frustration was evident and after one appearance in September, Montgomery was shut down for the rest of the season. It was thought at first that rest might be enough to curb swelling in the shoulder, but eventually surgery was recommended.

The surgery was intended to shave down a bone spur in Montgomery's shoulder, but Dr. Steve Joyce also found a frayed tendon in the rotator cuff and a partial tear in the labrum. It was more damage than anticipated, and while everyone was optimistic, it was still major shoulder surgery.

Montgomery made Opening Day 1997 his goal. To get there, he needed to go through extensive rehab in the offseason. He worked to strengthen his shoulder every day, and starting in January and going into spring training, the Royals carefully monitored his velocity any time he threw.

It was encouraging, and Boone noted that Montgomery's arm slot had returned to where it had been years ago. While Montgomery usually worked around 90 mph with his fastball, in spring training he was regularly around 92 or 93 mph. In mid-March he threw his first inning in a spring-training game without holding back. Still, he remarked that he wasn't entirely convinced he'd make it back to the big leagues. His goal was to make the big-league roster, but the Royals conceded that he might need more work at the spring-training facility before joining the big-league club. However, Montgomery suffered no setbacks and joined the Royals as the season started in April.

In his first five games of 1997, Montgomery gave up three homers in 4⅓ innings and had an ERA of 16.62. Boone and others suggested the conditioning wasn't there yet, and his breaking pitches were flat. Montgomery spoke with Boone and pitching coach Bruce Kison about potential retirement, but they persuaded him to go on the disabled list to work through it instead.[28] On April 18, he was placed on the DL.

The setback was particularly frustrating after the work he'd put in, but Montgomery persisted. While throwing a simulated game toward the end of April, Montgomery threw "free and easy" without a radar gun for a change and felt the familiar command of his pitches again. He returned to Omaha for a brief stint before returning to the Royals on May 4.

In his first appearance back, he gave up four runs, but Montgomery's next four outings were scoreless appearances and once June started, he was showing signs of returning to form. From June 4 through the rest of the season, Montgomery put up a 1.45 ERA over 43⅓ innings, including a stretch of 32 straight batters retired over a three-week stretch. New manager Tony Muser (who replaced Boone over the All-Star break) remained committed to Montgomery as the closer. The strong second half led the Royals to exercise their option to keep Montgomery for the 1998 season, and with surgery and rehab behind him, the club had high expectations for him to be as good as ever.

Montgomery had the same high expectations heading into 1998, stating that he felt as good physically as he had in 1993, before any bursitis issues. On Opening Day he closed out a win in Baltimore for his first save. In his second appearance, Montgomery gave up four runs in two-thirds of an inning. The rest of his first half featured stretches of scoreless pitching marred by strings of games in which he gave up multiple runs. After giving up three runs on June 15, he had an ERA of 8.10.

Muser suggested that Montgomery was suffering from dead arm. Montgomery expressed shaken confidence.

Multiple issues were cited. Rushing pitches. Mechanics. But his repaired shoulder felt fine. After refocusing on stride length and arm slot, Montgomery felt confident he'd sorted things out.

The results suggested that to be the case. From June 17 through August 6, Montgomery converted 15 consecutive save opportunities, allowing just one earned run in 16⅔ innings. He finished the season with a 4.98 ERA with 36 saves, but in the second half, he'd put up a 3.46 ERA. The season earned him the honor of being named the Royals pitcher of the year for 1998, the only time he won the award.

Montgomery was a free agent again, and the Royals made him a one-year offer. However, out of the offers Montgomery had received by late November, the Royals had offered the lowest salary.[29]

With no experience in the postseason, and with Kansas City amid a perpetual rebuild, Montgomery's decision was a difficult one. His family and home were in Kansas City, and the same concerns about uprooting his children that had led him to stay for less money after 1995 were still present. But contenders were offering him more money and the opportunity to set up or close by committee in their bullpen. Montgomery posed the dilemma thusly to the Kansas City Star: "I, personally, would prefer to be a closer. But do I want 35 or 40 saves, or do I want to be playing in October?"[30]

Montgomery ultimately stayed with the Royals on a one-year deal with a base salary of $2.5 million (after the Royals had initially offered a reported $2 million). He was close to signing with Baltimore, though, going so far as to compare schedules to see when his travel might overlap with the opportunity to see his children back in Kansas City. One factor that steered him back to Kansas City was that Baltimore had already signed reliever Mike Timlin and the Orioles couldn't guarantee that Montgomery would close for them. He returned to Kansas City eight saves short of 300 for his career and as the only pitcher in baseball to lead his team in saves in every season of the 1990s to that point.

Montgomery got save number 293 early in the 1999 season, but the Royals bullpen struggled early, and he often went two or more days between outings. After blowing saves on April 17 and 23, the Royals went to rookie Jose Santiago for their next save chance. In May, Montgomery worked four save opportunities, converting three but blowing a save on May 31 that would put his ERA above 5.00. It remained above that level the rest of the year.

As the Royals and Montgomery struggled, they went to a bullpen-by-committee approach. For Montgomery (who always felt sharper with more consistent work) he often spent days between outings. Montgomery was critical of manager Tony Muser, but local media columns pointed out that his performance didn't warrant much more work either.[31]

In early July, Montgomery's hip started to give him trouble, and after two blown saves, he went on the disabled list on the 9th. He had saved five games and blown five saves to that point with a 7.54 ERA.

Montgomery had often said in the later years of his career that he'd think about retirement when his wife or the batters told him it was time. In 1999 the hitters of the American League were shouting the message. While rehabbing ahead of a return from the DL, Montgomery hinted that 1999 would likely be his last season.[32] General manager Herk Robinson told a reporter that the Royals would be unlikely to be able to fit Montgomery into their 2000 budget.[33] It was also reported that Montgomery hadn't talked to the Royals about the next year either.

On August 10 Montgomery returned from his rehab assignment and pitched in three games before his first save opportunity. On August 18 he threw a scoreless inning against the Yankees for career save number 298. The next night he earned save 299 with a scoreless 11th inning.

Montgomery wouldn't pitch again until August 24 but gave up a run on three hits and blew a 3-2 lead against the Orioles. The next night the Royals led Baltimore 8-5, but Brad Rigby opened the ninth inning by surrendering a home run. Lefty Tim Byrdak came in to retire Rich Amaral and Brady Anderson. Montgomery was summoned for the right-handed-hitting Mike Bordick.

One of the hallmarks of Montgomery's career was the tense save. Number 300 was no different. Bordick singled to center on a 2-and-1 pitch, then B.J. Surhoff followed with a single to right. With the Royals leading 8-6, Albert Belle stepped to the plate, representing the go-ahead run. The night before, Belle had homered in the 10th inning to give the Orioles the win.

Montgomery's first pitch was a called strike. Belle chopped the second pitch to shortstop, where Rey Sanchez fielded and threw him out.[34] Montgomery shook hands with his teammates after save number 300, the 10th pitcher to reach the milestone and the first to do so with every save coming with one team. Again, the topic of retirement came up and this time Montgomery was more direct, stating that 1999 would be his final year.

On September 20, Montgomery retired all four batters he faced to earn his 12th save of the year and 304th (and final) save of his career. Four days later he confirmed that he would retire at season's end.[35] Montgomery entered an October 2 game against the Tigers at Kauffman Stadium – the 700th appearance of his career – with one out in the ninth, struck out Dean Palmer and induced a groundout from Damion Easley. That turned out to be his final appearance, as the final game of the year was rained out.

Montgomery finished his career with 304 saves, a franchise-leading 686 appearances, and a 3.27 ERA in 868⅔ innings pitched. He was named an All-Star three times. While he was honored to be on the ballot for the Baseball Hall of Fame in 2005, he conceded that he wasn't likely to be inducted (he received two votes).[36] The Royals did honor him with induction into their team Hall of Fame in 2003, and Montgomery threw out the ceremonial first pitch to his father before an August 3 game. [37]

While Montgomery had mentioned the possibility of becoming a baseball agent upon retirement, his post-baseball career has been more involved with the media than player negotiations. He bought a share of Kansas City's Union Broadcasting in 1998 and as of late 2018 was their acting vice president of internet and new media. Montgomery was also a co-host of Royals Live! on Fox Sports Kansas City, appearing on the pregame and postgame show, and occasionally appearing on game broadcasts as a color commentator. As of 2018 Montgomery and his wife, Tina, lived in Kansas City.

Sources

Along with sources cited in the Notes, the author also consulted the yearly game logs and player pages on Baseball-Reference.com as well as the following book:

Jacobs, Dr. Andrew, Jeff Montgomery, and Peter D. Malone. *Just Let 'Em Play: Guiding Parents, Coaches, and Athletes Through Youth Sports (*Olathe, Kansas: Ascend Books, 2015).

Notes

1 Dennis Eckersley had 320 saves for the Oakland A's.

2 "Wellston Senior Wins Award," *Chillicothe* (Ohio) *Gazette*, May 21, 1980.

3 Jeff Montgomery, telephone interview, September 8, 2018 (Montgomery interview).

4 "Haywood Top Coach," *Greenville* (South Carolina) *News*, June 3, 1981.

5 Montgomery interview.

6 Montgomery interview.

7 Montgomery interview.

8 Dave Trimmer, "Montgomery's Arm Needs Little Relief," *Billings* (Montana) *Gazette*, August 20, 1983.

9 Montgomery interview.

10 Jeff Montgomery, *If These Walls Could Talk: Stories From the Kansas City Royals Dugout, Locker Room, and Press Box* (Chicago: Triumph Books, 2017), 199.

11 Bud Burns, "Montgomery Likes Lind, His New Club," *The Tennessean* (Nashville), April 8, 1987.

12 Montgomery, *If These Walls Could Talk*, 201.

13 Montgomery interview.

14 Bud Burns, "Reds' Murphy No Longer an 'Untouchable,'" *The Tennessean*, November 8, 1988.

15 *The Sporting News*, October 9, 1989: 17.

16 Tracy Ringolsby. "Mark Davis at the Top of KC's Shopping List," *Glens Falls* (New York) *Post-Star*, November 26, 1989: 41.

17 *The Sporting News*, January 1, 1990: 50.

18 "Royals to Give Mark Davis Nod as Starter," *Macon* (Missouri) *Chronicle-Herald*, July 6, 1990.

19 Montgomery interview..

20 Montgomery interview..

21 "Kansas City Royals at Cleveland Indians Box Score, July 24, 1992" baseball-reference.com/boxes/CLE/CLE199207240.shtml.

22 Dick Kaegel, "Montgomery Signs for Three Years," *Kansas City Star*, February 16, 1993.

23 Jeffrey Flanagan, "Royals Report," *Kansas City Star*, June 20, 1994.

24 Jason Whitlock, "OK, Herk, Keep 'em Coming," *Kansas City Star*, August 13, 1995.

25 Dick Kaegel, "Montgomery Backs Off," *Kansas City Star*, July 16, 1995.

26 Jeffrey Flanagan, "Royals Retain Closer," *Kansas City Star*, December 16, 1995.

27 LaVelle E. Neal III, "Montgomery Passes Friend on His Way to Saves Record," *Kansas City Star*, July 21, 1996.

28 Montgomery interview.

29 Howard Richman, "Montgomery Pitcher of Year," *Kansas City Star*, November 20, 1998.

30 Ibid.

31 Dick Kaegel, "Appier's Streak Ends," Kansas City Star, June 3, 1999; Joe Posnanski, "Please Keep Comments, Pitches Down," *Kansas City Star*, June 4, 1999.

32 Steve Rock, "Monty Starts Rehab," Kansas City Star, August 1, 1999.

33 Jeffrey Flanagan, "Royals' Plans for 2000 Season Won't Include Montgomery," *Kansas City Star*, August 27, 1999.

34 "Baltimore Orioles at Kansas City Royals Box Score, August 25, 1999" baseball-reference.com/boxes/KCA/KCA199908250.shtml.

35 Dick Kaegel, "Monty Says He's Out," *Kansas City Star*, September 24, 1999.

36 Dick Kaegel, "Montgomery Honored by Candidacy," web.archive.org/web/20121006110838/http://kansascity.royals.mlb.com/news/article.jsp?ymd=20041223&content_id=925571&vkey=news_kc&fext=.jsp&c_id=kc (accessed October 30, 2018).

37 David Boyce, "Royals Induct Montgomery/Ex-Closer Relishes Hall of Fame Honor with His Family," *Kansas City Star*, August 3, 2003.

AMOS OTIS

BY BILL LAMBERTY

Late in the evening of May 15, 1973, Amos Otis lifted a Nolan Ryan fastball to Royals Stadium's spacious right-center-field gap. Angels right fielder Ken Berry "pulled it down," Otis told the *Kansas City Star*. "Right there on the warning track. If Bob Oliver (whom Berry had replaced for defensive purposes) had been out there, I'd have had it, I'd have broken it up."[1]

Instead, with Otis's help, Ryan took a major step on the path that led him to immortality. The no-hitter was the first of seven fired by the famed Ryan Express. Ryan's career would lead him to the Hall of Fame, while Otis played for another decade and remains one of the most productive and popular players in Royals history.[2]

While no one could have known it at the time, Otis and Ryan remain linked for another reason. The two came to symbolize the futility of the 1970s New York Mets, and are widely considered parts of the two worst trades ever made by the Mets.[3] Ryan brought shortstop Jim Fregosi to the Mets, but Otis netted New York's National League entry much less in return. The fledgling Royals received Otis and pitcher Bob Johnson for third baseman Joe Foy, who played only 140 more games in the majors, while Johnson was later shipped from Kansas City in a package of players that brought the Royals Freddie Patek.

Otis, however, was stellar. Sandwiching short stints with the Mets at the beginning of his career with a partial season in Pittsburgh at the end, Otis became a Royals legend. The five-time All-Star finished in the top 10 among AL players in OPS twice, was among the best 10 players in the junior circuit in runs created four times, and as of 2018 stood in the top five in games played (third, 1,891), runs scored (second, 1,074), RBIs (third, 992), walks (second, 739), and stolen bases (second, 340), and ranked in KC's top five in every offensive career category except batting average. He helped lead the Royals from the futility of its brief expansion era to one of baseball's most successful in less than a decade, and inspired the chants of "Aaaay-Oh! Aaaay-Oh!" that reverberated across the shimmering turf of sparkling Royals Stadium.

And while every Mets fan knows that the organization let Amos Otis slip through its hands, few know that he actually got away twice. In 1964, the year before the major leagues instituted the amateur player draft system, Otis was among 35 players flown to Shea Stadium for a workout during a Mets road trip. Sending Otis home to Mobile, the Mets told him they would contact him.[4]

Otis heard from a major-league team several months later, but it wasn't the Mets. The Boston Red Sox drafted him with the 95th selection of the first draft. Like his hometown hero Hank Aaron, Otis was drafted as a shortstop. Mobile produced Hall of Famers Aaron and Billy Williams and major-league regulars like Tommie Agee and Cleon Jones, Otis's future Mets teammates, but Otis remains the only player ever drafted out of the city's Williamson High School who made it to the major leagues. Otis hit .329 with 9 home runs and 10 stolen bases on the

Appalachian League's Harlan club in 1965, leading third basemen in fielding (.910), chances accepted (134), and double plays (13).

The success on the diamond masked a tumultuous summer off the field. One of two African Americans on the squad, Otis recalled in a 1969 *New York Times* feature that he received an anonymous phone call several weeks into the season admonishing him to leave town in strongly-worded, racially-inflamed language. The Red Sox chose not to heed Otis's pleas for reassignment, and he and teammate Bobby Mitchell endured sporadic threats and harassment not uncommon in the 1960s American South through the rest of the summer.[5]

If Otis needed a change in scenery, it would arrive soon. He advanced to Oneonta of the New York-Penn League the next season, and responded by earning all-star honors. He hit .270 with three homers, drawing 39 walks in 419 at-bats while stealing 14 bases. After the season ended, though, Otis received a jolt. The Mets, two years after working him out at Shea Stadium, drafted him from Boston's farm system on November 29, 1966, in that year's minor-league draft.[6]

Taking the move in stride, Otis hit .268 in 407 at-bats for Triple-A Jacksonville in 1967, with 11 doubles, 7 triples, and 3 home runs. He stole 29 bases, earning a September call-up to Shea Stadium. Otis indicated in a 1996 *Sports Collectors Digest* interview that he arrived in the majors with a clear sense of his defensive role, although New York manager Wes Westrum initially played him at third base. "I was a jack-of-all-trades in high school," Otis said. "I could play all nine positions. I started out my pro career at shortstop, kind of lost interest at shortstop and moved over to third base for a while. Then I was the fastest guy in the outfield for the Mets and then I wanted to be an outfielder."[7]

Returning to Jacksonville in 1968, Otis settled in for an outstanding season. He hit 15 home runs, matching his previous career total as a professional, and stole 21 bases. He again earned all-star honors and played in the Triple-A all-star contest.

Otis's 1968 season landed him in an awkward position entering spring training in 1969. The 22-year-old was lauded as "the best piece of property we've got"[8] by Mets farm director Whitey Herzog, who would be instrumental to Otis's career in Kansas City, and New York general manager Bob Murphy tagged Otis as "untouchable" in trade negotiations with Atlanta for Joe Torre before the 1969 campaign.[9] Drawing scorn from Braves GM Paul Richards (who asked, a few months early, "If they got so many 'untouchables' on that club, how come they haven't won any pennants?") as well as the New York sporting press, that untouchable list included Tom Seaver, Jerry Koosman, and Bud Harrelson.[10] Howard Cosell even asked Otis in one spring-training interview if he expected to win Rookie of the Year honors.[11]

If trying to break into a lineup for a New York major-league team wasn't pressure enough, the label of untouchable was. "That untouchable label was a terrible burden," Otis told sportswriter Arthur Daley in 1971.[12] Although seen as a utility infielder during the winter months, he broke camp as a third baseman. Veteran Ed Charles earned time at third to begin the season, but when opportunity knocked Otis responded. He told the *St. Petersburg Independent* in 1971 that "the season started and I didn't play for three weeks. After they had a losing streak I finally got to play and we broke the streak. Then (the press) started coming out with all this 'phenom Otis breaks streak' and all that stuff. I played three games in a row," then returned to spot duty, playing primarily as a defensive replacement for the next several weeks. His bat went cold.[13]

On June 15, with only six hits to his credit in 66 at-bats, Otis was farmed out to make way for Donn Clendenon. Otis saw some action in September, but his September 2 recall eliminated him from consideration for the postseason roster. In fact, Murphy said that "Gil liked what he saw of him in the final series in Philadelphia," saying Gil Hodges claimed Otis "looked like the player we always said he was." Otis's teammates appreciated his performance enough to vote him a World Series share, although he didn't receive a championship ring.[14]

Significantly, Otis earned a second look from Hodges while playing center field. He also opened the eyes of Cedric Tallis, Kansas City's general manager. Tallis built those teams by acquiring young talent, and the Mets stood as Tallis's first victim.

Immediately after the December 3 trade that moved him to the American League, the Royals installed Otis in Municipal Stadium's spacious center field. Kansas City manager Charlie Metro said Otis's acquisition was made to plug Kansas City's hole in center field.[15]

Tallis correctly read New York's displeasure with 35-year-old Ed Charles and Wayne Garrett, and the organization's desperation to plug a hole at third base that had been a sore spot since the organization's inception in 1962, and hawked the Mets through the summer and fall with the idea of moving Foy. "During the World Series, we sent a lot of people to Baltimore and New York. I assigned two men to each of the other 23 clubs to sound out their needs and what they would give in a trade," Tallis said.[16] He said the Mets had tried to acquire a young third baseman from Cleveland, but the teams didn't match up. Negotiations began between the Mets and Royals at the World Series, according to Tallis, with talks heating up at the general managers meetings in Colorado Springs. "That was a kind of four-day outing, mostly golfing. Murphy didn't play golf but we got together at night. We couldn't agree at that time, but promised to talk again at the Winter Meetings in Miami. Bob Scheffing (who succeeded Murphy) and Whitey Herzog (farm system director for the Mets) was there, too. We finally made the deal with Foy going to New York and Otis and Johnson coming here."[17]

Evaluating the opportunity facing him, Otis celebrated in ironic fashion. "December third was the happiest day of my life. I didn't get to drink any of that World Series champagne, but on the day I was traded my wife and I went out and bought our only bottle," he said in 1970.[18] Otis never meshed with New York's stoic manager Gil Hodges. When wished good luck by his former boss at the 1970 All-Star Game, Otis commented later that the salutation was about half the number of words Hodges had spoken to him in his entire time with the Mets.[19] Still, Otis headed to America's Heartland with mixed emotions: "The disappointment came from being traded from a World Series champ to an expansion team; it had only been around one year. The best thing about that was there were no superstars over there; the only name recognized there was Lou Piniella. He was Rookie of the Year that year. So it was like I went from being on top of the water barrel to being under the water barrel. That was probably my biggest thrill in baseball, getting a chance to play more in Kansas City and I stayed there for 14 years."[20]

He also continued to hold mixed emotions about his opportunity in New York. In an August 1970 interview Otis said, "I didn't want to play third with the Mets, but I think I could have played it if I'd really gotten a shot at it. But three games? That's no test. I never got an explanation from anyone why I was benched."[21] Hodges showed little remorse in letting Otis go, commenting after the deal that it may have been "unfair to the boy to ask him to play third. He didn't like the position and he didn't play well there."[22] Comments by Hodges in the spring of 1969 offer further clues to the uneven career and limited opportunity Otis experienced in New York. "Lackadaisical is the word people in our organization use" to describe Otis, Hodges said in March 1969. "Seems like I play my best ball when they're pushing me," Otis admitted in that same article.[23]

Otis's impact in Kansas City was immediate and unquestionable. In 1971 he recounted an incident during spring training in 1970. "I was standing in the outfield not far from the right-field foul line when I saw Charlie Metro walking toward me. I didn't even know what to say to him and so I headed toward center field. I looked again and he was coming my way. Finally he pinned me against the left-field fence. 'Amos,' he said, 'you're my center fielder for as long as you can hold the job.'"[24]

On his way to hitting .284 in 1970 with 36 doubles, tied for the league lead, Otis reached base by hit or walk in 135 of his 159 games. He became the Royals' second All-Star and was involved in one of the best-known plays in All-Star Game history. Otis made the throw to the plate on which Pete Rose collided with Ray Fosse. That throw, Otis recalled in 1996, spawned the nickname Famous Amos "because I made that great throw from center field. It was a one-hop throw. ... That's the way baseball's supposed to be played."[25]

If 1970 announced Otis's arrival, the next year marked his coming-out party. Playing in 147 games, Otis stole a league-leading 52 bases in 60 attempts to set a stolen-base percentage record, and hammered 15 home runs with 26 doubles. His 1971 honors included the Kansas City Sports Personality of the Year Award from the city's Jewish Community Center. The Royals continued to improve, adding Patek, Cookie Rojas, and John Mayberry to the infield mix through trades and matriculating George Brett and Paul Splittorff through the farm system, and battled Oakland through the Athletics' five-year run of division crowns (1971-75). Otis played well through this period, earning renown for his speed and glove. He led AL outfielders in putouts (404) and total chances (418) in 1971, and on September 7 that season stole five bases in a nine-inning game against Milwaukee, one short of the major-league record. He became the first player since 1927 with five swipes in a game, and only the fifth since 1900 to do so. Otis and Patek swiped 101 stolen bases between them that season, the highest total by two American League players with 49 or more stolen bases on the same team since 1917.[26] In 1973 Otis finished third in AL MVP voting, behind Reggie Jackson and Jim Palmer.

Otis's production slipped some in 1974, a season in which some hard feelings emerged on both sides in his relationship with Royals fans. "I can't help it if I make things look easy," Otis said early in 1975 about the perception that he occasionally coasted. "Even in 1973, when I had my best year, people said I could do better. Last year I didn't have the year I wanted to have. I got to pressing. It was just something I couldn't overcome. Everything I do on this team, I'm first or second. I can't do much more than that. I know I didn't have the year I wanted, but you can't always do it. I got so I hated to come to the park. It was embarrassing. ... As soon as you came out of the dugout, they were on you. After a while, you just hated to play."[27]

On April 30 and May 1, 1975, Otis tied an AL record for most steals in two consecutive games (seven), but he struggled with injuries and a midseason tonsillectomy during the season and finished with a .247 average, although his walk total spiked to 66 in 470 at-bats and his on-base percentage held at .342. Otis rebounded in 1976, and Kansas City finally outraced Oakland to the American League's West Division championship. The postseason brought heartache, however. Leading off the bottom of the first in Game One of the ALCS at Royals Stadium, Otis severely sprained his ankle running out a grounder at first base and missed the remainder of the series. Kansas City was locked into a 6-6 tie with the Yankees in the deciding Game Five when Chris Chambliss's home run off Mark Littell launched New York into the World Series for the first time in a dozen years, and also began a string of three straight American League Championship Series where New York beat the Royals for the AL pennant.

Otis nearly made another career move after Kansas City's first divisional crown. The Royals completed a deal sending Otis and Cookie Rojas to Pittsburgh over the winter, but Rojas voided the transaction.[28] Even then, Otis was a fixture in the Royals outfield. He won Gold Glove Awards in 1971, '73, and '74, and was Kansas City's Player of the Year in '71, '73, and '78. He led AL outfielders in fielding average in 1978 and '79, and in 1980 the Royals finally beat the Yankees to advance to the World Series. Otis belted three home runs and hit .478 in a losing effort against the Phillies.

Throughout his Kansas City career, one of Otis's calling cards was his one-handed style of catching fly balls in center field. Bucking a century of conventional wisdom that called for two-handed catches, Otis came upon his unique style early in his Royals career. While trying to help raw, athletic outfielder Pat Kelly, who tended toward nervousness in the field, Otis demonstrated that waiting on a fly ball after reaching its approximate landing spot in the outfield called for patience, not nerves. "I was trying to show him he didn't have to be nervous or tense while waiting for the ball," Otis said. "After a while, it felt awkward going back to two hands. I decided to go ahead and catch everything one-handed. I feel more comfortable, and I think it helps my throwing."[29]

While his smooth defensive play and cool demeanor were occasionally misdiagnosed as hot-dogging or loafing, Otis became a fan favorite in Kansas City. He was also noted for acts of kindness and compassion. On September 12, 1977, with Kansas City cruising to its second straight American League West crown, a game in Royals Stadium was postponed because of a drenching storm. As 16 inches of rain swamped the city and flooded many areas, eventually resulting in 25 deaths, Otis came across eight wet, frightened boys. He piled them into his Lincoln Continental, fed them, and lodged them for the evening. One of the youngsters to whose aid Otis came, Richard Brown, eventually became a Missouri state legislator and in 2017 sponsored a proclamation commemorating the flood and honoring Otis as a Good Samaritan and humanitarian. "I was doing what any other dad would have done," Otis said.[30]

After Otis played the two guaranteed seasons on a $1.27 million contract, the Royals declined to exercise a club option prior to the 1984 season in order to make room for Willie Wilson in center field. Otis hooked on with the Pirates, but was released in August, ending his career. Otis remained sporadically active in baseball after his playing days, working in the Rockies organization as a hitting instructor for a time in the late 1990s. Along with pitcher Steve Busby, Otis was in the Royals Hall of Fame's inaugural induction class and remained a Royals icon.

Notes

1 Sam Mellinger, "Amos Otis Remembers the Last No-Hitter Thrown Against the Royals," *Kansas City Star*, May 19, 2008.

2 Ibid.

3 Jocelyn Taub, "New York Mets: The Team's 10 Worst Trades Ever," BleacherReport.com, December 14, 2011. The trades are also linked in several other online sites, including "The 15 Worst Trades in New York Mets History" on sportster.com, January 5, 2006, and a Fangraphs.com analysis "The Best and Worst Teams of the Trade," from February 10, 2005.

4 "Otis, Met Rookie 'Untouchable,' Is Forced to Third Base by Mobile Neighbors," *New York Times*, March 23, 1969.

5 Ibid.

6 Ibid.

7 Gary Herron, "Another Famous Amos (Otis) Offers Some Pretty Startling Revelations … for the Record," *Sports Collectors Digest*, February 9, 1996.

8 Jack Lang, "Versatile Otis – Mets Blue-Chip Prospect," *The Sporting News*, November 23, 1968: 52.

9 Jack Lang, "Mets' Otis Available – And Murphy Enjoys Dig at Richards," *The Sporting News*, November 15, 1969: 44.

10 Ibid.

11 Jack Lang, "Versatile Otis – Mets Blue-Chip Prospect."

12 Arthur Daley, "The Mets Had Him and Let Him Get Away," *New York Times*, August 18, 1971.

13 Ibid.

14 Lang, "Mets' Otis Available – And Murphy Enjoys Dig at Richards."

15 Joe McGuff, "Otis Loosens Up – He's One of the Royals' Elites," *Kansas City Star*, March 27, 1971.

16 Joe Trimble, "Ex-Met Otis Spurs Royals," *New York Daily News*, August 26, 1970.

17 Ibid.

18 Ibid.

19 Murray Chass, "Steady Work Agrees with Otis," *New York Times*, August 28, 1970.

20 Herron.

21 Paul Ballot, "Otis Feels Royal in Kansas City," *Newsday*, August 15, 1970.

22 Joe McGuff, "Royals Counting on Big Lift from Otis," *The Sporting News*, December 20, 1969: 38.

23 Jack Lang, "Mets to Put a Burr Under Otis' Saddle," *The Sporting News*, March 22, 1969: 19.

24 Daley.

25 Herron.

26 Joe McGuff, "101 Heists: Royals' Otis, Patek, Now Steal Kings," *The Sporting News*, October 23, 1971: 16, 40.

27 Joe McGuff, "Next MVP Could be Otis, Asserts Royals' McKeon," *The Sporting News*, May 10, 1975.

28 Joe McGuff, "Cookie Balks – Royals' Trade Collapses," *The Sporting News*, December 27, 1975: 50.

29 Sid Bordman, "Royals' Otis En Route to Super Star Status," *The Sporting News*, August 14, 1971: 3.

30 Eric Adler, "I Was Doing What Any Other Dad Would Have Done': Royals Star Helped Kids in KC Flood," *Kansas City Star*, September 8, 2017.

FREDDIE PATEK

BY JEFF BARTO

"How does it feel to be the smallest player in the majors," a Houston reporter asked Fred Patek in 1968. "A heck of a lot better than being the tallest player in the minors," countered the rookie shortstop.[1]

Patek's quip matched his quickness on the field and the basepaths for 14 years in the major leagues. At 5-feet and change tall, he stood as the smallest player of his time. Patek often claimed that he was 5-foot-5, but throughout his career most sources listed him at 5-foot-4. The origin of his lost inch began with Bob Prince, the Pittsburgh Pirates radio announcer. Prince measured Patek on TV shortly after he debuted in 1968. "I came out 5-4," chuckled Patek, "but I think Bob wanted me to come out 5-4."[2] Others stretched the truth the other way. When Patek joined the California Angels as a free agent in 1980, their PR director asked, "How tall are you?" "I'm around 5-6," Fred said. "How come you were listed at 5-4?" "I guess 5-6 sounded better." "Well" said the director, "from now on you're 5-6."[3] Whatever his height, Patek beat back several challenges. He played only one year in high school and caught the attention of scouts while playing ball in the Air Force. He was drafted in the 22nd round of the 1965 amateur draft, yet he posted a career WAR second to only one first-round draftee that year.[4] And he battled an all-star shortstop for playing time as a Pirate, yet became a three-time All Star for the Kansas City Royals.

Frederick Joseph Patek was born on October 9, 1944, in Oklahoma City. His family soon moved to Seguin, Texas, where he grew up. "Three or four weeks later my dad left to go overseas, and my mom went back home."[5] Her sister's brother – Freddie's uncle Joe Faldik – lived in Yoakum, Texas, so she stayed with him until her husband came back.

Freddy preceded two brothers and two sisters. Kenny, born next, nearly tried out for the Pittsburgh Pirates. Instead, he chose to serve his country in Vietnam. He earned two Purple Hearts after twice enduring serious wounds to his chest and legs.[6] Cathy, Anthony, and Annette filled out the rest of the family parented by Joe and his wife, Annie (Faldik). Joe Patek ran a butcher shop that kept his wife and children busy. As youngsters Fred and his siblings made hamburger meat in the mornings. In the afternoons they stuffed sausage to sell the next day at the Seguin meat market.[7] At age 7, Fred helped on his uncle Joe's bread truck. At 4:00 A.M. each morning he woke up at 965 E. Weinert St. to stack bread trays for 12 hours at $2.00 a day. His early work ethic matched his hard-nosed play as a kid. Uncle Joe would drive the 7-year-old to nearby Yoakum, to be regularly picked first among the older kids in sandlot games. "I was better than all of them," Fred crowed.[8] He excelled for six years in Little League for the Lions Club and two years in American Legion in preparation for high school.

Patek played third base his junior year at Seguin High School. Earning all-district and all-state honors, he was poised to lead the Matadors his senior year.[9] However, the school made a coaching change and the new coach refused to allow Fred to try out.[10]

After graduation in 1963, Patek received a few scholarships, but went to Houston to work instead. On

July 13 he played in the South Texas All-Star game in San Antonio. At that game, former third baseman Pinky Whitney scouted and selected Patek to play in the annual Hearst Sandlot Classic.[11] This tournament pitted invited players across the country to play a team of all-stars from New York. St. John's University freshman baseball coach Lou Carnesecca watched Patek blast several home runs in practice. Carnesecca, who later coached the school's great basketball teams of the 1980s, offered Patek a scholarship.[12] "I wasn't going to go to New York," Fred said with a chuckle. Instead, "My mom called me, she said, 'You need to come home. ... You got your draft induction notice.'"[13]

On January 1, 1964, Patek joined the Air Force in San Antonio, Texas.[14] At Grater Field on Randolph Air Force Base, he played a 140-game schedule for two years. "It was the best thing that could have happened to me because the scouts got a chance to see that I could play," Fred said. "Had I gone on to college out of high school and played 30, 40, or 50 games a year, I probably would have never made it."[15] His play captured the eyes of two major-league scouts, Bob Zuk and Larry DeHaven of the Pittsburgh Pirates.[16] On June 8, 1965, the Pirates drafted Patek in the 22nd round of the major leagues' first amateur draft. Of all the first-round draftees that year, only Rick Monday, the first-ever pick, would score a better career WAR (33.1) than Patek's 24.1.

After the draft, Patek's father fell ill and the Air Force gave him a hardship discharge. The Pirates allowed Fred to tend to family business the rest of the year. The next spring he began his professional career, with Gastonia (North Carolina) of the Class-A Western Carolinas League. His hitting (.310/.401/.401) and 38 stolen bases placed him in the league's all-star game, where he was named the MVP.[17] The next day the Pirates promoted him to the Triple-A Columbus Jets of the International League. On August 10 the Pirates sent him to Double A to finish the year with Asheville (North Carolina) of the Southern League. Patek played all of 1967 at Columbus. His play at shortstop and center field along with leading the league with 42 stolen bases earned him another nickname, the Flying Flea.[18]

Patek began 1968 in Columbus and continued to burn on the bases, stealing 18 bags at a 90 percent clip. The Pirates called him up for his major-league debut on June 3. In Los Angeles, Dodgers lefty Claude Osteen collared Patek in four at-bats and he remained hitless in his first 12 plate appearances. On June 14 at Forbes Field, he got his first hit. He dropped a bunt single off Houston left-hander Denny Lemaster and got his first stolen base.[19] The next day Patek slammed his first home run. Houston right-hander Don Wilson yielded the drive, which produced his first three RBIs.[20] Soon after, Patek earned a nickname that stayed with him the rest of his career. Pirates announcer Bob Prince began calling him the Cricket during broadcasts. Patek chuckled, "[T]hey'd punch a bunch of ... I guess they were selling crickets (metal noisemakers) all over Pittsburgh. So, at the ballpark you'd hear all the cricket sounds when I came to bat."[21]

Just as Patek settled in, a fastball on June 18 stalled his season. "I got hit on the wrist by a Don Drysdale pitch and I played a month without knowing I had a cracked bone in my wrist. I knew something was wrong, but the first X-rays were negative and I kept playing."[22] He played a week with a heavily taped left wrist when new X-rays revealed the broken bone. He lost 33 games to the disabled list. The injury also affected Patek's bat; he ended the season with five hits in his last 45 at-bats (.114).[23]

Soon after the season, Fred married Geraldine "Jerri" Freeze on October 12. They lived in Sarasota that winter while he played in the Florida Instructional League in preparation for spring training.[24]

Despite his injury, playing time looked brighter for Patek in 1969. Pirates manager Larry Shepard reluctantly inserted him full time at shortstop over incumbent Gene Alley. Alley, a two-time All-Star, suffered a sore right shoulder that forced him into a utility role. Patek played hot and cold all year, never feeling the confidence of Shepard, who doubted him.[25] "I was a seven-inning ballplayer in 1969," Patek complained. "I'd bat two, maybe three times a game and I was out of there for a pinch-hitter. They took away my aggressiveness. ... So I batted eighth and you don't get many chances to steal when you're the eighth man in the order."[26] Patek finished with an anemic slash line of .239/.318/.296 with only 15 extra-base hits and 15 steals. He struck out a career-high 86 times. The

Pirates saw his lackluster play as reason to platoon him in the coming season.

In 1970 the Pirates replaced Shepard as manager with the return of Danny Murtaugh. The Bucs moved from aging Forbes Field to Three Rivers Stadium on July 16. A new Tartan Turf surface required quickness and a strong arm from the shortstop position; Patek had both. But his 30 errors the year before led Murtaugh to lean on the veteran Alley. Patek played only 65 games and pinch-hit more times (13) than in the rest of his career combined (11). The Pirates won the NL East, but in the NLCS the Cincinnati Reds swept them in three games. Patek went hitless in the only game he played. As the year ended, Patek expressed his unhappiness with Pittsburgh. "They treat me like a kid," he fumed. "They don't say things in words. It's in actions. They indicate they don't think I can play every day. Baseball is no longer fun to me."[27]

Early in his career, baseball was fun for Patek. He attracted much attention by other clubs. In 1968, the Mets offered left-hander Jerry Koosman for him; the Bucs turned them down.[28] Dodgers manager Walt Alston believed Patek to be the National League's most underrated player.[29] Preston Gomez, skipper for San Diego, said, "If the Pirates ever want to trade him, I hope they speak to us."[30] Gomez nearly got his man late in the '70 season as he and the Bucs flirted with an exchange of Patek for pitcher Pat Dobson.[31] The deal fell through. Patek and the Bucs had to wait until December to find a trading partner.

On December 2, 1970, the Pirates traded Patek at the Winter Meetings. He found out from his manager, Roberto Clemente, while playing winter ball in Puerto Rico.[32] They packaged him in a six-player trade with the Kansas City Royals. Pittsburgh acquired right-hander Bob Johnson along with shortstop Jackie Hernandez and backup catcher Jim Campanis. The Royals obtained spot starter Bruce Dal Canton, catcher Jerry May, and Patek. Surprisingly, the Pirates offered the Royals a choice between Patek and Alley, hoping they would take the older, injury-prone vet.[33] The Royals wisely picked Patek, who was pleased he could now bat leadoff and steal more bases. "I want to go someplace where I can utilize my speed," he said. "I did a lot of running in the minors. When I came to Pittsburgh from Columbus ... I was aggressive. Everybody said I gave the club a big lift."[34] He soon gave a lift to the Royals with a career year in 1971.

The trade rejuvenated Patek. Batting leadoff, he stole 49 bases, beginning a string of eight consecutive years of 30 or more steals. He posted career highs in batting average (.267), at-bats (591), runs (86), hits (158), home runs (6), and triples (11, which led the American League). On April 30, he beat Baltimore with the first of six career walk-off hits. On July 9 at Minnesota, Patek became the first Royal to hit for the cycle. In the field he teamed with second baseman Cookie Rojas to form a remarkable double-play combo that included a four-year streak in which Patek led AL shortstops in double plays. As of 2018 only three shortstops have matched the record, George McBride, Roy McMillian, and Rafael Ramirez. Patek's 301 putouts also led the league. For much of the season writers considered him an MVP candidate. However, he started pressing at the plate, hitting only .157 with three steals in September. He still finished sixth in the MVP voting, garnering 77 points. His play helped to elevate the Royals to second place in the AL West.

In November Patek went through a life-changing experience. At home one night he thought, "If I die right now on the spot, where would I go? The only answer I had was, 'Straight to hell! ... It was like God was saying, 'This is your last chance, if you want eternal happiness in heaven, it's up to you to go get it.'"[35] Patek thought about quitting baseball after his spiritual epiphany but decided baseball was his way to do God's work. He has embraced his Christianity ever since, but his faith would be tested over 20 years later by a family tragedy.

Patek dropped in nearly every offensive category in 1972, but he did deliver two walk-off hits in less than a week. On August 5 his single beat California, 2-1. Three days later his game-winning hit handed a 4-3 loss to Oakland's future Hall of Famer Rollie Fingers. Patek's modest offense did not affect his glove. He led the AL in Defensive WAR with a 3.2 mark, bolstered by a league-leading 510 assists, 18 Total Zone Runs, and 113 double plays, that again led all shortstops. Despite producing his weakest career slash line (.212/.280/.276), Patek's stellar defense and 33 steals secured his selection to his first All-Star Game. The Royals fell back to fourth place, but they looked forward to a new home in 1973.

The Royals acquired Patek knowing they'd soon switch from grass to artificial turf. They did so in 1973, moving from Kansas City's old Municipal Stadium to Royals Stadium (renamed Kauffman Stadium in 1993.)[36] On April 10 Patek christened the new park with its first walk, stolen base, and run scored. On the new turf, Patek excelled defensively. "When I left Three Rivers, we were playing on it, but it was really hard, really fast, and I thought, 'This is tough,' Fred recalled. "The balls were just like lightning, so I changed my game. I moved deeper and I moved more parallel to the third baseman and it increased my range a lot."[37] At bat, Patek improved his slash lines slightly from '72 while chipping in 36 steals and a 10th-inning hit to beat the Yankees on August 22. The Royals rebounded to second place in the AL West.

In up-and-down fashion, the Royals fell to fifth place in their division in 1974, their poorest showing since they began in 1969. Patek delivered another mediocre year with the bat, but did draw a career-high 77 walks along with his best hitting streak, 12 games. Again he paced the AL in double plays with 108. But team chemistry suffered between the players and manager Jack McKeon. Tension and conflicts foreshadowed a change to challenge the Oakland A's dominance of the AL West.

McKeon battled his players and the media early in 1975. By July 23, the team replaced him with Whitey Herzog.[38] The Royals reclaimed second place, but Patek continued to struggle at the plate. An ankle injury on July 10 sidelined him for 17 days. He returned to deliver a 10th-inning hit to beat Minnesota, 6-5, on August 4. Three days later he stung the Twins again, hitting his sixth and final leadoff home run, an inside-the-park round-tripper to start a 10-2 romp.[39] On the bases he extended his streak of 30-plus steals with 32 thefts. The Royals finished as bridesmaids again to the Athletics, who won their fifth straight division crown. Oakland's streak spanned all five of Patek's years as a Royal. Kansas City pushed them often, finishing second three times. But under Herzog's guidance, the Royals were on the verge of controlling the AL West for the next three years.

By mid-May of 1976 the Royals claimed first place in the division for the rest of the year. The team jelled with the emergence of future Hall of Famer George Brett, stars Amos Otis and Hal McRae, and pitchers Dennis Leonard and Paul Splittorff. They also ran wild on the bases. Patek stole over 50 bases for the first time (he had 51) and six other players stole 20 or more bases for a franchise record (218). The increased thefts were part of an early version of Whiteyball, a strategy Herzog perfected later with St. Louis. He built the roster to fit Royals Stadium with its artificial turf and challenging fences. Speed, defense, and line drives played better on the Royals' carpet than fly balls that wilted in its huge power alleys. Herzog saw Patek as vital to his strategy. Artificial turf demanded deeper positioning, greater range, and a cannon arm from a shortstop. Herzog saw Patek as the prototype to play the position in the '70s. "Patek, Bud Harrelson, and Larry Bowa are the three best I've seen at playing shortstop on the carpet," Whitey exclaimed, "...but no one can play it any better than Fred."[40] Herzog's praise endured even after managing Ozzie Smith in St. Louis during the 1980s. Patek's play also earned him his second All-Star Game appearance.

Whiteyball propelled the Royals to win their first AL West crown in 1976. The night the Royals clinched the division, Patek and Rojas, in full uniforms, famously jumped into the right-field fountains to celebrate. "We jumped in there with our cleats and everything on," Patek recalled. "If (Royals PR director Dean Vogelaar) hadn't had the electricity in the fountains turned off, we could've been swimming out there like a couple of dead goldfish."[41]

Patek hit well in the ALCS. He drove in four runs on seven hits with two doubles to bat .389; it was not enough. In the final game, Yankees first baseman Chris Chambliss led off the bottom of the ninth inning with a pennant-winning homer. Despite the loss, the Royals were poised to control their division and return to the postseason.

Before the 1977 season, Patek sought a five-year contract with the Royals. The team eventually signed him to a three-year deal worth $500,000.[42] The 32-year-old shortstop then helped the club to a franchise-record 102 wins. They blended their usual speed and pitching with unusual power by slugging 146 home runs, more than double the 65 hit the year before. Patek produced his second-best season as a Royal. He generated career highs in doubles (26), RBIs (60), and steals (a league-leading 53). His steal of home on June 19 produced the 2-1 margin over Minnesota.[43] On June 22 Patek got his "biggest thrill in baseball" when he belted his 1,000th career hit in a 4-3 win over Seattle.[44] He recalled the fans' standing ovation — "[T]hat was the first time I ever felt that people were applauding me for what I had accomplished instead for just being a little guy."[45] He played a career-best 154 games. A postseason rematch with the Yankees was next.

In the five-game ALCS, Patek repeated his .389 batting average, adding more power. He produced three doubles, a triple, and five RBIs. In the final game a brawl broke out between Brett and Yankees third baseman Graig Nettles. Both scuffled after Brett slid hard into Nettles on a first-inning triple. As the fight swelled, Patek felt someone pull him away from the scrum. Billy Martin dragged him to the pitcher's mound and put an arm around him as the two watched the melee together. Billy's protection of Fred mirrored a similar time when Martin managed in Texas. When a fight broke out then, "the next thing I knew, someone grabbed me by the back of my jersey. I thought. 'Oh, man, this isn't going to be good!' I turned around and it was Billy Martin. ... I knew he was going to lay me out. But no, instead he pulled me by the collar to the pitcher's mound and said, 'You just stay here with me. We'll be out of trouble up here.'"[46]

Surprisingly, no one was ejected after the fight. "(Umpire Marty) Springstead told me he wasn't going to throw Brett out," Martin recalled. "This is a championship game and not the time to be throwing players out. If this game had been played in July, Brett would have been gone."[47]

The game edged to the top of the ninth with the Royals leading 3-2. Three pitchers later the Yankees led 5-3 going into the bottom of the ninth. Frank White got a one-out single to bring Patek's hot bat to the plate. His slash line positioned him to win the MVP of the series (.389/.400/.667). But on his 33rd birthday he hit Sparky Lyle's slider sharply to Nettles who started a pennant-winning double play. As the Yankees celebrated, Tony Triolo from *Sports Illustrated* snapped the poignant photo of Patek sitting in the dugout alone, head in hands, in disbelief. "I just can't believe we lost," he sighed.[48]

The Royals rebounded to claim their third straight AL West crown in 1978. In the first half Patek played well, hitting .274 with 23 steals to earn his third trip to the All-Star Game. He batted for the first time in the midsummer classic, singling in three at-bats. He finished with 38 steals, the last time he would swipe over 30 bases. But his second-half struggles at the plate (.216/.284/.281) led to his final season as a full-time shortstop. In the playoffs the Royals tried to claim the pennant for the third consecutive year against the Yankees; it was not to be.

In the two prior ALCS meetings, the Royals lost in five games. In 1978 the Yankees ended the series in four games. After hitting .389 in both of the previous two playoffs, Patek cratered at the plate. His two-run homer helped rout the Yankees, 10-4, in Game Two, but it was his only hit in 13 at-bats. By next spring the Royals had plans for a change at shortstop.

In 1979 Patek started fewer than 100 games for the first time as a Royal. The 34-year-old lost a third of his playing time to youngsters U L Washington and Todd Cruz. Injuries plagued him. He played most of May with a hyperextended shoulder. On August 22 he suffered a sprained right ankle, putting him on the disabled list. He returned on September 14, only to play two innings on defense, his final appearance that year. After the season he was asked why he lost his job at short. Patek responded, "It was given away. I never had a job last year. ...When I lost my job, I was playing well. ... I was shuffled in and out of the lineup."[49] His Royals career was over at that point. The club finished second behind the California Angels, Patek's new team for 1980.

Unhappy in a utility role, Patek tested free agency for the first time.[50] On December 5, 1979, he signed a three-year deal for $550,000 with the Angels.[51] He started strong at the plate. By mid-June, his OPS surged over .800, including two four-hit games, the first of which shocked the league. On June 20 he led off the game against the Red Sox with a double off the top of Fenway Park's left-field wall; it was his shortest hit that day. By the end of the 20-2 blowout, Patek had joined Ernie Banks as the only two shortstops at the time to slug three home runs in a game. "You know, the thing I remember most from that game," Patek recalled, "is that the fans in Boston gave me a standing ovation after the third home run. They did it so long that I went back out and tipped my hat. That's really unique for a visitor, but Fenway and the Boston fans were special."[52] His outburst also produced a career-high seven RBIs. Days later, Patek talked about his playing bonus to manager Jim Fregosi, who reminded GM Buzzy Bavasi. "I had a contract, if I played 100 games," Fred recalled. "It was a $25,000 or $50,000 bonus and when I got close to 100 games, they sat me on the bench."[53] He realized that Bavasi had ordered his playing time to rookie Dickie Thon to save the bonus money. The Angels packed it in and fell to sixth place.

In 1981 the Angels acquired Rick Burleson in a trade with the Red Sox to play shortstop. Before the players strike on June 12, Patek played sparingly, mainly at second base. After the season resumed on August 10, he played in only 10 games, batting just six times. With Burleson set at short, the Angels released Patek, the following April.[54]

Soon after Patek's release, Burleson injured his right rotator cuff and his season was ended. Bavasi scrambled for a fix by contacting Patek to come back, but was immediately turned down.[55] Patek remembered the bonus snub Buzzy pulled in 1980. "Bavasi was not a very good person. He was kind of nasty about stuff. ... I did not care for that man at all," he recalled.[56] Instead, Dick Enberg hired Patek as a part-time color analyst for NBC's backup Game of the Week. He analyzed six Saturday games in 1982 and three more in 1983. In 1984 he worked with Don Drysdale and Ken Harrelson on television for Chicago White Sox road games. In his last stint as an analyst, he paired with Phil Stone on KTVT for the Texas Rangers in 1985.[57]

In the late 1980s, Patek owned six Grandy's home-style-cooking restaurants in the Kansas City area. All of them went under by the early '90s.[58] In 1992 he worked as a roving minor-league coach for the Milwaukee Brewers. Soon after returning from a road trip that year, tragedy struck the Patek clan on July 21. A car crash left their 20-year-old daughter, Kimberlie, a quadriplegic.[59] For three years she battled her spinal-cord injury on a respirator, mostly at home. A very religious family, the Pateks — Fred, wife Jerri, and daughter Heather — supported Kim with prayer and frequent trips to Hickman Mills Church of Christ. Former teammates and the Baseball Assistance Team (BAT) also helped with medical bills. After Kim died in 1995, Fred isolated himself for several more years. "I was in a shell, hurt, sad, angry, and you don't understand," he reflected. "The only thing I can tell you is that I was never the same; I was totally different."[60] Soon after, Heather gave birth to Jordan, the Pateks' first granddaughter. "She saved my life," Fred exclaimed. "She's the one God gave me to keep me going."[61]

And going he did; he formed the Kim Patek Foundation to fight paralysis and raised funds for the Spinal Cord Society through fishing and golf tournaments as well as charity basketball games. Besides coaching American Legion ball, he worked with Little League teams for over 30 years.[62] Health issues caught up with him in 2005, when he had a cobalt shoulder replacement for all those throws he made as a player.

Months later he had triple-bypass surgery on his heart.[63] By 2017 he decided to retire from coaching completely and enjoy his family and grandchildren in Lees Summit, Missouri, near Kauffman Stadium.[64]

Thankfulness filled Patek's heart after that day in 1971 when he took inventory of his life. "If it hadn't been for the good lord, I wouldn't have made it," he reflected. "And I could see that in my whole life, where God was taking care of me, he was looking out for me. That's the only reason I ever made it to the big leagues. ... I can see God's hand in all of that."[65] Some of "that" includes many honors Patek received in retirement. Bill James rated him the 14th greatest Royal. A number of halls of fame inducted him, including the Royals Hall of Fame (1992) and the Missouri Sports Hall of Fame (1999). In 2018 the San Antonio Sports Hall of Fame nominated Patek for membership. Despite these earthly recognitions, Fred Patek might value his highest honor as induction into his Fathers Hall of Fame.

Sources

In addition to the sources cited in the Notes, the author also consulted Baseball-Reference.com

Notes

1 Fred Patek, telephone interview with author, September 25, 2018. (September 25 interview).

2 Dave Anderson, "Patek Adds 2 Inches as an Angel," *New York Times*, March 13, 1980: D19.

3 Ibid.

4 Dan Holmes, "Little Freddie Patek Made Immediate Impact on Royals," *Baseball for Egg Heads,* April 25, 2012. baseballegg.com/2012/04/25/little-freddie-patek-made-immediate-impact-on-royals/, retrieved July 17, 2018. Rick Monday, the first overall pick posted a 33.1 WAR, Patek produced a 24.1 WAR.

5 Fred Patek, telephone interview with author, November 2, 2018. (November 2 interview).

6 September 25 interview.

7 Ibid.

8 Ibid.

9 Joe McGuff, "Big Heart Chief Ingredient in Tiny Patek's Comeback," *The Sporting News*, May 20, 1972: 4.

10 Bill Ballew, *The Pastime in the Seventies: Oral Histories of 16 Major Leaguers* (Jefferson, North Carolina: McFarland Publishing, 2002), 166.

11 Alan Cohen, "The Hearst Sandlot Classic: More than a Doorway to the Big Leagues," *Baseball Research Journal*, Society for American Baseball Research, Fall 2013: 27.

12 Alan Cohen, "The Hearst Sandlot Classic – Part Nine: 1963-1964. One Little Guy and One Big Guy," June 28, 2016. linkedin.com/pulse/hearst-sandlot-classic-part-eight-1963-1964-alan-cohen?articleId=6153567872460341249, retrieved September 13, 2018.

13 September 25 interview.

14 November 2 interview.

15 Bill Ballew.

16 Joe McGuff, "Big Heart."

17 September 25 interview.

18 "International Items," *The Sporting News*, July 29, 1967: 31.

19 Les Biederman, "Veale Missed Turn," *The Sporting News*, June 29, 1968: 18.

20 United Press International, "Pirates Win by 13-2 on Veale's 6-Hitter," *New York Times*, June 16, 1968: S4.

21 September 25 interview.

22 Charley Feeney, "'They Treat Me Just Like a Kid!' Fumes Patek, the Unhappy Buc," *The Sporting News*, November 21, 1970: 47.

23 Les Biederman, "Buccos Used the Broom, Now Kids Can Kick Up Some Dust," *The Sporting News*, November 2, 1968: 38.

24 September 25 interview.

25 Charley Feeney, "Bucs Hold Pat Hand at SS, It's Patek," *The Sporting News*, November 22, 1969: 36.

26 Charley Feeney, " 'They Treat Me ...'"

27 Ibid.

28 Dick Young, "Young Ideas: Cardenas Tosses Barb at Reds," *The Sporting News*, April 12, 1969: 14.

29 Jerome Holtzman, "Vet Ump Barlick May Retire," *The Sporting News*, October 3, 1970: 6.

30 Charley Feeney, "Weather Torrid ... So Are Alley, Patek," *The Sporting News*, September 6, 1969: 18.

31 Paul Cour, "Padres May Give Zoilo New Shot at Shortstop," *The Sporting News*, November 14, 1970: 57.

32 September 25 interview.

33 Charley Feeney, "Johnson Puts New Sheen on Corsair Hill Staff," *The Sporting News*, December 19, 1970: 41.

34 Charley Feeney, "'They Treat Me ...'"

35 Charlie Smith, "Swifties Otis, Patek Carry Royals' Title Bid," *The Sporting News*, March 4, 1972: 21.

36 The Official Site of the Kansas City Royals. History of Kauffman Stadium. mlb.mlb.com/kc/history/ballparks.jsp, retrieved August 29, 2018.

37 September 25 interview.

38 Joe McGuff, "Tiffs with Players, Press End McKeon Reign at K.C.," *The Sporting News*, August 9, 1975: 9.

39 Sid Bordman, "Tiny Patek a Mighty Atom Fueling Royals' Late Surge," *The Sporting News*, August 30, 1975: 11.

40 Joe McGuff, "Patek Sheds Suet and Scoots in Old-Time Style," *The Sporting News*, July 10, 1976: 14.

41 Curt Nelson, "This Date in Royals History – October 1, 1976," *Royals Then, Now & Forever: The Official Blog of the Royals Hall of Fame*, royalshof.mlblogs.com/2009/10/01/this-date-in-royals-history-october-1-1976/#comment-36, retrieved September 3, 2018.

42 Baseball Reference salary data 1977-79 for Fred Patek, baseball-reference.com/players/p/patekfr01.shtml, retrieved July 14, 2018.

43 Bob Fowler, "Thor Removing Thunder from Enemy Bats," *The Sporting News*, July 9, 1977: 3.

44 Herman Weiskopf, "The Week (June 19-25)," *Sports Illustrated*, July 3, 1977: 45.

45 Dave Anderson, "The Shortest Shortstop: 5-4 and 140," New York Times, October 7, 1977: 33.

46 Matt Fulks, "Composure: Fred Patek," *C You in the Major Leagues Foundation*, August 31, 2017, cyouinthemajorleagues.org/composure-fred-patek/, retrieved October 12, 2018.

47 Rustin Dodd, "40 Years Ago, George Brett Punched Graig Nettles in the ALCS. Then the Game Continued," *Kansas City Star*, October 18, 2017, kansascity.com/sports/mlb/kansas-city-royals/article179483061.html, retrieved September 20, 2018.

48 Joe Posnanski, "From the Archives: Royals and Yankees Didn't Play Nice in '77," *Kansas City Star*, April 22, 2015, kansascity.com/sports/mlb/kansas-city-royals/article19219905.html, retrieved September 20, 2018.

49 Dick Miller, "Patek 'Grows' as Angel Shortstop," *The Sporting News*, March 8, 1980: 35.

50 Del Black, "Washington Earning Royal Raves," *The Sporting News*, September 22, 1979: 7.

51 Dick Young, "Young Ideas," *The Sporting News*, December 22, 1979: 16.

52 Matt Fulks, "Composure: Fred Patek."

53 November 2 interview. See also Charlie Smith, "Former Royal Patek Proud to Be Among Ryan Victims," *TulsaWorld.com*, September 23, 1989, tulsaworld.com/archives/former-royal-patek-proud-to-be-among-ryan-victims/article_f2db3503-08c2-55c1-8c73-e119d521546c.html, retrieved October 2, 2018.

54 "Pro Transactions. Baseball," *The Sporting News*, April 24, 1982: 33.

55 Keith Thursby, "Viewpoint: A Look at Those Colorless Color Commentators," *Orange Coast Magazine* (Irvine, California), July 1982: 138.

56 November 2 interview.

57 Barry Lewis, "Rangers Won't Keep Carpenter," *TulsaWorld.com*, January 12, 1990, tulsaworld.com/archives/rangers-won-t-keep-carpenter/article_d165aaf6-82f6-5dbc-b7d9-6c6aac3f9558.html, retrieved August 12, 2018.

58 Charlie Smith, "Former Royal Patek."

59 Ira Berkow, "Baseball; For Pateks, the Safety Net Fails," *New York Times*, March 14, 1993: 81.

60 Matt Fulks, "Composure: Fred Patek."

61 Ibid.

62 Bill Althaus, "My Idol Patek Giving Back to Young Players," *The Examiner* (Eastern Jackson County, Missouri), July 29, 2009, examiner.net/article/20090729/NEWS/307299719, retrieved October 23, 2018.

63 Matt Fulks, "Composure: Fred Patek."

64 November 2 interview.

65 September 25 interview.

DARRELL PORTER

BY GLEN SPARKS

St. Louis Cardinals catcher Darrell Porter leapt into the waiting arms of relief pitcher Bruce Sutter after the last out of the 1982 World Series. Fireworks lit up the sky above Busch Stadium. Fans roared with delight; many jumped onto the field and joined the celebration.

Porter, voted the Series MVP, said afterward, "I didn't know I'd ever feel this good again. I didn't think I'd ever be in this position." He added, "What happened in the past is in the past. I've got a wonderful wife, a beautiful little girl 6½ months old. I haven't had a drink in 2½ years. I haven't had any pot or any pills, either."[1]

Maybe Porter had conquered his demons. Maybe he no longer needed alcohol or other recreational drugs. Maybe he could put that rehab stint in 1980 behind him and just focus on baseball and family. He and his loved ones hoped, and sometimes prayed, that he could.

The four-time All-Star played another five seasons. He retired in 1987 with 188 home runs and 826 RBIs. Whitey Herzog, who managed Porter both in St. Louis and for the Kansas City Royals, said, "He played for me eight years, and we won four times, so he had to be a pretty good player."[2]

Porter wrote a book published in 1984 titled *Snap Me Perfect!: The Darrell Porter Story*. He admitted that staying sober wasn't easy. "I still have moments when I don't think I can make it. ... Sometimes, I wish the Lord would snap me perfect."[3]

Darrell Ray Porter was born on January 17, 1952, in Joplin, Missouri, located in the state's southwest corner. His father, Raymond, hailed from Gracemont, Oklahoma, a town of just a few hundred people. Ray met Twila Mae Conley at a square dance in 1947. The two fell in love at first sight. "He looks like Clark Gable!" Twila Mae said after taking one look at the athletic, dark-haired Ray.[4] Soon after, they were married. Ray found a job driving for United Transport in Joplin.

The youngest of four Porter children, Darrell began playing organized baseball as a Little Leaguer. Within a few years, he grabbed a catcher's mitt, a chest protector, and a mask. "It was when I began to concentrate exclusively on catching that I really blossomed," Porter wrote. "Even in those days, I hustled my butt off behind home plate. I was a fiery catcher.[5]

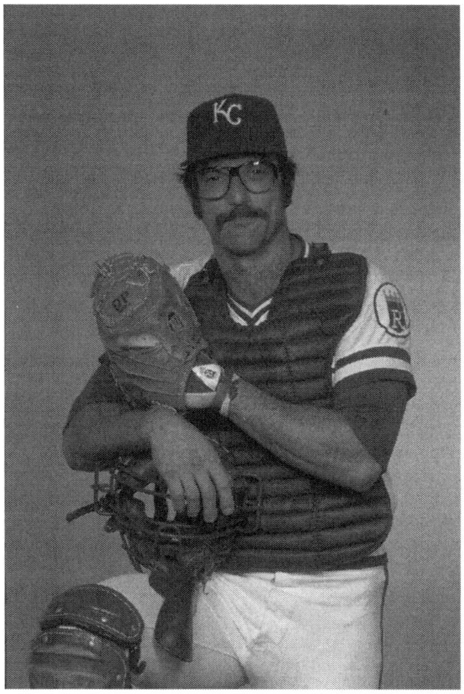

Darrell followed his siblings to Southeast High School in Joplin. He went out for football, basketball, and baseball. Football scouts liked his strong throwing arm. Nearly 40 universities — including Oklahoma, Arkansas, and Southern Methodist - wanted him to play quarterback. Agents, though, said that Porter could expect a $100,000 signing bonus — or more — if he chose professional baseball. The Milwaukee Brewers drafted Porter fourth overall in the June 1970 amateur draft.

The Brewers didn't give him $100,000. They offered $70,000 and assigned Porter to the Clinton (Iowa) Pilots of the Class-A Midwest League. "We feel this young man is our number-1 catcher of the future," Milwaukee general manager Marvin Milkes said after the signing.[6]

Milkes told Porter to stop off in Baltimore for a couple of days before reporting to Clinton. The Brewers were playing a series against the Orioles. One look at that major-league clubhouse, and the 18-year-old prospect felt shocked. He saw ballplayers drinking beer and smoking cigarettes. "The illusions I had always cherished about clean-living jocks were shattered in that clubhouse for good," Porter lamented.[7]

His rookie season in pro ball didn't get much better after that disappointing introduction. Porter batted just .200 in 185 at-bats. Like many young players, he struggled to hit professional changeups and curveballs. And the long season tired him out. And, finally, Porter took a drink. He put away four bottles of beer that first night. The rest of the season, he went out a few nights every week. The drinking helped him relax.

Porter reported back to Class-A ball in 1971, this time to Milwaukee's new Midwest League affiliate, the Danville (Illinois) Warriors. His sophomore season went much better than his freshman campaign. He hit 24 home runs, drove in 70 runs, and batted .271 as a 19-year-old. The Brewers called him up in September. Porter made his major-league debut on September 2 and went hitless in three at-bats against the Kansas City Royals at Milwaukee's County Stadium. The Brewers won 1-0 behind Marty Pattin's five-hit shutout. A few nights later, at home against the California Angels, Porter collected his first major-league hit, a single off Angels starter Tom Murphy that scored Jose Cardenal. Later, he added a sacrifice fly. The Brewers beat the Angels, 6-4. Porter batted .214 with two homers and nine RBIs in 22 games with Milwaukee.

Over the offseason, Porter met Teri Brown. He was quickly smitten, and the two began dating. Soon enough, they set a wedding date for May 30, 1972. Porter also started using Quaaludes, a barbiturate. "They eventually became my drug of choice," Porter said. "With a 'lude, nothing bothered me."[8]

The Brewers expected Porter to share starting catching duties with veteran Ellie Rodriguez in 1972. But major-league pitching still baffled Porter. He played in 18 of Milwaukee's first 25 games and batted just .125 with one home run and two RBIs. The Brewers sent him to the team's Triple-A affiliate in Evansville, Indiana. "We felt that major-league pitching was just a little too tough for him," said Frank Lane, who took over the GM duties in Milwaukee after the 1970 season. "So we went sent him down to the minors to develop more batting experience."[9] Porter hit just .216 with 13 home runs and 45 RBIs as an Evansville Triplet. He did not get a late-season call-up to the big club but looked forward to establishing himself as a regular in 1973 and joining other talented prospects, including infielder Pedro Garcia and outfielder Gorman Thomas.

The Brewers also counted on quality veterans like first baseman George Scott, third baseman Don Money, outfielder Dave May, and pitcher Jim Colborn. Ellie Rodriguez broke his hand in spring training, making Porter the starting catcher as a 21-year-old with a .175 batting average in 40 big-league games. When Rodriguez returned, the two shared duties behind the plate.

Porter cut down his swing in 1973. "I have natural power, so I don't have to cut hard," he told a reporter in June.[10] The change in approach worked. Porter smacked 16 homers, drove in 67 runs, and batted .254 with a .363 on-base percentage. The Brewers backstop tied for third in the AL Rookie of the Year voting, along with pitchers Steve Busby of the Royals and Doc Medich of the Yankees. The Baltimore Orioles' Al Bumbry won the honor, while Pedro Garcia, Porter's Milwaukee teammate, took second. The Brewers finished 74-88, in fifth place in the AL East.

The Brewers traded Ellie Rodriguez in the offseason. Porter went on to make his first AL All-Star team. He said that Money, Scott, and Briggs deserved the honor more than he did. Even so, he added, it was "the greatest thing that has ever happened to me."[11]

Porter, batting .272 at the midsummer break, struggled as the season wore on. He finished at .241 and hit 12 home runs. The Brewers ended up 76-86, once again in fifth place. A late-season incident put a damper on Porter's first All-Star campaign. Near the end of a twin bill against the Cleveland Indians on September 23 at Cleveland Municipal Stadium, Porter jumped onto the top of the dugout and punched a fan who had been razzing him for several innings.

"I'd rather not say anything about what happened," Porter said afterward. Brewers manager Del Crandall told reporters, "The fans were on him all night. It was one of those quick-reaction things. It certainly didn't take him long to get up there (to the top of the dugout)."[12] Newspapers across the country printed photos of several Brewers restraining Porter. Baseball fined Porter and suspended him for three games.

Porter put together another solid year in 1975. He slugged 18 home runs and drove in 60 runs. His batting average slipped to .232 but, thanks to 89 walks, he raised his on-base percentage over the previous year, from .326 to .371. Even so, Milwaukee still could not get into the pennant race and fell to fifth place for the third straight season, this time with a 68-94 mark. The Brewers fired Crandall in late September.

Porter's 1976 season turned into a mess. He batted only .208 with 5 homers and 32 RBIs. Off the field, his life spiraled out of control. Porter's marriage to Teri ended in divorce, and his drug problems continued. A friend introduced him to cocaine at a party. "I wanted to fit in, really fit in," Porter said. "And coke did that for me."[13] He wrote that he contemplated suicide but not seriously. "There was always pot and Quaaludes, beer, cocaine to dull the agony of living," he wrote.[14] The team also had spiraled downward and muddled through a 66-95 campaign, in last place in the AL East.

Porter's career in Milwaukee ended December 6, 1976. The Brewers dealt him and Colborn to the Royals for infielder Jim Wohlford, infielder Jamie Quirk, and a player to be named later (Bob McClure). Porter hoped for a new start in Kansas City and admitted that "my mind just wasn't 100 percent on baseball" the previous season.[15] When he arrived at the team's spring-training facility in Fort Myers, Florida, he noticed some changes from his Brewers days, such as the team camaraderie and family atmosphere. "There's a feeling of togetherness that we didn't have in Milwaukee," Porter said.[16]

Porter joined a franchise that began playing in the American League as an expansion club in 1969, two years after the Kansas City Athletics left for Oakland. The team finished above .500 in just its third year of existence (85-76 in 1971) and won a division title in 1976, going 90-72 before losing to the New York Yankees in the AL Championship Series.

Kansas City boasted talented players like third baseman and future Hall of Famer George Brett, first baseman John Mayberry, second baseman Frank White, and outfielders Amos Otis and Al Cowens. The strong starting pitching staff included Dennis Leonard, Paul Splittorff, and Colborn.

Porter got off to a solid start with his new team, winning Royals Player of the Month honors in April with a .365 batting average, one homer and 11 RBIs. Kansas City went 11-8 in April but stumbled through a 10-15 mark in May. The Royals finally got hot as the weather warmed and cruised to a 102-60 record by season's end, the best mark in baseball. And then they lost again to the Yankees in the playoffs. Porter batted .333 (5-for-15) during the postseason after hitting .275 with 16 home runs and 60 RBIs in 130 regular-season games.

Kansas City celebrated another division crown in 1978. Porter ripped 18 homers, drove in 78 runs and hit .265 with a .358 on-base percentage. The 26-year-old catcher earned a spot on the AL All-Star team for a second time and plenty of admiration from Herzog. On June 4 Porter smacked two triples, a double, and two singles in leading Kanas City to a 13-2 pasting of the Chicago White Sox. "That might be as fine as I've ever seen a guy have," Herzog said. "He swung hard at every pitch and hit the ball well to all fields."[17]

Once again the Yankees ended Kansas City's hopes for postseason glory in the ALCS. Porter went 5-for-14 for a .357 batting average and drove in three runs against Yankees pitching in October. Porter told *Sports Illustrated* that not much separated the Yankees and the Royals. "But that small difference," he said, "is what makes KC a good team and New York a great one."[18]

Porter spent his offseason in the fast lane. "I went wild," he said.[19] Then he stepped on the brakes and posted the best numbers of his career. Early in the 1979 campaign, when Porter was batting .379, Herzog declared him "the best catcher in the league."[20]

By mid-June Porter carried a .305 average with 9 home runs and 53 RBIs. He beat out popular Boston Red Sox catcher Carlton Fisk for starting catcher on the AL All-Star team. He finished with career highs in most offensive categories, including home runs (20), RBIs (112), batting average (.291), runs scored (101), on-base percentage (.421), and slugging percentage (.484). He led the AL with 121 walks and played in 157 games. The writers voted him ninth in the MVP race. He might have finished higher, but the Royals slumped to 85-77 and slipped to second place, missing out on the playoffs for the first time since 1975.

Over the winter, Porter settled into another self-destructive routine. "Get up and make coffee, do a Quaalude, drink beer, sniff cocaine, and smoke cigarettes," he wrote.[21] Finally, in the spring of 1980, he checked into The Meadows drug treatment center in Arizona. Royals general manager Joe Burke told reporters, "Darrell Porter has a very confidential and personal problem. I cannot betray his confidence, but I don't expect him to be back with us until he has had treatment for his problems."[22]

After a six-week program, the catcher returned to Kansas City, and to a new manager. The Royals had fired Herzog and signed Jim Frey as the new skipper. Despite some nervousness, Porter started his season strong. He lifted his batting average above .300 at one point and was still hitting .274 when Orioles manager Earl Weaver named him to the All-Star team as a reserve. The Royals earned another division title, finishing 97-65, 14 games better than the runner-up Oakland A's. Brett led the way for Kansas City with his .390 batting average, the highest season-ending average since Ted Williams hit .406 for the 1941 Boston Red Sox. Porter batted .249 with 7 homers and 51 RBIs.

This time the Royals finally knocked off the Yankees in the ALCS, sweeping them in three games. They faced the Philadelphia Phillies in the World Series. Porter, who hit just .100 against New York (1-for-10), batted only .143 in the fall classic as Philadelphia won in six games.

Over the offseason, Porter remarried. He also signed a five-year, $3.5 million contract with the Cardinals. The deal made sense for Porter and his bride, Deanne. They'd be going to a new city but one just a few hours away from Kansas City, and St. Louis had hired Porter's old boss, Whitey Herzog, as manager.

Then, the Cardinals made life tough for their new player. They traded popular All-Star catcher Ted Simmons to Milwaukee. "From day one, a few of the Cardinals fans took an instant dislike to me," Porter wrote. "This vendetta by the St. Louis fans really hurt me. Things got worse and worse, and gradually it affected my game to the point that I hated come to the stadium."[23]

Porter began the season in a slump that lasted for months. He batted just .173 through April and May. On June 12, 1981, the players went on strike. As the work stoppage wore on, Porter did some fishing. One day, he drank a beer and then drank a few more. "An alcoholic (and a drug addict for that matter) is never cured," Porter wrote. "All his life, he is only a recovering alcoholic/addict. One taste of beer, one snort of coke (or whatever), can put him back into the gutter."[24]

The season restarted on August 10 in a split-season format. Porter played in just 61 of the team's 102 total games. He batted .224 with 6 home runs and 31 RBIs and did not top the .200 mark for good until August 23. The Cardinals, who stood in second place with a 30-20 record when the strike began, also wound up as division runner-up in the second half (29-23) and missed the postseason.

Porter enjoyed a slightly better year in 1982. He ripped 12 homers, drove in 48 runs, and batted .231. St. Louis won the division with a 92-70 mark and beat the Atlanta Braves in the NLCS. Porter hit .556 (5-for-9) and walked five times for a .714 on-base percentage against Atlanta. Next, the Cardinals met the Milwaukee Brewers in the World Series. Porter batted .286 (8-for-28) with one homer and five RBIs; St. Louis won the Series in seven games. "Bruce (Sutter) and I grabbed one another and did a victory polka"[25] after Gorman Thomas struck out to end the Series, Porter wrote.

Maybe Porter could extend that postseason glory into 1983. He did put up his best numbers as a Cardinal — 15 homers, 66 RBIs, a .262 batting average, and a .363 on-base percentage. St. Louis, though, finished in fourth place with a record of 79-83. A frustrated Porter spoke to reporters about the team's struggles and his ongoing battles with addiction. "I guess I keep talking about it because it might be some kind of safeguard against me doing it again," he said, but added, "I could get back into drugs again and no one would know, because they didn't know before."[26]

St. Louis improved a bit in 1984, going 84-78 and winding up third in the NL East. Porter, though, once again struggled to find any offensive consistency. He hit 11 homers with 68 RBIs but batted a modest .232 in 127 games. Maybe the veteran catcher had started to wear down at age 32. "Darrell Porter was just not producing," Herzog wrote. "He'd gotten his life turned around after kicking his drug habit, but in the process, he'd lost his aggressiveness."[27]

Porter split catching duties with Cardinals prospect Tom Nieto in 1985 and batted .221 with 10 homers. St. Louis beat the Los Angeles Dodgers in the NLCS and met Porter's former team, the cross-state Royals, in the World Series. Porter managed two hits in 15 at-bats. St. Louis released him shortly after the Series ended. He signed a two-year deal with the Texas Rangers.

Porter got into 68 games, hit 12 homers, and batted .265 in 1986. The Rangers finished in second place with an 87-75 record. The following year, he played 85 games, batted .238, with 7 homers and 21 RBIs. The Rangers did not offer Porter a contract for the 1988 season, making him a free agent. No other team made him an offer.

In retirement, Porter began to speak about his Christian faith and his struggles with drug addiction. He dabbled in real estate and several businesses and also hosted a weekly radio show in Kansas City, with hopes of joining the Royals radio booth. Along with a friend, Bill Stutz, Porter worked with Enjoy the Game. Stutz founded this youth program, which encourages good sportsmanship at athletic events and a positive environment for students and parents. "What it teaches is respect for your teammates or peers, the coaches or teachers, and to respect authority and the rules and to do what's right," Porter said.[28]

On the worrisome side, Porter's weight ballooned from about 225 pounds to nearly 300. He died on August 5, 2002. He had driven from his house in the Kansas City suburb of Lee's Summit to a park in nearby Sugar Creek. His body was found next to his car that afternoon. He was 50 years old. The chief of the Sugar Creek Police Department said Porter's car went off the road and hit a tree stump. Police theorized that Porter tried to push the car off the stump and "the heat got to him"[29] on a 97-degree day. No foul play was suspected.

A few days later, the Kansas City medical examiner, Dr. Thomas Young, reported that Porter had cocaine in his system, "typical of someone who uses (cocaine) recreationally." Young said that Porter did not die from an overdose, but from excited delirium, which causes "behavior that is agitated, bizarre, and potentially violent," and stopped his heart."[30] He left behind his wife, Deanne, and three children, Lindsey, 20; Jeff, 18; and Ryan, 14.

Nearly 1,000 people attended Porter's memorial service on August 9 at Noland Road Baptist Church in Independence, Missouri. A smaller service was also held that day at First Baptist Church in Raytown, Missouri. Longtime friend and former Royals teammate Jerry Terrell said, "So, all I've got to say is this: Darrell, I love you, man. I really miss you. Thanks for the memories."[31]

Sources

In addition to the sources cited in the Notes, the author also consulted Baseball-Reference.com.

Notes

1 "Porter Delivers the Goods," *The Sporting News*, November 1, 1982: 28.

2 Rick Hummel, "Cardinals Family Mourns Again After Porter's Death," *St. Louis Post-Dispatch*, August 7, 2002: 38.

3 Darrell Porter and William Deerfield, *Snap Me Perfect! The Darrell Porter Story* (Nashville, Tennessee: Thomas Newson Publishers, 1984), 219.

4 *Snap Me Perfect*, 26.

5 *Snap Me Perfect*, 40.

6 Tom Flaherty, "Porter Rides Around and Learns," *Wisconsin State Journal* (Madison), August 3, 1970: 29.

7 *Snap Me Perfect*, 64.

8 *Snap Me Perfect*, 87.

9 Associated Press, "Scoreless Streak at 19," *Fond du Lac* (Wisconsin) *Commonwealth Reporter,* May 22, 1972: 26.

10 "Porter Puts It All Together," *Wisconsin State Journal,* June 10, 1973.

11 AP, "Surprise! Brewers' Porter Is an All-Star," *Wausau* (Wisconsin) *Daily Herald,* July 19, 1974: 18.

12 AP, "Brewers Split in Battle for 4th," *Green Bay* (Wisconsin) *Gazette,* September 24, 1974: 23.

13 *Snap Me Perfect,* 103.

14 *Snap Me Perfect*, 112.

15 Joe McGuff, "Porter Finds Royals Better Tippers than Brewers," *The Sporting News*, April 16, 1977: 7.

16 Ibid.

17 AP, "Darrell Porter Has a Royal Day," *Journal Times* (Racine, Wisconsin), June 5, 1978: 15.

18 Peter Golenbock, *The Spirit of St. Louis: A History of the St. Louis Cardinals and Browns* (New York: William Morrow, 2000), 534.

19 *Snap Me Perfect* 139.

20 *Snap Me Perfect,* 140.

21 *Snap Me Perfect*, 155.

22 AP, "Everybody Wonders Just What's Wrong with Darrell Porter," *Statesman Journal* (Salem, Oregon), March 18, 1980: 27.

23 *Snap Me Perfect*, 237.

24 *Snap Me Perfect*, 238.

25 *Snap Me Perfect*, 251.

26 Mark Whicker "Baseball's Newest Spy Scheme a Shot in the Dark," *Hartford Courant*, June 11, 1983: 98.

27 "Baseball's Newest Spy Scheme," 154.

28 Rob Rains and Alvin Reid, *Whitey's Boys: A Celebration of the '82 Cards World Championship* (Chicago: Triumph, 2002), 88.

29 Heather Hollingsworth, "Cause of Porter's Death Not Yet Available," *Daily Oklahoman* (Oklahoma City), August 7, 2002: 27.

30 AP, "Autopsy Shows Cocaine in Darrell Porter's Body," *Courier-Journal* (Louisville), August 13, 2002: 36.

31 Amy Shafer, "Memorial Honors Porter's Friendship," *Salina* (Kansas) *Journal,* August 10, 2002: 27.

DAN QUISENBERRY

BY STEVE WULF

LOOKIN UP

It lasted so long
it went so fast
it seems like yesterday
it seems like never

--"A Career" – from *Days Like This*,
by Dan Quisenberry[1]

Sigh.

There never was, and maybe there never will be, a major-league pitcher quite like Dan Quisenberry. He literally and figuratively came out of nowhere. Because he was a right-handed submariner, hitters had to turn their heads to pick up his pitches as they materialized out of the third baseman's jersey and shot across the plate with a cartoonish sink.

Undrafted and signed on a whim by the Kansas City Royals, he became an integral part of their first two World Series teams (1980 and 1985), set the major-league record for saves in a season (45 in '83) and retired with 244 career saves and a stat line remarkably similar to that of Hall of Famer Bruce Sutter. Perhaps his most amazing number is under the column heading BB9: In 1,043⅓ innings, he averaged 1.4 walks per nine innings.

He revolutionized relief pitching, yes, but he was so much more than a closer. He was a funnyman, a man of faith, a quote machine, a poet, a loving husband and father, a cherished teammate, a player rep, a humanitarian, a tenacious competitor, and a source of inspiration. He died on September 30, 1998, at the so-unfair age of 45 from a rampaging form of brain cancer. But even then, he had perfect timing: it happened in the bottom of the ninth month.

In his obituary for the *Kansas City Star*, the estimable Joe Posnanski wrote, "He made everyone who knew him feel alive. ... People needed to be near him, needed to feel his arm on their shoulders, needed to tell him a story, needed to hear the wild hunches and beautiful thoughts that clattered around in that amazing mind of his."[2]

Even now, more than 20 years later, his teammates dearly miss him, and some wonder why he's not enshrined in Cooperstown. With the help of the Royals Alumni Director Dina Blevins, who's also the daughter of former Royals catcher and manager John Wathan, here's a small chorus of the men who played beside him.

John Wathan: "Dan was one of the best people I ever met in baseball. He was a great teammate and friend who didn't take the accolades he received as individual awards, but as ones that should be shared by all his teammates. Even though he looked more like a professor on the mound than a bulldog, he was a tremendous competitor. I still keep his book of poetry on my night stand by my bed."

Pitcher Charlie Leibrandt: "Probably my favorite teammate. We drove to the park every day for several years, and some of the lines he came up with, well, you would swear he spent hours the night before thinking of them, but they were off the cuff. Once, on a road trip to Toronto, we played golf, and Dan took several shots to advance a ball out of the high rough. From that day forward, we started calling him 'Chopper,' and it always made us laugh. I still think about him a lot. ... A very underrated pitcher, too. He could pitch almost every day and for more than an inning."

Catcher Jamie Quirk: "Some of my favorite memories of Quis are about our times in the bullpen. On hot Sunday day games in K.C., he would water down the fans with a hose from the bullpen because he was the 'fireman.' He also had a routine of going to the bathroom in the fourth inning, so one night in Boston, where the bathroom is basically an outhouse, we lit a bunch of newspapers on fire and threw them under the door. ... He came out with his pants down. For such a humble guy, he had no fear as a pitcher. He trusted his stuff and his infielders. Take Game Three of the 1980 ALCS against the Yankees. He went three and two-thirds to get us to our first World Series. I wish the Royals would retire his number."

Outfielder Willie Wilson: "I called him Mr. Wizard. Here's a memory. He came in with the bases loaded and no outs against the White Sox once. He picks off the man on first, and the batter hits a line drive right at him that he turns into a double play. I can still hear him say, 'I knew I'd get out of that inning.' He did things you don't see relievers do in today's game, coming in with the bases loaded, pitching multiple innings. His mind was very special, but he had a great heart, too."

Infielder Greg Pryor: "He was one of the nicest, most humble players that I ever played with or against. Everybody loved Dan. I just wrote a book, and I titled one of the stories 'The Day That Dan Quisenberry Yelled at Me.' Whenever he threw with you, he liked to make a loud. popping sound when the ball hit his glove. We often came into the game together, me for defense, him to close. Well, one night, I'm at third, and I decided to come underneath to him and let one fly at about 85 mph so he could make that familiar 'Pop!' sound. It startled him so much that he yelled, 'Pryor, stop that! You're throwing harder than I am. ... You're showing me up.' We both had the biggest laugh on the field."

Pitcher Mark Gubicza: "He was one of the funniest people I've ever been around. But he was also an amazingly caring person. He was a perfect example for all of us young players who wanted to be as good off the field as on. On the mound, he was a fierce competitor who pitched multiple innings and never asked for a day off. Personally, I think he was a Hall of Famer."

Hall of Famer George Brett: "One thing I remember about Dan is that he never took credit for saves, and always took the blame for losses, regardless of what happened."

"Here's another thing. About one month before his passing, I went to have lunch at his house with him, and he knew he was not going to win this battle. I asked him, 'Why you?' And he responded, 'Why not me? I can handle this.' That speaks volumes about the type of person he was."

I practiced my whole life
from day dream days
in social studies
to sandlot games
little league games
hardball
tennis ball
whiffle ball
rock ball

When Quisenberry was in his heyday, Royals bullpen coach Jim Schaffer would pick up the phone 100 times a year, listen to the voice at the other end, then hang up and announce, "The Australian." That's because his bullpen ace came from down under.[3]

He actually came from Santa Monica, California. His more common nickname, "Quiz" or "Quis," was a natural offshoot of the seamstress-challenging name above the 29 on his jersey. But it also spoke to both his inquiring nature and the riddle of his success. He looked up the derivation of his name once and discovered that there was no such fruit as a quisenberry - the name was an English mutation of the German surname Questenberg.

He and his older (by two years) brother, Marty, were very close. Their mother, Reberta, and father, John, had divorced when the kids were 9 and 7, and because Reberta worked as a color consultant for Revlon, the boys ran through a gauntlet of babysitters. Then Mom remarried a man named Art Meola, who put a little discipline into their lives. "He used to make us work around the house all the time," Dan told *Sports Illustrated* in a 1983 profile written by yours truly. "We were forever changing white rocks into redwood chips, or the other way around. We got pretty sassy. We needed to be spanked."[4]

But the brothers grew to love Art, a North American Rockwell engineer who encouraged them to play baseball and saved them from the ballroom-dancing careers that Reberta had in mind for them. Although Marty and Dan never played on the same organized team together, they played imaginary ballgames together, outside and inside. The indoor game was Strat-O-Matic. "When I got to the majors," said Dan, "it was like déjà vu. There I was facing Carl Yastrzemski and Rico Carty again after all these years. Why should I be scared, after I had already been chased down the street by Harmon Killebrew?"[5]

They both played baseball at Costa Mesa High. Marty was actually considered the better athlete, a submarine pitcher long before Dan dropped down. He played at Orange Coast Community College and Southern California College, where he was scouted by Rosey Gilhousen of the Royals. But then Marty threw his arm out and abandoned baseball for the ministry.

Dan followed his brother to Orange Coast, where he was named the team MVP his second year, 1973. The baseball coach at LaVerne College, Ben Hines, recruited him to play there. True to his restless mind, Dan kept switching his majors, from business to religion to sociology to psychology to history. But his most fateful class was square dancing, which was a course Hines encouraged his players to attend because it improved their balance and footwork. It was in that class that Dan met Janie Howard, his future bride and soulmate.

At the time, Dan was considered something of a hothead. In later years, when asked what calmed him down, he replied, "Janie and Christianity."[6] In his two years at LaVerne, Quis went 12-2 and 19-7, pitching an astounding 194 innings his senior year and making the NAIA All-America team. But all that work took the edge off his fastball and lowered his delivery point to side-arm. "The scouts were not exactly flocking around the house," he recalled.[7]

Hines gave Gilhousen a call and asked him if might be interested in Marty's younger brother. The scout said that, yes, there was an opening for a pitcher in Class-A Waterloo, Iowa, but that the kid would have to be at Gilhousen's house within the hour. So Dan drove 10 minutes to Santa Ana in his battered Gremlin, rang the bell, walked in and signed. "I got $500 a month, and the special-covenants clause was left blank. My bonus was a Royals bat that Rosey had in the house, a Royals pen, and a Royals lapel button. I was really pretty excited, especially about the lapel button."[8]

much gets blurred
wins, losses, races
mostly I had my head down
down in the trenches
I missed stuff
sometimes the shrapnel
but sometimes I looked up

On June 22, 1975, Quisenberry had an unusual twin bill. That morning, he was formally baptized at a church in Waterloo. That afternoon, in his first game for Waterloo, he pitched a seven-inning, complete-game 5-3 victory over Wausau in the opener of an actual doubleheader.

Read that again. Quisenberry's professional debut was a complete game. It was also his last start as a minor- or major-league pitcher. Waterloo manager

John Sullivan told him right after the game that he was moving him to the bullpen because he needed a reliever who could throw strikes. Dan thought he was being demoted. "I figured that was his best chance to make it," said Sullivan. "But I didn't think he'd ever be in the majors."[9]

One of his teammates agreed with that assessment. "I didn't see him going to the big leagues," said Willie Wilson, who was then 19.[10]

But Quis did well enough at Waterloo (2.45 ERA with four saves) to be called up to Double-A Jacksonville for eight innings at the end of the season. The next year, 1976, he divided his time between A and Double A, and while he was effective, nobody seemed to notice. After the season was over, he and Janie were married and ended their honeymoon in Coeur d'Alene, Idaho, where they decided to spend the offseason. They lived in an apartment behind a funeral home. By day Dan would work in a sporting-goods store, and by night he worked for the mortuary. In his own words, "Me and another guy would go around picking up dead bodies and throwing them – I'm sorry – putting them in the back of a hearse."[11]

He pitched solely for Jacksonville in '77, appearing in 33 games to a 1.34 ERA, then spent the winter in Mexico, where he and Janie grew closer together in sickness. Back in Jacksonville for the '78 season, he saved 15 games and had a 4-2 record with a 2.39 ERA, but got the feeling he was stuck. "I made up mind that if I didn't get to Triple A that next spring, I was going to quit."[12] He even went to Fresno Pacific College that winter to get his teaching certificate.

Luckily for him and the Royals – and unluckily for some California high school that missed out on a very cool history teacher and baseball coach – Quis was assigned to Triple-A Omaha in the spring of '79. In the beginning of July, when infielder Jerry Terrell went on the disabled list and the Royals were desperate for another arm, they called up Quisenberry.

Years later, when Royals general manager John Schuerholz was asked to identify Dan's champion within the organization, he said, "The truth of the matter is that we didn't have anybody else. Necessity is the mother of invention, and in this case, she was the mother of Dan Quisenberry."[13]

I was lookin up when I took the ball
for the first time my rookie year
from Whitey Herzog
my knees shook
like I was getting married
Lamar Johnson drilled a two hopper
that Frank White snared with a bound to his right
that I never saw in minor leagues

On July 8, 1979, Quisenberry made his major-league debut. He came into the game against the White Sox in the top of the seventh to face big Lamar Johnson with a man on and one out, and on the second pitch, Johnson grounded the ball to second baseman Frank White, who started a double play – a scene that would be oft repeated in the next few years.

Quis finished the game, giving up two hits, no walks, and no runs, but the White Sox won anyway, 4-2. Nobody at the time thought they were looking at the future. "I'd never heard of him," said Brett. "He looked funny, he threw funny, he was funny, and I wanted to know why we didn't go out and trade for somebody."[14]

But he did reasonably well the rest of that season, finishing with five saves, a 3-2 record, and a 3.15 ERA. Not bad for a side-armer with one good pitch, a sinker. In a revealing interview for *Inside Sports* in 1981, Quis told Mike McKenzie, "I wasn't supposed to stack up by visual standards. Friends couldn't wait to face me, no heat at all. But I got them out. Having to prove myself became a way of life."

One proof came courtesy of Topps, which put him on a 1980 rookie card alongside fellow pitchers Renie Martin and Bill Paschall.[15] Quis would later immortalize the triptych in a poem entitled "Baseball Cards": *I am the older one/the one on the right/game-face sincere/long red hair unkempt/a symbol of the '70s/somehow a sign of manhood/you don't see/how my knees shook on my debut/or my desperation to make it* [16]

Fate also played a hand early in the spring training of 1980. Jim Frey had replaced manager Whitey

Herzog a week after the Pirates beat the Orioles in the '79 World Series. Well, one of the heroes for Pittsburgh was submariner Kent Tekulve, who had three saves. Frey knew him, and the Royals and Pirates trained not far from each other. So when Quis had a bad outing against the Pirates, Frey went to Tekulve and asked him if wouldn't mind working with Quisenberry, and Tekulve said sure. Quis, however, was reluctant: "I didn't think I needed to change."[17]

Here's how he described their first session in Bradenton for Roger Angell in his epic 1985 profile of Quis in *The New Yorker*: "When the day came, Jim said to Tekulve, 'We want this guy to be like you. He throws a little like you already, but basically, he doesn't have shit.' So (said Quisenberry) it was a total makeover. ... Well, I didn't like this at all. Frey and a lot of our coaches were watching, and I was throwing all over the place and bouncing the ball before it got to the plate. Teke kept saying, 'Hey, that's a good pitch, that's the way to throw,' and I'm thinking I have *no idea* what I'm doing. But Jim liked it, and two days later, he put me in another game ... and I did real well. I was on my way."[18]

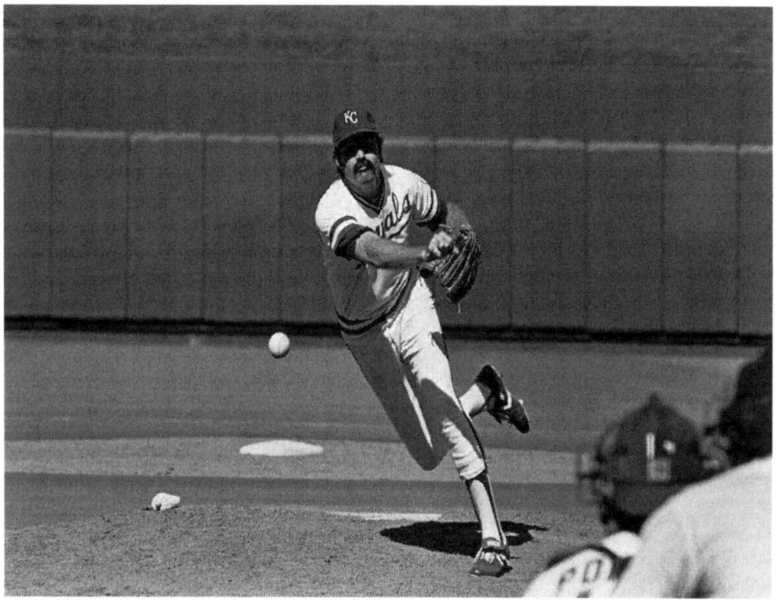

Still throwing his sinker, but now with a motion that resembled a flamingo falling over as it releases the ball, Quisenberry baffled American League hitters in much the same way he baffled the Royals' front office. His numbers also went against type for relievers: In 128⅓ innings, he struck out only 37 batters while giving up 129 hits, but he also walked only 27. He had 12 wins and 33 saves, and most tellingly, he entered 41 games in which the Royals were leading, and they won all but two of them as they easily won the AL West. And whenever he finished a game with John Wathan catching, Wathan, would say, 'Way to mix 'em up,' and Quis would respond, 'Way to call 'em.'"[19]

Credit Frey not only for enlisting Tekulve's help, but also for entrusting so much responsibility to a rookie reliever. The 1980 Royals were a remarkably loose bunch with exemplary leaders like Hal McRae and Brett, who hit .390 that season and came within just five hits of .400. They provided a welcoming environment for Quis – and for a *Sports Illustrated* writer who was on the baseball beat for the first time. That's when I first got to know Dan, who was kind of in the same rookie boat as I was, and I couldn't help but fling away journalistic objectivity. He had a great story to tell, and he told it with a smile on his face.

As a whole, the Royals had as much to prove as he did. Stuck in their craw were the three straight losses to the Yankees in the '76, '77, and '78 playoffs, and they had to face the Bronx Bombers again.

I was lookin up when
George Brett hit a Ruthian blast
off a guy who threw as hard as God
Willie Randolph took a called third
why didn't he swing?
it was right there
and we were series bound

The Royals took the first two games in Kansas City, 7-2 and 3-2, the latter victory coming after Quisenberry got Graig Nettles to hit into a 4-6-3 double play with the tying run on first. Asked what pitch he threw, a deadpan Quis said, "An overhand curve."[20] He hadn't thrown one in years, of course, but reporters who didn't know him dutifully took him at his word.

With history and a Yankee Stadium crowd on their side, the Yankees and George Steinbrenner were not expecting to be swept. And for one inning of Game Three, it looked as if they might rally. With the Royals holding a slim 1-0 lead in the bottom of the sixth, Reggie Jackson hit a one-out double off Paul Splittorff, and Frey called for Quis. The wheels promptly fell off when Oscar Gamble singled in the tying run and advanced to third on an uncharacteristic error by Frank White. Quisenberry then gave up the go-ahead run on a single by Rick Cerone before retiring the side.

After Tommy John gave up a two-out double to Willie Wilson in the top of the seventh, Rich Gossage came on. The Yankees had the Royals just where they wanted them. But then U L Washington singled, bringing Brett to the plate. The best closer in the game vs. the best hitter.

Fans will forever remember Brett launching Goose's first pitch high and far into the third deck in right to give the Royals a 4-2 lead.

What they may not remember, though, is what Quisenberry did to shut the door. After a 1-2-3 seventh, he gave up a leadoff triple to Bob Watson in the eighth, then walked the next two batters to load the bases with no outs. "Sometimes, magical things happen when I let it go," he used to say, and in that instance, they did – Cerone hit into a line-drive double play (6-4) as Watson held his ground, and Jim Spencer grounded out to second to keep the Yankees off the scoreboard.

With two outs in the bottom of the ninth, Quis struck out Willie Randolph looking at a 3-and-2 pitch.

Alas, the magic ran out in the World Series against the Phillies in a matchup of teams that had never won the fall classic. Frey had come to rely on Quisenberry *too much,* asking him to pitch in every one of the six games, which in retrospect seems insane since four of his appearances were for multiple innings. As Pete Rose of the Phillies said at the time, "The guy [Frey] is giving us the World Series by letting us look at Quisenberry's delivery so much."[21]

Quis did lose two of the games, but one of the losses came on a two-out single off his glove in the ninth inning of Game Five after he had put out a fire in the seventh and shrugged off a leadoff error in the eighth. As the Phillies celebrated after Game Six, Dan stood at his locker in the visitors' locker room and graciously offered to take the blame.

He could handle it.

I was lookin up when Janie and I
had a girl and a boy
a fifty-day strike, Marvin Miller said
"let's show em our muscle"
I learned to hang wallpaper
change diapers
grow tomatoes
lose golf balls

After the 1980 World Series, the Royals and the Phillies appeared as opponents on the quiz show *Family Feud,* and it was small consolation that Kansas City won. Quis also went up against the host, Richard Dawson. Dawson approached him at one point, imitated his underhand delivery and asked, "You throw this way, don't you? I think it's effeminate to throw that way."

Dan laughed, grasped Dawson by the lapels of his sport coat and said, "Is this more comfortable than the popular style?"[22]

It's a measure of his wit that when two competing baseball quote books came out in the early '80s,

Quisenberry had seven in each, and only two were repeated.[23] And he had only been in the majors for a couple of years. He once explained his humor this way: "There is a correlation between a sinkerball pitcher and being funny. If I try to force my sinker, it doesn't do a thing. No velocity, no sink. Same with humor."[24]

And he was just plain fun, as well as funny. He could keep the denizens of the bullpen amused by conducting a panel to name a hypothetical All-Star team of players they would be most afraid of rooming with. While Renie Martin, his best friend, sang songs about the game in progress, Dan would play Renie's protuberant teeth as it they were xylophone keys. Once, as he was leading this writer to his house, he pulled up to the gates of a huge mansion in Mission Hills, got out and walked up to them as if he were about to open them. The house actually belonged to Royals owner Ewing Kauffman.

But the 1981 season was not fun, at least not at the start. He came into spring training unhappy about his contract negotiations, and the defending AL champions played dreadfully, costing Jim Frey his job. With a players strike looming, Quis had to juggle his responsibilities as player rep, new father, and closer, and he lost the last of those responsibilities at one point. When the season was interrupted on June 12, the Royals were 20-30. Fortunately for them, the slate was clean when the second half resumed on July 27. After going 10-10, Frey was replaced by Dick Howser on August 31. They won the AL West second half with a 30-23 record and Quisenberry "found a delivery in my flaw" to reclaim his closer role.[25] Alas, they were swept by the A's in the best-of-five Division Series, with Dan getting only one inning of work, a shutout ninth in Game Two.

He again led the league in saves in '82, with 35, but the Royals, beset by drug problems, finished second in the division. Quis might have once been considered a fluke, but now he was one of the best closers in the game, and it wasn't just because of his funky delivery. He could get ready in a hurry, so he was often called upon before the eighth or ninth, and he could pitch every day. His fielding skills played into his out pitch, the sinker. And he acquired other pitches for his repertoire: a slider, a changeup, and a knuckleball he found on a tour of Japan. Tigers starting pitcher Milt Wilcox became an admirer: "The smartest thing Dan does is come with a variation of pitches every year. I watch him. He plays the chess game real well. I don't care what the hitters say, they're up there guessing."[26]

Quisenberry also kept a detailed scouting notebook on each of his outings for future reference. All that hard work paid off in 1983, when he set the major-league record for saves with 45. Take your pick of his incredible stats: 69 games, 139 innings, or better than two an outing! 11 walks, two of them intentional, no hit batsmen, no wild pitches! One HR for roughly every 26 innings! Had WAR been a popular metric back in '83, Cy Young voters might have made him the second AL reliever to win the award rather than 24-game winner LaMarr Hoyt – Quisenberry's was 5.5, Hoyt's was 3.7. Then again, Hoyt's White Sox did finish 20 games ahead of the second-place Royals.

That summer, shortly before the infamous Pine Tar Game, *SI* sent me to Kansas City to do a long takeout on Dan. Together, we decided to divide the story into nine innings, and to give him the ninth. His "outing" was mostly humorous, but there was one passage that came from his more serious side:

"I feel a lot of responsibility, more than I used to. If I lost, I used to be able to think it away easier. I could accept the result if I'd thrown a good pitch."

"It's not that easy anymore. I feel more guilty if things don't go right. I think about the starting pitcher and the fans and the owner and the general manager and the friends and relatives who are going to read the paper the next morning, and the guys who built up the lead. Everybody expects me to close up shop nicely, and I feel guilty when I don't."

"I don't want to sound depressing, and I'm only talking about maybe 10% of the games I'm in that I don't do the job. It's just that I've come to expect a lot more out of myself. So when everything goes right, and I get the save, I'm the one who's saved."[27]

I was lookin up when it was a cool night
in October
Darryl Motley caught
A lazy fly off Andy Van Slyke's bat
Kansas City delirious as champs
we poured champagne on sweat-soaked heads
it burned our eyes
we didn't care
we screamed we sang we laughed
drunk with victory

He and Janie had always been active in charities, but in May of 1984, they went a step further by establishing the Quisenberry Relief Fund to benefit the Harvesters Food Bank, a Kansas City organization established in 1979 to combat hunger.[28] "I feel like we all ought to do our part to better our community or alleviate some problems."[29] Besides making his own generous contribution, he enlisted the help of Warner-Lambert, sponsor of the Rolaids Award he had already won three times.

Quis would win the award again in 1984, with 44 saves and six victories, as the Royals finished first in the AL West, only to get swept by the Tigers in the ALCS. He was the hard-luck loser in Game Two after coming on to start the ninth with the score tied 3-3 – thanks to an error, Detroit broke through for two runs in the 11th.

That ALCS victory helped justify the Cy Young Award and MVP for Tigers reliever Willie Hernandez. But consider this: Quisenberry, who finished second in the Cy Young voting and third on the MVP ballots, saved 12 more games than Hernandez.

The 1985 season began on a high note when co-owner Avron Fogelman signed Quisenberry, Frank White, and Willie Wilson to "lifetime" contracts tied to his real-estate holdings.[30]

The Royals took years off the lives of their fans, though, by going down to the wire to win the AL West in the regular season, then coming back from 2-0 and 3-1 deficits in the ALCS against Toronto. Quis saved 37 games in the regular season to lead the league for the fourth straight year, but he had blown 12 saves and Howser started losing trust in him, especially after he faltered in Game Two of the ALCS. Still, he did get the final outs in Games Six and Seven.

That set up the I-80, Show-Me State Series against the Cardinals and old friend Whitey Herzog. Once again, the Royals dug themselves a hole, losing the first two games at home. In Game Two, Howser left the southpaw Leibrandt in too long, thinking he had a better chance against the Cardinals' left-handed hitters than his closer did.[31] Dan was not happy about his late arrival.

As it happened, my wife, Bambi, was in St. Louis for Game Three to celebrate our first anniversary, and I was able to secure two seats in the first row of the upper deck in left field, right above the Royals bullpen. In the third inning, we heard our names being called from down below. We looked down, and there were Quis and John Wathan and Jamie Quirk waving to us.[32]

Even the Cardinals fans around us couldn't help but be impressed – not by our who-are-you? celebrity, but rather by how loose the team they hoped to sweep seemed to be. Bret Saberhagen pitched a complete-game 6-1 victory, so that was about the extent of the bullpen action that night. Looking up.

John Tudor threw a five-hit shutout as the Cards won Game Four, which turned the Royals' hopes of winning their first World into prayers – they would need to win three straight elimination games. But Danny Jackson answered with his own five-hitter in a 6-1 victory to send the Series back to Kansas City.

The rest is history ... and infamy. The Cardinals had a 1-0 lead in the bottom of the ninth inning in Game Six, and hadn't coughed up a lead in the ninth all season when Jorge Orta led off the inning with a groundball to first baseman Jack Clark, who tossed the ball to reliever Todd Worrell, racing over to cover first. Umpire Don Denkinger said that Orta had beat the throw, though replays clearly showed that he had not. That opened the door for a rally that ended with former Cardinal Dane Iorg singling home the tying and winning runs. Denkinger was the goat and Iorg the hero in the 2-1 victory, but lost in the hysteria was the lesson learned by Howser, who kept the score close by replacing Leibrandt with Quisenberry at the right time this time.

Game Seven turned into an 11-0 coronation for the Royals, thanks to Saberhagen's five-hitter and three

RBIs by Darryl Motley, who made the final out in right field, unleashing a joyous riot on the field while etching an indelible memory for the Royals faithful cheering in the ballpark and watching at home. President Ronald Reagan made a call to the victorious clubhouse, congratulating, among others, "Jim Quisenberry."[33]

Even in victory, there was still an air of disbelief. At the subsequent parade through downtown Kansas City, Quis said from his open convertible, "Sometimes I still think we need to play someone else. It's hard to believe we don't have anyone else left to beat."[34]

When the Royals visited the Rose Garden of the White House on Halloween, just four days after the final out, President Reagan told them, "You proved to America what a never-say-die spirit can do."[35] He also personally apologized to Quis for calling him Jim.

The pitcher replied, "That's okay, Don."[36]

He almost didn't make the trip, though. Dan needed to be reassured that the charter flight back to Kansas City would arrive in time for him to trick-or-treat with Alysia, 6, and David, 4. "I would have missed more if I'd missed Halloween than if I didn't go to the White House," he said.[37]

I was lookin up when Dick Howser told us
he couldn't manage anymore
go on without him
more to life than baseball
he died that summer
we froze and played like statues

The roses faded all too quickly. There was bound to be a letdown after such a tremendous high, but 1986 was a total bummer. The team played with a hangover, and though Quisenberry didn't pitch that badly, he fell into a closer rotation with Bud Black and Steve Farr. But the real shock came at the All-Star break. Howser, who had been feeling sick and messing up signals, was diagnosed with a brain tumor after leading the AL to a 3-2 victory.[38] It was the last game he would ever manage – Mike Ferraro took over the club, which finished with a desultory 76-86 record.

After recovering from brain surgery, Howser tried to come back the next spring training in Fort Myers, but he quickly discovered that he was too weak to do the job. Here's how Quis described him telling the team he was quitting in "Ode to Dick Howser": *this small man/who fought big/now looked us in the eyes/just a man/who no longer talked of winning/but hinted at life beyond champagne.*[39]

Billy Gardner was hired to replace Howser, but nobody could. He died on June 17, 1987, at St. Luke's Hospital at the age of 51. With the team going nowhere at 62-64, Gardner was replaced by John Wathan, who gave it something of a spark. But the Royals still finished second, two games behind the Twins.

The writing was on the wall for Quis as well. Despite a decent ERA of 2.76, he pitched only 49 innings and had only eight saves. He was unhappy about his reduced role, and he made no bones about it. The Royals finally gave him his release on the Fourth of July, 1988 – Independence Day.

I was lookin up when the mirror showed
a red hat on my head
a different logo
it looked foreign
like in a prism
felt it too
like a defector in a new land
except Whitey again was manager

He promptly signed with the Cardinals. The National League appealed to him, and so did reuniting with Whitey Herzog, the first manager to show faith in him. He also drew inspiration from his old mentor, Kent Tekulve. "I watched him fall into disfavor in Pittsburgh and then resurrect himself in Philadelphia," he told Bob Hertzel of the *Pittsburgh Press*, "and that has given me a lot of hope."[40]

He made 33 appearances for the Cards in '88, and the results weren't pretty (a 6.16 ERA). But they brought him back the next year, and he did fairly well, saving six games with a more Quis-like 2.64 ERA. He even got his first – and only – major-league hit, an RBI single off Tim Belcher of the Dodgers, on July 6.

Later that summer, the Cardinals came to New York, and we had lunch. He even came by our apartment, where he threw Wiffle Balls to our baseball-mad 3-year-old son, Bo. Dan knew he was at the end of the line, but he was at peace with his career and looking forward to raising his own two children. The Cardinals released him at the end of the season.

But then, lo and behold, the San Francisco Giants signed him to a modest two-year deal on January 28, 1990.

I was lookin up when I sat at a table with reporters
telling them I quit
telling myself don't cry don't cry don't cry
I didn't want to break
the unwritten code of big leaguers

When Larry Stone of the *San Francisco Examiner* asked Quis what he still had to offer, he replied, "I can pitch any time in the game. I don't get riled. I throw strikes. I can get hitters out. I know how to get along in the clubhouse. I know how to help out the young kids. I throw 100 miles an hour. I hit home runs. I steal bases. You choose the ones that apply."[41]

The Giants and Quis were fooling themselves. He pitched in only five regular-season games. For the first time in his career, he had a sore arm. His last appearance came in a 13-3 blowout loss to the San Diego Padres on April 23, 1990. He came on to get one out in the second inning with the Giants already behind 5-0, breezed through the third, then gave up three runs in the fourth.

That was enough. On the day he announced his retirement, the Giants let him take the lineup card out to the umpires. "It's my turn," he told the reporters afterward. "A rite of passage. I'm doing what I have to do." When asked what his plans were, he replied, "I've got a big pile of laundry I've wanted to get to."[42]

It lasted so long
it went so fast
it seems like yesterday
it seems like never

As much as baseball meant to Quisenberry, it wasn't everything. Retirement gave him the freedom to pour himself into his family and community. The Harvesters Food Bank kept growing, and so did Dan. He took up poetry, eventually amassing enough material to fill a book, *On Days Like This*. The poems about baseball are under the heading "Covering First," and the poems about life are under "Stuff That Could Be True."

Roger Angell, who was the fiction editor at The New Yorker when he wrote about Dan, had this to say about the book: "Like his pitches, Dan Quisenberry's poems come at you unexpectedly, rising from a different part of the field, clear and unthreatening in their intentions, and then startling you with a late swoop or slant. ... [They] turn you back to the top of the page again, wanting more time with this good poet and sweet man."[43]

He and the family were on vacation in Colorado in January of 1998 when he noticed his vision had become blurry. He wasn't expecting the news he got from the doctors back in Kansas City: They found Grade IV malignant astrocytoma in his brain. Soon after surgery to remove the tumor, he and Janie gave a press conference at Royals Stadium. He tried to put everyone at ease. "Every day, I find things to be thankful for," he said. "My kids take me for rides, so I feel like a dog. I get to stick my head out the window and let the wind flap my ears. I love it."[44]

But there was no denying the dire prognosis, and the link to Dick Howser, not to mention the other players from the 1980 postseason who had died of brain cancer: Bobby Murcer, Johnny Oates, Tug McGraw, and John Vukovich. "Dick was such a feisty leader guy," said Quis. "And then he was this mellow man, saying, 'Don't worry about this stuff on the field. Do your best because winning and losing takes care of itself.' That was so strange to hear. I didn't really know how to process those words. Now here I am and I know what he was saying. It's like getting new eyes. So, in a way, it's a gift. The peace is incredible."[45]

On May 30, the Royals inducted Quis into their Hall of Fame.[46] He had to be coaxed into attending the festivities before the game with the A's, but as he and Janie circled Royals Stadium in an antique

Corvette convertible, the 30,000 fans and players on both sides showered him with love. "Wow," he said, "it's been a long time since I had a good year."[47]

Though his vision had diminished, and his shaved head bore the signs of his battle, his mind was as sharp as ever. At an ensuing press conference, a reporter asked him, "Is there a lesson in all this?"

Quis made him define "this," then begged off answering the question because he didn't want to come up with a cliché. Later, when another writer asked him about his accomplishments, he said, "I don't think about those things because I needed so much help. I needed a great wife. I needed Willie Wilson in center. I needed a great second baseman like Frank White."

Then he turned to the writer whose question he hadn't answered.

"We need each other. That's the lesson."[48]

Sigh.

Sources

In addition to the sources cited in the Notes, the author also consulted Baseball-Reference.com, the Kansas City Royals Alumni Association, and the National Baseball Hall of Fame Library and Research Center.

Notes

1 *On Days Like This*, by Dan Quisenberry (Kansas City, Missouri: Helicon Nine, Midwest Center for the Arts, 1998). All poems by Dan Quisenberry come from this book.

2 Joe Posnanski, "Quiz, a Royal Remembered," *Kansas City Star*, October 1, 1998.

3 Steve Wulf, "Special Delivery From Down Under," *Sports Illustrated*, July 11, 1983.

4 Ibid.

5 Ibid.

6 Mike McKenzie, "The Inside Track," *Inside Sports*, September 1981.

7 Wulf, "Special Delivery From Down Under."

8 Ibid.

9 Ibid.

10 Material supplied by Royals Alumni Director Dina Blevins, January 2019.

11 Wulf, "Special Delivery From Down Under."

12 Ibid.

13 Ibid.

14 Ibid.

15 1980 Topps #667, "Royals Future Stars."

16 *On Days Like This*.

17 Roger Angell, "Quis," *The New Yorker*, September 30, 1985.

18 Ibid.

19 Wulf, "Special Delivery From Down Under."

20 Ibid.

21 Roger Launius, "Phillies vs. Royals: Reflecting on the 1980 World Series," July 20, 2012. launiusr.wordpress.com/2012/07/20/phillies-vs-royals-reflecting-on-the-1980-world-series/.

22 Wulf, "Special Delivery From Down Under."

23 Kevin Nelson, ed., *Baseball's Greatest Quotes* (New York: Simon & Schuster, 1982); Bob Chiefger, ed., *Voices of Baseball* (New York: Atheneum, 1983).

24 Mike McKenzie, "The Inside Track."

25 Mike McKenzie, "Quisenberry Discovers 'Delivery in My Flaw,'" *The Sporting News*, June 6, 1981.

26 Wulf, "Special Delivery From Down Under."

27 Ibid.

28 Mike Fish, "Quisenberry Launches Campaign to Battle Hunger in the Community," *Kansas City Times*, May 24, 1984.

29 Ibid.

30 Associated Press, "Three Royals to Sign Lifetime Pacts," *New York Times*, April 3, 1985.

31 Jeffrey Spivak, *Crowning the Kansas City Royals* (New York: Sports Publishing LLC, 2005), 31.

32 Steve Wulf, "Echoes of the '85 K.C. Royals," ESPN.com, October 22, 2014.

33 Ibid.

34 Jeffrey Spivak, 117.

35 Pete Grathoff, "Royals Were Served Cake When They Visited the White House in 1985," *Kansas City Star*, July 20, 2016.

36 Wulf, "Echoes of the '85 K.C. Royals."

37 Krista Fritz Rogers, "Royal Father," *Kansas City Parent*, June 1986.

38 Sarajane Freligh, "Howser Showed Early Signs of Illness," *Chicago Tribune*, July 25, 1986.

39 *On Days Like This*.

40 Bob Hertzel, "Quisenberry Hoping It Works Out for Best With the Cardinals," *Pittsburgh Press*, July 27, 1988.

41 Larry Stone, "Quiz Is Still a Quip Wiz," *San Francisco Examiner,* March 11, 1990: 35.

42 Rod Beaton, "Quisenberry Says Cheerful Goodbye," *USA Today*, April 30, 1990.

43 *On Days Like This*, back cover.

44 Thomas Boswell, "Quiz Faces the Toughest Test," *Washington Post*, January 30, 1998.

45 Ibid.

46 "Pop(ular) Quiz in KC," *USA Today Baseball Weekly*, June 3-June 9, 1998.

47 Steve Wulf, "Saving Grace," *ESPN The Magazine*, October 3, 1998.

48 Ibid.

JOE RANDA

BY MAX RIEPER

The life of a ballplayer is a life on the road. Half of your season is spent traveling around the league, and even your "home" can be temporary, uprooted by a trade at any moment. Some players are lucky enough to stay in one place for more than a season or two, and it is the rare player who stays in one place long enough to set down roots and become part of his adopted community. It took several seasons shuttling around the league for Joe Randa to find his home, but he eventually found it in Kansas City.

Randa was a sure-handed third baseman who consistently hit for average and had solid gap power. He had a good reputation in clutch situations and was cited as a clubhouse leader who had a positive attitude. He was known for always smiling on the field, even as he stood at the plate, causing Pittsburgh broadcaster Bob Walk to give him the nickname "The Joker."[1]

Joseph Gregory Randa was born on December 18, 1969, in Milwaukee and grew up 30 minutes west of there in the city of Wales, Wisconsin. His parents divorced when he was 4 years old, leaving him to be raised by his mother, Donna Lexa, who was an art therapist committed to working with people with disabilities.[2] Randa grew up playing lots of sports, excelling at tennis and baseball.[3] He attended Kettle Moraine High School, leading the baseball team to a state title his senior season.[4] Randa attended a workout with his hometown Brewers, but turned down an offer of $1,200 to sign with them.[5]

Randa worked out at an indoor baseball facility owned by former Milwaukee Brewers first baseman Mike Hegan. There he befriended Hegan's son, who persuaded Randa to travel down to Florida with him to work out for schools there.[6] In Florida, he was recruited to Broward County Community College by a coach named Allard Baird, who would one day be general manager of the Kansas City Royals.[7] Baird immediately left for another school, so Randa transferred to Indian Rivers Community College, where he was drafted by the California Angels in the 30th round.

He turned down the Angels, instead opting to move on to the University of Tennessee, where he hit .342 with 10 home runs his junior season. Leading up to the June 1991 amateur draft, the Red Sox and Brewers expressed interest in Randa.[8] In the 11th round, Randa's hometown Brewers took USC third baseman Jeff Cirillo. Two picks later, the Royals selected Randa.

Randa got his professional career off to a hot start, hitting .338 with 11 home runs in 72 games for the Eugene Emeralds, earning Northwest League MVP honors. He would not hit for that kind of power again in the minors, but he consistently hit for a high average. He hit .301 the next season back in his native Wisconsin for the Appleton Foxes in the Midwest League before being promoted in midseason to the High-A Florida League. By 1993, in just his second full season in the minors, he was in Double A playing for the Memphis Chicks. He hit .295 for the Chicks and met his wife, Bethany, that year.[9]

Randa was on the cusp of the big leagues by 1994, playing for the top Royals affiliate in Omaha. His numbers slumped that season and with the players strike that summer, he did not get a September call-up. But when play resumed the next spring, the Royals found themselves in austerity mode. Owner Muriel Kauffman had died, leaving the team in the hands of a board of directors tasked with making the team financially attractive for a sale. This meant an emphasis on young, homegrown players like Randa, who was one of seven rookies to make the Opening Day roster that year.[10]

However manager Bob Boone still found a preference for playing veteran third baseman Gary Gaetti, who was rejuvenating his career with a big power season. Randa spent his time riding the pine, and actually made his major-league debut at second base, a position he had never played before. When regular second baseman Jose Lind unexpectedly left the team in June, it seemed an opportunity opened up for Randa. But the Royals went with two journeymen with more experience at the position in Keith Lockhart and Edgar Cáceres. With his batting average well under .200 through July, Randa was demoted to Omaha, not to return until rosters expanded in September.

"I've tried to change my swing around to become a power hitter, and it's just not my game," he said. "I'm a line-drive, gap hitter, and I think my home runs are going to increase – but I'm not going to be a 25-30 homer guy."[11]

Gaetti departed in 1996, but Randa's offensive woes the previous season caused Boone to platoon him at third with the left-handed-hitting Keith Lockhart. A knee injury kept Randa out of action for three weeks in May, but he got hot over the summer, hitting .367 in June. He ended the year hitting .303 with 6 home runs and 13 steals in 110 games. The season was bittersweet, however, as Randa's mother was killed in an automobile accident.[12]

The Royals had finished dead last in the American League in runs scored that year, and sought more offense. They found an opportunity to pick up two veteran hitters from the cost-cutting Pittsburgh Pirates, acquiring first baseman Jeff King and shortstop Jay Bell in exchange for four players – Randa and pitchers Jeff Granger, Jeff Martin, and Jeff Wallace.

Randa was going from one youth movement to another, with the Pirates saving $7 million on the deal. But at least he would get an opportunity to play every day in Pittsburgh. After a slow start, Randa heated up and got his average over .300 by June. He missed a month with a broken finger, but managed to end the 1997 season over .300 for the second year in a row with 7 home runs and 60 RBIs in 126 games as the Pirates flirted with postseason contention.

Pittsburgh's top prospect was third baseman Aramis Ramirez, so the club felt it could risk leaving Randa unprotected for that winter's expansion draft despite his solid season. The Cardinals called hoping they could work out a deal for Randa with first baseman John Mabry discussed as a potential return, but no trade was made.[13] During the expansion draft, the Royals tried to get the Tampa Bay Devil Rays to select Randa to trade him back to Kansas City, but the teams couldn't agree on a deal.[14] Pirates general manager Cam Bonifay would later admit, "I didn't feel like either Arizona or Tampa Bay was going to take him, to tell you the truth."[15] But he was wrong. Eventually, the Arizona Diamondbacks selected him with the 57th pick, immediately trading him with infielder Gabe Alvarez and pitcher Matt Drews to the Tigers for third baseman Travis Fryman.

Randa missed being with his teammates in Pittsburgh and expressed some disappointment when a rumored deal to send him back there for pitcher Esteban Loaiza didn't come to fruition.[16] He struggled with the bat much of the year, and lost his starting job in June to Alvarez. He finished the year hitting just .254 with 9 home runs, a sharp decline from his career numbers to that point. However, he had a 40-game errorless streak and credited Tigers coach Perry Hill with helping him dramatically improve his defense.[17] "Offensively it wasn't clicking for me, but defensively I was a stud," he said.[18]

The Tigers signed free agent Dean Palmer to upgrade third base, making Randa expendable. He found himself on the move once again, acquired by the Mets in December. However it was a salary-dump deal, done so the Mets could rid themselves of pitcher Willie Blair. With veteran Robin Ventura at third, general manager Steve Phillips had no intention of keeping Randa.[19] Less than a week later, they shipped him back to the Royals for minor-league outfielder Juan Lebron.

Randa was back with his original franchise, playing near the house he had purchased back in 1996. That same week he and Bethany welcomed their first child into the world, son Jacob.[20] Randa was thrilled to be back, telling reporters, "Ever since I've been traded, I've always followed the Royals. I've always had the Royal blue inside me that never really went away."[21]

Randa got off to a slow start with the Royals in 1999, but he worked with Hall of Famer George Brett on his swing and caught fire that summer.[22] In early June he tied a franchise record with hits in nine consecutive at-bats. He enjoyed the first five-hit game of his career that week, and a month later he achieved his second. Over the months of June and July, Randa hit .404/.441/.644 with 9 home runs in 51 games. He had a breakout season, hitting a career-high .314 with 16 home runs and 84 RBIs. His 197 hits were sixth most in the American League and the most by a Royals hitter in over a decade. *Kansas City Star* beat writer Jeffrey Flanagan named Randa the team's most valuable player.[23]

Randa got off to a blazing start in 2000, as the Royals had a bevy of talented young hitters around him like Johnny Damon, Carlos Beltran, Jermaine Dye, and Mike Sweeney. The team set a club record for runs scored, and Randa did his part with a career-high 106 RBIs. A second-half slump brought his average down to .304, but it was still his fourth season out of five with an average over .300.

The next season was going to be Randa's last season before free agency, but he signed a two-year, $8.5 million contract extension in spring training to keep him in Kansas City. He acknowledged that the deal was below market value, but he was willing to take less money to stay, saying, "I only picture myself wearing Royal blue. That weighed very heavily into my decision."[24]

Randa battled back and hamstring injuries in 2001, and his offensive numbers sank to .253/.307/.386, the worst of his career. He bounced back in 2002 to hit .282 and reached the 80-RBI plateau for the fourth consecutive season. But the perpetually rebuilding Royals were becoming cost-conscious again, and began looking to move Randa and his multimillion-dollar salary. General manager Allard Baird had a potential deal to send him to the Cubs for two minor-league prospects, but Royals club President Dan Glass nixed the deal.[25] Randa denied a report that he used his limited no-trade clause to veto a deal to the Mets.[26] He grew discouraged at the lack of direction from the franchise, saying, "I'm not the type of person who likes to complain. ... But sure, it's frustrating. We're in a division that we could be competitive in, but we're really not sure where we're going."[27]

The Royals were thankful they never worked out a deal for Randa, as the team got off to an unexpectedly hot start in 2003, and found itself in first place through August. Randa would be a big part of the quick start, hitting .316 with five home runs in April. But he hit just .152 in May and missed three weeks in July with an oblique injury. Upon returning, Randa went on another tear, hitting .381 in August as the Royals clung onto first place for dear life. The red-hot Twins overtook the Royals and denied them their first postseason appearance since 1985. Randa finished his up-and-down season with a batting average of .291 with 16 home runs. He set a franchise fielding record, though, going 75 consecutive games without an error.

The taste of contention fueled the Royals to invest more in player payroll, signing free agents like Juan Gonzalez and Benito Santiago and re-signing pitcher Brian Anderson. The club also made sure to retain Randa, signing him to a one-year deal worth $3.25 million with a mutual option for 2005. Unfortunately for the Royals, those investments would not lead to more success on the field. With the team again in the cellar, they dealt superstar Carlos Beltran to the Astros in June in a three-way trade that netted them third-base prospect Mark Teahen from the Athletics. With a replacement in the wings, Randa's days in Kansas City seemed numbered. A slump and a knee injury that cost him a month of action kept him from being traded that summer, but he knew the end was near. He returned to have a six-hit game in September, becoming just the third player in franchise history to achieve that feat. At the end of the season, the Royals let Randa walk.

The 35-year-old Randa signed a one-year, $2.15 million deal with the Cincinnati Reds to be their starting third baseman in 2005. He got off to quite a start, becoming the first player in their long history to hit a walk-off home run on Opening Day.[28] But the Reds fell out of contention, and with young Edwin Encarnacion ready to come up, the Reds dealt Randa to the Padres for pitchers Travis Chick and Justin Germano in July. With the Padres, Randa got the only postseason action of his career. He hit .364 (4-for-11) as the Padres were swept in three games by the Cardinals in the National League Divisional Series.

Randa relished his postseason experience, but lamented that he was never able to have that success in Kansas City. "It would have been so much sweeter for me to have won with Mike Sweeney and all those guys in my hometown," he said. "I mean, don't get me wrong, it was incredible to win. But I did think a lot about Kansas City."[29]

As for why the Royals weren't able to win more, Randa defended GM Baird and put the onus squarely on ownership, saying, "[T]here's a lot of hidden agendas there," and adding, "[H]opefully the Glass family ... will try to sell the team and get somebody in there that cares and wants to win."[30] Randa later walked back those comments, but it was clear that years of losing and the lack of long-term commitment from the franchise had frustrated him.

Having reunited with a former team once before, Randa found it easy to return to another organization he had enjoyed, signing a one-year deal with the Pittsburgh Pirates in 2006. Again in rebuild mode, the Pirates looked to Randa to provide veteran leadership.[31] A stress fracture in his foot cost him six weeks and limited Randa to just 89 games. He hit .267 and his four home runs were the lowest of his career since his first season.

After the season, Joe decided he had enough of the mental grind of the game. He retired after 12 seasons, 1,543 hits, and 123 home runs. At the time of his retirement, he was seventh in Royals history in hits with 1,084. Upon retirement, Randa returned to his home in Kansas City to spend more time with his wife, Bethany, and two sons, Jacob and Justin. He served as a special adviser to the Royals front office, working with young players like Mike Moustakas.[32] He also started to work with Royals Charities and joined the board of directors of the Donna Lexa Art Centers, facilities dedicated to his mother that provide art classes to adults and teens with special needs.

Joe Randa showed that if a player loves playing in Kansas City, he will find that love returned by the fans many times over.

"I love Kansas City. I love the Kansas City Royals," he said. "I owe everything to this organization. They brought me back home. I told them I will give everything in my heart for this team, this city."[33]

Notes

1 Dick Kaegel, "Joker' Goes Wild at Plate," *Kansas City Star*, September 20, 2000.

2 Dick Kaegel, "Small Town Life Suits Randa," MLB.com, August 2, 2004. kansascity.royals.mlb.com/content/printer_friendly/kc/y2004/m08/d02/c817452.jsp.

3 Lee Warren, "This Blue-Collar Royal Has Priorities in Order," *The Pathway*, August 3, 2004. mbcpathway.com/2005/11/11/article20075-htm/.

4 Evan Frank, "Stu Pease, Who Guided the 1988 Kettle Moraine Baseball Team to a State Title, Dies at Age 77," *Milwaukee Journal-Sentinel*, July 21, 2017.

5 Dave O'Brien, host, "Joe Randa," *Clubhouse Conversation*, July 16, 2014. clubhouseconversation.com/2014/07/joe-randa/.

6 Ibid.

7 Ibid.

8 Ibid.

9 Kimberly Winter Stern, "The Good Life," *435 Magazine*, February 2010. 435mag.com/February-2010/The-Good-Life/.

10 Dick Kaegel, "Royals Rookies Learn Life Is Good at the Top/Big-League Ball Especially Sweet for Bunch and Nunnally, Two Who Moved Up from Class A," *Kansas City Star*, May 2, 1995.

11 Dick Kaegel, "Third Base Is the Place for Randa/Royals Infielder May Be Platooned but Could Win Job," *Kansas City Star*, March 12, 1996.

12 Chris Patterson, "Randa Putting On a Positive Spin," *Waukesha* (Wisconsin) *Freeman*, June 19, 1996.

13 Rick Hummel, "Teams Will Wheel, Deal After Today's Expansion Draft," *St. Louis Post-Dispatch*, November 18, 1997.

14 Dick Kaegel, "An Ozzie at Shortstop for the Royals? Or Joe Carter or Jeff Conine in Left Field?" *Kansas City Star*, November 20, 1997.

15 Ron Cook, "No Ordinary Joe – Royals' Randa Still Popular with Former Pirates Teammates," *Pittsburgh Post-Gazette*, June 4, 2000.

16 Ron Cook, "Randa Longs for Return to Third Base for Pirates," *Pittsburgh Post-Gazette*, May 26, 1998.

17 Dave O'Brien, *Clubhouse Conversation*.

18 Ibid.

19 Mike Vaccaro, "Mets Send Blair Back to Tigers," *Newark Star-Ledger*, December 5, 1998.

20 Dick Kaegel, "Randa Back in Comfort Zone," *Kansas City Star*, March 4, 1999.

21 Ibid.

22 Rick Plumlee, "With a Little Help from Brett, Randa Is a Hit in Kansas City," *Wichita Eagle*, July 24, 1999.

23 Jeffrey Flanagan, "Randa's Big Year Makes Him Worthy of Royals MVP Award," *Kansas City Star*, September 7, 1999.

24 Bob Dutton, "Randa Agrees to Contract Extension," *Kansas City Star*, March 18, 2001.

25 Dick Kaegel, "Randa Trade Vetoed/Dan Glass Puts Halt to Deal with Cubs," *Kansas City Star*, January 14, 2003.

26 Jeffrey Flanagan, "Randa Says He Didn't Have to Veto Mets Deal," *Kansas City Star*, January 24, 2003.

27 Ibid.

28 Paul Daugherty, "Randa 'Rakes,' Caps Wonderful Day in the Yard," *Cincinnati Enquirer*, April 5, 2005.

29 Joe Posnanski, "Randa's Postseason Bittersweet," *Kansas City Star*, October 6, 2005.

30 Mike Berardino, "Glass Family, Not GM Baird, Problem in Kansas City," *South Florida Sun-Sentinel*, August 21, 2005.

31 Jim Brockman, "Ex-Pirate Is Back, Expected to Lead Young Teammates," *Bradenton Herald*, March 28, 2006.

32 Jeffrey Flanagan, "Randa Is Impressed with Moustakas," *Kansas City Star*, July 27, 2008.

33 Joe Posnanski, "In His Heart, Randa Always Knew He Belonged with This Team," *Kansas City Star*, August 8, 1999.

COOKIE ROJAS

BY PETER M. GORDON

Cookie Rojas is one of a handful of major leaguers who played every position in his career including pitcher. Of that group, he is the only one to make both the American and National League All-Star teams. Rojas worked in the major leagues as a player, coach, manager, and broadcaster for more than five decades.

Octavio Victor (Rivas) Rojas was born on March 6, 1939, in Havana, Cuba, to an upper-middle-class family. His mother gave him the Spanish nickname Cuqui, meaning charming or adorable, when he was young. The name got anglicized to Cookie when he started in baseball, and stuck with him throughout his long career.

Rojas's father was a doctor who wanted his son to follow in his footsteps, but Cookie wanted more than anything to play baseball. Rojas was small, slight (listed at 5-feet-10 and 160 pounds), and wore glasses, three things that worked against many promising ballplayers during the 1950s. He wouldn't give up his dream, and turned himself into a major-league prospect.

The Havana Sugar Kings (Triple A, International League) were a Cincinnati Reds affiliate during the '50s, and as a result the Reds signed several Cuban players who played for them in the majors. They signed Cookie in 1956, when he was 17, and sent him to their West Palm Beach team in the Class-D Florida State League. Cookie made steady if unspectacular progress through the minors, playing at the Reds' Class-C affiliate in 1957 and Class A in 1958. In 1959 the Reds returned Cookie to Havana to play second base for the Sugar Kings, where he teamed with future Reds shortstop and fellow Cuban Leo Cardenas.

The Sugar Kings won the International League title in 1959, but the Cuban revolution interrupted the next season. The Reds moved the franchise to Jersey City, New Jersey, in midseason to avoid the possibility of Fidel Castro nationalizing the team, and Cookie moved with it. He spent 1960 and 1961 with the Jersey City Jerseys while the Reds played Johnny Temple, then Don Blasingame at second base. The Reds won the pennant in 1961 and didn't bring Rojas to the majors until 1962.

Rojas made his debut as a second baseman in the first regular-season game at Dodger Stadium, on Tuesday April 10, 1962, against the Los Angeles Dodgers' southpaw Johnny Podres before a crowd of 52,564. He went 0-for-3 though he did lay down a successful sacrifice bunt in the first inning in a 6-4 Reds victory. Rojas was 0-for-4 the following evening against Sandy Koufax. After another hitless game in which he went 0-for-2 with two bases on balls, Rojas was dropped from second in the batting order to eighth, and got his first hit on April 19, in the second inning, a single to center field off Sandy Koufax at Cincinnati's Crosley Field. Rojas saw limited action as a utility infielder and batted only .221 with two extra-base hits in 78 at-bats. The Reds sent him down to Dallas-Fort Worth midway through the season, although Cookie finished the season with the club.

After the season the Reds traded Rojas to the Phillies for relief pitcher Jim Owens. The Phillies had an all-star Cuban second baseman, Tony Taylor, and in 1963 Cookie played in only 64 games backing up second and playing outfield. He hit only .221 again, but fielded well, and hit his first major-league home run, a solo shot, on September 17 off of the Mets' Tracy Stallard at the Polo Grounds.

Rojas worked hard to improve his hitting and quickly developed a reputation as a player who would do whatever the team needed to win. During the 1964 pennant race, manager Gene Mauch used Cookie as a super sub, backing up short and second but also logging a great deal of time in center field when Tony Gonzalez was out, and worked at other positions as well. As Rojas put it, "When I was asked if I could play center field I said yes. When I was asked if I could play third base, I said yes. I never said no."[1]

Rojas played in 104 games in 1964, hit a solid .291, and made some key hits that helped the Phillies get a 6½-game lead going into the last two weeks of the season. At the All-Star break Rojas was hitting over .300 as the Phillies surprisingly surged into first place. During a game on July 23 he doubled in the winning run in the top of the tenth to beat the Milwaukee Braves.

A game on July 19 typified how Mauch used Rojas throughout the season. He started in center field, then moved to shortstop and finished the game as the catcher in the Phils' 4-3 victory over the Reds. During the Phillies' ten-game losing streak in September, Rojas hit only .200, but several teammates, including shortstop Bobby Wine, hit for a lower average. Rojas was bitterly disappointed that the Phillies' collapse prevented him from playing in the World Series.

The 1964 season provided Rojas with other unforgettable moments. In an article in *Baseball Digest*'s November 1979 issue, Rojas called his participation in Jim Bunning's perfect game "The Game I'll Never Forget." Rojas played shortstop during the game and said that the longer the game went the more nervous he was about making a mistake and ruining the game. Rojas made a fine play at shortstop, going to his knees to spear a line drive, but it was clear that he was just as happy as the game went on to not have the ball hit to him.

In 1965 Cookie played everywhere except third base and pitcher, and was the regular second baseman. He appeared in 142 games, batted .303, made his first All-Star team, and received some MVP votes from sportswriters. He was statistically the toughest player to strike out in the National League that year. Rojas had now improved his batting average in each of his major-league seasons. In 1966 his average fell to .268. He played in 156 games.

Even as the Phillies slipped out of the pennant races, Rojas continued to perform. In 1967 he played every position for the Phillies, including pitcher, for one inning during the second game of a doubleheader when the staff needed a break. He allowed no runs and never pitched again, so his lifetime ERA remains 0.00. He played in 147 games and hit .259. Mauch liked to bunt, and Cookie led the National League with 16 sacrifice hits. He finished second in double plays by NL second basemen, behind only Bill Mazeroski.

In 1967 Cookie teamed with shortstop Bobby Wine to make, as the reporters called it, "The Plays of Wine and Rojas," a takeoff of the popular film *The Days of Wine and Roses*. In 1968 Rojas supported his defensive reputation by leading all NL second basemen in fielding percentage with a .987 figure.

In 1969 the Phillies slipped toward the back of the NL East and Cookie's batting average slipped to .228, marking the fourth straight year his batting average declined. With hot prospect Denny Doyle coming up through the minor leagues the Phillies included Rojas in a postseason blockbuster trade that sent him, slugger Dick Allen, and pitcher Jerry Johnson to the St. Louis Cardinals for Curt Flood, Tim McCarver, outfielder Byron Browne, and pitcher Joe Hoerner. Curt Flood refused to report and demanded to be made a free agent after the trade. His subsequent suit to overturn the reserve clause made it all the way to the Supreme Court, where the reserve clause was upheld. Yet Flood's case laid the groundwork for eventual player free agency.

For Rojas, the trade was a personal disaster but ended up providing him with a great opportunity. He said, "I was 31 years old and didn't fit into their (the Phils) plans. When I got to St. Louis they had Julian Javier and didn't really need me."[2] In limited action, Rojas hit .106 with few highlights. He did win a game with a tenth-inning pinch-hit single on April 14. On June 13 the Cardinals sent him to the expansion Kansas City Royals for outfielder Fred Rico, another example of the

Royals' trading acumen in their early years that landed them players like Amos Otis and John Mayberry.

The Royals were a young team that benefited from Rojas's veteran leadership. Given an opportunity to play every day, and reinvigorated by his new environment, Cookie finished the year with a solid .268 average and played steady and sometimes spectacular defense for the young team. He teamed up with shortstop Freddie Patek to form one of the best double-play combinations in baseball. Longtime Royals broadcaster Denny Matthews said of them, "They were the first guys I ever saw work the play where, on a groundball up the middle, the second baseman gets to it, backhands it and flips it to the shortstop with a backhand motion of the glove."[3]

Despite his success, Cookie considered retiring after the 1970 season. His wife was ill, and he thought his family needed him. When his wife's health improved, he returned to the Royals and at the age of 32 had arguably the best season of his career, batting .300, leading AL second basemen in fielding percentage with a .991 mark, and finishing 14th in the MVP voting. He represented the Royals in the All-Star Game four consecutive years, 1971-74. In the 1972 midsummer classic, Cookie's pinch-hit home run in the eighth inning gave the AL a one-run lead, although they would go on to lose the game in extra innings.

Royals broadcaster Matthews said, "He brought the element of experience, class, and big-league smarts to the team. That really helped the expansion team at the time."[4] The Royals rewarded Cookie, increasing his salary from $30,000 in 1971 to $67,500 in 1975. In 1973 Cookie achieved his career high in RBIs (69) and doubles (29).

Cookie turned 36 in 1976 and started losing playing time to a promising young star, Frank White. In 1976 Rojas batted only 132 times, hitting .242. Although he wanted to play, Cookie understood the Royals' reasoning. "They had to give Frank White a chance," he said.[5] In Cookie's final season, 1977, he played even less as White became an All-Star for the Royals. Rojas did achieve his goal of playing in the postseason in 1976 and '77, hitting .308 (4-for-13), in part-time play in losses to the New York Yankees in the American League Championship Series. Rojas summed up his playing career like this: "I came in with a reputation of not being able to hit and I developed a reputation as a winning player who would do anything and play anywhere to help you win, who could not only contribute with his bat and glove but with the experience he passed along to the other players. And the more I played, the more determined I became to remain in the game when I retired."[6]

Rojas signed with the Cubs ostensibly as a defensive replacement in 1978, but never appeared in a game. After he retired from playing, the Cubs hired him to coach and scout, and as of 2013 he's been involved in baseball ever since. In the 1980s he moved to the Angels as a coach and advance scout. In 1988 the Angels made him the third Cuban-born manager in baseball history. He didn't last the season, however. The team fired Rojas with about two weeks remaining in the season and their record at 75-79.

The Angels still valued Rojas's baseball knowledge, and offered him his former job of advance scout after the season, which he accepted. In 1992 the expansion Florida Marlins hired him as the third-base coach for their inaugural 1993 season. He then became Bobby Valentine's third-base coach on the Mets from 1997 through 2000, participating in his first World Series. In the 1999 playoffs he got into an argument with umpire Charlie Williams over a ball hit down the left-field line that Williams called foul and Rojas thought was fair. He was suspended for five games for bumping Williams. Bobby Valentine hung Rojas's jersey in the dugout until he rejoined the club.

Rojas went to the World Series as a coach with the Mets in 2000. The next two seasons he served as bench coach for the Toronto Blue Jays. In 2003 Cookie Rojas joined the Miami Marlins radio broadcast team as a Spanish-language broadcaster, a and color commentator. His son Victor was also a broadcaster, for the Anaheim Angels. Rojas broadcast for the Marlins until he retired in 2016 at the age of 77. He was still making appearances at baseball camps and informally coaching players in the summer of 2018.

In addition to Victor, Cookie, and his wife (the former Candy Rosa Boullon) had three other sons – Octavio Jr., Miguel, and Bobby, and a number of grandchildren.

Rojas is a member of the Philadelphia Phillies, Kansas City Royals, and Cuba's baseball Hall of Fame, and played the second most games at second base in Royals history (789), after Frank White (2,151). Rojas continued to be a popular and revered figure in the game. In 2012, when Marlins manager Ozzie Guillen made a statement saying he admired Fidel Castro, which upset and alienated some of the Marlins' Cuban-American fan base and threatened to harm ticket sales, Rojas did his best to repair the damage and stem controversy. As a Cuban, he acknowledged that Guillen's comments "opened a wound."[7] Then he added some words that probably summed up not only his feelings about Guillen's remarks, but also how he dealt with many of his own professional disappointments:

"Let's get over it and play ball."

Sources

In addition to the sources cited in the Notes, the author also consulted *Huffington Post*, *Los Angeles Times*, *Miami Herald*, *Naples Daily News* (Naples, Florida), *Philadelphia Inquirer*, Philly.com, and RoyalsReview.com, and the following:

Bjarkman, Peter, *A History of Cuban Baseball* (Jefferson, North Carolina: McFarland Publishers, 2007).

Golenbock, Peter, *Amazin': The Miraculous History of New York's Most Beloved Baseball Team* (New York: St. Martin's Press, 2002).

Palmer, Pete, and Gary Gillette. *The Baseball Encyclopedia* (New York: Barnes & Noble Books, 2004).

Rossi, John P., 1964 *Phillies: The Story of Baseball's Most Memorable Collapse* (Jefferson, North Carolina: McFarland Publishers, Inc., 2005).

Thorn, John, et. al. *Total Baseball* (Wilmington, Delaware: Sports Media Publ., 2004).

Westcott, Rich. *Phillies Essentials* (Chicago: Triumph Books. 2006).

Rojas, Cookie, "The Game I'll Never Forget," *Baseball Digest*, November 1979.

Soderholm-Difatte, Bryan, "Gene Mauch and the Collapse of the 1964 Phillies," Baseball Research Journal (The Society for American Baseball Research), Fall 2010.

Notes

1 Ross Newhan, "Crunch Time for Cookie," *Los Angeles Times*, May 23, 1988. articles.latimes.com/1988-05-23sports/2201

2 *Nevada* (Missouri) *Daily Mail*, September 22, 1976.

3 Denny Matthews and Matt Fulk, *Denny Matthews' Tales from the Royals Dugout* (Champaign, Illinois: Sports Publishing, 2004), 95.

4 Ibid.

5 *Nevada Daily Mail*, September 22, 1976.

6 *Los Angeles Times*, May 23, 1988.

7 Ap report on Yahoo Sports April 23, 2012. www.yahoo.com/news/guillen-returns-suspension-tuesday-184613421-mlb.html

BRET SABERHAGEN

BY ALAN COHEN

"Times of adversity make you stronger. And sometimes those times make you so tired that when your son says to you, 'Dad, I want to be there at the last game you pitch,' you tell him, 'Kid, you might have been there already.'"[1]

- Bret Saberhagen – August 8, 2001 one day after his last major-league game.

Success came early for Bret Saberhagen. In only his second major-league season, 1985, the 21-year-old won the Cy Young Award with a 20-6 record and was named the Most Valuable Player in the World Series. With his Kansas City team winless in its first two games against St. Louis, he pitched the Royals to a 6-1 win in Game Three and, with everything on the line, pitched an 11-0 shutout in Game Seven to give Kansas City its first World Championship in baseball. For his efforts in 1985, he had been paid $150,000. At season's end, he was eligible for arbitration and won a third award, as the arbiter's decision yielded him $925,000 for the 1986 season.

He was on top of the world and was rated by writer Thomas Boswell as one of the three top pitchers in baseball (along with Dwight Gooden and John Tudor) going into the 1986 season. Saberhagen was heard to say, "I'm just going to do everything the same as last year. Take it one step at a time. Can't do too much too fast. I just have a feeling of confidence. Every time you go out there you have to think you're going to win or you won't. If I give the best Bret Saberhagen can give, then I'll be happy with it."[2]

However, in what was to become a pattern, the Saberhagen of the even-numbered years did not match up with the Saberhagen of the odd-numbered years.

He was born on April 11, 1964 in Chicago Heights, Illinois, but his formative years were spent in California. Bret is an only child. His parents Bob and Linda divorced when he was only 9 years old and, by then, the Saberhagens had relocated to the West Coast. Linda took a position in the accounting department of a retail store. Bob remained in his son's life, relocating to Chatsworth, California, and taking a position with a computer leasing firm in Encino, California.[3] Bret starred as a sophomore at Grover Cleveland High School in Reseda, California, and was selected the MVP of the West Valley League in 1980. However, he had an off-year the following season, although he also played a good shortstop and was one of his team's leading batters with a .333 average. In his senior year, when the basketball season extended into early spring, he rushed himself into shape, developing tendonitis in his shoulder. Just after Easter, he resumed pitching and put together a 6-0 record in his team's regular season. On the eve of the high school playoffs, the major-league draft was held. At this point, most scouts felt that his velocity was still suspect and this reduced his chances at being a high draft pick. But Royals scout Guy Hansen had seen Bret as he was rounding into form and Kansas City used its 19th round pick in the 1982 draft to select Saberhagen.[4]

Bret then went on to go 3-0 in the playoffs. His second playoff win came in the semifinals when he relieved in the first inning with none out and his team behind by five runs. Over the course of the remaining innings, he struck out 12 as his Cavaliers team came from behind to win, 7-6.[5] In the championship game, won by Cleveland 13-0, he pitched a no-hitter at Dodger Stadium to bring his overall high school record to 24-2, under the tutelage of coach Leo Castro. Were it not for a first-inning error by the Cleveland second baseman, Saberhagen, who struck out eight and retired the final 20 batters in a row, would have had a perfect game. After the game, he commented, "I didn't start thinking of it (the no-hitter) until the fifth inning (of the seven-inning contest). When I went out in the last inning, I was going for it."[6] His no-hitter was the first ever in the 44-year history of the city championship, and the last inning had its challenges. The first two of the final inning outs came on outstanding fielding plays by the first baseman and right fielder, respectively. After the final out, on a failed bunt attempt, Saberhagen said, "This is the best feeling I've ever had in my life. The rest of the team helped out and were with me all the way."[7]

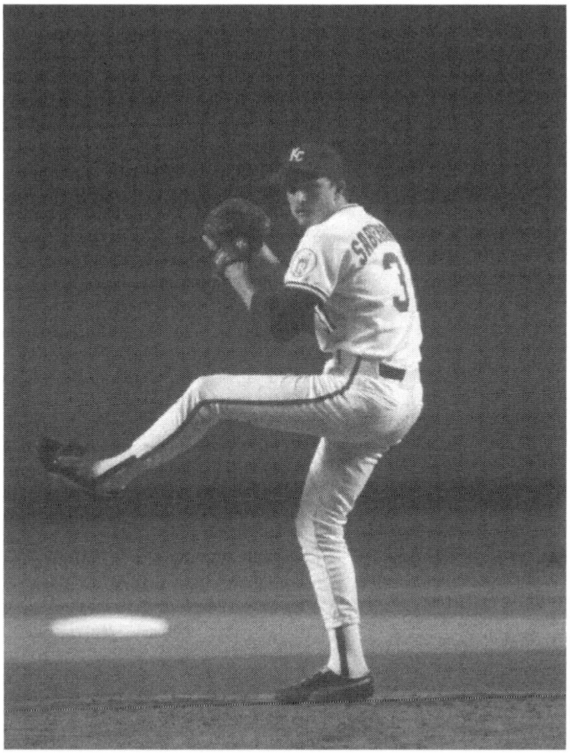

Shortly thereafter, he was named City Player of the Year, and he signed with the Royals. Bret married his high school sweetheart, Janeane Inglett, in 1984. Their first child, Drew William Saberhagen was born on October 26, 1985, eight hours before the start of Game Six of the 1985 World Series, and Saberhagen celebrated with a 2-0 win in Game Seven. They had two more children, daughter Brittany Nicole (born September 5, 1986) and son Daulton, before separating in 1992. Their divorce became final in 1994.

Saberhagen's minor-league career was brief. His first exposure to professional baseball was in the Florida Instructional League in the fall of 1982, where he pitched to a 7-2 record with a 2.36 ERA. He began the 1983 season with Fort Myers in the Class-A Florida State League, going 10-5 with a 2.30 ERA. He was named to the Southern Division team for the league's All-Star game. He was promoted before the end of the season to Class-AA Jacksonville in the Southern League where he won six of eight decisions and lowered his ERA to 2.91. In the Florida Instructional League that fall, he allowed only one earned run and walked only three batters in 47 innings.

He made it to the majors in 1984, becoming the youngest Royal ever, and got off to one of the rockier starts in major-league history. In his first appearances, he was called in from the bullpen to replace Paul Splittorff, who had been ineffective. The score was 4-2 in favor of the Yankees, and Butch Wynegar was standing on first base with only one out. Manager Dick Howser said, "Don't worry about the runner on first. He's not very fast and I don't think he'll be stealing. Just concentrate on the batter." To Saberhagen's surprise, catcher Don Slaught then called for a pitchout. However, Saberhagen was focused on the batter and threw a curve that crossed up his catcher and rolled to the back stop. The wild pitch advanced the runner to second base.[8] Saberhagen regained his composure and registered the next two outs. He went on to pitch 4 2/3 innings of scoreless ball that day, scattering three hits.

His first start came on April 19 against the Tigers, and resulted in his first career win. He went six innings, allowing only one run as the Royals defeated the Tigers 5-2, snapping a season opening nine-game winning streak by Detroit. He made a positive impression on Detroit pitching coach Roger Craig who said, "He's one of the best looking young pitchers I've seen. He's got as much poise as any young pitcher I've seen. I've seen guys with better stuff, but not many with as much poise."[9] In his first season, he went 10-11 with a 3.48 ERA.

In 1985, en route to a 20-6 record, becoming the fifth-youngest pitcher in major-league history to win 20 games, Saberhagen had a 2.87 ERA, third best in the league. He pitched with exceptional control and led the league with a 4.16 strikeout to walk ratio. He would go on to lead his league in that statistic two other times during his career, and his career ratio of 3.641 puts him at 18th place on the all-time list. He had gotten off to a slow start that year, but after May 12, he was 18-3 with a 2.54 ERA. His 20th win on September 30 put the Royals into a first-place tie with the Angels with six games left in the season. Five days later, they clinched the division and advanced to the League Championship Series. In the LCS, Saberhagen started Game Three but was knocked out of the box in the fifth inning. However, the Royals came back to win that game and Saberhagen was back on the mound in Game Seven. He bruised his thumb in the first inning and came out after three scoreless innings with the Royals leading 2-0. They went on to win the game and advanced to the World Series.

1986 was a disaster. As Peter Gammons wrong in *Sports Illustrated,* he went from "Cy Young to Die Young."[10] The season started out well for him. His second start and first decision of the season was at Fenway Park on the afternoon of April 16. It was not a typical Fenway game. Only 11,164 fans were in attendance, and if one dallied too long at the concession stand, he would miss an inning or two, as the game took only two hours and five minutes to complete. Steve Balboni gave Saberhagen all the support he would need, leading off the second inning with a home run. Although the Royals could only muster five hits off Red Sox pitcher Al Nipper, Saberhagen, working quickly, limited the Red Sox singles by Tony Armas and Don Baylor in the early innings. He retired the last 15 batters in succession for a 1-0 shutout win.

After that, things did not pan out well for Saberhagen. His overindulgence on the banquet circuit after winning the Cy Young Award caught up with him. He lost his next two starts in April before hurling his second and last shutout of the season, defeating Baltimore 5-0 at Kansas City on May 2. It was his only win of the month, and at the end of May, his record stood at 2-5. The season wore on and the losses continued to outnumber the wins. Arm troubles were such that he was on the shelf from August 10 through September 5, and his record for the season was 7-12 with an ERA of 4.15. Looking back on the season during a winter when the phone stopped ringing with invites, Saberhagen said, "I still don't have any answers. If I could figure out what I did wrong, I'd do something about it. It's tough to pinpoint. The big thing was the injuries. That didn't help for sure. I did so many different things (to improve); it's hard to say what went wrong. Who knows? I just know I was expected to win at least 20 last year and I was very, very upset at the year I had."[11]

His salary was cut to $740,000, but he went to spring training in 1987 determined to turn things around. After his first spring start he said, "I've been thing about this (his first spring start) for a long time, especially the last week. I was concerned because of what happened last year. But I know that if I can get through the spring like I did today, I should have nothing less than 17 wins this season."[12] But he came back with a good season in 1987 and was named the comeback-player-of-the year. He won each of his first six starts including a shutout of Cleveland on May 9 that brought his ERA down to 1.59. His 4-0 record in April garnered him Player of the Month honors. Over the course of the season, he won 18 games, losing only 10. He was second in the league in both shutouts (four) and complete games (15), and his ERA was 3.36. He was named to his first All-Star team, and started the game on July 14 in Oakland, pitching three shutout innings marred only by a double off the bat of Andre Dawson. The Royals in a hotly contested West Division race (10 games separated the seven clubs) finished in second place, two games behind the Detroit Tigers.

At the beginning of the 1988 season Saberhagen had signed a lucrative three-year deal with the Royals. At the conclusion of the negotiations he said, "It turned out excellent for both sides. Now I don't have to keep going through this every year. It was driving me crazy."[13] He received $1.1 million in 1988, $1.25 million in 1989, and $1.375 million in 1990.

He was healthy in 1988, but his record fell to 14-16 with high numbers in all the wrong places. He led the league giving up hits (271) and allowed 110 earned runs as his ERA rose to 3.80. The only injury he sustained that year was when he tripped in his hotel room in New York in May and required 16 stitches to close the gash on his forehead and another five to sew up the laceration beneath his one of his eyes. More embarrassed than bruised, he did not miss a start.[14] It was a year of streaks for Saberhagen. In June, he was 4-1 with a 2.68 ERA, and at the end of June his record for the season stood at 10-6. After that, he was winless in his next five starts, in which he was charged with four losses. Over the last three months of the season was 4-10 with an ERA of 4.27. Even if Saberhagen had had a good season, the Royals would not have improved much on their third-place finish as the Athletics romped to the AL West title leading the pack by 13 games.

Saberhagen's second Cy Young Award season followed in 1989 when he went 23-6 with a league-leading ERA of 2.16. The durable Saberhagen pitched in at least 250 innings for the third year in a row, hurling a league high 262 1/3 innings. His first start of the season on April 10 was a harbinger of things to come. During the course of the season, he only lost successive games on one occasion, and that was in April. After April, he was 21-4 with a 1.93 ERA. He was left off the All-Star team, although his record at the All-Star break was 8-4. After the All-Star break his record bordered on the sensational, as he was 15-2 with a 1.74 ERA. His control during the season was exceptional as he walked only 43 batters while striking out 193. Although he committed a career high four errors during the season, he was awarded the only Golden Glove of his career. The Royals were in contention for most of the season, and on September first were 1 1/2 games out of first place. They finished at 92-70, but the Oakland A's distanced themselves from the pack in the late going. The Royals finished in second place, seven games behind the division champions.

By now you have guessed it - 1990 was a disaster. However, largely due to his record in the prior season when he had been snubbed, he was chosen to pitch in the All-Star Game on July 10. He pitched scoreless ball in the fifth and six innings, retiring each of the six batters he faced, and was awarded the win when the American League broke a scoreless tie in the top of the seventh inning and went on to win 2-0. His record was 5-7 when he had surgery in late July to have two loose bone chip fragments removed from his right elbow. He returned to the lineup later in the season and his record for the season was 5-9 with a 3.27 ERA. Not only was the season a disaster for Saberhagen, but the Royals hit the skids as well finishing in sixth place. At the end of the season, general manager John Schuerholz resigned. He had assumed the role after the 1981 season and was at the helm during Kansas City's first World Championship in 1985.

Would Saberhagen return to his normal odd-year form in 1991? Not right away. He lost three of his first four decisions and after righting the ship winning each of his five decisions in May, his rollercoaster ride with the disabled list continued when he was placed on the D. L. in June due to tendonitis in his shoulder. He returned from the D. L. on July 13 and his record stood at 9-6 with a 3.10 ERA after he defeated the Yankees at Kansas City on August 21. He had recorded his first shutout of the season on August 2, defeating Cleveland 4-0.

Six weeks after coming off the DL he pitched the game of his career. On August 26, 1991, he pitched the first no-hitter of his major-league career, defeating the Chicago White Sox, 7-0. He received help from official scorer Del Black. Black had initially rule a line drive by Chicago's Dan Pasqua a double, much to the chagrin of the 25,164 fans in attendance. However, after viewing several replays, he ruled that left fielder Kirk Gibson had misplaced the fifth-inning line drive. When the H changed to E on the scoreboard, the crowd erupted and Saberhagen, who was looking towards home plate at the time, knew that his ho-hitter was still intact. "You can pretty well tell by the crowd's reaction. I heard the crowd and figured what happened." He settled down, got out of the inning and when Frank Thomas grounded to second base with two outs in the ninth inning, Saberhagen had the fourth no-hitter in Royals history. Reflecting on his achievement, he said, "This is terrific, but there will never be anything better than the (1985) World Series."[15]

For the season, his record was 13-8, and his record during eight seasons with the Royals was 110-78. He had been paid $2.95 million in 1991 and would be going into the second year of an expensive longterm contract with a "small-market" team. He was "on the block," and after the 1991 season, he was traded to the Mets along with Keith Miller and Bill Pecota for Kevin McReynolds and Gregg Jefferies.

His first two seasons in New York were disappointing. Not only was his record disappointing but there were once again health issues. His first two starts in 1992 were a collective nightmare. In neither game did he make it past the fifth inning, and he allowed seven earned runs in each of those games. He was 0-2 and his ERA was18.00. In his third start, he allowed five runs in the third inning against the Expos and then turned things around. The Mets came from behind and take him off the hook as he pitched three innings of scoreless ball before leaving the game in the for a pinch-hitter in the seventh inning.

He then became the Saberhagen the Mets were expecting. On April 23, he pitched nine shutout innings in a game that the Mets went on to win in the 13th inning, and on April 29 he spun a three-hit shutout as the Mets defeated Houston 1-0. His streak of consecutive scoreless innings ended at 26 in his next start when the Astros tallied a single run in the sixth inning. By then the Mets had a 5-0 lead and they went on to win 5-1, evening Saberhagen's record at 2-2.

However, he would only win one more game in 1992. In his first season with the Mets, he was only 3-5 as tendonitis, this time in his right index finger, resulted in his being on the shelf from May 16 through July 20 and starting only 15 games over the course of the season, the lowest number in his career to date.

In his new baseball home, he found new love after the breakup of his marriage to Janeane. They separated at the end of 1992, and he soon met his second wife, Lynn Critelli, who he married in 1996. They subsequently divorced.

After the 1992 season, he was awarded a three-year contract extension by the Mets, estimated at $15.4 million, but 1993 turned into a year of frustration. The Mets of 1993 were most definitely not the Mets of 1986, and by season's end their record was an unenviable 59-103. Frank Cashen and Davey Johnson were gone and the new regime of General Manager Joe McIlvane and manager Dallas Green were not receptive when it came to Saberhagen's clubhouse pranks. Two pranks during July 1993, one involving setting off a firecracker near reporters and another, involving spraying bleach, got him in trouble with management and in August a tirade in the clubhouse made headlines. Eventually he was suspended for the bleach spraying incident, and he missed time at the beginning of the 1994 season. He also was fined $15,384, a day's pay, which was contributed to the Eye Research Foundation of Central New York. For the season, Saberhagen was 7-7 with an ERA of 3.29 in 19 starts.

That season was abbreviated when he underwent surgery on August 3 for a tear in the medial collateral ligament in his right knee. The knee injury was sustained when he inadvertently stepped on a ball when he was jogging in the outfield. In September, he once again had elbow surgery.

In 1994, there were many changes. The National League went from two divisions to three and the Mets found themselves in a restructured Eastern Division with the Phillies, Expos, Braves, and Marlins. And the biggest change was Bret Saberhagen who reverted to his former self. He was still the prankster, but his actions showed a newfound maturity. "I've tried to change my habits around the clubhouse, not screw around so much. That's tough for me to do, because I've always been a practical joker. But now before I do something, I think of the ramifications."[16] In the early part of the season, Saberhagen was receiving good run support and through June 25, his record was7-4 with a 3.58 ERA. After that, it was lights out. He won each of his seven decisions and registered a 1.51 ERA in his final nine starts. During this time, he walked only five batters in 71 2/3 innings, and his strikeout to walk ratio was an eye-popping 11.00. For the season, which ended for him and everyone else in August, he was 14-4 with a 2.74 ERA with only 13 walks in 177 1/3 innings. He was third in the Cy Young Award voting and was named to his third All-Star team. This time around, he did not pitch as the game went into extra innings. He and José Rijo were the only pitchers left in the National League bullpen when the NL pushed across a run to win the game in the 10th inning. Oddly enough he was not named to the All-Star team in either of his Cy Young Award seasons.

In 1994, he also appeared in a movie. *The Scout* featured Brendan Fraser and Albert Brooks. Brooks, the scout, hired Saberhagen, playing himself, to throw pitches to Fraser, who played a baseball prospect in the film.

The 1995 Mets went from bad to worse and by August of that year, Saberhagen was 5-5 on a team that was going nowhere. He and his big money contract were gone from New York on August 1 as he was traded along with Dave Swanson to the Colorado Rockies for Arnie Gooch and Juan Acevedo. With Colorado, he was 2-1 in nine starts and spent two weeks on the shelf from August 27 through September 9.

He missed the entire 1996 season, undergoing surgery on May 28 that involved a titanium anchor being drilled into the bone of his right shoulder to hold together his rotator cuff. He signed a minor-league contract with the Boston Red Sox for the 1997 season. He pitched his way back to the majors and was 0-1 with a 6.58 ERA in 26 innings at the end of the 1997 season. He returned to the Red Sox in 1998.

And return he did. However, the durability wouldn't be there. The man who had hurled 76 complete games in his first 12 major-league seasons would go no further than the seventh inning in any of his 31 starts. He put together a 15-8 record with a 3.96 ERA. The Red Sox finished in second place with a 92-70 record, and advanced to the Division Series against the Cleveland Indians.

Saberhagen pitched the third game of the series and allowed three runs on only four hits in his seven innings of work, walking one and striking out seven. He took a no-hitter into the fifth inning when Jim Thome led off the inning with a homer for Cleveland's first run of the game. It tied the score at 1-1. The next two Cleveland hits were also solo home runs — a sixth-inning blast by Kenny Lofton and a seventh-inning shot by Manny Ramirez. The Red Sox were unable to come from behind, losing 4-3, and Saberhagen was tagged with the loss. It was Saberhagen's last appearance in 1998. Cleveland won the best-of-five series in four games.

His success in 1998 led to his being awarded the Tony Conigliaro Award by the Boston chapter of the Baseball Writers' Association of America for overcoming adversity.

In 1999, Saberhagen was unable to duplicate the success of the prior season, but he wasn't far off, going 10-6 and cutting his ERA to 2.95. He only started 22 games and paid three visits to the disabled list. The Red Sox once again finished second in the AL East and advanced to postseason play. Saberhagen started the second game of the Division Series against the Indians and had a rare bad day. His undoing came in the third inning and was initiated when Saberhagen's control abandoned him. He walked two batters and, with one out, gave up a triple to Omar Vizquel and a double to Roberto Alomar. Harold Baines, the eighth batter of the inning, came up with two on and two out and his three-run homer knocked Saberhagen out of the game. Cleveland won the game to take a 2-0 lead in the series, but the booming Boston bats won the next two games to force Game Five.

Saberhagen, given a chance to redeem himself, was once again ineffective. Given a two-run lead, he gave up three runs in the first inning and before an out was recorded in the second inning yielded two more. The knockout blow was a home run off the bat of Travis Fryman. But the booming Boston bats, which had generated 32 runs in Games Three and Four, were not about to be silenced. The Sox came back to win Game Five, 12-8, and it was on to the League Championship Series against the Yankees. The Yankees won two of the first three games and in Game Four, Saberhagen took the mound against

Andy Pettitte. Saberhagen was effective in his six innings, allowing three runs, only one of which (a Darryl Strawberry homer) was earned. However, he left the game on the wrong end of a 3-2 score. The Yankees broke the game open with six ninth-inning runs to take a commanding 3-1 lead in the series. The Red Sox were eliminated in five games.

But by 2000 Saberhagen was 36 years old and the pain had returned to his shoulder, causing him to miss the entire 2000 major-league season. He rehabbed that year, appearing in seven minor-league games, and also rehabbed in five games in 2001, returning to the mound at Fenway on July 27, 2001. He pitched six innings in a 9-5 defeat of the White Sox. It was his last major-league win. He followed up this outing with two losses and was placed on the disabled list one last time. He announced his retirement at the end of the 2001 season.

After baseball, Saberhagen retired to California, where he coached son Drew at Calabasas High School. He also did some film work. With Kevin Costner and former players Johnny Bench and George Brett, he appeared in Field of Dreams Roundtable in 2004, and he appeared as himself in the 2009 film, *The Open Road* with Justin Timberlake and Ted Danson.

In 2004, he established the Bret Saberhagen Make a Difference Foundation to help children fighting diabetes and other illnesses. In 2005, he was inducted into the Kansas City Royals Hall of Fame.

Sources

In addition to the sources listed in the Notes, Baseball-Reference.com and the articles listed below were used by the author.

Antonen, Mel, "Unique Surgery Saves Saberhagen's Shoulder, Career," *USA Today*, April 29, 1998: 1C.

Attner, Paul. "Common Work Habits Mark Return to Royalty: Saberhagen Has His head, Body Back into the Game," *The Sporting News*, May 25, 1987: 4.

Durso, Joseph, "Saberhagen is Near Perfect in Cy Young Voting," *New York Times*, November 16, 1989.

Frey, Jennifer, "Saberhagen Sounds Off at Mets' Management," *New York Times* June 22, 1994.

Frey, Jennifer, "The Joke's Up for Bret Saberhagen," *New York Times* February 27, 1994.

Kravitz, Bob, "Saberhagen Decision Offers No Guarantees," *Rocky Mountain News*, January 18, 1996: 2B.

Martinez, Michael, "Saberhagen Still the Same Old Kid: '85 Success Has Not Led to '86 Excess," *New York Times News Service*, February 23, 1986.

Moran, Malcolm, "On a Rainy Day, Saberhagen Throws a Tantrum," *New York Times*, August 7, 1993: 31.

Nightengale, Bob, "Saberhagen Signs for 3 Years, Riches," *The Sporting News*, February 22, 1988.

Nightingale, Dave, "Even in Odd Year, Saberhagen's No. 1," *The Sporting News*, July 9, 1990: 8.

Ocker, Sheldon, "Royals Get Breaks to Slip by Indians and Post 5-4 Win," *Akron Beacon-Journal*, May 4, 1987: D4.

Notes

1 Gordon Edes, "Towel May End Up as His Next Throw," *Boston Globe*, August 9, 2001

2 Thomas Boswell. *The Heart of the Order* (New York, Doubleday, 1989), 278.

3 Lorenzo Benet. "Bret's Team – From the time he was 7, Baseball was Bret Saberhagen's Dream – His Parents helped make it Come True," *Daily News* (Los Angeles, California), November 6, 1985.

4 Vincent Bonsignore, *Daily News* (Los Angeles, California), May 7, 2002.

5 Joe Koenig, "Palisades Reaches the City Final Against Cleveland," *Los Angeles Times*, June 11, 1982: E15.

6 Randy Sparage, "Saberhagen's No Hitter Decides It," *Los Angeles Times*, June 15, 1982: D4.

7 Paul Vercammen, "Cavaliers Cradle City Baseball Crown After Hoping for a Lot Less," *Los Angeles Times*, June 17, 1982: V4

8 Bruce Nash and Allan Zullo, *The Baseball Hall of Shame 4* (New York, Simon and Schuster, 1990), 76-77.

9 "K. C. Rookie 1st to Tame Tigers," *Chicago Tribune*, April 20, 1984: C5

10 Peter Gammons, "Return of the Royal Nonesuch," *Sports Illustrated*, June 8, 1987.

11 Bob Nightengale, "Homework by Saberhagen gives him new Hope for 1987," Kansas City Times, January 14, 1987: 1-B.

12 Bob Nightengale, "Saberhagen Blots Out Past, Follows Plan in Spring Debut," *Kansas City Times*, March 11, 1987: E-1.

13 Bob Nightengale. *The Sporting News*, February 22, 1988.

14 *The Sporting News*, May 9, 1988: 17.

15 *The Pentagraph* (Bloomington, Illinois), August 27, 1991: B1.

16 *New York Post*, May 13, 1994.

KEVIN SEITZER

BY PAUL HOFMANN

During a late season call-up in 1986, Kevin Seitzer burst upon the American League looking like the next Kansas City Royals star, the heir-apparent to future Hall of Famer George Brett at third. He arrived with his trademark hunched-over batting stance that produced sensational batting averages in the minor leagues and a brash attitude that shaped his aggressive approach at the plate. A pure hitter who had the ability to spray the ball to all fields and draw walks, Seitzer never fulfilled the promise of super-stardom his first few seasons in the big leagues suggested might have been in the offing.

A wizard with the bat during his early years with the Royals, he was average or below-average in many other aspects of the game – modest power, slow-footed, and a defensive liability.[1] Known for a prickly personality, fiery temper, and demeanor that came off as abrasive in the clubhouse, Seitzer at times found himself at odds with teammates and managers alike.

Kevin Lee Seitzer was born in Springfield, Illinois, on March 26, 1962. He was the oldest child of three born to Clifford and Carolyn Seitzer. Cliff, a jack of all trades, worked as a millwright for the Caterpillar Company in East Peoria, Illinois, for 40 years. Carolyn was a secretary at the Logan County Soil and Water Conservation District in nearby Lincoln.[2]

Kevin grew up in Middletown, Illinois, a village in Logan County in the central part of the state with a population of about 500. He attended New Holland-Middletown elementary, middle, and high schools and grew up playing sports of all kinds on the Middletown playgrounds. He moved up the ranks of Junior League, Little League, and Pony League and was often coached by his father, Cliff, whom Seitzer called his "best coach."[3] At New Holland-Middletown High School, Kevin starred on the baseball diamond and basketball court. According to Seitzer, basketball was his first love.[4] On the hardwood he averaged 20 points per game and shot 52 percent from the field.[5]

Seitzer began drawing the attention of college coaches during his sophomore year when he set four records as a member of the Lincoln American Legion baseball team. He said his American Legion experience was critical in his development and that without taking a step-by-step approach, he might not have achieved the success he did. In Legion ball, "I got to play much better competition than I did in high school," Seitzer said. "What was important about Legion baseball is until you play at that high level, you really aren't going to develop."[6]

After his junior year, the Seitzer family moved to Lincoln, Illinois, a city 30 miles northeast of Springfield. The city was named for and by Abraham Lincoln before he became president.[7] In addition to Seitzer, the town of fewer than 15,000 inhabitants produced major leaguers Dick Reichle, Bill Sampen, Emil Verban, and Dennis Werth. Seitzer attended Lincoln Community High School during his senior year and was an All-Conference and All-State pitcher. He was the sixth man on the school's basketball team that finished in fourth place in the 1980 Class-AA Illinois High School Association basketball tournament. An all-around athlete, he ran track as well.

Seitzer drew some college interest as both a baseball and basketball player, but was not a deemed a blue-chip recruit. He was recruited by Hawaii, Illinois State, and Eastern Illinois University. Seitzer accepted a partial scholarship offer from EIU. "I liked the campus because it's small and easy to get around," he said. "And Coach (Tom) McDevitt treated me very well when I was down there visiting."[8]

Seitzer enjoyed a standout baseball career at EIU. A member of the Panthers' 1981 NCAA Division II runner-up team, he is the school's only baseball player to bat over .400 for three consecutive years (1981-83). He left EIU with a career batting average of .418 and as of 2018 ranked in the top five in career hits, doubles, triples, runs scored, and RBIs.[9] Seitzer was elected to the EIU Athletics Hall of Fame in 1992 and his number-2 jersey was retired by the Panthers in 2012.[10] Seitzer earned a degree in Industrial Electronics in 1985.

Seitzer credited Panthers coach McDevitt for making him a complete player and transforming his game. "He pretty much taught me how to hit to the opposite field," said Seitzer. "I was a straight pull hitter. And he was annually detailed about how to play the game the right way. We worked on cutoffs, relays, bunt defenses, first-and-third situations. But he would take it to the nth degree."[11]

Seitzer decided to forgo his final season of eligibility at EIU. In June of 1983 he was selected by the Royals in the 11th round of the free-agent draft and was assigned to the Butte (Montana) Copper Kings of the rookie Pioneer League. Seitzer immediately showed what kind of player he could be, hitting .345. His performance earned him a promotion for the 1984 season. In 141 games with the Charleston Royals of the Class-A Sally League, Seitzer batted .297, the only minor-league season he failed to hit .300, with 8 home runs and 79 RBIs. He also demonstrated patience at the plate, compiling a team-leading 118 walks.

Seitzer started the 1985 season with the Fort Myers Royals of the Class-A Florida State League. In 90 games he hit .314 and drew a team-leading 85 walks before being promoted to the Memphis Chicks of the Double-A Southern League. He had no difficulty hitting Double-A pitching and finished with a .348 average. He started the 1986 season in Memphis before being promoted to the Omaha Royals of the Triple-A American Association. In 129 games with the Royals' top farm club he hit .319 with a team-leading 13 home runs and 74 RBIs. The effort earned him a call-up to the Royals when Omaha's season ended.

Seitzer made his major-league debut on September 3, 1986, against the Chicago White Sox at Royals Stadium. He started the game in left field before moving to third base in the top of the 10th inning. With the Royals trailing the White Sox 1-0, he collected his first major-league hit with a leadoff single off right-hander Joe Cowley in the top of the ninth inning. He scored the game's tying run when Steve Balboni doubled to center field. Seitzer capped off his 2-for-5 major-league debut with a 10th-inning walk-off single that scored Willie Wilson to give the Royals a 2-1 victory.

Looking back on his first day in the majors, Seitzer remembered how he was given a locker next to Royals closer Dan Quisenberry: "I was scared to death. I had never been on the 40-man roster before, so I wasn't in big-league camp in spring training, and I didn't really know anybody. I was petrified, but if it wasn't for Quiz, I don't know if I would have been able to do what I did. He talked to me and calmed me down."[12]

Two and a half weeks later, on September 21, Seitzer belted his first major-league home run, off Seattle Mariners right-hander Mike Brown. The two-run shot to left center in the top of the eighth inning came in the Royals' 8-1 shellacking of the Mariners in the Kingdome. In his 28 games with the Royals in 1986, Seitzer finished with a .323 batting average, 2 home runs, and 11 RBIs.

In 1987 the right-handed-hitting Seitzer picked up right where he left off the previous year. Breaking camp as the Royals' starting first baseman, Seitzer got off to a fast start, collecting nine hits in the team's first four games and finishing April with a .382 batting average. In mid-May he and Brett swapped positions in an effort to keep the aging star's bat in the lineup. The defensive move had little impact on Seitzer at the plate. His average remained over .300 for the entire season except for one day in June when it dipped to .299. He ended the first half of the season at .305 and earned a trip to the All-Star Game in Oakland.

Seitzer replaced Wade Boggs at third in the sixth inning of the midsummer classic. Facing right-hander Rick Reuschel and leading off the bottom of the eighth inning, he hit a pop fly to shallow center that was caught by Phillies second baseman Juan Samuel. His second plate appearance, in the bottom of the 10th, resulted in a long fly ball to center field off of right-hander Lee Smith. After the American League All-Stars fell behind by two runs in the top of the 13th, Seitzer was walked by Mets left-hander Sid Fernandez to lead off the bottom of the inning. With two outs Dave Winfield grounded to third, forcing Seitzer at second to end the game, a 2-0 National League victory.

Seitzer's performance after the All-Star Game was even more impressive. He batted.343 with 11 home runs and 45 RBIs. On August 2 he was 6-for-6 (including two home runs and seven RBIs) in a 13-5 victory over the Boston Red Sox at Royals Stadium. He wrapped up the year with a season-high 12-game hitting streak. Defensively, he was raw and led AL third basemen with 22 errors.

Although he finished the season with a .323 average and compiled a league-leading 207 hits, the Royals third baseman was overshadowed by another Royals rookie, left fielder Bo Jackson. However, it was Seitzer who finished second in the American League Rookie of the Year balloting to the Oakland Athletics' Mark McGwire, who belted a league-leading 49 home runs. On the surface, it appeared that things couldn't have been going better for the Royals rookie. However, things are not always as they appear.

While he enjoyed a career year in 1987, Seitzer struggled off the field. He became so despondent during his first full year with the Royals that he contemplated suicide. "I never loaded a gun and put it to my head, but there were times I thought I'd be better off dead than to continue like this," he said. "The only time I was happy was when I was on the baseball field, between the lines, in war. As soon as it was over, I started to drink."[13]

While his emotional struggles and drinking problem may not have been evident in his play, it certainly affected his marriage to his first wife, Lisa Seitzer. "I never hit my wife, but I'd have her up against the wall, drawing back on her," Seitzer said. "She was petrified. I'd back her into a corner, raging, like I was going to kill her."[14] On the field, all appeared well. Seitzer enjoyed another fine season at the plate in 1988. In 149 games the Royals third baseman hit .304 with 5 home runs and 60 RBIs. Defensively, he continued to struggle and made a league-leading 26 errors at third.

By the end of the 1988 season, separation from Lisa appeared inevitable.[15] However, during the offseason the Seitzers attended the Pro Athletes Outreach Conference in Orlando, Florida. Seitzer wasn't aware it was a Christian gathering but when he learned the true purpose of the conference, his interest was piqued. Seitzer would find relief at the conference and on November 2, 1988, he became a born-again Christian, a turn of fate that possibly saved his life.[16]

Seitzer played in a team-high 160 games for the Royals in 1989. While his offensive production dropped (he hit .281 with 4 home runs and 48 RBIs), he did draw 102 walks and finished with a .387 on-base percentage. He also improved defensively and cut his errors at third base down to 20. While he was far from winning a Gold Glove Award, he did improve his fielding percentage to a respectable .950, which was slightly higher than the .943 fielding percentage for all AL third baseman that season.

After three full seasons in the majors, Seitzer was now arbitration-eligible. On January 26, 1990, he and the Royals avoided arbitration and agreed to a one-year contract worth $1,001,250, a significant increase over the $340,000 he earned the previous season.[17] Seitzer led the Royals in 1990 with 158 games played, 622 at-bats, 91 runs scored, and 67 walks while batting .275 with 6 home runs and 38 RBIs. Notably, his OBP dipped to .346.

Seitzer was again arbitration-eligible after the 1990 season. Contract talks turned a bit contentious when he sought a raise to $1.8 million while the Royals countered with $1.25 million. The two sides again avoided arbitration and settled on a two-year contract worth $1.625 million per year.[18]

Seitzer struggled mightily to begin the 1991 season. He was hitting an anemic .182 on April 26, when he broke a hamate bone in his hand after being plunked by a pitch by Red Sox right-hander Greg Harris. The injury caused Seitzer to miss 30 games. When he returned on May 31, he continued to struggle at the plate. It wasn't until June 17 that he raised his average above .200 for the remainder of the season.

To start the second half of the season, new Royals manager Hal McRae decided to shake things up, benching Seitzer, shortstop Kurt Stillwell, and first baseman Jim Eisenreich in favor of reserves Bill Pecota, David Howard, and Warren Cromartie. McRae wanted to emphasize defense, and Seitzer's erratic arm was no fit, particularly when he was no longer hitting as he did in 1986 through 1988. Referring specifically to the benching of Seitzer and Stillwell, McRae said the moves were made to "basically see if he can catch the ball."[19] The move did not sit well with Seitzer, who testily responded by saying, "All I can do is play as hard as I can. I'll never be Brooks Robinson."[20] For the remainder of the season, Seitzer was relegated to spot appearances at third and pinch-hitting. He played in only 85 games and finished the year with a (then) career-low .265 average, with one home run and 25 RBIs.

At the end of his disappointing season, Seitzer revealed he was having knee problems and on October 1 had arthroscopic surgery on both knees to address the thickening of the joint lining under each kneecap. "What's hard on me was that I was supposedly benched because my range and speed were no good," he said. "I couldn't say anything because I didn't want teams to know about it and bunting on me, and there was a possibility that I could be traded. Now I'm happy I wasn't traded because I couldn't have played for anybody anyway."[21]

During the offseason the Royals made a blockbuster five-player trade with the New York Mets, shipping ace pitcher Bret Saberhagen and Pecota to the Mets for third baseman Gregg Jefferies, outfielder Kevin McReynolds, and utilityman Keith Miller. It was clear that Seitzer was no longer in the Royals' future plans.

Seitzer's offensive decline was puzzling. He did not attribute it to injury. "Mentally, emotionally, I put a lot of pressure on myself," Seitzer said. "And when my goals and expectations weren't met, you start trying harder, pressing more."[22]

On March 26, 1992, Seitzer's 30th birthday, he was released by the Royals. The club decided that $1.625 million was too much to pay a utility infielder, and by releasing him before the start of the season they were obligated only to give him $401,785 in termination pay.[23] After clearing waivers, Seitzer signed a one-year contract for the major-league minimum salary of $109,000 with the Milwaukee Brewers, who were looking for a third baseman to fill the void created by the trade of Gary Sheffield to San Diego Padres.[24]

In 148 games with the Brewers, Seitzer hit .270 with 5 home runs and 71 RBIs, his highest RBI total since his rookie year in 1987. Defensively, he had his best season ever at third base. In 146 games at the hot corner, Seitzer made only 12 errors and had a fielding percentage of .969. It was a solid bounce-back season for a guy less than a year removed from double knee surgery. At the end of the year, he opted for free agency.

On February 1, 1993, Seitzer agreed to a nonguaranteed one-year contract for with the Oakland A's for the major-league minimum $109,000. The contract called for called Seitzer to be paid $600,000 if he made the Opening Day roster. In essence, Seitzer was betting on himself. He won the bet, starting the season as the A's everyday third baseman. But a May slump relegated him to a utility role. He was hitting .255 with 4 home runs and 27 RBIs when he the A's designated him for assignment on July 16. When he refused to go to the minors, the A's released him. It was the second time in 16 months that Seitzer had been released.

A standout pitcher in high school, Seitzer made his only major-league pitching appearance on May 2, 1993. With the Athletics trailing the Indians 10-2, Seitzer came in from third base to pitch to Carlos Martinez in the bottom of the eighth inning. The right-handed-throwing third baseman ended the inning when the Indians' designated hitter was caught looking at strike three.

Three days after he was released by the Athletics, Seitzer re-signed with the Brewers and began resurrecting his career. He returned in a utility and pinch-hitting role, but by late August he was once again the team's everyday third baseman. In 47 games with the Brewers, he batted .290 with 7 home runs and 30 RBIs.

During the offseason, Seitzer and the Brewers agreed to a two-year, $1.3 million contract. Primarily playing third base to start the 1994 season, Seitzer got off to a hot start. He was batting .324 with 3 home runs and 17 RBIs when a torn left hamstring landed him on the disabled list. After missing five weeks, he returned to hit safely in his first 13 games back. He was enjoying his best season since his rookie year, hitting .314 with 5 home runs and 49 RBIs when the season abruptly ended after the players struck.

In 1995 Seitzer proved that his resurgence at the plate was not a fluke. The right-handed-hitting corner infielder was hitting .345 as the month of June closed and earned a second trip to the All-Star Game. Just as he had in 1987, he replaced Boggs at third. Pinch-hitting for Boggs in the bottom of the seventh inning, Seitzer was retired on a fly ball to right by Expos rookie left-hander Carlos Perez. Chicago Cubs closer Randy Myers retired Seitzer on a groundball to second in his only other plate appearance of the game. Having been released twice, Seitzer took amazing pride in making it back to the All-Star Game.

Seitzer continued to swing a consistent bat for the remainder of the 1995 season. He finished the year with a .311 average, 5 home runs and 69 RBIs. For his efforts he was rewarded with a $1 million contract with a player option of $1.2 million for the 1996 season. The pact turned out to be a good investment for the team. In 132 games with the Brewers in 1996, Seitzer hit .316 with 12 home runs, 62 RBIs, and a .406 OBP. However, the Brewers were going nowhere in the AL Central and needed to begin thinking about the future.

On August 31, 1996, the Brewers traded Seitzer to the Cleveland Indians for outfielder Jeromy Burnitz. Seitzer, who was resigned to the fact that he would retire without playing in the postseason, was excited to have the opportunity to the join the AL East-leading Indians. Used primarily as a designated hitter and spot starter at first base to spell Jim Thome, a rejuvenated Seitzer responded by hitting .386 in 22 games for the Tribe. He started all four games of the ALDS against the Baltimore Orioles (three as a designated hitter and one at first base). He hit .294 with four RBIs as the Indians dropped the series, three games to one.

Having finally had a taste of postseason play and coming up short of his goal of winning the World Series, Seitzer returned to the Indians in 1997 as a part-time designated hitter, corner infielder, and pinch-hitter. In 64 games he hit .268 with 2 home runs and 24 RBIs as the Indians won the AL Central Division title with an 86-75 record. Seitzer and his teammates would get one more chance to capture a World Series title.

The Indians beat the New York Yankees three games to two in the ALDS. (Seitzer started and played first base in the Indians' 6-1 Game Three loss, going 0-for-4 against Yankees left-hander David Wells.) The Indians advanced to the ALCS and faced the Baltimore Orioles. Seitzer got into four games during the Series. He was the starting first baseman in Game Two and had pinch-hitting appearances in games Three, Four, and Five. He went 0-for-4 with a walk and a sacrifice in six plate appearances as the Indians beat the Orioles, four games to two. The Indians winning the pennant was one of Seitzer's best memories in baseball. "That was probably my greatest moment," he said in 2018. "I had worked my whole career to go the World Series."[25]

The Indians met the Florida Marlins in the World Series. Seitzer finally realized his goal to play in the World Series when he pinch-hit for pitcher Paul Assenmacher in the top of the ninth inning of Game Six. With runners on first and third with two down and the Indians leading 4-1, Seitzer grounded out to Marlins third baseman Bobby Bonilla to end the inning. It was Seitzer's only appearance in the Series, which the Indians lost in seven games. Reflecting on coming so close to winning a World Series ring, Seitzer said, "You know the satisfaction of being able to say you've been there and went seven games. That was pretty cool."[26]

After the World Series, Seitzer retired. He finished his 12-year major-league career with a .295 batting average, 74 home runs, and 613 RBIs. While his career numbers may pale in comparison to what was expected after his rookie season of 1987, Seitzer earned the reputation of being one of the best situational hitters in baseball. His ability to make consistent contact and the patience he demonstrated at the plate prepared him well for a second major-league career as a hitting coach.

Seitzer was a hitting coach for a number of major-league teams. In October of 2006 he was named hitting coach for the Arizona Diamondbacks. Halfway into his first season, he was fired and replaced by Rick Schu. In 2009 he returned to Kansas City and was the Royals' hitting coach for four seasons. In 2014 Seitzer was the hitting coach for the Toronto Blue Jays. He was hired as the Atlanta Braves hitting coach after the season.

Under Seitzer's guidance, the Braves' team batting average improved in each of his first three seasons. In 2018, the club batted .257, second highest in the National League. Preferring to remain humble and unwilling to take credit for any players' successes, Seitzer pointed to his success and struggles as a player as great preparation for his current role. "Guys who never struggle in their career have a hard time relating to those who are struggling," he said. "Those who never enjoyed success don't know what it takes to maintain it. I've been fortunate that I've experienced both."[27]

For youngsters, Seitzer and former Royals teammate Mike Macfarlane opened a hitting facility in Kansas City called Mac-N-Seitz Baseball and Softball.[28]

As of 2018, Seitzer and his wife, Beth, resided in Leawood, Kansas, where they liked to "hang out and watch movies together."[29] Together they raised four sons, Tyler, Brandon, Nick, and Cameron. His stepson, Nick Graffeo, was drafted as a pitcher by the Royals in the 38th round of the 2010 Amateur Draft. He was released by the Royals in the spring of 2013. Cameron was drafted as a corner infielder and outfielder in 11th round of the 2011 Amateur Draft by the Tampa Bay Rays. In 2017 he joined the Chicago White Sox organization and in 2018 made the transition to pitcher.

Sources

In addition to the sources cited in the Notes, the author also relied on baseball-reference.com and Retrosheet.org.

Notes

1 Max Rieper, "The 100 Greatest Royals of All-Time – number 19 Kevin Seitzer." royalsreview.com/royals-history-trivia/2016/11/11/12662244/the-100-greatest-royals-of-all-time – 19-kevin-seitzer.

2 Kevin Seizer, personal correspondence, October 8, 2018.

3 Bill Flick, "Seitzer Enjoys Life of Balls, Hits and Strikes," *The Pantagraph* (Bloomington, Illinois), June 6, 1980: 18.

4 Kevin Seitzer, personal correspondence.

5 Bill Flick.

6 Jason Blasco, "A Pathway to Success," *The Courier* (Lincoln, Ilinois), June 12, 2013. lincolncourier.com/x1002423462/A-pathway-to-success.

7 Abraham Lincoln practiced law in Lincoln, Illinois, from 1847 to 1859.

8 Bill Flick.

9 Hall of Fame: Kevin Seitzer. eiu.touchpros.com/hallofFame.asp?sectionName=hof&sectionID=4&letterID=S

10 Ibid.

11 Missouri Sports Hall of Fame Inductee: Kevin Seitzer. Mosportshalloffame.com/inductees/kevin-seitzer/.

12 Ibid.

13 Reality is Sobering for Brewers' Seitzer. washingtonpost.com/archive/sports/1995/07/04/reality-is-sobering-for-brewers-seitzer/ae288c22-226b-46ba-ac5f-9024f4b750e4/?noredirect=on&utm_term=.4da54b87f487.

14 Ibid.

15 The 20-year marriage ended in divorce.

16 Kevin Seitzer, personal correspondence.

17 "Baseball," *Springfield* (Missouri) *News-Leader*, January 27, 1990: 22.

18 "Royals, Seitzer Agree on One-Year, $1,625,000 Pact," *Springfield News-Leader*, February 16, 1991: 17.

19 Rick Hummel, "Mets Are Making a Run, Even Without Coleman," *St. Louis Post-Dispatch*, July 14, 1991: 61.

20 Ibid.

21 Rick Hummel, "Free Agent Flops Are a Chewy Problem," *St. Louis Post-Dispatch*, September 15, 1991: 46.

22 Kevin Seitzer, personal correspondence.

23 "Kansas City Releases Seitzer," *Springfield News-Leader*, March 27, 1992: 45.

24 Seitzer, Bell Are the New Kids on the Block: Brewers Sign Former Royal for Minimum," *Springfield News-Leader*, April 1, 1992: 31.

25 Kevin Seitzer, personal correspondence.

26 Ibid.

27 Ibid.

28 macnseitz.com/.

29 Kevin Seitzer, personal correspondence.

PAUL SPLITTORFF

BY JOHN DIFONZO

Some would call Paul Splittorff the "original Royal" because he was selected in Kansas City's first amateur draft, started in the franchise's first game and the first game at Kaufman Stadium, pitched for 15 seasons, and served as a broadcaster for 24 years. The bespectacled blond left-hander with the high leg kick appeared to squint on the mound, giving the impression that he had trouble seeing the catcher's signs, and this proved disconcerting for hitters. Splittorff did not possess an overpowering fastball, instead relying on finesse, a variety of pitches, and control to get batters out. He remains the team's all-time leader in wins.

Splittorff was intelligent and iron-willed, had a strong work ethic, and prepared meticulously for each start. He was a reliable workhorse who took the mound every fifth day. From 1972 to 1980, he averaged almost 30 starts, 217 innings pitched, and an ERA between 3.13 and 4.24. Never flamboyant, Splittorff was unassuming and preferred to fly under the radar. Splittorff was prepared, gave 100 percent, and was good enough to keep his team in games. He was a student of the game, studied hitters, and paid attention to the game when he wasn't playing in the days before videotape. He had remarkable intelligence, former managers and coaches marveling at his ability to attack hitters' weaknesses.

Splittorff was known as a Yankee killer because of his 2-0 record and 2.68 ERA in six playoff appearances. A college graduate who majored in business, Splittorff dabbled in real estate, bought rental property and sold rookie George Brett his home in Blue Springs, Missouri.

In his second career, Splittorff through his intelligence and hard work, became an insightful, respected broadcaster. He was also a respected member of the community, known for his charitable work. He was named Heart Fund chairman for its annual Blue Springs drive.

Paul William "Splitt" Splittorff was born on October 8, 1946, in Evansville, Indiana, to Paul Splittorff Sr., a salesman, and Bettye (Reckner) Splittorff, who were of German descent and met while attending Indiana University. The couple raised three children, Louis, Anne, and Paul Jr. Paul Sr.'s job required him to travel throughout the Midwest, and he was able to watch his son pitch at many American League ballparks. "He was very into sports and spent a lot of time with me as a kid," said the pitcher. "He encouraged me to me to play sports, not just baseball, basketball and football also. Maybe I'm in baseball because that's the one thing he could not do. He played basketball and football in high school and could shoot the eyes out of a basket, but he liked baseball more than any other sport. I guess he was just a sports nut."[1] Bettye was employed by Town District High School 214. She loved to travel, and was a licensed pilot.

Splittorff attended Arlington High School in Arlington Heights, Illinois. He went out for the baseball team as a first baseman, but coach Bob Baker groomed the 6-foot-3 left-hander as a pitcher. Because he attended a high school with a large student body, there wasn't an opportunity to play varsity baseball in his freshman or sophomore years. He posted a 6-3 record in his junior year. Splittorff was the captain of the baseball team in his senior year and recorded a 7-1 with a 2.10 ERA.[2] Splittorff was an All-Suburban Valley selection and was named the team's most valuable player. In basketball, Splittorff averaged 18 points per game and was named to All-Conference and All-Chicago teams.[3]

That same year Splittorff played American Legion ball for Merle Guild Post 208 of Arlington Heights and won 12 and lost 2 with a 2.10 ERA, leading his team to a berth in the Legion World Series. Art Stewart, senior adviser for the Royals, recalled Splittorff during his high-school days remarked in 2011, "He was a fierce competitor. He didn't throw hard enough to be drafted out of high school, but he was a real intelligent guy with a lot of savvy, a lot of moxie for his age and he pitched that Legion team all the way to the World Series. He had a lot of heart."[4]

Splittorff caught the attention of one of the Legion World Series umpires, Don Protexter, who was also a baseball coach at Morningside College in Sioux City, Iowa. Splittorff enrolled at Morningside, studying business administration, and played on the varsity baseball and basketball teams. In 1967 he went 5-3 with a 1.95 ERA and in 1968 he went 6-2 with a 2.80 ERA.[5] He was named All North Central Conference both seasons. In one season, Splittorff averaged a conference-record 13 strikeouts per game. During the summers of 1966 and 1967, Splittorff played semipro baseball for the Valentine (Nebraska) Hearts of the Basin League. In 1966 he went 3-1 with a 3.96 ERA. In 1967 Splittorff played on the US baseball team that won the Pan-American Games title in Winnipeg. While attending Morningside, Splittorff met and married Lynn Litterick of Sioux City Iowa.

During his junior year, Splittorff was drafted by the expansion Kansas City Royals in the 25th round of the June 1968 amateur draft. Even though he had one year of eligibility left, he was signed by Lou Gorman, the Royals' farm director, and accelerated his studies and completed his degree early in February 1969 in order to concentrate on baseball come spring training. Splittorff started his baseball career in 1968 with the Corning Royals of the short-season New York-Penn League.

The Royals didn't begin playing until 1969, so when Splittorff took the mound for Corning in Williamsport, Pennsylvania, he started the first game in the history of the Royals organization. Splittorff posted an 8-5 record and a 3.45 ERA, tied for the league lead in strikeouts (136), complete games (11), and innings pitched (120), and led the league's pitchers in home runs allowed (11), hits allowed (127), and wild pitches (17). Splittorff won the praise of his manager, Bobo Osborne, who said, "He learned real fast. He progressed as rapidly as any player I've ever seen. You tell him something once and he remembers it."[6]

In 1969 Splittorff started spring training assigned to Double-A High Point-Thomasville but was quickly promoted to the Omaha Royals of the Triple-A American Association, who were managed by Jack McKeon. The first draftee from the Royals first draft to reach Triple A, Splittorff became one of the team's workhorses, and was among the league leader in innings pitched and victories. On October 24, 1969, he was the first of the original draftees to be placed on the Royals' major-league roster. Of the difference between college and professional ball, he said, "You play baseball, that's your job. That's the only thing you have to do. You get to concentrate on it. You're always talking baseball in the clubhouse. You can pick up a lot from that."[7]

After receiving some consideration for a bullpen spot with the Royals in 1970, Splittorff instead spent a second season with Omaha, who won their second consecutive American Association title. He posted an 8-12 record with a 3.83 ERA, and earned a September call-up to the Royals. Splittorff was the first of the 48 players signed by the club from the 1968 draft to make it to the Royals.[8]

Splittorff made his major-league debut on September 23, 1970, starting against the Chicago White Sox in Comiskey Park. Splittorff pitched seven innings, striking out eight, walking three and giving up five runs, three of them earned, as he took a 6-0 loss. He singled in his first major-league at-bat. On the 29th, when starter Al Fitzmorris injured a shoulder while warming up, Splittorff replaced him and was roughed up for four runs in 1⅔ innings. (The Royals took him off the hook with a five-run fourth.)

After the season, Gorman, then the Royals director of minor-league operations and scouting, gave this assessment: "Splittorff does not have overpowering stuff, but his fastball and breaking ball are both good enough. He started to put everything together the last month of the season at Omaha and he has pitched as well as he ever has. In the past he was inconsistent, but once he got in the groove, he set hitters up well and pitched like a man who knew what he was doing. He has a definite chance to make our staff in [1971] spring training. If he doesn't do it, I think he'll make it later in the year."[9] After the season, Splittorff pitched in the Florida Instructional League on the Royals team managed by McKeon.

Splittorff did not make the major-league roster out of spring training in 1971 and reported to Omaha for a third season. "When they sent me down near the end of spring training I was jolted," he said. "Jack [McKeon] told me it was better to go back to Omaha, perfect my pitches and stay in the majors a long time instead of getting rocked before you are ready. Every player feels he must rush things. It's a battle of time. I was 23. I thought time was running out. I felt I should get up here or find something else to do. You feel you have to move up a level every year in the minors and make it up here by the time you're 24."[10]

Perfect his pitches he did. In his first six starts at Omaha in 1971, Splittorff went 5-1 with a 0.40 ERA. In one game he tied the team's strikeout record at 14. That was out of character, he acknowledged; he was more of a control pitcher who moved the ball around the strike zone and changed speeds. "That's an unusual night for me. I don't consider myself a strikeout pitcher. I figure if I strike out six or seven, that is average for me. I just concentrate on getting ahead of a hitter in the count, then make a good to pitch to get him out."[11] Splittorff earned a second call-up in June and stayed with the Royals for good. He started 22 games, going 8-9 with a 2.68 ERA. Splittorff was runner-up to Bill Parsons of Milwaukee as *The Sporting News* Rookie Pitcher of the Year for the American League.

In 1972 Splittorff established himself as a major-league starter. He began 9-4 and had a streak of 23 consecutive scoreless innings.[12] He slumped but broke out of it in late August when he hurled five complete games in his last six starts. He ended the season 12-12 with a 3.13 ERA in 33 starts and struck out a career-high 140 batters. Splittorff's slump was attributed to three factors, he was hit in the right shoulder on a line drive by Willie Horton which affected his motion; he was suffering from an illness; and he was working on a new pitch, a slider, to the detriment of his curveball. When he needed to throw a curve in a game, he could not locate it. In 1973 Splittorff turned 26 and set out to be more consistent. He didn't throw as hard and had greater control of his pitches. It seemed to pay off. Splittorff won six of his first eight starts with a 2.61 ERA. On April 10 the Royals opened Royals Stadium (now called Kauffman Stadium). Splittorff was the starting pitcher and tossed a complete game to get a 12-1 win over the Texas Rangers. At the All-Star break he was 12-5, but did not get named to the All-Star team. He had hurt his back and AL manager Dick Williams was worried that he could not pitch. Splittorff was disappointed and was never named an All-Star in his career. During the season he was overall more consistent with the exception of a slump in August. Splittorff won his last five starts of the season and finished with 20 wins, the first Royals pitcher to reach that plateau. He said of his achievement, "It certainly was the biggest thrill of my baseball career. I did have my usual August slump, but the first 3½ months I was as consistent as can be. To win 20 games again, I'll have to fight the same thing – consistency – and again have a good team behind me."[13] McKeon remarked, "Paul never takes anything for granted. He has great self-discipline, confidence and dedication."[14]

The Royals were runners-up to the Oakland A's in 1973 and critics pointed to their lack of pitching as evidenced by an American League 10th-worst 4.19 team ERA, down from 3.24 (ninth-worst) in 1972. Splittorff thought the criticism was unfair and said the new ballpark had some effect: "People do not stop and think how much conditions changed when we moved from Municipal Stadium to our new ballpark. In Royals Stadium, the fences are shorter, the lighting is better and you have artificial turf. The old park was a pitchers' ballpark, the new stadium is a hitters' park. ... How can you use the same set of statistics to compare a pitcher who pitched in Fenway Park with a pitcher who pitched in our old park? Last season there were more total runs given up in Royals Stadium than anywhere else. That means pitchers from other clubs gave up a lot of runs, too. ... People should remember we're playing a different game in our new stadium than in our old one."[15]

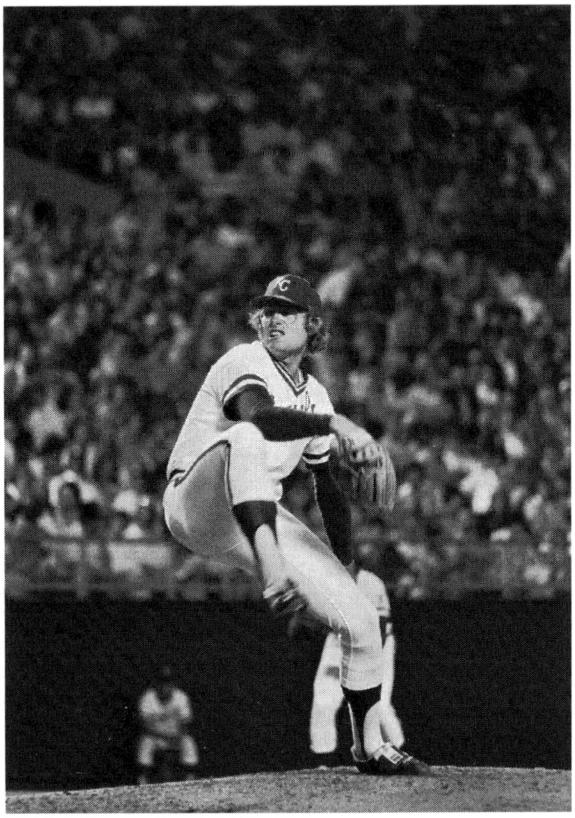

In 1974 Splittorff had a down year: 13-19, 4.10 ERA, 252 hits allowed in 226 innings pitched. He attributed his failures to minor injuries and inconsistency. Once again, he tried to develop a slider, but remained a two-pitch pitcher. Splittorff critiqued himself: "I did not throw well consistently over any period of time. I'd be good for two weeks and bad for two weeks. I had some minor injuries which weren't publicized, but I can't use them as an excuse. I wasn't actually wild, but I was getting behind batters more than I had in the past. I was just off the corner where before I had been on it. My breaking ball was poor and I developed poor arm motion. I was throwing my fastball with normal arm motion, but when I threw my curve, I was choking the ball way back in my hand and slowing down my motion."[16] Opposing batters would wait on his fastball and had time to adjust to his curve. On the plus side, Splittorff credited himself for improving his ability to pitch inside and said he had developed what he called a "hard curve for 1975."[17]

But Splittorff got off to a bad start in 1975, starting 1-4 with a 5.08 ERA. After a bad outing on May 3 against the Minnesota Twins, McKeon demoted him to the bullpen to change his routine and build up his confidence. McKeon had confidence in his lefty, saying, "As far as his stuff is concerned, he's throwing as well as he ever has. The year he won 20, he had excellent control. He could put the ball on the outside corner when he wanted to. Somewhere along the line, he got out of his groove. I had him in the minors when no one believed in him. I did then and I still do."[18] For his part, Splittorff said, "Right now, I'm just confused. I'm throwing the ball well at times but I'm not consistent. When I was winning, I was always ahead of the hitter. I've been hot enough now that I've become a nibbler. I have a tendency to be timid. Instead of throwing for the middle of the plate, I get behind."[19] But he agreed with McKeon's decision to take him out of the rotation.

Splittorff got himself together in the bullpen, appearing in 12 games, giving up 19 hits and allowing only six earned runs for a 2.25 ERA. Returning to the rotation on July 29, he started 13 games, went 7-4, and lowered his ERA to 3.17 at the end of the season. He had a 24-inning scoreless streak and pitched a masterpiece against the Oakland A's, whom the Royals were chasing for the division crown. Splittorff walked Phil Garner with one out in the first inning, then gave up a hit to Claudell Washington on a chopper toward third that bounced off home plate. Then he retired the next 26 batters for a 5-0 one-hitter. On September 15, Splittorff was credited with another victory, the 62nd of his career, passing Dick Drago as the team leader.

Splittorff started the 1976 campaign with an 11-6 record and a 3.55 ERA, with an eight-game winning streak. On July 27, after a loss to the Angels, he was diagnosed with a torn tendon sheath on the middle finger of his pitching hand. He was out until September. Returning on September 10, he gave up five runs in 2⅓ innings in relief. He started against the Twins on October 3, the last game of the regular season, lasted four innings, and took the loss. But the Royals had captured the American League West title for the first time, holding off the Oakland A's. New manager Whitey Herzog, still not confident Splittorff could contribute in the postseason, sent him to the rookie league for some work. Splittorff looked sharp and Herzog decided to use him out of the bullpen in the playoffs.

The Royals faced the New York Yankees in the ALCS. In Game Two, Splittorff relieved Dennis Leonard in the third inning with the Royals trailing 3-2 and held the Yankees scoreless for the next 5⅔ innings. The Royals won 7-3 with Splittorff picking up the win, the Royals' first-ever playoff victory. In the deciding Game Five, Splittorff relieved Leonard in the first inning with runners on second and third, nobody out, and the Royals trailing 1-0. He allowed an inherited runner to score, but kept the Royals in the game, allowing two runs in 3⅔ innings, leaving the game with the Royals trailing 4-3. The Royals tied the game, 6-6, in the top of the eighth, but Chris Chambliss won the game on a walk-off home run in the bottom of the ninth to send the Yankees to the World Series.

Splittorff started slowly in 1977, going 1-4 with a 4.72 ERA. But he went 15-2 from May 20 on and finished the season 16-6, 3.69. Splittorff pitched his second one-hitter, against the Milwaukee Brewers on September 2, losing a no-hitter in the eighth inning on a two-out single by Charlie Moore. The Royals captured their second AL West title and again faced the Yankees in the ALCS.

Splittorff started Game One, pitched eight innings, gave up two runs, and earned the victory. He also started the deciding Game Five. In a much debated move Billy Martin sat his superstar Reggie Jackson, who was 2-for-12. Herzog pulled Splittorff in the eighth inning with the Royals leading 3-1 after the leadoff batter got a hit. The Yankees rallied in the ninth to win 5-3. Splittorff defended his manager, saying that he told Herzog he was tired.

In 1978 Splittorff was 31 and the ace of the Royals staff. "The last three years I believe I pitched to my potential," he said. "I'm doing things I couldn't do the first five years in the majors. By that I mean pitching inside, getting the breaking ball over consistently, and changing speeds."[20] Splittorff's best years coincided with the years the Royals were contenders. From June 5, 1976, through 1978 he compiled a 43-21 record. His pitching coach, Galen Cisco, observed, "I'd call Splitt a heady pitcher. He doesn't try to strike guys out, but when he needs a strikeout, he goes after it. He stays on top of the situation. He never gets rattled."[21] Whitey Herzog appreciated his frankness, saying, "What I like about Paul is that he tells me the truth. When I go out there during a game, he'll say whether he's got good stuff or if he can go any longer in a game. He'll give you all he's got, and he'll always get everything out of his ability."[22] His catcher, Darrell Porter, commented, "He's got a fastball, slider, curve, and changeup. When he puts them where he wants them, it's a thing of beauty. He knows how to set up hitters. He never tries to overpower anybody, but just with control he can be overpowering."[23]

Splittorff finished the season 19-13, falling short of 20 wins when he lost his last start. The Royals won the AL West for the third season in a row and again faced the Yankees. Splittorff was scheduled to start the first game of the ALCS, but his father, Paul Sr., died of lung cancer at age 57 and the funeral was on the day of the game. Splittorff started Game Three in Yankee Stadium with the series tied at one game apiece. He pitched into the eighth inning and was relieved with a runner on and the Royals leading 5-4, but Thurman Munson hit a two-run home run off Doug Bird to give the Yankees a 6-5 victory. The Yankees won the series, three games to one.

The next season, 1979, the Royals were dethroned in the AL West by the California Angels. Splittorff started 35 games and finish the season at 15-17 with a 4.24 ERA. In 1980 he finished 14-11 with a 4.15 ERA. The Royals ran away with the AL West over the Oakland A's by 14 games. They again faced the Yankees, and this time swept the series. Splittorff started Game Three and was relieved by Dan Quisenberry in the sixth inning with the Royals ahead 1-0 and two runners on. The Yankees scored two runs to take the lead. George Brett hit a three-run home run and Quisenberry shut the door for the pennant. Splittorff exulted: "To me the World Series is as high as you can go. I've watched the World Series on TV for years and hey, now Paul Splittorff is going to be playing in it and a lot of guys don't ever get that opportunity. And to me that means more than anything else — that someone out there is going to be watching me play in the World Series. I can't explain how much that means to me."[24]

It would be bittersweet. Manager Jim Frey decided to go with a three-man rotation and opted for sore-shouldered Rich Gale over Splittorff. Splittorff didn't pitch in the first five games and was openly critical of his manager, saying, "It's not the time of year to be making waves, but it's not fair to me or my teammates. Based on what I have done in the past and this year, I should get a chance to pitch."[25] Splittorff finally appeared in relief in Game Six, in mop-up duty, allowing one run in 1⅔ innings as the Phillies won 4-1 to win the World Series. There was speculation that the veteran left-hander would not be back with the Royals in 1981.

Splittorff did return to the Royals in 1981 but started out slowly. Because of rainouts he was skipped for two starts. Splittorff was not used to the irregular schedule and at one point did not pitch for nine days. He didn't get his first victory until May 27. Then the players struck and there was no major-league baseball for almost two months. Play resumed on August 10. Splittorff didn't pitch longer than five innings in his first three starts after the strike. Frey banished him to the bullpen in favor of rookie Mike Jones. When Frey was replaced by Dick Howser, Splittorff did not hold back his feelings, saying, "I never enjoyed playing for him, he is the first manager I never really cared for."[26] Howser was open to the idea of Splittorff starting again, but at the time wanted him coming out of the bullpen, where he remained for the rest of the season. Because of the strike, the major leagues played a split-season format in which the division winners of the first and second half played in a best-of-five Division Series. The Royals, despite finishing fourth overall, won the AL West in the second half and played the Oakland A's for the division crown. They were swept in three games. Splittorff did not make a postseason appearance and was amenable to a trade.

Because Royals ace Larry Gura was left-handed, as were prospects Mike Jones and Atlee Hammaker, it did not appear there was room for the 35-year-old Splittorff. "I have to turn things around at this point in my career," he said. "I have been a starter all my life, and I'm sure there's probably baseball people who are questioning my ability because of age and the number of innings I've worked and stuff. And after what happened last year, people are probably thinking, well, he can't start anymore."[27] But in the offseason, Jones suffered a broken neck in a car accident. Howser employed a five-man rotation and Splittorff competed for one of the open spots. He was determined to make the most of his opportunity and changed his offseason regimen, starting to throw before spring training began. Then just before spring training, Howser told him he was going to be the number-three starter.[28]

Splittorff started 28 games and went 10-10 with a 4.28 ERA. Throughout his career, Splittorff had nagging injuries such as back spasms during the season that caused him to miss a start, but often the injuries did not cause him to miss significant time. On May 19, 1982, Splittorff lost to the Yankees for the ninth straight time in the regular season as the fortunes of the one-time Yankee killer were reversed. (He ended his career 14-16 with a 4.68 ERA against New York.) Splittorff was one of the more consistent pitchers the Royals had in the second half of the season and re-signed with the Royals for 1983. His contract would be renewed for 1984 if he started 27 games or pitched 180 innings.

In 1983 Splittorff started 27 games, went 13-8 with a 3.63 ERA. He led the staff in wins and ERA at age 36 on a staff that ranked ninth in the American League with a 4.25 ERA as the Royals suffered their first losing season since 1974.

But the future was bright for the team. In 1984 a trio of bright young pitching prospects made the squad out of spring training: Mark Gubicza (21 years old), Danny Jackson (22), and Bret Saberhagen (19). Splittorff's first start of the season, on April 4, was against the Yankees in Royals Stadium. After allowing four earned runs in

3⅓ innings, Splittorff was relieved by Saberhagen in his debut game. Saberhagen pitched 4⅔ scoreless innings as Splittorff took the loss. In Splittorff's next start, the pattern was the same. He gave up five runs in two innings, Saberhagen relieved him and allowed one run in five innings. Splittorff was replaced in the starting rotation by Danny Jackson. After being idle for 17 days, in his first relief appearance on April 28, Splittorff came in for Saberhagen. He pitched in relief eight more times before appearing in his last game. Splittorff started on June 26 in Kansas City against Oakland, gave up seven runs (four earned) in 4⅔ innings, and was relieved one last time by Saberhagen.

Splittorff was struggling with a 7.71 ERA. Faced with being released, he announced his retirement in the clubhouse on July 1 after the Royals defeated the Yankees in what was described in *The Sporting News* as an emotional farewell to a popular veteran who was influential both on and off the field. Though he would leave as the Royals' all-time leader in wins (166), innings pitched (2,554⅔), games pitched (429), and starts (392),[29] his teammates remembered him for more than just the steady production he put up in his 12½ seasons with the Royals. George Brett said, "I think a lot of people look up to him. Buddy Black got teary-eyed and he has only been his teammate for two years."[30] John Wathan said, "He probably epitomizes the name Kansas City Royals. Just a super guy to have on the club. You never heard any complaints."[31] In 1993 Splittorff was named on the Royals 25th-anniversary team and was voted into the Royals Hall of Fame.

Splittorff had planned for a career in broadcasting, covering football for Blue Springs, Missouri, radio station KKJC and University of Missouri-Kansas City basketball. He used the same hard work ethic and preparation as he did as a pitcher and became regarded as a professional. The Royals also used Splittorff as a part-time radio announcer, then signed him to join the club's TV crew as a play-by-play commentator and analyst. Splittorff also served as a commentator for Big Eight and Big Twelve college basketball.

Splittorff also enjoyed watching his children excel in sports. Jennifer was a scholarship-level softball player. Jamie was a right-hander pitcher who played in the College World Series for Kansas on the same field his father had played on in Omaha. Jamie played three years of minor-league ball in the Minnesota Twins organization.

Royals TV analyst Ryan Lefebvre said of his partner, "There are many former players who get into broadcasting in whatever sport, who in the very end don't get regarded as a professional broadcaster. There's probably a whole generation of kids in Kansas City who don't realize that Paul Splittorff pitched for Kansas City and won 166 games. He's just a Royals broadcaster who gives them great information, great content every game."[32]

Opening Day 2009 listeners noticed that Splittorff's speech was slurred and he took time off to regain his voice. Former teammate Frank White took over in the booth and Splittorff did pregame and postgame interviews. Splittorff was a mentor to White, who said, "He was very good at what he did, not only baseball but in basketball. He prepared well and when I came on to start doing Fox broadcasts, he was very helpful to me, showing me how to study, how to prepare for games, what periodicals to read. He actually gave me his books first year. He was very helpful, very informational. He wasn't a selfish person. We did a couple of games together which I thought was very good."[33] Splittorff, a private man who did not want people feeling sorry for him, did not disclose the serious nature of his illness and just said he had a virus. But he began to lose weight and people noticed. He worked some basketball games and pregame and postgame shows for the Royals for two seasons.

Splittorff died on May 25, 2011, of complications from melanoma. He also suffered from oral cancer. He was survived by his wife, Lynn, his daughter, Jennifer Lynn, and his son, Jamie. His family carries on his legacy of community service as active fundraisers for the Saint Mary's Medical Foundation. They also work to raise awareness and prevention of melanoma.

Notes

1 Associated Press, "Splittorff Has More Than Pitching on His Mind," October 5, 1978.

2 Bob Williams, "Omaha's Splittorff Baffles A.A. Batters," *The Sporting News*, August 23, 1969: 37. This article reports a 12-4 record.

3 Splittorff player file at the National Baseball Hall of Fame library.

4 Dick Kaegel, "Splitt, from beginning to end, the real royal," MLB.com, May 25, 2011, wap.mlb.com/kc/news/article/2011052519572168/?locale=en_US, accessed on October 31, 2018.

5 Stats come from Splittorff's Hall of Fame player file. *The Sporting News* reports 6-3 records both seasons.

6 "Omaha's Splittorff Baffles A.A. Batters."

7 Ibid.

8 Jim York was drafted in the June 1969 draft and made his major-league debut on September 21, 1970, becoming the first Royals draftee to make it to the major leagues by two days over Splittorff.

9 Joe McGuff, "Sharp Kid Hurlers Give Royals a Quick Return," *The Sporting News,* October 10, 1970: 18.

10 Joe McGuff, "'Established' Splittorff Eyes a Higher Plateau: Stardom," *The Sporting News*, June 2, 1973: 11.

11 Joe McGuff, "Control, Confidence Making Splittorff a Winner at Omaha," *The Sporting News*, June 5, 1971: 37.

12 From the third inning of his April 16, 1972, start to the third inning of his May 3 start, Splittorff allowed only one unearned run. On April 22 Splittorff pitched an eight-inning complete game and lost 1-0 on an eighth-inning error.

13 Bob Wirz, "Splittorff Named Royals Top Pitcher," Kansas City Royals Baseball Club – News Release, November 28, 1973.

14 Ibid.

15 Joe McGuff, "Royals' ERA an Unfair Yardstick, Says Splittorff," *The Sporting News*, March 30, 1974: 39.

16 Joe McGuff, "Splittorff Cites Slider for '74 Woes," *The Sporting News*, April 5, 1975: 41.

17 Ibid.

18 Joe McGuff, "Slump in Confidence Takes Toll on Splittorff," *The Sporting News*, July 5, 1975: 9.

19 Ibid.

20 Del Black, "'Split' Giving Royals a 10-Strike on Mound," *The Sporting News*, May 6, 1978: 19.

21 Del Black, "Royal Family United on Splitt – He's Great," *The Sporting News*, July 1, 1978: 3.

22 Ibid.

23 Ibid.

24 Dick Kaegel, "They're A.L. Royalty," *The Sporting News*, October 25, 1980: 13.

25 "Splittorff Wants to Pitch," The Sporting News, November 1, 1980: 12.

26 Blair Kerkhoff, "Royal Great Paul Splittorff Dies," *Kansas City Star*, May 25, 2011.

27 Dave Renbarger, "Splittorff – After 2,209 Innings of Wear, This 35-Year-Old Left-hander Must Prove Baseball Doubters Wrong," *Fort Myers* (Florida) *News-Press*, date unknown.

28 Mike McKenzie, "Splittorff a Starter in Royals New Plan," *The Sporting News*, February 13, 1982: 42.

29 As of the 2018 season, Splittorff was still the team leader in career wins, innings, and games started. He has been surpassed in game appearances.

30 Mike Fish, "A Royal Original Bids the Club Goodbye," *The Sporting News*, July 16, 1984: 30.

31 Ibid.

32 "Royals Great Paul Splittorff Dead at 64," *Associated Press*, May 25, 2011.

33 Dick Kaegel, "Splitt from Beginning to End, the Real Royal," MLB.com, May 25, 2011, wap.mlb.com/kc/news/article/2011052519572168/?locale=en_US, accessed on October 31, 2018.

MIKE SWEENEY

BY BILL LAMBERTY

Kansas City designated hitter Mike Sweeney strode to the plate with two men on base and two outs in the bottom of the ninth on Father's Day in 2003. Reliever Tim Worrell stood on the mound for San Francisco, on its way to a 100-win season and its third playoff appearance in four years. By contrast, Kansas City was in the midst of a surprising revival, sitting at 32-32 when the day began but without a winning season since 1994.

Angel Berroa, who had reached on a bloop double, stood at third and Aaron Guiel, after drawing a walk, edged off first. Sweeney swung at the first pitch and missed. Then he took strike two. Then, with Guiel in motion, Sweeney hammered Worrell's 0-and-2 fastball into the right-center alley. Berroa jogged home with Guiel not far behind him, and the crowd of nearly 30,000 rejoiced in a dramatic win. As it turned out, the Royals won their next three games, and nine of the next 11, and, including the game on the other side of the All-Star break, rolled to a 19-9 record that boosted the team into playoff contention into September.

Sweeney said after that game that he knew "the team was relying on me to get the job done,"[1] and that stood as a microcosm of his Kansas City career to that point. In the middle of the surprising 2003 surge, Sweeney stood as the team's most recognizable star after the trades of Johnny Damon and Jermaine Dye, and then Carlos Beltran on June 24, 2004. Sweeney had signed a $55 million contract extension in May 2002, and was viewed as the player willing to stay in Kansas City and restore the organization's once-proud history.

In the days after reveling in the excitement of that series win over San Francisco, the Royals scored 31 runs in winning the first three games of four against division rival Minnesota. Sweeney finished the first two games 4-for-8 with two walks and four runs, but he left the third game of the series in the early innings with an injury. That would be his last game action for nearly two months, and it would be a problem that came to define his final seasons with the Royals. He finished 2003 with 108 games played, and played in at least that many only once more in his career (122 in 2005).

Upon his induction into the Royals Hall of Fame in 2015, Sweeney was a five-time American League All-Star who held the team's single-season RBI record (144, in 2000). To that point he was in the conversation as the organization's second-best hitter of all time, after George Brett. His .340 in 2002 narrowly missed the American League lead and remains as of 2019 the second-highest average in Royals history; and his .299 batting average and 197 home runs were also second on KC's all-time list.

Michael John Sweeney was born on July 22, 1973, in Orange, California. Of his father, Michael Peter Sweeney ("Big Mike"), Royals historian Curt Nelson said, "'Little Mike' is always quick to say his father 'Big Mike' has always been his hero – and still is to this day."[2] Big Mike played in the California Angels organization in 1971 but abandoned major-league dreams after he and his wife, Maureen, welcomed what would be the first of their eight children into the world. Big Mike took a job as a beer truck driver in Southern California. He was also later a very successful high-school baseball coach.[3]

"Little Mike" graduated from Ontario (California) High School.

Sweeney's rise to stardom with the Kansas City Royals was simultaneously probable and unlikely. As a 10th-round draft choice in 1991, the odds were stacked against him. The 6-foot-1, 195-pound right-hander was drafted as a catcher, a position known historically for a high attrition rate due to its physical and mental demands. He hit just .216 in the Gulf Coast League in 1991, and the next season hit .221 for Eugene in the short-season Northwest League.

Still, Sweeney's minor-league career indicated the possibility of greatness. Although his batting average didn't rise above .250 until his third season, his power and patience both increased in a repeat stop in Eugene in 1993, then broke out in 1994 at Rockford (Midwest League), when he batted .301 with a .504 slugging percentage. Prospect analyst John Sickels wrote that Sweeney's "power was clearly developing, and for the second year in a row he made major strides with his strike zone judgment, increasing his walk rate while reducing his strikeouts."[4]

Sweeney's development as a prospect mirrored the progress in the Royals organization, which had been absent from postseason play since the 1985 World Series championship team. Sweeney was part of the restocking of the Royals system. At Wilmington in the Class-A Carolina League in 1995, he was one of seven future major leaguers on the squad. Sweeney continued to impress in Wilmington's difficult offensive environment that year, logging a .972 OPS in 99 games. Sickels rated him as "a solid A- prospect" after the season, although he remained absent from Baseball America's top 100 prospect rankings.

The 1996 campaign began a two-season roller-coaster ride for Sweeney. He continued to bash minor-league pitching (slugging over .500 in 550 plate appearances in 1996 and 1997 in Double A and Triple A without gaining real traction in the majors. Sweeney played the entire 1998 season in the majors, seeing action in 92 games with a .259 batting average and all but one of those games at catcher. His breakout season came in 1999, when he batted .322 with a .907 OPS, in spite of minor-league coach Tom Burgmeier telling Sweeney in spring training that his chances of sticking with the team were "zero percent." It took a lucky break to vault him into an everyday role.

In late May, regular first baseman Jeff King suddenly retired from baseball. He was hitting .236 on May 21, his last day in the majors. The next day the Royals' lineup featured Carlos Beltran, Joe Randa, Johnny Damon, Jermaine Dye, and Sweeney, but the team lost its second straight game, and after salvaging the finale of the three-game set with Seattle lost 12 of its next 13 games to fall to 23-32. Sweeney got regular at-bats, with Jeremy Giambi and Larry Sutton also rotating through designated hitter and first base.

June 10 dawned with the Royals 25-32 and enjoying an offday before an evening flight to Pittsburgh. Sweeney, Giambi, and Jed Hansen headed to Kevin Appier's farm outside of Paola, Kansas, for fishing and recreation. Near the day's end, Giambi jumped on a four-wheel all-terrain vehicle, similar to those he'd raced years before, and after a spin around the property hit an embankment and ended up with a gash in his head. With staples in his head and stitches in his eye, he told manager Tony Muser a story about a toolbox falling on his head in Sweeney's garage, rendering him unable to play and vaulting Sweeney into a full-time role.[5] Hitting .309 as the team's primary designated hitter when he unwittingly became Kansas City's permanent first baseman, Sweeney got hits in six of his next 11 at-bats and finished the season hitting .322 with a .907 OPS.

The 1999 campaign was Sweeney's first unencumbered by catcher's gear. Baseball analyst Rob Neyer wrote that "Mike Sweeney could catch, and Mike Sweeney could hit. He just couldn't seem to do both at the same time," and added that while playing catcher, Sweeney "hit like a catcher."[6] In his 25-year-old season of 1999 (he turned 26 on July 22), Sweeney began a four-year run of batting over .300. He hit .322 with a .907 OPS and anchored a lineup that featured rising stars Damon, Beltran, Dye, and solid contributors including Randa and Rey Sanchez. Kansas City finished third in the American League with 1,584 hits that season, and the team's 856 runs scored was seventh. But while the team's lineup was following an upward trajectory, its pitching staff scrambled. The Royals' 5.72 runs allowed per game were worst in the league, and the team ranked in the bottom five in all meaningful pitching statistics.

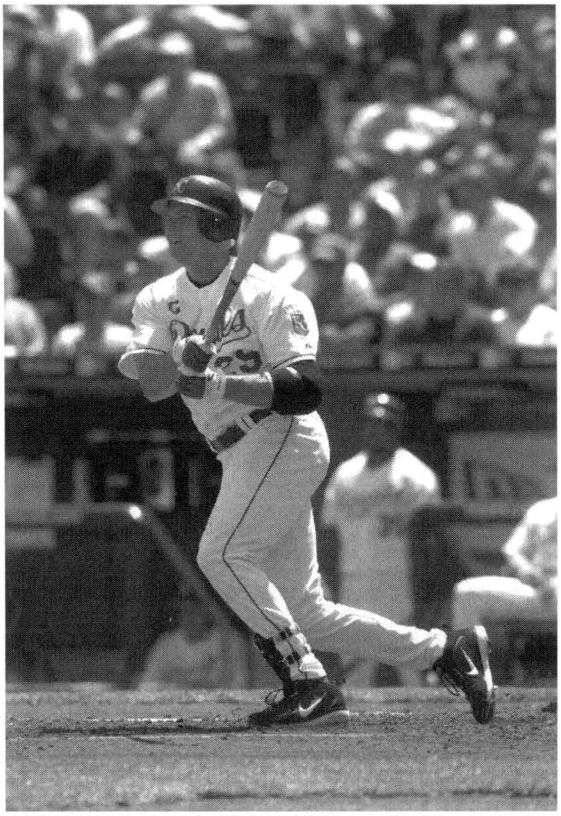

That 1999 season foreshadowed Kansas City's next half-decade. The promising young core flowered, but by 2002 the important members were traded away. The team finished fifth in the American League in runs per game in 2000, and slipped to 10th in 2001 and 11th in 2002 before rebounding to fourth in 2003. With Sweeney serving as the only truly consistently productive hitter (David DeJesus was establishing himself as a fine, if underrated, player during these years), Kansas City finished 12th of 15 in the AL in average runs in 2004 and 2005. During that stretch, Royals pitching finished 11th in runs allowed per game in 2001, below that in every other season.

The team's record followed that trend, as well. After winning 64 games in 1999 Kansas City improved to 77 wins the next year. That 2000 campaign and the 83-win effort in 2003, when the Royals were in playoff contention into September, proved to be mirages. Between the resolution of the 1994 strike and the team's 86 wins in 2013, the 2000 and 2003 seasons were the organization's two best in terms of wins.

Through the Royals' lean years, Sweeney was one of the bright spots. Through his peak years, 1999 to 2005, he was either first or second on the team in adjusted OPS each season. He accumulated 21.8 WAR during that time, and finished in the top 10 in the AL batting race in 2000 (.333, seventh) and 2002 (.340, second). He was fifth in the league in OPS in 2002, and was in the top 10 in slugging twice.

Sweeney's primary shortcoming as a player was durability. His first stint on the disabled list came in July 2002, when he missed 30 games with a hip strain. He missed at least that many games in each of the next three seasons, and after 2005 never again played in more than 74 games or logged 289 plate appearances in a season.

After partial seasons in 2006 and 2007 (541 plate appearances combined), Sweeney signed a deal in 2008 to join the Oakland Athletics. He had just 136 plate appearances (hitting .286 with a .728 OPS), then played for Seattle in 2009 and the Phillies in 2010 before finishing the 2010 season with the Mariners. He retired at the end of that campaign.

Sweeney's career ended with him in the top 10 in every Royals offensive category (including second in slugging and OPS and third in batting average), and was capped with induction into the team's hall of fame. But at the very beginning, his aspirations were modest. "My dream growing up was to some day be like my dad," Sweeney told the Kansas City Star before his hall of fame induction. Mike Sweeney Sr. was nearly lost to esophageal cancer in the months leading to the induction, but vowed to his son that he would be at Kauffman Stadium on August 15, 2015, for the ceremony.[7]

He was. Mike said during his induction speech that his goal in baseball when the Royals drafted him in 1991 was to accomplish what his father had. "I thought: I'm going to give it everything I can, maybe play a couple years of minor-league ball. Just to say I could be like my dad."[8] Throughout his baseball journey Sweeney was known as a person "who treated the parking lot attendant the same way he treated (Royals owner David) Glass," Kansas City broadcaster Ryan Lefebvre said.[9] Stories surfaced during and after his time with the Royals of Sweeney's regular and sincere interactions with fans. That began early. During his time with Class-A Wilmington Sweeney's conversation at a motel swimming pool with a family from Kansas City was interrupted by a phone call. "I'd like to talk to you guys a little longer, but ... my agent's calling; I'm going to the big leagues." When approached by that same family at Kauffman Stadium years later, Sweeney remembered them by name.[10]

Sweeney's Kansas City career was punctuated by memorable moments. The most unlikely came on August 10, 2001, when Sweeney charged Detroit pitcher Jeff Weaver after the hurler had lobbed obscenities toward Sweeney in the batter's box. Sweeney was ejected for the only time in his career, but not before returning to the batter's box and receiving an attempted punch from Tigers catcher Robert Fick.[11] On August 14, 2002, in the sixth inning, Sweeney drilled a double to right-center field to drive in Carlos Beltran and tied the game at 1-1. Moments later he took his lead off third base, and knowing that the batter, Guiel, had struck out against Andy Pettitte in his previous at-bat, Sweeney broke for the plate and narrowly beat Jorge Posada's tag to complete the steal of home. The Royals ended up losing the game in 14 innings.[12]

The bedrock of Sweeney's life has remained his faith as a Catholic. He was raised by "praying parents and grandparents" who promoted faith-related causes while calling love "the foundation necessary to make an impact on someone's life."[13] That impact showed up in small ways as well as large. While in Florida during his first season in professional baseball, Sweeney learned Spanish from a Mexican roommate, and made an acquaintance with a Catholic priest originally from Cuba, Rev. Domingo Gonzalez, who helped teach him the language through Spanish Catholic Masses and whom Sweeney continues to call his "spiritual father."[14] He has remained active in the Kansas City community in the Fellowship of Christian Athletes, the Boys and Girls Clubs of Greater Kansas City and many other charity and nonprofit organizations.[15]

The ability to speak Spanish aided Sweeney throughout his Royals playing career, as well as in his role as an assistant in baseball operations with Kansas City. He rejoined the organization in February 2014, calling himself a "deckhand" in contrast to the captain's "C" he wore during his later years there as a player. The player who purchased a full-page ad in the Kansas City Star after the 2007 season thanking fans for their support as his five-year contract ended,[16] and who has called the Royals' back-to-back pennant and 2015 World Series victories his favorite moments in baseball,[17] continued to make positive contributions. He won the 2007 Hutch Award, presented to the player annually who most reflects the "fighting spirit of the legendary leader Fred Hutchinson," a major-league player and manager who died of cancer shortly after the 1964 season.[18] During the 2018 season rookie Ryan O'Hearn attributed positive affirmations from Sweeney as a factor in his breakout campaign.[19]

Sources

In addition to the sources cited in the Notes, the author relied upon Baseball-Reference.com for statistical information.

Notes

1 "Bonds Hits HR No. 632 Against Recalled Lima," ESPN.com, June 15, 2003.

2 Email from Curt Nelson on January 22, 2019.

3 Ibid.

4 John Sickels, "Career Profile: Mike Sweeney," Minorleagueball.com, March 27, 2011.

5 Rustin Dodd, "Mike Sweeney Sheds Some Tears and Tells Story of His Big Break as He's Inducted into Royals' Hall of Fame," *Kansas City Star*, August 15, 2015.

6 Rob Neyer, "Remembering Mike Sweeney," SBNation.com, March 25, 2011. sbnation.com/mlb/2011/3/25/2072242/remembering-mike-sweeney.

7 Rustin Dodd, "Mike Sweeney's Royals Career: Losses, Yes, but Also Lots of Love," *Kansas City Star*, August 14, 2015.

8 Dodd, "Mike Sweeney Sheds Some Tears and Tells His Story of His Big Break as He's Inducted into the Royals' Hall of Fame."

9 Dodd, "Mike Sweeney's Royals Career: Losses, Yes, but Also Lots of Love."

10 Rustin Dodd, "Even as a Minor Leaguer, Mike Sweeney Was a Standup Guy," *Kansas City Star*, August 16, 2015.

11 Matt Galloway, "Mike Sweeney, Whose 2001 Brawl Lives in Perpetuity, Relates to Fighting Royals," *Topeka Capital-Journal* On-line, April 25, 2015.

12 Dodd, "Mike Sweeney's Royals Career: Losses, Yes, but Also Lots of Love."

13 Trent Beatie, "Mass-Going Mariner Suits Up," *National Catholic Register*, March 22, 2010.

14 Elizabeth Merrill, "Speaking Spanish Helps K.C.'s Sweeney Relate to Teammates," ESPN.com, September 20, 2007. espn.com/espn/hispanicheritage2007/news/story?id=3025837.

15 Mike Sweeney player biography, royals.com. web.archive.org/web/20070507105448/http://kansascity.royals.mlb.com/team/player_career.jsp?player_id=123041.

16 "Sweeney Purchases Full-Page Ad to Thank Fans, Organization," ESPN.com, September 30, 2007. espn.com/mlb/news/story?id=3043675.

17 Louis Brewster, "World Series Title Wraps a Very Eventful Year for Ontario's Mike Sweeney," *Daily Bulletin* (Ontario, California), November 2, 2015.

18 FredHutch.org.

19 Pete Grathoff, "How Mike Sweeney's Quiet Support has Been a Boon to Royals' Rookie Ryan O'Hearn," *Kansas City Star*, August 27, 2018.

DANNY TARTABULL

BY CHARLES F. FABER

For several years baseball was very, very good to Danny Tartabull. The game gave him honors and recognition, though not quite as much as he thought he deserved. Baseball paid him millions of dollars, enabling him to live a luxurious life style that most people could barely imagine. But it wasn't enough. He was unable or unwilling to support his youngest sons. His photograph had once graced the cover of *Sports Illustrated for Kids*. More recently it has appeared on Most Wanted posters in post offices throughout the state of California.

Danilo Tartabull Mora was born on October 30, 1962, in San Juan, Puerto Rico, a son of Antonia Maria Mora and José Milage Tartabull Guzman. His family had been prominent in Cuba until Batista was overthrown by Fidel Castro in 1959. Maria's father had owned a sugar factory in Cienfuegos, José's father was a college professor; his grandfather was a judge.[1] Factory owners and supporters of the Batista regime did not fare well under the new order.

José Tartabull was a professional baseball player. After five years of semipro and minor-league experience, he made his major-league debut for the Kansas City Athletics a little more than six months before Danny was born. During the baseball season, the family lived wherever José's club was based. They spent their winters in South Florida. Danny's earliest memories were of romping in the ballpark in Winter Haven during spring training.

As the son of a ballplayer, Danny learned the game of baseball at a very early age. During the summer of 1967, the Tartabulls lived in Brookline, Massachusetts, while José played for the Boston Red Sox. There was a park near their residence, where José was often seen playing catch with his four-year-old son.[2]

The youngster developed his skills on the sandlots of Miami. "I grew up in baseball because of my father, not because of Miami," he said. "I thought everybody's dad went to the ballpark every day at 3 o'clock and played a game of baseball."[3] Danny didn't just play baseball at 3 o'clock. Sometimes he played in three leagues at once. He could play a game in the morning, another after lunch, and a third in the evening. His teammates on one Little League team included José and Ozzie Canseco, Rafael Palmeiro, and Junior Valdespino. Who was the star? "I hate to say this," he said, "but I was. I think my development was quicker because of being around the game more than all of them."[4]

In 1978 15-year-old Danny played American Legion baseball in suburban Miami for Hialeah Post 32 and helped the club win the American Legion World Series. He played high-school ball for Miami's Carol City High School. At age 17 he was selected, as a second baseman, out of high school by the Cincinnati Reds in the third round of the 1980 amateur draft.

The Reds sent Danny to Billings, Montana, in the Pioneer League. He hit .299 in 59 games for the Mustangs in 1980 and played mainly at third base (34 games), although he logged one game at second and 22 in the outfield. In 1981 Tartabull hit .310 for the Tampa Tarpons in the Class-A Florida State League, while playing 46 games at second base and 78 at third. He led the league in batting and doubles, was tied for fourth in home runs, and tied for third in triples and RBIs. He was named the circuit's Player of the Year. Hal Keller, Seattle's director of player personnel, was enthusiastic about the youngster. He told a reporter for *The Sporting News*, "I must have checked with a dozen people who saw this guy play and there was little doubt he could play in the big leagues. I think he'll be a second baseman, but as a fallback, he has enough pop to be a legitimate third baseman."[5]

In 1982 Tartabull hit a career-low .227 for the Waterbury Reds in the Double-A Eastern League, while playing exclusively at second base. That was his final season in the Cincinnati farm system, as the Seattle Mariners chose him on January 20, 1983, as a compensation pick after the loss of Floyd Bannister to free agency. At that time clubs could prevent the loss of players to the draft by putting them on a "protected list." Years later, Cincinnati's farm system director said the failure to protect Tartabull was the most regrettable decision the Reds had made in his quarter-century with the team.[6]

In 1983 the Mariners shipped Tartabull to Chattanooga, their affiliate in the Double-A Southern League. He hit .301 for the Lookouts and played the entire season at second base. The following year the Mariners promoted him to Salt Lake City in the Triple-A Pacific Coast League and switched him to shortstop He hit .304 for the Gulls, earning a late-season callup to the big leagues.

Tartabull made his major-league debut on September 7, 1984, at Royals Stadium in Kansas City. He was 21 years old, stood 6-feet-1, weighed 185 pounds, and batted and threw right-handed. He entered the game as a pinch-runner for Alvin Davis in the ninth inning of a 5-3 loss to the Royals. His next appearance came in Seattle's Kingdome on September 11. The Mariners and the Texas Rangers were tied, 3-3, in the bottom of the ninth inning. The bases were loaded with two outs. Tartabull hit a game-winning RBI single. In his first major-league at-bat he had a walk-off hit.

On February 18, 1984, Danilo Tartabull and Monica Anita Cusseaux were married in Hillsborough County, Florida. In compliance with Florida law at the time, the race of the bride and groom was shown on the marriage certificate. Both were identified as "black." The marriage lasted about 5½ years. The couple divorced in Pinellas County, Florida, on August 4, 1989.

In 1985 Tartabull played a few major-league games for Seattle, mainly at shortstop, but he spent most of the season with the Calgary Cannons, who had replaced Salt Lake City as the Mariners' affiliate in the Pacific Coast League. What a season he had! He hit .300, scored 102 runs, and batted in 109, the first time he had topped the century mark in either category. He experienced a real power surge, blasting 43 home runs. In five previous seasons in professional baseball, Tartabull had never clouted more than 17 homers in a season. He ranked second in the league in runs scored, led in both home runs and runs batted in, and was named the league's Most Valuable Player.

After that performance, Tartabull could no longer be kept down on the farm. He never returned to the minor leagues, playing 12 more years at the major-league level. In 1986 Tartabull hit .270 with 25 homers for the Mariners. He ranked fifth in voting for the American League Rookie of the Year Award. Although he had been primarily an infielder throughout his earlier career, Seattle converted him into an outfielder and he roamed the outer garden the rest of his career. On December 10, 1986, the Mariners traded Tartabull along with minor-league pitcher Rick Luecken to the Kansas City Royals for outfielder Mike Kingery and pitchers Scott Bankhead and Steve Shields. Many Seattle fans were stunned by the trade, as they envisioned the young power hitter as a possible superstar of the future.

Tartabull made an immediate impact in Kansas City. In 1987 he hit .309 with 34 home runs and 101 RBIs. The next year he hit .274 with 26 homers and 102 runs batted in. Those performances earned him a big boost in pay. In 1989 he received over a million dollars for the first time in his career. He got nice raises the next two seasons, even though his productivity fell off slightly. However, he came back in 1991 with one of his best years ever. He hit a career-high .316 with 31 home runs and 100 runs batted in. He led the league with a .593 slugging percentage. He was twice named the American League Player of the week, once in June and once in July. Tartabull was selected for the 1991 All-Star Game.

Despite his success at the plate, Tartabull was not universally popular among his teammates. Some Royals thought Tartabull had a bad attitude. He was regarded as aloof, arrogant, selfish, interested only in his own hitting, not a team player, and a lackadaisical outfielder. Some resented his ostentatious style of living. He certainly showed off his new-found wealth. One example was how he splurged on his proposal to his girlfriend, Kellie Van Kirk. One April night in 1989, he sent a limo to pick up Kellie, along with a dozen roses, and a note requesting that she wear his favorite dress and asking that she go with the driver to Wyandotte County Lake, just across the state line in Kansas. When she arrived, she found he was waiting for her in a rented tuxedo, accompanied by caterers and a harpist. A four-course meal with champagne was served, while the harpist played romantic music. After the meal Danny suggested they go for a walk up a nearby hill. When they reached the crest of the hill, they saw a fireworks display that spelled out in letters 25 feet high, "Kellie, will you marry me?" She said. "Yes." Tartabull said, "I'll get married, I'll have kids, and I'll have a lot of things happen in my life, but that was a night I'll treasure as long as I live."[7] Little could he imagine the things that would happen in his life.

After the wedding, Kellie and Danny lived during the offseason in a lavish mansion in the Santa Monica Mountains near Malibu, California. The couch was made of Italian leather, the sound system was floor-to-ceiling, the works of art were well-chosen, the 300-gallon saltwater tank was filled with exotic fish, the wine cellar was stocked with expensive fine wines, including 50 bottles of 1985 Chateau Lafite Rothschild, valued at $450 each. "I enjoy making other people feel great," he said. "I want to make my wife happy, and my kids happy, get them things they want."[8] In view of what happened later, how ironic were those words! In the garage were parked two luxury automobiles. The vanity license plates reflected the ego and talents of their owner: SLUGGER and I CAN HIT.

Tartabull professed to not know why some of the Kansas City players found him aloof and a poor teammate. He thought perhaps it was jealousy. "I don't know where it came from, and I don't waste my time trying to find out. It's not true. I brush it off like dust."[9] Kellie said, "It bothers me more than Danny. I know he's none of those things I hear about, not even close. He's a family man, a person who enjoys having fun, going to nice restaurants. He always includes my whole family in the things we do."[10] Kellie accompanied Danny on every road trip. When he was with his wife, he wasn't with his teammates, contributing to the feeling that he was aloof.

Tartabull thought the high opinion he had of himself was justified. "I've always felt I'm a great player. I am great. I know that in certain situations I can do things that a lot of other guys can't," he said. "Let's say I do tell everyone that I'm great. What does that have to do with having a bad attitude?"[11]

At least one of Tartabull's Kansas City teammates defended him. Brian McRae said, "Some people say he had a bad attitude. People think he is arrogant, but that's just the way he is. Not everybody can be your normal run-of-the-mill person. He likes fancy cars, he likes dressing nice, he has a lot of nice jewelry. That might rub some people the wrong way, but that's just Danny.[12]

Kansas City granted Tartabull free agency on October 28, 1991. Several clubs were interested in obtaining the services of the young star. During the early part of the recruiting process, the California Angels, Chicago White Sox, and the Texas Rangers appeared to the frontrunners. The White Sox dropped out of the bidding when Tartabull insisted on a five-year contract. Chicago general manager Ron Schueler said, "Five years is too long for me."[13]

Tartabull had been the Angels' primary target, but their ardor cooled when the club's vice president, Whitey Herzog, became bitter about the way Tartabull's agent, Dennis Gilbert, had behaved during earlier negotiations involving Bobby Bonilla. (Gilbert represented both Tartabull and Bonilla.) [14]

Although they had not been mentioned among the early contenders, the New York Yankees made Tartabull an offer he couldn't refuse. On January 6,

1992, he signed a five-year contract with the Yankees for $25.5 million, the most lucrative contract in club history to that point. He was guaranteed an additional $1.5 million in an endorsement clause that covered the life of the contract. "Texas and the Angels were both very attractive to me," Tartabull said. "But the New York Yankees, man, they're something else. How can you not get excited about that tradition? There's a great mystique to it. Everyone and everybody would love to have that prestige."[15]

Tartabull expected that playing for the Yankees would be a joyful experience, but fate deemed otherwise. He was hampered by injuries every year he was in pinstripes, never logging more than 138 games in a season for New York. Some Yankees officials thought, perhaps unfairly, that he should have played through his injuries.

At first Danny was thrilled at the opportunity to play in New York. He and Kellie purchased a home in Saddle River, New Jersey, within commuting distance of the city. When he signed with the Yankees, they had two children, Danica Janelle, 5, and Danny Jr., 4. Kellie was pregnant with their third child, Zachary, who would be born in Teaneck, New Jersey, on June 23. "New York is the greatest city in the world," Tartabull said. "I can live here (in California) in the winter and play in New York during the season. It's the ultimate."[16] In New York he and Kellie could attend the opera, see Broadway shows, and visit world-class art galleries. "You can't do that in Kansas City or Seattle," he said. "I've always been interested in culture. I like going to plays, my wife and I love the ballet, and we both love art. You can tell just walking through my house. We spend a lot of time in galleries."[17]

The house in Malibu was nice, but Tartabull wanted bigger and better. He had some property in Rancho Santa Fe Farms in the San Diego area. He hired an architect and planned to spend $30 million to build an 11-room, 27,000-square-foot house next door to the home of pop star Janet Jackson. The house would feature a batting cage with a viewing platform, a saltwater aquarium, a scaled-down train to take the family or visitors on a tour of the estate, with stops at a game room, Tiki bar, basketball and tennis court, putting green, and an indoor/outdoor swimming pool, with a 14-foot waterfall, and a water slide descending from the children's bedrooms. He planned to also have a sports training center, with an exercise room and a health bar, a two-story movie theater, a pinball and video arcade, and an aviary.[18] How many of these plans actually came to fruition is not known.

Although he missed 39 games his first year in New York due to injuries (strained left hamstring, lower-back spasms), Tartabull was the Yankees' most productive hitter with 25 home runs and 85 runs batted in. The next year he was even better with 31 homers and 102 RBIs. However, he was unable to match those figures again, and he never hit more than .266 in New York. He struck out more than 100 times each season he wore pinstripes, with his 156 K's in 1993 being second highest in the league. Because of a shoulder injury, incurred when he was making a throw on July 15, Tartabull was unable to play in the field during the second half of the 1993 season, being restricted to the designated-hitter slot.

After the season Tartabull elected to have cosmetic facial surgery and then spend the first three weeks of November vacationing in Europe, delaying his shoulder surgery for more than a month. Dr. Frank Jobe performed the operation at Centinela Hospital in Inglewood, California.[19] Some Yankee officials thought Tartabull should have given higher priority to the shoulder surgery.

In 1994 Tartabull played in only 104 games, mostly as a designated hitter. He hit .256, with 19 home runs and 67 RBIs. He appeared twice on the *Seinfeld* TV show and once on *Married ... With Children.*

Unhappy with Tartabull's attitude, the Yankees tried to trade him during spring training, 1995, but found no takers, even when they offered to eat as much as $2 million of his contract. On Opening Day the much-criticized slugger hit a homer and an RBI single. Yankees owner George Steinbrenner said, "I'm still disappointed in Tartabull. Very disappointed."[20]

Upset by Steinbrenner's criticism, in June Tartabull asked to be traded. He needn't have bothered. The Yankees had been trying to unload him for months.

"It's easy for him to ask, but it's not easy to move him," general manager Gene Michael said. "Clubs don't want to take that kind of money (Tartabull's $5.3 million salary). I've tried to move him."[21]

Disappointed with his performance, Yankee fans started booing Tartabull whenever he failed to deliver. Tartabull thought Steinbrenner encouraged the boos. The owner was famously hard to get along with, but Tartabull carried their feud to an extreme. His days in New York were numbered. The long-anticipated trade occurred on July 28, when the Yankees dealt the disgruntled slugger to the Oakland Athletics for veteran Ruben Sierra and minor-league pitcher Jason Beverlin. The Yankees sweetened the deal by agreeing to pay half of Tartabull's salary. "I feel like I've been released from jail," Tartabull said.[22]

With the deal completed, Tartabull was able to vent his bottled-up feelings. "It's a zoo there. No I take that back; it's a joke. The sad part is that the only reason for that is the owner. He wants to be the center of attention so bad he just destroys that team. It's so hard for those guys to win because of that man. ... The guys won't say it on the record, but they're just miserable there. ... I'd still be there if it weren't for George. I had no problems with anyone else, but when you've got an owner like him, he makes it impossible to play up to your capabilities. I mean why would an owner keep downgrading his own product? It'd be like Lee Iacocca telling people not to buy cars. That's just stupid. He's an idiot for doing that."[23]

Tartabull played only 24 games for Oakland. On January 22, 1996, the A's traded him to the Chicago White Sox for pitcher Andrew Lorraine and minor-league outfielder Charles Poe. The Sox had to pick up only half of his $5.3 million salary.

On January 31, 1996, Kellie gave birth to the family's fourth child, Quentin Riley Tartabull. In 1996 Danny had a good season on the South Side of Chicago. Although he hit only .254, he clubbed 27 home runs and knocked in 101 runs. He became a free agent on November 18, and the Sox were willing to re-sign him only if he would accept a huge pay cut. He was unwilling to do so and went on the open market. Few clubs were interested in him. One exception was Philadelphia. Hal McRae, who had managed Tartabull one year in Kansas City, was now the Phillies hitting coach and lobbied on Danny's behalf. Tartabull rejected the Phils' first overture, saying he was insulted by the "lowball offer."[24] After months of negotiations and no better deals tendered, Tartabull signed with Philadelphia for $2 million on February 25, 1997.

On Opening Day, April 1, 1997, Tartabull was in the Phils' starting lineup, playing right field and batting cleanup in a game at Dodger Stadium. During the game he fouled a pitch off his left foot. He was removed from the game and sat out the next three contests, thinking he had a contusion. He was back in the lineup for the games in San Francisco on April 5 and 7. He was unable to complete the latter game and was taken out in favor of Derrick May in the seventh inning. He didn't know it at the time, but his major-league career was over at the age of 34. An MRI revealed that his foot was fractured, and he would be out for the season. For their $2 million investment, the Phils got virtually nothing in return. Tartabull drew four bases on balls and scored two runs, but he made no hits in his seven official trips to the plate.

The Phillies declined to renew his contract, and Tartabull opted for free agency on October 10, 1997. He worked out during the winter, getting himself in shape, and hoping for a return to the big leagues. The San Diego Padres offered him a minor-league contract, but he turned it down. His baseball career was over. He returned to California, and stayed out of the limelight for a few years.

The next time Tartabull was in the national news involved family problems. He and Kellie split up around 2007, and a family court judge ordered Danny to pay child support for the two youngest children, Zach and Quentin. (Having passed the age of 18, neither Danica nor Danny Jr. was entitled to support.) Both boys were star football players, Zach at Valencia High School and Quentin at Bishop Alemany High School in Mission Hills. Zach graduated from high school in 2010 and became a male model. Quentin graduated in 2014 and accepted a football scholarship at the University of California, Berkeley.

Tartabull fell far behind on his child-support payments. On January 24, 2011, he entered a no-contest plea to charges that he willfully disobeyed the court order.[25] Zach had already reached the status of "emancipation" and Quentin would soon join him in that category. Danny would not be liable for child support in the future, but he was liable for payments missed in the past, amounting to $276,204.93. Tartabull was placed on probation, but he violated the terms of the probation. On May 2, 2012, he was sentenced to 180 days in the Los Angeles County jail. He failed to report to jail, and the court issued a warrant for his arrest with bail set at $200,000. When authorities were unable to locate him, he was declared a fugitive from justice.[26]

If anyone knows where Danny is hiding out, they're not talking. "Most Wanted" posters went up in California post offices in July 2013. When Danny Tartabull was a baseball star, he was called "The Bull." Now he is called a "deadbeat dad."

Notes

1 Joanne Hulbert, "Jose Tartabull," sabr.org/bioproj/person.54213446.

2 Ibid.

3 Craig Davis, "Yanks' Danny Tartabull Has $25.5 Million, Wants More: A World Series Paycheck," *Sun-Sentinel* (Fort Lauderdale, Florida), April 5, 1992.

4 Ibid.

5 Tracy Ringolsby, "No-Trade Clauses Create Contract Woes," *The Sporting News*, January 31, 1983.

6 Mike Bass, "Cincinnati Reds," *The Sporting News*, January 20, 1992.

7 "Best of Plans Made for Night to Remember," *Los Angeles Times*, April 29, 1989; Bruce Newman, "Bright Light, New City," *Sports Illustrated*, March 23, 1992: 76.

8 Michael Martinez, "Bronx Is Up, but Tartabull Will Take Manhattan," *New York Times*, February 6, 1992.

9 Ibid.

10 Ibid.

11 Newman.

12 Ibid.

13 Joe Goddard, "Chicago White Sox," *The Sporting News*, January 13, 1992.

14 Dave Cunningham, "California Angels," The Sporting News, January 6, 1992.

15 Moss Klein, "Yanks Give Tartabull a Record Number," *The Sporting News*, January 13, 1992.

16 Martinez.

17 Ibid.

18 "Yanks' Danny Tartabull Building a $30 Million House in California," Jet, May 11, 1992: 48.

19 Jack Curry, "Tartabull Has Operation Yanks Preferred," *New York Times*, December 1, 1993.

20 Jon Heyman, "New York Yankees," *The Sporting News*, May 22, 1995.

21 Jon Heyman, "New York Yankees," *The Sporting News*, June 19, 1995.

22 Bob Nightengale, "Tartabull Loves New York but Loathes Steinbrenner," *The Sporting News*, August 7, 1995.

23 Ibid.

24 cornerpubsports.com/2015/06/phillies-all-train-wreck-team.

25 Sam Gardner, "Call him Deadbeat Danny Tartabull." foxsports.com/mlb/story/danny-tartabull-former-mlb-allstar-shows-up-atop-deadbeat-dad-list-n-la, July 9, 2013.

26 Ibid.

FRANK WHITE

BY RICHARD BOGOVICH

It's easy to find high praise about Frank White from members of the Baseball Hall of Fame, ranging from managers and executives for whom he worked (John Schuerholz and Whitey Herzog) to longtime players on opposing teams such as Reggie Jackson.[1] Still, there may be no more significant comment about White than from Hall of Famer George Brett. During spring training in 1991, Brett was openly emotional about losing teammates. "This game's a business and I understand that," Brett said. "But it really strikes you hard when [it's] someone close to you, someone that you have a lot of respect for, not only as a player but as an individual."

"Frank White and I were teammates for 20 straight years," Brett continued. "We started off in 1971 together in the instructional leagues and played every year together from 1971 up until this spring." Brett hadn't felt White's absence through mid-March because the few familiar faces in spring-training camps get lost among the long shots who flood the lineups. "But come Opening Day, when I'm out there and Frank's not there, then it's going to hit me: Frank's no longer on our team."[2]

At that point, Frank White had lived half of his life in the Royals organization. How he got into it in the first place was rare and remarkable.

Frank White Jr. was born on September 4, 1950, in Greenville, Mississippi to Frank White Sr. and Daisie Vestula (Mitchell) White.[3] Daisy's parents, Roosevelt and Bertha Mitchell, were sharecroppers about 20 miles to the north near Grapeland, Mississippi. Frank Jr. reported vivid memories of picking cotton there during several summers.[4]

Frank White Sr. was also born in Greenville. He served in the military during World War II in Germany. He played amateur baseball as a young adult, and may have had professional aspirations. "The Negro Leagues were just winding down and I think he had a shot at going down and playing with the Memphis Red Sox," Frank Jr. wrote in his 2012 autobiography.[5] It so happened that in early 1950, Red Sox manager Homer "Goose" Curry ran a baseball school for African-American players in Memphis. The school's assistant director was Boyce Jennings, manager of the Greenville Delta Giants of the Negro Southern League. The school opened in late February.[6] Only a few of the 40-plus participants were ever named in local newspaper accounts, but three were from Greenville,[7] and one history of the NSL lists "Frank White, 3b" on the roster of the Greenville Delta Giants in 1950.[8] Also, before the start of the NSL season, the Delta Giants faced another team in the league, the New Orleans Creoles, and a preview of the game reported that Jennings planned to have Frank White among his infielders. The Greenville daily made a big deal about the fact that female player Toni Stone was with the Creoles, but the day after the game it printed only one paragraph about the contest and didn't name any of the players.[9]

Though born in Greenville, Frank White Jr. said he lived in Benoit, about two miles north of Grapeland, until his parents moved the family to Kansas City when he was 6 years old. Despite his old and new homes being about 600 miles apart, Frank Jr. said his parents continued to send him and three siblings to their grandparents every summer; "our folks thought maybe if they sent us back there it would keep us out of trouble."[10]

It was a tradeoff, due to the racial tensions of the 1950s and 1960s. "It was tough being black anywhere in the United States back then," White said, "but it was really tough in Mississippi."[11] His mother's sister Louella was the first relative to try moving to Kansas City for a better job and a higher standard of living. Daisie White spent her entire working life there pressing clothes in the city's Historic Garment District. Her husband worked for various car dealers.[12]

Their son Frank's first school in Kansas City was Wendell Phillips Elementary. For fourth grade he started being bused Linwood Elementary.[13] It was around that time, at the age of 9, that he first played baseball in an organized league. Frank started learning the game simply by playing with neighborhood kids, without adult coaching. His first glove was a first baseman's mitt because that was his main position early on. When he started playing organized ball his father never missed a game, but anger management was an issue at times, and he was asked to leave some of his son's games. "When I was playing a position he was fine," Frank White Jr. recalled, "but when I pitched he didn't always see eye to eye with the umpire, so he watched a few games from the car."[14]

After Linwood Elementary, White attended Lincoln High School, a historically significant institution founded for African-American students in the 1800s and the only high school in the region they could attend until at least 1950. It was integrated about a decade after White graduated.[15] Lincoln is a block from the site of Municipal Stadium, home of the Royals for their first four seasons as well as the A's while the franchise was located in Kansas City. Lincoln didn't have a baseball team but White played football and basketball. It was through Connie Mack, Ban Johnson, and Casey Stengel leagues that he honed his baseball skills into his teens.[16] He was on a Hallmark Card team made up of 14-year-olds that won a Connie Mack League championship, and at the age of 18 he was on a Safeway grocery store team led by Hall of Famer Hilton Smith. White represented the latter team in a Casey Stengel League All-Star Game played in Municipal Stadium.[17]

The assassination of the Martin Luther King Jr. on April 4, 1968, happened shortly before White graduated from Lincoln. The worst rioting occurred only two blocks from the family's home. In the midst of that, Frank White Sr. managed to drive his pregnant daughter Mona to a hospital because she'd just gone into labor.[18]

Frank White's first job after high school was as a stock handler for Hallmark Cards, for which he made $100 a week. He later worked for the Metals Protection Plating company. He also briefly attended Southern University in Baton Rouge, Louisiana.[19]

On September 11, 1969, the course of Frank White's life shifted dramatically. During the Royals' first season, owner Ewing Kauffman announced a detailed plan to open a "baseball academy" in Florida in 1970 for about 50 recruits primarily 17 and 18 years old. Syd Thrift, Kaufmann's director of scouting for the Eastern half of the United States, was named director. "This is the only way Kansas City can have a winning team right away," Kaufmann said.[20]

"I always wanted to play baseball, but I never thought I could play and get paid for it," White said. "I dreamed about it, but you dream about a lot of things that never happen." He heard a little about tryouts for the academy, but doubted he could get off work to attend. But Hilton Smith and White's high-school science teacher and basketball coach, Bill Rowan, urged him to make the effort. He also received encouragement from scout Bob Thurman and brothers Don and Bob Motley, significant figures in Negro Leagues history.[21]

White went to Municipal Stadium on the first day of a two-day tryout, and found about 300 other young men with similar dreams. After sprints and fielding exercises on the field, some of the applicants were sent to a doctor inside the building for coordination tests. When White was later in the batting cage, he overheard former A's first baseman Norm Siebern say, "You need to take a chance on this kid." White didn't know who the other man was, but when the two talked about White's age, Siebern said it was only important that White was obviously an athlete. Moments later, though, White was crushed when he also overheard that the plan was to send only unmarried players to the academy. White was married, and he and his wife, Gladys, had a baby, Frank III. When his tryout concluded, he thought his baseball playing days were over.[22]

"Then, something that only happens in movies happened to me," White's 2012 autobiography says. "Later that day, I was at my parents' house and I hear this commotion outside. I look out the window and there is a big blue limo parked in front of our house." It was Kauffman's, but the owner wasn't in it. He didn't send it to take White somewhere; he only wanted to speak with White on the limousine's car phone (decades before there were such things as cell phones). "I'd never talked on a phone in a car before – I didn't even know there was anything like that – and we started our conversation," the book says. Kauffman said another married player, catcher Art Sanchez, agreed to attend the academy, and Kauffman would give Frank's wife, Gladys, a job in the camp's ticket office if that would enable White to enroll. White replied that he'd need to discuss the offer with his wife and parents first, and soon agreed.[23]

Thrift, Kauffman, and his wife held a press conference at Municipal Stadium to name the academy's first 15 students, and seven were present. White can be seen in a photo from that announcement, standing near the Kaufmanns. The Royals listed him as 5-feet-11, 167 pounds, and an outfielder.[24] About two months later, an academy team played its first game, against the semipro Sarasota Grays. White started the scoring in the first inning with a two-run homer, and his team won, 10-0.[25]

By the spring of 1971 White was officially a professional ballplayer, with the Royals' team in the rookie-level Gulf Coast League. Before that, players who had completed the academy's first year made a 16-day tour of Central and South America. White was one of eight players on that tour who hadn't played an inning of baseball in their high schools.[26] By the start of the 1972 season the academy had put 14 players into the Royals' minor-league system, and White had already played some exhibition games for Triple-A Omaha and Double-A Jacksonville before being assigned to San Jose in the Class-A California League.[27] He was told that Omaha manager Jack McKeon wanted to keep him, but White ended up splitting the 1972 season between San Jose and Jacksonville. He found the city of San Jose to be "exciting" but he was very uncomfortable when he returned to Florida. The academy at Sarasota was a self-contained community, but with Jacksonville his team traveled much more, and he quickly grew uncomfortable seeing signs supporting the Ku Klux Klan. He was the only African-American player with Jacksonville at the time, so at various stops his teammates got in the habit of bringing food and drinks to him while he remained on the bus.[28]

White started the 1973 season with Omaha. He was batting .280 when in early June it was announced that an injury would keep Royals shortstop Freddie Patek inactive for at least 10 days, and suddenly White found himself in the majors.[29]

White heard much later that there was resistance within the Royals' front office to calling him up, but that Jack McKeon, who had advanced from Omaha to managing Kansas City, reportedly said, "Send me Frank, or don't send me anyone." White made his major-league debut on June 12, 1973, in Baltimore. He replaced Bobby Floyd at shortstop in the bottom of the sixth inning. "The first ball that was hit to me was a high chopper that I lost in the lights and it hit me in the chest," White recalled. "I was thinking to myself, 'I'm glad that didn't happen in Kansas City.'"[30]

White grounded out to second in his only time up in the game, and went hitless in four at-bats as leadoff hitter the next night. His first two hits came against Doyle Alexander in his third game. In his sixth game he had three hits and a sacrifice fly in five plate appearances against Gaylord Perry. White led off the game with a triple, and his next time up Perry threw a pitch at

White's head. "He flipped me good," White recalled. "I didn't know about things like that. Gaylord thought I was showing him up, so he threw at my head." This was presumably when White batted for the second time, in the top of the second inning. White singled off Perry and drove in a run. Then in the bottom of the frame, Royals pitcher Dick Drago struck out catcher Dave Duncan and then hit Chris Chambliss on the hand. "He did it for me," White said. Drago "was protecting me and the rest of our hitters."[31]

White played his first game as a pro in Kansas City on June 18, in a 9-5 loss to the Oakland Athletics. In his 2012 autobiography he admitted that he didn't remember the game, in which he went hitless. He had two hits in five at-bats the next game. He did retain vivid memories of having been a construction worker at Royals (now Kauffman) Stadium, which had opened weeks earlier. Ewing Kauffman had arranged for White to work there during the previous offseason.[32]

On June 28, numerous newspapers printed an Associated Press story that profiled White as the academy's first graduate to reach the major leagues. In it he credited Gladys for encouraging him to try out for the academy and acknowledged Siebern's crucial praise. "I have no intention of sending White back to Omaha with Patek coming off the disabled list," McKeon emphasized. "I think White can help us. He can play shortstop, and he can play second base. He has proven that."[33]

A few weeks later the Royals acquired pitcher Joe Hoerner, and on July 20 White was returned to Omaha. In 27 games he batted .236.[34] He played 86 games for Omaha in 1973 and batted .264; he never played another game in the minors. He was one of the players called up from the minors when rosters expanded on September 1, and the *Kansas City Times*, writing about the September 18 "Farm Phenoms Night," highlighted White's 2-for-4 performance at bat along with George Brett's fielding. White and Brett batted first and second in the lineup.[35] White ended 1973 with 51 games for Kansas City and a .223 batting average. He then played winter ball in Venezuela under teammate Cookie Rojas, whose starting job at second base White ended up taking in 1976. White described in detail in his autobiography the help Rojas provided.[36]

On April 6, 1974, the Royals' second game of the season, White hit his first major-league home run. They hosted Minnesota and pounded six Twins pitchers, 23-6. White led off the seventh inning with a blast off Tom Burgmeier.[37] That season he started 25 games at second base, 17 at shortstop, and 10 at third base. In 1975 he started 57 times at second, 26 at short, and 2 at third base. In 1975 only Sandy Alomar and Pedro Garcia had better fielding percentages among second basemen who played in more games than White, and then only by a single percentage point, at .985.[38]

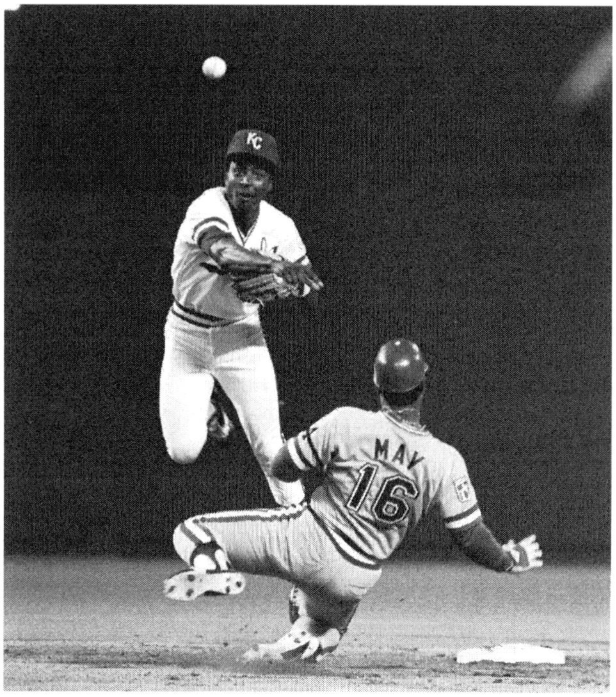

In 1976 White became the Royals' second baseman full time and also had his first postseason experience. Though Cookie Rojas had no longer been the team's starting second baseman, he and White split that duty in the American League Championship Series against the Yankees, who won the series three games to two. White didn't play in the final contest but still called it "one of the most heartbreaking games" of his entire life when Chris Chambliss homered to break a 6-6 tie in the bottom of the ninth inning.[39]

The ALCS outcome was the same in 1977, between the same two teams, and White found that the fifth game was even more gut-wrenching than a year earlier.[40] At least in the 1977 ALCS White was able to play full time, and showed up well with a .278 batting average. For that season he was awarded the first of six consecutive Gold Glove Awards. (He earned his seventh and eighth Gold Gloves in 1986 and 1987.) White said a last big leap forward as a student of fielding occurred when he played ball in Puerto Rico after the 1976 season.[41]

In mid-1978 White was named a reserve on the AL All-Star Team. He was also an All-Star in 1979, 1981, 1982, and 1986. In the 1978 All-Star Game he batted once and he popped out against Rollie Fingers. Decades later White didn't recall much about the experience, except that "it was so much fun being around the stars of the game." He noted that players "didn't fraternize much back then, but at the All-Star Game you could talk to the guys you played against and you could talk to the National League players you never saw."[42]

In 1978 the Royals faced the Yankees in their third consecutive ALCS, losing in four games. In hindsight, White suspected that he actively tried to forget that rematch.[43] The Royals didn't win their division in 1979, but White was selected by fans as the AL's starting second baseman in the All-Star Game. That season he achieved one personal best of note: His 28 stolen bases that season were the highest total of his career. He first reached 20 steals in 1976, and then had 23 in 1977. His best success rate was in the latter season, when he was caught only five times.

The Royals achieved a major milestone in 1980 by sweeping the Yankees in the ALCS. White was named the MVP of the series with a .545 batting average. He and the Royals played in their first World Series, against the Philadelphia Phillies.

Toward the end of the World Series, the *Jackson* (Mississippi) *Clarion-Ledger*'s Steve Doyle called White "a refreshing change" in an era of "the aloof superstar," and added, "He's a scholar and a gentleman, quiet and unassuming, confident, yet, not cocky." Doyle invoked two familiar names who were covering that World Series. "He is one beautiful person," said NBC-TV sportscaster Tony Kubek. Doyle noted that at least twice Sparky Anderson, working the Series for CBS Radio, proclaimed White the best in all of baseball. White laughed off the latter claim, saying, "I heard Sparky, and he said Willie Randolph is the best."[44] The Phillies won the World Series in six games.

The Royals returned to the playoffs in 1981 and 1984 but both times they were swept in three games. In between, White had a particularly good year in 1982 with 45 doubles and a .298 batting average, both career highs, and in 1983 he was named Royals Player of the Year for the first of two times. He also led AL second basemen in putouts for both 1982 and 1983. In 1984, for the seven days starting August 5, he was named AL Player of the Week.[45]

Then came 1985. During the regular season he hit a career-high 22 home runs, and on defense he led all AL players, regardless of position, with 490 assists.[46] The Royals won their division for the last time in his tenure, and beat the Toronto Blue Jays in the ALCS, four games to three. In preparation for the World Series against the St. Louis Cardinals, Royals manager Dick Howser summoned White into his office. "We can't use the DH, and since you had those 22 home runs during the season and have hit fourth a few times, I'd like you to hit cleanup," Howser said. "You gotta be kidding me," White replied. Howser wasn't joking.[47]

The Royals lost the first two games at home but in Game Three found themselves up 2-0 in the top of the fifth inning. George Brett led off with a single against St. Louis starter Joaquin Andujar, and then White knocked Andujar out of the game with a blast over the wall in the left-field power alley. Not surprisingly, White wrote at length about it:

"That was the longest home run I ever hit – and the most special. When I hit it, I watched (Tito) Landrum in left field and he never moved. When you're not known for hitting home runs, and you get one like that you're always going to remember it. I knew it was gone, so I wanted to make sure I ran the bases just right – not too fast and not too slow. I tried to be the ultimate professional and not show up the other team or the other pitcher. I still get chill bumps just thinking about it. I'd hit that home run a thousand times in the alley behind my house and in the park in our neighborhood, but now it really happened."[48]

The Royals won the game, 6-1, but were shut out in Game Four, so each remaining game was do-or-die. In Game Five, White drove in the first run in another 6-1 victory, and that sent the Series back to Kansas City for one or two more games. The Royals eked out a 2-1 win in Game Six to knot the Series at three games each. Much attention has been focused on first-base umpire Don Denkinger's botched "safe" call in the bottom of the ninth inning,[49] but two decades later Jason Roe of the Kansas City Public Library noted that "many fans have forgotten another call – one that benefited the Cardinals. In the fourth inning of Game Six, the Royals' Frank White appeared to have stolen second base, but was called out," Roe wrote. "The next batter, Pat Sheridan, hit a single to right field that would have allowed White to score the go-ahead run for the Royals."[50] Instead, the Royals didn't score until that memorable bottom of the ninth, which White called his "single greatest moment as a Royal. When we scored that run, we all knew we were going to win Game 7."[51]

The Royals won the World Series the next night, with an 11-0 blowout. White had a batting average of .250 in the World Series with a Series-leading six RBIs, four runs scored, three doubles, that important Game Three homer, and three walks.[52]

In 1986 the Royals slid to third place in their division, and didn't have a winning record, but that season may have been White's best. He was an All-Star again, and his homer in the seventh inning provided the decisive run. White achieved lifetime bests with 84 RBIs and 76 runs scored, and tied his career high with 22 home runs. He was named Royals Player of the Year for the second time and received his only Silver Slugger Award.[53] After the season he was among the players who traveled to Japan for a seven-game exhibition series.[54]

White's All-Star Game home run was a big thrill at the time, but soon became bittersweet. The AL manager was his own, Dick Howser. "My first all-star hit was a homer – and it was for Dick. I was so happy running around the bases," White wrote. "It looked like we were finally going to win my first All-Star Game and I was going to be able to share it with Dick and George [Brett]. Dick was so happy after we won." White knew at the time that Howser was battling cancer, but added, "[W]e had no idea how bad it all was. But the smile on his face when we won that game 3-2 was something I will always remember."[55]

In 1987 White became the first American League second baseman to be awarded an eighth Gold Glove.[56] A final milestone came at home on September 11, 1990, when he doubled home two runs with his 2,000th hit. More than 18,000 fans gave him a prolonged standing ovation. White stepped off second base and responded to the warm cheering with a smile and tip of his cap. "I respect them so much, I had to give them a bow," White said of the crowd. "They've been so good to me for so long."[57] He played his final major-league game at the end of that month, not by choice. The end of his career was awkward, to say the least.

A month after White's last game as a Royals player, Gib Twyman of the *Kansas City Star* expressed frustration about the aftermath. "It would be nice to see the Kansas City Royals not drop the ball on the departure of another of their fixtures, Frank White," he wrote. He observed that "the Royals have had a pretty tough time with these kinds of things over the years." Twyman alluded to a certain irony for "a club that has prided itself on organization, family, togetherness." How many of their great players, he wrote, "have wound up working here as scouts, coaches, instructors, front-office personnel? Some. Precious few, really."

"White's feelings are hurt, no matter what he says for print," Twyman concluded, and implied that White didn't make it easy on his team toward the end. "But White has meant too much to the team and town to just let him go away. Somehow, you'd like to see the club be creative enough that their longtime stars still seem part of them."[58]

White's relationship with the Royals swung from positive to negative and back over the years. In 1992 he jumped to the Boston organization, beginning with a season as manager of their Gulf Coast League rookie team. From 1994 to 1996 he was the first-base coach for the Red Sox. In the midst of that he was inducted into the Royals Hall of Fame in 1995 and his uniform number 20 was retired. He returned to the Royals in 1997, initially as the club's community outreach representative, but during the 1997 season he took over as first-base coach and continued in that role through 2001.[59]

Around the time White left Boston's organization, he and Gladys divorced after about 25 years of marriage. His first job after returning from Boston was with Blue Cross Blue Shield. There he met Teresa, who became his second wife on October 7, 2000.[60] In 2002 he entered the Royals' front office as special assistant to the general manager and in 2003 added manager of the Arizona Fall League's Peoria team to his duties. In 2004 a statue of White was erected on the ballpark grounds.[61] "That was one of the most special moments in my life because my father passed away a few months after that ceremony," White wrote. "I am so proud and honored that he lived long enough to see my statue, because I know it made him proud of me."[62]

From 2004 through 2006 White coached the Royals' Wichita team in the Texas League, and then switched to community relations, among other things by engaging with MLB's RBI (Reviving Baseball in Inner Cities) program.[63] In 2007 White became a senior adviser to the Royals, and in 2008, he added a part-time role with Fox Sports Kansas City as part of the team televising Royals games. From 2009 through 2011 that role increased to almost full time as broadcaster and former teammate Paul Splittorff slowly succumbed to cancer. White resigned the senior adviser position early in 2011 and declined a community-relations position.[64]

White's mother died in February 2010, so when his autobiography was published two years later, that personal loss was still very fresh in his memory, as was the erosion of his relationship with the Royals. "You'll never see me in that stadium again," White wrote in the book. However, his concluding words in it were, "Will I step back in that stadium? Never say never."[65]

In 2012 White joined the Kansas City T-Bones in the independent American Association and he continued in that role through 2016.[66] His relationship with the Royals started to revive in 2014,[67] and on September 1, 2015, when the Royals held their "Franchise Four" event honoring George Brett, White, Bret Saberhagen, and the late Dan Quisenberry as the four best players in team history, White attended and appeared to enjoy himself.[68]

In 2014 White ran and was elected to the Jackson County Legislature. On January 11, 2016, the county legislature appointed him county executive.[69] As a result, he took part in the Royals meeting with President Barack Obama after they won the 2015 World Series.[70]

White received considerable negative publicity in 2018 as a result of thousands of dollars in unpaid taxes and related financial problems, which led him to sell some of his memorabilia.[71] He had admitted in his autobiography that the players strike during the 1981 season caused financial hardship for him, and that being fired in late 2011 did likewise.[72] The news didn't seem to affect voters' attitudes about him much. On August 7, 2018, he received 68 percent of the vote in the primary for county executive, and on November 6 he was re-elected easily.[73]

So what exactly did John Schuerholz, Whitey Herzog, and Reggie Jackson say about Frank White? "Frank White is the best second baseman I have ever seen play," said Schuerholz. "He was like [dancer] Rudolf Nureyev at second base. Frank's athletic ability, agility, and physical play was unparalleled to me. In addition, he's a really classy guy." Herzog's assessment began similarly: "Frank White was the best defensive second baseman I have ever seen. I've seen second basemen that were pretty darn good such as Bobby Richardson and Bill Mazeroski. Frank played second base for me for five years and I just don't see how you play the position defensively any better than he played it."[74] Reggie Jackson took his praise in a somewhat different direction: "Frank White saved as many runs as I drove in," said Jackson. But leave it to George Brett to sound more like his bosses Schuerholz and Herzog: " 'It`s like that song by Carly Simon: 'Nobody Does It Better.'"[75]

Sources

In addition to the sources cited in the Notes, the author consulted Baseball-Reference.com.

Notes

1 See Denny Matthews with Matt Fulks, Denny Matthews's Tales from the Royals Dugout: *A Collection of the Greatest Stories Ever Told* (Champaign, Illinois: Sports Publishing, LLC, 2004), 106 and 107, for quotes by Schuerholz and Herzog. See Frank White with Bill Althaus, *One Man's Dream: My Town, My Team, My Time* (Olathe, Kansas: Ascend Books, 2012), 2, for a quote by Jackson and a different but equally strong quote by Schuerholz.

2 Claire Smith, "Brett's Fading Friends: It's All in the Game," *New York Times*, March 27, 1991: B11. Brett's baseball-reference.com stats for 1971 are limited to Billings in the Pioneer League, but toward the end of that year he and White were in the Florida Instructional League together. For example, see "Red Sox Pitchers Blank FIL Pirates," *Sarasota* (Florida) *Herald-Tribune*, October 16, 1971: 3-C. White and Brett were in opposing lineups and the latter homered as "the Kansas City Royals outslugged the Kansas City Baseball Academy 10-9 at the KC Complex."

3 David L. Porter, ed., *Biographical Dictionary of American Sports: Baseball, Q-Z* (Westport, Connecticut: Greenwood Press, 2000), 1660.

4 Frank White with Bill Althaus, *One Man's Dream: My Town, My Team, My Time* (Olathe, Kansas: Ascend Books, 2012), 23.

5 White, 29, 30.

6 "Baseball School May Save Sports," *Plaindealer* (Kansas City, Kansas), February 24, 1950: 4.

7 For example, see "Negro Baseball School to Meet Martin on Friday," *Delta Democrat-Times* (Greenville, Mississippi), March 15, 1950: 8. Players from Greenville who were mentioned were brothers Joe and Tom Barnes, both right-handed pitchers, and slugger Sid Wright.

8 William J. Plott, *The Negro Southern League: A Baseball History, 1920–1951* (Jefferson, North Carolina: McFarland & Company, Inc., 2015), 237. Greenville was also home to a "Colored" semipro team, the Brown Bombers, in 1948 and 1949 at a minimum. See "Cinderellas Face Greenville Team," *Monroe* (Louisiana) *Morning World*, April 25, 1948: 10, and large ad for a game in the *Delta Democrat-Times*, May 1, 1949: 5.

9 "Girl Star with Creoles Sunday," *Delta Democrat-Times* (Greenville, Mississippi), April 6, 1950: 6. The other three infielders were Alvin Taylor, Mike Hobbs, and Johnny Green. Jennings' planned outfield was Big Mules Depha, Charlie Walton, and Ike Newsom, but his battery was to be determined. See also "Orleans Creoles Beat Giants, 5-1," Delta Democrat-Times, April 10, 1950: 7. Attendance was estimated at 300.

10 Paul Borden, "Royals' White Not Fond of Magnolia Memories," *Jackson* (Mississippi) Clarion-Ledger, March 11, 1986: 19.

11 White, 24.

12 White, 25.

13 White, 28, 37.

14 White, 25, 28, 39.

15 See kcpublicschools.org/Page/1016.

16 Porter, 1660.

17 White, 29, 39, 238.

18 White, 37.

19 White, 31, 41, 44. During the 1970s he attended Metropolitan Community College-Longview in Lee's Summit, Missouri. See Christina Medina, "Video: MCC Is Proud to Call Royals Hall of Famer Frank White an MCC Alumnus," June 30, 2015: blogs.mcckc.edu/newsroom/2015/07/30/100-years-100-stories-frank-white-mcc-is-proud-to-call-frank-white-an-mcc-alumni/.

20 "Kauffman Has Academy Plans," *Panama City* (Florida) *News*, September 12, 1969: 2B. For more information, see Richard Peurzer, "The Kansas City Royals' Baseball Academy," *The National Pastime*, Number 24, 2004: 9-10.

21 White, 41.

22 White, 42.

23 White, 42-43.

24 Ed Fowler, "Royals Line up 15 for Academy," *Kansas City Times*, July 4, 1970: 17. In his autobiography White described his academy experience in detail (pages 44-51).

25 "Academy Starts with 10-0 Victory," *Kansas City Times*, September 8, 1970: 36.

26 "Royals Baseball Academy to Hold Tryouts in P.C.," *Playground Daily News* (Fort Walton Beach, Florida), June 4, 1971: 13.

27 "Academy Sends 14 Into System," *Kansas City Times*, April 13, 1972: 57.

28 White, 51-52.

29 "Royals Call Frank White," *Kansas City Times*, June 12, 1973: 23.

30 White, 53-54. At baseball-reference.com/boxes/BAL/BAL197306120.shtml it shows two balls were hit to him. In the bottom of the eighth inning he threw out Al Bumbry on the first, but in the bottom of the ninth Tommy Davis reached on an infield single hit toward White. White wasn't charged with an error in his debut.

31 White, 54. He said Drago broke Chambliss's hand but Chambliss didn't leave the game, nor did he miss any time in subsequent games. However, Chambliss remained in a prolonged slump and went a week without driving in a run. See "Aspro Knows Feeling," *Sandusky* (Ohio) *Register*, June 26, 1973: 24.

32 White, 59-60, 67.

33 "Dream Comes True for KC's 'Academy Frank,'" *Neosho* (Missouri) *Daily News*, June 28, 1973: 11. In the article he named two baseball idols, Hank Aaron and Jackie Robinson, though on page 53 of his 2012 autobiography White said he chose uniform number 20 because Frank Robinson was his favorite player.

34 "Frank White Sent to Omaha," *Kansas City Times*, July 21, 1973: 51.

35 Gib Twyman, "Royals Keep 'Em Down with Farm," *Kansas City Times*, September 19, 1973: 26.

36 White: 54-56.

37 See baseball-reference.com/players/event_hr.fcgi?id=whitefr01&t=b.

38 See baseball-reference.com/leagues/AL/1975-specialpos_2b-fielding.shtml.

39 White, 75-76.

40 White, 77.

41 White, 108.

42 White, 160.

43 White, 78.

44 Steve Doyle, "White Shines Bright," *Jackson* (Mississippi) *Clarion-Ledger*, October 20, 1980: 6B. The article started on page 1B. Not surprisingly, White wrote at length in his autobiography about the 1980 postseason. See pages 83-91 about that ALCS and pages 21-22 and 92-95 about the World Series.

45 See kansascity.royals.mlb.com/kc/history/awards.jsp and https://www.baseball-reference.com/players/w/whitefr01.shtml#all_leaderboard.

46 See baseball-reference.com/players/w/whitefr01.shtml#all_leaderboard.

47 White, 12.

48 White, 14-15.

49 See mlb.com/news/don-denkinger-players-recall-blown-call-in-1985-world-series/c-99040244.

50 kchistory.org/week-kansas-city-history/championship-season.

51 White, 19.

52 See mlb.com/royals/hall-of-fame/members/frank-white.

53 See kansascity.royals.mlb.com/kc/history/awards.jsp and slugger.com/en-us/silver-slugger-awards.

54 "All-Stars Top Japan," *Daily Sitka* (Alaska) *Sentinel*, November 3, 1986: 6.

55 White, 163.

56 See mlb.com/royals/hall-of-fame/members/frank-white.

57 "Blue Jays Thump KC; White Gets 2,000th Hit in Loss to Toronto," *Macon* (Missouri) *Chronicle-Herald*, September 12, 1990: 2.

58 Gib Twyman, "Royals Bobble Ball with Treatment of White," Salina (Kansas) Journal, October 30, 1990: 11.

59 See mlb.mlb.com/kc/team/exec_bios/white_frank.jsp.

60 White, 125, 191.

61 See mlb.mlb.com/kc/team/exec_bios/white_frank.jsp.

62 White, 34, 138.

63 White, 147. He also engaged with the RBI program a decade later; see David Brown, "Former Player White Gives Kids a Boost at Clinic," July 15, 2017, mlb.com/news/royals-frank-white-helps-kids-at-rbi-clinic/c-242376764.

64 See Jason M. Vaughn, "Royals Boot Frank White Off Broadcast Team," WDAF-TV, December 2, 2011; fox4kc.com/2011/12/02/frank-white-out-of-royals-broadcast-team/.

65 White, 35, 174, 241.

66 See baseball-reference.com/bullpen/Frank_White.

67 See Jeff Passan, "Why Royals Great Frank White No Longer Associates with the Team Whose Stadium He Built," Yahoo Sports, October 19, 2014; sports.yahoo.com/news/why-royals-great-frank-white-no-longer-associates-with-the-team-whose-stadium-he-built-044453095.html.

68 Karen Kornacki, "Frank White: Return to Kauffman Stadium Was Awesome," KMBC 9 News, September 1, 2015; kmbc.com/article/frank-white-return-to-kauffman-stadium-was-awesome/3555744.

69 See jacksongov.org/395/County-Executive.

70 See jacksongov.org/794/Royals-White-House-Celebration.

71 For example, see Tom Dempsey, "Records: Jackson County Executive Owes $45,000 in Unpaid Taxes," KSHB-TV News, September 27, 2018; kshb.com/news/region-missouri/jackson-county/jackson-co-executive-owes-45000-in-unpaid-taxes.

72 White, 98, 166, 213.

73 See ballotpedia.org/Frank_White_Jr.

74 Denny Matthews with Matt Fulks, *Denny Matthews's Tales from the Royals Dugout: A Collection of the Greatest Stories Ever Told* (Champaign, Illinois: Sports Publishing, LLC, 2004), 106, 107.

75 Jack Etkin, "Royals' White Isn't Ready to Quit Just Yet," *Chicago Tribune*, October 7, 1990: Section 3, page 8. (Etkin was a reporter for the *Kansas City Star* at the time.)

WILLIE WILSON

BY ALAN COHEN

"I always hope he hits the ball to left so I can watch him run, because I've never seen anything like him turning second."

— Dwight Evans of the Red Sox, talking about Willie Wilson in 1980[1]

"Having Willie Wilson in center field is like having four outfielders."

— Billy Scripture (Wilson's first minor-league manager) in 1974[2]

Willie Wilson did not know his father.

Willie James Wilson was born in Montgomery, Alabama, on July 9, 1955 and as a young boy lived with his grandmother, Annie Mae (known as Madear). Uncle Tim, Aunt Sally, and his great-grandmother. His other aunts and uncles lived nearby and included Aunt Martha, who taught him life's early lessons. They all lived in the Jackson Heights section of Montgomery, and Willie's first schooling was at the segregated George Washington Carver Elementary School. He was there through the first grade, when he went to live with his mother in Summit, New Jersey. He was escorted on the long bus trip by his grandmother and his uncle Tim. After moving north, he would return to the South during the summers and work on the family farm.

At the end of the long bus trip from Montgomery to Newark, New Jersey, Willie met his mother, Dorothy, for the first time. By then, she was Dorothy Lynn, having married Gene Lynn and had a baby, Willie's younger brother, Anthony. George earned a living in Summit, New Jersey, where they settled, washing windows, but Willie's mother and stepfather divorced while Willie was in elementary school.

New Jersey was a new experience for young Willie, who was enrolled at Lincoln Elementary School. The school was predominantly white, with only a handful of black students. He played youth football in the Pop Warner League and by the time he got to high school, the athletic youngster was ready to excel. His football coach, Howie Anderson, and baseball coach, Dominic Guida, guided him through four formative years, and Art Cottrell coached him in baseball at Summit High School.

Although the picture of a fleet-footed Willie Wilson manning the outfield is familiar to most fans, he was a catcher during his high-school years. His hero among major-league players of the time was catcher Manny Sanguillen of the Pittsburgh Pirates. His other hero was running back Gale Sayers of the NFL Chicago Bears. Knowing of how Willie felt about Sayers, coach Anderson arranged to have Sayers visit Wilson in the hospital when Willie was recovering from a football injury. Part of championship teams in both baseball and football, Willie had thoughts of going to the University of Maryland on an athletic scholarship.

But after signing a letter of intent to go to Maryland, Wilson was drafted in the first round by the Kansas City Royals in the June 1974 draft. Accompanied by his mother, football coach Anderson, and lawyer Gil Owren, Wilson went to Kansas City and signed with the Royals for $90,000, some of which went to pay bills that his mother, a single woman who had lost her job, had accrued.

Wilson's first stop as a professional ballplayer was Sarasota in the Gulf Coast League. Rookie League was a time of adjustment for him. Not only was he away from home for the first time, but he was learning to play the outfield and facing hard throwers, some with not much control, in every game. After a slow start, he finished well to raise his batting average to .252. He stole 24 bases in 47 games.

In 1975 Wilson was at Waterloo in the Class-A Midwest League. His team ran away with the divisional title, posting a 93-35 record. He led the league in hits (132), set a Midwest League record with 76 stolen bases, and was named the league's player of the year. The next season, he was at Jacksonville in the Double-A Southern League. In early August, the Royals scouting director and director of player development, John Schuerholz, said, "We believe he is playing center field as good or better than anybody in the organization. Defensively, Willie is a major-league center fielder right now."[3] After 107 games, Wilson was batting .253 with 37 stolen bases when he was sidelined with a hamstring injury. When he came off the DL on September 2, he was called up to the Royals and made his major-league debut against the Texas Rangers on September 4, entering the game in Kansas City as a defensive replacement for Amos Otis in the ninth inning.

Wilson's next appearance, on September 9, was a harbinger of his basepath wizardry at the big-league level. In the bottom of the ninth inning at home against the Angels, with the Royals trailing 5-3, John Mayberry singled in Tom Poquette and advanced Fred Patek to third base. Wilson was inserted as a pinch-runner for Mayberry. Pitcher Mike Overy tried to pick off Wilson and his throw eluded first baseman Tony Solaita. Patek raced home with the tying run and Wilson advanced to second. Willie had his first steal in a game the Royals would win in 10 innings.[4]

The next day, in a blowout at Minneapolis, Wilson had his first at-bats in the majors. The score was already 10-0 when he entered the game in the bottom of the fifth inning as a defensive replacement. By the time he came to bat in the seventh inning, the score was 17-0. With two out and a runner on first, Wilson hit a grounder between the shortstop and third base. By the time shortstop Roy Smalley fielded the ball, Wilson was approaching first base. Smalley held on to the ball and Wilson had his first-major league hit. That was his only hit in 12 at-bats in September 1976.

In spring training for the 1977 season, the decision was made to convert Wilson into a switch-hitter. As a right-handed hitter, he had had difficulty with the slider from right-handed pitchers. Hitting from the left side would counter the effectiveness of that pitch. Also, hitting from the left side would give him the opportunity to better utilize his speed going to first base. The season was spent at Triple-A Omaha. Wilson batted .281, his highest average in four minor-league seasons. At the end of the minor-league season he again was called up to the Royals, with much better results than 1976.

On September 15 at home against Oakland, he starred in a doubleheader sweep. In the first game, after entering the game in the ninth inning as a pinch-runner, he stayed in the contest, singling and scoring the winning run in the 11th inning. He made his first start in the second game and went 2-for-5 with a double, scoring the first two of his team's runs in a 5-4 win. In 13 games, he batted .324. As a late season callup, Wilson was not eligible for the postseason and was a spectator as the Royals lost in the ALCS to the Yankees.

In the offseason between 1977 and 1978, Wilson played winter ball in the Dominican Republic and his hitting was aided when he worked with Licey Tigers teammate Manny Mota.

Wilson's first full year in the majors was 1978, and he had his struggles adapting to big-league pitching. Although he played in 127 of his team's games, starts were rare after May 23. He started 14 games in April and was batting .291 at month's end. In May he went into a slump. After starting 15 games, during which he went 9-for-51 (.176), Wilson's average after the doubleheader on May 23 stood at .236. Thereafter, most of his appearances were as a pinch-runner or defensive replacement. Although he stole 46 bases, his batting average for the season plummeted to .217.

The Royals won the AL West for the third consecutive year advanced to the ALCS, once again against the Yankees. Wilson first saw action in Games Two and Three as a pinch-runner. In Game Four, he started in left field and in the top of the fifth inning, with the score tied 1-1, beat out a grounder to shortstop for his first postseason hit. He advanced to second on a groundball but was gunned down trying to steal third base. The Yankees won the game, 2-1, and advanced to the World Series.

There was a degree of uncertainty going into the 1979 season, but an injury to Al Cowens on May 8 gave Wilson an opportunity to play regularly. After starting only six of his team's first 30 games, he was given a start on May 11.

"It was a high fastball, and I just got on top of it. It went into the gap. It got through to the fence and I just kept running. When I got to third, they waved me in, and I just kept going."

— Willie Wilson[5]

On May 13 manager Whitey Herzog put Wilson atop the batting order for the first time, and he went 3-for-6. In the top of the seventh inning, he faced Steve Trout of the White Sox. The game was already decided as the Royals were leading 10-3. With a runner on third and one out, Wilson hit the ball to left-center field and scampered around the bases for his first major-league home run. It was the first of his 13 career inside-the park homers.

He played in each of his team's remaining games, all but two as a starter. A nine-game hitting streak from May 20 through May 29 pushed his average to .357. On a team based on speed, Wilson was the fastest and improved his base-stealing technique as he played alongside Amos Otis and Fred Patek.

During the season, Wilson and his wife, Kathy, had their first child, daughter Shanice Nicole. was born on August 29, after Wilson had been named AL Player of the Week for a six-game stretch during he went 13-for-24 (.542) and stole 8 bases.[6] The couple's second child, Donnel, was born on April 30, 1983.

The Royals won seven of eight games between August 22 and 30 and were briefly in first place. However, they were unable to capitalize on a good finish by Wilson (.336 with 18 stolen bases in September) and finished three games behind the Angels. For the season, Wilson stole a league-leading 83 bases and wound up batting .315. It was the first of four consecutive seasons in which his average was above .300. Although It was the only time he led the league in steals, it was the second of 15 consecutive seasons with 20 or more thefts.

In 1980 Wilson's 705 at-bats not only led the American League, but also made him the first major leaguer with more than 700 at-bats. His league-leading 133 runs scored were the most runs ever scored in a season by a switch-hitter in the American League. His league-leading 230 hits tied the major-league record for hits by a switch-hitter in a season. He had 184 singles, the most ever by a player in the American League.[7] He led the league with 15 triples, and his 79 steals were second in the league to Rickey Henderson's 100. For Wilson, it would be the last time he stole more than 60 bases in the season. Factoring into his decision to run less often was the fact that if first base was open, intentional passes would be given to teammates like George Brett, who batted .390 that year. Wilson's

.326 batting average was overshadowed by Brett's flirtation with .400. Wilson's mastery of the outfield was recognized with his only career Gold Glove Award.

The Royals returned to the postseason in 1980. Once again, they faced the Yankees. In the second game of the ALCS, Wilson tripled in his team's first two runs and scored the third Royals run as they took a 3-0 lead in the third inning. The Royals were clinging to a 3-2 lead when the Yankees threatened in the eighth inning. Willie Randolph was at first base with two outs when Bob Watson doubled down the left-field line. Wilson raced toward the corner, retrieved the ball and, as Randolph raced around the bases, threw the ball in. Brett relayed the throw to catcher Darrell Porter, who tagged out Randolph. The Royals won the game, took a 2-0 lead in the series, and traveled to New York to play in front of a crowd of 56,588 that included many of his hometown fans. New York took a 2-1 lead in the bottom of the sixth inning. Two Royals were retired in the top of the seventh inning when Wilson stepped to the plate against Tommy John. Wilson's double ignited a rally topped off by Brett's three-run homer that gave the Royals a 4-2 lead. There was no further scoring, and the Royals were in the World Series.

"It went from the highest high beating the Yankees in New York to the lowest low."

— Willie Wilson[8]

After defeating the Yankees on October 10, the Royals waited in New York to see whether they would be playing Houston or Philadelphia in the World Series. They took the short flight to Philadelphia for the Series opener on October 14. Wilson had a terrible Series, striking out 12 times. Nevertheless, the Royals had a chance to extend the Series to a seventh game when they mounted a ninth-inning rally in Game Six. Down 4-1 going into the ninth, they loaded the bases with one out. Frank White popped out, bringing up Wilson, who was 0-for-3 with a walk in the game. He fouled off two pitches and then swung at missed at a high fastball and the World Series was over. By the time of Wilson's next appearance in a World Series, his world had turned upside down. In the aftermath of the 1980 series, much was made of his 12 strikeouts, and the negativity extended into the following season.

The Royals got off to a bad start in 1981 and Wilson was batting .271 when the players went on strike after the games of June 11. The team was 20-30. When play resumed in August, Wilson and the Royals caught fire. In the 53 games after the strike, Wilson batted .332 and stole 26 bases. For the season, his average was .303. The Royals posted the best post-strike record (30-23) in the AL West and played a best-of-five series against Oakland to determine the AL West's representative in the ALCS. Oakland swept the Royals and advanced.

Wilson had one of his best seasons in 1982. After pulling a hamstring during spring training and missing 24 of his team's first 26 games, he returned to the lineup on May 9 and hit in 16 consecutive games. His hitting streak, including a start on April 19, stood at 17 games, and his batting average was .347 on May 26. It was his best start ever and he was selected for the All-Star Game for the first time. He entered the game in the fourth inning and was 0-for-2. At the All-Star break, he was batting .344, and the Royals trailed the division-leading Angels by one game. As the season drew to its conclusion, Wilson was contending for the league batting title with Robin Yount of the Brewers.

The Angels clinched the AL West on Saturday, October 2, the next to last day of the season. Going into the last game, Wilson had a four-point lead in the batting race (.332 to .328). Yount would need a 4-for-5 day to catch him. The Royals brain trust of Dick Howser and John Schuerholz advised Wilson to sit the day out. So, Wilson did not start in an otherwise meaningless game between Kansas City and Oakland. In his first four at-bats, Yount hit a pair of homers, a fly ball, and a triple while Wilson sat. Both games were in the late innings and if Yount got up a fifth time, a hit would put him in the lead.

That was when things got a bit dicey. The Royals began a stalling act with two outs in their half of the ninth inning. They were down by three runs and the outcome of the game did not matter. Manager Howser called batter Mark Ryal back to the dugout for a chat, and he was ready to insert Wilson into the game in the event Yount got the needed hit in his final at-bat. Opposing A's manager Billy Martin, fully aware of the motivation for the stalling, phoned the Royals dugout and agreed to go along with the stall, making an unnecessary and prolonged visit to the mound to talk with his pitcher, Dave Beard. When word came that Yount had been hit by a pitch in his final plate appearance, Howser signaled Martin, and Billy left the mound. Beard got Ryal out on a grounder, the game was over, and Wilson had won the batting title, .3316 to .3307.

The negative image that surfaced when Wilson struck out 12 times in the World Series was further fueled by his failure to play the final game of the 1982 season. The ghosts of each would stay with him. Then, an off-field ghost entered the picture. Wilson began to experiment with cocaine. The experimentation was over by the beginning of the 1983 season and Wilson got off to a good start. Through May 25, he had played in each of his team's 37 games and was batting .302. He was once again named to the All-Star team. In the All-Star Game, Wilson entered the game defensively in top of the seventh inning. He came to bat in the bottom of the seventh and drove in Lou Whitaker with a double. It was the 11th AL run as they won the game 13-3. It was Wilson's final All-Star appearance.

On July 24 at New York, Wilson injured his shoulder diving for a ball hit by Roy Smalley in the fifth inning and came out of the game for a pinch-hitter in the top of the sixth. He missed a couple of games but returned to the lineup on July 27. In those three days, his world turned upside down. His voice had been recorded in a call to his former cocaine supplier and he had been questioned by police on July 25. The team was informed that Wilson and several other Royals were involved in the investigation. The rest of the season went by as a blur for Wilson, who batted .276 with 59 stolen bases.

After the season, Wilson faced charges related to cocaine and plead guilty to a misdemeanor count of attempting to buy cocaine, the charges being based on the wiretap evidence. In a time when there was little tolerance for cocaine use, especially by an athlete, Wilson was sentenced to a year in jail, of which nine months was suspended. He began serving his 90-day sentence on December 5, 1983. He was released nine days early, on March 1, 1984, from the federal penitentiary near Dallas, Texas.

Wilson was suspended by Commissioner Bowie Kuhn on December 13, 1983. The suspension was for one year, but it was subject to review on May 15. While suspended, Wilson worked out and met with team owner Ewing Kauffman, who proved to be a pillar of support through the crisis. The suspension was lifted on May 16, 1984, 33 games into the season. In his first game back, Wilson walked in the first inning. With Frank White batting, Wilson stole second base without a throw. White Sox pitcher Floyd Bannister then tried to pick Wilson off second base. Second baseman Julio Cruz misplayed the ball and it went into short center field.[9] Wilson scored from second base, giving the Royals an early lead in a game they won 7-6. Wilson had another solid season, batting .301 and stealing 47 bases as the Royals won another AL West title. In the playoffs, Kansas City was swept by the Tigers in three games.

Despite his renewed success on the ballfield, Wilson's trials off the field continued. During the 1984 season, he and his wife, Kathy, separated. They were divorced on February 19, 1987. Although he felt stress from his marital problems and the lingering criticism by fans of him for his drug problems, Wilson continued to contribute on the field. When he was separated from Kathy, he had a child out of wedlock. Mallori was born on February 5, 1985. Wilson married for the second time in 1988. He and Catherine had two sons, Trevor in 1992 and Max in 1995.

Early in the 1985 season, Wilson signed a lifetime contract with the Royals that would ultimately yield him $27 million by some estimates.[10] The deal called for a four-year contract extension through 1989 with a salary of $1.25 million per year, of which $250,000 would be invested by a Royals minority owner. The money would effectively be used to provide an annuity to Wilson after his playing days. Within a couple of years of signing, Wilson, not feeling that he had made the best deal, elected to take a buyout.

On May 22, 1985, Wilson stole his 400th base, against the Texas Rangers. The Royals won the game, putting them two games above .500. The teams in the AL were tightly bunched but the Royals had trouble making headway. They were still two games above .500 as late as July 21 and were 7½ games out of first place.

A seven-game winning streak in late July moved the Royals into second place, and for the balance of the season they challenged the Angels for the AL West lead. Wilson was batting .285 at the end of August, and the Royals trailed the division leaders by 2½ games. But Wilson was not feeling well and, while his team was in Texas, took a penicillin shot. He had a bad reaction to the shot and missed the next 18 games. During the time he was absent from the lineup, the Royals went on a tear, winning 13 of 18 games and taking a two-game lead over the Angels.

When he returned to action, Wilson went into a slump, going 2-for-26 over six games. But by the time the Royals returned home for their last two series of the season, Wilson was back in stride with both his hitting and fielding. In the first of the two series, the Royals took three of four from the Angels at Kansas City and had a one-game lead going into their season-ending three-game series against Oakland. In the first two games, Wilson's season was redeemed. In the first game he led off the third inning with a double and came home on a single by Jorge Orta to make the score 2-0. The Royals won, 4-2, to clinch a tie for the division championship.

The next day, before a home crowd of 32,949, the game went into extra innings. The day did not start out well as the Royals fell behind 4-0. Never in the season had the Royals come back to win from such a deficit. Wilson legged out an infield hit, and George Brett homered to cut the lead in half in the sixth inning, and the Royals evened things up in their next at-bat. The game went into the 10th inning. Although Wilson set a career high with his league-leading 21 triples in 1985 (the third of five times he would lead the league in triples), it was a single that proved the most memorable hit of his day and season. He came to the plate with two on and two out in the 10th inning and sent a Jay Howell fastball up the middle. Howell got his glove on the ball but was unable to catch it. The ball rolled over second base and into the outfield. Wilson rounded first, pumping his fist into the air as Pat Sheridan came in from third with the winning run that sent the Royals to the playoffs.[11]

In the ALCS, the Toronto Blue Jays won the first two games. In Game Three of the best-of-seven series, Wilson's sixth-inning single was followed by George Brett's game-tying homer, and the Royals won, 6-5. However, Toronto won the next game to take a 3-1 lead in the series. The Royals had to win the next three games, including the final two in Toronto, to advance to the World Series, and they did precisely that. Wilson had the most hits (9) of any Royals player in the series.

Against St. Louis in the World Series, the Royals lost the first two games at home. In Game Three, behind a strong pitching effort by Bret Saberhagen, the Royals won 6-1. The Cardinals won Game Four to go up 3-1 in the Series and once again the Royals had a formidable task. In game Five, Wilson's first two at-bats proved productive. In the first inning, his single advanced Lonnie Smith to second and Smith subsequently scored the first run of the game. By the time, he came to bat in the second inning, the Royals led 2-1 and there were runners on first and second. Wilson, batting left-handed, tripled into the gap in right-center field, giving the Royals a 4-1 lead. Pitcher Danny Jackson shut down the Cardinals from that point.

The Royals' 6-1 win took the Series back to Kansas City. They won Game Six with two runs in their last at-bat to force Game Seven and manhandled the Cardinals 11-0 in the finale to win their first World Series. They broke the game open with six runs in the fifth inning, during which Wilson got a run-scoring infield hit. His 11 hits in the Series led the Royals, and he was relieved that he cut his strikeouts down from 12 in 1980 to four in 1985. After the Series the Royals went to Washington and met with President Reagan and Vice President Bush.

In 1986, any problems of Wilson and his teammates were secondary, as manager Dick Howser's illness left its mark on the team. It was brain cancer. After he managed the American League in the All-Star Game, it was evident that Howser could not continue.

An 11-game losing streak from June 27 through July 8 took the Royals out of contention. Mike Ferraro took over as manager on July 17 and the team limped to a third-place finish, 16 games out of first place. Wilson hit .269 with 34 stolen bases.

The 1987 Royals were a bit younger with the addition of Bo Jackson and Kevin Seitzer. The team mourned Howser's death on June 17. The core of older players who had been there when Wilson first arrived was further depleted when Hal McRae was released. Billy Gardner managed the Royals for most of the season, but the team was two games under .500 when Wilson's former teammate John Wathan was named manager August 27. No team was dominating the AL West and the Royals were still in contention on Labor Day. They won nine of their last 11 games and finished the season in second place, two games behind the AL West champion Twins. Wilson led the league in triples with 15 and batted .279.

In 1988 and 1989, the Royals continued to add new talent to the mix. In 1988 they finished third. Wilson led the league in triples (11) for the last time and his batting average sank to .262. In 1989 Wilson played in fewer games (112) than in any season other than the strike-shortened 1981 season. The Royals posted a 92-70 record and finished in second place. In neither season had they made a serious run at the championship. And Wilson seemed to be nearing the end of the line. In 1989, at age 33, he batted only .253.

As the 1990 season began, Wilson was no longer playing regularly as Bo Jackson, Danny Tartabull, and Jim Eisenreich were the starting outfield. However, an early-season injury to Tartabull gave Wilson the opportunity to get into the lineup. In April he started 16 of his team's 18 games and batted .345. Tartabull did not return to the lineup until May 19. By then Wilson's bat had cooled off a bit and his average had slipped to .293. For the season, his last with the Royals, Wilson batted .290 and had 24 stolen bases, bringing his career total with the Royals to 612.

Under the terms of the contract Wilson had signed with the Royals, the team could pick up his option for the following season or release him. They elected to release him. The Oakland A's wasted no time in signing Wilson and he was with them for two years. In 1991 he was a situational player, as the team was set with Dave Henderson, Jose Canseco, and Rickey Henderson in the outfield, and Wilson, primarily a singles hitter, was rarely asked to DH. He got into 113 games with 64 starts. He batted only .238 as the A's, after three consecutive trips to the World Series, finished fourth in the AL West.

In 1992 Wilson became an important cog in the A's machine as Dave Henderson hurt himself in spring training and was out for most of the season, getting into only 20 games. Wilson, at age 36, started 100 games, batted .270, and stole 28 bases. The A's went 19-10 in August and took a 6½-game lead into September. They coasted to their fourth division championship in five years. In the best-of-seven ALCS, Oakland was defeated by Toronto in six games. Wilson played in each game, going 5-for-22 with seven stolen bases.

After the season, the A's did not offer Wilson a contract extension and he signed with the Chicago Cubs. The Cubs were a younger team and Wilson was playing in the National League for the first time. He was also playing before fans who were far more boisterous than what he had experienced in Oakland over the prior two seasons.

Early in the season, Wilson received word that his grandmother, who had raised him in the early years of his life, had died. He returned to the team after the April funeral, but his playing time with the Cubs was not significant. He started only 39 games and had 237 plate appearances, his lowest total since 1978. He stole fewer than 20 bases in a season for the first time, and he played for a team that had finished below .500 the prior three seasons. On September 2 the Cubs were six games below .500 and 19½ games behind the division leaders.

Wilson was never a big home-run hitter, but his most memorable moment of 1993 involved the long ball. On September 6 the Cubs, having won three straight games, started a three-game series in Philadelphia. The fans, remembering Wilson's being the goat of the 1980 World Series, were heckling him severely. That day he got a bit of revenge. In the top of the fourth inning, he doubled and scored a run that put the Cubs ahead 3-2. Two innings later, the Cubs scored three runs on consecutive homers by Steve Buechele, Wilson, and Steve Lake to make the score 7-2 in a game they won 7-6. The home run was the last of Wilson's 41 career homers, and the only one he hit after leaving the Royals.

The Cubs went 20-8 over their last 28 games and finished the 1993 season over .500. Wilson batted .258. The Cubs released him on May 16, 1994. He had started only three games. His last appearance came on that day, and he went out with a flourish. He entered the game at San Diego as a pinch-runner in the bottom of the eighth inning and finished the game in center field. With the Cubs leading 4-2 and one out in the bottom of the ninth, Dave Staton of the Padres hit a fly ball to deep left-center field. Wilson, in full gallop, reached out and grabbed the ball. Pitcher Randy Myers struck out the next Padres batter to end the game.

Wilson finished his 19-year career with 2,207 hits. His 668 stolen bases rank him 12th on the all-time list. His lifetime batting average was .285.

By the time Wilson left baseball in 1994, he had remarried and lived in Kansas City. He invested in a Toronto-based telecommunications company, and that turned out to be a bad investment. Other investments, including a restaurant in New Jersey, also did not work out, and he was bleeding financially. Wilson tried his hand at coaching in the minor leagues but was unsuccessful. He was a coach for the Syracuse Chiefs, Toronto's Triple-A affiliate, for most of 1997 before being reassigned to Dunedin in the Class-A Florida State League.

By 1999, Wilson was on the verge of bankruptcy. He was also using cocaine. He sought help for his drug problem at the Shawnee Mission Medical Center and got clean. In 2000, not long after his drug rehab, he was inducted into the Royals Hall of Fame, but his problems with money were far from over. He filed for bankruptcy, and during the process was stripped of his baseball memorabilia. An auction in April 2001 raised $30,570. Wilson's World Series ring was sold for $16,250.[12] The problems he faced during this period put a stress on his marriage, and his wife and children moved to Toronto to be closer to her family.

Wilson got back into baseball in 2001 as a coach in the Arizona Diamondbacks organization. He was with the South Bend Silver Hawks in the Class-A Midwest League. The team did well, and in 2002 Wilson was promoted to a higher-level Class-A team, the Lancaster JetHawks in the California League. Toward the end of the season, he was released after a confrontation with one of the players.

Wilson relocated to Toronto and lived near his wife and children, but in the summer of 2004, he returned to New Jersey and established a baseball camp. His camp proved to be a success and he stayed with it for several years, bringing in former teammates to work with the children. He moved back to Kansas City, where he became more involved with the Royals, gave clinics to youngsters, and worked with the Negro League Baseball Museum. In 2008 the Royals named their minor-league baserunning award in Wilson's honor.

In September 23, 2014, at a book signing and talk after the release of his autobiography, Wilson received a surprise. Helen Mohr, who oversees the Willie Wilson Foundation, presented him with a 1985 World Series ring. About 100 of his friends had funded a recasting of a new ring to replace the ring that had been auctioned off in 2001.[13]

At age 63 in 2018, Wilson was at peace with himself and spent as much time with his five grandchildren as his schedule allowed.

Sources

In addition to the sources shown in the notes, the author used Baseball-Reference.com, the Willie Wilson file at the National Baseball Hall of Fame and Museum, and the following sources:

Black, Del. "Royals Outfield to Depend on Willie Wilson," *The Sporting News*, March 25, 1978: 53.

Bordman, Sid. "Royals' Speedy Wilson Setting Hot Bat Pace," *The Sporting News*, August 18, 1979: 13.

Fish, Mike. "Wilson Is Basking in Second Chance," *The Sporting News*, May 6, 1985: 17.

Kaplan, Jim. "Will He Be Willie Again?" *Sports Illustrated*, February 9, 1981: 78, 81.

Looney, Douglas S. "Fleetest of the Royal Fleet," *Sports Illustrated*, April 24, 1978: 34.

McKenzie, Mike. "Wilson's Fuse Always Burning," *The Sporting News*, October 11, 1982: 49.

Rock, Steve. "Bittersweet Blessing: Wilson Glad to Go in Royals' Hall, but Expected More from Team," *Kansas City Star*, June 26, 2000: C1.

"Our Opinion: Some Mixed-Up Priorities," *The Sporting News*, October 18, 1982: 6.

Notes

1 Peter Gammons, "Continual Spur Necessary for Whippet Willie Wilson," *The Sporting News*, May 24, 1980: 23.

2 Mike DeArmond, "Injuries Fail to Quell Enthusiasm for Royal Farm Hands," *Kansas City Star*, August 6, 1974: 10.

3 Del Black, "Royals Farm Teams Play Follow Their Leader," *Kansas City Star*, August 4, 1976: 18A.

4 Associated Press, "Royals Win Squeaker in 10th on Clutch Brett Hit," *Baton Rouge Morning Advocate*, September 10, 1976. 4-C.

5 Willie Wilson (with Kent Pulliam), Inside the Park: Running the Base Path of Life, (Olathe, Kansas: Ascend Books, 2013), 75.

6 Jim Kaplan, "K.C. Takes Off on Willie's Wings," *Sports Illustrated*, September 10, 1979: 26.

7 The Sporting News, October 18, 1980: 41.

8 Wilson with Pulliam, 100.

9 Kaplan, "Taking Steps to Solve the Drug Dilemma," *Sports Illustrated*, May 28,1884: 36.

10 Bob Nightingale, "Wilson's Struggles Extend Beyond the Baseball Field," *Kansas City Star*, June 30, 1986: 1B.

11 Mike Penner, "Royals Win West Again — Angels Don't Again: Kansas City Wraps It Up in 10th, 5-4," *Los Angeles Times*, October 6, 1985: 1.

12 Associated Press, "Wilson Auction Fetches Big Bucks," *Springfield* (Missouri) *News-Leader*, April 24, 2001: 3C.

13 Blair Kerkhoff, "Former Royal Willie Wilson Surprised with New World Series Ring," *Kansas City Star*, September 24, 2013.

EWING KAUFFMAN

BY DAN LEVITT

Like many successful owners, longtime Kansas City Royals magnate Ewing Kauffman could be highly demanding, both publicly and privately. Yet he was one of the few also celebrated by the community and his players for his generosity and obvious caring for their wellbeing. Kauffman made his fortune as a pharmaceutical entrepreneur in the decades after World War II, primarily on the strength of his drive, sales skills, and his active, creative mind. His compelling personality along with his ability to connect with a diverse range of individuals made him one of baseball's more beloved owners.

"When he walked in that first meeting, I don't know how to put it other than there was as presence in the room, even among accomplished baseball men," longtime Royals scout Art Stewart remembered. "He just carried himself with this dynamic air of confidence. ... He sort of glided into the room and introduced himself to those of us who hadn't met him. Then he takes his coat off, rolls up his sleeves and addresses the room with the perfect blend of confidence and humility. ... The motivation was amazing. Sitting there you got a special feeling about him and the group he assembled. He was a terrific leader, and the way you knew that was because he made you want to work hard for him, and would give you whatever you needed to be successful."[1]

Ewing Marion Kauffman was born on September 21, 1916, just southeast of Garden City, Missouri, on his parents' farm. According to his biographer's research of family lore, Kauffman was named after State Senator Ewing Cockrell and his maternal grandfather, John Marion Winders. Winders was a locally famous stonemason of Scotch and Irish heritage who believed strongly in education for his six children. Kauffman's mother, Effie Mae, graduated from Missouri State Teachers college with a strong background in the classics.[2]

Kauffman's father, John Samuel Kauffman, was of German heritage and grew up on a farm, the youngest of the family's seven children. John's six older siblings were all female, and they helped raise and support him, even into adulthood. Though John had little formal schooling, he was something of a mathematical prodigy, often challenging Ewing on math problems, and the youngster embraced his father's joy of mathematics.

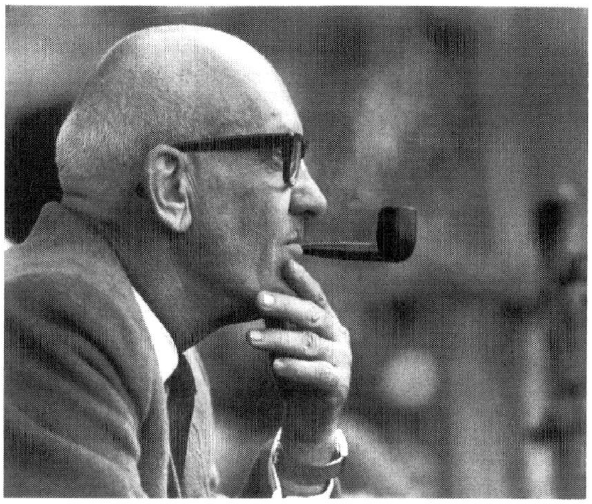

Effie and John met while he was selling door-to-door and she was a schoolteacher. After they were married, the newlyweds lived on John's family farm. To establish their own home and allow Effie to escape the mostly German-speaking household, the couple moved nearby to a small rental where first Ruth was born and then Ewing three years later. The young family upgraded to a leased farm with a nice farmhouse while Ewing was still a baby. Unfortunately, after several apparently prosperous years, the land flooded, and the family was forced to give up farming. Adding to the insecurity, John's ability to make a living had been further hampered when he lost an eye in a freak accident several years earlier.

Ewing's family moved to Kansas City, where his father's sisters and parents helped them buy a house. John eventually turned to selling life insurance, and Effie took in boarders to help cover household expenses. Ewing exhibited an early aptitude for sales, selling eggs from his grandparents' farm to the neighbors. Kauffman's father never flourished as a salesman, and the family could rarely afford more than the bare necessities. Nevertheless, Kauffman grew up with a loving family, a mother who taught him the value and love of learning, an outgoing father who encouraged his mathematical interests, and an early exposure to the thrill of successful selling.

When he was 11, Kauffman was diagnosed with endocarditis, a heart ailment, for which the treatment at the time was absolute bed rest for an entire year. As awful as this must have been for a young boy, Kauffman read up to 20 books a week and learned to quickly perform complicated mathematical calculations in his head. Shortly after he recovered, John and Effie separated and then divorced. The two had been struggling for some time, and Ewing and Ruth moved in with their mother. "(Dad) was close to the earth," Kauffman remembered. "Mother was spiritual and mental. Mother was fastidious. Dad was not. She liked to stay home and he liked to travel."[3]

Once back up and healthy, Kauffman joined the Boy Scouts, winning a scholarship so he could attend Scout camp one summer and eventually earning Eagle Scout, the highest achievement level in Scouting. Anxious to make up for his lost year, Kauffman also played football and worked at a laundry to help support his family. After graduating from Westport High, Kauffman spent a little time out on the road – this was 1934 and the heart of Depression – before returning home to earn an associate's degree at Kansas City Junior College.

Over the next half-dozen years Kauffman worked at a number of jobs, including managing laundry drivers, selling insurance, and selling training courses. He was also briefly engaged to the daughter of one of his insurance-company bosses.

For many American men still searching for their place in American society as the country began to climb out of its economic doldrums, World War II changed their trajectory, and for Kauffman it was no different. In December 1941 before heading into the military Kauffman secretly married Marguerite Blackshire, a woman he had met at Sunday school, his primary social circle. Not until later that spring did he send his mother a letter alerting her to his new bride.

Kauffman joined the Navy, where he was trained as a signalman. While at sea, with some encouragement from the ship's captain, he developed an interest in astronomy, and on his own he occasionally checked the calculations of the ship's navigation officer. At one point he determined that the calculations provided by the navigation officer were wrong and that several ships in the convoy might run aground due to the error. At some personal risk he sidestepped naval regulations and reported his concerns directly to the captain. Kauffman's calculations were correct, and the captain later made Kauffman his navigation officer.

Kauffman's time in the Navy also proved extremely profitable. Over his enlistment he won roughly $90,000 playing poker and would often send a large percentage to Marguerite to save for after the war.[4] When he returned home they used much of Kauffman's winnings to purchase a house in Kansas City. After two miscarriages the couple decided to adopt, adding Larry to the household in 1947 and Sue a year later.

By this point Kauffman had matured into an interesting, complex individual. He was extremely competitive, hard-working, and driven, and very much believed in people having to earn their rewards. But he also was generous and caring. His extraordinary sales skills came from the former tempered by his obvious openness and genuineness in wanting to help the clients he was selling to.

Shortly after the war Kauffman joined a pharmaceutical company as a salesman and "simply fell in love with the business."[5] At the time medications were typically dispensed by doctors either on house calls or at their offices, so salesmen called on doctors at their offices. Moreover, the industry was much less regulated and concentrated than it is today, with many regional suppliers of common drugs. Kauffman read constantly to educate himself about the industry and demonstrated a knack for building relationships with the doctors. He quickly became one of the highest-grossing producers in the company, and grew disillusioned when they arbitrarily reduced his bonus because they felt he was making too much.

Kauffman decided to strike out on his own. In June 1950 he took what remained of his savings and launched Marion Laboratories. Though it didn't have any research capabilities at the time, Kauffman imagined that "Laboratories" added a gravitas to the corporate name. Critically, he managed to hold onto a number of existing clients. To save money Kauffman initially operated out of his basement, which he quickly outgrew, and began adding sales and management staff. He also introduced a couple of new drugs, effectively reformulations or recombinations of existing compounds; for his first drug he concocted a pill for chronic fatigue.[6] Kauffman himself came up with the designs for these early drugs from his extensive reading of medical journals and probing of doctors. Maybe most importantly, he labored to create a quality sales staff, and in typical Kauffman fashion, he researched and experimented with ways to identify and then train salesmen. (They were all men at the time.) Kauffman also introduced significant profit-sharing for his salesmen – generally structured as equity in the company – soon broadening the plan to include all employees. He often expressed pride later in life over all the "millionaires" created by the growth of his company.

Kauffman was an attentive, inquiring, and engaged boss. To screen sales candidates, he began using skills and psychological assessments well before they were standard in industry. Moreover, he examined the results and tinkered with the tests to try to improve their accuracy. To motivate his sales force once they came on board, Kauffman introduced sophisticated sales-recognition programs. Nevertheless, though the compensation was significant, succeeding as a high-producing pharmaceutical salesman required long hours and enduring a high-pressure work environment. Turnover was a constant problem. "His cardinal rule of business is: 'Produce or get out,'" wrote Allan Demaree in *Fortune*. "Sometimes if a salesman fails to increase the volume of business in his territory, says Kauffman, 'we call him in and say, "Before we leave this room one of three things is going to happen. Either you're going to get fired, or you're going to quit, or you're going to change."' The first time a salesman hears this pitch it constitutes a warning; the second time he's canned."[7] Demaree went on to discuss Marion's business: "What Marion does best is to find products in the research of others, prepare them for market, and, above, all, motivate salesmen and sell."[8]

Kauffman built a solid management team to support his sales staff, and the company prospered throughout the 1950s: By 1959 Marion achieved $1 million in annual sales. His family life, however, was more troubled. Marguerite struggled with depression and continuing back problems following a car accident years earlier. In December 1960 Kauffman found her dead in her car in their closed garage with the engine running. There was no note, and neither Kauffman nor the children sensed she had been particularly despondent. The authorities ruled her death accidental.

A little over a year later Kauffman remarried, tying the knot with Muriel McBrien on February 28, 1962. Kauffman had first met the twice-widowed Muriel at a conference in Miami in March 1961. A native of Toronto, Muriel was highly accomplished in business and brought a daughter to the combined family. Muriel would become a force in her own right in the Kansas City community.

As the company flourished in the early 1960s, Kauffman wanted to take it public to bring in additional capital and create liquidity for his shares and those of many of his longtime employees. By 1965 company revenues were almost $5 million and net income had surpassed the $500,000 target set by his investment bankers. Initially, the company went public as over-the-counter stock, eventually listing on the New York Stock Exchange in 1969.

After decades of stability, the 1950s and 1960s saw a flurry of long-standing baseball teams moving to new cities and baseball expanding three times, adding two AL teams in 1961, two NL teams in 1962, and two in each league in 1969. The 1969 expansion was precipitated when Charlie Finley moved the Kansas City Athletics to Oakland in October 1967. Facing legal pressure, the American League responded by awarding franchises to Kansas City and later Seattle. Unlike more recent expansions in the 1990s, baseball chose the cities first, and then searched for ownership groups.

With the initial public offering of Marion Laboratories, Kauffman now had both significant net worth and the liquidity necessary to purchase and bankroll an expansion franchise. Marion Laboratories had a market value of roughly $156 million, and Kauffman and his family owned 31 percent.[9] Moreover, he had become a sportsman in the old-fashioned sense of the word, owning a stable of several race horses and enjoying the associated lifestyle. Sportswriter and local booster Ernie Mehl pushed Kauffman to pursue the franchise, telling him, "We need to show the American League there is somebody in Kansas City that is somewhat interested in baseball and financially can afford it."[10] With encouragement from his wife, Kauffman entered the sweepstakes to own Kansas City's expansion team.

With his typical resourcefulness, as he contemplated his bid Kauffman traveled to Anaheim to meet with California Angels owner Gene Autry and team President Bob Reynolds, who had been through the process with their 1961 expansion team. While on the trip Kauffman also met Cedric Tallis, an Angels executive who greatly impressed him. As Kauffman finalized his bid for his team, he invited Tallis to join his group as its general manager. Kauffman thought Tallis not only a smart baseball man, but also someone who could be a champion and overseer for the new stadium complex under consideration in Kansas City.

Four groups, including Kauffman, presented to the American League's owners at the December 1967 winter meetings. Kauffman's earlier lobbying and natural sales skills helped him in winning over the owners. More important, perhaps, were his demonstrated financial capabilities and his stated intention to own the franchise himself. When asked about his connection with gambling due to his race horses, Kauffman stated he never bet on baseball or football, and earned a chuckle when he said he would continue to gamble but only at golf and cards. On January 11, 1968, the league announced it was awarding the team to Kauffman.[11] "I've always said it was the greatest trade in the history of baseball [getting Kauffman instead of Finley as the city's franchise owner]," said sportswriter Joe McGuff.[12] The Royals initially cost Kauffman roughly $6 million, and he signed a lease to play at Municipal Stadium until a new $43 million sports complex for the Royals and the football Chiefs would open in 1972. (Royals Stadium eventually opened a year late.)[13]

While pursuing the franchise, Kauffman told the owners he would bring in professional management, just as in his pharmaceutical business. Tallis, awarded a four-year contract and with a new major-league team to build, received the same memo. "Outside of finances, he will run the club," Kauffman told reporters.[14]

"Kauffman did not dabble in day-to-day team management," wrote his biographer. "He had decided early in his involvement with baseball that he would either have to trust the executives he hired or fire them. That had been his policy at Marion Laboratories where he understood the pharmaceutical business."[15] That said, Kauffman would get involved if he felt he needed to. To increase sales he mirrored his Marion sales recognition programs on the baseball side, creating an exclusive booster club with high-test perks for local businessmen who sold at least 75 season tickets.

At the ballpark Kauffman could be similarly engaged, sitting behind the dugout at home games and dissecting his manager's decisions. "I'd have taken out the kid [Hedlund] and brought in Moe [Drabowsky] a little sooner than [manager] Joe [Gordon] did," Kauffman remarked after one game in 1969. After learning that Drabowsky wasn't "completely warmed up," Kauffman backpedaled, "That's why he's the manager and I'm the owner."[16] But he remained attentive and unafraid to demand explanations from his senior management.

Though Kauffman allowed his baseball men to build his team, he was unafraid to think unconventionally and push to implement his ideas. He kept a copy of Earnshaw Cook's *Percentage Baseball* on his desk, the first serious statistical look at the game written by an outsider. He even followed up by meeting with Cook to discuss his concepts. Kauffman also introduced one of baseball's first computer systems, which by the end of the 1971 season contained statistics like "the nature of every pitch thrown by a Royal ... what happened to every ball hit ... [and] even the humidity." One writer who witnessed Tallis and his staff reviewing some of this information exclaimed: "I felt I had walked in on a conclave of madmen. Here were six or seven grown men around a table piled high with computer cards, mulling over every pitch thrown and every ball hit in what is supposed to be a game." This information was fed to the manager so that it could be applied. Thirty years before Michael Lewis wrote *Moneyball*, Kauffman believed that statistical analysis could provide a competitive advantage when added to traditional evaluation methods.[17]

Kauffman also had new ideas on how the team should find talent. He had publicly stated that he wanted a pennant within five years, a wildly aggressive prediction given the history of the four previous expansion franchises. To accomplish this goal, Kauffman realized that the usual methods of finding young players would not be sufficient: The amateur draft offered all teams equal access to top prospects, Latin and Caribbean countries were being scouted (though untapped opportunity was later to be uncovered there), and Japan was not yet considered a source for major-league players.[18]

Kauffman's brainstorm was to create the Kansas City Baseball Academy, a school operating outside the traditional farm system where undrafted great athletes with little baseball background could learn the game. Kauffman's academy applied a scientific approach to scouting and training: Figure out which raw skills best translated into baseball success and then how to best develop and hone those skills to create ballplayers. To house it, Kauffman purchased a 121-acre site in Sarasota, Florida. The complex cost roughly $1.5 million and required a further $600,000 or so in annual operating expenses.

In mid-June 1971 the Academy faced its first public test when a team of its cadets was placed in the seven-team, rookie-level Gulf Coast League, pitting the recruits against drafted ballplayers in other organizations. The team finished 40-13 and led the league in both batting average and ERA. This early validation of his concept was one of Kauffman's greatest thrills in baseball.

Yet the Academy had detractors within the organization, as many in the front office begrudged the huge allocation of resources to something outside of their traditional farm system, which in tandem had built a first-rate scouting and development system. By 1973, while the Academy had produced several prospects, it had become clear that Kauffman's brainchild needed to be revamped. The Royals' original thesis – that great young athletes with little baseball background could be molded into major-league baseball players – had not proven out. Despite all its creative ideas and intense testing, the Academy could not create enough ballplayers from raw, unskilled athletes. The top prospect in the Academy, infielder Frank White, had significant previous baseball experience. The other noteworthy problem with the Academy was the huge cost. When Marion Laboratories stock collapsed during 1974 due to the recession and concerns over forthcoming FDA approval for a new drug (between February and August the stock price dropped from $52 per share to $11) Kauffman decided to shutter the academy and integrate its facilities into the overall minor-league system.[19] He would later say his greatest regret in baseball was closing the Academy. "If I knew then what I know now," Kauffman later lamented, "I would have kept it going. And we would have had a dynasty here."[20]

That the Academy did not succeed in turning athletes into baseball players testified to the fact that traditional scouting was already finding most – though not all – of the potential major leaguers in the US. However, Kauffman's philosophy of always looking for new sources of talent is one of the foundations of successful organizations. Of the Academy's innovations in scouting and player development, some were transferred to the Royals farm system and many others were carried by the Academy's coaches and trainers as they migrated within the organization and to other teams. Like most successful organizations, Kauffman's Royals showed a sincere willingness to experiment with new ideas and methods. As a result they found a few valuable players and learned useful player development and scouting lessons.

The 1972 season was marred by a players strike that began during spring training and lingered into the season, canceling a week's worth of games. As the players union had never taken such an action before, the events stunned many longtime baseball people, and Kauffman developed into a semi-hawk on player issues. He was a paternalistic owner in the best sense of the word, offering free career counseling and financial advice to his players or occasionally handing out hundred-dollar bills to players in the locker room after a tough game, telling them to take their wives out for dinner.[21] As an owner Kauffman had spent a lot of money to acquire and build the franchise, which was still not profitable, claiming he had invested roughly $19 million in the franchise: Beyond the initial investment he had sunk $5 million into Royals Stadium and annual losses were significant. For example, in 1971 the team lost $2.2 million; $600,000 was depreciation, a noncash charge, but the other $1.6 million was operating losses.[22] Kauffman couldn't see why the players should be allowed any more of the overall baseball revenues.

In response to Marvin Miller and the players association filing to arbitrate the McNally-Messersmith challenge to the reserve clause in the fall of 1975, Kauffman filed suit, supported by the other major-league clubs, arguing that the reserve clause was not arbitrable under the collective-bargaining agreement. The court allowed the arbitration to move forward, telling Kauffman he could come back if he wanted to dispute the decision. When Kauffman led the owners back into court to overturn the famous Seitz decision that invalidated the reserve clause, the court ruled that the arbitrator's ruling would stand. Kauffman's frustration with free agency can be seen is his reaction to it: Through 1980 the only free agent signed off another team was utility infielder Jerry Terrell.

On the field, the Royals backslid in 1972 after a surprising 1971 season, and the impatient Kauffman decided to fire manager Bob Lemon over Tallis's objections. As justification, Kauffman publicly mentioned a mishandled August benching of Amos Otis and Freddie Patek for not hustling and also suggested that he wanted to hire someone younger. This last comment exposed Kauffman to age-discrimination protection, causing him to have to pay Lemon an extra year's salary. Kauffman's impatience and unrealistic expectations were also laid bare. "Starting in 1974," he bragged, "we expect to win (the American League championship) five out of ten years."[23]

Kauffman further exasperated Tallis by hiring Jack McKeon, the manager at Triple-A Omaha, with whom Tallis had quarreled in the past. In particular, McKeon was a vocal advocate for the Baseball Academy, and hence a favorite of Kauffman's. McKeon would go on to a successful career in baseball as both a manager and general manager, but in 1972 he owed his allegiance to Ewing Kauffman alone. The impatient Kauffman had journeyed a long way from the putatively hands-off owner of 1969.

Despite a strong second-place finish in 1973, principally due to a number of great trades and smart drafting by Tallis and the front office, Kauffman became frustrated with his mounting financial losses. Between the financial drain of the Academy and the Royals' top-notch minor-league system, the team reportedly lost hundreds of thousands of dollars annually. Notwithstanding a strong season on the field, the opening of their new ballpark, and a near-doubling of attendance, Kauffman lost roughly $900,000 in 1973. Late in the season he hired Joe Burke to run the financial side of the Royals. Burke had spent years in the front office of the Washington Senators and, after the club's move to Texas, two years as the club's GM. Kauffman was clearly preparing for a change in his GM.

By the middle of the 1974 season, as the Royals hovered near .500, "Kauffman's irritation with the costs of owning a baseball team was beginning to show."[24] He had sunk somewhere around $20 million into the club and had yet to turn a profit in any season, and his net worth was sinking due to the Marion stock slide. Kauffman bounced Tallis and promoted Joe Burke to general manager, giving him full control over both the baseball and business sides. In another cost-saving move, after the season Kauffman directed Burke to join the newly formed Major League Scouting Bureau, enabling the Royals to lay off 20 full-time and 50 part-time scouts.[25] A couple of years later, as the impact of this decision began to be felt in the farm system, Kauffman reversed course and began rebuilding his scouting staff. As with the sales employees at Marion, he offered the Royals scouts better perks and profit-sharing, but they "were expected to generate more leads and baseball talent than [their] rivals."[26] In late July 1975 Burke and Kauffman again changed managers, firing McKeon, and bringing on Whitey Herzog. Herzog had managed for Burke in Texas and at the time was the third-base coach for the California Angels.

After four seasons of pursuing the Oakland A's, in 1976 Kauffman's team finally broke through with a 90-72 record and won the division title before losing a tightly contested ALCS with the Yankees. Of the eight expansion teams that began play in the 1960s, the Royals attained and sustained success the quickest, and Kauffman's willingness to hire good baseball people and put money into his team was a big reason.

The team won division titles in 1977 and 1978 as well, again losing to the Yankees in the ALCS both years. Despite his success, Kauffman and Muriel never really warmed to Herzog, and the manager felt as though he was tolerated only as long as he was winning. Once when Angels owner Gene Autry asked Muriel how his "old friend Whitey was," she responded, "Who gives a shit?"[27] After falling to second place in 1979, Kauffman and Burke jettisoned Herzog, bringing in Jim Frey. Under Frey in 1980 the team finally beat the Yankees in the ALCS to win the pennant. "That was my greatest thrill in baseball," Kauffman remembered. "And the moment was made all the more memorable because it had come at the expense of the New York Yankees."[28]

After a disappointing 1981 season, Kauffman promoted John Schuerholz to GM and Burke to president. The team still boasted a talented nucleus, led by third baseman George Brett, and remained competitive in the early 1980s. The Royals finally won the World Series in 1985, bolstered by three young pitching aces.

For Kauffman, 1981 was something of a watershed year. He turned 65 and had a tumor removed from his chest along with part of a rib. On the baseball front, the Royals slumped as Kauffman believed Frey lost control of his players (Burke replaced him with Dick Howser), and the long players strike began to sap baseball's appeal for him.[29] Kauffman started searching for a partner willing to buy a 49 percent interest in the team with rights to acquire full ownership down the road. He reached an agreement with a man named Michael Shapiro in early 1983 for $11 million, but when Shapiro could not come up with the required deposit by the required deadline, Kauffman canceled the deal.[30]

Later that spring Kauffman cut a similar deal with Memphis real-estate developer Avron Fogelman. The two stipulated the value of the franchise at $22 million, and Fogelman paid $11 million for a 49 percent interest. Kauffman had the right to put the remaining 51 percent to Fogelman between 1988 and 1991, at which time Kauffman would be obligated sell to if he hadn't yet done so. In early 1988 the two recut the agreement. Fogelman paid $220,000 to bring his share up to 50 percent and Kauffman's put obligation went away; he could now remain a partner in the team. Their partnership agreement was extended through 2012 with the provision that if Kauffman died before then, Fogelman could purchase the Kauffman's 50 percent for $11 million.[31] His frustration with baseball's economics blinded Kauffman — like many others — to the massive increase in franchise values that was about to occur.

As Kauffman aged and with some of Fogelman's purchase capital now infused into the team, the team became more willing to pursue free agents to keep it competitive, particularly toward the end of the decade. But several high-profile signings — notably Mark Davis, Storm Davis, Kirk Gibson, and Mike Boddicker — did not live up to the hype.

In 1989 Kauffman found himself forced to reorganize his businesses. As the pharmaceutical industry evolved, Marion's executive leadership team felt a merger with another drug company was required for its long-term survival. Kauffman hated to surrender control of the company he had built from his basement, but he acquiesced to the recommendation. Later that year Marion Laboratories merged with Merrell Dow, a subsidiary of Dow Chemical, to create Marion Merrell Dow and a nice but unwelcome payday for Kauffman. In 1988 Forbes estimated his net worth at $740 million, an amount certainly increased through the merger; now much of that was liquid as well.[32]

At the same time, Fogelman's real estate empire was unraveling in the commercial real-estate lending and liquidity crisis of the late 1980s and early 1990s. Fogelman was under tremendous pressure from his lenders and needed his equity in the franchise to bail himself out. Somewhat cornered to support Fogelman lest the franchise get entangled is his messy finances or an out-of-town buyer get a hold of his purchase option, Kauffman agreed to recut their deal. Under the new agreement, Kauffman loaned Fogelman $34 million and effectively regained full ownership of the team. In addition he would have to cover roughly $20 million in failed real estate investments awarded to players George Brett, Dan Quisenberry, and Willie Wilson, originally backstopped and advocated by Fogelman as part of their contract extensions. Moreover, Kauffman would have to fund $5 million to cover the previous year's asset contribution defaulted on by Fogelman and the entire $7 million in operating losses for the current year, typically split between the partners. Not surprisingly Kauffman said, "I feel like I have been taken advantage of."[33] Kauffman used the franchise uncertainty created by Fogelman's troubles to leverage a more attractive new 25-year lease on the ballpark and lock the team to Kansas City for the foreseeable future.

When four Royals players pleaded guilty to misdemeanor drug charges and were sentenced to 90 days in a federal penitentiary after the 1983 season, Kauffman was shaken and distressed. It also stimulated his charitable impulses to address the drug problem and support disadvantaged youth. Most notably, for the class entering his alma mater Westport High in 1988, he offered to pay for college, technical, or vocational training for any students who graduated, and stayed away from drugs and pregnancy. In 1992, when the class graduated, 115 of the original 240 freshmen qualified and took advantage of the offer.[34] He later extended the program to other schools and classes. The Kauffman Foundation, whose mission was later expanded to promote and encourage entrepreneurship, would be a lasting legacy to Kauffman's philanthropic vision.

By the early 1990s Kauffman was aggressively spending on his roster while at the same time seething at the players union. In 1990 as the two sides battled over the collective bargaining agreement, Kauffman said, "If they don't settle soon, it would be my nature to withdraw everything offered and close the season down. You cannot keep giving and giving and giving."[35] Nevertheless, he still desperately wanted to win, and by 1993 after signing David Cone and Greg Gagne, Kansas City had the fourth highest payroll in the game.

His health had also begun increasingly to fail, and Kauffman began to fear for his mortality. He wanted to sell the team to a local ownership committed to keeping the team in Kansas City, but no one stepped up to the roughly $90 million price tag he hung on the franchise. Alternatively, he came up with a convoluted, tax-advantaged plan to donate the team to a charitable limited partnership upon his death, with the eventual sale proceeds going to his philanthropic interests. Kauffman also funded enough cash to cover annual operating losses, estimated at $3 million per year, for several years and required local business leaders to post $50 million, from which the interest would also be used to subsidize operating losses.

Kauffman died on August 1, 1993, from bone cancer and had a private funeral and burial three days later. A month before his death, Royals Stadium was renamed Kauffman Stadium in his honor. The franchise was turned over to the limited partnership with Kauffman's longtime friend and Walmart CEO David Glass named managing general partner. The team would flounder under this provisional ownership but remain tethered to Kansas City until Glass finally purchased the franchise outright in 2000.

Since his death Kauffman's stature has continued to grow. His foundation has grown to over $2.1 billion in assets and makes more than $65 million a year in grants and donations.[36] It has also become one the foremost research and support organizations for entrepreneurship. The first 25 years of the Royals under his ownership also hold up well. The team was consistently competitive, had top-notch front-office executives, often maintained a payroll in excess of its market size, and showed creativity and original thinking when approaching problems. That the team didn't quite live up to Kauffman's initial predictions of quick and consistent greatness simply highlights his competitive fire and occasional impetuousness.

Editor's note:

For a more detailed look at the full ownership history of the Royals, please see Dan Levitt's article on the subject:

https://sabr.org/research/kansas-city-royals-team-ownership-history

Notes

1 Art Stewart, *The Art of Scouting: Seven Decades Chasing Hopes and Dreams in Major League Baseball* (Olathe, Kansas: Ascend Books, 2014), 127.

2 The principal source for Kauffman's pre-baseball life is Anne Morgan, *Prescription for Success: The Life and Values of Ewing Marion Kauffman* (Kansas City, Missouri: Andrews and McMeel, 1995); also helpful were Phil Koury in Sid Bordman and Jim Reed, *Expansion to Excellence: An Intimate Portrait of the Kansas City Royals* (No other publication information presented), iii-viii, and Phil Koury, "Kauffman Puts Winning Record on Line," *Kansas City Star*, January 14, 1968.

3 Phil Koury, "Kauffman Puts Winning Record on Line," *Kansas City Star*, January 14, 1968.

4 Morgan, 46-7.

5 Morgan, 49.

6 Allan T. Demaree, "Ewing Kauffman Sold Himself Rich in Kansas City," *Fortune*, October 1972: 101.

7 Demaree, 100.

8 Demaree, 101.

9 Joe McGuff, "Kauffman Goal: Flag in Five Years; Royals' Boss Weighs Daring Plan," *The Sporting News*, June 7, 1969; Demaree.

10 Roger D. Launius, *Seasons in the Sun: The Story of Big League Baseball in Missouri* (Columbia, Missouri: University of Missouri Press, 2002), 93.

11 Joe McGuff, "Four Kaycee Groups Seek Franchise," *The Sporting News*, December 16, 1967: 29.

12 Gene Fox, *Sports Guys: Insights, Highlights, and Hoo-hahs from Your Favorite Sports Authorities* (Kansas City, Missouri: Addax Publishing, 1999), 82.

13 Jerome Holtzman, "A.L. Vote to Expand Marks 1967 History," *Official Baseball Guide For 1968* (St. Louis: The Sporting News, 1968), 180-81; Jerome Holtzman, "Expansion, Canadian Club, Feature 1968," *Official Baseball Guide For 1968* (St. Louis: *The Sporting News*, 1969), 181.

14 Dickson Terry, "Kaycee 'Will Never Lose This Team,'" *The Sporting News*, January 27, 1968: 23-24.

15 Morgan, 266.

16 Mark Mulvoy, "KC Is Back with a Vengeance," *Sports Illustrated*, May 26, 1969: 16.

17 Frank Deford, "It Ain't Necessarily So, and Never Was," *Sports Illustrated*, March 6, 1972.

18 Joe McGuff, "Kauffman Goal: Flag in Five Years; Royals' Boss Weighs Daring Plan," *The Sporting News*, June 7, 1969, 16.

19 Morgan, 176.

20 "Inside Mr. K," The Squire, March 9, 1989.

21 Denny Mathews and Fred White with Matt Fulks, *Play by Play: 25 Years of Royals Radio* (Kansas City, Missouri: Addax Publishing, 1999), 86.

22 Joe McGuff, "'Players Must Learn Facts of Life' — Kauffman," *The Sporting News*, April 22, 1972.

23 Joe McGuff, "'Blame Me for Lemon's Exit,' Says Kauffman," *The Sporting News*, October 21, 1972: 23; Joe McGuff, "Tallis-Kauffman Split Linked to Lemon Firing," *The Sporting News*, July 6, 1974: 15.

24 Morgan, 260.

25 Morgan, 261.

26 Stewart, 149.

27 Whitey Herzog with Kevin Horrigan, *White Rat: A Life in Baseball* (New York: Harper & Row, 1987), 111.

28 Morgan, 268.

29 Jonathan Rand, "Kauffman Finds Outlet in Baseball," Kansas City Times, undated clipping.

30 "Lawyer Says Shapiro Held Up Royals Suit in Hopes of Settlement," *Kansas City Times*, February 13, 1985.

31 Bob Nightengale, "A Partnership Is Anchored in K.C.," *The Sporting News*, January 25, 1988: 48.

32 Morgan, 294. "Royals Co-owner Bails Out; Highest Bidder Gets Club," *USA Today*, August 1, 1990.

33 Charles R.T. Crumpley, "Kauffman OKs Loan to Fogelman," *Kansas City Star*, undated clipping.

34 Erik Brady, "Graduation a Thrilling Payoff for Royals Owner," USA Today, June 4, 1992.

35 "KC Owner Suggests Canceling Season," Associated Press, March 11, 1990.

36 990finder.foundationcenter.org/990results.aspx?990_type=&fn=kauffman+foundation&st=MO&zp=&ei=&fy=&action=Search.

WHITEY HERZOG

BY ADAM FOLDES

In the annals of baseball dating back to when it first became a game played by professionals, the great teams have always taken on the persona of their managers. This includes the old Chicago White Stockings of the National League led by their first baseman-manager Adrian "Cap" Anson, and continues with managers such as Ned Hanlon of the Baltimore Orioles in the 1890s, and a couple of Hanlon's protégés, John McGraw with the New York Giants and Hughie Jennings of the Detroit Tigers.[1]

Toward the middle of the twentieth century, there were Mel Ott with the New York Giants, Leo Durocher's Dodgers and Giants, and Al Lopez's "Go-Go" White Sox of the late '50s.

Since free agency began, two managers have stamped their game on their teams and largely contributed to their success. They were Alfred Manuel "Billy" Martin, famous for Billyball, and Whitey Herzog, whose Whiteyball focused on speed, pitching, and defense.

Dorrel Norman Elvert Herzog was born on November 9, 1931, the second of three boys, to Edgar and Lietta Herzog in New Athens, Illinois, 40 miles east of St. Louis.[2] Edgar worked at the Mound City Brewery and Lietta worked in a shoe factory.

To help make ends meet and make some extra money, young Dorrel, or "Relly" as he was called, dug graves, worked at the Mound City Brewery, delivered baked goods, and delivered newspapers.[3]

Young Herzog would sometimes skip school, hitchhike on Route 13 to Belleville, and then take a bus to Sportsman's Park, home to the Browns and Cardinals. Herzog would not only watch his idols Stan Musial, Vern Stephens, and Enos Slaughter but would snatch up batting practice balls by sneaking into the ballpark early. He would bring the balls back to the New Athens sandlots, sell some and keep some to play with.[4]

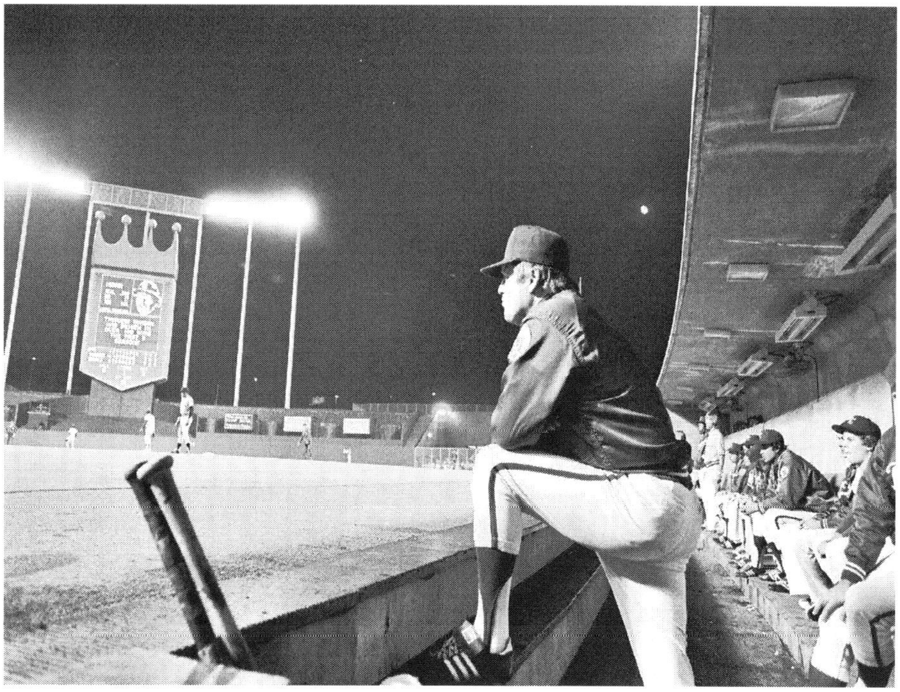

At New Athens High School, Herzog, a left-handed thrower and batter, was a first baseman, pitcher, and outfielder. He also played guard on the basketball team.[5] During his senior year, Herzog led the Yellow Jackets to the regional playoffs and had interest from colleges including the University of Illinois and St. Louis University. As a junior he batted .584, was named a second-team all-stater, and led the team to a spot in the championship game against Granite City. (New Athens lost, 4-1.) He was named second team all-state in baseball.

After graduating in 1949 Herzog bypassed college and signed a contract with the New York Yankees. Another Yankees recruit that year was Mickey Mantle.[6] Herzog was recommended by scout Lou Maguolo and cross-checked by Tom Greenwade.[7]

In his first year in the minors, playing for the Yankees' Class-D Sooner State League team in McAlester, Oklahoma, Herzog hit .279; the following year he hit .351. While at McAlester he acquired the nickname Whitey, bestowed on him by a sportscaster in the McAlester area because his light blond hair resembled that of a pitcher on the Yankees, Bob "White Rat" Kuzava.[8]

In 1951 Herzog hit a combined .276 for Class-C Joplin and Class-B Piedmont. The next season, 1952, after playing for Quincy in the Three-I League and Beaumont in the Double-A Texas League, he reached Triple A with Kansas City in the American Association. After the season, with the Korean War still raging, he was drafted into the US Army and spent two years in the Corps of Engineers.

The same year Herzog joined the Army, he married his high-school sweetheart, Mary Lou Sinn. As of 2018, they had been married 66 years and had three children, Debbie, Jim, and David.[9]

While stationed at Fort Leonard Wood in Waynesville, Missouri, Herzog got his first experience running a ballclub, when he managed the company baseball team.[10]

Discharged from the Army, Herzog played in 1955 for the Yankees' Triple-A team in Denver. In 149 games he hit .289 with 21 home runs and 98 runs batted in.

After his success in 1955, Herzog hoped to spend the 1956 season with the Yankees. He made the majors, but with the Washington Senators. On April 2 Herzog was traded to the Senators in a seven-player deal that saw pitcher Mickey McDermott and shortstop Bobby Kline head to the Yankees.[11]

For the Senators in 1956, Herzog played in 117 games, all in the outfield except for five at first base. The 5-foot-11, 182-pound Herzog batted .245 with 4 home runs and 35 RBIs. In May of 1958 he was sold to the Kansas City Athletics. Before the 1961 season the Athletics traded him to the Baltimore Orioles, and after the 1962 season the Orioles traded him to the Detroit Tigers.

Over the next six years, Herzog bounced back and forth between the majors and the minors and played with three other American League clubs, the Kanas City Athletics, the Detroit Tigers, and the Baltimore Orioles. He appeared in 634 career games, batting .257 with an on-base percentage of .354, and with 25 homers and 172 RBIs.

After batting only .151 in 52 games for the Tigers in 1963, Herzog retired as a player. Of his playing career, Herzog was known to say that baseball had been good to him once he stopped trying to play it.[12]

Herzog scouted for Kansas City in 1964 and was a coach in 1965 under Mel McGaha and Haywood Sullivan.[13] Following the 1965 season, Herzog left the Athletics organization and was hired by the New York Mets organization. His first position in 1966 was third-base coach under Wes Westrum, on a team that went 66-95 and finished in ninth place ahead of only the Chicago Cubs. They finished 28 1/2 games behind the pennant-winning Los Angeles Dodgers.

The following year Herzog was named the Mets' director of player development but also got his first taste of managing in professional baseball, when at 35 he guided the Florida Instructional League Mets for 50 games. Over the next six years, Herzog oversaw a number of players who played important roles in the pennant-winning Mets teams of 1969 and 1973, including Jerry Koosman, Gary Gentry, Jon Matlack, John Milner, and Wayne Garrett as well as players who had successful careers on other teams including

Amos Otis, Nolan Ryan, and Ken Singleton. After seven years in the Mets organization Herzog, who disliked Mets Chairman M. Donald Grant, left the organization upset when the Mets passed him over for manager in 1972 after Gil Hodges died. (First-base coach Yogi Berra got the job.[14])

Herzog quickly rebounded. On November 2, 1972, at the age of 40, he was named the manager of the Texas Rangers, replacing Ted Williams. Team owner Bob Short said general manager Joe Burke believed Herzog would help develop the team's young talent.[15]

On April 7, 1973, Herzog made his managerial debut with the Rangers with a 3-1 loss to the White Sox. He did not get his first win until April 12, 4-0 over the Kansas City Royals.

The 1973 Rangers were a somewhat dysfunctional team. In the June amateur draft, the team drafted pitcher David Clyde number one overall ahead of future Hall of Famers Robin Yount and Dave Winfield. As part of the contract Clyde signed, he was to make two major-league starts before going to the minors. He pitched fairly well in the first couple of starts, but then batters began to get to him. Herzog was unable to get Bob Short to agree to send Clyde to the minors to get his footing. Herzog later said it was "a travesty." Teammate Tom Grieve called it "the dumbest thing you could ever do to a high-school pitcher," and said Short had effectively ruined Clyde's career.[16]

At 138 games into the season with the Rangers sitting at 47-91, Herzog was fired and replaced by Billy Martin, who had recently been fired by the Detroit Tigers. Short knew Martin from his time as a Twins executive while Martin was manager. Short had allegedly once quipped to Herzog that he "would fire his grandmother for the chance to hire Billy." A few days after his ouster, Herzog said, "I'm fired. I'm the grandmother."[17] Herzog was not the only member of the Texas Rangers staff to be fired late in the 1973 season; General Manager Joe Burke was also let go.

The following year, 1974, Herzog stayed in the American League West, becoming the California Angels' third-base coach under manager Bobby Winkles. Herzog became the interim manager for four games after Winkles (30-44) was fired. After Dick Williams became the manager, Herzog stayed on as coach the rest of the year.

During the 1975 baseball season, Kansas City Royals GM Joe Burke was sensing that something was wrong despite the team being 50-46. He sensed a divide between team manager Jack McKeon and the team. On July 24, he fired McKeon and hired Herzog as manager on a deal worth $50,000 through the end of the 1976 season.[18]

Herzog inherited a solid Royals team with players like George Brett, John Mayberry, Paul Splittorff, Hal McRae, Frank White, Freddie Patek, Cookie Rojas, Doug Bird, Amos Otis, Dennis Leonard, and 39-year-old Harmon Killebrew. He managed the Royals to a second-place finish, seven games behind the Oakland Athletics.

Starting with his tenure with the Royals and continuing with the Cardinals, Herzog implemented a system of baseball well suited to the turf of both Royals Stadium and Busch Stadium and the antithesis of winning baseball via home runs. Whitey Ball was predicated on great fielding, line-drive hitting, speed on the basepaths, and solid pitching.[19]

The 1976 season was a turning point in Herzog's managerial career. Whitey Ball worked especially well on Royals Stadium's artificial turf.[20] The team hit only 65 home runs, 11th in the American League, but George Brett and Hal McRae finished 1-2 in the AL batting race with batting averages of .333 and .332 respectively, and the team had eight players with 10 or more stolen bases, led by Freddie Patek (51 SB's). On the pitching side, the Royals had four pitchers with 10 or more wins and Mark Littell and Steve Mingori each had 10 or more saves.

This team led the Royals to their first AL West title with a record of 90-72, edging out Oakland by 2½ games. The 1976 American League Championship Series pitted the Royals against the Yankees, with the teams splitting the first four games. In the pivotal Game Five at Yankee Stadium, with the Royals down by three in the eighth inning, George Brett hit a game-tying three-run home run off Grant Jackson. But in the bottom of the ninth inning, Yankees first baseman Chris Chambliss hit a home run off Littell to win the pennant.

The next year, 1977, the Royals were paced by a career year by Al Cowens, who batted .312 with 23 home runs and 112 runs batted in. Combined with strong pitching that included 20-game winner Dennis Leonard, the team won 102 games and finished eight games ahead of the Texas Rangers. The ALCS was a rematch against the Yankees. The Royals took a two-games-to-one lead and seemed poised to advance to the World Series when an issue arose with first baseman John Mayberry, who after dropping a foul ball, was pulled by Herzog and never played for the Royals again. After the Royals lost Game Four, 6-4, Herzog refused to play Mayberry in Game Five, despite the pleas from his teammates, and the Royals lost, blowing a 3-2 ninth-inning lead.

In 1978 the Royals won 90-plus games for the fourth year in a row and finished 92-70, five games ahead of the Rangers and Angels. In their third consecutive matchup with the Yankees, the Royals lost again, in four games.

The 1979 Royals finished with 85 wins, good enough for second place, three games behind the California Angels. This step back cost Herzog his job. The firing had less to do with on-field performance than the fact that there had been friction between Herzog and Royals owner Ewing Kauffman. Herzog got a $50,000 bonus each year if the Royals drew 2 million fans, which they did in 1978-1979, but Herzog felt that Kauffman and the front office did not really want to improve the team through free agency. (The next season, under Jim Frey, the Royals won the AL West with a record of 97-65, swept the Yankees in the ALCS, and lost to the Philadelphia Phillies in six games in the World Series.)

In June of 1980 Herzog moved east on I-70 to take over the beleaguered St. Louis Cardinals from Ken Boyer, with the team's record at 18-33 and having gone 5-22 over the previous 27 games.[21] Under Herzog the Cardinals were 38-35. On August 17, he was promoted to take over for John Claiborne as the Cardinals GM; his successor as manager was Red Schoendienst.

After the season Herzog acquired Bruce Sutter and Darrell Porter, who had played for him for three years in Kansas City. He also demoted Red Schoendienst to coach and took over the dual role of general manager and manager, the first person to serve in both roles since Connie Mack was GM and manager (and owner) of the Philadelphia Athletics in 1950.[22]

The 1981 season was interrupted by a 50-day players strike. When the games resumed in August, the season was split into two halves, with each half's winner advancing to the playoffs. This ended up hurting the Cardinals, who had the best overall record in the NL East, 59-43, but finished second in both halves, to Philadelphia and to Montreal.

The 1981 offseason saw the acquisitions of Lonnie Smith, Steve Mura, Willie McGee, and Ozzie Smith, as well as the re-signing of Joaquin Andujar. These acquisitions along with the players already in place led the 1982 Cardinals to a 92-70 season, edging out the Phillies by three games. They swept the Atlanta Braves in the National League Championship Series. Three games into the season, Herzog gave up his position as GM to focus on managing. He was replaced by Cardinals assistant GM Joe McDonald, three games into the 1982 season.[23] On April 10, 1982, the stress of being general manager and manager was beginning to take away from Herzog's abilities on the field so he turned over the general manager duties to McDonald, who had been hired by the Cardinals in 1981 as an executive assistant and assistant GM. McDonald had not only worked with Herzog when they were both with the New York Mets, but McDonald had previous GM experience with the Mets as he had been their GM from 1975-1980.

The 1982 World Series presented a stark contrast between the Cardinals and the Milwaukee Brewers, known as Harvey's Wallbangers after manager Harvey Kuenn. Milwaukee led the AL with 216 home runs. The Cardinals hit only 67 homers, last in the NL, but their team batting average was .264, tied for second, and the led the league with 200 stolen bases. The Series went the full seven games, with the Cardinals coming back after going down three games to two, to win Game Six, 13-1 and Game Seven, 6-3, giving the

Cardinals their first World Series championship in 18 years, and Herzog his first.

The Cardinals were unable to repeat and finished the 1983 season 79-83, fourth in the NL East. The major event of the season came at the June 15 trade deadline, when the Cardinals shocked the baseball world by trading former MVP and reigning Gold Glove winner Keith Hernandez to the New York Mets for Rick Ownbey and Neil Allen. Herzog said he made the move because the Cardinals needed more pitching, and that the plan was to bring Andy Van Slyke up from Triple A and move George Hendrick to first base.[24] It was later discovered that the trade was due to the longtime personality conflict between Hernandez and Herzog.[25] There were rumors of Hernandez's cocaine use, which turned out to be true. This also affected Joaquin Andujar and Lonnie Smith, leading to the trade.[26]

After finishing in third place (84-78) in 1984, the Cardinals went to the World Series in both 1985 and 1987.

In the 1984-85 offseason George Hendrick was part of a four-player trade for John Tudor and first baseman Jack Clark was acquired from San Francisco. This trade was done to stabilize the first-base position for the Cardinals. Also, 1985 saw the emergence of left fielder Vince Coleman, who stole a rookie-record 110 bases en route to Rookie of the Year honors and also led to the trade of Lonnie Smith to Kansas City.

The 1985 season in the National League East came down to a battle the last couple of weeks of the season between the Cardinals and the New York Mets. The Cardinals ended up with a record of 101-61, edging out the Mets by three games. They were led by Jack Clark's 22 home runs, and also stole 314 bases; besides Coleman's 110 steals, Willie McGee contributed 56 and Tommy Herr and Ozzie Smith each had 31. Pitchers John Tudor and Joaquin Andujar each won 21 games and Jeff Lahti, Ken Dayley, and Todd Worrell combined to save 35 games, to make up for the loss of Bruce Sutter who had signed in the offseason with the Braves.

In the NLCS, against the Dodgers, with the series tied at two games apiece, and the score 1-1 in the bottom of the ninth, Ozzie Smith hit a solo home run off LA's Tom Niedenfuer to win the game, 2-1. The call from Jack Buck – "Go crazy, folks, go crazy, it's a home run" –was ranked by mlb.nbcsports.com as number 21 of the 32 best calls in sports history.[27] Two days later, in Dodger Stadium, Jack Clark hit a three-run home run in the ninth inning off Niedenfuer to capture the pennant for the Cardinals. The win came at a cost: Before Game Four, Vince Coleman's leg was fractured in a freak accident with the tarp at Busch Stadium.[28]

With both teams from Missouri, the 1985 World Series was known as the I-70 Showdown Series and the Show-Me World Series, The Cardinals faced Herzog's former team, the Royals. Many of the Royals' leaders that year were holdovers from the Herzog era. The Royals had won 10 fewer games than the Cardinals, and St. Louis was the heavy favorite.

The Cardinals won the first two games, 3-1 and 4-2, and Kansas City took Game Three, 6-1. After John Tudor shut out Kansas City, 3-0, the Royals staved off elimination by winning Game Five, 6-1. Game Six was one of the most memorable games in World Series history. The game was scoreless through seven innings. In the bottom of the ninth, with St. Louis leading 1-0, Herzog called on rookie closer Tim Worrell to give the Cardinals their second championship in four years. The leadoff batter, pinch-hitter Jorge Orta, hit a bouncer to Jack Clark, who threw to Worrell covering first base. Orta was called safe on the play by umpire Don Denkinger.[29] Replays showed that Orta was out by half a step, but in the days before instant replay, Denkinger chose not to overrule himself and the call stood. The Cardinals proceeded to self-destruct. Steve Balboni hit a popup in foul territory that neither Darrell Porter nor Jack Clark could come up with; he subsequently singled. After Jim Sundberg's bunt forced Orta at third, a passed ball moved the runners up to second and third. Hal McRae was then intentionally walked. Pinch-hitter Dane Iorg singled to right and the tying and winning runs scored, to force a seventh game. After the drama of Game Six, Game Seven was anticlimactic as the Royals' Bret Saberhagen shut out the Cardinals, 11-0, to win the World Series.

The only drama in Game Seven was that Herzog became the first manager since Billy Martin (in 1976) to be ejected from a World Series game.

The next season the Cardinals slumped to a record of 79-82, 28½ games behind the first-place New York Mets, the only positives being that both Ozzie Smith and Willie McGee captured Gold Gloves and pitcher Todd Worrell earned Rookie of the Year Honors.

During the 1986-1987 offseason, the Cardinals, in an effort to improve their catching, traded catcher Mike LaValliere and outfielder Andy Van Slyke to the Pirates for four-time All-Star Tony Peña. This trade along with the 35 home runs from Jack Clark, the 109 stolen bases of Vince Coleman, and a pitching staff that had four winners of 10 or more games, helped the Cardinals improve by 16 wins and narrowly overtake the Mets and Expos. In the NLCS the Cardinals came from a three-wins-to-two deficit to defeat the San Francisco Giants in seven games and advance to their third World Series in six years.

Herzog's Cardinals faced the Minnesota Twins in a World Series played entirely on artificial turf (as had occurred in 1985). The Twins came back from a three-games-to-two deficit and won Game Six, 11-5, and Game Seven, 4-2.

Over the next couple of years the Cardinals slumped. In 1988 they finished with a record of 76-86 in fifth, ahead of only the Philadelphia Phillies, and 25 games behind the East-leading New York Mets. In 1989 they improved by 10 games to finish 86-76, but finished seven games behind the Chicago Cubs.

The 1990 season proved very difficult for Herzog and the Cardinals, and culminated in his resignation when the Cardinals, with a 33-47 record, were in last place in the National League East.[30]

The end of Herzog's Cardinals tenure also ended his managerial career, with a record of 1,281-1,125, a .532 winning percentage. He had a postseason record of 26-25, with the one World Series championship in 1982, three AL West titles, three NL East titles, and three National League pennants.[31]

Herzog's departure from the Cardinals did not end his career in baseball. In 1992, after holding various positions with the California Angels, he was named general manager. Over the next two years, the Angels fell short of expectations, finishing 72-90 in 1992 and 71-91 in 1993. In January 1994 he resigned, citing the opportunity to do other things.[32] He had spent 45 years as a player, coach, manager, and general manager.

As recently as 2018, Keith Hernandez, despite having been traded by Herzog, had nothing but the highest praise for Herzog's managerial and overall baseball acumen. "He was a great manager, best I ever played for," Hernandez said.[33]

Herzog was inducted into the National Baseball Hall of Fame in 2010. On a more local note, the baseball field at New Athens High School was renamed Whitey Herzog Field in honor of Herzog, who donated money to have the field renovated.

Herzog took the talent of his teams and where they played, to their full capacities. He took two teams from smaller markets to great heights.

Notes

1 On Anson, see David Fleitz; Cap Anson: sabr.org/bioproj/person/9b42f875; on Hanlon, see "The 'Inside' Scoop on Inside Baseball: Plus 'Inside Joke,' 'Inside Job,' and other 'inside, words. merriam-webster.com/words-at-play/the-inside-scoop-on-inside-baseball. Retrieved July 1, 2018.

2 Dan O'Neil, "Whitey Herzog: The Pride of New Athens," USA Today, July 18, 2010. stltoday.com/sports/baseball/professional/whitey-herzog-the-pride-of-new-athens/article_88fad913-7b40-5683-88f9-417f30044412.html; Retrieved July 15, 2018.

3 Ibid.

4 Ibid.

5 Ibid.

6 Ibid.

7 Scouting information thanks to Rod Nelson, chair of SABR's Scouts Committee.

8 Ibid.

9 Transcript of Whitey Herzog's Hall of Fame Speech. stltoday.com/sports/baseball/professional/transcript-of-whitey-herzog-s-hall-of-fame-speech/article_fec87545-dd96-52e2-9038-f2aa37d9ff5d.html; July 26, 2010; retrieved July 15, 2018.

10 O'Neil.

11 baseball-almanac.com/players/trades.php?p=herzowh01; retrieved July 15, 2018.

12 Glenn Liebman, "Here Are Some New Names for Humor Hall of Fame," *Baseball Digest* March 1992: 23.

13 John E. Peterson, *The Kansas City Athletics: A Baseball History, 1954—1967* (Jefferson, North Carolina: McFarland, 2003), 308.

14 Richard Sandomir, "Leaving Mets Put Herzog on a Path to the Hall," New York Times, July 23, 2010. nytimes.com/2010/07/24/sports/baseball/24herzog.html?ref=sports. Retrieved August 8, 2018.

15 "Texas Rangers Name Herzog Manager," *New York Times*, November 3, 1972. nytimes.com/1972/11/03/archives/texas-rangers-name-herzog-manager.html. Retrieved August 8, 2018. See also Paul Rogers, *The Impossible Takes a Little Longer* (Dallas: Taylor Publishing Company, 1990).

16 Brad Townsend, "40 Years After Memorable Debut, Ex-Ranger David Clyde Reflects on Career Cut Short," *Dallas Sports Day News*; June 22, 2013; sportsday.dallasnews.com/texas-rangers/rangersheadlines/2013/06/22/townsend-40-years-after-memorable-debut-ex-ranger-david-clyde-reflects-on-a-career-cut-short; retrieved August 8, 2018. The contract also included a $125,000 signing bonus.

17 Jimmy Keenan and Frank Russo, "Billy Martin," SABR BioProject, sabr.org/bioproj/person/59c5010b.

18 United Press International, "Royals, Fire McKeon, Hire Angels' Herzog," *Milwaukee Sentinel*. July 25, 1975.

19 Whitey Herzog and Kevin Horrigan, *White Rat — A Life in Baseball.* (New York: Harper and Row, 1987), 145.

20 Herzog and Horrigan.

21 William Nack, "They've Committed Cardinal Sins. Bad Fortune and Worse Playing Have Put Hard-Hitting St. Louis in Last Place — And Beleaguered Ken Boyer Out of a Job," *Sports Illustrated*, June 16, 1980.

22 Cardinals Clinch Eastern Title," *New York Times*, September 28, 1982. nytimes.com/1982/09/28/sports/cardinals-clinch-eastern-title.html.

23 baseball-reference.com/teams/STL/1982-schedule-scores.shtml; Retrieved December 9, 2018.

24 Kevin Paul Dupont, "Keith Hernandez Sent to Mets for Allen, Ownbey," *New York Times*, June 15, 1983: 46.

25 Jeff Pearlman, *The Bad Guys Won* (New York: ITBooks, 2011), 32.

26 Harold Friend, "Keith Hernandez Used Cocaine and Was Forced to Name Others," *Bleacher Report*, February 17, 2012. bleacherreport.com/articles/1070283-keith-hernandez-used-cocaine-and-was-forced-to-name-others; Retrieved August 10, 2018.

27 Joe Posnanski, "The 32 Best Calls in Sports History (and a Scully vs. Buck Debate," mlb.nbcsports.com/2013/10/16/the-32-best-calls-in-sports-history-and-a-scully-vs-buck-debate/; retrieved August 10, 2018.

28 Benjamin Hochman, "The Day the Tarp Ate Vince Coleman," *St. Louis Post-Dispatch*, October 12, 2015.

29 mlb.com/video/denkingers-missed-call/c-13062921; Retrieved August 11, 2018.

30 Associated Press, "An 'Embarrassed' Herzog Quits as Cardinals' Manager," *New York Times*, July 7, 1990. nytimes.com/1990/07/07/sports/an-embarrassed-herzog-quits-as-cardinals-manager.html. Retrieved August 26, 2018.

31 baseball-reference.com/managers/herzowh01.shtml. Retrieved August 26, 2018.

32 Bob Nightengale, "Angels GM Herzog Out in Surprise Resignation," *Los Angeles Times*, January 12, 1994.

33 David Jordan, "Keith Hernandez on his Cardinals Career, the Modern Game and a Mets Trade That Never was," *The Sporting News*, May 23, 2018.

DICK HOWSER

BY ALAN COHEN

"I will remember Dick Howser making that rush toward Bret Saberhagen the October before last, smiling like a kid, grabbing the most shining moment of a worthy baseball life."[1]

— Mike Lupica, June 18, 1987.

"Well, I just recruited me a shortstop."[2]

— Legendary FSU baseball coach Danny Litwhiler remembering the 1955 tryout of unheralded walk-on player Dick Howser

"He makes everything look so easy, and his attitude makes him easy to teach. He's the kind who can be a success in anything he tries."[3]

— Danny Litwhiler, March 12, 1958.

Dick Howser stood only 5-foot-7 and weighed 150 pounds as an adult. The mighty mite, as he was called, had been encouraged to participate in sports by his father, H. D., and played American Legion ball at an early age. However, he was very short and didn't try out for his high school team until he grew about six inches early in his junior year. Although he excelled in his junior and senior years at Palm Beach High School, with his Wildcats team winning the Class-AA State Championship in his junior year, the then 125-pounder was not heavily recruited by colleges. In 1954, as Howser recounted in 1979, he and two high school classmates, Burt Reynolds (the future actor) and pitcher Fred Kenney, "belonged to the same high school fraternity and one of the things we did was raise money to provide a scholarship of $500 for two years to a member who wanted to go on to school but couldn't afford to. The other guys had athletic scholarships so I kind of won the money ($500) by default."[4]

Although offered a minor-league contract, he elected to go to college expecting to go into teaching. But he still kept his dream about playing baseball. The baseball program at Florida State was relatively new, but when he first tried out at Florida State, coach Danny Litwhiler (who was in his first year at FSU) said to pitching coach/team trainer Don Fauls, "That one is not big enough to be a batboy." But Litwhiler said to Howser, "You got a glove. You got shoes. We'll give you a tryout."[5] Dick returned to the field with his gear, snatched up each ball hit to him and stung each ball pitched to him. In a manner of minutes, he evolved from walk-on to recruit.

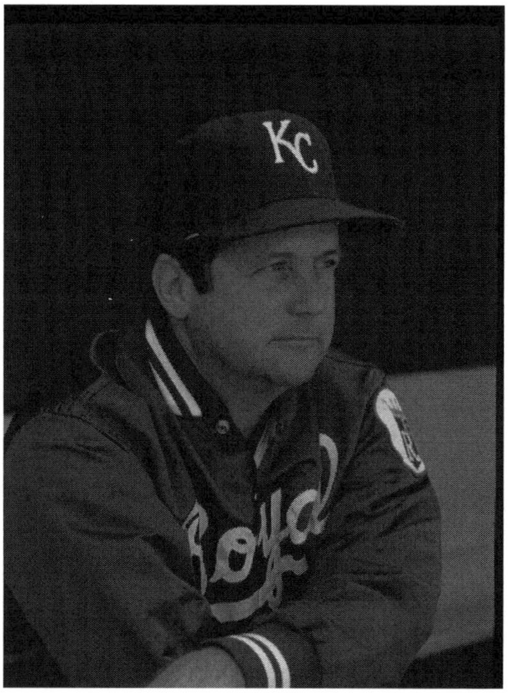

He hit .422 with an FSU record 38 hits as a sophomore in 1956 and became the first-ever consensus All-America student-athlete from the State of Florida in 1957. He was a repeat honoree in 1958. FSU Baseball's new home, which opened in 1983, was renamed Dick Howser Stadium in 1988, and a bust of Howser is on the stadium grounds. The field in 2005 was named Mike Martin Field at Dick Howser Stadium to honor longtime FSU coach Mike Martin. Since 1987, the Dick Howser Trophy, established by the St. Petersburg Area Chamber of Commerce, has been awarded to the College Baseball Player of the Year.

In 1985, Howser was at the top of the world after his Kansas City Royals won the World Series, defeating the St. Louis Cardinals in seven games. The following August, shortly after the All-Star game, he was diagnosed with brain cancer. He died within a year of the diagnosis. On July 3, 1987, his number 10 was the first number retired by the Kansas City Royals. In 2008, while renovating their ballpark, the Royals commissioned a spectacular bronze statue of Howser that is at Kauffman Stadium behind the fountains in right-center field. It was unveiled on Opening Day, April 10, 2009.

Richard Dalton Howser was born to Hubert Dalton "Dutch" Howser and his wife Marjorie Felton Howser in Miami, Florida on May 14, 1936. Dick was the oldest of four children. He had a sister, Joyce, and two brothers, Tom and Larry. Tommy, one year younger than Dick, signed with the Kansas City A's in 1956 and played two minor-league seasons. He started his first season at Fitzgerald, Georgia in the Georgia-Florida League and was, in mid-year, sent to Cincinnati's Class-D affiliate, West Palm Beach, where he got to play in front of his family. The next season, he was with Port Arthur, Texas in the Class-B Big State League. The Howsers moved to West Palm Beach when Dick was a youngster. Dick's father moved the family to West Palm Beach when Dick was a toddler. The elder Howser had been a baker in Miami but changed jobs when he took over an auto body shop after the move to West Palm Beach. Dick's mother served as PTA president when he was in Junior High School.

Dick Howser, in three years at FSU, batted .375. After his senior year at Florida State, he signed, on June 13, 1958, with scout Clyde Kluttz of the Kansas City Athletics for a reported $22,000 and spent the balance of the 1958 season with the Winona, Minnesota A's[6] in the Class-B Illinois-Indiana-Iowa League, batting .288. In the fall of that year, he played in the Florida Instructional League. The following season, the Class-B team relocated to Sioux City, and Dick batted .278. After batting .349 in 44 games with Sioux City in 1960, he was promoted to Double-A Shreveport in the Southern Association where his bat stayed healthy (.338), and he was on his way to Kansas City, becoming the first product of the Kansas City Athletics farm system to become a regular with the major-league squad.

He made his debut with the Athletics on Opening Day in 1961, starting at shortstop against the Red Sox at Fenway Park. After going hitless in his first four at-bats, he doubled off Mike Fornieles in the eighth inning for his first major-league hit.

He cemented his place in the lineup with an eight-game hitting streak (13-for-34) at the end of April and made a name for himself on the basepaths, challenging Chicago's Luis Aparicio for the league lead in stolen bases. He eventually finished second to the White Sox shortstop, as Aparicio won his sixth straight stolen base title. After 60 games, manager Joe Gordon was dismissed and replaced by Hank Bauer on June 19. One of Bauer's first decisions was to install Howser as team captain.[7] Dick was named to the All-Star team and played in the first of the season's two All-Star Games. He entered the game, played in the winds of San Francisco's Candlestick Park, as a defensive replacement in the eighth inning and struck out in his only at-bat.

On September 10, in the first game of a doubleheader against the Twins at Kansas City, Howser had the first five-hit game of his career. His two-out third inning triple launched a three-run rally that gave the A's a 4-0 lead. When the A's broke the game open with eight runs in the seventh inning, Howser singled to lead off the inning and, later in the inning, drove in a pair of runs with a double. The double came off back-up first baseman Julio Becquer who took the mound when the game got out of hand.

For the season, Howser posted what were to be career highs in batting average (.280), doubles (29), and stolen bases (37) and finished second to Boston's

Don Schwall in the rookie-of-the-year balloting. He was named the league's best rookie by *The Sporting News* and was selected for the Topps All-Rookie team. But the A's were years away from contention, finishing ninth in the American League.

"The kid is a good runner. He's got a good pair of legs and I can tell he loves to lay ball. He's the kind of player that will improve from year to year. He's the best I've seen. Every time I see him, he's stealing."[8] — Luis Aparicio, 1962.

The next season, Howser played each and every inning of his team's first 72 games before sustaining an injury to his glove hand while taking a throw in a game against Chicago. In the first inning of the game on June 23, he tagged out Luis Aparicio who was trying to steal second base. After finishing that game and playing a doubleheader, in pain, the next day, x-rays showed that Howser had sustained a broken bone in his left thumb. He was out of the starting lineup for the balance of the season. The best game of his abbreviated season came on June 16. The A's beat the Twins 6-2 for their fifth consecutive win and Howser's three hits included a second-inning RBI triple and a fifth-inning inside-the-park homer. Little more than a week later, things had changed. The A's had hit a cold snap, losing seven straight and falling from seventh to ninth place. And Howser had felt the snap in his left hand. Dick came off the DL in August, but only made 11 appearances as a pinch runner during the season's remaining weeks. His batting average for the season was .238 at the time of his injury, he had 19 stolen bases, and Aparicio had 13 swipes. Although he missed most of the season, Howser finished fifth in the league in stolen bases. The A's finished in ninth place, 24 games from the promised land.

He was healthy as the 1963 season began, appearing in each of his team's first 10 games before again falling prey to injury. Howser was batting only .211 and was given the day off on April 21. The following day, in batting practice, he injured himself taking a swing, cracking two ribs, prompting a return to the DL. By the time he had healed, Wayne Causey had taken over at shortstop, making Howser expendable. He was dealt, on May 25, 1963, along with Joe Azcue, to the Cleveland Indians for catcher Doc Edwards and $100,000. In his first 27 games with the Tribe, the team went 18-9 with Howser stealing eight bases and scoring 19 runs. But then a series of pulled leg muscles caused him to miss several stretches of games.

In the offseason, Howser subscribed to a training regimen to strengthen his leg muscles and, in his first full season with the Indians, 1964, he rebounded and posted a .256 batting average with a career-high 52 RBIs in a career high 162 games. He was also the only Indians player to score more than 100 runs. His 101 runs scored placed him second in the American League. He also led his team in hits (163) and triples (4). He was a bunter par excellence, tying Bobby Richardson for the league lead with 16 sacrifices. Manager Birdie Tebbetts in speaking of Howser said, "This kid runs, he handles the ball, he's coachable, knowledgeable ... He suits me fine. I'll tell you something else about him. He's a 100 percent effort guy – and I appreciate that kind."[9] Unfortunately, the Indians lacked for offense and finished in a sixth place tie with the Minnesota Twins, 20 games behind the first place Yankees.

Howser was not able to replicate his 1964 success in the two following seasons in Cleveland. In 1965, his hitting tailed off, he injured his ankle on July 20, and he lost the shortstop position to Larry Brown. For the season, Howser played in only 107 games, and batted .235. The following season, he was given an opportunity to regain his old position when Brown was injured in a collision with Leon Wagner on May 4. Howser started 16 consecutive games at shortstop from May 5 through May 22, batting .241.The Indians only played .500 ball during that span and opted to move Chico Salmon into the position. Over the balance of the season, Howser only played in 46 games (22 starts), and his batting average shrunk to .229 for 1966.

On December 20, 1966, he was traded to the New York Yankees for minor-league pitcher Gil Downs and cash. The Yankees' need for a new shortstop, at least in a backup role, was hastened by the resignation of Tony Kubek and the unavailability of prospect Bobby Murcer, who was in the Army, at the position.

When Howser first suited up with the Yankees in 1967, the franchise was in the third year of its fall from greatness. Mickey Mantle, at age 35 a shell of his former self, led the team with 22 homers. Howser proved a more than ample fill-in when injuries sent regulars to the bench. He filled in for Horace Clarke at second base and Charley Smith at third in the early going and appeared in 24 of the team's first 30 games, batting .300. With Ruben Amaro taking over at shortstop, and the return of Clarke and Smith, Howser only started 16 games (filling in for Clarke in July) after May 21. His season was abbreviated, once again by injury, when he broke his arm when making a double play in a game against the Orioles on July 16. For the season, he played in 63 games, batting .268. His average was better than virtually all of the regulars. Only Clarke (.272) was higher amongst those players with more than 100 at-bats. The Yankees finished in ninth place.

The following year, 1968, was Howser's last as a player. He appeared in 85 games, mostly as a pinch-hitter, and only batted .153. For his career, he batted .248 in 789 games. He stole 105 bases in 139 attempts.

In 1969, Howser took over as the Yankees' third-base coach and served in that capacity through 1978. The first few years coaching with the Yankees were marked by a painful rebuilding process and many of the pieces were in place when George Steinbrenner took over the team in 1974. Howser first managed the Yankees, for one day, in 1978 after Billy Martin was fired and Bob Lemon came on board as manager.

In the fall of 1978, Howser left the Yankees and returned to FSU to coach the Seminoles, replacing Woody Woodward, who had taken a position with the Cincinnati Reds organization. Howser and wife Nancy relocated to Tallahassee and became a vital part of the community over the next several years, although Howser returned to New York after only one year at the helm of FSU. During the 1979 season, Howser's team went 43-15-1 and was selected to play in the East Regional of the NCAA Tournament. Unfortunately, the squad lost to Florida and Delaware, ending Howser's only season as coach at his alma mater.

"It would be hard for anyone to turn down the New York Yankees' managing job, especially when you've been part of the organization for12 years. I'm a Yankee. I know the players fairly well. I read the box scores everyday this summer and tried to follow the team very closely."[10]— Dick Howser, October 29, 1979.

While Howser was at FSU, Billy Martin returned as Yankees manager, replacing Bob Lemon 65 games into the 1979 season. Martin, in and out of controversy, was dismissed after the 1979 season, pursuant to a brawl with a marshmallow salesman, and Steinbrenner lured Howser back to the Yankees as manager.

"Dick was an intense competitor who played beyond his ability. We may not have had the right chemistry, but I admired him greatly. He battled cancer the same way he battled the opposition. Even though we couldn't work together, our friendship remained. I'm going to miss him greatly."[11] — George Steinbrenner, June 18, 1987

In parts of seven seasons as a manager at the major-league level, Howser was highly successful, never finishing lower than second place during the first six years of his managerial career. His final season as a manager, 1986, was abbreviated by a foe far greater than any baseball opponent, and the Royals were in fourth place when Howser was forced to step aside in July due to illness. His teams won three divisional championship and one World Series.

In 1980, buoyed by Tommy John's 22 wins and Reggie Jackson's 41 homers, Howser led the Yankees to the AL Eastern Division championship with a 103–59 record. For most of the season, the ride was smooth and there was little in the way of controversy between owner and manager, a very unusual circumstance for the Yankees. There was also the leadership displayed by a new Yankee, 34-year-old Bob Watson, who was acquired in the offseason after 16 major-league seasons in which he had never been to the postseason. On August 15, after the Yankees had lost four of six games and seen their league lead shrink to 2.5 games, Watson called a team meeting. It lasted only 19 minutes, and there was a general feeling that the players would do what had to be done to win. That evening, they defeated the second-place Orioles 4-3, the win going to John, and the big blow being a two-run homer by Jackson. A beaming Howser said after the win that "We may have another meeting tomorrow. It was probably part of what happened in the game. There was a little more enthusiasm on the bench. It's bad to start feeling sorry for yourself in this game."[12]

Only the Baltimore Orioles stood in the way of the Yankees winning the AL East, and New York clinched the division title in their 160th game. However, the team lost three consecutive games to the Kansas City Royals in the best-of-five American League Championship Series, and it was in the LCS where Howser and owner Steinbrenner feuded.

Steinbrenner was highly critical of Yankee third-base coach Mike Ferraro's decision to send Willie Randolph home on a double by Watson with two outs in the top of the eighth inning and the Yankees down 3-2. Randolph was thrown out at the plate. Steinbrenner wanted Ferraro fired, but Howser supported his coach. Steinbrenner fired Howser shortly after the team lost the ALCS.

"Dick didn't say a lot; he just expected us to work hard. His famous words when we got down were, 'just get it done.'"[13] — John Wathan

The next year, the Kansas City Royals, his post-season rival in the previous season, hired Howser to manage on August 31. After play had resumed following that season's work stoppage, the Royals had gone 10-10 under Jim Frey. Howser managed the last 33 games of the season as the Royals went 20-13 to finish in first place in the AL West for the second part of the split-season. At the end of the season, the Royals and Oakland were matched up in a best of five series to determine who would go on to the American league Championship Series. The overmatched Royals lost to the A's in three games.

With the Royals, Howser was a quiet leader.

In his time with the Royals, Howser's teams went 404-365 (.525). They finished second in 1982 and 1983. Although they finished second in 1983, their record was a disappointing 79-83, and they finished 20 games behind the White Sox. During the offseason between 1983 and 1984, a drug investigation led to the arrest, incarceration and suspension of four 1983 Royals players including two starters, Willie Wilson and Willie Mays Aikens. Wilson's suspension was lifted in May 1984, but Aikens did not return to the Royals. The Royals obtained first baseman Steve Balboni from the Yankees in what turned out to be a fortuitous move.

As the 1984 season began, the Royals were in a bind. Not only was Wilson out of the lineup, but George Brett was coming off an injury and didn't see action until May 18. The pitching staff included three young pitchers (rookies Bret Saberhagen and Mark Gubicza, joined 1983 September call-up Danny Jackson) and not much was expected of the team. As late as June 23, the Royals were in seventh place. By Labor Day, they had moved into second place, and a 16-9 record after Labor Day propelled them to the AL West championship. Unfortunately, Howser, whose teams had been swept in 1980 and 1981, saw his postseason record go to 0-9 when Detroit swept the Royals in the best-of-five ALCS to advance to the World Series.

"If we do have the Cy Young Guy (Bret Saberhagen) and the MVP guy (George Brett), it'll keep me around longer."[14] — Dick Howser, October 5, 1985 in the clubhouse after the Royals clinched the AL West.

In 1985, the Royals repeated as AL West champions, clinching the title with a come-from-behind 6-4 win in 10 innings on the next to last day of the season, and faced the Toronto Blue Jays in the ALCS. The Blue Jays, in their first postseason appearance won the first two games, which were played in Toronto. Game Three at Kansas City was dominated by George Brett of the Royals. Prior to Game Three, Dick Howser, as a manager, had lost 11 consecutive postseason games, and it looked for a while, that it would be an even dozen. It was not Bret Saberhagen's night. Staked to a 2-0 lead, the 20-6 Cy Young Award winner imploded in the fifth inning yielding two singles, a double, and a pair of homers. He only recorded one out the Blue Jays took a 5-2 lead. The Royals, on George Brett's sixth-inning two-run homer tied the game.

The Royals lineup included Steve Balboni, who had begun his career with the Yankees, but had proven expendable when Don Mattingly joined the team. Balboni's tendency to strike out was annoying to some, but Howser displayed patience in letting the big 6-foot-3 guy play. Balboni had 36 homers and 88 RBIs for the 1985 Royals. During the series against Toronto, Balboni said, "I've got a chance to play now, and that's the whole thing."[15]

Balboni came up in the eighth inning of Game Three and, with two out singled in Brett with what turned out to be the winning run. Brett, the offensive star of the game, had reached base with his fourth hit of the encounter. The Royals stayed alive and, after falling behind in the series three games to one, won the final two games at Toronto to advance to the World Series.

In the World Series, the Royals were matched up against the St. Louis Cardinals. The heavily favored Cardinals were put at a disadvantage when leadoff batter Vince Coleman suffered a leg injury when the automatic tarpaulin at St. Louis inadvertently came into his path when he was running off the field prior to the fourth game of the NLCS. Although the Cardinals' run production was seriously hindered by Coleman's absence, they won the first game of the World Series by a 3-1 margin.

The Royals' top reliever in 1985 was Dan Quisenberry, who led the American League with 37 saves. It was a game in which Quisenberry was not used that temporarily caused headaches for Howser. In Game Two of the World Series, the Royals took a 2-0 lead into the ninth inning and Howser elected to stay with starter Charlie Leibrandt. The left-handed Leibrandt was pitching a masterpiece. Over the first eight innings he had given up only two hits and had retired the last 13 batters he faced. When Willie McGee doubled to lead off the ninth inning, Leibrandt retired the next two batters he faced and was one out away from the win. Up stepped righty Jack Clark. Rather than bringing in the right-handed Quisenberry, Howser chose to stay with Leibrandt. The move, or lack thereof, backfired as Clark singled and the Cardinals went on to score four ninth- inning runs to take a two-games-to-none lead in the series.

The Royals eventually were down three games to one but rallied behind the strong pitching of Danny Jackson to avoid elimination in Game Five.

Howser wasn't worried when his team was down in what was known as the I-70 Series against the cross-state rival Cardinals. After the Royals 6-1 win in Game Five, Howser said, "I can't explain it. It's not me and it's not the organization. They respond well to this pressure. I don't say anything. I just line them up and let them play."[16] In Game Six, Leibrandt was back on the mound facing Danny Cox and the game was scoreless through seven innings. The Cardinals broke the ice in the eighth inning and loaded the bases with two out. Howser brought in Quisenberry who put out the fire. Quisenberry pitched a scoreless top of the ninth to keep the score at 1-0. In the bottom of the inning, the Royals had runners on first and second with two out. Hal McRae was at the plate, and Quisenberry was in the on-deck circle. After a passed ball advanced the runners to second and third, Cardinal manager Whitey Herzog ordered an intentional walk. Howser countered with a move of his own, ordering Dane Iorg to pinch hit for Quisenberry. This moved worked out just fine as Iorg singled to right field, scoring two runs and forcing Game Seven.

The Royals scored early and often, but Darryl Motley's two-run homer in the second inning was all that World Series MVP Bret Saberhagen would need as he pitched an 11-0 shutout and the Royals won the World Series. At a White House ceremony, Howser presented President Ronald Reagan with a Royals jacket, hat, and bat. For the Royals, it was their only World Series win until 2015.

As the 1986 season began Howser's 364 wins as a Royals manager put him in second place behind Whitey Herzog's 410. It was pretty much a foregone conclusion that he would eclipse the record by the end of the season. But that would not happen. As June turned into July, the Royals went into a skid losing 11 consecutive games between June 27 and July 8. But Howser remained calm, as he always did, as his team slipped to fourth place in the AL West, 8 1/2 games behind the division leaders. Speaking with reporter Bob Gretz, Howser said, "But it's coming (the end of the team's futility). It (the team's performance) will get there. I don't know when. Maybe tomorrow." Gretz went on to say:

"Always Tomorrow: That could be the epitaph on Howser's tombstone. How better to explain the methods of a man whose team was twice just a game away from elimination last year in the playoffs and World Series? Still it won."[17]

The Royals won three of their next five games and headed into the All-Star break. The All-Star Game was played on July 15, and Howser led the American League to a 3-2 win. After the game, Howser, who had been having headaches for the prior two weeks, was examined on July 17 and it was determined that he had a brain tumor.

"I look at this as just another ballgame. He's the batter, he's the runner, and he's got to score. And he's going to win this game. I talked to him on the phone the other day and he didn't even sound like he'd been through anything. He sounded like he was back to normal."[18] — Marjorie Howser, July 30, 1986

On July 22, 1986, Howser underwent surgery at St. Luke's Hospital in Kansas City. Surgeons had found a malignant tumor in the left frontal lobe of Howser's brain.

"I've been pushing and pushing since the first operation in Kansas City and the second operation in Los Angeles (December 1996). I couldn't do it."[19] — Dick Howser, February 1997.

Howser attempted a comeback the following season. He arrived at spring training on February 21. He quickly found he was physically too weak and abandoned the attempt after just two days. He resigned his position and Billy Gardner took over as manager of the Royals. Experimental brain surgery was performed on Howser on March 20 in Pasadena, California. Surgeons injected cancer-killing cells known as lymphocytes, into the surgical cavity.[20] Less than three months later, Dick Howser was dead.

Howser was survived by his wife Nancy and his twin daughters from a previous marriage. He met his first wife Michelle Ann Metzger in 1961, while with the Kansas City Athletics. They were married in February 1964 and had twin daughters Jana and Jill on November 28, 1964. Dick and Michelle (who died in an automobile accident in 1980) subsequently divorced, and Dick married Nancy Kate Stephenson, an interior designer, on January 15, 1972. Jana became the Executive Vice-President of Development at the National College Baseball Museum and Hall of Fame in Lubbock, Texas, and Dick was named to that Hall of Fame in 2008. Jill and her husband are the parents of two daughters, Melody and Michelle.

After his death on June 17, 1987, Dick Howser was laid to rest at Memory Gardens Cemetery in his adopted hometown of Tallahassee, near the campus of his alma mater, Florida State University, and the stadium which bears his name.

Sources

In addition to the sources shown in the Notes, the author used Baseball-Reference.com, Newspapers.com, GenealogyBank.com, Ancestry.com, and:

Donnelly, Joe. "Dick Howser: Kaycee Captain," in *Baseball Stars of 1962* (New York, Pyramid Books, 1962), 122-132.

"FSU Soph Howser Tabbed for Bright Diamond Career," *Palm Beach Post*, April 27, 1956: 18.

Henry, Jim. "Seminole Scrapbook: Jana Howser celebrates Dad's Legacy," *Tallahassee Democrat,* April 14, 2016.

Mehl, Ernest. "A's Farm System Takes Bows Over Kid Howser," *The Sporting News*, November 8, 1961: 25.

Schneider, Russell. "Howser Shuts up Critics with Slick Plays at Shortstop," *The Sporting News*, April 15, 1965: 25.

Stilley, Aaron. "25th Anniversary: Remembering Dick Howser," I-70 Baseball, October 23, 2010.

Stilley, Aaron. "A Conversation with Jana Howser," I-70 Baseball, November 21, 2010.

Twyman, Gib. "Howser Has Learned to Roll with Punches," *Kansas City Star*, October 22, 1985: 1C.

Notes

1 Mike Lupica, "A Full Baseball Life Graced by Dignity," *New York Daily News,* June 18, 1987: 78.

2 Gerald Ensley, "Dick Howser: He Won Friends with his Savvy, Wit, and Loyalty," *Tallahassee Democrat*, June 18, 1987: D1.

3 "Deceptive Dick Howser Set for Final Spring at FSU," *Palm Beach Post*, March 13, 1958: 14.

4 Larry Fox, "Howser a Legend in Tallahassee," *New York Daily News*, November 1, 1979: 23C.

5 Ensley.

6 The Three-I League added three new teams in 1958. They were Rochester, Green Bay, and Fox Cities. The Rochester team relocated to Winona on June 29.

7 John E. Peterson, *The Kansas City Athletics: A Baseball History 1954-1967* (Jefferson, North Carolina, McFarland Publishers, 2003), 144.

8 Jerome Holtzman, "Two Greyhounds Threaten Theft-King Looey; Howser, Wood Endanger Six-Year Reign of Chisox Swifty," *The Sporting News*, June 2, 1962: 5.

9 Russell Schneider, "Birdie's New Ballad: We'll Win with Howser," *The Sporting News*, January 2, 1965: 9.

10 "Howser to Manage Yanks," *Tallahassee Democrat*, October 29, 1979: 1A.

11 Bill Madden, "Boss's Mistake: Firing Howser," *New York Daily News*, June 18, 1987: 79.

12 Phil Pepe, "Quiet Meeting May Have Saved Yank's Year," *New York Daily News*, August 17, 1980: Sports-8.

13 Denny Mathews (with Matt Fulks), *Denny Matthews's Tales from the Royals Dugout* (Champaign, Illinois, Sports Publishing, 2006), 65.

14 Bob Nightengale, "Royals Bask in the Glow of their Championship Season," *Kansas City Star*, October 6, 1985: Sports-12.

15 Rich Chere, "Balboni Handling Playoff Pressure," *Newark Star-Ledger*, October 9, 1985: 90.

16 John Sonderegger, "Royals' Reverse Logic Works with Another Win," *St. Louis Post Dispatch*, October 26, 1985: 6C.

17 Bob Gretz, "Howser Remains on an Even Keel as Royals Ship Goes Off Course," *Kansas City Star*, July 8, 1986: 1B.

18 Dave George, "Howser's Mother Says Tumor Like 'Just Another Ballgame'," *Palm Beach Post*, July 30, 1986: 1C.

19 Robert MCG, Tomas, Jr., "Dick Howser Dies at 51; Ex-Manager of Royals," *New York Times*, June 18, 1987.

20 Dave George, "Howser 'Alert' After Third Surgery for Tumor," *Palm Beach Post*, March 21, 1987: 1C.

DENNY MATTHEWS

BY CURT SMITH

Growing up in downstate Illinois, between Chicago and St. Louis, a midcentury youth was blessed by time and place. By radio, born in 1920, and television's relatively new wonderwork, baseball could be followed through the art of play-by-play. If you grasped the pastime's rhythm, the Voices often became as arresting as being at the park.

At Comiskey Park, cultivated Bob Elson – "The Old Commander" – patented *he's out* and perfected the on-field interview. Crosstown, two Jacks, Brickhouse and Quinlan, conjured the Second City and embodied the beloved Cubs. In St. Louis, Harry Caray crowed *Holy Cow!* and sang of a home run *It might be! It could be! It is!* If the sky was "right," recalled Denny Matthews, still manifestly the Voice of the Royals after a half-century of radio/TV, "I could pick other games" – from Milwaukee, Detroit, or Cleveland by the wireless – only later knowing "that I was under their influence, as well."[1]

Matthews was born on November 14, 1942, in Jacksonville, Florida,[2] soon moving to Bloomington, Illinois, where at home the dial was always turned to baseball – especially to longtime Cardinals affiliate WJBC, Caray, Jack Buck, and Joe Garagiola forging a *nonpareil* cast.[3] His father, George, had been Illinois State University's "first All-American baseball player [1938] who might have signed with the Reds or White Sox but for World War II,"[4] said Denny. Instead, he and his wife, Eileen, worked at State Farm Insurance's company offices in Bloomington, their son inheriting pop's baseball genes.

As a freshman at Illinois Wesleyan University in Bloomington, Denny even got a tryout at nearby Decatur with the affiliate of the big-league San Francisco Giants. At Wesleyan, he also belonged to Sigma Chi fraternity, manned the varsity middle infield with future major leaguer Doug Rader, and tried football – his receiving yardage eighth in the nation after not even playing in high school.[5] Matthews concedes to "liking all sports, not just baseball, but I didn't know what I wanted to do with them."[6] Recalling Dad and the radio, what seemed natural to do was what he hadn't yet tried – airing the pastime of his youth.

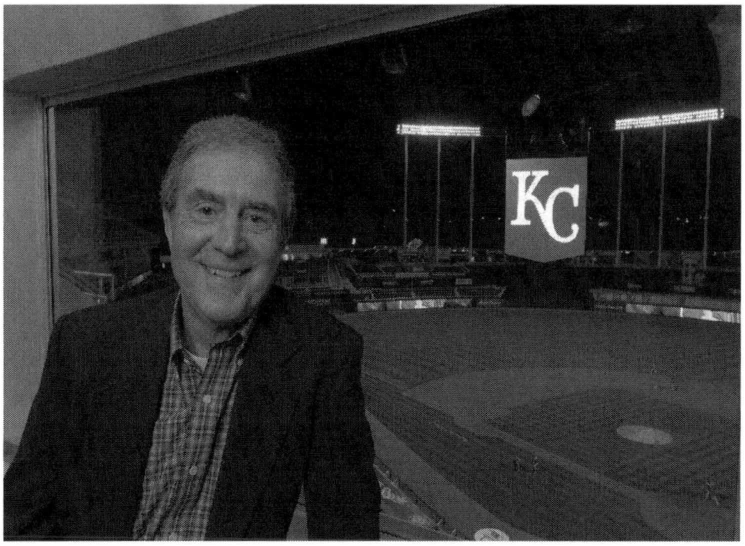

The part-time college basketball announcer began by working for State Farm in Bloomington, then Peoria radio, next St. Louis TV. Then, in 1968, he eyed the next-year expansion draft that upped each major league from 10 to 12 teams. That September, having never called an inning, Denny got the Cardinals' OK to bring a recorder, find a spare booth, and on reel-to-reel tapes describe a regular-season game at Busch Stadium. Later, applying for the 1969 American League Kansas City job, he sent the three half-innings that sounded best.

"This was early '69," said Matthews, "and the Royals were looking for a second banana" after hiring iconic Bud Blattner as lead announcer. "A friend said: 'A lot of people'll [more than 300] apply. Make yours unique. It's not enough that they like your tape. They gotta *remember* you.' Schlitz beer was primary Royals sponsor — that's why a Milwaukee agency had the account. So, I go to a local Schlitz distributor and pick up menus they gave bars and restaurants."[7] A Schlitz ad filled the outside flap. The inside was blank, for the local place to print its menu. They also had serving trays with a Schlitz logo.

Denny printed his résumé, put a menu on the tray, enclosed a tape, and sent them off. "That was my packaging — pretty corny, I'll admit — that, and a letter I'm ashamed of," he said. Matthews penned, "I hope you don't think I'm a bush-leaguer for having done a Cardinal game, but here is my final pitch for the Royals' job."[8] Ambition can be brutal — owner August A. Busch's Cardinals had given him his chance. Several months later Denny met Blattner, was among three finalists, and got interviewed.

Blattner invited Matthews to Kansas City, telling him to arrive on a Friday at about 3 or 4 P.M. Denny left home in Illinois at 10 A.M., he said almost half-a-century later, arriving on time. From the start, "Buddy and I hit it off. We chatted, got acquainted and talked baseball, broadcasting, and the job."[9] They went out for pizza "and before you know it, it's real late," Denny overnighting at Bud's home. "I got home at 10 — 10 the next *morning*, looked at my mother and said, 'Mom, I told you I'd be back at 10!"[10] Several days later the offer became official.

Later, Matthews asked Blattner why he had chosen a big-league neophyte. "The audition was a [baseball], not a minor-league game," Bud explained. "It's how [you] filled time between pitches, covering strategy and anticipating moves on the playing field. In other words, [adding] insight — beyond mere play-by-play. [Your] on-the-field experience in high school and college was a help. The Royals were a new team and wanted a fresh face and voice. Those in charge wanted someone with no bad habits."[11] In a sense, inexperience helped.

Blattner, a native Missourian, was already a household name in millions of Midwest homes when he joined the Royals — world doubles table tennis champion at 16, big-league infielder at 22, athlete-turned-announcer with the Browns, Mutual and Liberty Broadcasting System, then sidekick to as Falstaffian a legend who ever lived. On 1953-54 ABC and 1955-59 posher CBS, Bud and Dizzy Dean pioneered network TV's first sport series, the monumental *Game of the Week*.[12] "In the hinterlands and small towns, watching Ol' Diz was an absolute religion," said CBS sports head Bill MacPhail."[13] Each weekend Pleasantville closed down.

Entering the Hall of Fame in 1953, ex-pitcher Dean had thanked God for "a strong body, a good right arm, and a weak mind."[14] Broadcasting, he made baseball a regular-season *national*, not just *local*, product. If *Game* failed, "maybe TV sports has a different future," MacPhail marveled.[15] Instead, debuting on Saturday and adding Sunday in 1957, *Game* lured more than one-half of all sets in use.[16] Ol' Diz sang *The Wabash Cannonball* and called the viewer *pod-nuh* and mangled English like no one had or will. Runners *slud*. Fielders returned to their *respectable* positions. A hitter stood *confidentially* at the plate.

Middle America loved the 300 pounds, string tie, and Stetson — the whole rustic goods. But — this is key — Dean's insanity relied on "pod-nuh" restoring sanity. "Viewers loved the songs, the craziness," Blattner said, "but Diz wouldn't even give the score."[17] Bud gave the score — also analysis, reminiscence, and humor. Weary of Dean's ego, he resigned in late 1959, replaced by Pee Wee Reese. Blattner aired the 1960-61 Cardinals and 1962-68 Angels before returning home, where Denny saw another skill: observation. "Bud hated if I wasn't listening [in his innings] because he might say something, and I'd come on the air and repeat the same thing!" said Matthews. "Listening is smart. Not listening to others is also rude. God gave us one mouth but two ears. Maybe we're supposed to be listening two-thirds of the time."[18]

Blattner said, "Diz brought the audience to the game before we said a word."[19] Bud brought like credibility to the 1969 Royals – "people'd come up to him everywhere and talk about his *Game* with Diz" – and discretion. *Off* air he told of doing Mutual Radio when Pat Mullin's late-inning 1951 home run for Detroit tied the Yankees. Bud was exhausted, Mullin due to hit again in the 10th. Except for him, Blattner would have been home, writing "the bastard" beside his name. Bud's partner read: "Now to the bastard, I mean batter."[20] *On* air peers later fondly recalled how as a game was set to begin before a small crowd on the West Coast starting in the Midwest at 9:35 or, as one mused, "any other game with people disguised as empty seats," Bud would cry before airtime: "Hi, anybody!" To Denny's knowledge, no one answered.

Many players on the 1969-70 Royals gave anonymity new connotation, with a collective 134-190 record. Each day Matthews hosted a 10-minute star of the game show "featuring the Royals star of the previous day," he said. "We had to have one, even if no player had played well." By August 1969 every "Royal had made it except a utility infielder who rarely played," Juan Rios.[21] One day he made a game and got three hits. Driving to the park next day, Denny decided to have Rios as his guest – *finally*, Juan wished upon a star.

As usual, shortstop Jackie Hernandez offered to interpret Spanish over the Royals' 1969 46-station KMBZ radio network.[22] Municipal Stadium housed Kansas City's two franchises – the lowly 1955-67 Athletics, missing the first division *every* year before vamoosing to Oakland in 1968, replaced by the expansion Royals. Matthews hosted his guest in the dugout bullpens down the right-field line. "Jackie, ask Juan for his feelings on last night's game," he began. In Spanish, Rios seemed a chatterer, Denny feeling "There must be some terrific stuff." Rios then handed Hernandez the mic. "Juan said he feels great," the translator said. As producer Ed Shepherd dropped his recorder, Denny dripped sweat. "His life story and that's it – five seconds in English."[23]

A major radio/TV sponsor was a local food manufacturing firm, Guy's Foods, that made a panoply of snacks: pretzels, nuts, Doritos, potato chips. One 1970 Friday night in Milwaukee, the Royals' producer/engineer handed Matthews a card reading, "Guy's Foods," Denny's task to think of an apt one-liner. Wheels began spinning: Friday was July 3 – Saturday the Fourth – a long holiday weekend. People would be outside. Below, Royals-Brewers unfolded. Properly strategized, Matthews said, "For those of you planning a Fourth of July picnic, take those good Guy's potato chips." A nice drop-in. Unfortunately, the K.C. hurler took an eternity to pitch, which gave Denny an eternity to fill. Pleased with his plug, he tried another – for a time, he feared his last. "And fans, while you're in the store, be sure and grab Guy's nuts."[24]

Hearing it, said Denny, Blattner whitened, his face saying, "Heavens, what have my young men done now?" Matthews returned to Kansas City afraid that a pink slip might precede him. Yet, improbably, Guy's head Guy Caldwell had already heard the story – and the junior partner's all-time blooper had made him howl! "Here's to a sense of humor," Denny hailed. "It can save careers."[25] Little saved the early Royals, locals uncomplaining after the quisling 1967 A's had beat the sheriff out of town. A year later Royals owner Ewing Kauffman signed a four-year lease on Municipal at 21st and 22nd Streets, Euclid Avenue, and 2128 Brooklyn Avenue. By bus, car, or taxi it took 20 minutes from downtown to the park. Seats were bright, ushers kindly, and rest rooms clean. Nothing beat the heat. "During midsummer days," *Sports Illustrated* had written, "it is quite possible to be baked alive."[26]

The memory of Kansas City's first big-league act clouded the second in the October 15, 1968, AL expansion draft. Assuming patience, the Royals eschewed age. The first choice, Orioles pitcher Roger Nelson, 24, had finished 4-3 with a 2.41 earned-run average. His 1969 suggested promise before 1970-71 injuries struck: 7-13, 3.31 ERA, 29 starts, 8 complete games. Other pitchers selected were Ike Brookens, Wally Bunker, Tom Burgmeier, Bill Butler, Jerry Cram, Moe Drabowsky, Dick Drago, Al Fitzmorris, Mike Hedlund, Steve Jones, Dave Morehead, Don O'Riley, Jim Rooker, Jon Warden, and Hoyt Wilhelm. Position players were Jerry Adair, Mike Fiore, Joe Foy, Billy Harris, Bill Haynes, Fran Healy, Hernandez, Pat Kelly, Joe Keough, Scott Northey, Bob Oliver, Ellie Rodriguez, Paul Schaal, and Steve Whitaker.[27] Kansas City opened April 8, 1969, edging Minnesota, 4-3, on Keough's 12th-inning sacrifice fly, before 17,688 at Municipal. Its lineup read: Lou Piniella, leading off, in center field; Adair, at second base; Ed Kirkpatrick, left field; Foy, batting cleanup, third base; Chuck Harrison, first base; Oliver, right field; Rodriguez, catcher; Hernandez, shortstop; and Bunker, pitching.[28]

K.C.'s first hit, run batted in, and victory were Piniella's, Adair's, and Drabowsky's. Its first home run was Fiore's on April 13 against Oakland.[29] The Royals placed fourth in the six-team East and drew 902,414, the best in their tenure at the makeshift park (next year luring a Municipal-low 693,647). Rookie of the Year Piniella, temper as searing as Sahara heat, played a makeshift left field. "He was a character here [1969-73] before he was a Yankee," Denny said. The early Royals wore button-down jersey tops, Lou so irate making an out that he grabbed his jersey by the collar, pulled violently, and tore the buttons off — "a wonder he didn't put out someone's eye."[30] One Saturday, he hit into an inning-ending double play, profaning and kicking dirt and grass. Shortstop Freddie Patek brought out his glove and sunglasses, which Piniella threw to left field, where they landed in a heap worthy of a rugby scrum. Still fried, Lou got there, picked up and put on the glove and glasses — and would have seen the second batter fly to left had he not, flipping down his glasses, popped a lens out when it hit the ground.

"Lou's blinded in one eye by the sun!" Matthews bayed much later. "And he starts spinning like a top to get an angle, yet amazingly made the catch!"[31] A fine hitter, 1969-71's Piniella averaged .282, .301, and .279, the '71ers reaching second with a shocking 85-76 record. Everything was relative: A year later Tigers catcher Tom and umpire Bill Haller faced the Royals — said 1968-82 Hall of Fame librarian Jack Redding, "the first such sibling act in big-league history."[32] Next year, Municipal's last as K.C.'s chateau, Piniella hit .312. He retired with a .291 average, then managed for the Yankees, Reds, Mariners, Devil Rays, and Cubs, where, thankfully, sunglasses were no longer a concern. Handclapping feted Oliver's 27 and John Mayberry's 25 homers in 1970 and 1972, respectively; Big John's 100 RBIs in Municipal's final year; Piniella's 18-game hit streak in 1971; and Roger Nelson's six shutouts in 1972. Oliver and Amos Otis got six hits and stole five bases in a game, respectively — all exceptions to expansion's rule.[33]

From 1969-72, K.C. drew as many as 32,728 for an April 12, 1971, night opening game against Minnesota; 30,035, May 24, 1970 day, Milwaukee; 31,872, April 20, 1969, doubleheader, Oakland; 16,406, June 13, 1970 non-opener night, New York; and 18,248, June 18, 1969 twi-night doubleheader, Oakland.[34] The '72ers left Municipal October 4, blanking Texas, 4-0. To many, they still seemed merely the A's' successor — the local team once owned by Arnold Johnson, crediting Yankees brass for getting the AL to let him move from Philadelphia in late 1954. All decade Johnson kept trading fine players to his old Bombers benefactor who later starred in the Bronx — Art Ditmar, Ralph Terry, Roger Maris — the relationship, they believed, miming its former vassal state — major-league Kansas City still the "Yankees' cousins." What could change such servitude? The only major-league sports site built solely for baseball between 1962 and 1991.

The nearby chapter on Royals, later renamed Kauffman, Stadium describes a vote of local citizens in 1967 approving bonds for the Truman Sports Complex, including a stadium for pro football's Chiefs and a park for the Athletics.[35] This flouted the 1960s mania a.k.a. multisport stadia that dissimilar baseball and football could somehow live as one. In turn, A's owner Charles O. Finley flouted his word, breaking a lease to move cross-country in 1968. Irate, the US Senate vowed to revoke baseball's antitrust exemption if Kansas City wasn't given another team. The offshoot was 1969 expansion: the Royals and Seattle joining the AL; Montreal and Seattle, swelling the National League; K.C.'s owner to be pharmaceutical czar Kauffman.[36] Then, in 1973, the Royals got a new skipper, "Trader Jack" McKeon, new road uniform — "powder blue" — and new home — a 40,733-seat baseball park, 12-story-high crown-shaped scoreboard near a fountain, waterfall, and pool complex, and accent on defense, alley power, and speed. The Sports Complex built two houses, not one. No longer did everything seem up to date here — except its park.[37]

"Everything changed here when we moved into our new place," said Matthews. "We became a trailblazer. We began to draw."[38] 1,345,341 its first year, 1973; 1,680,265, the team's first West title, 1976; and 2,255,493, 1978's third straight crown. In 1975, Blattner reached a flagship WIBM Topeka 50-outlet radio network, aided by Denny and Fred White, and KMBW TV seven-affiliate arrangement, aides Matthews and Gene Osborne.[39] That winter the Royals' first-liegeman behind the mic retired or was axed, depending on which paper you read or announcer you believe. Most saw Blattner's hand at work, tired of the travel but regretting that his exit deprived the Royals of a familiar, easy name, leaving for his home and business in Lake of the Ozarks, Missouri. Matthews "succeeded, not replaced, my mentor," Denny said carefully, rolling lucky 7 from the start.

The adopted Illinoisan inherited three Western Division titlists in a row. Like other prior almost-dynasties — think postwar Brooklyn — the Royals found the Yankees in their way, New York taking each 1976-78 skin-of-its-teeth American League Championship Series. A kinder, gentler end graced K.C.'s greatest comeback: Friday night, June 15, 1979, in Milwaukee. After the Brewers took an 11-2 fourth-inning lead, skipper Whitey Herzog yanked his starters and sent them back to the Pfister Hotel for a good night's sleep, the Royals had a game scheduled next afternoon, a Saturday. "Incredibly, the subs rally, winning, 14-11," said Denny. "Around 11 P.M., the guys who'd left to get some sleep were still in the hotel lounge, telling stories and having a few cool ones." The team bus arrived, one sub saying, "We don't need you guys, we won!"[40] The starters needed a little convincing. A few more drinks helped.

In 1980, Mid-America toasted George Brett — on August 17, reaching .401. Could No. 5 become the first batter to average .400 since Ted Williams in 1941? He missed 45 games — but hit .390 as league MVP.[41] "He was a one-man warrior," said Matthews, but the Royals were not a one-man team. Dennis Leonard won 20 games for the third time in four years. Saving 33, reliever Dan Quisenberry was nicknamed The Quiz. An answer was center fielder Willie Wilson's Gold Glove, then-record 705 at-bats, and 230 hits.[42] K.C.'s reply in that year's LCS was new, beating the Yankees twice, 7-2 and 3-2. The Bronx Zoo hosted Game Three: New York, 2-1, in the seventh inning. Yankees bullpen ace Goose Gossage threw a fastball. "Swing and a high fly ball!" White said on Royals wireless. "Deep right field! There she goes!"[43] Royals Stadium's scoreboard could use more than 16,000 bulbs. Brett's three-run titan into Yankee Stadium's upper tier still hangs in lights: final, 4-2, K.C.'s first pennant. "Making the World Series," said Matthews, "threw off all that frustration."[44] The Series renewed it — in Game Six, the 97-year-old Phillies franchise won its first title, 4-1.

Having climbed one rung, the Royals had not yet scaled the final. Ahead — that elusive Series victory, also photographs and memories. Anecdotist more than statistician, Denny liked to reminisce. *Exempli gratia:* Amos Otis was a superb 1970-83 center fielder acquired from the Mets who ranks among the top 10 Royals in at-bats, bases on balls, caught stealing, doubles, double plays grounded into, extra-base hits, games, hits, home runs, plate appearances, runs, runs batted in, sacrifice flies, singles, stolen bases, steal percentage, total bases, triples — and first in power/speed quotient.[45] To Matthews, he exceled as a basestealer by studying pitchers. The A's' famed lefty, Vida Blue, was a special subject, relying on rhythm. To break it, Amos stepped out of the box or asked the umpire to check the ball, so irking Blue that he threw the ball directly *at* him. "Vida faced first base in the stretch, yet

Amos took the biggest lead I've ever seen," Matthews said. Kauffman Stadium's then-artificial turf had dirt around the bases. Otis would plant both feet on the carpet – about an 18-foot lead – and ask a teammate if he saw a wrinkle. What wrinkle? Denny said Amos answered: "'That wrinkle in his pants. When that's there, he's going home.'"

Two players occupied opposite poles of Denny's radar. Hal McRae was Kansas City's clubhouse enforcer. In 1979 George Scott arrived after 13 years with Boston and Milwaukee, Herzog using him to pinch-hit or sub at first base. Matthews said that Scott's nickname, Boomer, was at variance with his high-pitched voice – "Mike Tyson before Mike Tyson." Wanting his Boston number 5 with the Royals, Scott found *another* George wearing it. Inexplicably, Boomer couldn't grasp why Brett got to keep it, complaining 24/7. "I'm George Scott!" he said in a voice Denny dubbed Scott's "Tiny Tim" contralto. "I deserve number 5! Boomer gets no respect!" Mates tired of Scott's rhetoric and hitting into double plays: "I'm number 5!" (He wore No. *0.*) Finally, after Scott went 0-for-4, again whining, McRae, the club enforcer, exploded. "*Boomer, shut up!* I'm sick of listening to you talk about number 5. We have another number we're going to give you ... *6-4-3!*"[46] Silence. Scott was released, then briefly signed by the Yankees, who wouldn't give him number 5, either. As Denny said, it belonged to some guy named Joe.

In 1971-81, the Royals and Athletics won the AL East 10 of 11 years. Having stolen the A's, Oakland was viewed by Kansas City as the Capulets would the Montagues. In Oakland, an A's fan, leaning over the Royals bullpen railing, was struck by a player, "like putting your head through a carnival hole and meeting a water balloon," said Denny.[47] The next fan to do so met a fate in kind. McRae, a 1973-87 Royal whose 133 RBIs led the league in 1982, grabbed a fan's umbrella and hit the bystander on the head. Next morning an Oakland paper showed Hal holding this umbrella, about to strike him. According to Matthews, "Charlie Lau, our hitting coach, always got on Mac because Hal's top hand dominated his swing, the top wrist rolling over too soon. At breakfast, Lau pointed to the picture. 'See,' he told Mac, 'I keep telling you – too much top hand.'"[48]

Once the would-be player almost *became* a player. At K.C., the first four A's hit safely: 3-0, nobody out, runners on, "and Whitey strolls toward the home-plate umpire, everybody puzzled." As they talk, Matthews thinks, "'They got good swings,' and a light went on. Does Whitey think they're stealing signs and know what pitches are coming?" Later, Denny conceded, "I shouldn't have done this – no proof – but I say on air that Whitey may think they've got his signs," citing how a club could flash a sign to the hitter, using binoculars in the bullpen. "You'd have a pitcher who puts a towel over his right leg for a fastball. Little towel: a breaking ball." Suddenly, Herzog and the umps start for the A's pen. Matthews "feels like the guy with a huge fish on his line." They reach the pen, go through the gate, and get to the bench's end, where Whitey picks up the binoculars. "I'm watching with *my* binoculars, and suddenly a heady feeling hits me. Whitey and I may have been the only people in Royals Stadium who were on to the A's ruse." For one game, Denny "knew exactly what was going on, as much a part of it as anyone on the field, feeling like a player."[49]

In 1981 players felt like striking, an abbreviated regular season siring a best-of-five-games divisional playoff series. Fittingly, the A's and Royals met: Oakland swept. Next year Denny called his first LCS on CBS Radio – Brewers-Angels. In 1983 Brett's home run against the Yankees in the Bronx was ruled illegal because pine tar on his bat topped the rule book's 18-inch limit. Later, an AL president for the first time overruled an umpire, Brett's homer was restored, the game continued, and Kansas City won the 5-4 "Pine Tar Game."[50] Blattner had warned Matthews not "to be a bad imitation of some original."[51] His first full year, 1974, Brett held his bat high above his head, a bad imitation of Carl Yastrzemski. He was blessed to have a great work ethic and hitting coach. Midseason, Charlie Lau asked if he wanted to work on his swing. Slumping, George absorbed Lau's "extension through the ball and having a weight shift."[52] Investment in Lau's advice reaped spectacular returns.

Ageless: The Royals captain won batting titles in 1976, 1980, and 1990 — the only player to lead in three decades.[53] *Peerless*: the 13-time All-Star became the 18th player to get his 3,000th hit, in 1992.[54] *Timeless*: Some still debate which 1985 Brett game mattered most. "Many say it's in that World Series," said Matthews. "Actually, it's LCS Game Three. We'd lost the first two in Toronto. Lose the next, at home, and you're dead." It was arguably Brett's best-ever game. "A position player, say shortstop, rarely dominates baseball, since it's not a one-man game, you can't control what's hit your way, and at most bat five times. George made huge plays in the field and went 4-for-4, homering twice." Somehow Lau, an average hitter, made Brett a superb hitter, using a teaching *tool*, his "incredibly soft-spoken manner," to *teach* hitting. A commercial went, "When E.F. Hutton talks, people listen." When Charlie spoke, "people listened," Denny said. "Brett, most of all."[55]

In 1985 George wed 30 homers, 112 RBIs, and a .335 average. Wilson, *the* star on almost every other American League club, lashed 21 triples, topping Brett's 20 in 1979 and the most in the majors since 1949. The Quiz led a fifth/final time in saves (37). Cy Younger Bret Saberhagen went 20-6. Still, Kansas City trailed the LCS, three games to one, despite Brett's third game of two homers, a bravo stop to throw out a Jay at the plate, and making the final out — a rare "one-man game." Before 1985, the series consisted of best-of-five; under that format, K.C. would have been kaput. Best-of-seven gave the Royals breath. Using it, they swept Toronto three straight. "The War Between the States" followed, Kansas City extending its trend of not wanting to peak too soon. St. Louis launched it, 3-1 and 4-2, no team having won a Series after losing the first two at home. Saberhagen ignored the past, 6-1, the Cards then replying, 3-0, before Danny Jackson countered, 6-1.

This backdrop preceded the play that more than any other led baseball to later sanction instant replay. To the 1985 combatants, a more immediate goal was to win Game Six. St. Louis led, 1-0, in the home half of the ninth inning, three outs from a title, as Royal Jorge Orta led off by rolling to first baseman Jack Clark. Pitcher Todd Worrell took his throw and beat Orta to the bag — except that umpire Don Denkinger called him safe. Steve Balboni then popped out in foul ground — except that Clark lost the ball. The Cards still led — until a passed ball, intentional walk, and pinch-hitter Dane Iorg's game-winning 2-1 hit. Next evening, mentally bent on chaining Denkinger in Leavenworth, St. Louis sleepwalked through Saberhagen's Game Seven five-hit jewel and Darryl Motley's seeming blast onto adjacent Interstate 70. "One out to go in the ninth inning," Denny said. "Eleven to nothing. The one-oh pitch. Fly ball! Motley going back to the track! No outs to go! The Royals have won the 1985 World Series! And they converge on the mound in celebration!"[56] As usual, Matthews aired the Series on the Royals radio network — and also CBS wireless.

By the '80s, Denny led the American League's largest radio network — 120 stations in 11 states[57] — the Voice of Cardinals Nation's Radio Free AL, preferring radio to TV "for the obvious reasons," he said, later. "You're your own boss. No director or producer in your ear. On TV, you're never going solo. What I miss, though, about [doing radio] is the ability to be instructive. You can't call for a replay on radio."[58] Matthews reached far beyond greater Kansas City. Similarly, Kauffman's original artificial turf absorbed rain, reducing postponement, key to pilgrims trooping from hundreds, even thousands, of miles away. The team drew chiefly from its own Central Time Zone — but also the next-door Mountain Zone. Then, in 1993 the NL gave an expansion franchise to Denver, heretofore not represented by a big-league baseball team. "Until then we'd been their closest franchise," said Denny of pulling weekenders from Arizona to Montana.[59] Now the new Colorado Rockies began "crowding us," luring radio/TV outlets in Colorado's Durango; South Dakota, Lead-Deadwood; Utah, Salt Lake City; and Wyoming, Cheyenne — many of whose listeners previously cheered the Royals.

Kansas City's radio network still consists of 60 teams in six states: Eureka Springs, Arkansas; Cherokee and Humboldt, Iowa; Coffeyville and Emporia, Kansas, names even apart from places redolent of a *Gunsmoke* TV episode; Miami, Oklahoma;

North Platte, Nebraska; Moberly, Missouri, the sites of suburbs and farmhouses and sleepy small towns. Ratings have bloomed despite, not because. For the team's, the quarter-century after 1985 fused one saw ("It's always darkest before the – dark") with another (William Bendix as 1950s TV's hard hat with a heart of gold, Chester A. Riley, who regularly boomed, "What a revoltin' development *this* is!")[60] In 1990, general manager John Schuerholz left for Atlanta after a decade of K.C. taking or vying for the AL West title. The Royals promptly plunged, never near a '90s West or realigned Central Division crown. In 1993 Kauffman died after assuring a succession plan to keep the team in town. He could not assure success.

In 1994 team payroll had been $40.5 million. In 1999, it fell to a paltry estimated $16.5 million, wrote the *Kansas City Star*.[61] That year the Royals set a franchise-low .398 losing percentage, Carlos Beltran became Rookie of the Year, Matthews and Fred White wrote *Play by Play: 25 Years of Royals on Radio* – and Ryan Lefebvre replaced White. The new millennium began with beloved Mike Sweeney's club record 144 RBIs and Johnny Damon's league-leading 136 runs – as good as the Royals' then-getting got. In 2001 the Voice of the Royals contracted to air 130 games a year. "It recharges the battery," Matthews hailed his schedule. "You get away from it for a few days and come back strong." Mirage lightened the Royals' 2003: their first .500 (64-51) record since 1994. Misery resumed in 2004, K.C.'s first of nine straight losing years, five in the cellar.[62] Denny did his first TV play-by-play since 1986. "I had to remind myself you don't need to paint the picture," Matthews said. A few writers scored him for placing thought above emotion behind either mic, hating to promote or schmooze, thinking it "not my job to scream," said Denny. "I tell what happened and then *you* can scream."[63]

Ironically, *away* from a microphone, Denny was a baseball Bible when it came to opinion: Ask, and ye received, as the below views show.[64]

Realignment: "Create four geographic divisions," he proposed. "We'd be with the Cubs, White Sox, and Cardinals." Instead, the bigs once briefly eyed *contraction* before sanity returned.

Favorite park: Wrigley Field, Denny said, "by a mile, the atmosphere inside and out fantastic. The Cubs have made the most of its charm and history, almost creating the feeling of a pilgrimage to a holy shrine." To Matthews, Fenway Park was its equal until "the Red Sox forgot what they were trying to sell."

Performance-enhancing drugs: "You'd have to be on Mars in the last two decades to miss players trying to get a legal and illegal edge through steroids, growth hormones, and other performance-enhancing drugs. I don't condone their use, though risking future health is a player's business."

October scheduling: "As kids, we raced home to watch postseason, brought a radio to hear at school, and took an extra-long lunch break to catch some innings. Loving baseball, we found a way to listen." Earth to baseball: Make October count again. "Let kids catch daytime coverage. There's a new generation to attract."

Designated Hitter: "The AL created the DH in 1973 because interest was down, the NL having better players. So what do we do? Add offense! Sadly, the DH made ours a standaround kind of game. So end it – now!" Some announcers think the hymn "How Great Thou Art" refers to them, personally. To Matthews, storytelling meant team, not self. "Listening, you don't learn about his life,"[65] Fred White had said – Denny working out with the Green Bay Packers, catching passes from All-Pro quarterback Len Dawson, or tossing to a rather well-known wide end in a touch football game.

"Denny, thank you," said that receiver, radio's Rush Limbaugh, eyes turning moist. "That was the first touchdown I ever had."[66] Listening to Denny, a Royals listener never knew. You had to hear it elsewhere. Matthews' emotion was conveyed quietly, graciously – having been brought up, like Middle America, not to brag on himself, diverting conversation to a visitor.

In 2004, the Royals held Denny Matthews "Talking Bobble Head" Day, named him to their Hall of Fame, and helped pack a special K.C. to Wellington, Kansas, train. For Denny, the day was redolent of his grandfather, working for the Chicago and Alton Railroad. Matthews became a "train nut" – and Midwest grade-crossing safety spokesman. "The crews were terrific," Denny saluted the thank-you ride. "The only problem was that they wanted to talk baseball — and I wanted to talk trains!" Matthews loved their lure — also, the flat, fall-grass, and endless Plains. "That alone would keep me here."[67]

In 2005 Missouri named Denny to *it's* Hall of Fame. Then, in 2007, he received the ultimate honor any baseball Voice can — the Ford C. Frick Award for broadcast excellence at the National Baseball Hall of Fame and Museum, topping other finalists Tom Cheek, Dean, Ken Harrelson, Bill King, Tony Kubek, France Laux, Graham McNamee, Dave Niehaus, and Joe Nuxhall. "It's pretty heady stuff," the 31st Frick honoree said. "You stop and look at the previous recipients and, gosh." In his acceptance, Denny quoted Jack Brickhouse, who in his 1983 induction at Cooperstown, had conceded, "Today, I feel like a man 60 feet, six inches tall."[68] Matthews became only the eighth big-league Voice to spend his career with one club and at that time work for 35 or more straight seasons. A year later, he lightened his schedule, making fewer trips. Bob Davis and Steve Stewart replaced Lefebvre on radio, Ryan turning to TV.

Denny still held forth on home radio, his voice "having a pleasant timbre which suggests a cheerful occasion," as stats guru Bill James said. "His inflection varies naturally so it's neither falsely enthusiastic nor boring. He has a dry, understated humor that drifts through much of his audience undetected. One cannot learn these things at a microphone; they are given."[69] By now, a given for many was to focus on an individual, not the team — to wit, '09 Zack Greinke of the 65-97 Royals named a Cy Young honoree, like 1980s Saberhagen and 1994's David Cone. In 2012 the All-Star Game visited Kansas City for the third time, vaunting Kauffman at its refurbished best. Then: In quick succession, jewels for the Royals' diadem joined 1985's and lesser baubles, now almost Paleozoic to some.

In October 2014 Kansas City helped stage a seven-game classic Series, losing by a run to San Francisco. A year later, baseball's smallest big-league market won its second World Series by besting the pastime's largest, Kansas City clinching in Game Five at the Mets' Citi Field.[70] (See Kauffman Stadium chapter.) Matthews aired each on radio, signing a four-year pact on the last day of the 2015 FanFest to keep him with the Royals in its and his 50th year in 2018. "He has delivered the word pictures of virtually every important moment in team history," said team vice president Mike Swanson.[71] With the Dodgers' Vin Scully's 2016 *adieu*, Denny became the bigs' second-longest tenured Voice, behind only LA's Spanish-language Jaime Jarrin (1959-present).

To Matthews, two early personae still especially resound. Ewing Kauffman was a casual-turned-fervent fan trying to better his product, as he had in pharmaceuticals. In 1970 his Royals Baseball Academy, founded in Sarasota, Florida, and designed to train good athletes into good baseball players, opened to skepticism.[72] In the Academy's two-year program, including Manatee Junior College, players attended daily Ewing-mandated courses in personal finance and public speaking. After school, they studied baseball basics for the rest of the day. The Academy closed in 1974, due largely to a recession, alumni Frank White and UL Washington forming much of K.C.'s 1970s and '80s middle infield. "The biggest mistake I made in baseball was letting them talk me into closing the Academy," Kauffman said a year before he died. Each big-league team now advises players in public relations, speaking, and finance. The image evokes class, exactly as Kauffman hoped.

The other persona is former Royals farm director and director, player development Lou Gorman's. Joe Garagiola wrote a best-selling book, *Baseball Is a Funny Game*.[73] Lou made Royals baseball funny, malapropping, to quote Denny, via *Gormanisms* of which Casey Stengel would be proud. One spring, Matthews noted, Lou was unsure about the fate of prospect Joel Bishop, noting, "We were faced face to face with the face of Joel Bishop." Other somersaults included "That burns gas like it's eating peanuts, "I'll keep my ears posted," "I vaguely and vividly remember in my own mind," and "We're glad to have you with you." Once Lou said, "He looked like he threw real good listening on the radio."[74] That has been Denny

Matthews, making baseball a game to be enjoyed and recalled, the pastime looking good on the air.

A personal note. I grew up in perhaps the last generation for whom trains trekked slowly through small-town America, children gathered on each side to await their last car, the caboose. Open to God and sky, the blue-suited and -capped conductor aboard waved to us like a wizard, the train then leaving to vanish like Oz into back country and tomorrow — now gone. Like Matthews, my grandfather worked on a railroad — with me, the New York Central. With Denny at the throttle, Royals Radio/TV has seldom gone off the tracks.

Sources

Grateful appreciation is made to reprint all play-by-play and color radio text courtesy of John Miley's The Miley Collection. In addition to the sources cited in the Notes, most especially the Society for American Baseball Research, the author also consulted Baseball-Reference.com and Retrosheet.org websites box scores, player, season, and team pages, batting and pitching logs, and other material relevant to this history. FanGraphs.com provided statistical information. In addition to the sources cited in the Notes, the author also consulted:

Books

Angell, Roger and Walter Iooss Jr. *Baseball* (New York: Harry N. Abrams, 1986).

Coffrey, Michael. *27 Men* (New York: Atria Books, 2002).

Cohen, Richard M., David S. Neft, and Roland T. Johnson. *The World Series* (New York: Dial Press, 1976).

James, Bill. *The Bill James Historical Baseball Abstract* (New York: Villard Books, 1985).

Koppett, Leonard. *Koppett's Concise History of Major League Baseball* (Philadelphia: Temple University, 2015).

Matthews, Denny, Fred White, and Matt Fulks. *Play by Play: 25 Years of Royals on Radio* (Lenexa, Kansas: Taylor, 1999).

Smith, Curt. *Mercy! A Celebration of Fenway Park's Centennial Told Through Red Sox Radio and TV* (Washington, D.C.: Potomac Books, 2012).

___. *Voices of The Game: The Acclaimed History of Baseball Radio and Television Broadcasting* (New York: Simon and Schuster, 1992).

Newspapers

The *Kansas City Star* has been a primary source of information about Denny Matthews' career. *The Sporting News* and *USA Today* also were extremely helpful. Other contemporary sources include Associated Press, *Baseball Digest*, *Chicago Tribune*, *Los Angeles Times*, and the *Miami Herald.*

Interviews

Bud Blattner, with author, December 1975.

Bill MacPhail, with author, September 1977.

Denny Matthews, with author, February 2007, November 2015, and August 2018.

Jack Redding, with author, January 1981.

Fred White, with author, May 1998.

Notes

1 Denny Matthews interview with author, August 2018.

2 Ibid.

3 sportsbroadcastjournal.com/denny-matthews-hall-of-fame-voice-of-royals. David Halberstam, "Denny Matthews, Hall of Fame Voice," *Sports Broadcast Journal*, July 13, 2018: 2.

4 Matthews August 2018 interview.

5 Halberstam.

6 Matthews August 2018 interview.

7 Matthews interview with author, February 2007.

8 Ibid.

9 Halberstam, 4.

10 Ibid.

11 Halberstam, 5.

12 Ron Powers, *SuperTube: The Rise of Television Sports*. (New York: Coward-McCann, 1984), 71-76.

13 Bill MacPhail interview with author, September 1977.

14 Acceptance speech, National Baseball Hall of Fame and Museum, Induction Day 1953, Cooperstown, New York.

15 MacPhail interview.

16 Powers, SuperTube, 74.

17 Bud Blattner interview with author, December 1975.

18 Matthews February 2007 interview.

19 Blattner interview.

20 Ibid.

21 Matthews February 2007 interview.

22 "Radio/TV Rundown," *The Sporting News*, April 12, 1969: 31.

23 Matthews November 2015 interview.

24 Ibid.

25 Matthews February 2007 interview.

26 "Analysis of this year's Athletics: Spectator's Guide," *Sports Illustrated*, April 15, 1957, 61.

27 worldcat.org/title/official-major-league-baseball-fact-book. *Official Major League Baseball Fact Book 2001 Edition* (St. Louis: The Sporting News, 2001), 383.

28 Ibid.

29 Ibid.

30 Matthews November 2015 interview.

31 Ibid.

32 Jack Redding interview with author, January 1981

33 *Official Major League Baseball Fact Book 2001 Edition*, 381: All statistics in paragraph from Oliver's home runs to Otis's stolen bases.

34 Bill Shannon and George Kalinsky, *The Ballparks* (New York: Hawthorn Books, 1975), 255.

35 royalsreview.com/2013/4/10/4207434/today-in-royals-history-royals-stadium. Craig Brown, "Kaufman Stadium Turns 40," Royals Review, April 20, 2013: 5.

36 www.royalsreview.com/2018/4/12/17230714/here-are-your-kansas-city-royals. Bradford Lee, "Here Are Your 1969 Kansas City Royals." *Royals Review*, April 12, 2018: cover.

37 Lowry, *Green Cathedrals* (Reading, Massachusetts: Addison-Wesley, 1992), 49-50.

38 Matthews February 2007 interview.

39 "Broadcasting Batteries for 1975," *The Sporting News*, April 10, 1975: 38.

40 Matthews, August 2018 interview.

41 kansascity.royals.mlb.com/kc/history/all_stars.jsp.

42 kansascity.royals.mlb.com/kc/history/single_game_records.jsp.

43 Play-by-play courtesy of The Miley Collection.

44 Matthews February 2007 interview.

45 kansascity.royals.mlb.com/kc/history/all_time_leaders.jsp.

46 Matthews November 2015 interview.

47 Ibid.

48 Ibid.

49 Ibid.

50 Official Major League Baseball Fact Book 2001 Edition, 332.

51 Blattner interview.

52 Matthews August 2018 interview.

53 kansascity.royals.mlb.com/kc/history/single_game_records.jsp.

54 Ibid.

55 Matthews August 2018 interview, quotations throughout paragraph.

56 Play-by-play courtesy of CBS Radio.

57 "American League Broadcasting Batteries," The Sporting News, April 11, 1981: 42.

58 Halberstam, 7.

59 Matthews August 2018 interview.

60 Tim Brooks and Earle Marsh, The Complete Directory to Prime Time Network TV Shows, 1946-Present (New York: Ballantine, 1988), 449. From 1953-58, William Bendix starred as Chester A. Riley on NBC's The Life of Riley — a blue-collar hardhat with a heart of gold.

61 Bob Dutton, "2010 Royals to Open Season with $70.1 Million Payroll," *Kansas City Star*, April 4, 2010.

62 kansascity.royals.mlb/com/kc/history/timeline.jsp.

63 Matthews November 2015 interview.

64 Ibid.

65 Fred White interview with author, May 1998.

66 Ibid.

67 Matthews August 2007 interview.

68 Matthews' acceptance speech at Hall of Fame, Cooperstown, July 7, 2007.

69 baseball-reference.com/bullpen/Bill_James_Historical-Abstract; Bill James, *The Bill James Historical Abstrac*t (New York: Villard Books, 1985).

70 kansascity.royals.mlb/com/kc/history/timeline.jsp.

71 kansascity.com/sports/mlb.kansas-city-royals/article8875085.html. "Royals Broadcaster Denny Matthews' New Contract Ties Him to Team Through 50th Season," *Kansas City Star,* January 31, 2015.

72 kansascity.com/sports/spt-columns-blogs-sam-mellinger/article940797.html. Sam Mellinger, "Forty Years Later, Royals Academy Lives On in Memories," *Kansas City Star*, August 2, 2014.

73 goodreads.com/book/show/3981587-baseball-is-a-funny-game. Joe Garagiola, *Baseball Is a Funny Game,* (New York: HarperCollins, 1960).

74 Matthews February 2007 interview.

JOHN SCHUERHOLZ

BY DAN LEVITT AND MARK ARMOUR

John Schuerholz spent 26 seasons as a big-league GM, winning 16 division titles, six pennants, and two World Series. In Kansas City he oversaw that franchise's first World Series. After moving to Atlanta, he took over a team that had lost more than 90 games four consecutive years and won the next 14 division titles (excepting the truncated 1994 strike season) and five pennants. Schuerholz displayed an uncanny knack for retooling his team, knowing which holes could be filled by integrating prospects and which needed outside solutions. In recognition of his front office accomplishments, Schuerholz was unanimously voted into the Baseball of Fame in 2016 by the Today's Game Era Committee.

John Schuerholz with Dick Howser

John Boland Schuerholz was born on October 1, 1940, into one of Baltimore's most famous athletic families.[1] His parents, John, Sr. and Maryne (Rinny) Schuerholz, brought him up among some great athletes and coaches. His grandfather William Schuerholz coached at Loyola College in Baltimore from 1912 to 1926 and had 10 children; he occasionally put together a basketball team with his sons as the players. John's uncle Gilbert (his godfather) was an All-American soccer goalie and member of the US Olympic team; his uncle Wilson was a football star at East Carolina Teachers College; and uncle Don was a captain of the University of Maryland basketball team right after World War II. John Sr. was also a great basketball player and manned second base in the Class-D minor leagues in the years leading up to WWII.[2]

Though relatively small, John was also a stellar athlete. He starred at Baltimore City College High and then at Towson State University in Maryland, where he played soccer and baseball all four years. Schuerholz was all-conference in both sports, and in 1962, his senior season, he was named the school's athlete of the year. In 1974 he was inducted into the Towson Athletics Hall of Fame.[3]

After graduation Schuerholz took a job at North Point Junior High in Baltimore teaching eighth grade English and world geography. He also went back to school to earn a Master's degree in Administration and Supervision of Secondary Schools. Nevertheless, just two courses short of his master's, Schuerholz remained drawn by baseball, and on a whim sent a letter to Baltimore Orioles owner Jerry Hoffberger asking about an entry-level position in their front office. Hoffberger passed the request along to executive vice president Frank Cashen, who had once been a Baltimore sportswriter. Cashen recognized the Schuerholz name and called the young schoolteacher in for an interview, where he met with Cashen, GM Harry Dalton, and farm director Lou Gorman. Gorman and Dalton liked Schuerholz, and they hired him as Dalton's administrative assistant.[4]

Two years later, in 1968, Gorman joined the front office of the expansion Kansas City Royals, taking Schuerholz along with him. In Kansas City, GM Cedric Tallis assembled a strong front office that, over the first several years, included several other future general managers, notably Gorman, Syd Thrift, and Herk Robinson. Once again Schuerholz started in an administrative assistant position, but he slowly worked his way up.

In the mid 1970s Tallis, now in the Yankees front office, courted Schuerholz with a promotion to farm director. When Schuerholz informed the Royals he was joining the Yankees, Royals GM Joe Burke counter-offered with an expanded role (also farm director) and presumably more money. Schuerholz decided to stay in Kansas City. "Cedric was irate," Schuerholz recalled, telling him, "'I can't believe you would go against your word.'" Although Schuerholz felt he had made the right decision, he never managed to rebuild his relationship with Tallis.[5] In 1979 the Royals promoted him to vice president of player personnel; in October 1981 they named him GM, elevating incumbent Joe Burke to president.

When Schuerholz left Baltimore the O's were just embarking on a historically notable run of success. One of the keys to the Orioles' success was the refinement of the Oriole Way, a systematic approach throughout the organization to the team on and off the field—items such as scouting, teaching of baseball skills, approach to talent acquision, management of the farm system, player evaluation, and how players were expected to behave off the field. Gorman and Schuerholz brought this discipline to Kansas City where it eventually evolved into the Royals Way.

And the Royals Way helped Kansas City become successful more quickly than any other pre-free agency-era expansion franchise. The team won its first division title in 1976, winning again in 1977 and 1978. The Kansas City team eventually broke through to the World Series, winning the AL pennant in 1980, but slipping back below .500 in the strike-shortened 1981 season.

As Kansas City GM in the fall of 1981, Schuerholz inherited a talented manager in Dick Howser. "Dick had a great ability to appreciate how hard it is to play the game of baseball," Schuerholz said. "He knew how hard you had to work and how you had to prepare. He also knew what it took to be a member of a winning team."[6]

Schuerholz felt his squad was relatively close — despite their overall fourth-place finish in 1981, the Royals made the expanded playoffs by winning the division over the second half of the split season. In one of his first moves, Schuerholz hoped to fill a couple of needs for his mostly veteran team by swapping several young players for Vida Blue and outfielder Jerry Martin. While no longer the pitcher he had been in the early 1970s, Blue was still one of baseball's top pitchers, and the team rebounded to 90 wins in 1982. But cocaine was becoming a problem in baseball in the early 1980s, and Blue and Martin proved a distraction in 1983, as a cocaine investigation dogged them and other players. Moreover, Schuerholz later wrote that, according to the federal drug investigation, it was Blue that introduced the drug to the Royals.[7] After the season Blue and Martin, along with star center fielder Willie Wilson and first baseman Willie Mays Aikens, pleaded guilty and were each sentenced to three months in prison.

Despite the lost 1983 season, the Royals still had a strong nucleus, particularly of position players. Along with Wilson, the team had George Brett at third, Frank White at second, Hal McRae at DH, plus fireman Dan Quisenberry in the bullpen. Rather than try to rebuild his aging rotation with veterans, Schuerholz promoted a trio of young starters in 1984: Bret Saberhagen (20), Mark Gubicza (21), and Danny Jackson (22). For 1985, he acquired veteran catcher Jim Sundberg to help his young staff acclimate. A couple of great trades, landing first baseman Steve Balboni in late 1983, and left fielder Lonnie Smith in May 1985, further augmented his roster. In 1985 the revamped Royals won the franchise's first World Series. In recognition of the Royals season, *The Sporting News* named Schuerholz Executive of the Year.

Over the remainder of the 1980s, the Royals sat on the fringes of the division race but could not capture another title. The team made some astute draft picks, such as outfielder and football star Bo Jackson, but Schuerholz also made what he considered his worst deal--swapping pitcher David Cone for catcher Ed Hearn--and some suspect free agent signings, such as reliever Mark Davis, towards the end of the decade.

By this time the Royals' executive suite was becoming a little unwieldy: In 1983 longtime owner Ewing Kauffman had brought in a partner, real estate mogul Avron Fogelman. The latter had been trying to put his stamp on operations, principally by leaning on Schuerholz to act as his proxy within the front office, which led to some friction. Moreover, by 1990, the value of Fogelman's real estate investment portfolio was crumbling in the wider commercial real estate crisis, and he was looking to use his half of the franchise as loan collateral. In this uncertain environment, Kauffman was considering selling the team altogether.[8]

In the summer of 1990, Schuerholz happened to be talking to Atlanta president Stan Kasten, who mentioned that the team was planning to move incumbent GM Bobby Cox back to manager and bring in a new GM. Kasten asked Schuerholz if he had any recommendations. Schuerholz, after contemplating the shifting sands within the Royals' front office, let Kasten know that he would be interested. Kasten quickly agreed, and in October 1990, Schuerholz joined the Atlanta Braves as GM with full authority over baseball operations. Schuerholz also received a pay raise, reportedly to $400,000 per year under a five-year contact, up from $180,000 (plus some shares in real estate investments through Fogelman) in Kansas City.[9] As he had in Kansas City, Schuerholz also inherited a great manager in Atlanta. A Hall of Famer in his own right, Bobby Cox in the dugout gave Schuerholz a leg up as he refashioned his ballclub.

Schuerholz took control of a franchise coming off a last-place finish that had not been relevant for some time, having lost at least 97 games in each of the past three seasons. Nevertheless, the team had a solid core of young pitchers in John Smoltz, Tom Glavine, and Steve Avery, plus outfielders Ron Gant and David Justice. As he had back in Kansas City, Schuerholz went to work to support his young hurlers, acquiring four solid defensive players: first baseman Sid Bream, shortstop Rafael Belliard, third baseman Terry Pendleton, and centerfielder Otis Nixon. In 1991 Pendleton also turned in a great hitting season, winning the league MVP, and the Braves won their first pennant since 1958, before losing in the World Series. For this historic single-season turnaround, Schuerholz received the Executive of the Year award from United Press International.

At spring training in 1992, Schuerholz worked out a deal with Pirates GM Ted Simmons for Barry Bonds, with one year left on his contract, in exchange for pitcher Alejandro Pena, outfielder Keith Mitchell, and a player to be named later. Unfortunately for the Braves, Simmons was overruled internally, and the trade fell through.[10] The Braves returned with pretty much the same lineup as the previous season, and the team once more captured the league flag, but again fell short in the World Series.

Schuerholz was not typically a participant in the big-name free agent auctions, but prior to the 1993 season, the Braves rocked the baseball world by signing free-agent Greg Maddux, the 26-year-old ace of the Chicago Cubs, to bolster a pitching staff that was already the envy of the league. Maddux responded with the second of his four straight Cy Young awards, but the team fell to the Phillies in the NLDS.

After his quick success in Atlanta, other teams pursued Schuerholz to oversee their baseball operations. Baltimore reportedly reached out to him in late 1993 regarding a chief executive position, and the Cubs contacted him for a similar role late in the 1994 season before hiring Andy MacPhail for the job. The Braves, responding to the market demand for their GM, extended Schuerholz's contract through 1999. In early 1998 they extended his contract again, this time though 2003 with a club option for 2004.[11]

The Braves could not have maintained their success for a decade without a continual influx of talent. The team that won the World Series in 1995 was much different than the one that had lost four years earlier: five of the eight position players, two starting pitchers, most of the bench and all of the bullpen had turned over. When the Braves lost the World Series in 1999, five of the eight position players, two starters, and all of the bench and bullpen were different from the champions of 1995.

Most importantly, Schuerholz continually addressed aging and ineffective players with internal solutions (if available) as opposed to trading his prospects for more aging veterans. Good teams are often reluctant to give significant roles to untested players. The Braves of the early 1990s had several veteran journeymen that needed replacing within a few years. What set the Braves apart from other great teams of the past generation was their willingness to give regular roles to the jewels of their farm system. When Terry Pendleton or Ron Gant needed replacing, Schuerholz did not trade his young talent for veteran solutions. In 1994 the Braves gave starting positions to Javy Lopez and Ryan Klesko, and within two years both Chipper Jones and Andruw Jones were key players. Later still, Rafael Furcal, Marcus Giles, and Adam LaRoche claimed jobs.

Schuerholz also made several impressive trades to keep his team competitive. During his first two years Schuerholz made a couple of minor late-season trades that bolstered the Braves for the stretch run and playoffs, picking up reliever Alejandro Pena in 1991 and Jeff Reardon in 1992, though the latter struggled in the World Series after a stellar September. In perhaps his best and most timely deal, Schuerholz landed Fred McGriff from San Diego for prospects in July 1993. The Braves went 51–17 after the acquisition to capture their third straight division title.

Whether on trades or free agent signings, Schuerholz and his staff generally displayed sound judgement in identifying veteran solutions, often securing very good players for a reasonable return. For 1998 he added still-productive first baseman Andrés Galarraga, and the next season he brought in outfielder Brian Jordan and second baseman Bret Boone. In 2002 he landed Gary Sheffield, and when the outfielder bolted as a free agent two years later after finishing third in the MVP voting, Schuerholz traded for J.D. Drew to replace him. Drew finished sixth in the MVP voting, and he, too, then departed as a free agent. In retrospect, the inclusion of then-prospect Adam Wainwright in the swap makes it seem less advantageous. Regarding moves that received criticism, Schuerholz often defended them by highlighting the need to manage to a budget, though he also maintained that ownership rarely forced him to cut payroll.

On the pitching side of the equation, Jaret Wright may have represented Schuerholz and the Braves organization at its most astute. Wright had been the tenth overall pick in the 1994 draft but was often injured and from 2000 through 2002 had pitched only sparingly; when he had been on the mound, he threw poorly. Nevertheless, when Wright was available on waivers late in the 2003 season, Schuerholz claimed him on the advice of his scouts, and Cox and renowned pitching coach Leo Mazzone helped Wright turn in a great 2004 season.[12] Unfortunately, Wright jumped to the Yankees after the season for an impressive free agent contract.

One of the reasons the Braves' magnificent run eventually ended was because the farm system could not continue to produce stars the way it had in the mid-1990s, putting additional pressure on Schuerholz's trades and free agent signings. Nevertheless, even in 2002 and 2003, 12 years after Schuerholz's first division title, the team was still winning 101 games in both years.

Schuerholz often liked to note that the Braves on average turned over ten players on their roster every year. "One of the key responsibilities we have as general managers is managing change effectively," he said. "I think it's true in any business. We exist in an environment where change occurs in a bizarre fashion at a bizarre pace. We have to keep our antennas up and keep our minds open. We have to understand that change is inevitable, especially in our business, where we rely on human beings to perform physically, and we have to be able to manage the changes that are required in an effective manner."[13]

Schuerholz was forced to handle several controversies during his tenure in Atlanta, though none rose to level of legal consequences of the early 1980s drug trials, including Cox's arrest for allegedly striking his wife in 1995, *Sports Illustrated*'s infamous profile of John Rocker in December 1999 in which the reliever callously demeaned a whole host of minorities and ethnic groups, and Furcal's DUI arrest in 2004 (his second).

After the 2007 season the 67-year-old Schuerholz intended to retire from the front lines of baseball operations, but the Braves asked him to stay on as team president and he happily agreed. To direct the front office, he promoted his longtime assistant Frank Wren to GM. After a few mediocre years, the Braves returned to the postseason in 2010, followed by appearances in 2012 and 2013. But after missing the playoffs in 2014, Schuerholz dismissed Wren and brought in veteran GM John Hart to oversee baseball operations. More recently, he and Hart promoted John Coppolella to GM, and Schuerholz was elevated to Vice Chairman.

In 2013 the Braves announced their intention to leave Fulton County's Turner Field and move to Cobb County. Though Schuerholz was not the driving force behind the move or the development of the new stadium itself, as team president he was highly supportive and involved. "We wanted to [develop and control the commercial space] in the area surrounding Turner Field," Schuerholz said. "When we found out that that was impossible, we were told that it would not happen, that we had no choice. But the concept of building a major league ballpark and mixed-use development, we believed was valid."[14] The new stadium, SunTrust Park, opened in 2017.[15]

Schuerholz and his wife Karen live in Atlanta where the couple moved when John accepted the Atlanta GM job. The two have been married over 35 years and have two children, Jonathan and Gina. Jonathan played for several years as a second baseman in the Braves organization, peaking at AAA and an invitation to major league spring training. After his playing career ended, he followed in his father's footsteps, taking a job in the Braves organization in 2014. He is currently an assistant director of player development.

Along with baseball and teaching, Schuerholz had two other loves: clothes and music. He dates his interest in dressing well to a pair of "electric blue" pants with "saddle stitching down the side, [and] a matching belt," that his uncle gave him. Much of his musical taste dates to his formative years, and "with my apologies to Beethoven," Schuerholz contends that "Come and Go with Me" by the Del-Vikings is the greatest song of all time.[16]

The Atlanta Braves from 1991 to 2005 enjoyed one of the most impressive runs of success by a franchise in sports history. The team has been underrated because it navigated through the post-season unscathed only once, in 1995, but Schuerholz's maneuvering that kept this team at the top for 14 years is truly remarkable. When added to his legacy in Kansas City, Schuerholz clearly merits a ranking among the best general managers ever.

Notes

1 www.wbal.com/article/209758?title=brett-hollander-talks-to-baseball-legend-and-baltimore-native-john-schuerholz.

2 articles.baltimoresun.com/2009-05-11/news/0905100079_1_university-of-maryland-schuerholz-maryland-basketball-team; www.wbal.com/article/209758?title=brett-hollander-talks-to-baseball-legend-and-baltimore-native-john-schuerholz; www.legacy.com/obituaries/baltimoresun/obituary.aspx?n=maryne-schuerholz-rinny&pid=98287943&fhid=4134.

3 www.towsontigers.com/news/2016/12/5/schuerholz-inducted-into-baseball-hall-of-fame.aspx; *1984 Kansas City Royals Media Guide*, 5; www.wbal.com/article/209758?title=brett-hollander-talks-to-baseball-legend-and-baltimore-native-john-schuerholz; www.towson.edu/news/2016/schuerholz_hof.html.

4 www.wbal.com/article/209758?title=brett-hollander-talks-to-baseball-legend-and-baltimore-native-john-schuerholz.

5 John Schuerholz, *Built to Win: Inside Stories and Leadership Strategies from Baseball's Winningest GM* (New York: Warner Books, 2006), 127-28.

6 Richard Justice, "Schuerholz a Baseball Institution after Almost 50 Years," MLB.com, December 1, 2014.

7 Schuerholz, *Built to Win*, 239.

8 Joe Strauss, "New GM Schuerholz Likes to Think Positive but Faces a Major Task," *Atlanta Journal*, November 4, 1990; Schuerholz, *Built to Win*, 123-24.

9 Strauss.

10 Schuerholz, *Built to Win*, 1-4.

11 Joseph A. Reeves, "Twins' MacPhail in Line To Replace Cubs' Cook 'Down the Line,'" chicagotribune.com, September 4, 1994; John Steadman, "Schuerholz Puts Stamp on Game after Chance Letter," *Baltimore Sun*, September 23, 1994; Rod Beaton, "NL Alters Method to Pick Chiefs for Umpiring Crews," *USA Today*, March 5, 1998.

12 Schuerholz, *Built to Win*, 42-44.

13 Russell Adams, "The Culture of Winning," WSJ.com, October 5, 2005.

14 Joe Mock, baseballparks.com/2016/09/26/turning-the-page-on-turner-field/

15 I. J. Rosenberg, "Whatever Happened to…Jonathan Schuerholz," ajc.com, February 27, 2016; I. J. Rosenberg, "Looking Back: John Schuerholz," ajc.com, March31, 2016.

16 Thomas Stinson, "Model for Success," *Atlanta Journal Constitution*, April 2, 2000.

CEDRIC TALLIS

BY DAN LEVITT

When the expansion Kansas City Royals hired Cedric Tallis as the team's GM, he assumed an almost impossible task. Before the first expansion season was even half over in 1969, Kansas City owner Ewing Kauffman was proclaiming that a glorious future was not far away. A hard-driving yet generous pharmaceutical entrepreneur, Kauffman publicly stated that he expected a pennant within five years, a wildly aggressive prediction given the development of the four expansion franchises in the early 1960s.[1]

Moreover, the rules of the time made building a team particularly difficult. Between the onset of the amateur draft in 1965 and the introduction of free agency in 1976, there were fewer avenues to compete for players than at any point in history.

Tallis didn't deliver a pennant in five years. Nevertheless, he built one of baseball's best organizations. Through a series of brilliant trades, Tallis boosted the Royals' talent level remarkably quickly, such that the Royals were competitive and winning division titles well before their three expansion counterparts. "Cedric was the right person at the right time for those Royals," wrote longtime scout Art Stewart. "He was naturally aggressive. ... And Cedric had guts. That's what you need to navigate the trade market when you're a general manager."[2] Unfortunately, Tallis was sacked before the franchise's first division title in 1976. But the key players on that team and the competitive ones that followed were almost entirely amassed under his watch.

Cedric Nelson Tallis was born on July 29, 1914, in New York City. His mother, Annabelle Peters, was Canadian, and his father, Walter, who was born in England, immigrated to the United States in 1898. Walter was an accountant by occupation, and the family, including an older brother and sister, moved several times while Tallis was young. They lived in Belleville, New Jersey, in 1915 and later moved to St. Lucie, Florida, where Walter was president of a land company, though this was likely less of an executive role that it sounds. Eventually the family migrated to Penacook, New Hampshire, where Tallis seems to have spent the bulk of his formative years.[3]

Like other men his age, Tallis, now 6-feet and 170 pounds, joined the armed services in World War II, enlisting in the Army in October 1940. After the war he remained in the service for several years, marrying Barbara Neal in England in 1946. When he returned to the States, Tallis spent two years coaching basketball at Fort Benning, Georgia, where his squad won the Southeastern AAU championship.

In early 1948, 33-year-old Captain Cedric Tallis decided it was time for a life beyond military service. Switching to baseball, he landed a job as general manager at Thomasville in the Class-D Georgia-Alabama League, the lowest rung in Organized Baseball and a perfect place to learn the baseball business from the ground up. At this time a minor-league GM was responsible for just about everything: finding players, managing the business affairs, and, once for Tallis, helping to contain a pack of unruly fans trying to attack the umpire while waiting for the police.[4]

Tallis spent several years running minor-league teams, interrupted by a two-year Army recall during the Korean War. Back in baseball in 1953, he was overseeing a Single-A Detroit farm club in Montgomery, Alabama, three notches below the major leagues. His first year there was a disaster on and off the field. The club finished last, and Tallis was forced to sell off several players, including ex-major leaguers Kirby Higbe and Grady Wilson, to survive financially. He rebuilt his squad, and in 1955 they made it to the Southern League finals. While in Montgomery, Tallis also formed a long-term bond with his manager, Charlie Metro.[5]

After the 1955 season, Oakland Oaks owner Brick Laws moved his financially stressed Pacific Coast League franchise to Vancouver, British Columbia. Laws brought in Tallis to run the team, and Tallis signed a working agreement with the Baltimore Orioles. After one year in Vancouver and a last-place finish, Laws decided to sell, and Tallis spearheaded a group of local businessmen to finance the $150,000 purchase price and an additional $125,000 in operating funds. He brought in Metro to manage, and the team jumped to second place and led the league in attendance.[6]

Despite its Baltimore affiliation, in those days a minor-league club like Vancouver still needed to find many of its own players. Tallis organized a six-day tryout camp for 17- to 19-year-olds. The Mounties accepted 42 candidates for the clinic, where youngsters received instruction from several ex-major leaguers including outfielder Earl Averill and pitcher Earl Johnson.[7]

When the Orioles terminated their agreement with Vancouver after the 1959 season, Tallis moved to the Seattle Rainiers, another PCL team, which affiliated with the Cincinnati Reds. Tallis brought in a new manager and the team improved from seventh to fourth. When the Boston Red Sox purchased the Rainiers after the 1960 season, Tallis again moved on. Now 46 and with more than a decade as a minor-league general manager, he was ready for a major-league challenge.[8] He had hopes of landing the GM job in Cincinnati, where Gabe Paul had just resigned. "I would be honored to have the opportunity to appear before Powell Crosley Jr. and the Cincinnati club's board of directors," Tallis told the press.[9] The Reds instead chose Bill DeWitt and went on to win the 1961 pennant.

Determined to get into the major leagues, Tallis accepted a job as an assistant to general manager Fred Haney with the expansion Los Angeles Angels and over the next few years his role evolved into that of business manager.[10] Tallis worked for the Angels for six years, successfully overseeing the club's 1966 move to Anaheim and its new ballpark. Tallis met Kauffman in 1967 when the latter visited Anaheim to learn what went into building an expansion franchise. In early 1968 when Kauffman won the rights to the expansion Royals, he wisely brought in Tallis as GM. The 53-year-old Tallis signed a four-year contract and had a new major-league organization to build. "Outside of finances, he will run the club," Kauffman told reporters.[11]

In Tallis, Kauffman recognized not only a smart baseball man, but also someone who could be a champion and overseer for the new stadium complex under consideration in Kansas City. He was a driven, determined leader who took charge immediately. "Tallis had a booming laugh, a hot temper and the ability to turn any day into Armageddon," one writer remembered.[12] Moreover, Tallis was comfortable in the limelight, a key attribute for someone who would be the face of the team, second only to Kauffman himself. Years later, when Tallis was working in the Yankees front office, owner George Steinbrenner was looking for him. When told that Tallis was giving an interview, Steinbrenner joked, "Hell, we'll never get him out of there. You know how Cedric loves those TV cameras."[13]

Longtime baseball GM Gabe Paul believed that Tallis "was probably the best in baseball when it came to details and trivia."[14] In Kansas City, Tallis did not just sit on his hands waiting for the October 1968 expansion draft, which would get him his first players, but focused on the details of team building. He brought in two trusted lieutenants: Charlie Metro, recently the chief scout for Cincinnati general manager Bob Howsam, as director of scouting; and Lou Gorman, out of the well-respected Orioles organization, as director of minor-league operations. Taking a page from the Orioles and the Dodgers before them, Tallis, Metro, and Gorman put together the *Kansas City Royals Instructional Manual* to highlight how each defensive play should be executed. Gorman, with his Orioles background, advocated consistent instruction throughout the Royals organization.[15]

Tallis let Gorman bring along an assistant from Baltimore named John Schuerholz, just two years removed from teaching junior high school. Schuerholz would go on to become one baseball's greatest general managers, first in Kansas City and later in Atlanta. Two other future general managers also joined the Royals. Syd Thrift, an original thinker who later ran the Pittsburgh Pirates and Baltimore Orioles, started as a scout. Herk Robinson, also from the Baltimore organization, became Metro's assistant. Years later, Robinson led the Royals front office for a decade.

To manage the Royals, Tallis hired Joe Gordon, who had previously led three major-league teams, though none since 1961. "My main aim," Tallis had said, "is to pick a man who can motivate young players." Tallis gave Gordon free rein to pick the coaching staff, subject only to his final approval.[16]

Shortly after being awarded their franchise, the Royals petitioned the other owners to be allowed to participate in the June 1968 amateur baseball draft, a request that was not part of the original expansion arrangement. When the owners relented (although the four new teams were not allowed to select until the middle of the fourth round), the Royals drafted two quality future major leaguers, Paul Splittorff and Dane Iorg; none of the other expansion teams landed any. Tallis established two minor-league working relationships to place his draftees and minor-league free agents.[17]

On October 15, 1968, the Royals and Seattle Pilots had their chance to draft players from the other American League ballclubs. (The NL held a separate draft for its new teams.) As opposed to the Pilots, Tallis focused almost exclusively on young players. As researcher and historian Steve Treder has pointed out, the first 10 picks for the Pilots averaged 27.6 years old, 1,920 major-league at-bats, and 247 major-league innings. The Royals on the other hand averaged 24.2 years old, 332 major-league at-bats, and 164 major-league innings.[18]

Around the 20th pick the Royals changed their strategy to also target older players with trade value, realizing that many of the better, younger players had been protected by that point in the draft. (Their most famous draftee, veteran relief pitcher Hoyt Wilhelm, was traded to the Angels for two young players a few days later.) For the day, Kansas City selected a number of players who still had meaningful major-league seasons in front of them; measured by WAR, they ended up with nearly 50 percent more future talent than the Pilots.

Outside of the regular minor-league organization, Kauffman conceived and developed the Kansas City Baseball Academy in Sarasota, Florida. Recognizing the limited avenues available for finding major-league-caliber players, Kauffman's brainchild was to sign and develop great athletes who were not baseball players – and therefore undrafted and available – and turn them into baseball players. He also commissioned sports psychologists and scientists to develop new scouting and training techniques. In the end, however, he was forced to shutter the operation in 1974 and the facilities themselves were amalgamated back into the overall minor-league system.

While the Academy had some successes, most notably Frank White, it was extremely expensive to operate and finding potential candidates was becoming more difficult. Maybe just as importantly, Tallis and others in the front office were somewhat resentful of the resources that were being siphoned off into the Academy that could have been allocated to the regular farm system and skeptical of some of the new-fangled evaluation and training techniques being used. Nevertheless, Tallis worked to integrate the Academy into the larger organization, including rotating players from the farm system through the Academy and revising some of the instruction. Tallis recognized the value of keeping an open mind to new training techniques, including "purchasing a new stop action camera to help our hitters and pitchers. This camera can stop any action without blurring or fuzzy lines. It's expensive, but we feel it will be of considerable help to both our pitchers and hitters."[19]

Just prior to the 1969 season, Tallis made the first in a series of deals that would ultimately build a contending club. The Royals swapped outfielder Steve Whitaker, drafted from the Yankees, to the Pilots for Lou Piniella, who would go on to win the AL Rookie of the Year award that season.

In December 1969 Tallis made one of his most famous deals, securing 22-year-old outfielder Amos Otis from the Mets for third baseman Joe Foy. Foy had played well in his one season with the Royals, but Otis would become Kansas City's first star, holding down center field for the next 14 seasons. "The Mets wanted a third baseman and they were trying to get Ken McMullen from Washington," Tallis later related. "Washington wanted two starting pitchers and the Mets didn't want to give that much. When they saw they couldn't make the McMullen deal, they turned to Foy."[20] If the trade wasn't yet good enough, Tallis also got the Mets to include starting pitcher Bob Johnson. Johnson had one good year with the Royals and proved a valuable trade chip the next winter.

In June 1970 Tallis sent a minor leaguer to the Cardinals for 31-year-old second baseman Cookie

Rojas. Tallis did not generally look for older players, but second base had been a gaping hole on the club and Rojas seemed a reasonable stopgap. In fact, Rojas rejuvenated his career in Kansas City, playing in four All-Star Games.

The team had played surprisingly well in its inaugural 1969 season but Gordon resigned after the season due to the stress of the job. Tallis named his old friend Charlie Metro to skipper the team in 1970. Metro proved to be a disaster. He ran spring training like boot camp, and the players, only half-jokingly, referred to it as "Stalag 17." With the Royals at 19-33 in early June, Tallis fired Metro, promoting another longtime friend, pitching coach Bob Lemon.

After the 1970 season Tallis and his staff recognized that the team needed to improve at shortstop and decided that one of their targets should be Freddie Patek, an undersized, under-appreciated player backing up Gene Alley in Pittsburgh. For Johnson, displaced shortstop Jackie Hernandez, and a minor leaguer, Tallis landed Patek, pitcher Bruce Dal Canton, and a decent catcher in Jerry May.[21] Patek held down shortstop for nine years in Kansas City, teaming with Rojas as one of the league's top double-play combinations.

The 1971 Royals astonished everyone by finishing second with a record of 85-76, although 16 games behind the powerful Oakland A's. For his efforts, Tallis was named Executive of the Year by The Sporting News. Kauffman believed the team was on the verge of the playoffs, but the club had overachieved in 1971 and the talent was not really sufficient to capture a division title, even in the weaker West Division. Kauffman also felt that the Royals should be in contention annually. This sentiment placed Tallis in the difficult position of knowing he needed more talent to win, but also trying to fill specific holes to give him the best chance to win each particular season. A brilliant trader, Tallis walked this thin line remarkably well.

One of the stars of the Royals 1970 club, first baseman Bob Oliver, fell from 27 home runs and 99 RBIs to just 8 and 52 in 1971. Accordingly, Tallis looked for a power-hitting first baseman that winter. His scouts liked Houston's young first baseman John Mayberry, who had struggled in a few trials, so Tallis explored that option at the winter meetings. Dealing from strength, Kansas City sent two young pitchers to Houston for Mayberry, who broke through in 1972 with 25 home runs and 100 RBIs, and had several more fine seasons for the Royals.

The 1972 season was marred by a players strike that began during spring training and lingered into the season, canceling a week's worth of games. As the players union had never taken such an action before, the events stunned many longtime baseball people, including Lemon. "We asked the players to get on a bus, and they refused," Tallis said, recounting the start of the strike. "Then Lemon and I went into our office and Bob began to cry. He could not believe what was happening to his game."[22]

The Royals backslid in 1972 to 76-78, though the fall to fourth place likely overstated their regression. They were a young team that was still well ahead of the other three 1969 expansion teams. Nonetheless, the impatient Kauffman, disappointed that the club's 1971 improvement had not been sustained, decided to fire Lemon. Tallis disagreed, arguing that Lemon had done a fine job managing the club for 2½ years. In the October 3 press conference, Kauffman made the announcement while Tallis, when asked, indicated his disapproval. More ominously for Tallis, Kauffman's impatience and unrealistic expectations were laid bare. "Starting in 1974," Kauffman bragged, "we expect to win (the American League championship) five out of ten years."[23]

Kauffman further exasperated Tallis by hiring Jack McKeon, the manager at Triple-A Omaha, with whom Tallis had quarreled in the past. In particular, McKeon was a vocal advocate of the Baseball Academy, and hence a favorite of Kauffman's. His hiring of McKeon, knowing the feelings of Tallis – in theory the person in charge of running the baseball team – drove a further wedge in the organization. McKeon would go on to a successful career in baseball as both a manager and general manager, but in 1972 he owed his allegiance to Kauffman alone. The impatient Kauffman had journeyed a long way from the putatively hands-off owner of 1969.

At the winter meetings in November 1972, Tallis targeted Reds outfielder-third baseman Hal McRae, a player the Royals scouts felt could hit but lacked a defensive position. After some negotiation, Tallis offered Roger Nelson, their first pick in the expansion draft, who finished 1972 at 11-6 with a 2.08 ERA. The Royals braintrust was not really sold on Nelson's ability to stay healthy. To sweeten the pot, Tallis also proposed outfielder Richie Scheinblum, coming off an All-Star season in which he had hit .300, though he was already 29 and 1972 was his first season as big-league regular. Tallis asked for and received Wayne Simpson, a young pitcher with a history of arm problems, to help balance the expanded trade.[24]

The Royals opened the 1973 season strong, sitting at 30-23 on June 3, but after four straight losses, McKeon vented his frustration to the press. He felt the team was close but that Tallis had failed to land several key pieces that had been available earlier in the season. McKeon's actions were unusual, to say the least. Here was a first-year manager publicly berating one of the game's most respected GMs, less than two years removed from an Executive of the Year Award. Tallis was in an awkward situation. His rebellious manager had been imposed by the owner, limiting his disciplinary options and the chance of creating a harmonious relationship. Instead, Tallis gave a surprisingly blunt and honest public explanation of why he hadn't made the advocated moves.[25]

The team's solid finish validated Tallis's approach. The Royals ended the season 88-74, six games behind the eventual world champion A's. The club had great years from Mayberry and Otis and excellent starting pitching from Splittorff and Steve Busby. The club opened Royals Stadium, whose spacious outfield and artificial playing surface placed a premium on speed, something that players like Otis, Patek, and Rojas – all Tallis additions – had brought to the club. The club also began to feature some of the talent they had selected in the annual June draft. Both Splittorff and Busby (1971) were draftees, as was George Brett (1971), a 20-year-old third baseman from El Segundo, California.

After the 1973 season Tallis was typically active in the trade market, though he did not find any stars. In one of his few unfavorable deals, essentially forced on him by the fallout between Piniella and McKeon, Tallis sent Piniella and Ken Wright to the Yankees for Lindy McDaniel, a 37-year-old relief ace who had pitched 160⅓ innings in 1973, his most since 1957.[26] Piniella went on to several productive years with the Yankees, while McDaniel provided little to the Royals.

Cedric Tallis and Royals Players Obtained in Early Trades

Despite the Royals' strong second-place finish in 1973, Kauffman became frustrated with his mounting financial losses, magnified by the recession and the accompanying decline in the stock price of his pharmaceutical company. The strain of these losses triggered a rift between Tallis and the Royals vice president on the business side, Charles Truitt, leading to further divisions in an already inharmonious front office.[27] Late in the 1973 season, Truitt retired and Kauffman hired Joe Burke to replace him. This was an ominous hire for Tallis – Burke had spent years in the front office of the Washington Senators and, after the club's move to Texas, two years as the club's GM.

By the middle of the 1974 season, as the Royals hovered near .500, Kauffman decided to make a change at the top. In June he promoted Joe Burke to general manager, giving him full control over both the baseball and business sides, demoting Tallis to an unidentified position and bouncing him shortly thereafter. Kauffman never publicly identified why he fired Tallis, but it seems clear that his frustration had been building for some time. He knew that he was going to have to abandon his beloved Academy for financial reasons, and surely resented Tallis for never fully embracing it. When he fired Lemon and imposed McKeon as manager — an early sign of his growing irritation — Tallis, rightly or wrongly, would not publicly buy into the decision. The continuing friction between Tallis and McKeon led to a situation where Kauffman had to choose one or the other. With Joe Burke already on board, Kauffman had an executive ready to step into the position. In a further attempt to foster harmony and stability, Burke gave McKeon a two-year contract extension.

After four seasons of pursuing the A's, in 1976 the Royals team finally broke through with a 90-72 record and won the division title, before falling in a tightly contested ALCS. For the team's success *The Sporting News* named Burke Executive of the Year. In truth, Burke's key decision was the hiring of manager Whitey Herzog. He made one excellent trade - dealing backup catcher Fran Healy to the Yankees for pitcher Larry Gura - but otherwise did not materially alter the team that Tallis had left him. In fact, this core would win three more division titles over the next four years, finally reaching the World Series in 1980.

To evaluate Tallis's remarkable trading record a little more tangibly, Table 1 summarizes his key deals and calculates how much WAR each of the involved players accumulated over the remainder of their careers. In total, the trades made by the Royals during Tallis's tenure as general manager brought in nearly twice as much talent as defined by WAR as he surrendered. Tallis credited others in the organization for the evaluation involved in making each of these deals, but the final decision rested with the general manager, and Tallis was the one who bore the ultimate responsibility for the deal's success or failure.

Table 1 - Key Tallis Trades

Date	To KC (key players)	Rem WAR (all players in trade)		From KC (key players)	Rem WAR (all players in trade)
Dec-12-68	Ed Kirkpatrick	9.3		Hoyt Wilhelm	3.7
Apr-01-69	Lou Piniella	12.5		Steve Whitaker	1.7
Dec-03-69	Amos Otis	50		Joe Foy	2.9
Jun-13-70	Cookie Rojas	7.2		Fred Rico	0.0
Dec-02-70	Freddie Patek	27.3		Bob Johnson	1.0
Dec-02-70	Tom Hilgendorf	3.5		Ellie Rodriquez	13.0
Dec-02-71	John Mayberry	24.4		Two young pitchers	-1.6
Oct-25-72	Gene Garber	17.7		Jim Rooker	17.2
Nov-30-72	Hal McRae	26.7		Nelson/Scheinblum	1.8
Apr-02-73	Fran Healy	5.7		Greg Minton	17.9
Oct-24-73	NA	0.0		Tom Burgmeier	16.6
Dec-07-73	Lindy McDaniel	0.8		Lou Piniella	9.3
Total		**185.1**			**83.5**

After being let go, to keep his hand in the game Tallis acted as a consultant to a group of Louisiana businessmen and politicians hoping to bring major-league baseball to New Orleans, a natural role for a between-jobs veteran baseball man who knew and was on good terms with many executives throughout baseball.

Shortly thereafter, his old friend Gabe Paul, president of the Yankees, hired him as his assistant to watch over the completion and reopening of the remodeled Yankee Stadium, scheduled to open in April 1976, and act as his trusted assistant on baseball matters. Tallis's name was naturally associated with various top baseball positions. Early in his career with the Yankees, Tallis reportedly came in second in the Blue Jays' search for a team president to lead their expansion effort.[28]

In late May 1978 Tallis missed his scheduled trip with the Yankees to Kansas City because of a severe car accident leaving him hospitalized for five days with three fractured ribs.[29] Tallis drove like a maniac, and it's unlikely his friends and acquaintances would have been surprised when they heard of the accident. Once while giving a ride to the owner of the Tokyo Giants in Florida, Tallis took off down a two-lane highway, careening past the orange construction cones, and the owner became so agitated he kept his feet pressed against the floorboards the entire ride. The next morning when he reluctantly climbed back into Tallis's car for a lift to the ballpark, he immediately buckled his seat belt – in an era well before this was common practice – and clung to the dashboard with both hands. When surrounded by the Kansas City press who all knew about Tallis's driving habits, he told them, "Mr. Tallis is a kamikaze taxi driver."[30]

When Paul left after the 1977 season, owner George Steinbrenner promoted Tallis to GM, and the team repeated as world champions. This was at the height of Steinbrenner's micromanagement, however, leaving Tallis in a much-reduced GM role and the Yankees with a chaotic and disjointed front office. Not surprisingly, Tallis was rumored in the running for a number of other front-office positions. The first popped up after the 1979 season when the Mets made indirect contact. Tallis, uncertain of his role within the Yankees organization and tiring of Steinbrenner's constant abuse, showed interest but reportedly demanded full control of baseball operations. The Mets eventually went elsewhere. Later that year Tallis was reported to be aligned with Marvin Davis when the Denver oilman was about to secure the Oakland A's franchise and move it to Denver, a deal that eventually fell though. A year later Tallis's name popped up in connection with the Padres general manager search, and late in the 1981 season his name was floated regarding the Cubs job. Neither of these opportunities ever materialized either.[31]

After two years as GM, perhaps to dissuade him from jumping to one of the rumored positions, in early 1980 Steinbrenner promoted Tallis to executive vice president, putatively the top baseball executive, with Gene Michael taking over as GM. The next year, while Tallis's title remained the same, Lou Saban was hired as president, effectively the new head baseball man, though Steinbrenner remained highly engaged in all aspects of the team.

After another division title in 1980 and pennant in 1981, Tallis and Steinbrenner eventually broke up in late 1983 with Tallis becoming the executive director of the Tampa Bay Baseball Group, a collection of Tampa area businessmen looking to bring baseball to the region. Their target at the time was the Minnesota Twins and team owner Calvin Griffith, unhappy with his initial reception in the new Metrodome. Tallis was a logical choice for the Tampa Bay businessmen: he knew nearly everyone in baseball and was widely respected after roughly 35 years in the game. Moreover, he had experience building franchises and stadiums.

From Tallis's perspective, however, the move to Tampa seems a little curious. He loved wheeling and dealing and had spent most of the past 15 years as a key front-office employee of two different major-league baseball clubs. When other opportunities had presented themselves, he had expressed interest, though with little success. Most likely Tallis believed he would land the top spot in the front office of whatever franchise the group landed.

Once on board, Tallis found several major-league teams that appeared very close to moving — most notably the White Sox and Rangers — only to pull back at the last instant. Tallis's ownership faction subsequently expected to be short-listed in late 1990 for the 1993 National League expansion. When finally released, the short list did include Tampa but designated a rival ownership entity. Tallis was crushed. He felt betrayed by friends he had known most of his adult life.[32] Shortly after being notified of the decision, he suffered a heart attack and died several months later, on May 7, 1991, when struck with a second one.

Tallis was an avid golfer and often used the game to deal with stress or uncomfortable situations. To avoid an unpleasant conversation with an office visitor, he was known to pull out a putter and talk about his grip or practice his putting. Alternatively, a difficult day could lead him to grab a club, head down to the field and drive golf balls into the bleachers.[33]

"Tallis was a gentle bear of a man," one of his subordinates once wrote. "He was kind, personable, compassionate and fun-loving. He could be stubborn when he made up his mind and it would take a great deal of tactful persuasion to change. However, he was always willing to listen to your point of view, argument or opinions. He loved life and truly loved having a good time. He had a marvelous sense of humor, which made it fun to work for him. He was not afraid to delegate responsibility or authority, nor was he afraid to stand his ground on any issue he felt strongly about – no matter what the pressures brought to bear upon him. I admired his guts and also his compassion in dealing with subordinates."[34]

It's unfortunate that Tallis never had another chance with an expansion franchise or a losing team. He not only built a competitive team under the most difficult circumstances, but he also possessed the personality to run an organization. In addition to fashioning creative tension among capable subordinates, Tallis felt comfortable dealing with the press and enjoyed the limelight, key attributes for someone atop a baseball franchise. Very few men could match his extraordinary trading record and organizational abilities.

Disclaimer: All figures for wins above replacement (WAR) are based on the statistics per Baseball-Reference. These figures have been rounded for presentation purposes. The reader should be aware that if one were to look up these wins-above-replacement figures on Baseball-Reference, the actual results may vary slightly.

Notes

1 Joe McGuff, "Kauffman Goal: Flag in Five Years; Royals' Boss Weighs Daring Plan," *The Sporting News*, June 7, 1969: 16.

2 Art Stewart, *The Art of Scouting: Seven Decades Chasing Hopes and Dreams in Major League Baseball* (Olathe, Kansas: Ascend Books, 2014), 251.

3 Information on Tallis's family is principally derived from the public records available through Ancestry.com.

4 "Army Captain Gets G.M. Post," *The Sporting News*, February 18, 1948: 23; "Near Riot at Thomasville," *The Sporting News*, June 23, 1948: 36.

5 "Henry Aaron Aims at RBI Mark," *The Sporting News*, June 24, 1953: 33.

6 Keith Mathews, "Tallis Drafts Plan for New Coast League," *The Sporting News*, September 18, 1957: 9.

7 "Mounties Seek Home-Grown Talent, Hold Six-Day Clinic," *The Sporting News*, August 13, 1958: 34.

8 Hy Zimmerman, "G.M. Tallis Resigns His Seattle Post," *The Sporting News*, October 12, 1960: 24.

9 Earl Lawson, "Tallis, Ex-Boss of Seattle, Top Choice for Post," *The Sporting News*, November 2, 1960: 5.

10 Ross Newhan, "Angel Finale – Chavez Quiet as Tomb," *The Sporting News*, October 9, 1965: 15.

11 Dickson Terry, "Kaycee 'Will Never Lose This Team,'" *The Sporting News*, January 27, 1968: 23-24.

12 Steve Cameron, *Moments Memories Miracles: A Quarter Century with the Kansas City Royals* (Dallas: Taylor Publishing, 1992), 208.

13 Dave Nightengale, "Free-Agent Draft: It Was a Farce," *The Sporting News*, November 28, 1981: 53.

14 Bob Andelman, *Stadium for Rent: Tampa Bay's Quest for Major League Baseball* (Jefferson, North Carolina: McFarland, 1993), 77.

15 Charlie Metro with Tom Altherr, *Safe by a Mile* (Lincoln: University of Nebraska Press, 2002), 331 Lou Gorman, *High and Inside: My Life in the Front Offices of Baseball* (Jefferson, North Carolina: McFarland, 2008), 81-82.

16 Unidentified clipping, Cedric Tallis Hall of Fame file.

17 Gorman, *High and Inside*, 83; Allan Simpson, ed., *The Baseball Draft: The First 25 Years, 1965-1989* (Durham, North Carolina: American Sports, 1990), 65.

18 Steve Treder, "The Royals of Sir Cedric," hardballtimes.com, December 21, 2004.

19 Joe McGuff, "Pay Cuts on Tap for Royals Who Slumped in 1970," *The Sporting News*, January 30, 1971: 41.

20 Joe McGuff, "Tallis' Shrewd Trades Fuel Royals' Fast Start," *The Sporting News*, June 26, 1971: 12.

21 Metro, *Safe by a Mile*, 324-35; Gorman, *High and Inside*, 116.

22 Ralph Ray, "Instead It's No Season," *The Sporting News*, June 27, 1981: 3.

23 Joe McGuff, "'Blame Me for Lemon's Exit,' Says Kauffman," *The Sporting News*, October 21, 1972: 23; Joe McGuff, "Tallis-Kauffman Split Linked to Lemon Firing," *The Sporting News,* July 6, 1974: 15.

24 Metro, Safe by a Mile, 332; Gorman, *High and Inside*, 128-29.

25 Joe McGuff, "McKeon Sees Red Over Royal Dearth of Deals," *The Sporting News*, June 30. 1973: 16.

26 Cameron, *Moments Memories Miracles*, 106.

27 Sid Bordman, "Royals Promote Burke to G.M. Post," *The Sporting News*, June 29, 1974 12.

28 Dick Young, *The Sporting News*, July 10. 1976: 12

29 *The Sporting News*, June 3, 1978: 9.

30 Jack McKeon and Kevin Kernan, *I'm Just Getting Started: Baseball's Best Story Teller on Old School Baseball, Defying the Odds, and Good Cigars* (Chicago: Triumph, 2005), 88; Gorman, *High and Inside*, 117-18.

31 The Sporting News, October 27, 1979: 16; *The Sporting News*, November 17. 1979: 16; *The Sporting News*, December 1, 1979: 16; *The Sporting News*, March 1, 1980: 46; *The Sporting News*, September 27, 1980: 35; *The Sporting News*, August 1, 1981: 25.

32 Bob Andelman, Stadium For Rent: Tampa Bay's Quest for Major League Baseball (Jefferson, North Carolina: McFarland, 1993), 161.

33 Bill Madden, Steinbrenner: *The Last Lion of Baseball* (New York: HarperCollins, 2010), 202; McKeon and Kernan, *I'm Just Getting Started*, 106.

34 Gorman, *High and Inside*, 117

GEORGE TOMA

BY JOHN STAHL

Former Cleveland Indians and St. Louis Browns owner Bill Veeck once said, "A good groundskeeper was the 10th man on the field and was worth five to seven victories a season."[1] George Toma is often ranked among the greatest groundskeepers of all time, creating and maintaining professional baseball, football, soccer, and Olympic playing fields all over the world.[2]

His work philosophy was simple: Work as hard as you can, and then try to do a little more. He once noted that "the cheapest insurance for an athlete is a good, safe playing field." Toma believed sports fields could be maintained inexpensively in a way that could be beneficial for both the players and the team owners.[3]

Nicknamed the "nitty gritty dirt man" and/or the "sod god," by both the players and the baseball press, Toma was born February 2, 1929, in Edwardsville, a small, poor coal-mining town in Pennsylvania.[4]

His father worked as a breaker in a coal mine but died of black-lung disease when George was 10. To help address the financial challenges his family now faced, he began working at a tomato farm.[5]

At 5-feet-4, he felt he was too small to play baseball. Toma's interest in groundskeeping may have started when he and his friends annually cleared an area near his house to play sports. As part of the clearing process, they would use the springs from discarded mattresses and then drag/pull them by hand to smooth into a makeshift playing field.[6]

One of George's neighbors was a groundskeeper at Artillery Park for the Wilkes-Barre Barons of the Class-A Eastern League. When George's father died, his neighbor began taking Toma with him to help drag the infield.

When Bill Veeck became the owner of the Cleveland Indians and their farm system, he also became the Barons owner. He changed the club's name to the Indians. He also made a few cost-cutting moves, including making Toma the new head groundskeeper. Veeck also sent George to work with Emil Bossard, the Indians' head groundskeeper, who was nationally known for his groundskeeping acumen.[7]

From 1951 to 1953, Toma served in the US Army, deploying to Korea. After his discharge he resumed his job as the head groundskeeper for the Barons, continuing his excellent work at Wilkes-Barre. More importantly, his work was noticed by several major- and high-level minor-league clubs.

In 1955 Toma became the head groundskeeper for Buffalo, the Triple-A club for the Detroit Tigers. When Detroit moved the club to Charleston, West Virginia, Toma followed the club. In 1957 he got two head groundskeeper offers: the Yankees' Triple-A affiliate in Denver and the Kansas City Athletics' major-league club. Many of his friends, including Bossard, urged him to take the Denver offer. Kansas City's field had a reputation of being horrible. Looking to his future, Toma expected to eventually advance to Yankee Stadium. However, he knew he would not like living under the microscope in New York. Toma went to both Kansas City and Denver to look over their fields. Kansas City's field was, as rumored, horrible.

He went back to Charleston and received some sage advice from one of the club officials. "George, the best thing for you to do is to go to Kansas City. If you screw up, nobody will notice it's so bad." Toma took his advice, called Kansas City, and took the job.[8]

In 1955 former President Harry Truman threw out the first pitch at Kansas City's Municipal Stadium. By the time Toma took over as head groundskeeper, it had significantly deteriorated. The stadium was a mess and the infield posed a real danger to the players.

Toma and his staff of one other groundskeeper started with one Toro professional lawnmower, an airifier, and an International tractor. They gathered up broken seats and discarded items from concession stands and took it all to a local junkyard. With the money they got for the junk, they bought fertilizer and manure. Under the constant care of Toma, by the next spring Municipal Stadium's field became a yardstick for measuring infield/outfield quality.

Charles O. Finley was one of most despised baseball club owners in baseball history. Yet Toma considered Finley the finest owner he ever worked for. Toma was impressed by Finley's compassion when the owner gave him a $3,000 gift to celebrate the birth of George's new son.

Finley was also a little eccentric/crazy and liked a good joke. In particular, he liked animals and established a small zoo near the Municipal Stadium fence. He stocked his field with a mule (Charlie O), monkeys, pheasants, rabbits, and sheep. The groundskeepers had to maintain all of them, including spray-painting the sheep different colors.

In addition, there were pregame water fights between the Athletics groundskeepers and several Yankees players. Finley even bought some perfume and had Toma spread it through the Yankees dugout to irritate their players.

At the end of 1967, Finley moved the Athletics to Oakland, where they prospered. They won three consecutive World Series (1972-1974). Then Finley did something extraordinary. He gave Toma an Oakland A' s Championship ring with a clover leaf, the years '72,'73, and '74, three S's for sweat and sacrifice equals success, and Toma's name on it.[9]

In 1963, Lamar Hunt moved the Dallas Texans to Kansas City where they became the Kansas City Chiefs and would also occupy Municipal Stadium. When Hunt first visited Municipal Stadium, Toma was on top of the center-field flagpole giving it a fresh coat of paint. Toma did not like anyone walking on his field and yelled at Hunt and his party to get off his field.

The transition from baseball to football was not always smooth, as both Finley and Hunt had strong personalities. Trying to irritate Hunt and perhaps trying to get Toma to join him in Oakland, Finley ended up paying the remainder of Toma's 1963 salary if he would totally stay away from Municipal Stadium. During his time off, Toma received and executed several short-term baseball and/or football-field turf-related consulting jobs. One of his assignments was field preparation work for the annual Thanksgiving Day game at the Cotton Bowl. His work drew praise from NFL Commissioner Pete Rozelle.

Based on Toma's Cotton Bowl success, the NFL and the AFL chose him to prepare the Los Angeles Coliseum for the first NFL-AFL championship game. (This game became the Super Bowl.)

One of Toma's favorite Super Bowl memories was when Emmitt Smith of the Dallas Cowboys came by after practice for Super Bowl XXX and asked him to autograph a piece of sod that he was going to put down in his front yard. Over his career, Toma ended up handling the field prep work for 50 Super Bowls. The NFL also contracted with him to do and/or supervise all the field prep work for 37 Pro Bowls.

The NFL also used Toma's field preparation expertise for special American Bowls held in various international cities, including London, Tokyo, and Mexico City.[10]

In 1969 Toma was named head groundskeeper for the Royals and Royals (later Kauffman) Stadium. He also maintained his position with the Chiefs and was named the director of landscaping at the Harry S. Truman Sports Complex.

Toma's position also led to him meeting and marrying his wife, Donna, also an avid baseball fan. He credited the Royals' bullpen pitchers and catchers with helping his young son to learn how to walk and potty-training him.

One of the highlights of Toma's baseball career was watching the Royals beat the Cardinals to win the 1985 World Series. During the postgame celebration, as the fans streamed across the field, his youngest son began to cry, "Get off my daddy's field!"[11]

Toma also oversaw the infield preparations for Summer Olympics held in the Los Angeles Coliseum (1994) and Atlanta's Olympic Stadium (1996). In Atlanta, their sod was dead in the area where the opening ceremonies were to take place. Olympic officials contacted Toma immediately and he led the installation of 13,500 cubic yards of sod in 24 hours with 12 hours of sod-bed preparation. After the job was finished, an exhausted Toma fell asleep in Chipper Jones's locker.[12]

In 2000 Toma was asked to "salvage" Hammond Stadium in Fort Myers, Florida. Worms had chewed up the roots of the grass. In eight days, the field was to be used for the Florida State League All-Star Game. Toma and his crew had to take out the infield and outfield grass, fill the hole back up with a mixture of sand and peat moss, grade it, water it down, and then put high-quality sod over it. The job was done in eight days and the field drew praise from league management and the players. His work was also noticed by the Minnesota Twins, who used him to annually help prepare their spring training practice fields in Florida.[13]

In addition to his football and baseball field expertise, he assisted in the field preparation for various World Cup venues, particularly Soldier Field in Chicago and the Silverdome in Pontiac, Michigan.

Over the years, Toma's field preparation work has resulted in many awards and accolades. In 2001 he received the Dan Reeves Pioneer Award at the Pro Football Hall of Fame in Canton, Ohio. He is also in the Kansas City Royals Hall of Fame and the Missouri Sports Hall of Fame, and has received numerous awards from the Sports Turf Managers Association. STMA named one its annual awards after him: the George Toma Gold Rake Award.[14]

When asked about the seemingly minor role as a groundskeeper, Toma would describe what was under the Chiefs' Arrowhead Stadium: five miles of electrical conduit, two miles of drainage pipe, and one mile of irrigation pipe. Layered over the subsurface is a 4-inch pea gravel base topped by a 12-inch root zone. The root zone comprises 5,000 tons of 85 percent regular sand, and 15 percent reed sedge peat. Then comes choosing the right mixture of grass to put down as the playing surface. "I'm just nobody," Toma once said. "But I appreciate a good field."

Notes

1 George Toma with Alan Goforth, *Nitty Gritty Dirt Man* (Champaign, Illinois: Sports Publishing, 2004), 181.

2 Ibid.

3 Missouri Sports Hall of Fame Inductee, George Toma, mosportshalloffame.com/inductees/5327/

4 Toma with Goforth, 5.

5 Toma with Goforth, 6.

6 Toma with Goforth, 12-13.

7 Toma with Goforth, 16-32.

8 Toma with Goforth, 28-32.

9 Toma with Goforth, 35-44.

10 Missouri Sports Hall of Fame, George Toma.

11 Toma with Goforth, 69-78.

12 Toma with Goforth, 110.

13 David Dorsey, "George Toma: Super Bowl 'Sod God' Rakes It Easy in Fort Myers," *Fort Myers* (Florida) *News-Press*, March 21, 2017. news-press.com/story/sports/2017/03/21/george-toma-god-hammond-stadiums-sod/98948536/

14 Kevin Burrows, "George Toma: From Single A to the Superbowl. … and Then Some," landscapeonline.com/research/article-a.php?number=11137.

NED YOST

BY KEN CARRANO

A major-league ballplayer gets called a lot of things during his career, and a manager probably more so. In the case of Edgar Frederick Yost III, some of those things include taxidermist, catcher, grinder, idiot, app developer, survivor, twitter hashtag (#yosted), clothier, pot scrubber, and hunter. Oh, and one more thing – World Series champion manager.

Ned Yost was born on August 19, 1954, in Eureka, California, the son of Edgar Yost Jr. and Lael (Prindle) Yost. The Yosts divorced while Ned was in elementary school. Yost's father played football at Santa Rosa Junior College where he was named a Little All-American.[1] His mother was a homemaker. In May 1971, when Yost was a junior in high school, his father, a tanker-truck driver for the Arco petroleum company, was killed when a car cut his truck off. "Right after you get drafted, and then you work your way up, the first day you make it in the big leagues, you're thinking, 'Man, I wish he could have seen this,'" Yost said in 2014. "And then in '82, when we made it to the World Series (as a player with Milwaukee), it was, 'Man, I wish he could have seen this.'"[2]

Ned Yost (in uniform) with Whitey Herzog

Around the time of his father's death, Yost's family had moved to Dublin, California, where Yost joined the high-school baseball team, with little to no effect. "I went a whole year in high school without getting a hit, 0-36 my sophomore year."[3] Yost would improve, thanks to a summer job. "I went to work at Kentucky Fried Chicken. I was a pot scrubber. I'd sit there and scrub pots all summer long and my arms got strong."[4]

Yost's improved strength translated to the field as he earned all-league status as a senior, but didn't translate to any college scholarship offers, so he decided to walk on at Chabot Junior College in Hayward, California.

Chabot had produced several major-league players, including Dick Tidrow and Von Joshua, but coach Gene Wellman didn't think too much of Yost's chances after he was drafted seventh by the New York Mets in the first round of 1974 June Secondary Phase Draft. After deciding to sign with the Mets, Wellman told Yost to take care of himself for the next week. Wellman then told him why a just a week – "Because that's how long you're going to last, son. You're going to be back on the first bus. You think you're a professional player? You ain't going to make it. Good luck. See you later."[5]

Yost went to Batavia of the New York-Penn League in the summer of 1974 to try to prove Wellman wrong. He played in 44 games and hit .252, splitting time behind the plate and struggling with his defense, allowing six passed balls and 11 errors. Still, his performance gained him promotion to Wausau of the Midwest League for the 1975 season. Yost's hitting was more challenged at the higher level; he hit only .192 while handing most of the catching duties for the Mets' Single-A club. In spite of these troubles, Yost advanced to Double-A ball in 1976, with the Jackson (Mississippi) Mets of the Texas League. In Jackson, Yost improved his defense enough to catch most of the team's games even though he hit only .199 in 83 games.

While with Jackson Yost opened a taxidermy studio during the offseason, behind his uncle's bowling alley. "And that was my winter job. We'd go deer hunting and we'd do taxidermy in the back of the bowling alley back there. It was a lot of fun."[6] Yost would list taxidermy as his current occupation on the National Baseball Hall of Fame questionnaire that players complete when they make the major leagues.

The 1977 season changed the direction of Yost's life. After a great start with Jackson, he was promoted to Tidewater of the Triple-A International League. He continued his good play, hitting 12 home runs in 60 games while batting .291. Once the season ended, he married the former Deborah Ann Ferrell in September 1977. And finally, the Milwaukee Brewers acquired Yost in the Rule 5 draft during the winter meetings. Yost performed well with the Brewers' Triple-A affiliates in Spokane (1978) and Vancouver (1979), earning an invitation to the Brewers 1980 spring-training camp. Yost had confidence that he would make the major-league roster, whatever it would take, telling Brewers coach Larry Haney, "I'll warm up the pitchers, I'll wash the uniforms. I'll scrub out the clubhouse; anything."[7]

Yost made the team as the Brewers' third catcher behind Charlie Moore and Buck Martinez, and made his major-league debut on April 12, 1980, in the first game of a doubleheader against Boston. "We were blowing them out big, 14-0, 15-1, something like that, in the seventh inning and they put me in," Yost recalled. "The first hitter was Carl Yastrzemski. I remember just staring at his face, thinking that I can't believe this is happening."[8] After three appearances without a hit, Yost was sent back to Vancouver in May. His performance there (.309/2/41) earned him a trip back to Milwaukee in September. In his first at-bat back in the big leagues, Yost got his first major-league hit, off Albert Williams in a 15-2 drubbing of the Brewers at the hands of the Minnesota Twins. Yost wound up the season hitting .161 without a home run or RBI.

In December 1980 the Brewers acquired Ted Simmons from the St. Louis Cardinals, seemingly burying Yost deep in the Brewers roster. However, the Brewers traded Martinez in May, and Moore spent time on the disabled list and in the outfield, giving Yost an opportunity to learn from the experienced Simmons. Simmons wanted to pass on what he had learned in the majors, and found Yost a willing, if not skeptical, student. Simmons told Yost that he would have something for him every day to learn. Yost thought, "Yeah, right. And then for the next two and a half years, Simmons had something for me every day."[9] Yost got only 30 plate appearances in 1981 but experienced postseason baseball for the first time as the Brewers won the second half of the strike-shortened 1981 season, losing the Division Series to the New York Yankees.

Yost served as Simmons's primary backup behind the plate during the Brewers' 1982 campaign that took them to Game Seven of the World Series. Yost saw limited action, playing in 40 games with 107 plate appearances. He hit only one home run during the season, but it was one of the most important homers in the Brewers' season. They had taken over first place at the end of July and led the Baltimore Orioles in the AL East by three games with six to play going into their game at Boston on September 29. Yost entered the game in the bottom of the eighth and came up with two on and two out in the top of the ninth inning after Cecil Cooper was intentionally walked. Yost's home run gave the Brewers the 6-3 win and a four-game lead with five games to go over the Orioles. He was so sure he wouldn't be playing on the road trip that he had not packed a bat for the road trip, using Moore's bat to hit the game-winner. "It's a dream come true. You think about it, then you saw 'Naw. That would never happen.'"[10] The Brewers lost their next four, allowing the Orioles to tie for the division lead going into the last game of the season, in Baltimore. Milwaukee defeated the Orioles in game 162 to win the division flag. Yost did not play in the League Championship Series against the California Angels, and walked in his only appearance (in Game Six) of the World Series against the Cardinals.

The home run against Boston was the pinnacle of Yost's playing days. In 1983 he started 57 games behind the plate for the Brewers, 30 more than in 1982. He added six home runs in 1983, but his average dropped to .224 and he continued to struggle throwing runners out, nailing only 8 of 65 would be stealers for a 12 percent rate (the league average was 33 percent). The Brewers decided to move on from Yost, trading him to the Texas Rangers for veteran catcher Jim Sundberg.

Rangers manager Doug Rader thought Yost would be his starter for the 1984 season. "I believe Yost will be a top catcher," Rader said. "But because of the situation in Milwaukee – where Ted Simmons had a lock on the job – he has not been able to prove it. He will get that opportunity with the Rangers."[11] For his part, Yost was excited about the chance to be a number-one catcher. "I'm happy as heck about it," Yost said. "From everything I've heard, I think it's going to be fun."[12] Yost was the Opening Day catcher in 1984, but did not take advantage of the opportunity, hitting only .182 in 80 games. His hitting woes and continued difficulty with baserunners saw him lose time to Donnie Scott, and in April of 1985 he was released by the Rangers, catching on later that month with Montreal, who sent him to their Indianapolis affiliate for the season. Yost's numbers came up a bit at the Triple-A level, and he was called up to Montreal to finish the season and his major-league career. Yost signed with the Braves organization, where he bounced between Triple-A Richmond and Double-A Greenville for the next two seasons.

Knowing his playing days were over, Yost wondered what his next move would be when the Braves asked if he would work with the young players on their minor-league team in Sumter, South Carolina. He wound up being appointed manager in Sumter, and worked with some of the Braves that would go on to success at the major-league level, including Ryan Klesko, Ron Gant, and Mark Wohlers. After three years working in the South Atlantic League, Yost was again promoted to the big leagues, this time as the bullpen coach in Atlanta. "I was in the right place at the right time," he said. "It was just pure luck."[13] Phil Niekro had been the bullpen coach and was named the manager at Richmond, opening up the bullpen-coach job for Yost, working for manager Bobby Cox.

Yost joined Atlanta at the start of one of the most remarkable team runs in sports history. In every year Yost with the Braves (save the strike-shortened 1994 season), they won the National League East title. Yost spent eight years in the Braves bullpen and then moved to the third-base coach's box in 1999. Bobby Dews, who had been the third-base coach, was moved to the bullpen by Cox after the 1998 season.

Yost didn't spend all of his time in Atlanta studying box scores. In May 1993 he opened a clothing store, Major League Image, whose customers were helped to match their wardrobes using a dress-by-the-numbers strategy. The store had evolved from a computer program that Yost and local retailer Mac McLemore had developed. Yost used the system himself – "Hey, my wife can't travel with me everywhere," Yost once joked.[14] He also spent time outdoors with friends, including NASCAR legend Dale Earnhardt. The two were introduced by a mutual friend, Jody Davis. "We hit it off. Hunted together every year," said Yost.[15] Yost even worked on Earnhardt's pit crew during the 1994 baseball strike. Earnhardt was a huge Braves fan, and often pestered Yost to help him get into the Braves dugout so he could help manage. Earnhardt died in a crash near the end of the Daytona 500 in 2001. "There'd be times when we'd have an exciting play on the field and I'd think, 'Boy, I bet that fired Dale up.' I'm gonna miss knowing he's there watching us do our thing. There's a lot to miss when a man like him's not around anymore."[16] Yost began to wear uniform number 3 as a tribute to Earnhardt after his death.

The Brewers were looking for a new manager after the 2002 season. Jerry Royster had been fired after leading the team to a 106-loss season that saw attendance at Miller Park drop by nearly a million. The Brewers had looked at a number of candidates, and had offered the job to Ken Macha, who turned them down to take the Oakland A's open position. Brewers general manager Doug Melvin had not considered Yost until Yost's agent, Alan Hendricks, spoke with him. Melvin also spoke with Cox and Braves general manager John Schuerholz and gave Yost an interview. After he made the hire, Melvin said that Yost's "work ethic, energy and enthusiasm" set him apart from the other candidates.[17] Brewers fans would have been expected to wonder if a guy with no major-league managerial experience was ready for this job, but Yost believed that he was. "I don't have any apprehension about being a major-league manager," he said. "I don't have much experience managing but I've been around a Hall of Fame manager (Cox) for 11 years."[18]

The 2003 Brewers showed improvement in Yost's first year, improving to 68-94. Melvin was pleased with the team's improved play. "I guarantee you he talked our team into 15 or 20 wins last year just by telling the players they were better than they actually were. They believed him and went out and did it," Melvin said.[19] The Brewers continued to improve under Yost, and their record of 81-81 in 2005 was the first time since 1992 that the team did not have a losing record. After a slight step back in 2006, the Brewers rebuild was in full form for the 2007 season. They started the season 16-9 in April and by mid-May had an eight-game lead in a weak National League Central Division. They kept the lead until mid-August when a five-game losing streak knocked them to second place. The Brewers stayed in the hunt and moved into a tie for first on September 18. But the heat of the pennant race seemed to take its toll on Yost and the players. Yost was ejected from three games during a four-game stretch and served a one-game suspension on September 27 for retaliation in a game against the Cardinals. Yost was defiant, stating, "What happened in the past doesn't really concern me right now, but to answer your question, no, I wouldn't do a thing differently."[20] GM Melvin supported Yost, but admitted, "This is a situation we haven't been in before, and it's a situation Ned hasn't been in before as a manager. We handle all these things together as a team."[21] Brewers fans had been filling the sports airwaves and message boards looking for Yost's removal after the team lost an 8½-game lead in June, but Brewers owner Mark Attanasio confirmed Yost's status when he said, "Ned is fine."[22]

The 2008 version of the Brewers played better than they did in 2007 but found the division race more challenging with the improved play of the Chicago Cubs. Still, the Brewers were in the hunt for the playoffs after going 20-7 in August, finishing the month with a record of 80-56 and a 5½-game lead for the wild card over the Philadelphia Phillies. A poor homestand to start September saw the wild-card lead shrink to four games with a key four-game set coming in Philadelphia. The series was a disaster for the Brewers, who lost all four games and their wild-card lead. Attanasio and Melvin had seen enough after the Phillies series, and decided to fire Yost with 12 games left in the season. "When we talked to (Ned), he didn't have all of the answers to what's gone on the last two weeks," Melvin said.[23] Yost said he did not see the move coming, stating, "The timing of it surprised me. It's the nature of the business, but it's gotten a little strange. Two bad weeks (and you get fired)."[24] Yost's bench coach, Dale Sveum, took over the team, and while the results improved only slightly (7-5 over the final 12 games), it was enough for the Brewers to end their postseason drought and claim the wild card. The Brewers were eliminated by the Phillies (who had overcome the New York Mets to win the NL East) three games to one in the Division Series.

Yost spent 2009 on his 210-acre farm in Georgia but was not out of baseball long. In early 2010, Kansas City Royals general manager Dayton Moore hired him as a special assistant to baseball operations. Many saw it as an insurance policy for the Royals, whose manager, Trey Hillman, had taken a lot of criticism after a 97-loss season in 2009. "That's not the motive," said Moore. The motive is hiring good people to impact the organization. Trey was as much on board bringing in Ned as I was."[25] It didn't take long for the insurance policy to be cashed in, as Moore fired Hillman on May 12, 2010, and replaced him with Yost. "Ned has been through what we're going through (in terms of building a club). He has a lot of similarities to Trey, actually as far as their energy and relationship skills with people."[26] Yost later said that managing in the big leagues is mostly about three things: You must manage the personalities of the players, the games, and the media. Thinking he did okay with the first two while in Milwaukee, he decided that he wouldn't read, listen, or watch any coverage of the Royals. Some of the decisions he would make as the Royals returned to respectability would challenge this.

The Royals whom Yost inherited were in many ways like the Brewers in 2003, or even the Braves in 1991. After an 83-win season in 2003, they had three straight 100-loss seasons. Hillman was able to get them out of the AL Central cellar in 2008 with a 75-87 campaign. A promising 18-11 start in 2009 fell apart as the Royals crashed to a 65-97 final record in 2009, setting the table for Hillman's demise. But the poor record translated into high draft choices, and Moore and his staff made some good choices in these years, including first-round picks Alex Gordon (2005), Mike Moustakas (2007), and Eric Hosmer (2008). This infusion of young talent and a manager experienced in growing young talent led to improvements in the standings, from 67 wins in 2010 (Yost was 55-72) to 71 in 2011 and 72 (and a third-place finish in the division) in 2012.

Offseason moves to add pitchers James Shields and Wade Davis lifted expectations for the 2013 season, and The Sporting News predicted a second-place finish for the Royals and Manager of the Year honors for Yost. Yost shrugged off the pressure of these expectations, saying, "There's pressure with everything that you do, there really is, whether it's expectation and pressure. But there are so many variables. You can't get too carried away, because there are a lot of things that have got to happen right."[27] The season got off to a fair start, but by the end of May the Royals were 22-30 and in last in the division again. Speculation began to rise regarding Yost's job security, but Moore came to his defense, stating that Yost "was the least of the club's problems.[28] The team responded to Moore's defense of their skipper, going 64-46 the rest of the season to finish in third place with a winning record for the first time since 2003 and a contract extension for Yost, setting up several very exciting years of baseball in Kansas City.

Yost realized by the start of the 2014 season that the strict boundaries he had learned from Cox in Atlanta needed to be adjusted for the player of today. "I've gotten much better results than just coming in and trying to be the tough guy," he said. "The authoritarian. Yelling, screaming. That doesn't work with kids nowadays."[29] Billy Butler noticed the change in Yost. "He's been easier to talk to," Butler said.[30]

The Royals got off to another slow start in 2014, and in early June were three games under .500, bringing up discussion of Yost's job again. But just as in 2013, the young Royals found their form in the summer. They stayed in race for the division crown as well as the wild card. They could not catch the Detroit Tigers for the AL Central, but clinched a spot in the wild-card game after beating the Chicago White Sox on September 26.

The wild-card game cemented Yost's growing reputation as a manager who would manage his way, and not how convention would have him manage. In the top of the sixth inning, the Royals clung to a 3-2 lead, but starter Shields put the first two hitters on. Convention said that Yost should bring in Kelvin Herrera, as he usually did in the seventh inning, but instead he chose Yordano Ventura, a starter who had pitched two days earlier. Ventura promptly gave up a three-run home run and the lead. Fans in Kansas City had taken to Twitter to express their displeasure in similar Yost moves with the hashtag/verb #yosted, describing what happens when a choice goes horribly wrong. When Yost pulled Ventura three hitters later for Herrera, the Royals fans gave Yost rousing disapproval of the moves. "I'd never in my life heard anything like it,' said broadcaster Ryan Lefebvre.[31] "It didn't bother me. I still felt like we were going to win the game. I had no doubt that we would," Yost said. [32] They did, coming from behind with three runs in the eight and one in the ninth to tie, and then with two runs in the 12th after the A's scored one in the top of the frame. So inspired were the Royals after this multiple come-from-behind win that they swept the Los Angeles Angels in the Division Series and then the Baltimore Orioles in the AL Championship Series.

Suddenly the guy who couldn't handle the pressure of pennant race in Milwaukee and had nearly thrown away the Royals' first playoff appearance since 1985 became the first manager in history to start a postseason 8-0. "I've been called a dunce (Wall Street Journal), an idiot (Chicago Tribune) and everything else. It just doesn't bother me. I'm really comfortable with who I am. I know who I am," said Yost after the season.[33] The Royals faced Yost's favorite team growing up, the San Francisco Giants, in the World Series and came as close as you could to winning, leaving the tying run on third base in the bottom of the ninth inning in Game Seven. Yost spent time during the offseason doing exactly what one would never think he would do – develop an app for iPhone and Android. Ned Yost's Baseball Academics was launched at the American Baseball Coaches Association conference, where it won best in show. "It just teaches kids to think, teaches them to think quick and where to properly throw the ball. Even college coaches said, 'I would make my kids do that,'" Yost said.[34]

The 2015 Royals would not leave anything to chance. Avoiding the slow start that plagued the previous two seasons, they jumped out to a 15-7 record by the end of April, took over the Central Division lead for good on June 9, and won the division by a comfortable 12 games. Yost became the Royals' all-time winning manager on June 18 with his 411th victory. The Division Series against the Houston Astros went the distance, but trade-deadline pickup Johnny Cueto pitched a gem to win the series for the Royals. The Toronto Blue Jays were the opponent in the ALCS, and were dispatched in six games, leaving the Royals in the World Series in consecutive years for the first time. In the 1985 Series, the Royals had to battle back from a 3-1 deficit to claim the title. The 2015 Royals avoided this drama, winning the Series over the New York Mets in five games when they scored two runs in the top of the ninth inning to tie Game Five, then five more in the 12th to win the series.

Yost and the Royals perhaps used up all of their magic in their 2015 run to the title and could not replicate it in 2016. This version of the Royals briefly flirted with first place in May but fell to third in the division with a record of 81-81. The 2017 version was no better, finishing with an 80-82 record. Perhaps the most excitement that 2017 provided Yost nearly cost him his life. On November 4, while in a tree stand on his property in Georgia, Yost fell 20 feet when the stand collapsed as he was trying to attach a safety strap. He broke his pelvis and severed his iliac artery. The trauma doctor told him that he was lucky to be alive, as this type of injury has a 25 to 30 percent mortality rate. "I had my cell phone in my pocket, which was my key to the whole thing and being in a spot on my farm that had service was key," Yost said.[35]

After two mediocre seasons, the Royals decided to rebuild in 2018, and their record fell to 58-104, their second-worst performance in franchise history. Moore hired former Cardinals manager Mike Matheny as a special adviser in November 2018, perhaps as another insurance policy, especially with Yost under contract for only one more season.

In May 1983, after hitting home runs in consecutive games in Oakland, Yost saw his old coach Wellman for the first time since he left Chabot. "I was dead wrong about you," Yost recalled him saying. "The one thing I didn't take into account is that you can't keep a good man down."[36] Yost has been called many things during his career, many not fit for print. But he helped build one of the great teams in baseball history, then transformed two small-market losers into winners. Perhaps the best thing said about Yost came from a man who both hired and fired him, Doug Melvin: "He took a franchise that had not been to the playoffs in 25 years, built it up and got it to the playoffs. Then he took a franchise in Kansas City that hadn't been to the playoffs in 30 years and did the same thing. I don't care what anyone says about him. How many managers have done that?"[37]

Sources

In addition to the sources listed in the Notes, the author accessed Retrosheet.org and Baseball-Reference.com.

Notes

1 Vahe Gregorian, "Ned Yost Has Been Making 'Most of What He Has' Since Growing Up a Giants Fan," Kansas City Star, October 20, 2014, kansascity.com/sports/spt-columns-blogs/vahe-gregorian/article3185608.html.

2 Ibid.

3 Dick Kaegel, "Yost Recalls Hitless Season in High School," MLB.com, April 22, 2014 mlb.com/royals/news/royals-manager-ned-yost-recalls-hitless-season-in-high-school/c-72993074.

4 Gregorian.

5 Ibid

6 Chris Fickett, "Yes, Royals Manager Ned Yost Was a Taxidermist," *Kansas City Star*, October 27, 2015.

7 Tom Flaherty, "Kid Yost Mentally Ready, So Are Brewers," *The Sporting News*, April 26, 1980: 18.

8 Chuck Greenwood, " '82 World Series Yost's Career Highlight," *Sports Collectors Digest*, July 18, 1997: 60

9 Gregorian.

10 Tom Flaherty, "AL East Notes — Yost an Unlikely Brewers Hero," *The Sporting News*, October 11, 1982: 33.

11 Jim Reeves, "Deals for Ward, Yost Please Rader," *The Sporting News*, December 19, 1983: 42.

12 Jim Reeves, "Yost Promises Plenty of Hustle," *The Sporting News*, December 26, 1983: 47.

13 Greenwood.

14 I.J. Rosenberg, "Getting Dressed by the Numbers," *Atlanta Journal-Constitution*, February 18, 1993: E2.

15 Bruce Schoenfeld, "How Ned Yost Made the Kansas City Royals Unstoppable," New York Times Magazine, October 1, 2015.

16 Steve Hummer, "When NASCAR Lost an Icon, Yost and Others Lost a Friend," *Atlanta Journal-Constitution*, February 20, 2001: F5.

17 Michael Cunningham, "Yost Gets Two Years to Show Brewers He's the Man for the Job," *Milwaukee Journal Sentinel*, October 30, 2002: 1C.

18 Drew Olson, "Yost Looks to Catch On in Milwaukee," *Milwaukee Journal Sentinel*, October 29 2002.

19 Tom Haudricourt, "Yost Offers Brewers a Fresh Approach," *Milwaukee Journal Sentinel*, February 22, 2004.

20 Gary D'Amato, "Tumultous Week Finally Ends for Yost," *Milwaukee Journal Sentinel*, September 29, 2007: C1.

21 Ibid.

22 Rick Braun, "Players Not Surprised Yost Returning," *Milwaukee Journal Sentinel*, September 27, 2007: C5.

23 Tom Haudricourt, "Brewers Fire Manager Yost," *Milwaukee Journal Sentinel*, September 15, 2008.

24 Ibid.

25 Sam Mellinger, "Royals Hire Ex-Brewers Manager Yost as Special Advisor," *Kansas City Star*, January 13, 2010.

26 Bob Dutton, "Royals Fire Hillman, Select Yost as Replacement," Kansas City Star, May 13, 2010.

27 Pete Grathoff, "Ned Yost, Manager of the Year," Kansas City Star, February 6, 2013.

28 Bob Dutton, "Royals' Yost Says He 'Doesn't Listen' to Speculation Regarding His Job Security," *Kansas City Star*, May 29, 2013.

29 Andy McCullough, "Royals Manager Ned Yost Loosens the Reins as He Adjusts to a New Generation of Players," *Kansas City Star*, March 1, 2014.

30 Ibid.

31 Schoenfeld.

32 Ibid.

33 Joe Strauss, Royals' Yost Shrugs Off the Critics," *St. Louis Post Dispatch*, December 9, 2014.

34 Pete Grathoff, "Royals Manager Ned Yost Developed App to Teach Baseball Strategy," *Kansas City Star*, February 4, 2015.

35 Pete Grathoff and Rustin Dodd, "Royals Manager Ned Yost Says He Nearly Died as a Result of Fall from Tree," *Kansas City Star*, November 13, 2017.

36 Gregorian.

37 Schoenfeld.

CROWNING ACHIEVEMENT: THE MAN BEHIND THE KANSAS CITY ROYAL'S LOGO

BY JAMES FORR

At Kauffman Stadium a few years ago, someone introduced Shannon Manning to a fan and his young son. The boy had never heard of Manning and couldn't understand why he was supposed to be so impressed. The father just pointed to his kid's Royals cap and explained wryly, "Without this fellow, your hat would just be blue."

Many of us waste years, decades, sometimes a lifetime, figuring out what we want to be when we grow up. But Shannon Manning yearned to be an artist for as long as he can remember; nothing else ever seriously crossed his mind. Even when he was a boy in rural Indiana, his parents could hand him a crayon and a stack of brown paper bags and he would be set for the evening. "It was something I could do as a kid that made me kind of special," he recalled. "I wasn't particularly good at sports. I wasn't a particularly good student. But this was something I could do."

Rejected Logos

Manning graduated from Herron School of Art and Design in Indianapolis, spent five years as a graphic designer in Chicago, and then in 1967 trekked off to Kansas City, where he took a job creating retail packaging for Hallmark.

That winter, shortly after the Athletics relocated to Oakland, baseball awarded Kansas City an expansion franchise. Owner Ewing Kauffman had no in-house design talent in those hectic early days, so for a team logo he turned to Hallmark and the hundreds of talented artists under its roof. Hallmark opened the project to its entire staff. Any employee who wanted to devise a logo could do so, on company time, with company resources. Although Manning was only a casual baseball fan, the artistic challenge intrigued him. "It was pretty much up my alley."

The Royals had two requirements – they wanted to use blue and they insisted the logo incorporate a crown. Otherwise, Manning and his colleagues were free to go where their imaginations led them.

Twenty-one artists took a crack at it. Some concepts were straightforward (a simple crown perched squarely atop a baseball with the word "Royals" splayed across the seams). Others were more complex (crossed baseball bats and a shield beneath a fluttering "Royals" banner, all overseen by an imperious figure who vaguely resembled the King of Spades). And one design suggested a fanciful flight of Warholian whimsy. "There was a psychedelic cow," Manning chuckled. "That was kind of a strange approach."

Original Royals Logo

Manning's winning idea wove many disparate elements into a clean, elegant look. For the background, he chose what he described as, "a modified home plate shape that makes a shield, something that looks like a coat of arms." Resting atop the shield was a gold crown. Inside the shield, the letters "KCR" featured swing-down, curving flourishes called swashes, which were *au courant* in the late 1960s. The "R" was a standard font but Manning modified an existing typeface to allow the "K" and the "C" to meld into each other seamlessly. Until 2002, that white "R" remained the focal point, with the gold "KC" rendered in smaller font and set off to the upper-right. (The club wanted to emphasize the nickname "Royals," which was a nod to the American Royal, a livestock show, horse show, and rodeo that has been a fall tradition in Kansas City since 1899.)

Even after his design received the go-ahead, Manning still had to wrestle with the club over the nettlesome final details. "They kept trying to put images inside the 'R,' which was not a real good idea." Those images included horse heads and cow heads, an homage to the American Royal and the famous Kansas City Stockyards.

But Manning argued that level of detail was impractical. "When you think about how this thing is reproduced, sometimes it's huge and sometimes it's very, very small. If you get a small object inside the loop of that 'R,' it's going to be hard to reproduce in smaller sizes. So they did a wise thing and decided to leave all that stuff out, just use an 'R,' and let the simplicity of that design stand on its own. It just works better visually."

The Royals have tweaked the logo over the years, eliminating the giant "R" and shifting the "KC" front and center. But the foundation of the design is still Manning's. "The Royals' logo is one of the best in all of sports, in my opinion," proclaimed Curt Nelson, director of the Royals Hall of Fame. "If you silhouetted all the MLB logos to black, many of them would be difficult to distinguish from the others. Ours, however, would still stand out and be recognizable — simple, classic, and unique all at the same time."

ROYALS called on Hallmark artists to pinch-hit in designing of emblem

Psychedelic steers and lantern-jawed sluggers vied with royal symbols In friendly competition to select a logo for Kansas City's new team.

Manning, who retired from Hallmark more than a decade ago, never made a dime off the logo, but he has been compensated for it in other ways. Royals fans thanked him with a rousing ovation prior to the opening game in 1969, and the team awarded him four season tickets for that inaugural season. Even today, he can attend a game on the Royals' tab anytime he wants. "I can't tell you how many games I've been to and I've never bought a ticket."

However, a more profound reward is the deep pride that comes from creating something important, enduring, and tangible. "There's really not any higher way to make a contribution to your community than through your profession," Manning attested. "When my wife and I came here it was more rural; people didn't hustle and bustle quite as much. It was like coming home. So the ability to pay that back a little bit is something I'm really grateful for."

Original version of this article was published on the website Seamheads.com on December 7, 2011.

Rejected designs courtesy Hallmark and the Kansas City Royals Hall of Fame.

Different iterations of the original logo are Shannon Manning originals, courtesy Kansas City Royals Hall of Fame.

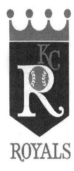

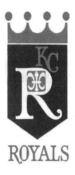

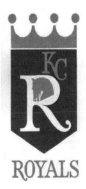

KAUFFMAN STADIUM

BY CURT SMITH

On April 12, 1955, the former Philadelphia Athletics, having moved that winter to Kansas City, opened their first season at Municipal Stadium: A's 6, Tigers 2, before a standing-room crowd of 32,147. Flanked by franchise progenitor Connie Mack, former President Harry Truman tossed the team's first ball in Missouri's first American League (AL) opener since April 23, 1902. Harry, recently retired to Independence, an hour away, made Opening Day, as he always did, a pip. "In Washington, Truman had become the first president to throw the first pitch of the season right- and left-handed," said 1946-60 Senators Voice Bob Wolff. "One year he threw with both arms successively. Another, Harry used both to cup the same ball and hurl it above his head."[1] Like most pitchers, he liked the A's sprawling new home, which housed the 1923-54 American Association Blues and 1923-31 and 1937-54 Negro League Kansas City Monarchs.

"For years we had a great Negro League and Yankees farm club tradition," said Kansas City Royals 1969-announcer Denny Matthews.[2] By the early 1950s, *Kansas City Star* sports editor Ernie Mehl persuaded Blues owner Arnold Johnson that Kansas City merited a big-league team. Johnson, owner of both Blues and Yankee Stadium, bought the A's from Mack in November 1954. He then moved them from Philadelphia, Yankees owners Del Webb and Dan Topping fueling the American League's okay. Kansas City bought Blues Stadium, renamed it Municipal, and leased it back to the new A's owner.[3] In 22 weeks, the city rebuilt and double-decked the park to a capacity of 30,716.[4]

Until 1955, baseball's most extreme geographic posts were Boston and St. Louis, train travel accessible and affordable. The Athletics' move to Kansas City made big-league rail kaput, ending at least one player's career. Jackie Jensen was a Red Sox perennial All-Star outfielder. "[He] drives home 100 runs every summer [*sic,* five times]," a writer said, "the way other men mow their lawns."[5] His problem lay above – he wouldn't, perhaps couldn't, fly. "I can see him now," said 1951-65 Red Sox Voice Curt Gowdy. "Jackie'd take the train all night to get to a game on time. By plane we'd get in the night before. He just had a fear of flying."[6] Worn, he retired in 1960, returned next year, and left again – for good.

The contrast in the effect of the Athletics' move on another well-known person could not have been more extreme. Less than a month after the A's debut, on Harry Truman's 71st birthday, May 8, 1955, his Presidential Library and Museum in Independence broke ground. "The boss is the real fan," Truman often said of wife Bess, as 1945-53 First Lady the greatest baseball student to be First Lady since 1923-29 Grace Coolidge.[7] They had met in Sunday School, Harry carrying her books to elementary school, gaping at her golden hair, blue eyes, and ability to whistle through her teeth – and "impressed," said Wolff, "by how she played baseball as a child with her brothers and their friends as the only girl on an all-boys team.[8]

Bess's childhood position was third base – baseball's "hot corner," perhaps an augury of Harry's fiery rhetoric. As First Lady, Mrs. Truman often went to D.C.'s Griffith Stadium on her own, with daughter Margaret, or with friends, using her scorebook for every game. A picture shows Bess casting a fan ballot for the annual All-Star Game.[9] In Washington, she watched, listened to, and scored as many games as possible even before her favorite spot was completed in 1948–the second-floor Truman Balcony, overlooking the South Lawn of the White House. In 1955, Mrs. Truman dusted off her scorebook for Missouri's first-year sixth-placers, their 1,393,054 attendance quadrupling the prior year in Philadelphia. Bess barely missed an Athletics' Opening Day. In 1956, she found it hard to forgive Margaret for picking the day after the A's home debut to be married "when they were 364 other days in the year!"[10] That season A's attendance barely hit one million for a club that berthed the second division each year before moving to Oakland in 1968.

In December 1960, Chicago insurance broker Charles O. Finley bought the A's. At one end, their new owner was cruel and stingy. At the other, Finley grasped baseball like a farmer senses rain. Catfish Hunter and John "Blue Moon" Odom got a bonus. Bert Campaneris arrived from Cuba. Sal Bando, Rick Monday, and Reggie Jackson helped forge baseball's amateur draft. "Charlie was his own scouting system," said Matthews.[11] In 1963, the Trumans left Independence on Opening Day to sit with Finley and his wife, the men wearing 10-gallon hats vaunting the A's new color scheme of Kelly green and gold—each an iconoclast, albeit Harry much smarter. Finley even built a children's zoo with a mule named Charlie O. and monkeys that ate Vodka-soaked oranges fed them by Tigers pitchers, based on the pragmatic notion that A's ineptitude was best viewed through a bottle.

While health allowed, the Trumans frequented the Athletics in person, Harry saying, pricelessly, "May the sun never set on American baseball."[12] A number of baseball books dotted his private collection, acquired year after year. America's last president to lack a college degree substituted a library for a classroom, owning more than *thirty thousand* books, the most of any president. Bess also read avidly, particularly about the pastime. In addition, she turned to the Athletics' four-state radio and TV network, usually in vain, Kansas City yearly ending between 19 and 45 games out of first. Merle Harmon was its 1955-61 play-by-play announcer, told by 1955-57 A's skipper and future Cubs Voice Lou Boudreau, "If your team is good, you can criticize. If it's lousy, show patience." In Missouri, Harmon rued, "Believe me, I was the most patient man in the world."[13]

Under Arnold Johnson, the ex-Yanks' farm club continued to send fine big-league players to New York – hence, called the "Yankees' cousins." Irate, Finley was so obsessed that their dynasty stemmed from Yankee Stadium's 296-foot right-field line that he built a Pennant Porch, a same-distance four-foot-high fence. (Municipal's right-field fence was originally 347 feet from the plate.)[14] When baseball countered (the pole had to be at least 325 feet away), Charlie scripted a 325 line (indenting it to 296 five feet from the pole). The AL cried foul, at which point Finley painted "K.C. One-Half Pennant Porch" at the 325-foot pole.[15] It didn't matter. The A's lost throughout.

On May 3, 1965, Finley himself greased the Bronx shuttle, acquiring pitcher Rollie Sheldon and catcher John Blanchard from New York for catcher John "Doc" Edwards. Former Pirates pitcher Steve Blass drolly tells how "Blanchard had been lucky, catching a little [behind Yogi Berra and Elston Howard], but cashing all sorts of World Series checks." The day of the trade Mickey Mantle entered the Yankees clubhouse, where his and Blanchard's lockers lay side-by-side.

> "Mickey sees Blanchard crying," said Blass," and he says, "'What's wrong?'" genuinely concerned.
>
> "Mick, today I got traded to Kansas City," Blanchard said.
>
> Mantle: "That's great, you'll finally get to play."
>
> Blanchard: "That's why I'm crying. You know I can't play."[16]
>
> Exposed, he hit .200 in 52 games, was that year sold to Milwaukee, and never again glimpsed the bigs.

Next season Jackson County, Missouri, commissioned a study on the viability of building a new stadium in Kansas City. In the 1943 Broadway musical by composer Richard Rodgers and librettist Oscar Hammerstein II, *Oklahoma,* a song proclaimed, "Everything's Up to Date in Kansas City!"[17] By 1966, Municipal Stadium, built in 1923, was still decidedly not: its baseball capacity remained 7,500 less than the city had promised when Johnson decided in 1954 that, paraphrasing W. C. Fields' reported epitaph, "On the whole, I'd rather [*not*] be in Philadelphia."[18] Municipal had scant parking, was hard to reach, and braved limited amenities. The American Football League Kansas City Chiefs, sharing the joint, were restless, too.

In retrospect, the County-commissioned study mirrored how "Kansas City was thinking big,"[19] wrote Craig Brown, proposing a multipurpose domed stadium for baseball and football, not excluding a smaller arena for hockey, basketball, and other events. The dome would have 49,000 fixed seats and 7,000 bleachers for a 56,000-baseball capacity – too large, history would show, in a building too huge. Two sites were suggested: the "Core Business District" (downtown) and the "Leeds area, nestled between Interstates between 70 and 435, deemed an option because of ease of access and availability of the site," said Brown. The second site was adopted. Thankfully, the multi-sport dome concept was not. In June 1967, a vote in Jackson County approved a $43 million bond issue for the Truman Sports Complex.[20]

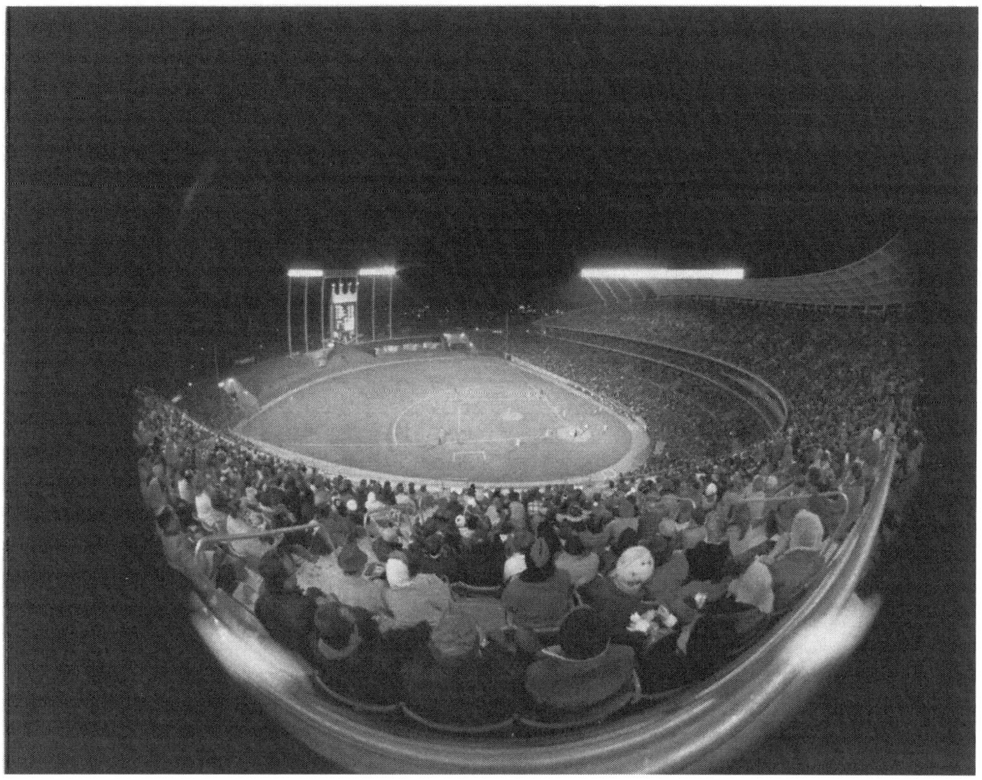

Royals Stadium Opening Night 1973

Soon consensus formed: "They didn't want a *single* multipurpose site," said Denny Matthews – instead, a *stadium* for the Chiefs and a *park* for the A's, who had signed a lease to stay in Missouri.[21] After Finley broke it by fleeing to Oakland, the County restated its support for two houses: 75,000-seat for football and 45,000 for baseball – showing ingenuity, since most locales then naively felt that one stadium could house both – Missouri U.S. Senator Stuart Symington vowed legislation to revoke baseball's anti-trust exemption if K.C. wasn't given another club. Ultimately, baseball expanded to four cities, including Symington's, in 1969: his Royals and Seattle to join the AL; Montreal and Seattle, swelling the National League; K.C.'s owner-to-be pharmaceutical czar Ewing Kauffman, whose Marion Laboratories had a market value of about $156 million and of which Kauffman and his family owned 31 percent.[22] His *community*-first mantra put *baseball* first.

The name Royals originated from the American Royal, a livestock show, horse show, rodeo, and championship barbeque competition held yearly in Kansas City since 1899.[23] In 1968, the team held a naming contest; more than 17,000 voting. Sanford Porte, a bridge engineer from suburban Overland Park, Kansas, won for "Royals," citing "Missouri's billion-dollar livestock income, Kansas City's position as the nation's leading stocker and feeder market and the nationally known American Royal parade and pageant."[24] The team's board first voted 6-1, team owner Kauffman dissenting, then supporting for unanimity.[25] By 1973, the Royals had a new home, turning heads, ground having been broken on Royals Stadium on July 11, 1968: park architect, Kivett and Myers; architect design associate, Charles Deaton; general contractor, Sharp-Kidde-Webb; cost, a 1972 players lockout and weather-delayed $70 million, or $386 million in 2017 change.[26] Original capacity was 40,733.[27] The footprint puta premium on pitching, defense, extra-base as opposed to home run-only swat, and speed.

The top two decks curled around home plate to each foul pole. A lower tier surpassed them to pens perpendicular to the field. Like them, every seat in smaller bleacher sections — here, "outfield plazas" — faced second base. No matter what your ticket, it was to *be* your supposed ticket to feeling part of the game. Royals Stadium's baseball-only core avoided a cookie-cutter's clang — remote seating, bad sightlines, and vast foul turf. In *The Ultimate Baseball Road Trip: A Fan's Guide to Major League Stadiums*, Kevin O'Connell and Josh Pahigian claimed that Royals hid such a core by limiting seats to those with a birds-eye view, few cursing a lively, baseball-only orb.[28] By some criteria it *did* define repetition, seeking "super blocks" to flank freeways, abut parking, and spur ease to help baseball and football, like oil and water, coexist. (Royals and football's Arrowhead Stadium stand next-door.) Like multi-sporters, Royals was concrete, with a smooth, largely roofless façade. Yet it was still the *sole* baseball-only park built between 1962 (Dodger Stadium) and 1991 (Comiskey II). Renamed Kauffman Stadium shortly before the Royals owner's August 1, 1993 death of bone cancer, "The K" kept baseball's faith in a dead-end ballpark age.

Unlike early parks with personality — Crosley Field, Comiskey Park, Ebbets Field—visual clones were rarely named for a person. Even here, Kauffman went back to the future. Unlike Riverfront, Three Rivers, or Veterans Stadium — seen one, seen 'em all, as in one too many — it was not dull, duller, dullest. The "K" also differed by flaunting *wearability* — the sole AL park named after a person and among the majors' 10 *sans* corporate name: their sixth-oldest field, hosting the 1973 and 2012 All-Star Game and World Series in 1980, 1985, 2014, and 2015. It prized the *history* of cathedrals like Fenway Park and Wrigley Field while adding *modernity*, renovated for $250 million in 2007-09 ($281 million now), including a new Royals Hall of Fame.[29] The result was *flexibility*: "The Royals are a small market," announcer Fred White said, explaining Kauffman's initial faster-draining AstroTurf. "Artificial turf cuts rainouts. We need to draw from hundreds of miles away."[30] For two decades the Royals drew heavily from the Mountain Time Zone, which lacked one big-league team, until the NL gave a 1993 expansion team to Denver.

[Bud Deck at Sunset Kauffman Stadium]

Overnight this made AstroTurf less necessary, letting famed Royals groundskeeper George Toma get high on grass. The greatest-ever Royal, George Brett, once said, "When a lot of people turn a certain age, they want to do certain things. Some people retire from being an accountant and all they want to do is play golf. Some people retire from being a doctor and all they want to do is fish. George Toma never retired. All he wants to do is work on fields. That's why he's the best groundskeeper in the world."[31] In fact, he retired at 70 full-time in 1999, but Brett's point rang. In 2012, Toma was an inaugural inductee in the Major League Baseball Groundskeeper Hall of Fame.[32] George still consults, a quarter-century after the Royals freed baseball's best in his field to tend grass at Kauffman beyond the cutaway [base] areas and Baja 125-foot forest beyond left-center field. Toma mixed five strains of bluegrass and one kind of rye, "The K" looking less new-age model than baseball park. Grass fit a park already deified in print and by the public. For one thing, the backstop was only 60 feet from the plate. For another, the park was fair—originally, each pole, 330 feet; alleys, 387 (later, 375; again 387 in 2004); and center field, 410 (400 in 1995; 410 by 2004) – and height (a 12-foot-high outfield fence dropped to nine in 1995 and eight today).[33]

"Municipal Stadium had served its purpose. It was a 1930s structure," said Denny Matthews. "From the start, Kauffman was a palace."[34] A key Ewing Kauffman hire was Cedric Tallis, a California Angels executive who became Royals general manager and point man for the new park, which opened April 10, 1973, 39,464, braving 39 degrees as the Royals spanked Texas, 12-1. First/winning pitcher: Paul Splittorf. Batter: Dave Nelson. Hit: Amos Otis. Run: Fred Patek. Homer: John Mayberry.[35] Seventeen days later, Steve Busby threw K.C.'s first no-hitter in Detroit. The Royals hosted the All-Star Game (NL, 7-1) and drew 1,345,341 (almost doubling Municipal in 1972). Otis and Mayberry started by nationwide vote.[36] A visitor got there by Interstate 70, liked a baseball-high 22,000-slot parking lot, and saw inside the stadium from a car. A sea of red wowed a passerby. Three tiers soared above the infield. Dick Allen said he would not play on its surface, since his horse could not eat off its *faux*, not real, grass.[37]

[Kauffman Stadium Fountains]

Inside, the park's symbol towered atop an incline beyond the outfield fence – a $2.7 million 12-story high crown-shaped scoreboard, with the Royals insignia, using more than 16,000 light bulbs. Beneath and to one side a 322-foot-side water complex cost $750,000 – the largest privately-funded fountain in the world – one 10-foot waterfall from an upper cascade pool serving as a backdrop for two water fountain pools, each 40 feet wide, and ending in front with five 10-foot-high horseshoe falls. As volume swelled, water rose, 19 pumps circulating 70,000 cubic feet. Nearly 700 500-watt lamps lit up to 50,000 gallons sailing skyward at a time[38] – noise seldom looked so fine. The Royals made postseason seven times in 1976-85, then had just one winning year from 1995-2012. For 28 straight seasons — 1986-2013 — K.C. missed even a wild-card berth. In 2014-15, it made and won the World Series, respectively. *W* or *L*, the fountain was there — also, the team's oneness with fundamental baseball, Kauffman built for hit 'em where they ain't, not sluggers treating its dimensions like a miniature golf arcade.

At Royals, the outfield egressed quickly from each pole, becoming a classic alley, almost National League, yard. In 1976, Brett trumped in triples, total bases, hits, and average, edging mate Hal McRae, .333 to .332, on a last at-bat inside-the-park homer. K.C. won its first division, infielders Patek and Cookie Rojas partying in the fountain. The League Championship Series (LCS) followed: New York, in a maximum best-of-five. "The Royals knew they'd be back," said Matthews — and were.[39] In 1977, Dennis Leonard (20-12), McRae (54 doubles), and Patek (53 steals) led the AL. If September waxed — a post-1953-high bigs 16-game win streak — for too long October waned. K.C. took a 2-1 LCS set edge, Mid-America atwitter, before New York won Game Four, whereupon the Royals led the final, 3-2, in the ninth inning, till "they hit us with three," said skipper Whitey Herzog. "It went slow motion." Patek cried in the dugout. K.C. again seemed the "Yankees' cousins"[40] — in 1978, too, the stripes beating their putative kin a third straight season in what seem "almost ... adventure chapters in a serialized novel," Stan Isaacs wrote of a kindred context.[41] That year Brett and McRae ranked 1-2 in doubles. Next year Willie Wilson whipped a most-since-1925 five-inside-the-park dingers in a season. Factors aiding speed included but were not limited to soft outfield padding, which contained drives in each foul corner; curving corners, fueling unpredictability and making it hard to guess the carom; and an almost concrete warning track, which kangarooed high hops off the wall past the fielder back toward the infield.

In 1980, Brett hit past and through it, averaging .390. As the Denny Matthews chapter tells, in the LCS Brett and the Royals finally made up for lost time. The World Series began with the Phillies accentuating the positive, 7-6 and 6-4. K.C. then won Game Three, 4-3, at Royals, Brett and Otis homering. Next day Willie Aikens homered twice for the home team to deep right field: 5-3. Kansas City led Game Five, 3-2, in the ninth inning, whereupon Del Unser and Manny Trillo drove in runs, pivoting the Classic, Tug McGraw over Dan Quisenberry, 4-3. Back at Veterans Stadium, the Phillies took a 4-1 edge into the ninth inning, McGraw loading the bases. Frank White fouled near the first-base dugout, catcher Bob Boone almost dropping the ball that Pete Rose nearby caught with his bare hand. At 11:29 p.m. ET, the 97-year-old Phillies won their first title, 4-1. The 12-year-old Royals lay ahead.

Once rain delays bred thousands of sawed web-worm moths, a frogman cleaning the right-center field pond. Left field promised a George Hamilton fan. A Heartlander mixed barbecue beef and local Boulevard beer. After each game a water show took exactly 9 minutes, 58 seconds. Before it the A's and Yankees usually sold out; box and reserved seats, gone for even the Brewers. By this time Middle America slowly sensed the Royals becoming the king of baseball's hill. On August 8, 1983, a regular-season record 42,039 saw them split a twi-night twin-bill with Milwaukee. At Yankee Stadium, Brett wafted a ninth-inning July 24 homer for a 5-4 victory but was called out because pine tar on his bat topped 18 inches, violating Rule 1.10 (b). Enraged, he bolted from the dugout like a lynx on speed.[42] For the first time an AL president (Lee MacPhail) overruled an umpire (Tim McClelland). The "Pine Tar Game" resumed on August 18, McRae making out to end the Royals' ninth. The Quiz retired the Yanks 1-2-3 before 1,245 in New York.

"It's tough to make predictions, especially about the future," Yogi Berra said.[43] The Hall of Famer might have reconsidered, had he seen the 1984 Royals win the East and lose a taut LCS to ultimate world titlist Detroit, 8-1, 5-3 in 11 innings, and 1-0. "You could see us coming," said Matthews. "Two of the three games were really close."[44] The pattern continued after an Opening Day record 41,086 greeted K.C. vs. Toronto April 8, 1985. (Other records: day, 41,329, Oakland, September 21, 1980; night, 41,860, New York, July 26, 1980.) Behind the Angels till September, the Royals won the West in the regular season's next-to-last set; trailed Toronto in the LCS, three games to one, and took three straight for the AL flag. In the World Series, Kansas City's habit of waiting lingered: losing three of the first four matches; beating St. Louis, 6-1, in Game Five; then using a 10th-inning pinch-single by Dane Iorg. "And there's a looper to right field for a base hit!" said ABC's Al Michaels. "[Onix] Concepcion scores! Here comes [Jim] Sundberg! Here comes the throw! He scores! And we go to the seventh!"[45] – the Royals surviving a Game Six of quiet desperation; a 2-1 near-death.

In Game Seven, K.C. scored three runs in the third inning and six in the fifth, imminent AL Cy Younger Bret Saberhagen scattered five hits and Brett reaped four, and the Cardinals batted a Series worst-ever .185. Romping, 11-0, the Royals avenged defeat in the 1976-77-78-84 league playoff, 1981 divisional series, and 1980 Series – only the fifth Classic team to U-turn a 3-1 set deficit and first after losing the first two games at home, taking their first title in the franchise's seventeenth year. Randy Galloway of the *Dallas Morning News* opined: "Move it on over, you Mets of '69. Way over. Go to the history board and rip out a page about the Miracle Braves of '14. And don't let anyone tell you about the Giants' Miracle of Coogan's Bluff in '51. The Royals of '85 are in an upset class of their own."[46]

Later, Michaels mused, "[Dick] Howser is to Billy Martin what the Salvation Army is to the SWAT team."[47] A brain tumor took Howser's life in 1987, his 404 victories behind only Ned Yost and Herzog among Royals skippers. Kevin Seitzer whacked a team six hits in a game vs. Boston. Saberhagen won another Cy Young in 1989. At 37, Brett won his third batting title – the sole player with 3,000 hits, 300 home runs, 600 doubles, 100 triples, and 200 steals. Under "all fame is fleeting," George got his 3,000th hit on September 30, 1992 – and was promptly picked off first base. Renamed Kauffman boasted a new JumboTron video-display board, amusement area with pitching booth, Royal Courtyard picnic and music area, and Fan-A-Gram, timing 14 tarp crew members cleaning up the infield after the home half of the fifth inning. All showed ownership's commitment to keeping the park up-to-date. Always in vogue there were famed barbeque and locally beloved Belfonte ice cream, the latter born, like the Royals, in 1969.[48] Sadly, across 1986-2014, nothing helped K.C. contend.

At first the patient deceptively seemed healthy, drawing a *still* record 2,477,700 (1989) attendance. The longer the illness lasted, the worse the condition turned. From 2004-12 the realigned AL Central team six times finished last, including 2005's Death Valley 56-106. Yet as its present got lousier, the future got ritzier. On April 4, 2006, Jackson County, Missouri, OK'd a 3/8 cent sales tax ballot for revenue to renovate the Truman Sports Complex.[49] A second proposal on the ballot for a portable roof was defeated.[50] Park renovation began with October 3, 2007 groundbreaking, complete by Opening Day 2009.[51] It continued an age of ballpark evolution begun in 1992 by Oriole Park at Camden Yards and 21 later "retro" parks trying to outdo the first's pastiche of quirk and angle—ivy backdrop like Wrigley Field, arched façade like old Comiskey Park, and right-field scoreboard like Ebbets Field.[52]

Again, Kauffman Stadium became the exception, not rule, *its* evolution siring a more contemporaneous yet even cozier feel than the original. Unlike others, it needed less a *new* park than to make a fine park *better*, adding a new high definition scoreboard a.k.a. "Crown Vision," themed restaurant, Hall of Fame and conference center, better concession, circulation, and concourse, and some seating closer to the field – thus, lower (37,903) capacity and better supply and demand.[53] The $8.3 million 84 feet wide by 105 feet tall high-definition scoreboard was among the first features installed.[54] It replaced the matrix board shaped like the team logo since the park's birth, was operated by 17 staffers on game day, and vaunted the world's then-largest HD LED display, since exceeded by Seattle's Safeco Field.[55] (Since 2008, a crown has graced it, strobe lights atthe top flashing each Royals home run.) About this time the team hailed its patrimony by placing four life-style bronze statues in the outfield plaza beyond the fountains – Ewing Kauffman and wife Muriel, waving; Brett, awaiting a pitch, bat cocked, right foot slightly raised; Howser, standing on the dugout steps; second baseman Frank White, artfully turning a double play.[56] Nearby is a site where youth practice their own pitch, field, and hit, including "a base path kids can run and be timed on," read the *Toronto Globe & Mail"* – "'Little K,' a miniature baseball field where big-league dreams are spawned ..!" What especially wowed Navin Vanswani, he wrote in 2018, were employees everywhere, saying, "Welcome to the K!"[57]

At Kauffman, Brett's statue is a cynosure. At Cooperstown, No. *5* is the sole member of the Baseball Hall of Fame and Museum whose plaque's cap reads *KC*. Seven more with another cap on their plaque spent part of a career in Kansas City: designated hitters Orlando Cepeda and Harmon Killebrew, skippers Joe Gordon, Herzog, and Bob Lemon, pitcher Gaylord Perry, and (no cap) General Manager John Schuerholz. At the Hall, Negro League baseball is ubiquitous, caps on Willard Brown's and Bullet Rogan's plaques hailing the Kansas City Monarchs. Other Monarch Negro Leaguers are: Cool Papa Bell, Andy Cooper, Jose Mendez, Satchel Paige, Jackie Robinson, Hilton Smith, Turkey Stearnes, Cristóbal Torriente, Willie Wells, and owner J.L. Wilkinson.[58] Buck O'Neil plays a special role. At Kauffman, the Royals fete the 1937-55 Monarch by placing a red seat among the blues behind home plate. Each game, said an official, a person "who embodies [his] spirit is selected from community nominees to sit" in the seat occupied by O'Neil. In 2007, Hall of Fame officials lauded the recently deceased's career by creating the Buck O'Neil Lifetime Achievement Award.[59] In 2012, Buck was evoked anew at the All-Star Game at Kauffman, the NL again winning, 8-0, as it had at Royals in 1973, 7-1. An All-Star guest could also see the Home Run Derby, All-Star Futures Game, and Taco Bell Legends and Celebrity Softball Game.

Next year's Royals topped .500 for the first time since 2003. Still, by July 21, 2014, Kansas City's postseason absence seemed same/safe again—almost three decades and counting/mounting. The 48-50 team trailed the Central lead by eight games when inexplicably it staged a 22-5 revival, temporarily took first place, and finished a game behind Detroit—even as amateur baseball historian Dave Webster, as historical figure "KayCee Baseball," began placing a blue *W* to mark each home victory under the Hall of Fame star on the ballpark roof, like Chicago hoisting a white flag with a blue *W* at Wrigley Field.[60] On cue, the Royals' first postseason since 1985, a home wild-card game – against all odds and teams, the *A*'s – became as wild as a heart should brave, Salvador Perez's 12th-inning single turning a once-7-3 hole into 9-8 glee.[61] K.C. then swept the favored Angels in the Division Series (DS). In the opener, Mike Moustakas's 11th-frame poke broke a two-all tie. A day later the Royals set a big-league postseason mark with three straight wins in overtime. Denny Matthews, who had seen it all, hadn't. "What role reversal!" he said. "And all since late July!"[62] The DS Series sweep brought relief – an 8-3 laugher.

Next, another favorite: Baltimore, in the LCS. In the opener, visiting K.C. bombed two 10th-frame homers, winning, 8-6 – in five 2014 postseason games of eight extra innings, a big-league record four dingers. Set Two scripted a different play, Lorenzo Cain's four inside-the-park hits fueling a 6-4 decision. The Royals came home up, two games to none. Pitching kept the O's down: Jason Frasor and Jason Vargas each won, 2-1. Dating to October 1985, the Royals had now taken *another* record: 11 straight postseason sets. The 2014 Fall Classic began less kindly, Giants starter Madison Bumgarner sailing, 7-1, before things began to ricochet, like ping pong or debate over Donald Trump. The Royals answered: 7-2, next, moving west, 3-2. Form then reemerged: 'Jints, 11-4, and behind Bumgarner again, 5-0. Back home, Yordano Ventura started in a 10-0 rout. The best of Game Seven's seven pitchers was Mighty Mouse to save the day – Bumgarner's five scoreless relief frames three days after a 117-pitch shutout: up in the ninth inning, 3-2, getting Perez to foul to Pablo Sandoval with the tying run on third base: game, and Classic, done.

How to pop the cork? For K.C., win the *next* World Series. Having endured one stopper, lacked their own, and needing what Earl Weaver termed "deep depth," the 2015 Royals dealt mid-year for pitcher Johnny Cueto and Ben Zobrist (Utility) Superstar. First, Kansas City finished 95-67 to gain home-field edge. In the DS, it eyed the chasm, down, 2-1, to Houston in games and 6-2 in the eighth inning of Game Four before scoring five runs to survive, 9-6. Warranting his addition, Cueto took a 7-2 final. In the LCS opener, Edinson Volquez beat Toronto, 5-0. Next day *another* five-spot erased the Royals' fourth multirun debt, K.C., 6-3. The best game was the sixth. Zobrist and Moustakas homered: 2-0. In the eighth inning, the Blue Jays tied at three. After a long rain delay preceded the home half, Cain reached first base on a walk, then raced around the bases to score the decisive 4-3 run on Eric Hosmer's single. Enos Slaughter scored the same-score run from first on a *double* to win the 1946 World Series, though memory often disagrees. The lauded 1974 Mobil Oil Corp. book *The Way It Was* refers to "Harry Walker hits single."

The Royals' prize was to meet another expansion team in the 111th World Series – the New York Mets, hatched in 1962 – whose first manager had been Casey Stengel, born Kansas City in 1890. "The trick is growing up without growing old," the Perfessor said.[63] By Series end, anyone who had ever rooted for the Royals must have felt age five. George Brett threw out the first ball at the opener, which took five hours and nine minutes, tying the longest-inning (14) Series game with 1916 and 2005.[64] The Royals starter, Volquez, lasted six innings, learning upon exiting that his father had died earlier that day. K.C.'s Alcides Escobar hit Matt Harvey's initial pitch for an inside-the-park home run –f irst in an Oktoberfest since 1929's Mule Haas.[65] In the 14th inning, Hosmer's sacrifice fly scored Escobar with the winning run. Having tallied his team's *first* run on the *first pitch*, Alcides plated its *last* run on the *last* pitch. The victor was the Royals' seventh pitcher, Chris Young. Next night they took a 2-0 set lead, Cueto hurling a complete 7-1 game of two hits. In Game Three, the Mets won for the only time, 9-3, at Citi Field: seven pitchers yielded 12 hits, David Wright and Curtis Granderson going yard.

Next evening, behind, two games to one, New York evoked the hapless 1962 Amazins' that made Casey say, "Can't anybody here play this game?"[66] Kansas City rallied in the eighth inning on two walks by Tyler Clippard, Daniel Murphy's crucial error, and run-produced singles by Moustakas and Perez to score thrice and give Jeurys Familia a blown save and the Royals a 5-3 victory. Game Five on November 1 was as tense, taking 12 innings and four hours and 15 minutes. Needing to win to return west, the Mets took a 2-0 lead. In the ninth inning, the Royals rallied – again. Cain drew a leadoff walk off starter Harvey. Hosmer, then scored him with a double. Manager Terry Collins brought in Familia, who got Moustakas to ground out, Hosmer advancing to third base. The game pivoted on Perez's grounder to third baseman Wright. The Mets captain, hurt earlier in the year, checked Eric toward the bag, then threw to first baseman Lucas Duda, who made the second out as Hosmer's two-all run broke for home.

Hurrying the throw, Duda flung wildly: two-all, forcing more extra innings. In the 12th inning, Perez singled, Jarrod Dyson pinch-running. Christian Colon singled, Escobar and Cain each doubled, Paulo Orlando reached on another Murphy muff, and Zobrist was intentionally walked, each scoring. To much of the Mets' crowd, the Royals' half-inning could have mimed "The Twelfth of Never"'s[67] "and that's a long, long time": final, 7-2, *another* five-spot profited winning pitcher Luke Hochevar. Wade Davis, postseason's definition of "deep depth," fanned Wilmer Flores to end the Series: in three games, four innings, three hits, and one save. K.C. outhit the Mets, .239 to .139. Perez batted .364 with eight hits and two doubles; Moustakas, .307, seven hits, and three RBIs; Zobrist, .261, six hits, four doubles, and 5 five runs; and Cain and Escobar, below or barely above .230, respectively, but teaming for 11 hits, seven runs, and eight RBIs.

On Tuesday, November 3, a day and a half after the final out, about 800,000 people of different age, race, and sex jammed downtown for the largest parade in Kansas City's history, waving hats, flags, and signs—"Thanks, Comeback Kids" referencing their record-setting eight postseason come-from-behind *Ws*.[68] The day went deep from the time it began in the Power and Light District till ending 2.3 miles later[69] at a rally at Union Station – one pickup truck after another, carrying players; cheers rippling from each side of the road; speeches following, politicians largely blessing by their absence – so suggestive of baseball's heartland Pleasantville that those beaten in the past month – the Astros and Blue Jays and Mets – had to smile at its success. It was a family feeling – different in look perhaps than that which Harry and Bess Truman bestowed sixty years earlier when they welcomed big-league baseball to Kansas City – but the same feeling, nonetheless.[70]

Sources

I wish to thank Dan Levitt for letting me read in advance his fine chapter on Ewing Kauffman which appears elsewhere in this book. My gratitude to Steve Friedman for reading my early draft, making suggestions, and letting me see his excellent early draft of a Kauffman Stadium biography. Mike Swanson, the Royals' Vice President, Communications & Broadcasting, was very helpful in finding material on Royals Stadium's birth. Grateful appreciation is made to reprint all play-by-play and color radio text courtesy of John Miley's The Miley Collection. In addition to the sources cited in the Notes, most especially the Society for American Baseball Research, the author also consulted: Baseball-Reference.com and Retrosheet.org websites box scores, player, season, and team pages, batting and pitching logs, and other material relevant to this history. FanGraphs.com provided statistical information. In addition to the sources cited in the Notes, the author also consulted:

Books

Coffin, Tristram Potter. *The Old Ball Game: Baseball in Folklore and Fiction* (New York: Herder and Herder, 1971).

Lowry, Philip L. *Green Cathedrals: The Ultimate Celebration of Major and Negro League Ballparks* (New York: Walker and Company, 2006).

Macht, Norman L. *Connie Mack and the Early Years of Baseball* (Lincoln, Nebraska: University of Nebraska Press, 1991).

O'Connell, Kevin and Josh Pahigian. *The Ultimate Baseball Road Trip: A Fan's Guide to Major League Stadiums* (Guilford, Connecticut: Lyons Press, 2012).

Rickey, Branch, and Robert Riger. *The American Diamond* (New York: Simon and Schuster, 1965).

Seymour, Harold. *Baseball: The People's Game* (New York: Oxford University Press, 1990).

Smith, Curt. *Storied Stadiums: Baseball's History Through Its Ballparks.* (New York: Carroll & Graf, 2001).

Westcott, Rich. *Philadelphia's Old Ballparks* (Philadelphia: Temple University Press, 1996).

Newspapers

The *Kansas City Star* has been a primary source of information about Royals, later Kauffman, Stadium. Other key sources include: Associated Press, *Baseball Digest*, *Chicago Tribune*, *SportsBusiness Daily*, *St. Joseph News-Press*, *The Sporting News*, *Toronto Globe and Mail*, and *USA Today*.

Magazines

Forbes SportsMoney

Interviews

Steve Blass, with author, March 2017.

Curt Gowdy, with author, May 1993.

Merle Harmon, with author, August 1995.

Denny Matthews, with author, February 2007; November 2015; and August 2018.

Mike Swanson, with author, October 2018.

Fred White, with author, May 1998.

Bob Wolff, with author, February 2012.

Notes

1 Bob Wolff interview with author, February 2012.

2 Denny Matthews interview with author, August 2018.

3 Bill Shannon and George Kalinsky, *The Ballparks* (New York: Hawthorn, 1975), 111.

4 *1955 American League Red Book.*

5 *Sports Illustrated*, April 14, 1958, 66.

6 Curt Gowdy interview with author, May 1993.

7 https://trumanlibrary.org. Harry S. Truman Presidential Library and Museum.

8 Wolff February 2012 interview.

9 http://www.firstladies.org/blog/first-ladies-at-the-old-ballgame/.

10 Gerry Van der Heuvel, "Remembering Bess," *Washington Post*, October 19, 1982. https://www.washingtonpost.com/archive/life-style/1982/10/19/remembering-bess./3ad55764-5296-4dd5-Bef1-8b2464067456/?utm_term=.fe21d025e32d.Thearticleerrantlysays that Margaret Truman was wed the day of the 1956 A's home opener. It was the day after.

11 Denny Matthews interview with author, August 2018.

12 Merle Harmon interview with author, August 1995.

13 Ibid.

14 https://ballparks.com/baseball/America/kcymun.htm.

15 Mark Armour, "Charlie Finley," Society for American Baseball Research. https://sabr.org/bioproj/person/6ac2ee2f.

16 Steve Blass appearance at broadcast media panel of Society of American Baseball Research convention, Pittsburgh, June 1, 2018.

17 https://broadwaymusicalhome.com/shows/oklahoma.htm.

18 John Bartlett, *Bartlett's Familiar Quotations*. Revised and enlarged, Fifteenth and 125th Anniversary Edition. (Boston: Little, Brown, 1980), 770.

19 www.royalsreview.com/2013/4/10/today-in-royals-history-royals-stadium. Craig Brown, "Kauffman Stadium Turns 40," Royals Review, April 10, 2013. www.royalsreview.com/2013/4/10/today-in-royals-history-royals-stadium.

20 Ibid.

21 Shannon and Kalinsky, *The Ballparks*, 111.

22 Allan T. Demaree, "Ewing Kauffman Sold Himself Rich in Kansas City," *Fortune*, October 1972, 101.

23 http://kxrb.com/how-did-the-kansas-city-royals-get-their-name/.

24 https://www.royalsreview.com/2018/4/12/17230714/here-are-your-favorite-kansas-city-royals. Bradford Lee, "Here Are Your 1969 Kansas City Royals," *Royals Review*, April 12, 2018, cover.

25 Ibid.

26 Mike Swanson interview with author, October 2018.

27 https://kansascity.royals.mlb.com/kc/history/ballparks/jsp. Official Royals Website: "Kauffman Stadium History."

28 Kevin O'Connell and Josh Pahigian, *The Ultimate Baseball Road Trip: A Fan's Guide to Major League Stadiums* (Guilford, Connecticut: Lyons Press, 2012).

29 https://kansascity.royals.mlb.com/kc/history/ballparks.

30 Fred White interview with author, May 1998.

31 Ian Wiseman, *The Harbinger Online*, December 16, 2009. https://smeharbinger.net/legendary-groundskeeper-George-Toma.

32 Dick Kaegel, "KC legend Toma earns groundskeeping honor," MLB.com, January 10, 2012.

33 https://kansascity.royals.mlb.com/kc/history/ballparks.jsp.

34 Denny Matthews interview with author, November 2015.

35 *The Sporting News Official Major League Baseball Fact Book 2001 Edition.* (St. Louis: The Sporting News Co.., 2001), 380.

36 https://kansascityroyals.mlb.com/kc/history/all_stars.

37 http://www.baseball-almanac.com/quotes/quoalin.schtml. "If a horse won't eat it, I don't want to play on it," said Dick Allen.

38 https://kansascity.royals.mlb.com/kc/history/ballparks.jsp.

39 Denny Matthews interview with author, November 2015.

40 Official Major League Baseball Fact Book 2001 Edition, 326. www.worldcat.org/title/official-major-league-baseball-fact-book.

41 www.worldcat.org/...was-great-sports-events-from-the-past/oclc/9158206. Stan Isaacs, The Last Subway Series: New York Yankees/Brooklyn Dodgers World Series, October, 1956," George Vecsey. Ed., The Way It Was (New York: McGraw-Hill, 1974), 174.

42 *Official Major League Baseball Fact Book 2001 Edition*, 332.

43 www.goodreads.com/author/quotes/79014.Yogi Berra.

44 Denny Matthews interview with author, November 2015.

45 Play-by-play courtesy of The Miley Collection

46 Randy Galloway, "Move It On Over," *Dallas Morning News*, October 29, 1985.

47 https://www.si.com/vault/issue/43503/35, *Sports Illustrated* staff, "Octobercasts Well Worth Celebrating."

48 https://www.thrillist.com/eat/nation/mlb-baseball-stadium-fast-food-snacks.

49 http://kansascity.royals.mlb.com/kc/history/ballpark_milestones.jsp.

50 https://www.revolvy.com/page/Kauffman-Stadium.

51 Ibid.

52 https://www.ballparksofbaseball.com/ballparks/camden-yards/.

53 https://www.revolvy.com/page/Kauffman-Stadium.

54 Ibid., footnote 12, "Daktronics Installs Largest HD Dish for Kansas City Royals," October 4, 2007."

55 Ibid., footnote 13, "Royals Fans to Watch Highlights and Replays on World's Largest HD Display"; 14, "Baseball Stadiums by the Board," *Chicago Tribune*, April 14, 2012; and 15, "Royals scoreboard is a vision of the future," *Kansas City Star*, April 8, 2008.

56 Navin Vasmani, "They're Real and They're Spectacular," *Toronto Globe and Mail*, May 8, 2018. Artist Harry Weber forged the statues of Dick Howser, Ewing and Muriel Kauffman, and Frank White. Artist Kwan Wu did George Brett's.

57 Ibid.

58 www.baseballhall.org. National Baseball Hall of Fame and Museum.

59 Ibid.

60 https://www.kctv5.com/a-great-nine-year-run---kaycee-the-w/article_3329db6f-f279-576b-8666-2596f11935213.html.Websterwas dismissed by KBMC Television, Kansas City, the "KayCee Baseball" tradition sadly ended. April 29, 2018.

61 https://kingsofkauffman.com. October 1, 2014.

62 Denny Matthews interview with author, November 2015.

63 https://www.brainyquote.com/authors/casey_stengel.

64 Ted Berg, "10 Crazy Facts About the Royals and Mets' Crazy Game 1," USA Today, October 28, 2015, 1Sports.

65 https://www.baseball-almanc-com/ws/yr2015ws.shtml.

66 http://www.baseball-almanac.com/quotes/quosteng.shtml . Originally, this quotation was more often and perhaps properly cited as the Perfessor's response to the 1962 expansion Mets: "Can't anybody play this here game!?"—an example of Casey's use of the language he was said to invent, Stengelese.

67 Julia Obert, *Postcolonial Overtures: The Politics of Sound in Contemporary Northern Irish Poetry* (reprinted). Poetry (Syracuse, New York: Syracuse University Press, 2015, retrieved 2017), 44. "The Twelfth of Never," written by Jerry Livingston and Paul Francis Webster in 1956.

68 Ryan Bort, "All of the Royals' Postseason Come-from-Behind Wins, Ranked from Least to Most Marvelous," *Newsweek*, November 2, 2018"—DS Game Four so seemingly decided that Texas Governor Greg Abbott prematurely hailed the Astros on making the ALCS.

69 https://www.mlb.com/news/royals-win-world-series/c-156205900.

70 The Truman Presidential Library and Museum has staged numerous baseball exhibits, including 2012's tribute to presidential-baseball history. https://trumanlibrary.org. Ibid

SYMINGTON'S REVENGE – BASEBALL RETURNS TO KANSAS CITY APRIL 8, 1969: KANSAS CITY ROYALS 4, MINNESOTA TWINS 3 (12 INNINGS) AT MUNICIPAL STADIUM

BY KEN CARRANO

Senator William Stuart Symington of Missouri was a fighter. A second lieutenant during World War I, he eventually became the first secretary of the Air Force, serving fellow Missourian Harry S Truman. After being elected to the Senate in 1952, Symington was a strong opponent of Senator Joseph McCarthy, took on the Pentagon over wasteful spending, and later opposed the Vietnam War. So when Kansas City A's owner Charlie Finley decided to move the Athletics from Kansas City, Symington saw another fight coming. On the Senate floor, Symington described Finley as "one of the most disreputable characters ever to enter the American sports scene."

Symington's appearance at the American League owners meeting in Chicago in 1967 and his threats to have Congress review baseball's antitrust exemption helped get Kansas City an expansion franchise for the 1969 season. The city would be without baseball for a year but, according to Symington, "This loss is more than recompensed for by the pleasure resulting from our getting rid of Mr. Finley." And Finley was most definitely gone. "There will be no parades down Main Street or promises of instant success, the sheep are gone from Lamb Chop Hill behind the outfield fence, and conservative blue and white uniforms have replaced Kelly green and gold."

In a year that promised firsts and new faces, something that wasn't new was the Royals manager, Joe Gordon. The manager of the Athletics in 1960, Gordon had the unenviable task of leading an expansion team filled with expansion-team players. "I'll have 16 different lineups before we open," Gordon told the *Minneapolis Star*. Making his major-league debut as a manager for the Twins on Opening Day in Kansas City was Billy Martin. The fiery Martin would lead the Twins to the newly formed American League West Division title in 1969 but would lose to Baltimore in the AL playoffs and be fired shortly thereafter.

Opening Days are always special, and for a new team in town, the pregame ceremonies are a time for speeches. First to speak was Royals owner Ewing Kauffman, who was greeted with a lengthy standing ovation. Once the crowd settled, Kauffman brought them to their feet again, stating, "As long as I am alive, this will be your team, forever and ever." American League President Joe Cronin, whose greeting was less enthusiastic due to the turmoil over the A's relocation, spoke next, and then Symington addressed the crowd. After telling the crowd that he was looking forward to the time in the not-so-distant future when there would be an all-Missouri World Series, he bounced the ceremonial first pitch to Royals catcher Ellie Rodriguez. Symington would leave the Senate in 1976, nine years before the first all-Missouri World Series he had hoped to see. With the ceremonies over, baseball could finally return to Kansas City.

Wally Bunker got the honor of throwing the first pitch in Royals history. Bunker was selected by the Royals from Baltimore in the expansion draft (skipping over Jim Palmer), and he retired the Twins in order in the first inning. Leading off the first for the Royals was Lou Piniella, who had been acquired from expansion partner Seattle toward the end of spring training. "We needed a right-handed hitter," explained Gordon simply. Piniella greeted Twins starter Tom Hall with a double down the left-field line. When Jerry Adair singled to left to score Piniella, the Royals had their first RBI and lead, and their faithful could be excused for thinking this baseball stuff was easy, at least the Royals version of it.

As was typical of expansion teams, though, the lead didn't last. After Bunker retired Harmon Killebrew to start the second inning, Graig Nettles homered to right field to tie the game. The score remained that way until the sixth inning, although both teams squandered chances in the fifth. The Twins led off the top of the fifth with a base hit by Rich Reese, but Reese was caught stealing second. Leo Cardenas then walked and John Roseboro singled to center, but Bunker retired the next two Twins to end that threat. The Royals had an even better chance to score in the bottom of the fifth when Bunker led off with a double to the right-field corner and moved to third on Piniella's third hit of the game. Adair followed with a fly to short center, but Bunker was held at third. Hall then retired Ed Kirkpatrick and Joe Foy to strand two runners in scoring position.

The Twins took the lead in the sixth but ran themselves out of a chance to score more. Rod Carew chased Bunker with a single to left, and Tony Oliva greeted reliver Tom Burgmeier with a single that moved Carew to third. Carew scored on Killebrew's groundout with Oliva taking second. Manager Martin brought in Cesar Tovar for Nettles, but Oliva was caught trying to steal third. Tovar singled to center, a hit that would likely have brought in the speedy Oliva. Reese followed with a double to score Tovar but was thrown out trying to stretch his hit to a triple.

The Twins brought their baserunning errors out to the field with them in the bottom of the sixth. With two out, Rodriguez hit a long fly to left field. Tovar, who had replaced Nettles in left, called for the ball but it carried over his head for a double. "You don't call someone off a ball to let it fall 10 feet behind you," Martin complained. Jackie Hernandez hit an easy grounder to Killebrew, who booted it, but did not incur Martin's wrath. "Killebrew made two exceptional fielding plays," Martin said. "Players are going to miss groundballs." In a meeting on the mound, Martin told Hall to throw curveballs to pinch-hitter Jim Campanis. After two curves and two strikes, Hall threw a fastball that Campanis drove to center to score Rodriguez. "I couldn't believe it when Hall threw a fastball down the middle on the next pitch. Hall's fastball was the pitch that lost the game for us," Martin said with his customary frankness. Martin replaced Hall with Bob Miller, who gave up Piniella's fourth hit of the game to tie the score, 3-3.

The score remained that way until the bottom of the 12th. After Ron Perranoski shut down the Royals for 5⅓ innings, Martin relieved him with Joe Grzenda to start the 12th. After one out, Foy beat out a grounder to deep short for a hit, although an error could have been charged. Foy went to second on Roseboro's passed ball, and Martin elected to intentionally walk Chuck Harrison. Both runners moved up on Grzenda's wild pitch, and Martin ordered Bob Oliver walked, loading the bases. Gordon brought in the Royals' leading hitter in the spring, Joe Keough, to face Grzenda. "I saved you for almost four hours, now go up there and rip one," Gordon told Keough. Keough took his manager's advice and hit the first pitch he saw over Oliva's head to end the game. "Keough's a real ripper," Gordon said after the game. "It was a tough game and I would have been disappointed if we lost it after battling all day long." Martin was understandably less pleased. "We beat ourselves," he said. "We had enough hard-hit balls to score nine runs in the first few innings. We made some mistakes, but there were two (in the sixth) that really killed us."

The Royals won another extra-inning, walk-off 4-3 win the next day, this time in 17 innings. But winning their first game was special. Gordon was asked what Ewing Kauffman said about the victory, and he answered, "The boss was too speechless for words."

Sources

In addition to the sources listed in the Notes, the author accessed Retrosheet.org and Baseball-Reference.com.

SECOND VERSE, SAME AS THE FIRST – ROYALS STAY UNDEFEATED APRIL 9, 1969: KANSAS CITY ROYALS 4, MINNESOTA TWINS 3 (17 INNINGS), AT MUNICIPAL STADIUM

BY KEN CARRANO

Opening Day is always a celebration, especially when it's your first one. Day two is usually just another day. For fans of the new team in town, though, excitement levels were still high, especially after they won their first game. The dignitaries had moved on, but there were still 161 games to be played, and the young Kansas City Royals were determined to enjoy them. However, after this 17-inning affair, which followed a 12-inning game the day before, everyone could have used a break.

Starting for the Royals was Roger Nelson, their first pick in the 1968 expansion draft. The right-hander had started six games for the Baltimore Orioles in 1968 and had an impressive 2.41 ERA in 71 innings. Countering for the Twins was the veteran Jim Kaat, only three years removed from leading the American League in wins. Kaat had been nursing a sore elbow, but Twins skipper Billy Martin was counting on him. "We need his pitching to win the Western Division," Martin said.[1]

The first couple of innings were uneventful. Nelson walked Twins leadoff batter Ted Uhlaender but retired the next six hitters, three by strikeout. Kaat was perfect through the first two innings. Nelson lost his control in the third and it was costly. The inning started with a walk to leadoff batter George Mitterwald, who moved to second on Uhlaender's single with one out. Rod Carew singled to center to score Mitterwald, and after a popout by Tony Oliva, Harmon Killebrew also walked to load the bases. Graig Nettles followed with a hard smash to Royals shortstop Jackie Hernandez, who booted it. Uhlaender scored easily, but Carew, trying to score from second, was cut down by Hernandez at the plate, limiting the damage to two runs.

The Royals got on the board the next inning. After Kaat struck out Jerry Adair, consecutive singles by Ed Kirkpatrick, Joe Foy, and Chuck Harrison plated a run. With Jim Campanis up, Foy stole third, and then scored on Campanis's fly to deep right. Twins manager Martin, never a fan of umpires, was unhappy that Harrison was called safe returning to first. "Tony (Oliva) made a great throw to Rich Reese at first and I thought Chuck Harrison was out by a wide margin. Martin said. "The ball beat Harrison to the bag but Marty Springstead called him safe."[2] Kaat walked Bob Oliver but ended the inning by getting Hernandez to foul out. The tie lasted for only two batters. Carew led off the fifth with a sharp double to left and made it to third on Oliva's fly to center. With Killebrew up, Carew stole home. "This is only the second time I have stolen home in the last two seasons," Carew recalled. "I got a big jump on the pitcher and made it easy."[3]

The Royals went to their bullpen in the sixth and started an impressive string of relief pitching. Steve Jones, Bill Butler, Moe Drabowsky, and Tom Burgmeier combined for 12 scoreless innings pitched with only five hits and two walks. That much relief pitching wasnecessary because the Royals tied the game in the eighth inning.

Besides the tying run, the eighth provided controversy, in the Twins half of the inning. With one out, Nettles singled off Butler, and Cesar Tovar ran for him. Tovar attempted to steal second but was called out by umpire Don Denkinger, bringing forth the wrath of Martin, who claimed that Tovar was safe because he kicked the ball out of Hernandez's hand. "There shouldn't have been any doubt about it," Martin said. "Cesar was safe as far as I'm concerned."[4] Tovar said, "I was safe all the way. I hit the bag before he put the tag on me."[5] Denkinger said, "I called Tovar out a few seconds before Cesar kicked the ball. That's all there is to say."[6] In the bottom of the inning, Adair singled to center and went to second on shortstop Leo Cardenas's error on the throw-in. Pat Kelly ran for Adair, moved to third on Kirkpatrick's grounder to second, and scored on Foy's single to left. Foy was cut down trying to take an extra base, but the game was tied, and it would stay that way for some time.

Butler, making his major-league debut, was magnificent in relief, retiring the Twins in order from the ninth inning through the 12th. The Royals mounted threats in the 11th and 12th. In the 11th, with Jim Kaat still on the mound for the Twins, the Royals' Juan Rios led off with a single and took second on a wild pitch, but after Foy was intentionally walked, Harrison grounded into a double play. The Royals had a better chance in the 12th. Kaat walked leadoff batter Campanis and was replaced by Dave Boswell.[7] Boswell got Oliver to ground into a double play, but walked Hernandez, Mike Fiore (intentionally, after Hernandez stole second), and Lou Piniella to load the bases. Ron Perranoski replaced Boswell and got out of the jam when pinch-hitter Joe Keough bunted in front of the plate, forcing out Hernandez. "Keough bunted on his own," Royals manager Joe Gordon said.[8] "(Third baseman Frank Quilici) was back," Keough explained. "When you see something like that, you take a chance."[9]

Drabowsky relieved in the 13th and was nearly as effective as Butler, allowing three hits and a walk in his 4⅔-inning stint. Drabowsky was the winning pitcher on Opening Day and after pitching one inning the day before and 4⅔ in this one, he was out of gas. "Cleaned and pressed," Drabowsky said after the game. "I was done."[10] The Royals did not put up much of a fight for the next few innings. Gordon was ejected by umpire Springstead in the 14th after arguing a close play at first. "I said one word to him and he kicks me out," Gordon complained.[11] "Some of these umpires are sure touchy these days."[12]

The Royals finally ended the festivities in the bottom of the 17th. Hernandez walked with one out and moved to second on Burgmeier's grounder to second. Piniella, the Opening Day hero but hitless in six at-bats thus far in this game, singled to left, scoring Hernandez with the winning run and putting the Royals in first place two games into the young season. "(This was) better than the four (hits) yesterday, believe me," Piniella said. "Seventeen innings to get a base hit. I was thinking why I wasn't hitting the ball. I made up my mind I was going to wait as long as I could and just go with the pitch."[13] "Winning a ballgame like this is just the greatest thing that could happen to us," Gordon bubbled. "Our kids hustled and it paid off for them. They lost some chances, but they didn't let it get 'em down."[14]

The Royals had played 29 innings in their first two days of competition and won both games by 4-3 scores. In 1970 they played another 4-3, 17-inning game in 1970, defeating the Cleveland Indians. The Royals' longest games (through 2018) were 18-inning affairs against the Texas Rangers in May 1972 (loss) and June 1991 (win). The score of both games – you guessed it – 4-3.

Sources

In addition to the sources listed in the Notes, the author accessed Retrosheet.org and Baseball-Reference.com.

Notes

1 Paul O'Boynick, "Martin Kicks on Call," *Kansas City Star*, April 10, 1969: 20.

2 Ibid.

3 Ibid.

4 Ibid.

5 Ibid.

6 Ibid.

7 Kaat's 11 innings pitched were one of 15 outings of 11 or more innings in the major leagues in 1969, including a second one by Kaat on May 20, against the Orioles. The last outing of 11 or more innings in the majors was by Dave Stewart of Oakland on August 1, 1990, when he shut out the Seattle Mariners, 1-0. There have been only 44 occurrences of a pitcher going more than nine innings since Stewart's outing.

8 Sid Bordman, "Royals and Piniella Star in Late, Late Show," *Kansas City Star*, April 10, 1969: 20.

9 Ibid.

10 Ibid.

11 "Gordon Gets Quick Thumb in Dispute at First Base," *Emporia* (Kansas) Gazette, April 10, 1969.

12 Bordman.

13 Ibid.

14 Ibid.

GEORGE BRETT MAKES HIS MAJOR-LEAGUE DEBUT AUGUST 2, 1973: KANSAS CITY ROYALS 3, CHICAGO WHITE SOX 1, AT COMISKEY PARK

BY RUSSELL BERGTOLD

In late July of the 1973 season, Royals third baseman Paul Schaal suffered an ankle injury that sidelined him for 19 games.[1] Utility infielder Kurt Bevacqua filled in at the hot corner during Schaal's absence. Searching for a replacement, the Royals placed a call to their Triple-A team in Omaha, Nebraska. Around noon on August 2, George Brett and his roommates, catcher Buck Martinez and pitcher Mark Littell, were getting ready to grill some hamburgers for lunch when they heard a knock on the door. It was Omaha manager Harry Malmberg who came over to inform the tenants that one of them was headed to Chicago to join the Kansas City Royals. Brett and Martinez assumed it was going to be Littell.[2]

Instead it was George Brett. Brett, who had competed in the Triple-A All-Star Game a month earlier, was caught off-guard. Brett was told to skip the burgers, gather his stuff, and drive to Rosenblatt Stadium to get his baseball equipment. Brett arrived in Chicago around 5 P.M. By the time he got to Comiskey Park it was too late to take batting practice, which wasn't a big deal since Malmberg told Brett that he wouldn't be playing that night. However, Brett noticed that the lineup card had him playing third and batting eighth.[3]

The game-time temperature was a pleasant 70 degrees with a gentle breeze. Before a crowd of 11,775, the Royals were facing right-handed pitcher Stan Bahnsen, which might explain why they wanted to get Brett's left-handed bat in the lineup. In the top of the first, Kansas City jumped on Bahnsen for two runs. Freddie Patek led off with a walk. A single by Cookie Rojas sent him to third, and he scored when Amos Otis grounded into a force play at second. John Mayberry walked, sending Otis to second. With Gail Hopkins batting, Bahnsen tried to pick off Otis at second. When Otis broke toward third, White Sox third baseman Bill Melton couldn't handle the throw, allowing Otis to scamper home with the second run. Mayberry chugged to third, where he was stranded. Hopkins grounded out second to first, and Lou Piniella grounded out to third to end the inning.

With one out in the top of the second, Brett stepped up to the plate for the first time in the major leagues. With a batting stance that resembled Carl Yastrzemski's, he lined out to Bahnsen as the Royals went down in order.

In the bottom of the second, the White Sox were retired in order. Brett handled his first chance at third base when Buddy Bradford grounded to him for the second out of the inning.

In the bottom of the third, the White Sox scored a run when Luis Alvarado led off with a triple off Royals starter Dick Drago and scored on a fly ball to center by catcher Ed Herrmann. Pat Kelly singled but was thrown out trying to steal second, and Jorge Orta struck out to end the inning.

With the Royals ahead 2-1, Brett came up again in the top of the fourth with one out and blooped a broken-bat single to left field for his first major-league hit. He was out at second when Fran Healy grounded into a double play.

In the top of the seventh, Brett struck out looking as the Royals went down in order.

It remained 2-1 heading into the top of the ninth. With Bahnsen still on the mound, Piniella singled to left. Ed Kirkpatrick sacrificed Piniella to second. Brett's grounder to second advanced Piniella to third. Healy singled to center to drive in Piniella, but then was picked off first by Bahnsen for the third out.

The White Sox' Jerry Hairston led off the bottom of the ninth with a single, but Kansas City reliever Gene Garber retired the next three batters to earn a four-inning save.

The Royals victory, along with the Oakland Athletics' loss to the Minnesota Twins, gave Kansas City sole possession of first place in the American League Western Division.

Postscript

Schaal returned to the Royals lineup on August 14.

On August 17 the A's reclaimed first place from the Royals on their way to winning their third division title in a row.

Stan Bahnsen, who began the season with a 4-1 start, went on to finish with an 18-21 record. Along with teammate Wilbur Wood, who went 24-20, the two pitchers combined to start 90 games for the White Sox in 1973. As of 2018 it was the last time that a team had two 20-game losers in the same season.

In the week that followed Brett's debut, he started three games at third base. From August 9 to September 7, Brett rode the bench for 24 consecutive games. In the second game of a doubleheader on Saturday, September 8, he entered the game in the sixth inning as a pinch-runner for Schaal and remained in the game. He sat on the bench for the next 10 games until September 18, when he played the entire game. He played in seven more games down the stretch.

Brett finished the season with five hits and a .125 batting average in 40 at-bats. He went on to collect 3,149 more hits over the next 20 years to earn a plaque in the Baseball Hall of Fame.

Sources

In addition to the sources cited in the Notes, the author also consulted Baseball-Reference.com.

Notes

1 Sid Bordman, "Royals Find a Fresh Beef Supply ... in McRae's Bat," *The Sporting News*, September 1, 1973: 9.

2 "Becoming George Brett: From the Beach to Billings and Beyond," interview by the *Kansas City Star*: youtube.com/watch?v=gXq2qtrL-p8.

3 "Welcome to The Show: George Brett Called Up to the Royals," interview by the *Kansas City Star*: youtube.com/watch?v=lo58I-aZgUPM&index=2&list=PL02VuT_SObZKgXiAols9l1rcXCe0X16O6.

ROYALS CLINCH TIE FOR AMERICAN LEAGUE WESTERN DIVISION TITLE SEPTEMBER 29, 1976 KANSAS CITY ROYALS 4, OAKLAND ATHLETICS 0 AT OAKLAND-ALAMEDA COUNTY COLISEUM, OAKLAND

BY THOMAS M. KNOSBY

On September 29, 1976, the Kansas City Royals clinched at least a tie for the American League Western Division title by defeating the Oakland Athletics, 4-0. It was a night game played at the Oakland-Alameda County Coliseum in Oakland, California.

Coming into the game, the Royals had lost four straight and could ill afford to lose another; the A's had cut their lead to 2½ games with a 1-0 victory behind Mike Torrez's pitching and Sal Bando's solo home run off Royals starter Marty Pattin.

The Royals did receive a bit of good news shortly before the crucial game. If they and the A's ended the season in a tie for first place, they would host a one-game playoff on October 5. This was determined by a coin flip in the league office to which Royals manager Whitey Herzog responded, "Let's not worry about that now." Herzog said, "Tonight is the one we need."[1]

Larry Gura was the Royals' surprise starting pitcher. The A's sent Paul Mitchell to the mound in hopes they could continue to shut down the Royals offense with his pitching. A crowd of 19,631 fans was in attendance for what one could argue was the most important game of the season thus far for either team.

In the first inning both the Royals and the A's went down in order. The Royals put across the first run of the game in the top of the second inning. Hal McRae led off with a single to left field and John Mayberry singled to right field, moving McRae to third base. Al Cowens hit a line drive to A's first baseman Ron Fairly, who doubled up Mayberry. Then Cookie Rojas surprised the A's by laying down a bunt along the third-base line that scored McRae. John Wathan recorded the last out of the inning lining out to Fairly. The A's were kept in check by Gura in the second.

The Royals added two more runs in the third. Fred Patek led off with a double to left field and went to third as Tom Poquette bunted past the mound and beat it out. Amos Otis doubled into the right-field corner, driving in Patek. With runners at second and third and no outs, A's manager Chuck Tanner pulled Mitchell in favor of Paul Lindblad. George Brett grounded to Phil Garner at second base and Poquette scored on the putout, making the score 3-0. Lindblad then got McRae to line out to Bert Campaneris at shortstop and Mayberry to ground out to Garner at second base. In their half of the third, the A's got their first baserunner when Claudell Washington was hit by a pitch. After Fairly flied to left fielder Poquette, Garner singled to left, bringing the tying run to the plate. The threat ended, though, with Bill North flying out to Cowens and Campaneris lining out to Otis. Both teams went in order in the fourth. But in the fifth inning, Otis hit a home run over the left-field fence, giving the Royals a 4-0 lead. The A's went three up and three down in their half of the fifth.

Two Royals reached base with one out in the sixth inning: Mayberry walked and Cowens singled to right field; when Don Baylor mishandled the ball, Cowens went to second and Mayberry to third. With runners at second and third and one out, Tanner called Stan Bahnsen from the bullpen. Bahnsen put the fire out by getting Rojas to pop up in foul territory to Campaneris and retiring Wathan on a drive to the warning track in right field that Baylor reached. In the A's half of the sixth, Mayberry and Cowens made great defensive plays off the bats of Garner and North. Campaneris followed with a single to right field but the threat ended when Joe Rudi flied out to Cowens.

Bahnsen retired the Royals in order in the top of the seventh inning and Gura continued to cruise, setting down the A's in the bottom of the inning. In the eighth inning, Bahnsen repeated his seventh-inning performance of three Royals up and three Royals down. In their at-bats in the eighth, the A's showed a bit of a promise of a comeback. Washington led off with a single to right field but Fairly grounded to Mayberry, who started a double play. Garner singled to left field but North flied out to Otis in center field.

In the top of the ninth the Royals went down in order. Bahnsen had retired 11 straight to keep the A's within striking distance, but they couldn't capitalize on his effort. In the bottom of the ninth, three players who played big parts in their championship years came up and all were retired. Campaneris grounded to pitcher Gura, Rudi flied out to right, and Gene Tenace popped out to Mayberry. With that the Royals clinched at least a tie for the AL Western Division championship.

There was more to the game than what went on in the field of play. A crowd of unruly fans near the Royals bullpen surfaced in the late innings. The Royals endured choice words and beverages thrown at them. Pitcher Steve Mingori described what he experienced: "Some guy tried to grab my cap. And I stood up to keep it. Then the guy told me to sit down or he would kill me. The stuff that went on down there made me sick. There were 10-year-old kids using four-letter words against us. I couldn't believe it."[2] Tanner, on the contrary, was gracious in defeat. About Gura's performance and Herzog's decision-making he said, "I'd give Gura a $25,000 raise. He deserves every bit of it. KC was looking for somebody, hunting for something to win, and Whitey pulled him out of a hat. He did a job under more pressure and adversity than that team has ever had. He kept us off balance and did the job in the most crucial game of the season."[3]

"This is probably the end of the team with things being the way they are," A's captain Sal Bando said after the game.[4] Tanner was not ready to concede the season. "It's not over yet," he said with about as much optimism one could muster in the situation.[5]

Two days later it was over. On September 30 both teams had the day off. On October 1 the Royals opened a three-game series against the Minnesota Twins at Royals Stadium while the A's traveled to Anaheim for a three-game series against the Angels. The Royals lost to the Twins, 4-3, their game ending before the A's-Angels game was completed. There is no doubt there was some scoreboard-watching on the part of the A's and knowing their postseason hopes were still alive had to have given them a boost. Pitchers Vida Blue of the A's and Frank Tanana of the Angels came through with stellar performances and the game remained scoreless into the 12th inning, when the Angels won it with one swing. Rusty Torres hit a home run to win the game and the Royals became American League West champions. Because the Royals did not learn of the Angels victory until after 2 A.M., they held off celebrating until later in the day. Among those celebrating in the Royals' clubhouse was owner Ewing Kauffman. "What a day!" He exclaimed. "This is what we've all been waiting for."[6]

Notes

1 Sid Bordman, "Otis and Gura Deliver as Royals Clinch Tie," *Kansas City Times*, September 30, 1976: 1D.

2 Del Black, "Amos Closes Tanner's Mouth with Bat," *Kansas City Star*, September 30, 1976: 17.

3 Dick Draper, "Gura Blanks Oakland," *San Mateo* (California) *Times*, September 30, 1976: 20.

4 Ed Schoenfeld, "A's Golden Era Almost Over," *Oakland Tribune*, September 30, 1976: 41.

5 Bob Stevens, "Royals Blank A's, 4-0, Clinch at Least a Tie," *San Francisco Chronicle*, September 30, 1976: 53.

6 Joe McGuff, "Gura Snatches Royals from Brink of Disaster," *The Sporting News*, October 16, 1976: 17.

ROYALS STAGE "COMEBACK FOR ALL SEASONS" IN DEFEATING BREWERS JUNE 15, 1979: KANSAS CITY ROYALS 14, MILWAUKEE BREWERS 11, AT COUNTY STADIUM, MILWAUKEE

BY MIKE HUBER

Yogi Berra is credited with saying the baseball truism "It ain't over till it's over."[1] Until the final out is made, don't count out any team. The *Garden City* (Kansas) *Telegram* aptly summed up the late-night heroics of the Kansas City Royals after they defeated the Milwaukee Brewers on June 15, 1979: "It was a comeback for all seasons – one nearly as swift as a Willie Wilson dash around the bases, as rare as a save by the gasoline splashers who inhabit the Milwaukee Brewers' bullpen."[2] Before a County Stadium crowd of 32,812, the Royals erased a nine-run deficit and stormed back in the ninth inning to shock the Brewers, 14-11. Wilson's inside-the-park home run with two aboard sealed Milwaukee's fate.

Left-hander Mike Caldwell, the *Sporting News* American League 1978 Comeback Player of the Year, got the starting nod for the Brewers. With an earned run average of 2.93, Caldwell was seeking his seventh win of the season. Opposite him for the Royals was southpaw Paul Splittorff (8-5, 3.66 ERA). The Royals had lost seven of their previous 10 games, while the Brewers had a mini-win streak of two games going for them. It appeared that the Brewers were on a roll.

Milwaukee jumped on Splittorff in the bottom of the first. Back-to-back singles by Paul Molitor and Cecil Cooper brought Sal Bando to the plate, and he wasted no time in propelling a ball over the fence for a three-run home run, his fifth of the year. The Brewers then started another rally, getting two more runners on base before Splittorff retired the inning's eighth batter, Dick Davis, on a groundout to third.

The Royals went quietly in the second; in fact, Caldwell cruised through the first three innings, allowing just two singles. In the bottom of the second, the Brewers started again. Molitor singled with one out. After Cooper flied out, Molitor stole second and then stole third. Bando walked and Gorman Thomas stroked a single to right, plating Molitor. In the third, Sixto Lezcano led off with a walk and was still aboard two outs later when Charlie Moore rocketed a home run, his second of the season. With the score 6-0, Royals skipper Whitey Herzog made the call to the bullpen. Eduardo Rodriguez, pitching in his final major-league season (even though he was just 27 years old), came on in relief and, after a single by Molitor, retired Cooper for the third out on a fly ball to center fielder Amos Otis.

The Kansas City bats finally came to life in the fourth. Darrell Porter's RBI single and a groundout RBI by designated hitter John Wathan brought in two runs. However, in the bottom half, the Brewers treated Rodriguez's pitching as if it were batting practice. Bando singled. An out later Ben Oglivie walked. Lezcano singled, driving in Bando. Robin Yount walked, loading the bases, and Davis crushed a grand slam. Suddenly, the score was 11-2 in favor of the home team. With the game seemingly out of reach, Herzog kept Rodriguez in the game.

The Royals scratched back a run in the fifth on consecutive singles by Wilson, George Brett, and Otis. In the sixth, Jerry Terrell (who had replaced Porter at third) and Frank White singled, and with two outs, Wilson hit his third home run of the season, his first homer to leave a ballpark in two seasons.[3] The score was now 11-6 in favor of Milwaukee.

Rodriguez survived the fifth and sixth innings and gave way to Steve Mingori in the seventh. Mingori faced the minimum in the two innings he pitched. Caldwell did not pitch the seventh. Recently acquired righty Paul Mitchell[4] set the Royals down in order in the seventh and eighth innings.

In the final frame, with Kansas City still trailing by five runs, Wilson started things with a single to right. Jamie Quirk, who had entered defensively for Porter in the fifth, copied Wilson with another single to right. Otis smashed the ball, but he hit it right to center fielder Thomas for the first out. Al Cowens singled, loading the bases. George Scott then singled to left, with Wilson and Quirk crossing the plate and Cowens scampering to third. Brewers manager George Bamberger called for Reggie Cleveland to pitch to Terrell. Herzog countered by sending up Pete LaCock, whose sacrifice fly brought in Cowens. Wathan then hit a seeing-eye single up the middle and into center field. White followed with the sixth single of the inning, driving in Scott from second base. With runners again on first and second, Bill Castro strolled in from the Brewers bullpen to take over. U L Washington greeted Castro with a hard single to left, and Wathan raced home with the game-tying tally. The Royals had batted around and had knotted the score, 11-11. Switch-hitter Wilson, batting left-handed, then sent the ball into the right-field corner and was off to the races. By the time Lezcano came up with the ball and relayed it to second baseman Molitor, who fired it home to catcher Moore, Wilson was sliding across home plate with an inside-the-park three-run homer. Kansas City led 14-11. Quirk doubled to right but was stranded when Otis lined out to center for the second time in the inning. Marty Pattin came in to close the ninth for the Royals, retiring the three batters he faced, and Kansas City had completed one of the greatest comebacks in franchise history.

The Royals saved nine of their 21 hits for their final at-bat. The Brewers allowed eight runs "against a Kansas City lineup dotted with reserves."[5] Former Brewer Quirk, who had six at-bats all season, and Terrell, who had 11, both played several innings. Quirk went 3-for-3 and Terrell 1-for-2. Scott, recently acquired by Kansas City,[6] collected two hits. Herzog used every nonpitcher on his roster, and the reserves (Quirk, Terrell, and Washington) came through with five hits. He explained his rationale after the game: "I took Brett and Porter out because they've been playing every day. And Caldwell's in there and it's 11-3."[7]

Six Kansas City batters had multihit performances, led by Wilson's 4-for-6 day at the plate. The Royals' leadoff hitter also scored four runs and knocked in six with his two three-run homers. The comeback left the "stunned fans booing and the principals groping for appropriate words to describe it."[8] The Brewers had banged out 14 hits of their own, led by three home runs (Bando, Moore, and Davis) and Molitor's 4-for-6 performance in the leadoff spot.

Wilson, the hero for the Royals, commented, "It was a weird game, that's for sure. I'm just glad it came out our way."[9] He added, "I popped one out – my first hit out of the park in two years. Then we started thinking we had a chance. But it was still 11-6 going into the ninth. It has to be a thrill."[10]

Milwaukee manager Bamberger had "exhausted his supply of spicy expletives on the bench while Wilson was streaking around the bases in the ninth." In the clubhouse, the somewhat composed, "noted nice guy"[11] Bamberger told reporters, "There's no sense in saying anything right now. What can I say? I did enough screaming on the bench. You can't print what I said. I'll tell you, you could put (the Royals) out there right now and tell them, 'Here's a fastball,' and throw it right down the middle. They wouldn't hit it any better."[12]

He added, "That is the worst, worst game I ever [have] been associated with in 34 years of baseball. That was worse than getting beat 25-0. And to lose a game like that after you have been winning 11-2, that's terrible for morale."[13] The press agreed. Thos. A Hawley of the *Wisconsin State Journal* wrote, "What happened to the Milwaukee Brewers Friday night was either the worst game ever played in franchise history or something close to it."[14]

Herzog shared with reporters that he'd "seen about four or five (comebacks) like that. But I was playing with Washington then."[15] He added, "And the funny thing is the three outs we got in the ninth were all hard hit. What kept us alive was that little dribbler over the mound by Wathan."[16]

Sources

In addition to the sources mentioned in the notes, the author consulted baseball-reference.com and retrosheet.org.

Notes

1 According to the BBC (bbc.com/news/magazine-34324865), Berra first uttered the phrase when speaking about the 1973 National League pennant race, as his 82-79 New York Mets rallied to win the divisional title, defeated the heavily favored Cincinnati Reds in the League Championship Series and eventually played in the World Series. Accessed July 5, 2018.

2 "Royals blast Brewers," *Garden City* (Kansas) *Telegram*, June 16, 1979: 8.

3 Wilson's first two home runs of the 1979 season were inside-the-park homers, against the Chicago White Sox on May 13 and the New York Yankees on June 9.

4 Mitchell had been traded by the Seattle Mariners to the Brewers on June 7 for Randy Stein.

5 Thos. A Hawley, "Wilson's Homer caps Brewers' Nightmare," *Wisconsin State Journal* (Madison), June 16, 1979: 13-14.

6 Scott had been traded by the Boston Red Sox to the Royals in exchange for Tom Poquette just two days earlier, on June 13, 1979.

7 Hawley.

8 *Garden City Telegram.*

9 Ibid.

10 Ibid.

11 Hawley.

12 Ibid.

13 *Garden City Telegram.*

14 Hawley.

15 Ibid.

16 Mike O'Brien, "Royal Rally Stuns Brewers," *Sheboygan* (Wisconsin) *Press*, June 16, 1979: 16.

GEORGE BRETT TOPS .400 AUGUST 17, 1980: KANSAS CITY ROYALS 8, TORONTO BLUE JAYS 3, AT ROYALS STADIUM, KANSAS CITY

BY JACK ZERBY

It was serendipity that George Brett even got his fifth plate appearance against the Toronto Blue Jays on Sunday night, August 17, 1980, as the Kansas City Royals closed out a brief homestand. It was the eighth inning. In the seventh, Brett had broken a tie with a double and the Royals, leading the American League West Division by 13 games,[1] were now coasting with a 5-3 lead against the moribund Blue Jays.[2] But even though Ken Schrom, Toronto's third pitcher of the night, quickly got two outs and three batters remained before Brett's spot in the order, the 30,693 fans rocking Royals Stadium had just seen U L Washington drill a single up the middle and Amos Otis and John Wathan both work Schrom for walks to load the bases for Brett.

The ballpark was rocking because the 27-year-old Brett had entered the game with a .394 batting average, was riding a 28-game hitting streak that dated back to July 18 in Yankee Stadium, was 3-for-3 with a walk, and would get to bat again. As he stepped in his average was .399, on the cusp of reaching the mystical .400 level generally considered unattainable so late in the season. If their guy was going to edge above the mystical mark, the fans wanted to see it done at home, not on the road against the Texas Rangers, where Kansas City would play the next three games.

In his seventh full season as the Royals' third baseman after a brief appearance at the end of the 1973 season and a permanent call-up in early May of 1974, Brett had missed a handful of games early in the 1980 season and 26 consecutive games from June 10 to July 10 with a collection of heel, ankle, and wrist injuries.[3] Except for reaching .364 after the third game of the season, he hadn't even topped .300 until May 31. When he injured his right ankle in a successful stolen-base attempt at Cleveland on June 10,[4] he was hitting .337. Healed and back in the lineup on July 10, he hit at a .515 clip with safeties in seven of eight games until lefty John Tudor of the Red Sox held him hitless in Fenway Park on July 17. Brett got the 28-game streak going the next night in New York, and he and the Royals were still red-hot as they hosted the Torontonians on August 17.[5]

Toronto manager Bobby Mattick had tabbed his co-ace, 24-year-old Jim Clancy,[6] as his starter. Clancy was a creditable 11-8 (3.14 ERA) and coming off a complete-game win at Milwaukee five days earlier. This night, though, he walked his way into trouble after his team went down in order in the first inning against bespectacled left-hander Paul Splittorff (8-8, 4.64), Kansas City manager Jim Frey's choice to start. Clancy walked Kansas City's leadoff hitter, Willie Wilson, who stole second base with John Wathan batting. Wathan popped out, but Brett, hitting third, also walked, as did Darrell Porter, the cleanup hitter. Willie Aikens drove in Wilson with a force out to second base before Clancy regrouped to strike out Hal McRae, stranding Brett and Porter and escaping further damage.

Toronto gained a 1-1 tie in the top of the third when Royals second baseman Dave Chalk booted Alfredo Griffin's groundball and Danny Ainge romped home from third base. Ainge had doubled with one out and moved to third on a single by Ernie Whitt. The Jays managed a 2-1 lead against Splittorff in the fourth on a squeeze bunt by Garth Iorg that scored Otto Velez; he had singled to open the half-inning, then wheeled to third base on Damaso Garcia's single.

Brett had efficiently singled off Clancy in the third to run his streak to 29 games, and Jamie Quirk tied the game at 2-2 in the Kansas City fourth as he led off with his fifth home run of the season. With the score still tied, Brett willed himself "an infield single in the fifth, beating a demoniacal path to the bag [and] arriving before the throw from first baseman John Mayberry to pitcher Jim Clancy."[7] Brett tried to keep the pressure on with an attempt to steal second base, but Whitt gunned him down for the second out of the half-inning.[8]

Splittorff rolled on through the sixth and seventh innings without damage. Clancy negotiated the sixth safely, but had to face Brett again in the seventh, this time with two outs but with White and Wathan on the corners via two more of the six bases on balls the big righty issued in the game. With a runner on first, the Jays took their chances, pitching to Brett in a potential game-altering situation. That potential became reality. Brett electrified the crowd with a ringing two-run double to right field that bumped the score to 4-2 and ended Clancy's night. Mike Willis came on to pitch for Toronto – Porter nicked him for a single that scored Brett. Aikens added another single to chase Willis as Mattick went to Schrom, who closed out the inning. The former 2-2 tie was now 5-2, Royals.

Toronto made a comeback of sorts in their eighth as Bob Bailor and Mayberry singled, chasing Splittorff and bringing on late-game specialist Dan Quisenberry[9] with no outs and runners on the corners. After a fly ball out too short to score a run, Bailor scored on a force out to close Kansas City's lead to 5-3. The side-arming Quisenberry then yielded a single but was able to snuff the rally with the help of some botched Jays baserunning.

Brett, benefiting from the eighth-inning turn of events that had brought him up with the bases loaded and another chance to edge over .400 at home, got to see a new pitcher this time – Mike Barlow. "I just don't like facing that guy," he said after the game.[10] "He's like facing Quisenberry. The only thing is, he throws harder than [Quisenberry]."[11]

Barlow had struck Brett out to end the seventh inning the night before.[12] Brett remembered as he stepped in: "If I hadn't chased a ball off Barlow [last night], I'd be hitting .400 right now."[13] This time, Barlow got two strikes on Brett, putting the left-handed hitter into "a survival stance. It was a sinker, away, and I just slapped it to left. I didn't want to let myself down, and I didn't want to let the fans down after the support they gave me."[14]

The opposite-field slap carried over left fielder Iorg's head and, with two outs, brought all three runners home. It was now 8-3, Kansas City, as Brett stood on second base and tipped his helmet to a standing ovation. Toronto reached Quisenberry for a pair of two-out hits and had runners at second and third in the ninth before the durable reliever shut things down for his 25th save of the season, sealing a win for Splittorff.

The eighth-inning double boosted Brett's average to .401. Any uncertainty was over for him, his teammates, and fans not only in Kansas City but all over the country who found it "extraordinary" that a hitter was "hovering at .400 in the third week of August."[15]

The hovering lasted another month. Brett's hit streak reached 30 games the next night on the road at Texas, but the Rangers stopped him on August 19. Brett reached a peak of .407 on August 26, and was at exactly .400 as late as September 19. Back at Royals Stadium on September 20, Matt Keough of the Oakland A's tossed a five-hit shutout against the Royals in which Brett went hitless in four at-bats. That dropped his average to .396. Brett ended the season at .390 and won the 1980 American League batting title by 38 points over Cecil Cooper of the Milwaukee Brewers. His epic year at the plate also brought George Brett honors as the 1980 AL Most Valuable Player.

Sources

In addition to the sources cited in the Notes, the author also used Baseball-Reference.com and Retrosheet.org for box scores, team and player pages, batting and pitching logs, and other pertinent material.

Notes

1 Kansas City, with a 74-42 record, also led the combined American League standings by 2½ games over the New York Yankees. The Oakland Athletics were in second place in the AL West.

2 Toronto was 48-67 and in seventh, last, place in the AL East. The club was in its fourth season after the American League expanded in 1977.

3 Phil Axelrod, "Brett Bats for Immortality," *Pittsburgh Post-Gazette*, September 24, 1980: 17, 21.

4 Associated Press, "Brett Injures Ankle in Slide," Tampa Bay (Florida) *Times*, June 11, 1980: 34.

5 The Royals were 21-7 and Brett hit .442 from July 18 through August 16.

6 Clancy finished the 1980 season with a 13-16 record and a 3.30 ERA in 250⅔ innings for the 67-95 Blue Jays. Dave Stieb, 22, nearly matched him at 12-15, 3.71, 242⅔. Clancy started 34 games; Stieb started 32.

7 Joel Bierig, "A Player's Player," *Minneapolis Star*, August 20, 1980: 13B.

8 After he returned on July 10 from the ankle injury sustained in a steal on June 10, Brett kept running and had stolen four bases in seven attempts through August 16. This unsuccessful attempt left him 4-for-8 since his return.

9 Quisenberry, 27, debuted with the Royals in 1979. He had a remarkable 1980 season, making all of his 75 appearances in relief, finishing 68 games, winning 12, and saving another 33 in 128⅓ innings. He pitched in excess of one inning 60 times.

10 Joel Bierig, "George Brett's Got Baseball's Number," *Minneapolis Star*, August 18, 1980: 10C.

11 Ibid.

12 Brett struck out only 22 times in 515 plate appearances in 1980, with 58 walks. He had a .454 on-base percentage, which led the American League by 27 points.

13 Bierig, "Baseball's Number."

14 Ibid.

15 Hubert Mizell, "One in a Million – George Brett Bucks Big Odds," *Tampa Bay Times*, August 19, 1980: 1C.

ROYALS ADVANCE TO FIRST WORLD SERIES AFTER SWEEPING YANKEES OCTOBER 10, 1980: KANSAS CITY ROYALS 4, NEW YORK YANKEES 2, AT YANKEE STADIUM II

BY GORDON GATTIE

The Kansas City Royals were on the threshold of experiencing their greatest franchise moment to date: their first World Series. The year before, the California Angels clinched the American League West Division crown during the season's last week, outpacing Kansas City by three games. From 1976 to 1978, the Royals lost three consecutive American League Championship Series to the New York Yankees, including two losses during the decisive fifth game. Now the Royals were positioned to sweep New York for their initial AL pennant.

The 1979 season ended bitterly for Kansas City, as California clinched their first division title on September 25 by defeating the Royals 4-1.[1] One week later, Royals manager Whitey Herzog was fired after 4½ seasons. Herzog had taken over midway through the 1975 season after Jack McKeon was fired on July 24.[2] Herzog had been the Royals' third-base coach; his previous major-league managerial experience consisted of guiding the 1973 Texas Rangers to a 47-91 record as the first of three managers, and leading California for four games in 1974. Although he endured strained relations with ownership during his tenure, Herzog received accolades from many within baseball on his ability to keep Kansas City competitive with below-average pitching and several rookies in key positions during the 1979 season.[3]

The 1980 Royals entered spring training with unheralded rookie manager Jim Frey, who worked for Earl Weaver for 10 years yet wasn't considered a Weaver protégé.[4] The Royals were expected to compete for the division crown, with strengths in team defense, scoring ability, and starting rotation. However, Kansas City faced challenges as the 1980 season began: John Wathan replaced All-Star catcher Darrell Porter, the bullpen was inexperienced, and the manager and coaching staff were unproven.[5] Baseball Digest predicted the Royals would finish first while the Baseball Writers' Association of America expected California to repeat as division champions with Kansas City finishing second.[6]

The Royals started slow, falling two games behind the surprising White Sox as April ended. However, Kansas City won eight games during a nine-game stretch between May 17 and 25, improving from 1½ games behind to 2½ games ahead; the Royals never relinquished the division lead after Memorial Day. They led by as many as 20 games, and finished the regular season with a 97-65 record, 14 games ahead of Oakland.[7] The offense was led by George Brett (9.4 Wins Above Replacement [WAR], .390 BA), Willie Wilson (8.5 WAR, 133 runs, 79 stolen bases), and Hal McRae (2.7 WAR, .825 OPS), while the pitching staff featured Larry Gura (6.0 WAR, 2.95 ERA over 283⅓ innings), 20-game winner Dennis Leonard, and closer Dan Quisenberry (33 saves).

The 1980 Yankees featured several stars from the 1977-1978 championship teams, although the team had tragically lost Thurman Munson in a plane crash the previous season. Willie Randolph paced the offense with a 6.6 WAR, .427 OBP, and 30 stolen bases; Reggie Jackson provided power with 41 home runs and 111 RBIs; and Rick Cerone admirably filled Munson's spikes. Ace Tommy John went 22-9 with a 3.43 ERA over 265⅓ innings, Rudy May won 15 games as a valuable swingman, and Rich Gossage intimidated hitters with 33 saves and 103 strikeouts in 99 innings. Like Kansas City, the Yankees were predicted to fall short of the division title, with Baltimore expected to win the AL East.[8] The Yankees were also guided by a rookie skipper, Dick Howser. New York finished with a 103-59 record, the best record in the majors and three games ahead of Baltimore.[9]

In ALCS Game One, the Royals won 7-2 behind Gura's complete game and Kansas City's seven unanswered runs.[10] In Game Two, an incredible relay from Wilson to Brett to Porter nailed Randolph at home plate in the eighth inning and preserved the 3-2 win.[11]

Frey sent veteran Paul Splittorff to the mound for ALCS Game Three. He completed the 1980 season with a 14-11 record and 4.15 ERA over 204 innings. Splittorff had joined Kansas City in 1970; he won least 12 games and pitched 200-plus innings in seven seasons (1972-1974, 1977-1980). In 31⅔ postseason innings, Splittorff was 2-0 with a 2.84 ERA. He was solid during the second half, as he had been throughout his career.

With 56,588 fans attending the damp Friday contest, Tommy John started Game Three by getting Wilson on a groundout. U.L. Washington singled to right field, Brett grounded into a fielder's choice, and McRae lined out to end the inning. Splittorff almost matched John's performance: Randolph grounded out to shortstop, Bucky Dent grounded out to second, Bob Watson doubled, and Jackson struck out. In the second, both teams exchanged harmless hits and stranded runners. During the third frame, John retired the Royals in order. Splittorff allowed a single to Randolph, who was erased when Dent hit into a double play. Watson singled and reached second on a balk. Jackson struck out swinging. After three innings, the game was scoreless.

Entering the fourth inning, John continued pitching effectively, though the Royals batters were hitting the ball farther: Brett flied out to left field, McRae singled to center, Amos Otis lined out to right, Willie Aikens singled to right, and Porter flied out to right. For the only time that evening, Splittorff retired the Yankees in order, relying on a fly out, line out, and groundout. After Clint Hurdle struck out to start the fifth inning, Frank White started the scoring on a solo home run – his first clout in postseason play. Wilson singled and advanced to second on Washington's groundout, but was stranded when Brett grounded out. Splittorff, who retired several Yankees on groundouts in the early innings, needed three fly outs around a walk to keep the Yankees scoreless.

Tommy John quieted Royal bats in the sixth inning, inducing McRae to ground out, striking out Otis, allowing a single to Aikens who advanced to second on a wild pitch, and ending the inning on a Porter fly ball. Splittorff returned for the bottom half; Watson lined out to second, where White leapt to catch the sharply hit ball. Jackson, who had struck out twice, doubled to left, prompting Frey to replace Splittorff with Quisenberry after 5⅓ innings. Quisenberry made his postseason debut the previous night; he allowed one hit in the ninth inning for the save. Only three previous times had Quisenberry entered a game during a sixth inning: the Angels' division-clinching game the year before, and April 20 and July 20, when he earned a four-inning save both times. Now he faced Oscar Gamble with Jackson on second base. Gamble singled a 1-and-2 pitch up the middle; White recognized that he didn't have time to throw out Gamble at first base, so he attempted to catch Jackson at third base. The ball sailed over Brett's head, allowing Jackson to score and Gamble to reach third.[12] Cerone followed with a single to left, plating Gamble and giving New York a 2-1 lead. The next two hitters grounded out, limiting further damage.

In the seventh, John retired the first two hitters and then Wilson doubled. Countering Frey, Howser summoned Gossage from the bullpen. Washington greeted Gossage with an infield single, advancing Wilson to third and bringing up Brett. Brett, hitless in his previous seven at-bats, preferred facing Gossage rather than John; after the game Brett commented, "In that situation, Tommy John (a sinkerballer) is very hard to hit a home run off. I know Gossage has one thing in mind – to throw it by you."[13] On the first pitch, Brett blasted a tremendous clout that reached Yankee Stadium's third deck and gave Kansas City a

4-2 lead.[14] McRae singled to maintain the rally, but was caught stealing to end the inning. Quisenberry set down Brown, Randolph, and Dent in order in the Yankees half of the seventh.

Tom Underwood relieved Gossage for New York in the eighth, and Otis singled. Aikens flied out, Otis was picked off, and Porter flied out as the Royals couldn't pad their lead. Quisenberry quickly ran into trouble in the bottom half, as Watson tripled, Jackson walked after an 0-and-2 count, and Gamble walked on four pitches to load the bases. However, Cerone lined out to short and Washington quickly flipped to White, catching Jackson off second base to complete a timely double play. With renewed confidence, Quisenberry retired pinch-hitter Jim Spencer on a groundout.

Neither team generated offense during the ninth inning. The Royals didn't hit the ball out of the infield; for New York, Nettles and Brown flied out and Randolph struck out looking to end the game. The Kansas City Royals won their first AL pennant.[15]

The ghosts of previous series were vanquished, and for longtime Kansas City fans, the win was especially gratifying as the Kansas City A's often served as a farm club for the vaunted Yankees teams of the late 1950s and early 1960s.[16] White, named ALCS Most Valuable Player for his .545 series batting average and spectacular fielding, commented, "This is the happiest three games of my life."[17] The Royals eventually lost to Philadelphia in the 1980 World Series, and remained a pennant contender throughout the 1980s.

Sources

Besides the sources cited in the Notes, the author consulted Baseball-Almanac.com, Baseball-Reference.com, Retrosheet.org, and the following:

James, Bill. *The Bill James Guide to Baseball Managers from 1870 to Today* (New York: Scribner, 1997).

Thorn, John, and Pete Palmer, et al. *Total Baseball: The Official Encyclopedia of Major League Baseball* (New York: Viking Press, 2004).

Notes

1 Dick Miller, "Angels Reach Realms of Glory," *The Sporting News,* October 13, 1979: 22.

2 Joe McGuff, "Tiffs with Players, Press End McKeon Reign at K.C.," *The Sporting News,* August 9, 1975: 9.

3 Del Black, "Why? Folks Ask at Whitey's Exit," *The Sporting News,* October 20, 1979: 29.

4 Dick Kaegel, "Nobody Noticed Jim Frey – Until He Led Royals to Top," *The Sporting News,* October 25, 1980: 14; Del Black, "Royal Relievers Frey's Big Headache," *The Sporting News,* November 17, 1979: 49.

5 Del Black, "Royals Tap Wathan to Fill Porter's Shoes," *The Sporting News,* April 12, 1980: 24.

6 George Vass, "How Major League Pennant Races Shape Up for 1980," *Baseball Digest,* April 1980: 29-37; Carl Clark, "Scribes Like Bucs, Astros, O's, Angels," *The Sporting News,* April 12, 1980: 7.

7 Mike DeArmond, "Royals Run, Run, Run Away with West Title," *The Sporting News,* October 25, 1980: 11.

8 Vass; Clark.

9 Phil Pepe, "Yanks Remain Calm – Get Set for 'Part Two,'" *The Sporting News,* October 18, 1980: 41.

10 Tom Barnidge, "Royals' Gura Times End of Slump Well," *St. Louis Post-Dispatch,* October 9, 1980: 43.

11 Tom Barnidge, "Yanks' Hopes Running Out," *St. Louis Post-Dispatch,* October 10, 1980: 21; Associated Press, "KC Edges Yanks 3-2, Goes 2-Up in AL Series," *Star-Gazette* (Elmira, New York), October 10, 1980: 15.

12 Associated Press, "Brett swings Royals to Series in 3," *Chillicothe* (Missouri) *Constitution-Tribune,* October 11, 1980: 3.

13 Rick Hummel, "Brett's 3-Run Homer Wipes Out Yanks," *St. Louis Post-Dispatch,* October 11, 1980: 5.

14 Mike DeArmond, "One Swing by Brett – A Moment to Savor," *The Sporting News,* October 25, 1980: 26.

15 Dick Kaegel, "Who Said Unknowns? They're A.L. Royalty!" *The Sporting News,* October 25, 1980: 13.

16 Mike O'Brien, "'Other' Missouri Baseball Team Turns Cardinal Fans 'Royal,'" *Springfield* (Missouri) *Leader and Press,* October 11, 1980: 5.

17 Associated Press, "No K.C. Blues This Time," *Chillicothe* (Missouri) *Constitution-Tribune,* October 11, 1980: 3.

GEORGE BRETT'S "BEST GAME" OCTOBER 11, 1985: KANSAS CITY ROYALS 6, TORONTO BLUE JAYS 5, AT KAUFFMAN STADIUM

BY BRIAN M. FRANK

The Kansas City Royals entered Game Three of the 1985 American League Championship Series against the Toronto Blue Jays in a postseason slump. The Royals had lost 10 consecutive playoff games, including the first two games of the ALCS. The Royals lost Game One of the ALCS, 6-1. They then lost a sloppily played Game Two in 10 innings. After the heartbreaking Game Two loss, All-Star third baseman George Brett, who'd been on the team for all 10 post-season losses, remarked, "I can't remember a loss that hurt worse than this. ... It's hard to take."[1]

Even though the Royals were struggling in the play-offs, their star player wasn't. Brett had gone 0-for-4, with a walk in Game Two, but was 3-for-4 off Blue Jays ace Dave Stieb and closer Tom Henke in Game One. He'd also helped carry the Royals into the play-offs during the final week of the regular season, going 11-for-23 (.478) with 5 home runs and 13 RBIs.

Kansas City turned to its ace for Game Three, 21-year-old hurler Bret Saberhagen, to try to stem the tide, against veteran Blue Jays right-hander Doyle Alexander. Saberhagen was coming off a tremendous regular season in which he went 20-6 with a 2.87 ERA.[2] The 35-year-old Alexander was no slouch himself, having led the American League with a .739 winning percentage, while going 17-6 with a 3.13 ERA.

The Royals jumped on top in the first inning. Willie Wilson lined a single to center field with one out, but was thrown out trying to steal. On the next pitch, George Brett drove an Alexander changeup just inside the right-field foul pole to give the Royals the lead, 1-0. The home run was Brett's seventh ALCS homer, pushing him past Reggie Jackson for most all-time.

Brett flashed the leather in the third inning. With one out, Blue Jays leadoff man Damaso Garcia doubled and went to third when Lonnie Smith misplayed the ball in left field. Lloyd Moseby then hit a screamer down the third-base line. Brett made a great back-handed stop and fired the ball off-balance to home, as Garcia raced to the plate. Brett described the play: "It was totally reaction and instinct. There was no time to think about which way to go. I just fired."[3] Catcher Jim Sundberg applied the tag on a sliding Garcia. "I thought for sure the throw was going to hit Garcia in the head," Brett added. "It only missed by a few inches. I was thinking, my God, that's all we needed now. ... Really, it was a do-or-die play."[4] The play preserved Kansas City's one-run lead. Brett proclaimed, "I've only made a play that good once before in my life. ..."[5] Royals manager Dick Howser added, "You'll never see a third baseman make a better play."[6]

Kansas City increased its lead in the fourth, and Brett was once again at the center of the action. He led off the inning by belting an Alexander slider just over right fielder Jesse Barfield's glove, missing his second home run of the game by inches, as the ball hit off the top of the wall. Brett ended up at second base with a double. He eventually scored on Frank White's sacrifice fly, on which Barfield made a terrific backhanded, sliding catch in deep right-center field.

The Blue Jays exploded for five runs in the fifth inning. Barfield drove a ball into the right-field seats for a two-run homer to tie the score, 2-2. With one out, Garcia doubled, and Moseby rocketed a ball off Saberhagen's left heel. The ball ricocheted into left field, driving home Garcia. After a visit from the trainer, Saberhagen remained in the game, but the next batter, Rance Mulliniks, drilled an 0-and-2 pitch into the right-field seats, chasing Saberhagen from the game and extending the Blue Jays' lead to 5-2. Bud Black relieved, but after getting the second out of the inning, he gave up back-to-back singles and a walk to load the bases.

Dick Howser turned to reliever Steve Farr to try to keep the Royals in the game. Farr had been released by Cleveland earlier in the year and signed a minor-league contract with the Royals. He'd already come in during a bases-loaded jam in Game One of the series and gave up a single, walk, and sacrifice fly, before finally settling in. This time, Farr had to face Barfield, who'd already homered in the inning. Farr retired Barfield on a sharp groundball to second baseman Frank White to end the inning.

Jim Sundberg blasted a solo home run in the bottom of the fifth to cut into the Blue Jays lead. In the sixth, Willie Wilson led off with a single, and Brett unloaded on an Alexander fastball, driving it to deep left-center field for his second home run of the game, tying the score, 5-5. The home run was Brett's eighth League Championship Series home run, tying him with Steve Garvey for the all-time lead.[7] Royals closer Dan Quisenberry said Brett's second home run of the evening prompted catcher Jamie Quirk to tell the bullpen: "We're in the driver's seat now. George has one more at-bat."[8]

Brett's next at-bat led off the eighth inning. Blue Jays manager Bobby Cox decided to have Jim Clancy, a right-handed pitcher and normally a starter, face the left-handed-hitting Brett. Cox's options were limited, as the only southpaws on the Blue Jays playoff roster were Gary Lavelle, who was suffering from a sore arm, and Jimmy Key, who would start Game Five. Coming into the at-bat, Brett was 23-for-53 (.434) with five home runs in his career off Clancy.

Clancy was able to get Brett to squib a grounder between first and second, on what Brett called "the worst swing I've taken all series."[9] But the ball was just out of the reach of a diving Damaso Garcia, and went through for a hit. Hal McRae sacrificed Brett to second, and Frank White's groundout moved him up another 90 feet. Clancy then intentionally walked Pat Sheridan to face the slumping Steve Balboni, who was 0-for-11 with four strikeouts in the series. Balboni blooped a ball into shallow center field. As three Blue Jays converged, the ball fell just out of the reach of shortstop Tony Fernandez, scoring Brett, and giving the Royals the lead, 6-5.

As the game moved to the ninth, Dick Howser decided to stick with the hot hand of Steve Farr rather than give the ball to closer Dan Quisenberry. Farr ended up facing the minimum in 4⅓ innings of relief. He allowed two singles, but they were erased on a double play and a caught stealing.

The final out of the game was appropriately hit to Brett, who squeezed a Moseby popup in foul territory to give the Royals their first win in the series and end their 10-game postseason losing streak.

Brett was surprised that Toronto continued to pitch to him: "Before the series, there was a lot of talk about how they'd pitch around me, like they did during the regular schedule when they walked me 10 times or something like that. But they've been coming right at me. I'm getting at least a chance."[10] Bobby Cox attempted to explain the failed strategy: "We thought we would get him out, sometime, but I guess we couldn't, because we didn't."[11]

Brett finished the game 4-for-4, with two home runs, a double, four runs scored, three runs driven in, and a spectacular play in the third to cut down a run at the plate. Brett said, "It was an awfully good time to have my best night of the year."[12] He later called it the "best game I ever played in my life."[13]

Royals outfielder Dane Iorg summed up what many players and fans were thinking after the game, saying, "The difference between us and everybody else is George Brett. ... He doesn't rise to the occasion. He's always in a class by himself."[14]

Sources

In addition to the sources cited in the Notes, the author also consulted Baseball-Reference.com.

Notes

1 Gib Twyman, "Royals Come Home After Signs of Life," *Kansas City Star*, October 10, 1985: 5C.

2 After the postseason, Saberhagen was named the 1985 American League Cy Young Award winner, his first of two Cy Youngs. He also won the 1985 World Series MVP, going 2-0 with a 0.50 ERA in two starts in the Series, including a shutout in Game Seven.

3 Jim Proudfoot, "Brett Has to Keep Up Heroics for Royals to Win," *Toronto Star*, October 12, 1985: 1.

4 Ibid.

5 Gib Twyman, "Brett Adds Another Chapter to His Memorable Moments," *Kansas City Times*, October 12, 1985: E-2.

6 Ibid.

7 Brett finished his career with nine Championship Series home runs. As of 2018 he is tied for third with Bernie Williams, behind Manny Ramirez (13) and Albert Pujols (10).

8 Tracy Ringolsby, "Brett Snatches Royals from Brink," *Kansas City Times*, October 12, 1985: E-2.

9 Garth Woolsey, "Boom Boom Brett!" *Toronto Star*, October 12, 1985: 1.

10 Proudfoot.

11 Twyman, "Brett Adds Another…"

12 Proudfoot.

13 Blair Kerkhoff, *Kansas City Star*, October 12, 1985. kansascity.com/sports/mlb/kansas-city-royals/article39354957.html

14 Ringolsby, "Brett Snatches Royals from Brink."

ROYALS COMPLETE COMEBACK AGAINST BLUE JAYS TO WIN AL PENNANT OCTOBER 16, 1985: KANSAS CITY ROYALS 6, TORONTO BLUE JAYS 2, AT EXHIBITION STADIUM, TORONTO

BY ADRIAN FUNG

When Game Seven of the American League Championship Series began, the temperature at Exhibition Stadium in Toronto was 44 degrees and rapidly dropping as a brisk wind blew across the outfield from left to right. The fading Blue Jays, in the postseason for the first time ever, handed the ball to ace Dave Stieb, the American League ERA leader, pitching on three days' rest for the second time in the series. The postseason-experienced Royals handed the ball to their ace, Bret Saberhagen, the AL Cy Young Award winner, pitching on normal rest. Toronto had built a three-games-to-one series lead but Kansas City then won the next two, necessitating this winner-take-all Game Seven.

In the top of the second inning, Pat Sheridan, batting .063 in the ALCS, bunted for a single and went to second on a groundout. Catcher Jim Sundberg (batting .100) drove him home with two outs on a soft, opposite-field single to right-center, giving the Royals a 1-0 lead. It was a sign of things to come from the light-hitting pair.

Two innings later Sheridan lined the ball to right field. Buttressed by the wind, it kept carrying and sailed over the Royals logo at the fence for a home run. Kansas City was now up 2-0, but abruptly right-hander Saberhagen's night was finished. His pitching hand had absorbed a hard comebacker by Willie Upshaw in the first inning. He pitched the second and third, but Kansas City manager Dick Howser brought in left-hander Charlie Leibrandt to start the fourth. The Blue Jays halved the Royals' lead in the fifth, on a single by Damaso Garcia, a groundout, and a double by Upshaw, but Leibrandt struck out pinch-hitter Cliff Johnson to end the inning.

Entering the top of the sixth, Stieb had thrown just 65 pitches, but he was approaching 280 innings overall and pitching on short rest in two straight starts for the first time all season. Reliever Jim Acker began warming up.

With one out, Stieb pitched around George Brett, walking the Kansas City third baseman on four pitches. In this series Brett led in runs, home runs, runs batted in, walks, on-base percentage, and slugging percentage, and would be named ALCS MVP hours later.

Stieb hit the next batter, Hal McRae, bringing Toronto manager Bobby Cox out of the dugout to check on his starter. Stieb stayed in the game as a surprised murmur rippled through the crowd. Sheridan was next and he slapped a bouncer into the hole between second and third. Shortstop Tony Fernandez backhanded the ball and threw to Garth Iorg at third to force out a sliding Brett.

Needing just one out to end the frame, Stieb continued to struggle with his control and walked Steve Balboni to load the bases. Stieb stepped in front of the mound, looked into the dugout and began flipping the ball up and down into his glove. Catcher Ernie Whitt got the message and slowly approached the mound, glancing into the dugout, too. Stieb began tapping the ball back and forth between his glove and right hand and looked into the dugout again, painstakingly trying to telegraph to Cox that he had nothing left in the tank.

Cox rose from the bench and conferred quickly with pitching coach Al Widmar. Acker was ready, as was relief ace Tom Henke, but Cox stayed in the dugout. It would be Stieb's inning to finish.

Sundberg stepped in. Earlier, his RBI single had opened the scoring. After the game he said, "I just knew I was going to do something good. I could feel it, especially after I got that hit in the second inning to drive in Pat [Sheridan] with the first run. That really got me loose."[1] Stieb started with a curve, low for ball one. His next pitch was a fastball over the plate. Sundberg swung and recalled that he "hit it real well, I didn't feel the ball hit the bat, which means you've hit it good."[2]

It looked like a catchable fly ball to the opposite field, but with the wind gusting out to right, it kept drifting deeper. In an image that would haunt Toronto sports fans for years, right fielder Jesse Barfield leaped in vain at the wall as the ball hit the top of the chain-link fence and slowly descended onto the right-center field warning track. Sundberg's wind-blown triple suddenly gave Kansas City a 5-1 lead.

In 1989, as the Blue Jays prepared to move from Exhibition Stadium to the SkyDome, their new home ballpark, Stieb blasted the Ex: "What a brutal stadium it is for a pitcher. [The] fly ball that Jim Sundberg hit pretty much ruined the year for me and the team in '85. In another ballpark, it's a routine fly caught by the right fielder. ... Matter of fact, if they reduce this place to a pile of bricks, I'd be willing to come around and help."[3] (Exhibition Stadium was demolished in 1999).

Whitt echoed Stieb's sentiments: "Stieb made a good pitch and Sunny just hit it. To me it was a routine fly ball at best ... [but] I looked up and saw Jesse drifting back and back and thought 'Wait a minute, what is going on here?' Then it hit the fence and there was just disbelief, really."[4]

Cox trudged to the mound as the shocked home fans erupted in boos. Manager and pitcher walked off the field together, dejectedly. After the game, Royals center fielder Willie Wilson complimented Stieb on his determination. "He didn't have that many days' rest. He didn't have what he's used to having but he tried to keep his club in this."[5]

Cox also defended his ace. "Stieb made the pitch on Sundberg. I thought it was a popup. It so happens it got up in the wind. I'm disappointed, frustrated. I thought we'd win it. I'm just sorry we lost on a popup."[6]

Frank White greeted Acker, now on in relief, with a bloop RBI single to make it 6-1 for the visitors. Sundberg crossed the plate and entered the dugout to effusive congratulations from his teammates. "I've never been a great hitter like George Brett, but I take pride in my hitting," Sundberg said during the post-game celebration.[7] Kansas City batting coach Lee May tipped his cap to Sundberg and Sheridan. "Everybody focuses on George Brett, but the bottom part of our batting order really came through with some big hits," May said. "Our pitchers kept us in the game until somebody got a key hit."[8]

The comeback series victory was especially sweet for White and McRae, both Royals since 1973. "This is by far the best," White started, reflecting on his seven postseasons. "We were down so far and counted out so we went out and played loose and came up big."[9] Said McRae, "This is the sweetest win for me. Everybody thought we were out, but we came back. We just didn't quit."[10]

The Blue Jays' cold bats, 1-for-9 with runners in scoring position and seven runners left on base in the first five innings, turned to ice after Sundberg's game-breaking triple. From the bottom of the sixth to the beginning of the ninth inning, Toronto batters went 0-for-10 with one walk. The season ended with a whimper for Toronto. Despite a single, double, and RBI groundout in the ninth, Royals closer Dan Quisenberry finished the game and earned Kansas City its second AL pennant in six seasons.

The Blue Jays denied that they cracked under pressure. "Nobody ever chokes. Not professionals. It's just a matter of the way things go sometimes," first baseman Willie Upshaw lamented.[11]

"It has nothing to do with pressure, nothing to do with choking. They beat us, they executed when they had to and their pitching was phenomenal, especially the last four games," agreed third baseman Rance Mulliniks.[12]

Brett disagreed, noting that pressure affected both teams. "When we lost that third game we came back relaxed and even though we lost, I said the pressure was on Toronto. I don't know why I said it, but I think I was right, the pressure was on them ... I don't feel they gave away any games. We just played better than they did. In fact, in the second game, we choked. Then we came back."[13]

Manager Howser credited his hurlers as the key factor, saying, "Our pitching was a much more important factor than experience or lack of experience. ... Seems to me that what happened was our pitching shut them down pretty consistently so that we could hang in and hang in until we got the runs we needed."[14]

The Royals became just the fifth team to win a postseason series after facing a three-games-to-one deficit. Kansas City played St. Louis in the first all-Missouri World Series in 41 years. (The Cardinals and St. Louis Browns faced each other in 1944.) Though the Royals were playing in their seventh postseason in 10 years, they had never won the World Series.

Sources

Besides the sources listed in the Notes, the author consulted the following:

baseball-reference.com/boxes/TOR/TOR198510160.shtml

retrosheet.org/boxesetc/1985/B10160TOR1985.htm

"American League Championship Series Game Seven: Kansas City Royals at Toronto Blue Jays," NBC Television (Buffalo, New York, WGRZ, October 16, 1985).

Notes

1 Tom Slater, "Sundberg's 'Feeling' Turns Into Jay-Slayer," *Toronto Star,* October 17, 1985: BJ3.

2 Ibid.

3 Kim Lockhart, "The View From the Dugouts," *Blue Jays Scorebook* (1988): 79.

4 John Kernaghan, "Stable Mates," *Blue Jays Scorebook* (1988): 34.

5 Garth Woolsey, "IT'S OVER! Blue Jays Drive of '85 Falls Just Short," *Toronto Star*, October 17, 1985: BJ1.

6 Woolsey.

7 Woolsey.

8 Neil MacCarl, "Jays Better Team, NL Scouts Agree," *Toronto Star,* October 17, 1985: BJ4.

9 Robert Brehl, "Missouri the Winner in World Series," *Toronto Star,* October 17, 1985: BJ5.

10 Ibid.

11 Allan Ryan, "Jays Look to Future to Ease Pain of Loss," *Toronto Star,* October 17, 1985: BJ4.

12 Ibid.

13 Woolsey.

14 Jim Proudfoot, "Let's look at Jays' Loss as a Positive Experience," *Toronto Star,* October 17, 1985: BJ1.

ROYALS FORCE GAME SEVEN AFTER CARDINALS COLLAPSE IN WAKE OF DENKINGER'S CALL OCTOBER 26, 1985: KANSAS CITY ROYALS 2, ST. LOUIS CARDINALS 1, AT ROYALS STADIUM

BY FREDERICK C. BUSH

Game Six of the 1985 World Series was played in Kansas City under a full moon, a fact that may have led people of a superstitious nature to believe it was an explanation for the events of the ninth inning. However, if a full moon were an adequate explanation, then the Royals would have to have played most of the past month under one. After all, they had won three of four from the California Angels in their next-to-last regular-season series to claim the AL West Division championship by one game over the Halos, and then they had come back from a three-games-to-one deficit against the Toronto Blue Jays in the AL Championship Series to make it to the World Series against the Cardinals. A more appropriate myth was that the Royals, perhaps channeling the former Kansas City Katz amateur team, appeared to have nine lives and it turned out that they still had at least one left.[1]

The Royals once again faced a three-to-one deficit against the Cardinals, but Danny Jackson's masterful effort in Game Five, a 6-1 triumph, had brought the World Series back to Kansas City. The home team pinned its pitching hopes on Charlie Leibrandt, who had thrown eight shutout innings in Game Two before unraveling and surrendering all of the Cardinals' runs in the ninth inning of a 4-2 loss. He would once again be opposed by Danny Cox, who had allowed two runs in seven innings and received a no-decision in Game Two. As Game Six progressed, it was clear that each hurler was determined to outdo his previous performance, and neither team scored until the eighth inning.

Although scoring opportunities were minimal, the Royals mounted an immediate threat in their half of the first inning. Lonnie Smith led off with a double and advanced to third on Willie Wilson's groundout to Cardinals second baseman Tom Herr. Cox bore down to quell the uprising, striking out George Brett and inducing Frank White's grounder to shortstop Ozzie Smith. After that Cox allowed only two Royals to reach second base in his seven innings; on both occasions, there were already two outs and the third out was made easily.

As for Leibrandt, he had pitched five perfect innings before Cesar Cedeño and Darrell Porter led off the sixth with back-to-back singles. The Cardinals' first scoring opportunity quickly vanished when Cox popped out to Brett at third base on a bunt attempt and Smith grounded into a double play.[2] Leibrandt retired the side in order for the sixth time in the top of the seventh inning.

In the bottom of the seventh, Cox struck out Leibrandt for the final out with Steve Balboni on second and Buddy Biancalana on first. Allowing Leibrandt to bat in such a situation seemed to be a questionable decision to some observers. Kansas City manager Dick Howser explained his rationale, saying, "If we'd had a guy on third with less than two out, I'd have hit for Leibrandt. But I wasn't going to take out a guy who was pitching a two-hit shutout for anything other than that kind of a situation."[3]

After such a vote of managerial confidence, Leibrandt ran into difficulty in the top of the eighth.

Tito Landrum flied out, but Terry Pendleton rapped a base hit and Cedeño drew a walk. Still, when Porter struck out and Cox was due to bat, it appeared that the Royals hurler might escape unscathed. However, St. Louis manager Whitey Herzog was not going to follow Howser's lead and allow Cox to bat for himself, shutout or no shutout. Nonetheless, his choice of Brian Harper as Cox's pinch-hitter seemed almost as puzzling as Howser's decision, since Harper had not registered a hit (or reached base) in 13 at-bats as a pinch-hitter since September 3.[4]

Perhaps the full moon was in full force against the Royals when Harper hit a broken-bat blooper to center field that drove in Pendleton with the first run of the game. Andy Van Slyke ran for the hobbled Cedeño, and Leibrandt walked Smith unintentionally to load the bases. At this point, Howser sent Dan Quisenberry to the hill in relief, and Quiz induced a grounder from Willie McGee to quell the uprising.

When the Royals failed to score against Ken Dayley in the eighth and Quisenberry kept the game at 1-0 in the top of the ninth, Kansas City appeared to be down to its final three outs of 1985. Howser and Herzog engaged in a managerial chess match in the bottom of the inning. First, Howser sent right-handed Darryl Motley to pinch-hit for Pat Sheridan against the lefty Dayley. Herzog countered by lifting Dayley and sending righty Todd Worrell to the mound. Next, Howser reciprocated by calling Motley back to the dugout and sending left-handed Jorge Orta to the plate. Herzog likely took comfort in the fact that his team had a 91-0 record (including the postseason) in games in 1985 in which they had a ninth-inning lead. Additionally, Worrell had tied a World Series record in Game Five by striking out all six batters he had faced.[5]

Orta hit a chopper that first baseman Jack Clark fielded and tossed to Worrell, who ran to cover the base. Umpire Don Denkinger called Orta safe, though television replays clearly showed that he had been out. Worrell said, "He stepped on the back of my foot, Orta did. The first thing Orta hit was my heel, not the bag. And I had the ball by then."[6] All the Cardinals' arguing was not going to change the call, though. When Herzog was asked later if the use of instant replay should be considered for close calls, he first responded, "They better use something," but then added, "No, they can't use instant replay on plays like that. It would take four hours to decide."[7]

It did not take four hours for the Cardinals to fall apart in the wake of the missed call. Balboni lofted a foul popup near the first-base dugout upon which Clark and Porter (the catcher) converged. As he ran, Clark first eyed Porter and then the TV camera near the dugout, by which time the ball dropped behind him. Clark admitted afterward, "It was a real catchable ball and it was misplayed."[8] Given new life, Balboni lined a single to left field, after which Onix Concepcion entered the game as his pinch-runner. Jim Sundberg then tried to lay down a sacrifice bunt, but Worrell reacted quickly and forced Orta out at third.

Hal McRae batted in place of the light-hitting Biancalana, and Porter allowed Worrell's second pitch of the at-bat to get by him for a passed ball that allowed both Concepcion and Sundberg to advance one base. Herzog then ordered an intentional walk to McRae to set up a double play. John Wathan ran for McRae, and Dane Iorg walked to the plate to bat for Quisenberry. Ironically, Iorg had been a World Series hero for the Cardinals in their 1982 triumph over the Milwaukee Brewers, having batted .529 as the designated hitter in that series.

This time, Iorg lined a 1-and-0 pitch from Worrell into right field to drive in Concepcion and Sundberg for a 2-1 Kansas City victory. Iorg, who may have been the most exultant of all the Royals, said, "These are the situations you dream about as a child. I've dreamed about that situation many times. To be here, to fulfill that dream, is very special."[9]

Iorg's dream was a nightmare for the Cardinals, most of whom chose to blame Denkinger's missed call for their loss. The lone exception was Worrell, who observed, "There's nothing you can do about it. I felt I had him, but I didn't. So you have to pick up and continue."[10] Herzog, on the other hand, steamed, "As far as I'm concerned, we had the damned World Series won tonight." In reference to Denkinger being the home-plate umpire for Game Seven, Herzog added, "We've got no more chance of winning than the man in the moon — not with that guy working behind home plate."[11]

Brett summed up the Royals' outlook by stating, "That is about as far to the wall as we can get. We looked like a dead team. ... We end up getting a break here, a break there, and then we get a big hit. You've got to take advantage of the breaks."[12] With Herzog's attitude prevailing among St. Louis's team members, the Kansas City Royals already had a psychological break for Game Seven. The outcome of the actual play on the field, and the 1985 World Series champion, would be determined the next night.

Notes

1 Kansas City's Katz Drugstore chain was in existence from 1914 to 1971. For many years, the company sponsored a team in the amateur Ban Johnson Baseball League. The team's name was the Katz, and its logo (appropriately) was a cat.

2 From 1976 through 1985, the designated-hitter rule did not apply in World Series played in odd-numbered years. Pitchers had to bat.

3 Dave Nightingale, "Full Moon, Controversy, Tied Series," *The Sporting News*, November 4, 1985: 19.

4 Ibid.

5 Worrell shared the record with Hod Eller of the 1919 Cincinnati Reds and Moe Drabowsky of the 1966 Baltimore Orioles.

6 Malcolm Moran, "Chance for Glory Instead Goes Awry," *New York Times*, October 27, 1985: S3.

7 Joseph Durso, "Herzog Inveighs Against Umpiring," *New York Times*, October 27, 1985: S3.

8 Nightingale, "Full Moon, Controversy, Tied Series."

9 Rick Hummel, "Ex-Teammate Iorg Downs Cards in 9th," *St. Louis Post-Dispatch*, October 27, 1985: 1.

10 Moran, "Chance for Glory Instead Goes Awry."

11 Nightingale, "Full Moon, Controversy, Tied Series."

12 Tracy Ringolsby, "Do You Believe in Miracles? Yes!" *Kansas City Star*, October 27, 1985: 1J.

ROYALS ROUT REDBIRDS TO WRAP UP FIRST WORLD SERIES TITLE OCTOBER 27, 1985: KANSAS CITY ROYALS 11, ST LOUIS CARDINALS 0 AT ROYALS STADIUM

BY FREDERICK C. BUSH

After the Royals narrowly escaped Game Six with a 2-1 victory, Kansas City's relief ace Dan Quisenberry remarked, "Every year the World Series should go seven games for the dramatics of it."[1] The 41,658 fans who packed Royals Stadium on October 27, along with a national television audience, certainly expected a thrilling end to the intrastate I-70 Series, especially with the Royals' 20-game winner Bret Saberhagen – the eventual AL Cy Young Award recipient – going head-to-head against the Cardinals' 21-game winner John Tudor, who had hurled 10 shutouts in the regular season. Tudor already had defeated Kansas City in Games One and Four while Saberhagen had bested St. Louis in Game Three. As this game unfolded, however, the only dramatics were of the theatrical kind on the part of the Cardinals as the Royals put an exclamation point on their first World Series championship in 17 years of franchise history.

The Cardinals were still fuming about umpire Don Denkinger's missed call in the ninth inning on the previous night, which they believed had cost them the game and a six-game Series victory. Game Six was not the first time that the Redbirds had been dissatisfied with the umpiring in this series either. Cardinals starter Joaquin Andujar had complained about balls and strikes in Game Three, and the team had also "hotly disputed" the Royals' Jim Sundberg being called safe at home in Game Five, a 6-1 Kansas City victory.[2] In regard to the Cardinals' prospects for Game Seven, manager Whitey Herzog had gone so far as to assert, "If John [Tudor] doesn't hit the corners, we're dead. If he doesn't get the calls from that guy [Denkinger], we're dead."[3]

Given the Cardinals' frame of mind, Herzog may as well have stated that his team was dead on arrival at the stadium as Tudor indeed failed to hit the corners, although Denkinger's ball-and-strike calls were not to blame. Tudor, who had walked only 49 batters in 275 innings during the regular season and three in 15⅔ innings in the World Series, lost his pinpoint control at the wrong time. In the bottom of the second inning, he issued a one-out walk to Steve Balboni that Darryl Motley followed with a blast into the seats in deep left field that gave the Royals a 2-0 lead.

The second inning provided foreshadowing to events in the bottom of the third. Lonnie Smith drew a leadoff walk and, after Willie Wilson flied out, advanced to second on George Brett's single. With Frank White at the plate, Smith and Brett then pulled off a double steal. After throwing eight pitches to White, Tudor surrendered a full-count walk to load the bases. Sundberg was up next and he drew the third base on balls, again on a full count, to force in Smith for the Royals' third run. At this point, Herzog pulled the plug on Tudor's evening, which at 2⅓ innings was his shortest outing in 1985. Tudor was so irate about his performance that he punched a cooling fan in the Cardinals dugout, incurring an injury to his left index finger that required stitches.

While a local hospital stemmed the bleeding from Tudor's digit, Bill Campbell took the mound for St. Louis to try to stop the flow of Royals runners across home plate. Balboni, the first batter he faced, had other ideas and stroked a single to left field that drove in Brett and White for a 5-0 lead. After Motley grounded out to first, Campbell intentionally walked Buddy Biancalana – the Royals' fourth free pass of the inning – in order to face Saberhagen, whom he struck out to end the frame.

Though Saberhagen was not a threat at the plate, he was cruising along against the hitters who stepped up to it to face him, having allowed only two harmless singles through the first five innings. In the bottom of the fifth, Saberhagen's teammates provided him with an even larger cushion than he already had, en route to turning a highly anticipated thriller into a laugher. The Cardinals, understandably, were not amused, and their tempers began to flare again in the fateful fifth inning.

Sundberg smacked a leadoff single that ended Campbell's stint on the mound. Jeff Lahti was the next fireman to take the hill, and he turned a brushfire into a raging inferno as Balboni and Motley hit consecutive singles, the latter of which plated Sundberg. Biancalana then struck out, and Saberhagen's bunt resulted in Motley being forced at second base for the second out; however, Lahti was not out of trouble yet. Smith belted a two-run double and advanced to third when left fielder Tito Landrum threw to home to try to nab Saberhagen. After Wilson drove in Smith with a base hit, Herzog inserted his third pitcher of the inning, Ricky Horton.

Brett greeted Horton with a single, prompting St. Louis's skipper to go to his bullpen once more. This time Herzog called for Andujar, another 21-game winner in the regular season, to enter the fray. Andujar fared no better than his predecessors as White worked an 11-pitch at-bat into an RBI single. The fiery Andujar, who was still angry about the umpiring in Games Three and Six, began to protest when Denkinger called a 2-and-2 pitch ball three against the next batter, Sundberg. When Denkinger called ball four on the next pitch, Andujar argued so vehemently that Denkinger ejected him, at which point the pitcher became so irate that "Mike Roarke, the St. Louis pitching coach, grabbed him and pushed and dragged him from the field and into the dugout."[4]

Herzog ran onto the field to argue with Denkinger and, according to one report, "all of a sudden, four-letter words were on sale for 99 cents a dozen," which resulted in the manager being tossed from the game as well.[5] Herzog tried to downplay the content of his tirade, admitting only, "I did say to Denkinger I didn't think we should be out there tonight, that we should be at home."[6] Shortstop Ozzie Smith agreed with Andujar's and his manager's tirades, asking, "When you're being cheated, how else are you supposed to react?"[7]

Outfielder Andy Van Slyke was the only Cardinals player to voice a dissenting point of view, opining, "I feel sorry for the kids around the country more than anyone else. Now they think this is the way a major-league ballplayer acts." In reference to the Cardinals' defeat, he added, "You swallow your pride, tip your hat, and come back to spring training next year."[8]

Once the dust settled, Bob Forsch became the fifth Cardinals hurler to take the mound – tying the World Series record set by the Baltimore Orioles in 1979's seventh game – and he promptly uncorked a wild pitch that allowed Brett to score what turned out to be the final run of an 11-0 Royals romp. The margin of victory tied the World Series Game Seven record, which had been set by Dizzy Dean and the 1934 St. Louis Cardinals, who had defeated the Detroit Tigers by the same score.

Saberhagen went the distance for a five-hit/no-walk shutout that gave him his second World Series victory. His two complete-game triumphs, in which he allowed a total of one run, garnered him the Series' MVP Award. The 1985 season was a banner campaign for the 21-year old pitcher: his wife had just given birth to their first child the previous day, he now was a World Series champion and MVP, and he soon would receive his first Cy Young Award.

Though Saberhagen was the hero of the moment, the entire Kansas City pitching staff had excelled. The Cardinals had led the NL in scoring during the regular season, but they managed only 13 runs against the Royals and batted a lowly .185, which was a record for the lowest team batting average in a seven-game World Series.[9] Royals manager Dick Howser noted, "It was a struggle, but we had good pitching. ... We played 14 pressure games [AL Championship and World Series] in a row, and our pitching was good."[10]

After losing three consecutive AL Championship Series to the New York Yankees from 1976 to 1978 and losing the 1980 World Series to the Philadelphia Phillies, the Royals had finally captured their first crown with a team that was considered to be weaker than any of their previous playoff squads. The fact that the 1985 Royals had become only the fifth team to overcome a three-games-to-one World Series deficit led Howser to assert, "This is a special club, and these are special players."[11] Longtime stars Brett, McRae, and White had suffered through those previous failures and no doubt shared their teammate Quisenberry's assessment about their World Series championship: "It's glorious. What else can you say but it's glorious."[12]

Notes

1 Murray Chass, "Triumph 2-1 Iorg's Hit: Royals Stun Cardinals in 9th and Tie Series," *New York Times*, October 27, 1985: S1.

2 Johnathan Rand, "Herzog Levels Blast at the Umpires as Cards Lose for First Time in Ninth," *Kansas City Star*, October 27, 1985: 2J.

3 Joseph Durso, "Herzog Inveighs Against Umpiring," *New York Times*, October 27, 1985: S3.

4 Murray Chass, "Royals Trounce Cardinals, 11-0; Take Series on 3rd Victory in Row," *New York Times*, October 28, 1985: C8.

5 Dave Nightingale, "Unheralded K.C. Romps to Throne Room," *The Sporting News*, November 4, 1985: 19.

6 Joe McGuff, "'85 Season: Wild and Glorious," *Kansas City Star*, October 28, 1985: 1C.

7 Ibid.

8 Ibid.

9 Nightingale, "Unheralded K.C. Romps to Throne Room."

10 McGuff, "'85 Season: Wild and Glorious."

11 Ibid.

12 Ibid.

DENNIS LEONARD'S COMEBACK APRIL 12, 1986: KANSAS CITY ROYALS 1, TORONTO BLUE JAYS 0 AT ROYALS STADIUM, KANSAS CITY, MISSOURI

BY BILL CARLE

Dennis Leonard was the ace of the Kansas City Royals' pitching staff in the late 1970s and early 1980s. Three times a 20-game winner, he was a true workhorse, leading the league in games started three times. In 1982 his season was derailed when he was hit in the pitching hand by a line drive, breaking two fingers, an injury that caused him to miss more than two months of the season.[1]

The next season, on May 28, 1983, he was delivering a pitch in a game against the Baltimore Orioles when he ruptured the patellar tendon in his left knee. Leonard immediately crumpled to the ground, thinking he had been hit with a line drive. The injury was so severe that it required four surgeries and caused him to miss the rest of the 1983 season, the entire 1984 season, and virtually all of the Royals' 1985 championship season.[2]

Leonard spent every day working out under the watchful eye of Royals trainer Mickey Cobb, striving to rehabilitate the knee. He strapped weights to his leg and performed leg lifts; he worked out on the Cybex machine; he ran in the outfield; he did sit-ups and trunk twists.[3]

By 1986 he was finally able to make it to spring training, where he battled to make the team. He wasn't going to be in the initial starting rotation although he made the Opening Day roster. On April 12 Danny Jackson was originally scheduled to start against Toronto, but he had twisted his ankle late in spring training, so manager Dick Howser named Leonard to start the game at Royals Stadium. The game was being nationally televised because it was a rematch of the 1985 American League Championship Series. This was to be Leonard's first start since he injured his knee three years earlier.[4]

The game began with the Blue Jays deciding to test how well Leonard moved off the mound, by bunting. Lloyd Moseby faked a bunt on the game's first pitch, but wound up grounding out to shortstop. Tony Fernandez followed Moseby with another bunt attempt, but bunted it too hard, and it went past Leonard to first baseman Steve Balboni, who was able to beat Fernandez to the bag.[5]

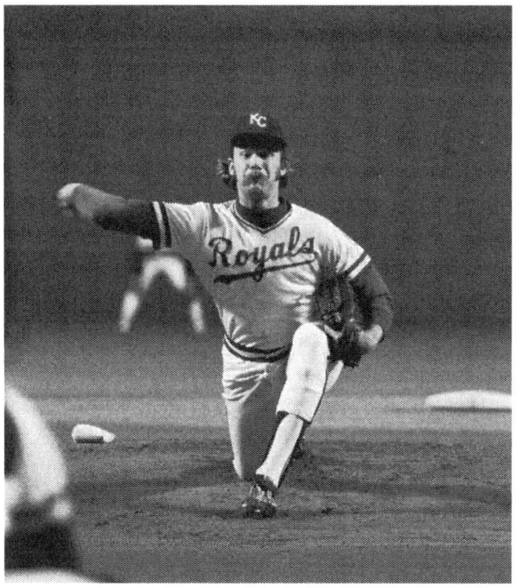

After that, Leonard settled into a nice groove. With two out in the second inning, the Blue Jays got their first hit when Jesse Barfield hit a ball to deep left that looked as though it was going to be a home run. A strong northwest wind caught the ball and kept it in the ballpark, where it bounced on the warning track and into the stands for a ground-rule double.[6]

In the third inning, again with two out, Moseby hit a dribbler down the first-base line that Leonard was unable to field, and Moseby had an infield single for the Jays' second hit. After stealing second, Moseby was stranded there when Leonard retired Fernandez on an infield grounder.[7]

Moseby proved to be the Jays' last baserunner for the next several innings, Leonard retired the side in order in the fourth, fifth, sixth, seventh, and eighth innings. Blue Jays starter Jim Acker proved to be equally as hard to solve for the Royals offense, and the game was scoreless as the Royals came to bat in the bottom of the eighth inning.

Acker retired the first two hitters quickly before Jim Sundberg managed a two-out single. Toronto manager Jimy Williams pulled Acker and brought in Don Gordon. Howser sent Buddy Biancalana in to run for Sundberg, and Jorge Orta to hit for shortstop Angel Salazar. On a 2-and-2 pitch, and with Biancalana running, Orta lined a double off the fence. Biancalana sprinted home to score the game's first run.

Leonard took the mound in the ninth inning trying to complete the shutout win. He retired Damaso Garcia and Lloyd Moseby on routine fly balls and with two out, Tony Fernandez stroked a single to break a string of 18 straight hitters retired by Leonard. Pitching coach Gary Blaylock emerged from the dugout to talk to Leonard amid a chorus of boos from the 24,332 fans who wanted to see Leonard finish the game. After a brief discussion, Blaylock left Leonard in to finish the job. After the game, Howser said, "I told Gary Blaylock, 'It's his ballgame.' I don't care who I brought in; nobody was going to pitch any better." Leonard fanned Rance Mulliniks with his 89th pitch to complete one of the most emotional games in Kansas City history. Leonard said later that the game was probably the biggest thrill he had in baseball. He gave the game ball to Royals trainer Mickey Cobb, who had guided him through the rehabilitation process.[8]

Unfortunately, Leonard was unable to recapture the skill that had made him one of the American League's best hurlers. He finished the 1986 campaign with an 8-13 record and a 4.44 earned-run average. He decided to retire in February of 1987. Leonard won 144 games in a Royals uniform, but none were more stirring than his comeback win against the Blue Jays.

Sources

In addition to the sources cited in the Notes, the author also consulted baseball-reference.com and retrosheet.org.

Notes

1 Interview with Dennis Leonard by Ryan Lefebvre, youtube.com/watch?v=O4cUBcmknfw.

2 Ibid.

3 Jill Lieber, "A Fight Against Pain and Doubt," *Sports Illustrated*, July 29, 1985.

4 Interview with Dennis Leonard by Ryan Lefebvre.

5 Jack Etkin, "Leonard Comes All the Way Back in First Start," *Kansas City Star*, April 13, 1986.

6 Ibid.

7 Ibid.

8 Ibid.

FRANK WHITE'S SEVEN RBIs OVERCOME RANGERS IN WILD 11-INNING GAME AUGUST 19, 1986: KANSAS CITY ROYALS 9, TEXAS RANGERS 8, AT ROYALS STADIUM, KANSAS CITY

BY RICHARD CUICCHI

Motivated by the unusual antics of opposing rookie pitcher Mike Loynd, Kansas City Royals second baseman Frank White took a frenzied game into his own hands and powered the Royals to a come-from-behind win over Texas on August 19, 1986. However, White's record-setting game would be squandered by the Royals in a disheartening season.

Mired in third place in the American League West Division, 12½ games behind the division-leading California Angels, the Royals were looking for something positive in their disappointing season. After all, they were the defending World Series champions.

The Royals had been playing near .500 through late June, before they suffered a disastrous 11-game losing streak. Then they lost popular manager Dick Howser at the All-Star break after it was discovered that he had a malignant brain tumor that required surgery.[1] Mike Ferraro filled in as interim manager for the balance of the season, but the Royals could never get back on a winning track.

The night game on August 19 was played before 26,716 fans in Royals Stadium. Division rival Texas was in second place, 4½ games behind the Angels.

Loynd was the starting pitcher for Rangers manager Bobby Valentine. It was his sixth major-league start since he was drafted out of Florida State University in June. The 22-year-old right-hander had won the Golden Spikes Award as the best college player and had two major-league wins to his credit going into the game.

Ferraro went with Alan Hargesheimer as his starter. The 31-year-old righty had not started a major-league game since October 3, 1981, although he had made four relief appearances for the Royals this season.

The rest of Royals' starting lineup featured several veteran holdovers from the championship season the year before: Lonnie Smith, George Brett, Willie Wilson, Frank White, Jim Sundberg, Steve Balboni, and Jorge Orta. Brett (13 HR, 61 RBIs), Balboni (26 HR, 75 RBIs), and White (14 HR, 62 RBIs) were pacing the team offensively.

In addition to Loynd, the Rangers had other recent college stars Pete Incaviglia and Oddibe McDowell, as well as 20-year-old rookie Ruben Sierra, in their lineup.

Each team scored a run in the first inning. Incaviglia drove in the Rangers' run with a single, while White's single plated the Royals' score. The fireworks started early in the game when Ferraro was ejected in the first inning. He had objected to a call by second-base umpire Richie Garcia, who called Smith out attempting to steal.

In the top of the second inning, Hargesheimer fell apart on the mound. Sierra doubled and Harrah was hit by a pitch. McDowell doubled to score Sierra, and Scott Fletcher singled Harrah and McDowell home. Hargesheimer was replaced by Steve Farr after walking Incaviglia. Ward's single scored Fletcher to make the score 5-1. An ineffective Hargesheimer gave up five earned runs on five hits and two walks in 1⅔ innings pitched. He would never appear in another major-league game.

Loynd struck out White to end the third inning, and, according to White, the rookie pitcher began yelling at him in what he thought was an attempt to show him up.[2] Loynd's supposed behavior would come back to haunt him later in the game.

The Rangers scored two more runs in the fourth inning with four singles off Farr, making the score 7-1. They appeared to have the game under control, and spectators began heading for the exits after the inning.[3]

But in the bottom of the fifth, Loynd gave up a double to Brett and walked Orta. Facing Loynd for the third time in the game, White slammed a double that scored both runners and cut the Rangers' lead to 7-3.

In the top of the sixth inning, the Royals again skirmished with the umpires. Replacing Farr, Royals pitcher Dennis Leonard faced Pete O'Brien as the first batter. On a 2-and-1 count, Leonard threw a pitch at which O'Brien began to swing and stopped. Home-plate umpire Rick Reed asked third-base umpire Dale Ford to make the call, and Ford signaled that O'Brien had held up his swing, calling it a ball. Arguments ensued with the umpires involving Leonard, Brett, and White, with Brett being ejected from the game by Ford.[4] After the imbroglio, O'Brien doubled and went to third on Incaviglia's grounder, but he was caught off third on Tom Paciorek's groundball and Paciorek was out trying to go to second.

After the game, Ford said, "(Brett) didn't like the no-swing call. He said three or four times it was a bad call. Then he called me a (obscenity). If my mother calls me that, she has to go."

The incident with the umpires seemed to light a fire under the Royals in the bottom of the sixth. Aided by a couple of Rangers miscues, Kansas City scored five runs and took an 8-7 lead.

Rangers reliever Jeff Russell replaced Loynd and walked Buddy Biancalana with one out. Smith doubled, sending Biancalana to third base. When Wilson hit a blooper to shallow center field, Biancalana waited to see if the ball would drop before running home. But Smith went to third immediately, and the Royals had two runners standing on the base. But when the ball dropped for a single, Biancalana scored without a throw from center fielder McDowell.[5]

Greg Pryor, who had replaced Brett, reached on an error by second baseman Harrah, who mishandled a flip from shortstop Fletcher on a groundball. Smith scored. After Orta hit into a force play, White came through again with a three-run home run into the left-field seats to give the Royals the lead, 8-7.

The Royals' lead didn't last long: Sierra tripled and Don Slaught singled to tie the score in the top of the seventh inning. The Royals got two runners on in the bottom of the inning but failed to push across a run.

Neither team scored again until the bottom of the 11th inning. White's heroics emerged once more as he led off with a dramatic walk-off home run off Dale Mohorcic to give the Royals a 9-8 victory.

Altogether, White had four hits in the game and drove in a career-high seven runs, tying a Royals record for the most RBIs in a game held by Brett in 1983, Willie Aikens (1982), and Jerry Grote (1981).[6] Smith, Wilson, and Brett each had two hits as part of the Royals' total of 14.

White commented after the game, "After (Loynd) struck me out he tried to show me up. It perked me up; it got my adrenaline going." He added, "It was a night where I thought I was concentrating, but I probably wasn't until then. After that I wanted to be at the plate all of the time."[7]

Ferraro said, "Their pitcher was making noises on the mound. He hollered something at White after he struck him out. White stared at him. That was the first time I'd seen White stare at a pitcher. Frank usually doesn't do that."[8]

Royals catcher Sundberg blamed Loynd for White's reaction. "I couldn't believe it," he said of Loynd's antics. "In my 13 years I've never seen anything like it. Not even for a veteran, let alone a college kid."[9]

The Rangers' offense was led by O'Brien's three hits, Sierra's four hits, and Fletcher's two RBIs.

Royals reliever Dan Quisenberry pitched two perfect innings to finish the game and claimed his first victory of the season. Mohorcic was charged with the loss.

Ferraro summed up the Royals' effort: "I've seen some wild games, but this has to be the wildest. Nothing amazes me what they do anymore. It shows everyone that even though we're 12 games out, no one's going to lie down."[10]

Despite Ferraro's optimistic outlook, the Royals finished the season in third place in the AL West, six games under .500 and 16 games behind the Angels.

Dick Howser underwent a second surgery on December 5 for additional cancer treatment known as immunostimulation.[11] He died on June 17, 1987.

White tied his career high for home runs (22) and set a career high for RBIs (84). He collected an American League record seventh Gold Glove for second basemen. He was named the Royals Player of the Year by the Kansas City chapter of the Baseball Writers Association of America.[12]

Sources

In addition to the sources cited in the Notes, the author also consulted Baseball-Reference.com.

Notes

1 *1987 Kansas City Royals Media Guide*, 12.

2 Bob Nightengale. "White's Homer Powers Royals in 11," *Kansas City Times*, August 20, 1986: E-1.

3 Ibid.

4 Ibid.

5 Ibid.

6 Ibid.

7 Ibid.

8 Bob Nightengale. "Royals Report," *Kansas City Star*, August 20, 1986: 1B.

9 Bob Nightengale. *Kansas City Times*.

10 Ibid.

11 1987 Kansas City Royals Media Guide, 12.

12 1987 Kansas City Royals Media Guide, 85.

KEVIN SEITZER GOES 6 FOR 6 AUGUST 2, 1987: KANSAS CITY ROYALS 13, BOSTON RED SOX 5, AT ROYALS STADIUM, KANSAS CITY, MISSOURI

BY BILL CARLE

The Kansas City Royals were undergoing a transition in 1986-87. The Royals had won the World Series in 1985, but were slow getting out of the gate in 1986. Shortly after the All-Star break, manager Dick Howser was diagnosed with a brain tumor. He stepped down as manager to undergo treatment, and Mike Ferraro finished out the lackluster season as Royals manager. Howser tried to come back in the spring of 1987, but soon discovered that he was too weak to put up with the strains of managing a major-league ballclub, and was replaced by Billy Gardner. Howser died in June of 1987.

The other big transition that occurred during this time was the shifting of future Hall of Famer George Brett from third base to first base with Kevin Seitzer taking over for Brett at the hot corner. Seitzer was drafted by the Royals in the 11th round of the 1983 draft out of Eastern Illinois University, where he hit over .400 all three years he was there.[1] Since being drafted, Seitzer had done nothing but hit in the minor leagues, posting on-base percentages of .453, .432, .456, and .442 in his first four years. This earned him a call-up to the big club in September of 1986. Seitzer didn't stop hitting when he reached the majors, posting a .323 average and .440 on-base percentage in 28 September games.

Seitzer opened the 1987 season as the starting first baseman, with Steve Balboni moving to designated hitter and Brett still entrenched at third. Third base was Seitzer's natural position, however, and by May, Seitzer was playing third on a full-time basis with Brett moving to first. Seitzer started the year red-hot, hitting .382 in the month of April. He continued to post solid numbers as the season wore on, and was hitting .313 when the Royals took the field on Sunday, August 2, to close out a three-game series with the Boston Red Sox.

The day was brutally hot with the temperature at game time a torrid 103 degrees. The Royals Stadium artificial turf made things that much hotter, and a thermometer placed near the third-base coach's box registered 160 degrees. A crowd of 29,154 hardy souls braved the heat to watch Mark Gubicza face off against Boston's Bob Stanley.[2]

Seitzer was hitting second for the Royals, and in the bottom of the first inning with one out, he beat out an infield single to shortstop. George Brett followed with a ground-rule double, and a grounder by Danny Tartabull drove in Seitzer with the game's first run.

The Red Sox scored two runs in the top of the second and led 2-1 when Seitzer came up to lead off the third inning. Seitzer belted a home run to tie the game at 2-2.

The score was still deadlocked when the Royals came to bat in the bottom of the fourth. Ross Jones led off with a single and, after a sacrifice bunt by catcher Larry Owen, Lonnie Smith singled, advancing Jones to third. Seitzer then singled to right, scoring Jones. After a fly out by Brett advanced Smith to third, Danny Tartabull rolled an infield single to score Smith and give the Royals a 4-2 lead. That was all for Bob Stanley as Red Sox manager John McNamara brought in Steve Crawford to get the final out in the fourth and keep Boston in the game.

Boston scored a run in the top of the fifth inning on a couple of singles and a sacrifice fly by Marc Sullivan to cut the Royals lead to 4-3. Crawford issued a leadoff walk to Bill Pecota to open the fifth, and Steve Balboni followed with a double to score Pecota. Ross Jones grounded to third baseman Wade Boggs, who looked up to see Balboni lumbering toward him.

Boggs easily tagged Balboni for the first out of the inning. After a fly out by Owen, Lonnie Smith banged out a single to bring Seitzer up with two on and two out. Seitzer launched a three-run homer for his fourth hit of the game and his third, fourth, and fifth RBIs. The Royals now led 8-3.

Gubicza retired the Red Sox in order in the sixth and seventh innings and the top of the order was due up for the Royals in the seventh with the Royals still up 8-3 and reliever Tom Bolton on the mound for the Red Sox. Smith flied to right, and Seitzer grounded a single to center for his fifth hit of the game. Brett grounded out and, following a walk to Danny Tartabull, Bo Jackson grounded out to end the inning.

Gubicza again held the Red Sox scoreless in the eighth inning. With the Royals up by five runs and Seitzer due up sixth in the Royals half of the eighth, Seitzer would need some help from his teammates if he was going to get his chance at a sixth hit. Calvin Schiraldi replaced Bolton on the hill for the Red Sox to face Bill Pecota, Steve Balboni, and Ross Jones. Pecota led off with a single, stole second, and scored when Balboni lined a single to left. Jones and Larry Owen both struck out, and that left things up to Lonnie Smith to get on so Seitzer could come to the plate. Smith doubled to left, putting runners on second and third to bring Seitzer to the plate for his sixth at-bat of the game. Only the specter of George Brett looming in the on-deck circle likely kept the Red Sox from intentionally walking such a hot hitter. Seitzer lifted a high fly to deep right that Mike Greenwell appeared to be moving under to catch. The sun was bright, and Greenwell lost sight of the ball. "I lost it in the sun," Greenwell said. "At any other angle, I would have had it. I saw the ball go right into the sun. I didn't see the ball again until it was like a foot from the ground. You can't fight nature. (The sun) was just too bright."[3] The ball bounced off the artificial turf and into the right field stands for a ground-rule double. Seitzer had his sixth hit of the game and his sixth and seventh RBIs. Brett followed with a homer, and the Royals romped to a 13-5 victory.[4]

After the game, Seitzer was modest about his accomplishment. "I was just trying to do my job," he said. "I'm not an RBI man. I'm not a home-run man. I'm what you call a set-up man. I hit in the second hole and allow guys to get into scoring position. I just kind of go in there with a job in mind every time and to accomplish whatever I'm asked to do. If nobody is on, I'll try and start it."[5]

Kevin Seitzer finished the 1987 season with a .323 average and 207 hits, a record that in most years would easily win the Rookie of the Year award. Unfortunately for Seitzer, Oakland first baseman Mark McGwire set a rookie record with 49 home runs and garnered all the first-place votes with Seitzer finishing second in the voting. After Seitzer's playing career, he was able to teach his hitting skills to others, becoming a respected hitting coach, and teaming up with former Royal Mike Macfarlane to open the Mac N Seitz Baseball and Softball Academy in Kansas City.[6]

Sources

In addition to the sources cited in the Notes, the author also consulted Baseball-Reference.com and Retrosheet.org.

Notes

1 Dennis Dodd, "Sun Helps Turn Seitzer's Fly Ball Into Hit," *Kansas City Times*, August 3, 1987.

2 Dodd.

3 Dodd.

4 "Kevin Seitzer Picks Up His Sixth Hit of the Game," youtube.com/watch?v=v0Guz52OsQI.

5 Larry Whiteside, "Seitzer Quiet, Unlike His Bat," *Boston Globe*, August 3, 1987.

6 macnseitz.com/.

BO KNOWS BASEBALL: JACKSON CLOUTS THREE HOME RUNS IN VICTORY OVER YANKEES JULY 17, 1990: KANSAS CITY ROYALS 10, NEW YORK YANKEES 7, AT YANKEE STADIUM

BY MIKE HUBER

One year after the debut of the "Bo Knows" Nike ad campaign,[1] Bo Jackson, the first modern athlete to play both professional baseball and football in the same year, led his Kansas City Royals team with three home runs and seven RBIs in a 10-7 win over the New York Yankees.

The Royals were playing the second of a three-game series against the New Yorkers, in front of 26,777 fans at Yankee Stadium on July 17, 1990. K.C.'s Storm Davis was seeking his third win of the season, opposed by New York's Andy Hawkins, who was in pursuit of just his second victory (Hawkins had not won since May 6). The two teams were struggling, each sitting in seventh place in their respective American League divisions. The Royals entered the contest with a record of 39-48, while New York had a 31-54 mark.

With two outs in the opening inning, George Brett drew a walk. On a 2-and-2 count, Jackson bashed the ball "well beyond the reach of a leaping [Deion] Sanders"[2] in straightaway center field and out of the park. The ball landed an estimated 412 feet from home plate. Sanders later said, "He swings the bat so hard that if the ball touches it, it's bound to go somewhere."[3]

New York answered in the second. Matt Nokes doubled and Jim Leyritz walked. Jesse Barfield forced Leyritz at second, but Nokes advanced to third and came home on Kevin Maas's single to right field.

In the third inning, Bill Pecota crushed a Hawkins pitch well beyond the left-center-field fence for a solo home run, getting Kansas City back its two-run lead. Two outs later, Brett walked for the second time, again bringing up Jackson. Hawkins grooved the first pitch to Bo and he crushed it. According to the *New York Times*'s Michael Martinez, "This one was clearly awesome, landing more than halfway up the bleacher section in right-center field"[4] and traveling 464 feet. Even Brett was impressed, saying, "The second home run was an eye-popper. I had to stop and watch that one, it got so small so fast."[5]

In the fifth, Kevin Seitzer led off for the Royals with a single to right. Kurt Stillwell popped out. Brett laced a ground-rule double, sending Seitzer to third. Jackson settled into the batter's box. Hawkins decided to face Jackson, rather than walk him with first base open. After taking ball one, Jackson hit something "that looked like a popup but sailed majestically over the fence in right."[6] This third round-tripper went a mere 328 feet. Jackson's 19th home run of the season was the 100th of his career. It also meant the showers for Hawkins. Yankees manager Stump Merrill made the call to the bullpen, and Greg Cadaret retired the next two batters. In three at-bats through five innings, Jackson had driven in seven runs, and the Royals led, 8-1.

As Bo trotted out to center field with the Yankees coming to bat in the bottom half of the inning, the New York fans gave him a standing ovation. The home team then gave the fans something else to cheer for. Roberto Kelly led off by doubling into deep left-center. Sanders' bunt rolled to second baseman Pecota and Sanders reached, with Kelly moving to third. Steve Sax swung at Davis's first offering and deposited the ball into the left-field bleachers, making the score 8-4.

An inning later, to start the bottom of the sixth, the Royals made a pitching change, with Mel Stottlemyre Jr. on in relief of Davis. Maas drew a one-out walk. Alvaro Espinoza lined a double to left, bringing up Sanders, who worked a full count before driving the ball into right-center. Jackson raced over and dove horizontally for the ball but missed, and the ball rolled to the wall. Sanders tore around the bases and was waved home by third-base coach Buck Showalter. Sanders tried to leap over Royals catcher Mike Macfarlane, who was trying to catch the relay throw, but the two players collided, and the ball got past the catcher. Stottlemyre, who was backing up the play, caught the ball and tossed it back to the plate, but Sanders reached out and touched home for the run before he could be tagged. Safe! The Yankees had now trimmed the lead to just one run. This was the first inside-the-park home run by a Yankee at home since Don Baylor accomplished the feat in 1984.[7] Sanders, understandably pumped, said, "I can't wait to get home and watch that play on TV. It was exciting; it was mean. The adrenaline was flowing."[8] As for Jackson, he felt his shoulder pop on the play and was taken to Columbia-Presbyterian Medical Center for x-rays. The diagnosis was a partial dislocation in which the bone popped out of the joint and then popped back in. Willie Wilson replaced Jackson in center field.

The injury cost Jackson an opportunity to tie the major-league record of four home runs in a game. Even Sanders remarked, "I'm hoping he wasn't hurt. I wanted to see him come up and hit again."[9]

In the top of the seventh, Seitzer doubled and two outs later, Brett walked (for the third time in the game). Jackson's position in the lineup was still magical, because Cadaret uncorked a wild pitch with Wilson at the plate, and both runners moved 90 feet closer to home plate. Wilson then grounded a single up the middle, driving them in and giving the Royals two insurance runs. The final score was 10-7 in favor of Kansas City.

Speaking of Jackson, Royals manager John Wathan said, "That's the best performance I've seen by an individual in a major-league game."[10] He added, "I think he would have electrified Yankee Stadium just coming up to the plate a fourth time." New York skipper Merrill also had praise for Jackson: "You give him the ball out over the plate and that's going to happen. He was a one-man wrecking crew tonight."[11]

Sanders, like Jackson a two-sport star (football and baseball), said Jackson was "one of the best athletes who ever put on a uniform."[12] Sanders had a productive night as well, with two hits, including the inside-the-park home run, and raised his batting average to .158.

The two teams combined for 17 runs and 25 hits. There were eight walks and eight strikeouts. Hawkins suffered his fourth defeat in four starts, lasting only 4⅓ innings and yielding four home runs. This game was the season's seventh in which a batter hit three home runs.[13] Wilson added a single in the ninth inning, giving the K.C. center fielders five hits and nine runs batted in. Brett was 2-for-2, but with the three walks, he scored four runs. Storm Davis improved his record to 3-6, and Jeff Montgomery earned his 11th save.

After the game and back at the ballpark, Jackson commented, "I certainly didn't expect a night like I had, especially getting hurt. But the x-rays came back negative and I should be all right in a few days. I felt great until the ball I tried to dive for. I didn't try to hit three home runs, but all three pitches were in my strike zone."[14] Jackson's slugging percentage jumped 36 points to .507. The Royals slugger was not all right in a few days; he did not return to the lineup until August 26. When he did return, he went 3-for-4 with a home run, two runs scored, and two runs batted in against the Seattle Mariners. But on this July night in the House That Ruth Built, Bo Jackson showed that he knew something about hitting the baseball, too.

Sources

In addition to the sources mentioned in the Notes, the author consulted baseball-reference.com, mlb.com, and retrosheet.org.

Notes

1 The first commercial spot for "Bo Knows" aired during the 1989 All-Star Game, just after the top of the first inning, when Jackson led off the midsummer classic with a home run.

2 Michael Martinez, "Jackson, Sanders Co-Star," *New York Times*, July 18, 1990: B7.

3 Ibid.

4 Ibid.

5 Ibid.

6 Ibid.

7 Ibid.

8 Ibid.

9 "Bo Hurt After Slamming 3 Homers in Royal Win," *Chicago Tribune*, July 18, 1990: 49.

10 "Jackson's 3 HRs, 7 RBI Lead Royals Past Yankees," *Baltimore Sun*, July 18, 1990: 16.

11 Martinez.

12 Ibid.

13 "Bo Belts 3 HRs to Pace Royals," *Philadelphia Inquirer*, July 18, 1990: 46. The other six were Detroit's Cecil Fielder (May 6), San Francisco's Kevin Mitchell (May 25), Atlanta's Jeff Treadway (May 26), Houston's Glenn Davis (June 1), Cecil Fielder again (June 6), and Baltimore's Randy Milligan (June 9). On September 29, two months after this game, Boston's Tom Brunansky also hit three home runs.

14 Baltimore Sun.

JUNE 6, 1991: ROYALS OUTLAST RANGERS IN MARATHON KANSAS CITY ROYALS 4, TEXAS RANGERS 3 (18 INNINGS), AT ROYALS STADIUM, KANSAS CITY

BY DARIN WATSON

One game in June counts as much as the other 161, but in practice they often don't feel that way. The newness of the season has dissipated, but the excitement of a pennant race is still weeks away. However, this game between the Royals and Rangers had a little extra shine to it. The teams were average (Texas entered the game at 26-20, in third place in the AL West, while the Royals were in last place with a 23-27 record), but Kansas City was sending two-time Cy Young Award winner Bret Saberhagen to the mound, while Texas was countering with the great Nolan Ryan, who at age 44 still had two seasons remaining in his Hall of Fame career. Little more than a month earlier, Ryan had thrown his seventh no-hitter.

Besides the pitching matchup, fans were also intrigued by the idea of a day game during the week. In 1991 those were a new experiment for the Royals. Team President Joe Burke said, "We did it last year because we had a number of requests to at least try one. It was successful, so we came back with another one this year." The team expected more than 30,000 fans for this game; more than 38,000 showed up.[1] Fans lined up for tickets early that morning and caused a traffic jam two hours before the 1:35 P.M. start time.[2]Ryan and Saberhagen were as good as anticipated in the first three innings, with Saberhagen collecting three strikeouts. Meanwhile, Ryan had racked up five K's without allowing a hit.

But Ryan was the first pitcher to allow a run. In the fourth, Brian McRae led off with a single. George Brett singled with one out, and Warren Cromartie doubled with two outs to score McRae. The Royals added another run in the fifth, with singles by Brent Mayne and David Howard ahead of a McRae sacrifice fly.

Saberhagen had allowed just three hits entering the seventh, but Texas tied the game that inning. Kevin Reimer led off with a single. Mike Stanley drew a two-out walk, then pinch-hitter Denny Walling singled to drive in one run. Pinch-hitter Brian Downing hit a grounder to third. Kevin Seitzer fielded it cleanly but made a bad throw to first, pulling Cromartie off the bag. Stanley scored from third and the score was even at 2-2.

Both Ryan and Saberhagen left the game after seven innings, turning things over to the bullpens.

The Rangers broke the tie in the ninth against Luis Aquino. With one out, Mario Diaz singled and took second on Rafael Palmeiro's groundout. The Royals intentionally walked Ruben Sierra, but Julio Franco smacked a grounder into left field. Diaz scored, and the Rangers took a 3-2 lead into the bottom of the ninth.

It took three pitches for closer Jeff Russell to give up the lead. Carmelo Martinez, batting for Cromartie, launched a 2-and-0 pitch into the left-field seats to tie the game. Although a good portion of the crowd had left after Ryan and Saberhagen were finished, the remaining fans demanded — and got — a curtain call from Martinez.

The first scoring chance in extra innings belonged to the Royals. In the 11th, Martinez drew a leadoff walk. Pinch-runner Gary Thurman stole second and advanced to third on a bad throw. The Rangers issued two intentional walks, loading the bases in hopes of a double play, or at least a force out at home. Kurt Stillwell hit a hard grounder toward left field, and third baseman Steve Buechele attempted a diving stop. The ball ricocheted off his glove ... right to shortstop Diaz, who fired home to cut down the winning run. Mike Macfarlane followed with a popup and McRae, trying to bunt for a hit with two outs, hit the ball a little too hard. Buechele's throw nipped him at first for the third out.

The Rangers had a chance to take the lead in the 12th. Franco singled to start the inning, and Reimer walked. Juan Gonzalez hit a line drive to third baseman Seitzer, who dropped it. He threw to second for one out, and the Royals had Franco in a rundown between second and third. But he eluded Seitzer and made it to third. Royals manager Hal McRae argued the call with third-base umpire Dale Scott, who said Seitzer had missed the tag. The KC skipper had barely returned to the dugout when Buechele popped up a squeeze bunt attempt. Mayne caught it and fired to third for the double play. When Scott ruled Franco had made it back safely, McRae charged out of the dugout and promptly earned the first ejection of his managerial career, 13 games in. As McRae and Scott argued, boos and trash rained down on the field. When play resumed, Walling grounded out to end the inning.

The Royals left the bases loaded in the 13th inning, and left two more on base in the 14th. The Rangers left the bases loaded in their half of the 15th. The Royals answered that by leaving three runners on in the bottom of the 15th.

It was becoming increasingly obvious that one run would win this game. So in the top of the 16th, when Reimer and Gonzalez started the inning with singles, Texas manager Bobby Valentine turned to small ball again. First, a sacrifice bunt to move the runners up. And then the Rangers attempted their second suicide squeeze of the game. This one turned out even worse for Texas than the first one. Stanley popped up his bunt attempt, Mayne snared it, and fired to third for an inning-ending double play.

"We made two lousy bunts and get outs.... Both times I'm thinking right-handed pitcher against right-handed hitter. It's a long game, people are tired, you get one run and you're going to win the game," Valentine said.[3]

The Royals had another chance to win in the 16th. Thurman led off with a single and moved to second on a bunt. Mayne — who caught all 18 innings, just like his Texas counterpart Stanley — hit a looping fly ball to center field. Sierra couldn't make the catch, but got close enough to it that Thurman stopped just before third base. Thurman tried to score anyway, but Sierra's throw home was in time. Despite a collision, Stanley held on to the ball and preserved the tie.

When the 18th inning arrived, both teams had used up their bullpens. Kansas City turned to starting pitcher Mike Boddicker, who had picked up the win in the first game of the series two days earlier. He continued to baffle the Rangers in this one, working a perfect inning against the heart of the Texas order.

Valentine put in left-hander Kenny Rogers to pitch the bottom of the 18th, although Rogers was scheduled to start in New York the next night.[4] Seitzer led off with a single and Mayne drew a walk. Stillwell came up in yet another bunt situation.

"It was about my 10th at-bat," Stillwell said. "I didn't think I could swing the bat anyway."[5] Stillwell bunted and Rogers quickly pounced on it. He had time to make a throw to third for a force out, but didn't get a good grip on the ball. His throw sailed well wide of Buechele and nearly hit third-base coach Adrian Garrett. "If that throw had hit me and dropped straight down and the run didn't score, I think people might have come down out of the stands and killed me," Garrett said.[6]

As the ball skipped up the left-field line, Seitzer headed home, stomping emphatically on the plate to finally bring the longest game (by time) in Royals history to an end. Six hours and 28 minutes after the first pitch, Kansas City had a 4-3 win.

The game featured 651 pitches, 157 plate appearances, 29 hits, 24 walks (seven of those intentional, including four by Rangers reliever Gerald Alexander), and 21 strikeouts. The two teams combined to go 4-for-34 with runners in scoring position, stranded 45 runners (28 of them in extra innings), and left the bases loaded seven times. Reimer picked up five hits and two walks, while Brett had four hits and three walks. On the other end of the spectrum, Stillwell went 0-for-7 and Palmeiro went 0-for-9, dropping his average from .325 to .310.

"It was the longest day of my life. It's funny. How can I go nine times and not get a hit? I could hit right-handed and get two hits," Palmeiro said.[7]

Understandably, frustration reigned in one locker room, while the other one was filled with hard-earned relief.

"We gave it to them in the end," Valentine said. "They didn't earn it. That was the disappointing thing."[8]

"It was a good day," Hal McRae said. "We played 18 innings and won. A lot of people got to play. George (Brett) had four hits. It was a helluva day."[9]

Sources

Besides the articles listed in the Notes, the author consulted baseball-reference.com and retrosheet.org.

Notes

1 Jack Etkin, "Big Bats to Come at Saberhagen," *Kansas City Star,* June 6, 1991: D1.

2 Steve Cameron, "Game Takes Crazy Turn After Star Pitchers Leave," *Kansas City Star*, June 7, 1991: D4.

3 T.R. Sullivan, "Rangers Throw Away Marathon Game," *Fort Worth Star-Telegram*, June 7, 1991: 1.

4 Sullivan, "Pitching Plans Unclear After 18-inning Duel," *Fort Worth Star-Telegram*, June 7, 1991: 5.

5 Dick Kaegel, "Long Day Leads to Happy Ending," *Kansas City Star*, June 7, 1991: D1.

6 "A Long Day at the Ballpark," *Kansas City Star*, June 7, 1991: D5.

7 Gerry Fraley, "Palmeiro Endures 'Longest Day' Of Life," *Dallas Morning News*, June 7, 1991: 4B.

8 Sullivan, "Rangers Throw Away Marathon Game."

9 Gary Bedore, "Royals Outlast Texas, 4-3," *Lawrence* (Kansas) *Journal-World*, June 7, 1991: 1D.

GEORGE BRETT JOINS 3,000 – HIT CLUB DURING FOUR-HIT PERFORMANCE SEPTEMBER 30, 1992: KANSAS CITY ROYALS 4, CALIFORNIA ANGELS 0, AT ANAHEIM STADIUM

BY GORDON GATTIE

George Brett entered the 1992 season as an accomplished veteran leading a rebuilding team. The 1991 Royals finished with an 82-80 record, 13 games behind the AL-West-leading Minnesota Twins and only one game removed from the basement. Kansas City hadn't reached the postseason since winning the 1985 World Series, although the Royals won 92 games during the 1989 season. They did have young stars returning, including homegrown staff ace Kevin Appier, who led the pitching staff with 13 wins and 207⅔ innings; Brian McRae, who paced the offense with 152 games, 663 plate appearances, and 20 stolen bases; and Tom Gordon, who recorded a team-high 167 strikeouts. Brett, entering his 20th season, had amassed 2,836 career hits, 163 shy of the vaunted 3,000-hit milestone. He won the 1990 AL batting title with a .329 average but struggled in '91 with a more pedestrian .255 average, 10 home runs, and 61 RBIs. Throughout the 1992 season and even before the 1991 season, questions arose about Brett's retirement, especially after longtime Royals Willie Wilson and Frank White departed Kansas City.[1]

After the 1991 season the Royals, continuing to contemplate life after Brett, made significant changes to their roster. All-Star Danny Tartabull was allowed to leave in free agency while first baseman Wally Joyner was signed from California. The Angels' senior vice president for player personnel, former Royals skipper Whitey Herzog, who twice thought a new deal with Joyner was approved, were now hoping to land Tartabull. The highly-popular Joyner,[2] who signed a one-year deal, was looking forward to his new environs though he was a fan favorite in California.[3] Two days later, the Royals traded two-time AL Cy Young Award winner Bret Saberhagen and versatile infielder Bill Pecota to the New York Mets for Gregg Jefferies, Kevin McReynolds, and Keith Miller.[4] The Mets gained instant credibility for the deal,[5] while Royals GM Herk Robinson noted, "What we did was a difficult thing. We have finished sixth the last two seasons so if Bret Saberhagen won four more Cy Young Awards and we didn't win it doesn't mean a thing."[6] The team also parted ways with first baseman Todd Benzinger and outfielder Kirk Gibson. The numerous offseason moves had far-reaching roster impacts, down into the minor leagues.[7]

Royals manager Hal McRae now looked forward to his first full season at the helm. He joined the 15-22 last-place Royals in May 1991 and attained a 66-58 record. McRae preached NL-style play, commenting, "We will force the action, create maximum pressure for nine innings, force the other team to make the perfect play."[8] *The Sporting News* predicted Kansas City would win the AL West based on its pitching, defense, and speed, noting "everything must work, but the material is there."[9] Kansas City struggled from the outset, losing its first seven games and becoming the last team to win a game. The Royals finished April with a 3-17 record, 9½ games behind the Oakland Athletics. As the summer dragged on, the Royals escaped the basement but focus gradually shifted from team success to Brett's milestone pursuit.[10]As Brett approached the milestone, rumors circulated about his desire to hit number 3,000 at Royals Stadium; he acknowledged the difficulty of timing the event: "I know it's going to get worse as I get closer. The toughest part is just trying to concentrate on the basics, just going out each night and forgetting about 3,000 and just hitting the ball hard."[11] Kanas City entered the September 30 game against the Angels with a 70-87 record, splitting the first two of the four-game series while Brett missed both games fighting a shoulder ailment.[12]

The Angels were not faring any better, two games behind the Royals. California struggled throughout May and June, spending most of the summer teetering between fifth and sixth place. The solid pitching staff was led by upcoming star Jim Abbott and veteran Mark Langston, but the offense struggled after Joyner left and several veterans endured subpar seasons.

Kansas City manager McRae selected Rick Reed for the start. Reed, who spent the previous four seasons with the Pittsburgh Pirates and was the 1991 American Association Pitcher of the Year, was signed as a free agent in April. He opened the season with the Omaha Royals in the American Association and was promoted to Kansas City in June. Reed was 2-7 with a 4.04 ERA over 91⅓ innings entering his final start of the season.

His mound opponent was Julio Valera, pitching his first full season in the majors and posting the best year of his career. He also was making his last start of the season, compiling an 8-10 record and a 3.69 ERA thus far. Valera's 3.2 Wins Above Replacement (WAR) in 1992 placed him third on the Angels' staff, just behind Langston. The Angels traded Dick Schofield and minor-leaguer Julian Vasquez to the Mets for Valera just after the season began.

Miller started the game by flying out to right field, and Joyner followed with a groundout to first base. Brett delivered the game's first hit, and career number 2,997, on a slicing double to left field. Jeffries singled home Brett for the game's first run. After two more singles, Jefferies was thrown out at home to end the half inning. Reed allowed one baserunner in the bottom half, Chad Curtis, who was caught stealing. Kansas City led 1-0 after one inning. Both sides allowed a lone hit and subsequent stranded runner during the second inning.

In the third frame, Joyner led off with a single, and Brett's 2,998th career hit was a single to center that advanced Joyner to third. Jefferies delivered another timely knock, scoring Joyner and giving Kansas City a 2-0 lead. The inning ended after a double play and infield groundout. The Angels threatened in the third with two outs when Damion Easley singled and Curtis was hit by a pitch, but Reed struck out Junior Felix to end the threat. In the fourth inning, both teams had baserunners though neither team scored.

Joyner began the fifth inning with a solo shot that gave Reed another insurance run and increased Kansas City's lead to 3-0. Brett followed with his third base hit that evening – and career number 2,999 – on a 1-and-0 forkball that he lined into center field for a single. He was erased when Jefferies hit into a double play. Valera allowed singles to Mike Macfarlane and Jim Eisenreich, then prevented further damage by striking out McRae. Tim Fortugno replaced Valera for the top of the sixth, and walked the first batter, Kevin Koslofski. But Fortugno retired the next three batters, stranding Koslofski. Reed continued his strong performance, setting down the Angels in order in the bottom half.

In the seventh inning, Joyner popped out to short for the first out. Brett approached home plate for the fourth time. On the first pitch, he singled, a line drive over second base to become the 18th major leaguer to get 3,000 hits. Brett reached the career milestone exactly 20 years after Roberto Clemente delivered his 3,000th hit.[13] Brett was mobbed by his teammates and received a five-minute ovation from the appreciative crowd. He became the second player to achieve the feat at Anaheim Stadium, following Rod Carew, who hit number 3,000 seven years earlier.[14] After the game he mentioned three people he hoped were watching "from a more heavenly seat": his father, Jack Brett, hitting instructor Charlie Lau, and manager Dick Howser.[15] After the festivities subsided and the game resumed, Jefferies flied out to right field. With two outs and the crowd still buzzing, Brett was picked off while talking with California first baseman Gary Gaetti. Brett commented, "He asked me if my wife was here and I said yes, and I had friends here from Kansas

City. ... He didn't even let me finish the sentence. Believe me, my mind wasn't on being picked off."[16]

After the prolonged top half, Reed took the mound for the bottom of the seventh and retired the Angels in order on a groundout and two fly outs. Macfarlane led off the eighth inning with his 16th clout to extend Kansas City's lead. Fortugno didn't allow any more baserunners in the eighth, but ran into trouble in the ninth when the Royals loaded the bases. Fortugno then got Mike Macfarlane on a grounder. Reed finished strong, allowing only one baserunner over the final four innings. Brett finished the game with four hits, supporting Reed's seven-hit shutout.

Brett was inducted into the Baseball Hall of Fame in 1999, elected on his first ballot with 98.2 percent of the vote. He had retired in 1993 after 21 seasons with the Royals as one of only four players with 3,000 hits, 300 home runs, and a .300 batting average, joining Stan Musial, Willie Mays, and Hank Aaron in truly rarefied company.

Sources

Besides the sources cited in the Notes, the author consulted Baseball-Almanac.com, Baseball-Reference.com, Retrosheet.org, and the following:

Hart, Stan. *Scouting Reports: The Original Reviews of Some of Baseball's Greatest Stars* (New York: Macmillan, 1995).

James, Bill. *The New Bill James Historical Abstract* (New York: The Free Press, 2001).

James, Bill, and Jim Henzler. *Win Shares* (Morton Grove, Illinois: STATS, Inc., 2002).

Notes

1 Associated Press, "New Faces Replace Old Stars for Kansas City," *Springfield* (Missouri) *News-Leader*, February 23, 1991: 25.

2 Jon Nalick, "Angel Fans Are Upset Over Joyner's Departure," Los Angeles Times, December 10, 1991: 179.

3 Ross Newhan, "Angels Will Be Left to Cry Over Deal," *Los Angeles Times*, December 10, 1991: 179.

4 Mike Lupica, "Mets Haul In," *New York Daily News*, December 12, 1991: 88.

5 Rick Hummel, "Acquisition of Saberhagen Makes Mets Front-runners," *St. Louis Post-Dispatch*, December 13, 1991: 17.

6 "Mets Make Huge Deal for KC Ace," *Press and Sun-Bulletin* (Binghamton, New York), December 12, 1991: 39.

7 Steve Buckley, "The Domino Theory," *The Sporting News*, April 6, 1992: 50.

8 Dave Nightingale, "No Repeat Business," *The Sporting News*, April 6, 1992: 54.

9 Nightingale, 54.

10 Tony DeMarco, "The Hits Keep Coming," *The Sporting News*, September 21, 1992: 9.

11 Jeffrey Flanagan, "Chasing 3,000: Brett Hopes H Gets Script Down Pat," *Indianapolis News*, September 18, 1992: 46.

12 Associated Press, "3,000, by George!," *Democrat and Chronicle* (Rochester, New York), October 1, 1992: 37.

13 Ibid.

14 Helene Elliot, "Brett's 3,000th: Easy as 1-2-3-4," Los Angeles Times, October 1, 1992: 218.

15 Ross Newhan, "The Swing for 3,000th: Brett's Goodby Wave?" *Los Angeles Times*, October 1, 1992: 221.

16 Elliot, 218.

GEORGE BRETT WALK-OFF AFTER ANNOUNCING RETIREMENT SEPTEMBER 26, 1993: KANSAS CITY ROYALS 9, CALIFORNIA ANGELS 8, AT KAUFFMAN STADIUM

BY STEVEN KUEHL

Major-league baseball saw four Hall of Fame careers come to an end after the 1993 season: George Brett, Carlton Fisk, Nolan Ryan, and Robin Yount. The Hall of Fame elected Ryan (491 votes), Brett (488), and Yount (385) to the Class of 1999 in their first year of eligibility. Fisk was elected in 2000, receiving 397 votes.

Lynn Nolan Ryan Jr. played 27 seasons for the New York Mets, California Angels, Houston Astros, and Texas Rangers. As one of the greatest pitchers the game has seen, the "Ryan Express" amassed 324 wins over the course of his storybook career, as well as countless records. Some lifetime benchmarks include 5,714 strikeouts, seven no-hitters, leading the league in strikeouts 11 times and fanning 300 batters in a season six times, including a record 383 in 1973.

Robin Yount played 20 seasons for the Milwaukee Brewers. "The Kid" was one of only three players to earn MVP honors at two positions, shortstop and center field. Yount was a prolific hitter who amassed 3,142 hits, batter over .300 six times, hit 40 doubles four times, smacked 20 home runs four times, and scored 100 runs five times.

Carlton "Pudge" Fisk played 24 seasons for the Boston Red Sox and Chicago White Sox. He caught more games (2,226) and hit more home runs (376) than any catcher before him. Fisk was the 1972 AL Rookie of the Year and was an 11-time All-Star. Most notably, true baseball fans remember Fisk's dramatic home run to win Game Six of the 1975 World Series, one of baseball's most unforgettable moments.

On Saturday, September 25, 1993, George Brett held a press conference to announce his retirement as a player. He was flanked on one side by his wife of two years, Leslie, and his 6-month-old son, named Jackson after his late father, and on the other side by Muriel Kauffman, widow of Ewing Kauffman, the founder of the Royals, and general manager Herk Robinson.[1] Brett's heart told him it was time to hang up number 5 for the last time. The Royals star always said he played for the fun of the game, not the money. "The game became a job," Brett said. "It wasn't a game anymore. And baseball shouldn't be treated that way. I wasn't getting that excited when I did something good, wasn't getting that down when I did something bad. I wasn't that happy when we won; I wasn't that sad when we lost. There was something missing."[2]

Even though there might not have been fireworks the day Brett announced his retirement, the next day proved different.

On Sunday, September 26, 1993, in front of 19,391 at Kauffman Stadium, the Royals (80-76) faced off against the California Angels (69-86). The Angels were managed by Buck Rodgers and Hal McRae was the skipper of the Royals. The game saw a starting pitchers were John Farrell of the Angels and Chris Haney of the Royals. Farrell came into the game with a record of 3-11 after four days' rest and Haney had a 9-9 record after resting for nine days.

In the Angels' first, Haney threw 13 pitches and got Luis Polonia to line out to third, Chad Curtis to line out to center, and Rene Gonzales to ground out to third.

After that quick one-two-three, the Royals' Kevin Koslofski led off the bottom of the inning with a fly ball to center. Félix José walked and stole second base.

Brett doubled to center, scoring José. Chris Gwynn walked, but Gary Gaetti and Bob Hamelin, struck out and lined out, respectively, to end the inning. The Royals were ahead 1-0 and Farrell had racked up a pitch count of 34.

The Angels returned the favor in the top of the second. After two quick outs (Chili Davis struck out swinging and Eduardo Perez grounded to short), Chris Turner singled to center and Stan Javier doubled down the left-field line to score Turner. Haney threw a wild pitch to Torey Lovullo, moving Javier to third. He scored when Lovullo hit a single to center. The Angels finished the inning ahead 2-1 after Rod Correia grounded out to third.

Both pitchers settled in and neither team scored again until the top of the fourth when Javier hit a two-out solo home run off Haney, making the score 3-1.

The Royals rallied in the bottom of the inning. After back-to-back singles by Brent Mayne and Jose Lind, Koslofski walked, loading the bases. Mayne scored on a sacrifice fly by José. Brett was up again. On the second pitch of his at-bat, Brett hit a line-drive home run to deep right-center field. Farrell was relieved by Ken Patterson, who retired the side with the Royals up, 5-3.

In the top of the fifth, the Angels tied the game at 5-5 on singles by Perez and Turner. McRae replaced Haney with John Habyan.

The Angels struck again in the top of the sixth. After doubles by Lovullo and Polonia, Habyan was replaced by Stan Belinda. This didn't stop the bleeding: Singles by Davis scored Polonia and Gonzales, giving the Angels an 8-5 lead, which still stood going into the bottom of the ninth.

The Angels' Steve Frey started the half inning by striking out Keith Miller and hitting Brett with a pitch. Hubie Brooks, pinch-hitting for Gwynn, flied to center. Frey walked Gaetti. Joe Grahe relieved Frey but things didn't get much better as he walked two straight batters, forcing Brett home. With the bases loaded, Mike Macfarlane tied the game with a single to center, scoring Gaetti and Phil Hiatt. With a chance at a walk-off, Terry Shumpert lined to second and the game headed to extra innings tied 8-8.

Jeff Montgomery relieved for the Royals in the 10th and got Curtis to fly out to center, J.T. Snow to ground out to second, and Davis to strike out swinging, all on 10 pitches.

The Angels' Paul Swingle relieved Grahe in the bottom of the 10th. After Brian McRae struck out swinging and Miller popped out to short, Brett stepped to the plate for the fifth time. Again on the second pitch, he hit his second home run of the night, into the Royals bullpen in right field. Brett took a little hop and pumped his arms as he rounded second. Bullpen coach Bruce Kison retrieved the ball for him. "I haven't been in that situation in a long, long time," Brett said. "If it's the last home run I ever hit, I'll have it inscribed in my trophy case."[3]

George Brett played 21 seasons for the Kansas City Royals. Brett was the first major leaguer to win a batting title in three different decades, with averages of .333 in 1976, .390 in 1980, and .329 in 1990. He is one of four players to have 3,000-plus hits, 300-plus home runs, and a batting average over .300. As a 13-time All Star, Brett holds the record for the longest time between hitting for the cycle at 11 years, 57 days; he did it the first time on May 28, 1979, and again on July 25, 1990. The Royals retired Brett's number 5 on May 14, 1994.

Brett ended his career the same season as Nolan Ryan, and his retirement was all but overshadowed by Ryan's as many news outlets, including *The Sporting News*, ran articles about Ryan at the end of the season. Brett was Kansas City Royalty and was one of the most productive hitters ever.[4]

Sources

In addition to the sources cited in the Notes, the author consulted Baseball-almanac.com, Baseball-reference.com, and the National Baseball Hall of Fame site at baseballhall.org/hall-of-famers.

Notes

1 Associated Press, "Emotional Brett Quits the Game," *Chicago Tribune*, September 26, 1993: 2.

2 Dick Kaegel and T.R. Sullivan, "Hall of Fame, Class of '98," *The Sporting News*, October 4, 1993: 18.

3 Associated Press, "Brett, 40, Swings His Bat Like Old Times," *Los Angeles Times*, September 27, 1993: C13.

4 Associated Press, "Brett Calls It a Career After 20 Years as a Royal," *New York Times*, September 26, 1993: 6.

A KANSAS CITY OPENING DAY TO REMEMBER APRIL 5, 2004: KANSAS CITY ROYALS 9, CHICAGO WHITE SOX 7, AT KAUFFMAN STADIUM

BY STEVE FRIEDMAN

There was an air of excitement on Opening Day at Kauffman Stadium in 2004. More than 41,000 fans packed the ballpark armed with Royals magnetic 2004 season schedules.[1] It was a comfortable 66 degrees, with clear skies, although winds were from the south at a potentially impactful 10 mph.[2]

The Royals' 2004 slogan was "We Believe,"[3] which carried over from their successful 2003 season, when they finished with an 83-79 record. It was their first winning season after eight consecutive losing seasons, and earned Tony Peña Manager of the Year honors.[4] In anticipation of a run at the AL Central title this season, they had signed former AL MVP Juan Gonzalez and five-time All-Star catcher Benito Santiago.[5]

In Chicago, the White Sox were a talented team that hadn't met its expectations in recent years. Ozzie Guillen, who replaced the fired Jerry Manuel, was hired to bring more fun to the dugout.[6] They were led by a powerful right-handed-hitting lineup that included Magglio Ordonez, future Hall of Famer Frank Thomas, Paul Konerko, and Carlos Lee. Their advantage in the AL Central was that their opponents were strong on left-handed starters and the White Sox had been successful hitting against lefties.[7] They further bolstered their lineup by signing catcher Sandy Alomar Jr.

The White Sox named Mark Buehrle their Opening Day starter, his third consecutive Opening Day start. The Royals countered with Brian Anderson, a veteran left-hander acquired during the 2003 season from the Cleveland Indians and re-signed as a free agent during the offseason.[8]

The game started at 2:10 P.M. with a Brian Anderson fastball strike to leadoff hitter Willie Harris.[9] After a scoreless first inning, the White Sox got four runs in the second. Frank Thomas and Carlos Lee led off with singles and were driven home by Paul Konerko's double. The next two batters were retired, but Alomar homered to drive in two more runs.

In the bottom of the inning the Royals countered with a run. Juan Gonzalez sent a line drive to center for the initial Royals hit. One out later, Ken Harvey dribbled a ball to pitcher Buehrle, who threw wide to first. Gonzalez went to third and Harvey to second. Benito Santiago followed with a groundball to short. Gonzalez scored but Harvey was thrown out trying to advance to third. Aaron Guiel struck out to end the inning.

The game settled in. Carlos Lee led off the fourth with a home run to extend the White Sox lead to 5-1, and Royals starter Anderson was relieved by Shawn Camp after five innings. By the seventh inning, the White Sox' lead was 7-2. In the seventh, Buehrle gave up two hits and a run and was replaced by Cliff Politte with two outs. Buehrle's pitched 6⅔ innings and surrendered three runs (two earned) and eight hits. Buehrle was not satisfied with his performance. "I really didn't think I had good stuff," he said, "I fell behind in the count a lot. If I have this outing the next time out [Saturday in New York], it's not going to go as well as it did. I got lucky."[10]

With a 7-3 lead, Politte came out to pitch the ninth. After he walked the first two batters, manager Guillen brought in righty Billy Koch to face the right-handed-hitting Benito Santiago, who had homered earlier in the game.

Santiago greeted Koch with a double down the left-field line, scoring Joe Randa and putting runners on second and third. "The pitch I threw to Santiago was in off the plate," said Koch. "It was thigh-high, so it was up a little bit, but it was off the plate. The only way he keeps it fair is because he was cheating."[11]

With the tying run now coming up to the plate, Guillen left Koch in to pitch to Aaron Guiel, whom he struck out. Powerful left-handed hitter Matt Stairs was on deck preparing to bat for light-hitting Tony Graffanino, so Guillen signaled for the left-handed Damaso Marte to replace Koch. "I wanted to get the best matchup," Guillen said. "I didn't want Stairs to tie the game [with a home run]. I'm going to play with my gut feeling."[12] Royals manager Peña countered the move by replacing Stairs with right-hander Mendy Lopez.

Lopez was an infielder who had spent most of his career in the minor leagues. His major-league career had spanned parts of six seasons, with only 384 at-bats and just five home runs. After Marte relieved, Peña recalled that Lopez had faced Marte in winter ball. "I just called him in and said hit a home run," said a grinning Peña.[13] Little did Lopez realize that this would be the greatest at-bat of his career.

On a 3-and-1 pitch, Lopez smashed a home run over the left-field wall, tying the game, 7-7. (It was Lopez's last major-league home run and he soon ended up back in the minors after hitting only .105 in 43 more plate appearances. He never made it back to the major leagues.)

Guillen stayed with Marte. A single by Angel Berroa brought up the Royals' best player, Carlos Beltran. Beltran dug in with the boisterous crowd imploring him to bring the game to a successful close. He took a 1-and-2 fastball from Marte because he felt he couldn't do anything with it. "It was very close," Beltran said after the game. "But I got a second chance."[14] The next pitch, another fastball, Beltran slugged over the left-field wall, the ball bouncing off the top of the wall in front of the fountains for a 9-7 Royals victory. Elated Royals fans cheered as Beltran smiled while he circled the bases, throwing off his helmet as he ran into a wall of teammates, who pushed him around and slapped his back and jumped on him.[15]

Beltran's home run made a winner of D.J. Carrasco, who had pitched the scoreless top of the ninth. The loser was Marte, who failed to retire any of the three batters he faced and surrendered the home runs by Lopez and Beltran.

Guillen's debut as a manager started strong, then faded with the Royals' ninth-inning comeback. "I started pretty good," said Guillen. "I don't know if people think I can manage or not. I'm going to have people second-guessing me from now on. (The Royals), you've got to pitch good every inning and that didn't happen today."[16] Guillen was second-guessed about his decision to pull Koch in favor of Marte, including by Koch himself. "There's no doubt in my head," Koch said. "I thought I threw the ball very well. For the velocity doubters, I saw a 97 [mph reading on the scoreboard]."[17] Just over two months later, he was traded to the Florida Marlins.

For the Royals, it was their first Opening Day game-winning home run. "This I'm going to remember for the rest of my life," Beltran gushed. "I'm going to live with this. Opening Day. A walk-off home run. It doesn't get any better."[18] The team was hopeful to build off their successful 2003 season, when they won their first nine games amid a run of winning 16 of their first 19 games. "We aren't saying this means we're going to start 9-0 again," said third baseman Joe Randa, who scored one of the six runs in the ninth. "But Mendy and Carlos did something magical today. It was a feeling none of us will ever forget."[19]

Sources

In addition to the sources cited in the Notes, the author used the Baseball-Reference.com and Retrosheet.org websites.

Notes

1 kansascity.royals.mlb.com/content/printer_friendly/kc/y2004/m02/d05/c634599.jsp.
2 wunderground.com/history/daily/us/mo/kansas-city/KMKC/date/2004-4-5.
3 Max Rieper, "Royals Slogans Throughout the Years," *SB Nation Royal Review*, February 6, 2015.
4 Bob Foltman, "Pena, Guillen Let Enthusiasm Show," *Chicago Tribune*, April 5, 2004.
5 Doug Tucker, "Pena and Guillen Center of Attention, Springfield (Missouri) News-Leader, April 5, 2004.
6 Bob Foltman, "Pena, Guillen Let Enthusiasm Show."
7 Phil Rogers, "Why the Sox Will Make the Playoffs," *Chicago Tribune*, April 5, 2004.
8 baseball-reference.com/players/a/anderbr02.shtml.
9 "Opening Game Firsts," *Chicago Tribune*, April 6, 2004.
10 Bob Foltman, "Royals Yank Rug Out from Under Sox in 9th," *Chicago Tribune*, April 6, 2004.
11 Ibid.
12 Ibid.
13 Doug Tucker, "Lopez Rewards Pena's Faith with Homer," *Springfield* (Missouri) *News-Leader*, April 6, 2004.
14 Joe Posnanski, "Making Most of 2nd Chance," *Kansas City Star*, April 6, 2004.
15 Ibid.
16 Doug Tucker, "Lopez Rewards Pena's Faith with Homer."
17 Phil Rogers, "Guillen's Gut Fails Him in a Gut-wrencher," *Chicago Tribune*, April 6, 2004.
18 Doug Tucker, "The Boys Are Back in Town," *Springfield* (Missouri) *News-Leader*, April 6, 2004.
19 Ibid.

THE WAIT IS OVER AS ROYALS EARN FIRST POSTSEASON APPEARANCE IN 29 YEARS SEPTEMBER 26, 2014: KANSAS CITY ROYALS 3, CHICAGO WHITE SOX 1, AT U.S. CELLULAR FIELD, CHICAGO

BY LARRY PAULEY

10,561 days is a long time.

And if you reduce that number to the major-league baseball seasons involved ... 29 seasons is still a very long time.

But September 26, 2014, had seen that much time pass since the Kansas City Royals had been a postseason team. It was long enough that four of the 10 players who started for the Royals against Chicago that evening were not even alive when the K.C. crew ended the 1985 World Series.

Gathering at U.S. Cellular Field that afternoon, the young team could bring all that history to an end. It was possible to start a chapter of postseason baseball under the Royals name. And K.C. fans were ready.

In May of 2010, Dayton Moore, the Royals GM since mid-2006, stated in an interview his ideas about what he coined "the Process."[1] He uncharacteristically revealed what he thought a timetable for the Royals resurgence might be:

> "Our goal by 2013, 2014 is to have the majority of our 25-man roster be homegrown players. That's what we're shooting for, that's been the long-term plan all along. ... Look what Colorado did, look what Minnesota did, look what the New York Yankees did. ... I'm not talking about getting to .500, I'm talking about winning the World Series when I say eight to 10 years."[2]

So, depending on whether Moore's 8- to 10-year window began with his hiring or the timing of the quotation, the Royals team playing that evening was either a few years early or right on time. Myriad Royals fans felt that a place in the postseason could not come soon enough.

The ballclub was certainly aware of its history and the fan base angst. It had been the subject of radio call-in shows and blog posts since before spring training.[3] Just the day before the September 26 game, a popular Royals blog site stated how many fans were approaching the possibility that the long wait might be over:

> "It's really hard – as a Royals fan – to believe something good is going to happen. If there's still a faint trace of a fraction of a chance that a pro sports team could defy 99.6 percent odds, it'd have to be the Royals. They do, of course, have the longest playoff drought in American sports after all ... until tonight ... maybe."[4]

Such skepticism was understandable. September saw the Royals play yo-yo with the idea of a postseason berth. Five of their first six games in the month were victories, but those were followed by five losses in seven games. Worse, two of the defeats were to the Detroit Tigers, the team just ahead of them in the Central Division.

Even so, when beginning play at 7:10 that evening, the Royals had a "magic number" of one to secure a postseason berth for the 2014 season. The host White Sox were out of the picture, fighting with the Twins to avoid last place. But 27,416 was the announced attendance on a comfortable late-season night. Part of that crowd was a large contingent of Royals fans who traveled to Chicago hoping to see their squad make history.

Those fans did not have to wait long to be rewarded. On the game's second pitch, Alcides Escobar lined a single off White Sox starter Hector Noesi. Two pitches later, Norichika Aoki blasted a triple to deep right field to score Escobar. Two pitches after that, Lorenzo Cain shot a single up the middle to bring in run number two. Eric Hosmer was a strikeout victim, but Cain stole second, his 28th stolen base of the year. Billy Butler, at age 28 a veteran of the team, worked a 3-and-2 count before hitting a single between shortstop and second base to allow Cain to tally the third run of the inning. The next two hitters made outs and the score after half an inning was 3-0 for the Royals.

Jeremy Guthrie, starting his most important regular-season game as a member of the Royals, began well. He gave up a bases-empty single to eventual AL Rookie of the Year Jose Abreu, and after that scattered three hits and one walk over seven innings pitched. The only time the White Sox managed multiple runners was in the fifth, but Guthrie stranded them at first and second. He never had a Chicago batter get as far as third.

For Royals fans the pitching was encouraging, but the lack of offense after the first inning had an unpleasant feel of déjà vu. In the second inning Mike Moustakas was on second and Escobar on first following a walk and a single with one out. They would stay there. Omar Infante's fourth-inning single was erased by a double play after a successful replay challenge by White Sox manager Robin Ventura. In the seventh the Royals struck out in order, and they also went down in order in the eighth. The score remained as it had been since the top of the first inning.

Throughout the season the Royals were never an offensive juggernaut. They were ninth in runs scored in the AL. But they boasted solid, if not spectacular, starting pitching; excellent defense (three Gold Glove players[5]); and a sensational bullpen corps known as "H-D-H" (Kelvin Herrera, Wade Davis, Greg Holland).[6] These were the ingredients of their history-challenging success, and they were potent on this night.

Wade Davis came in for the eighth inning (Herrera did not pitch). After Marcus Semien struck out to begin the inning, Adam Eaton laced a triple to deep center field. Alexei Ramirez singled to score Eaton, and the game became a 3-1 affair. There was one out and the slugger Abreu was up. It was here the Royals began to turn back time. Davis struck out Abreu and then Conor Gillaspie.

After the Royals failed to capitalize on a runner in scoring position in the ninth, manager Ned Yost gave two-time All-Star closer Greg Holland the chance to stop the clock on the team's postseason absence. Eleven pitches later the final out was recorded and the clock on Kansas City's playoff appearances was reset.

Naturally, bedlam ensued. The young ballclub began a raucous celebration that moved from the field to the locker room. The Royals would at least be a wild-card team. (They were one game behind the Tigers for the AL Central crown with two games to play.) They did become the wild-card club and would face the Oakland Athletics. But they were in.

The celebration moved back onto the field as the players wanted to show appreciation to the fans who had come to the game and, by proxy, all the fans who had stood by the Royals through 29 hard seasons. The players knew this was special to many people. Several of the players tossed their black and white playoff caps to cheering fans before finally walking off the field. Billy Butler remarked, "We're in Chicago, and look at all the Royals fans."[7]

10,561 days is a long time. Bringing that period to a close brought a surge of emotion throughout Kansas City and everyone connected to the Royals. George Brett, the Hall of Fame third baseman and greatest Royals player to date, shared that emotion. He said, "I got tired of the people criticizing the players on this team because they hadn't won a World Series since 1985. Ninety-five percent of these ... guys weren't even born in '85. It's not their fault. These guys played their (butts) off all year."[8]

Sources

In addition to the sources cited in the Notes, the author also consulted Baseball-Reference.com and Retrosheet.org.

Notes

1 An extended discussion of GM Moore's process by Craig Brown can be found at *Royals Review*. royalsreview.com/2014/1/29/5352466/process-2014-the-dayton-moore-timetable.

2 Craig Calcaterra, "Dayton Moore: 'The Process' Is 8-10 Years," NBCSports.com, Hardball Talk, May 20, 2010. mlb.nbcsports.com/2010/05/20/dayton-moore-the-process-is-8-10-years/.

3 Craig Brown, "Process 2014: The Dayton Moore Timetable," *Royals Review*, January 29, 2014. royalsreview.com/2014/1/29/5352466/process-2014-the-dayton-moore-timetable

4 Tyler Drenon, "The Royals Playoff Odds Are Pretty Good," *Royals Review*, September 25, 2014. royalsreview.com/2014/9/25/6842363/royals-playoffs-for-real-well-sorta-but-who-cares

5 Alex Gordon, Eric Hosmer, and Salvador Perez.

6 Jeffrey Flanagan, "2014 Royals Pitcher Grades: Wade Davis Is A Rare A+," FOXSports.com, Kansas City, October 20, 2016. https://www.foxsports.com/kansas-city/gallery/2014-royals-pitcher-grades-wade-davis-is-a-rare-a-110514?abTest=no-pin

7 Andy McCullough, "Royals Clinch First Postseason Berth Since 1985 With 3-1 Victory Over White Sox," *The Kansas City Star*, September 27, 2014.

8 "Royals Clinch First Postseason Spot Since 1985," *USA Today*, September 27, 2014. https://www.usatoday.com/story/sports/mlb/2014/09/26/royals-clinch-playoff-spot-with-win-over-white-sox/16307709/

THE WILD CARD GAME SEPTEMBER 30, 2014: KANSAS CITY ROYALS 9, OAKLAND ATHLETICS 8, AT KAUFFMAN STADIUM, KANSAS CITY, MISSOURI

BY BILL CARLE

From 1976 to 1985, the Kansas City Royals were one of the American League's best teams. In that 10-year span, they made the playoffs seven times, and finished second in the other three years. When Darryl Motley squeezed Andy Van Slyke's fly to right to clinch the 1985 World Series title, Royals fans had no reason to believe that postseason baseball wouldn't be almost a yearly occurrence. Much to the chagrin of the Royals faithful, it would be 29 years before the Royals again took the field in a postseason game. A 3-1 win over the White Sox clinched the postseason berth, and the Royals would host the wild-card Game against the Oakland Athletics.

Kansas City was abuzz as the Royals prepared to play their first postseason game in 29 years. Manager Ned Yost named James Shields as his starting pitcher. Shields had come to the Royals before the 2013 season along with Wade Davis in a trade with Tampa Bay and was considered the Royals' staff ace.

Oakland manager Bob Melvin named Jon Lester as his starting pitcher. Lester had come to the A's on the last day of the trading deadline in a deal with the Boston Red Sox. Lester had always been a Royals nemesis. In 13 starts against the Royals, he had allowed only 23 runs. He threw a no-hitter against the Royals in 2008, and had already beaten Kansas City three times in 2014.

A sellout crowd of 40,502 jammed Kauffman Stadium on an unseasonably warm 82-degree night for the much-anticipated game. Coco Crisp led off the game for the A's with a line single to left. After Shields retired Sam Fuld and Josh Donaldson, Brandon Moss belted a home run into the right-field seats to give the A's a 2-0 lead. The Royals came back in the bottom of the first when Alcides Escobar led off with an infield single. Nori Aoki forced Escobar at second and, with two out, stole second base. After Eric Hosmer walked, Billy Butler lined a single down the left-field line to score Aoki and cut the lead to 2-1.

The score was still 2-1 when the Royals came to bat in the bottom of the third inning. As the inning began, the A's had a new catcher. Starting catcher Geovany Soto had injured his thumb and was replaced by Derek Norris. This would later prove to be a fateful change. The Royals had led the American League in stolen bases by a wide margin, and in 2014 Soto had thrown out 43 percent of runners attempting to steal. Norris had thrown out only 17 percent and had allowed 60 steals during the regular season.

Mike Moustakas led off the third with a line single to left field. Escobar sacrificed him to second, and a groundout by Aoki moved him to third. Lorenzo Cain ripped a double to left to score Moustakas, and Eric Hosmer looped a single to short left to score Cain and give the Royals a 3-2 lead.

Both teams went down in order in the fourth and fifth innings, and the Royals still held a 3-2 lead as the A's came to bat in the top of the sixth. Ned Yost's strategy all season was to try to get through the sixth inning with a lead and then turn it over to his vaunted HDH bullpen of Kelvin Herrera, Wade Davis, and Greg Holland.[1]

Yost's normal plan ran into a bit of a snag. Sam Fuld led the sixth inning off with a single, then Shields walked Josh Donaldson. Yost headed to the mound to pull Shields and opted to go with 23-year-old rookie right-hander Yordano Ventura to get through the inning. Ventura had a fine year as a starter, but had relieved in only one game all season. The first man to face him was the dangerous Brandon Moss, who had already homered in the first inning. On a 2-and-0 pitch, Ventura came in with a low fastball, and Moss crushed a three-run homer to center field. A 3-2 lead had suddenly become a 5-3 deficit. Josh Reddick followed with a single and, after a wild pitch and a fly out, Yost replaced Ventura with Kelvin Herrera. Herrera got Stephen Vogt to foul out, but then three straight singles by Derek Norris, Eric Sogard, and Coco Crisp led to two more runs before Sam Fuld struck out to end the carnage. It was now 7-3, Oakland, and with Jon Lester on the mound, the Royals' chances seemed pretty bleak.

The score remained 7-3 when the Royals came to bat in the bottom of the eighth inning, six outs away from elimination. Alcides Escobar led off the inning with a seeing-eye single up the middle. He stole second and advanced to third on a grounder to second by Aoki. Lorenzo Cain grounded a single up the middle to score Escobar and cut the A's lead to 7-4. Cain stole second and Lester walked Eric Hosmer. With two on and one out, Bob Melvin brought in Luke Gregerson to pitch to Billy Butler. Butler lined a single to right to score Cain and send Hosmer to third. Yost brought in Terrance Gore to run for Butler.[2] Gore immediately stole second. Gregerson then uncorked a wild pitch, allowing Hosmer to score, and sending Gore to third. That was all the Royals could score, but they had cut the lead to 7-6.

Greg Holland wiggled through the ninth unscathed and A's closer Sean Doolittle was entrusted to protect the one-run lead in the bottom of the inning. Yost sent up veteran Josh Willingham to pinch-hit for Moustakas.[3] Willingham dropped a single into right field. Yost sent in his other pinch-running specialist, Jarrod Dyson.[4] Escobar sacrificed Dyson to second, and Dyson stole third, the Royals' sixth stolen base of the game, and their fifth against beleaguered catcher Derek Norris. Nori Aoki lifted a fly to the warning track in right field, easily deep enough to score Dyson and tie the game.

Having already used his three best relievers, Yost turned to southpaw Brandon Finnegan to start the 10th.[5] Finnegan held Oakland scoreless in the 10th and 11th innings. The Royals were also unable to score and it was still deadlocked entering the 12th.

Finnegan began by walking Josh Reddick. After a sacrifice by Jed Lowrie, Melvin called on Alberto Callaspo to pinch-hit for Nate Freiman. Yost countered by bringing in Jason Frasor from the bullpen. After a wild pitch moved Reddick to third, Alberto Callaspo poked a single to left to score Reddick and give the A's the lead once again.

Down 8-7 in the bottom of the 12th, with one out. Hosmer picked on a high fastball and hit a drive to deep left-center. Sam Fuld and Jonny Gomes converged on the ball, but neither could snare it as the ball hit the top of the wall and bounced back toward the infield. By the time Gomes had corralled it, Hosmer had pulled into third with a triple. Christian Colon chopped one off the plate that Donaldson tried to barehand, but it went for an infield single and Hosmer scored the tying run. With two out and Salvador Perez at the plate, Colon took off for second. The A's pitched out, but Norris dropped the ball before he could make a throw.[6] The sellout crowd was on their feet as Jason Hammel faced Perez. On a 2-and-2 pitch, Perez reached for a low outside slider and grounded it down the third-base line just out of the reach of a diving Josh Donaldson. Colon scored and the Royals had a stunning 9-8 win.

Delirium broke loose at Kauffman Stadium. Many said it was the greatest game they had ever witnessed. Rany Jazayerli wrote: "Just before midnight, as September fell into October, I hugged my friends. I hugged complete strangers. I screamed until what was left of my voice was completely hoarse. I spontaneously invented a dance that would embarrass Elaine Benes. I had entered that state of joyous delirium that I'm told only sports can bring, but that I'd never experienced. This was the greatest baseball game I'd ever witnessed live."[7] Raul Ibanez, who closed out his career with the 2014 Royals, said, "I'm telling you. It's the best game I've ever seen." Royals third-base coach Mike Jirschele concurred: "There hasn't been a game close to this tonight. The ups and downs in this game. And then to finish on top. You couldn't draw it up any better."[8]

The Royals would eventually lose the World Series in seven games, but made up for that disappointment in 2015 by winning the Series for their second world championship.[9]

Sources

In addition to the sources cited in the Notes, the author also consulted Baseball-Reference.com and Retrosheet.org.

Notes

1 The Royals had lost just four games all season that they led after the sixth inning, and only one that they led after the seventh. For the season Herrera sported a 1.41 ERA, Davis, 1.00, and Holland, 1.44. No team in history had ever had a bullpen with two relievers with a minimum of 60 appearances each having an ERA under 1.50, and the Royals had three. See Steve Gardner, "Royals Bullpen: 'There's No Better Weapon," *USA Today*, October 15, 2014.

2 Gore had been called up to the majors in September for one reason, to pinch-run.

3 Willingham had been acquired from the Minnesota Twins in August to provide an experienced bat.

4 Dyson was often used as a pinch-runner. Just as fast as Gore, he had stolen 36 bases during the regular season in a part-time role. An in-depth study of Dyson's stolen base appears at fangraphs.com/blogs/how-jarrod-dyson-stole-the-biggest-base-of-his-life/.

5 Just three months earlier, Finnegan had been pitching for Texas Christian University in the College World Series. The Royals had chosen him in the first round of the June free-agent draft and called him up to the big leagues in September. He had only seven major-league innings under his belt, although he had pitched well.

6 This was the Royals' seventh stolen base of the game. The seven stolen bases were by seven different players: Aoki, Cain, Colon, Dyson, Escobar, Gordon, and Gore

7 Rany Jazayerli, "K.C. Masterpiece," Grantland, October 1, 2014. grantland.com/features/2014-mlb-playoffs-kansas-city-royals-oakland-athletics-american-league-wild-card-classic/, accessed September 30, 2018.

8 Rustin Dodd, "In Afterglow of Wild Win, Royals Veterans and Youngsters Struggle to Explain What Happened," *Kansas City Star*, October 1, 2014.

9 The Royals swept the Los Angeles Angels in the American League Division Series, swept the Baltimore Orioles in the American League Championship Series, and lost to the Giants in the World Series. In 2015 they won the World Series, defeating the New York Mets to cap off a postseason that featured a number of stunning comebacks.

THE MIRACLE AT MINUTE MAID OCTOBER 12, 2015: KANSAS CITY ROYALS 9, HOUSTON ASTROS 6, AT MINUTE MAID PARK, HOUSTON

BY PAUL HOFMANN

The 2015 ALDS between the defending American League champion Kansas City Royals and the upstart Houston Astros was the first time the two teams met in the playoffs. The Royals finished the regular season with a 95-67 record, winning the AL Central Division by a comfortable 12 games. The Astros, making their first playoff appearance since 2005, finished with a record of 86-76, good enough for second place in the AL West and a wild-card berth in the playoffs. The Astros were leading the series two games to one and had a chance to close it out at Minute Maid Park.

Game Four was a matchup between two promising young right-handers. The Royals started right-hander Yordano Ventura. The 24-year-old Dominican finished the season with a 13-8 record and a 4.08 ERA. He started Game One, lasting only two innings and taking the loss. Twenty-two-year-old rookie right-hander Lance McCullers Jr. got the start for the Astros. McCullers, who was called up from Corpus Christi of the Double-A Texas League in May, was 6-7 with a 3.22 ERA. He was making his first postseason appearance.

With an afternoon high of 90 degrees, the roof of Minute Maid Park was closed when McCullers threw the first pitch at 12:07 P.M. in front of a sellout crowd of 42,387 roaring fans. Six pitches later, Royals shortstop Alcides Escobar was hit by a pitch and became the afternoon's first baserunner. McCullers quickly settled down and retired the next three hitters to end the top of the first. Similarly, Ventura hit Carlos Correa in the bottom of the first to give the Astros their first baserunner. After a single to right by Colby Rasmus, Ventura got Evan Gattis swinging to end a relatively uneventful first inning.

The Royals opened the scoring in the top of the second when Mike Moustakas drew a one-out walk and catcher Salvador Perez hit a two-run homer to right-center. The Astros quickly responded in their half of the second when center fielder Carlos Gomez led off with a homer into the Crawford Boxes[1] in left, cutting the Royals' lead to 2-1. Correa tied the game in bottom of the third when he launched a two-out, line-drive homer to left-center.

The game stayed tied, 2-2, until the Astros touched Ventura for another run in the bottom of the fifth. Right fielder George Springer drew a two-out walk and scored when Correa sent a slicing line drive down the right-field line that ricocheted off the stands for a double and his second RBI of the game.

McCullers responded with a shutdown inning in the top of the sixth. After retiring the Royals in order, McCullers rolled his shoulder and slapped two fingers across his neck. Some in the Royals dugout interpreted this as a throat-slashing gesture, a requiem for Kansas City's season. After the game the Royals' Edinson Volquez responded to McCullers' gesture with a simple reminder, "C'mon, man. You've got to get 27 outs. Not 17."[2]

The Astros added three in the top of the seventh. Right-hander Kelvin Herrera, who replaced Ventura in the sixth, issued a leadoff walk to Jose Altuve, and Royals manager Ned Yost summoned right-hander Ryan Madson from the bullpen. Madson struck out Springer for the inning's first out. Correa then hit his second home run of the game, a two-run bomb into the stands in left field. Before the buzz from Correa's blast had dissipated, Rasmus launched a solo shot that landed just inside the right-field foul pole. After back-to-back singles to Gattis and Gomez that put runners on second and third with one out, Madson managed to disentangle himself from further damage by getting Luis Valbuena on a fly to left and striking out Marwin Gonzalez. When the dust had settled, the Astros had a 6-2 lead and the Royals appeared all but beaten and eliminated.

Freeze that moment in time. The Royals had a 96.8 percent chance of their season ending and the Astros players and fans had a 96.8 percent probability of their team advancing to the ALCS.[3] Despite the improbability of a comeback suggested by the math, baseball is a game where anything can happen, even miracles.

Astros right-hander Will Harris, who came on relief of McCullers and recorded the final two outs of the seventh inning, started the bottom of the eighth. The Royals wasted no time mounting a comeback. Alex Rios singled to left, Escobar singled to center, and Ben Zobrist singled to center to load the bases. Lorenzo Cain hit a groundball single to left to plate Rios, prompting Astros manager A.J. Hinch to summon left-hander Tony Sipp from the bullpen. Eric Hosmer greeted Sipp with a line single to right, scoring Escobar and cutting the Astros' lead to 6-4. With the bases still loaded, Kendrys Morales sent a groundball up the middle that deflected off Sipp's glove and bounded over the glove of Correa at short. Zobrist and Cain scored and Hosmer went to third.[4] Jarrod Dyson ran for Morales and stole second before Sipp struck out Moustakas. Hinch again went to his bullpen and called on right-hander Luke Gregerson to face right-handed-hitting Drew Butera. Gregerson walked the Royals catcher to reload the bases. With the infield drawn in, left fielder Alex Gordon hit a groundball to second. Altuve made a diving stop to rob Gordon of a hit. As the Astros' second baseman completed the play, Hosmer crossed the plate with the go-ahead run. After walking Rios to load the bases again, Gregerson struck out Escobar to end the inning with the Royals leading 7-6. The season-defining workingman's rally featured five singles, an error, and a go-ahead groundout.[5]

With momentum in their favor, the Royals called on right-handed reliever Wade Davis for a six-out save. Davis, who was 8-1 with 17 saves and a microscopic 0.94 ERA, assumed the closer's role late in the season when Greg Holland suffered a partially torn elbow ligament.[6] Davis made short work of the Astros in the bottom of the eighth, retiring the side on seven pitches.

The Royals added a couple of insurance runs in the top of the ninth. Zobrist drew a leadoff walk and after Cain struck out swinging, Hosmer deposited a two-run homer into the seats in right-center to increase the Royals' advantage to 9-6.

Davis returned to the mound in the bottom of the ninth to close out Game Four. After yielding a leadoff single to Correa, the shortstop's fourth hit of the afternoon, Davis retired Rasmus and pinch-hitter Preston Tucker on called third strikes, then got Gomez on a fly ball to right to end the game. After 4 hours and 5 minutes and an improbable Royals comeback, the series was headed back to Kansas City for a decisive Game Five.

Royals manager Yost summed up the comeback in an almost disbelieving manner. "That kind of came out of nowhere, huh?" Shaking his head and still trying to process the result, Yost completed his thought, "Sometimes there's things that are meant to be."[7]

Indeed, things were meant to be. The Royals would go on to capture Game Five, 7-2, on the strength of an efficient outing by starter Johnny Cueto, solid relief from Davis, and a lineup that battled during every at-bat. The Royals went on to dispatch the Toronto Blue Jays in six games in the ALCS and defeated the New York Mets in five games to win the World Series. Only one World Series champion came closer to brink of elimination than the 2015 Royals.[8] In 1986 the New York Mets were down to a 1 percent win probability when they rallied in the bottom of the 10th inning of Game Six of the World Series and eventually captured the title in seven games. Like the Mets, the Royals were a team of destiny.

Sources

In addition to the sources cited in the Notes, the author also relied on Baseball-reference.com and Retrosheet.org.

Notes

1 The Crawford Boxes are so-called because they run parallel to Crawford Street, outside the ballpark.

2 Andy McCullough, "A Royal Miracle: Eighth-Inning Rally Gets KC Past Astros 9-6," *Kansas City Star*, October 13, 2015, kansas.com/sports/mlb/kansas-city-royals/article38855619.html. McCullers actually retired 19 batters before being lifted for Will Harris in the top of the seventh inning.

3 Joe Posnanski, "The Walking Dead: The Royals Were All but Beaten and Eliminated Monday, Until They Weren't," sportsworld.nbcsports.com/the-walking-dead/.

4 Despite not touching the ball, Correa was charged with an error.

5 A.J. Cassavell, "The Royals' Defining Moment," Sports on Earth, November 3, 2015, sportsonearth.com/article/156300198/royals-world-series-champions-comeback-rally.

6 Jeffrey Flanagan, "Holland Set for Tommy John Surgery Friday," MLB.com, September 29, 2015, mlb.com/news/royals-greg-holland-will-undergo-elbow-surgery/c-152290380

7 Andy McCullough.

8 The Royals actually had a 1.6 percent win probability after the Astros went ahead by four runs and put runners on second and third with one out in the bottom of the seventh.

OCTOBER 17, 2015: COMMUNICATION BREAKDOWN SPARKS ROYALS' LATE RALLY KANSAS CITY ROYALS 6, TORONTO BLUE JAYS 3 AT KAUFFMAN STADIUM, KANSAS CITY

BY DARIN WATSON

Once the Royals won the first game of the 2015 ALCS, the game plan for the rest of the series seemed simple. Win Game Two, pick up a win in one of the three games in Toronto, and come home needing to win just one of the last two games to advance to the World Series.

Of course, nothing in playoff baseball is simple. For starters, the Royals would have to figure out a way to beat longtime nemesis David Price, who took the mound for the Blue Jays in that second game with a lifetime ERA of 1.93 against the Royals. Price was battling his personal postseason losing streak (six starts without a win) but was a formidable opponent, with an 18-5 record and league-leading 2.45 ERA in 2015.

Going to Canada with a two-game lead in the series would be a big deal. The Blue Jays had gone 53-28 at home during the regular season, including a scorching 22-8 over the last two months. So there was some pressure on the slight shoulders of Royals starter Yordano Ventura. Despite his youth, the 24-year-old was a postseason veteran following Kansas City's playoff run in 2014, including seven shutout innings in the must-win Game Six of the World Series.

And Ventura looked dominant in the first inning of this sun-splashed but cool October afternoon, recording two groundouts and carving up AL MVP Josh Donaldson for a strikeout. In the bottom of the first, Alcides Escobar, whose proclivity for swinging at the first pitch of the game was already widely known, smacked a single to right on Price's first pitch. But then Price got three quick outs of his own.

Toronto began the second with consecutive singles, and with one out, Russell Martin lined a bullet toward center field. Escobar lunged to his left and snared it, then flipped the ball to second baseman Ben Zobrist for the inning-ending double play.

That saved a run right there, and it became a bigger deal when the Jays collected consecutive doubles to start the third inning. Ryan Goins was late on a Ventura fastball, but still guided it just inside the third-base bag, scoring Kevin Pillar. But Ventura retired the next three batters, keeping the Toronto lead at 1-0.

The score stayed the same into the sixth inning. Since Escobar's single, Price had retired 15 straight hitters. Meanwhile, Ventura had retired nine of the previous 10 after that Goins double.

But things fell apart for the Royals in the sixth. Donaldson narrowly avoided becoming the first out on a foul popup when home-plate umpire Laz Diaz correctly realized the ball hit a cable supporting the backstop on its way down to Salvador Perez. On the next pitch, Donaldson reached for a curve, hit a slow bouncer to shortstop, then beat Escobar's throw for an infield single. Jose Bautista followed with a walk. Edwin Encarnacion pulled a grounder into left field, just off the tip of Escobar's glove. Donaldson scored to put Toronto up 2-0. After a strikeout, Troy Tulowitzki hit a line drive toward the right-field corner. This one eluded Alex Rios by less than a foot, good for a double and another run. A walk to Martin loaded the bases. Although Ventura was less than two feet total from being out of the inning, manager Ned Yost had no choice but to bring in reliever Luke Hochevar. With the Royals' offense doing nothing, Kansas City needed to keep the score close.

"We stayed with him in the sixth inning because we felt like his stuff was good, but he battled his command. He kind of abandoned his fastball a little bit in that inning, facing the meat of the order, started going a little bit soft," Yost said.[1]

Hochevar did the job, retiring Pillar on a popup and Goins on a groundout. But things still looked grim for Kansas City, down 3-0. They looked worse when Price struck out the side in the bottom of the sixth.

But the Royals' luck was about to turn. Danny Duffy turned in a perfect seventh and Zobrist led off the bottom of the inning. The normally patient Zobrist swung at the first pitch. It was a popup into short right field, and he slammed his bat to the ground in frustration as Goins and Bautista converged. Goins waved his arms and Bautista slowed down, but at the last second Goins screeched to a halt, falling over backward. The ball dropped between them, and Zobrist had a leadoff single.

"I just thought I heard, 'I got it,' but it was nothing," Goins said later. "I should have gone in more aggressively. I put my glove up, like I always do. That means I got it. I just didn't make the play."[2]

Bautista would only say after the game, "There's video, you can watch it." He did add, "There was no confusion."[3]

Now Royals fans could sense another late-inning comeback. And the Royals could put their secret knowledge about Price to use. Advanced scouting by Tim Conroy and Paul Gibson had figured out that Price tipped his changeup. The catch was that he did so in the stretch position, taking a long breath after coming set and shrugging his shoulders a bit. They had also realized that Price rarely attempted pickoff throws to first (although no one had stolen a base against him in 2015), and that when he pitched from the stretch, he pointed the toes of his right foot down, making him unlikely to throw to first.[4]

"We needed more than one (hit), and we got it," Zobrist said.[5]

Lorenzo Cain lined a single to right. Eric Hosmer hit a changeup to center for a single, scoring Zobrist and moving Cain to third. Hosmer took off for second base on the second pitch to Kendrys Morales, meaning the grounder Morales hit to shortstop was good only for an out at first. Cain scored on the play, making it 3-2. Mike Moustakas lined a changeup into right for a single. Hosmer scored to tie the game and Moustakas took second on Bautista's throw home. Perez struck out, but Alex Gordon smashed a double to the right-center-field gap, breaking the tie and ending Price's day. Rios greeted reliever Aaron Sanchez with a single to center, scoring Gordon for a 5-3 Royals lead.

Kansas City tacked on one more run in the eighth, and Wade Davis recovered from letting the first two batters in the ninth reach base to strike out Ben Revere and Donaldson. A Bautista fly ball to right ended the game and sent the Royals to Canada with a 2-0 lead in the series.

The Blue Jays were left to wonder what might have been, as well as put on a brave face about their chances in the series, while the Royals were simply thankful for their good fortune.

"I just gave up hits at the wrong time," Price said. "I felt good. That's a very scrappy team. They put the ball in play, they continue to battle. That's a tough loss."[6]

"We have been down 2-0 before and came back. We go to Toronto and win three games. We are a resilient group of guys," Goins said.[7]

"It's the playoffs. We'll take anything. Any hit, any run, whatever. Guess they had a little miscommunication out there, and we'll definitely take it," Cain said.[8]

Sources

Besides the articles listed in the Notes, the author consulted baseball-reference.com, retrosheet.org, and YouTube, at youtube.com/watch?v=j_78tr2A_dQ.

Notes

1 Kathleen Gier, "Ace Ventura Fans Six," *Kansas City Star*, October 18, 2015: 7BB.

2 Andy McCullough, "KC Keeps It Going," *Kansas City Star,* October 18, 2015: 2BB.

3 Jordan Bastian, "Goins Takes Blame for Botched Popup in 7th," mlb.com, October 17, 2015; Accessed August 15, 2018.

4 Tom Verducci, "How Three Unheralded Contributors Helped Royals Repeat as AL Champs," si.com, October 24, 2015. Accessed August 17, 2018.

5 Vahe Gregorian, "Another Playoff Game, Another Royals Rally," *Kansas City Star*, October 18, 2015: 1BB.

6 "Blue Jays Left Stunned by Royals in Game 2 of ALCS," sportsnet.ca, October 17, 2015. Accessed August 18, 2018.

7 George A. King III, "Harmless Pop-Up Turns Into Disaster as Jays Fall in 0-2 ALCS hole," *New York Post*, October 17, 2015.

8 Ryan Fagan, "ALCS 2015: Stunning Seventh-Inning Meltdown Sinks Price, Jays in Game 2," The Sporting News, October 18, 2015.

CAIN RACES HOME, SENDS ROYALS TO WORLD SERIES OCTOBER 23, 2015: KANSAS CITY ROYALS 4, TORONTO BLUE JAYS 3, AT KAUFFMAN STADIUM, KANSAS CITY

BY ANDREW STOCKMANN

On a tense autumn evening at Kauffman Stadium, the Kansas City Royals won their second consecutive pennant by defeating the Toronto Blue Jays, 4-3. Exactly 30 years earlier, the Royals found themselves down 3-1 against the St. Louis Cardinals in the 1985 World Series after a Game Four defeat. But on this October night, after a 45-minute rain delay, the Royals became back-to-back American League champions.

After Toronto's 7-1 Game Five victory, Ned Yost and the Royals turned to 24-year-old Yordano Ventura, no stranger to October's bright lights. Ventura, in Game Six of the 2014 World Series, pitched seven scoreless innings to force a deciding game. Now, 360 days later, Ventura allowed a leadoff double to Ben Revere, but then settled in and retired the next 10 Blue Jays.

While Ventura looked to continue his postseason success, Blue Jays lefty David Price hoped to avenge his 0-7 record as a starter in the playoffs. (His two postseason wins had come as a reliever, one for Tampa Bay and one for the Blue Jays.) He had a 5.24 ERA in 56⅔ postseason innings.[1] The 2012 Cy Young Award winner had thrown 96 pitches in Game Two, allowing five earned runs and striking out eight Royals in 6⅔ innings.

After Ben Zobrist smacked a home run off of Price's cut fastball in the first inning, Mike Moustakas came up with one out in the second. Moustakas was batting .132 in the postseason but had hit lefties well in 2015, posting a .823 OPS. Off Price he crushed a changeup that was snatched off the top of the right-center-field wall by Caleb Humphreys, a 19-year-old from Blue Springs, Missouri. "I saw it coming right at me," he said. "This is Game 6 of the (ALCS), I played my baseball my whole life, I had a great time playing baseball, and for it to actually happen, and to get a home run ball. ..."[2] The drive was ruled a home run, but the umpire crew gathered to review the call. One couldn't help but remember the Jeffrey Maier escapade in the 1996 American League Championship Series. Asked by a writer if he knew the name Jeffrey Maier, Humphrey said he did not. "When the story was brought up, he interrupted. 'Oh yeah!' he said. 'Yeah, yeah, yeah.'"[3]

The Royals' early power surge in Game Six was deceiving. These 2015 Royals excelled at the little things, stealing bases and having excellent defenders while finishing next to last in the American League in home runs (139). By contrast, the Blue Jays relied on power, leading the major leagues in home runs and featuring three especially powerful hitters in Jose Bautista, Edwin Encarnacion, and Josh Donaldson. They led the major leagues in home run/fly ball rate, with 11.6 percent of their fly balls becoming home runs. The Jays tied for the league lead in walk rate at 9.2 percent, while the Royals were last with 6.3 percent.

Jose Bautista had not endeared himself too kindly to fans in Kansas City after pretending to toss the ball that made the final out of an inning into the stands in Game One. That incident, combined with the dust-ups the Royals and Jays had in their August series, and there was no surprise when Bautista faced thousands of boos after scorching a home run off Ventura in the bottom of the fourth. This was the first time Ventura ran into trouble, and the trouble continued when he walked Russell Martin and Kevin Pillar to begin the fifth inning. Further damage was averted when with two outs and Martin and Pillar still on first and second, Mike Moustakas dove to catch a 114-mph liner off the bat of Josh Donaldson. This was the third-hardest batted ball of the 2015 postseason, according to Statcast.[4]

After Ventura allowed a double to Edwin Encarnacion with one out in the sixth inning, Kelvin Herrera relieved him. A 2015 All-Star, Herrera induced three flyouts and struck out two Blue Jays in 1⅔ perfect innings. David Price went into his seventh inning facing a 2-1 deficit, and allowed a single to Mike Moustakas. After getting two outs, Price was removed in favor of Aaron Sanchez. Royals right fielder Alex Rios singled sharply to left field, scoring Moustakas. Kansas City took a 3-1 lead into the eighth inning.

The Royals had an embarrassment of riches in their bullpen during their run of postseason success. The "HDH" trio of Kelvin Herrera, Wade Davis, and Greg Holland that was so dominant during the previous pennant run had now been slightly modified with Holland's UCL injury. Ryan Madson, an effective free-agent signing with a 2.13 regular-season ERA, came to the mound in the eighth inning instead of Davis. That move would backfire. Bautista cranked a home run down the left-field line, tying the game at 3-3, and Madson walked Encarnacion. Wade Davis replaced Madson and retired the side. At that point a rain shower halted the game. Davis had once been the secondary piece to the James Shields trade, a reclamation project for the Royals, but now he was the best closer in the American League, armed with a devastating arsenal of pitches and a 0.94 ERA in 2015.

During the 45-minute rain delay, Davis did not throw off a mound, instead riding a stationary bike and keeping his arm loose with a heating pad.[5] Greg Holland, Davis's injured bullpen mate, approached Yost and told him, "Wade wants to go to the World Series. He's going to be fine."[6]

The Royals had to score a run to fulfill the wish of Davis and Kansas City. Lorenzo Cain walked to lead off the eighth inning. Eric Hosmer laced a 2-and-2 breaking ball from Sanchez down the right-field line, and Cain was off and running. Jose Bautista cut the ball off, stopping Hosmer at first base, but Cain kept on running, accelerating around third base and scoring the go-ahead run. Third-base coach Mike Jirschele had done his homework, participating in a similar situation in an earlier game of the series, just with a slower runner in Kendrys Morales.[7] "I knew if I had speed coming in there, I'd have that opportunity and it came at the right time," Jirschele said.[8] He sure had speed coming in. Cain advanced from first to home in 10.5 seconds, reaching a top speed of 20.7 miles per hour, according to MLBAM guru Mike Petriello, who also tweeted, "Lorenzo Cain had two of the top seven first-to-home times of the season, per Statcast."[9] Cain and the Royals were keen on the fundamentals of baserunning, and it came to fruition at the most pivotal of points.

The inning ended quickly when Moustakas flied out and Morales grounded into a double play. In the top of the ninth Davis ran into trouble. It had been over an hour since he had been out on the mound. Russell Martin singled. Dalton Pompey ran for him and stole second and third. With no outs, the Royals closer walked Kevin Pillar. Davis recovered to strike out Dioner Navarro, pinch-hitting for Ryan Goins. But Pillar stole second base on the strikeout pitch to Navarro. Davis fell behind 2-and-0 on Ben Revere. Revere had made an incredible catch in the seventh inning, leaping to snag a Salvador Perez extra-base-hit off the left-field wall. However, Davis fought back to strike out Revere. Fox's cameras caught Revere hitting a trash can with his bat in the dugout after his K.

Josh Donaldson, a few weeks away from being named the American League MVP, stepped up to face Davis with men on second and third and two outs. After a hard-fought battle, Donaldson grounded out to Mike Moustakas. He fired to Eric Hosmer, who with his game-winning single had tied George Brett for first in Royals postseason RBIs. The Royals had won the pennant for the fourth time in franchise history. It's fitting that for the second straight year, the final out to win the pennant was 5-3, Mike Moustakas to Eric Hosmer. These two players were general manager Dayton Moore's first two first-round selections in the major-league draft (Moore took over as GM right before the 2006 draft, but the outgoing group made that draft's selections). And it was the Zack Greinke trade that brought back the Game Six hero Lorenzo Cain, as well as ALCS MVP Alcides Escobar.

This win propelled the Royals to take on the New York Mets in the 2015 World Series, the 111th rendition of the fall classic. Showing resolve, using their trademark speed, and receiving heroic performances from Lorenzo Cain, Mike Jirschele, and Wade Davis brought Kansas City another pennant-winner after decades of not even getting close. After falling short in Game Seven against the San Francisco Giants in 2014, they became the third back-to-back AL pennant winners since 2000.

Sources

The author consulted Baseball-Reference.com for the game's box score and other details such as splits and play-by-play information, as well as Retrosheet. Watching the Fox broadcast on YouTube was also helpful in writing this article.

Notes

1 Jorge L. Ortiz, "Royals Win Wet, Wild Game 6 Over Blue Jays, Advance to World Series Again," *USA Today*, October 24, 2015. usatoday.com/story/sports/mlb/2015/10/24/royals-blue-jays-alcs-game-6/74514152/.

2 Rustin Dodd and Sam McDowell, "Royals Fan Nearly Interferes with Mike Moustakas Home Run in ALCS Game 6," *Kansas City Star*, October 24, 2015. kansascity.com/sports/mlb/kansas-city-royals/article41263632.html.

3 Ibid.

4 mlb.com/cut4/moustakas-robs-donaldson-in-alcs-game-6/c-155409246.

5 Andy McCullough, "Royals Beat Blue Jays 4-3, Win Back-to-Back American League Pennants," *Kansas City Star*, October 24, 2015. kansascity.com/sports/mlb/kansas-city-royals/article41289054.html.

6 Ibid.

7 Blair Kerkhoff, "Homework Gets Lorenzo Cain Home from First on Single," *Kansas City Star*, October 24, 2015.kansascity.com/sports/mlb/kansas-city-royals/article41314929.html.

8 Ibid.

9 twitter.com/mike_petriello/status/657768623021432832.

OCTOBER 27, 2015: KANSAS CITY WINS WORLD SERIES GAME ONE IN EXTRA INNINGS KANSAS CITY ROYALS 5, NEW YORK METS 4 (14 INNINGS)

BY THOMAS J. BROWN JR.

The New York Mets and the Kansas City Royals were ready to square off in the 2015 World Series. A crowd of 40,320 packed Kauffman Stadium on October 27. This date was significant for both teams because it was on that date that each had last won the World Series. The Royals' last championship came on October 27, 1985 and the Mets last won on October 27, 1986.[1]

The Royals were returning to the World Series for the second consecutive year, having lost in seven games to the San Francisco Giants in 2014. Manager Ned Yost chose Edinson Volquez to start the game for the Royals. Several hours before the game, Yost learned that Volquez's father had died. Volquez's family sent him a request: "Don't tell Eddie; let him go out and pitch Game One of the World Series." Yost honored their request although he worried about word getting to Volquez during the game and what might happen after that.[2]

Mets manager Terry Collins planned to start his star young pitcher Matt Harvey. Harvey had pitched 7 2/3 innings on his way to winning the first game of the NL Championship Series. The Mets did not trail the Cubs for a single inning in that series and were hoping to repeat their success in the World Series.

After Volquez got the Mets out in order in the top of the first, the Royals grabbed the lead on Harvey's first pitch. Alcides Escobar sent the pitch all the way to the warning track in center field. Michael Conforto and Yoenis Cespedes converged on the ball but neither one called for it. Cespedes tried to make a backhand catch at the last moment but the ball glanced off his leg and bounced away. The speedy Escobar noticed the misplay and immediately began to race around the bases. By the time that the Mets caught up with the ball, Escobar had an inside-the-park home run. Suddenly the Royals were up 1-0.

Strangely enough, this was not the first time that this feat had occurred. Patsy Dougherty, the leadoff batter for the Boston Americans in the second game of the 1903 World Series, hit a pitch by Pittsburgh's Sam Leever for a home run in the bottom of the first inning.[3]

But the Mets fought back. They scored a run in the fourth. Daniel Murphy led off with a single. A second single by Lucas Duda allowed Murphy to move to third base. Travis d'Arnaud hit a third single to score Murphy and tie the game.

In the top of the fifth, Curtis Granderson hit a solo home run and the Mets went ahead 2-1. They added a third run in the sixth inning when consecutive singles by Murphy and Cespedes set up Conforto, who hit a sacrifice fly that scored Murphy. The score was now 3-1.

The Royals fought back in the bottom of the sixth. Harvey had pitched well after giving up the first-inning home run but he quickly surrendered a double to Ben Zobrist and a single to Lorenzo Cain. Zobrist scored on Eric Hosmer's sacrifice fly and the score was 3-2. After Harvey got Kendrys Morales to ground out, he faced Mike Moustakas who hit a single to tie the game. Harvey had returned from elbow surgery. Even before the Mets' postseason run, he had pitched past the number of innings that he had planned for that season. Many wondered if those extra innings had taken a toll on his velocity. "I didn't feel great. I didn't have my best stuff," said Harvey after the game.[4]

The Mets took back the lead in the top of the eighth inning. With two outs, Juan Lagares battled set-up reliever Kelvin Herrera over nine pitches before hitting a single. He quickly stole second to put himself in scoring position. Lagares scored when third baseman Hosmer attempted a backhand on Wilmer Flores' routine grounder. The ball bounced past him. Flores had his single and the Mets had their lead. "I thought it was going to be an out," Flores said afterwards. "I thought he was going to get in front of it and that was it. It's a routine ground ball."[5]

The Mets sent their closer Jeurys Familia, to the mound in the ninth inning. Familia had not given up a run in the 2015 postseason. After getting Salvador Perez to ground out to shortstop to lead off the inning, Alex Gordon came to the plate.

Familia was recognized for his dominating 98-mph fastball and a concrete-heavy sinker. Tonight Familia decided to throw a quick, trick pitch to Gordon. "He tried to quick-pitch me and left the ball right there to hit," Gordon said after the game. "With a guy like that, you can't miss pitches that he gives you to hit." Gordon hit the pitch to center field and once again, the score was tied. "As soon as I let that pitch go, I say, Oh man," Familia said later, acknowledging his mistake.[6]

Gordon's home run was the first game-tying or go-ahead home run in the ninth inning of the first game of a World Series since the Dodgers' Kirk Gibson hit one off Oakland's Dennis Eckersley in 1988.[7] Gordon's home run was only the fourth time that a dramatic home run like this had occurred in the first game of a World Series.[8] Gibson's home run won that game. This game would now head to extra innings after Familia settled down and got the next two batters out.

It became a pitching contest as the game headed into extra innings. Batters on both teams stopped hitting and some of the best bats in baseball seemed to forget how to hit the ball. For the Mets, it seemed as if they had decided to turn into the team that could barely hit the ball in back in July. Over the next four innings, they struck out nine times. The Royals did not fare much better. Although they only struck out three times, they also had just three hits during that span.

In the 12th inning, Collins called on Bartolo Colon, who was usually a starter, to take over the pitching duties for the Mets. Colon pitched well for two innings. He kept the Royals off-balance and they repeatedly swung at his pitches in vain.

In the 14th, however, things changed. Escobar, who had ignited the Royals with his first inning home run, stepped to the plate. He hit a grounder to David Wright. The ball hit Wright's wrist, bounced off his midsection, and plopped to the dirt. Wright picked it up and whipped a sidearm throw to first. Escobar ended up on second base as Wright's throw was off the mark. "I got an in-between hop and the ball came up on me. I tried to rush the throw a little bit," Wright said afterwards.[9]

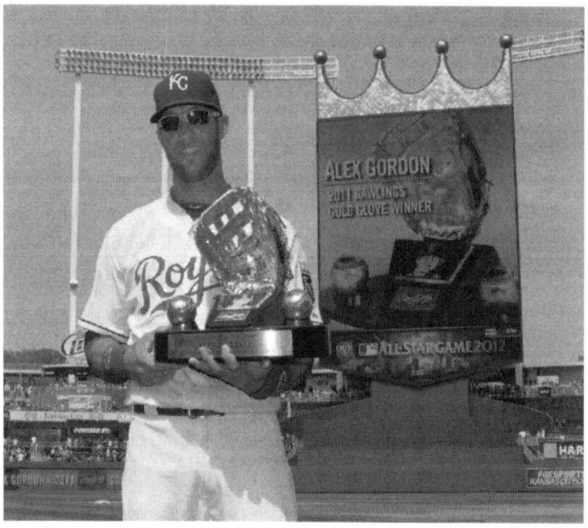

Alex Gordon, Gold Glove

Zobrist then stepped to the plate and hit a single to right field. Escobar moved to third. Colon intentionally walked Cain to load the bases and set up an out at any base. After Hosmer fouled off two of Colon's pitches, he hit a sacrifice fly to right field. Escobar scored and the Royals finally earned the win, 5-4.

As Escobar crossed the plate, the Royals rushed out of the dugout. Gordon ran straight to Hosmer. Then Perez lifted Hosmer off the ground. Hosmer had gone from goat to hero in a matter of hours or innings, depending on your perspective.[10]

Colon became the oldest losing pitcher in World Series history. He was 42 years, 157 days when he lost the game. Prior to this, the oldest losing pitcher was Grover Alexander, who was just over 41 years old when he lost to the Yankees while pitching for the Philadelphia Athletics in 1928.[11]

By the time the game ended after five hours and nine minutes, it had become the third game in World Series history to stretch for 14 innings. The last time that it had happened was back in 2005 when the Astros and White Sox battled against each other with the White Sox coming out on top, 7-5. The Royals took the lead in the series. Using the momentum of their marathon win, they never looked back as they eventually won the 2015 World Series in five games.

Sources

In addition to the sources cited in the Notes, the author also used the Baseball-Reference.com, Baseball-Almanac.com, and Retrosheet.org websites for box score, player, team, and season pages, pitching and batting game logs, and other pertinent material.

Notes

1 Ted Berg, "10 crazy facts about the Royals and Mets' 14-inning Game 1 marathon," *USA Today*, October 28, 2015.

2 Vahe Gregorian, "Drama fills Royals' 14-inning victory in World Series Game 1," *Kansas City Star*, October 28, 2015.

3 John Tattersall, "Hitting Leadoff Homers," *SABR.org*, accessed February 28, 2017.

4 Michael Powell, "Could Have, Should Have, Didn't: An Epitaph for Game 1," *New York Times*, October 28, 2015.

5 Mark Carig, "Mets lose in 14th inning after Alex Gordon's clutch HR in ninth," *Newsday*, October 28, 2015.

6 Michael Powell.

7 Vahe Gregorian.

8 Matt Snyder, "A look at all 15 walk-off home runs in World Series history," *CBS Sports.com*, October 18, 2013.

9 Michael Powell.

10 Sam Mellinger, "Eric Hosmer's late heroics in World Series Game 1 give Royals a shot of confidence," *Kansas City Star*, October 28, 2015.

11 Ted Berg.

NOVEMBER 1, 2015: KANSAS CITY EATS METS TO WIN WORLD SERIES KANSAS CITY ROYALS 7, NEW YORK METS 2 (12 INNINGS), AT CITI FIELD, FLUSHING, NEW YORK

BY THOMAS J. BROWN JR.

The Mets had their backs to the wall after a disappointing loss in Game Four of the 2015 World Series. They were ahead in that game through the seventh inning and lost it on costly mistakes that had shaken their confidence.

The Royals' confidence was growing as quick as the Mets' was disappearing. They just needed to win one more game to claim their first world championship since 1985. The Royals were also looking to redeem themselves after losing the 2014 World Series in seven games to San Francisco. "We think about [the 2014 World Series] quite often. I just think everyone kind of relates back to that and relates to how much that hurt," Royals first baseman Eric Hosmer said at the start of the 2015 Championship Series.[1]

Mets manager Terry Collins chose his young star Matt Harvey to pitch the fifth game. Harvey's presence fired up the home crowd. As the Mets took the field after the introductions, Harvey sprinted from the dugout and raced to the mound ahead of his teammates. He picked up the baseball as chants of "Let's Go Mets!" filled Citi Field.[2]

Harvey struck out the Royals' leadoff batter, Alcides Escobar, who had created difficulties for the Mets all throughout the series. Ben Zobrist then flew out to center field. He gave up a single to Lorenzo Cain, who quickly stole second base on Harvey's first pitch to Hosmer. But he then struck out Hosmer on five pitches for the third out. As he determinedly walked off the mound, Harvey pumped his fists while yelling along with the sellout crowd.[3]

The Royals chose Edinson Volquez to start Game Five. Volquez had pitched masterfully in the first game of the series. He learned after that game that his father Daniel had died earlier in the day and he flew to the Dominican Republic the following day for the funeral. Volquez had rejoined his teammates just before the start of Game Four.[4]

The Mets grabbed the lead in the bottom of the first inning. Curtis Granderson hit Volquez's third pitch over the right-field wall for a solo home run and the Mets were up 1-0.

Harvey pitched masterfully most of the evening. The Royals were able to get a single runner on base in the first three innings but Harvey shut down any hope of them scoring a run each time. When Harvey struck out the heart of the Royals batting order - Cain, Hosmer, and Mike Moustakas - in the fourth inning, the crowd of 41,165 stood on their feet and went wild. Harvey, who had gotten Moustakas to swing vainly at a 98-mph fastball, shook his fist and let out a loud scream before walking off the mound.[5]

Harvey struck out three more batters in the fifth inning. The last two batters in the fifth, Alex Rios and Volquez, were struck out looking at one of his fastballs.[6] Harvey kept the Royals off balance through the first eight innings using all four of his pitches (fastball, curveball, slider, and changeup).

The Mets scored again in the bottom of the sixth inning. Volquez walked Granderson to start the inning. Granderson moved to second on a David Wright single and then reached third when a Daniel Murphy ground ball couldn't be handled by the first baseman. Granderson scored on Lucas Duda's sacrifice fly to center field. The Mets were up 2-0 and it looked like this would be all that they would need to win.

When Harvey got out the Royals in order in the eighth inning, the Mets and their fans could taste a win. Harvey had given a performance that the Mets desperately needed to avoid elimination He had gotten nine strikeouts and had allowed the Royals to get just three hits up to that point.

As Harvey sat in the dugout in the bottom of the eighth inning, he could be seen telling Collins, "No way! No way!" as the manager and pitching coach Dan Warthen told him that they were contemplating taking him out and letting closer Jeurys Familia handle the ninth.[7]

"He just came over and said, 'I want this game. I want it bad. You've got to leave me in,'" Collins said after the game. Harvey said afterwards that "going into the ninth, I felt great. I felt like my mechanics, everything was right where I wanted it to be. As a competitor and as a person, I always want the ball. That's what I've said all year long. In this situation, I wanted the ball."[8]

Harvey ran to the mound for the ninth as the crowd roared "Har-vey, Har-vey." He battled Cain to a 3-2 count before he finally walked him. Collins didn't move and allowed Harvey to face the next batter. After Cain stole second base, Hosmer hit a double that scored Cain and cut the Mets lead to one run. "I let my heart get in the way of my gut," Collins said about his decision to let Harvey pitch the ninth inning.[9]

Collins now went to his bullpen and Familia trotted in. Moustakas took two balls from Familia before hitting the third pitch, a ground ball that moved Hosmer to third base.

Perez then hit a ground ball to Wright at third. Wright looked at Hosmer to keep him from running before throwing out Salvador Perez at first. As soon as Wright threw the ball, Hosmer took off for home. Duda tried to throw out Hosmer but his throw sailed to the right of the catcher. Hosmer scored and the game was tied. "You have to tip your hat. It took a lot of [guts] for him to make that play," Duda said afterwards.[10] The Citi Field crowd that had been so noisy all night was suddenly silent.

The Royals bullpen continued to shut down the Mets. They would limit the Mets to just one more hit, a two-out single in the bottom of the 12th inning.

In the top of the 12th inning, the Royals exploded. Addison Reed had taken over the pitching duties for the Mets. The first batter that he faced, Perez, singled to start the inning. Jarrod Dyson was brought in to run for Perez and immediately stole second base. Alex Gordon grounded out to the first baseman, which allowed Dyson to move to third. Christian Colon singled, his first postseason hit, to score Dyson. Murphy made an error on Paulo Orlando's grounder, giving the Royals runners at first and second. Escobar then doubled to drive in another run.

After Reed intentionally walked Zobrist to load the bases, Collins brought in Bartolo Colon from his bullpen. Colon promptly gave up a double to Cain that cleared the bases. By the time that Colon got the third out, the Royals were up 7-2.

Wade Davis, the Royals closer, came in to pitch the bottom of the 12th inning. Davis had pitched two scoreless innings the previous night for the save. Davis got the first two batters that he faced, Duda and Travis d'Arnaud to strike out swinging at his fastball. After giving up a single to Michael Conforto, he got Wilmer Flores to strike out. The Royals won the 2015 World Series, redeeming their heartbreaking loss in the 2014 World Series.

After the last 95-mph fastball from Davis whistled into backup catcher Drew Butera's glove, the team ran to the mound to celebrate. Thousands of miles away, fireworks popped in Kansas City and fans ran through the streets.[11]

"We never quit," Perez said as the champagne poured in the locker room. "We never put our heads down. We never think about, 'OK, the game is over.' No. We always compete to the last out."[12] As the Royals celebrated their first championship in 30 years, Mets manager Collins stated his feelings about the game to reporters: "I'm going to second-guess myself for a long time. I won't be sleeping much the next couple of days, I'll tell you that."[13] There would be no second guessing for the Royals this year. There would just be a celebration.

Sources

In addition to the sources cited in the Notes, the author also used the Baseball-Reference.com and Retrosheet.org websites for box score, player, team, and season pages, pitching and batting game logs, and other pertinent material.

Notes

1 Billy Witz, "Royals Rally Past Mets for First World Series Title Since 1985," *New York Times*, November 2, 2015.

2 David Lennon, "Matt Harvey brilliant in World Series Game 5," *Newsday*, November 2, 2015.

3 Ibid.

4 Billy Witz.

5 Ibid.

6 Ibid.

7 Phil Taylor, "Harvey's heroics for naught as Collins's Game 5 decision backfires," *Sports Illustrated.com*, November 2, 2015.

8 Adam Rubin, "Matt Harvey decision 'didn't work; it was my fault,' Terry Collins says," *ESPN.com*, November 2, 2015.

9 Mark Carig, "Royals win World Series after rallying against Mets to tie score in ninth," *Newsday.com*, November 2, 2015.

10 Phil Taylor.

11 Andy McCullough, "Royals are World Series Champs," *Kansas City Star*, November 1, 2015.

12 Ibid.

13 Phil Taylor.

ROYALS SCORE 7 IN THE NINTH TO BEAT THE WHITE SOX MAY 28, 2016: KANSAS CITY ROYALS 8, CHICAGO WHITE SOX 7, AT KAUFFMAN STADIUM

BY ROBERT P. NASH

After back-to-back World Series appearances in 2014 and 2015, including their first championship since 1985, the Kansas City Royals began the 2016 season with high hopes of a third straight trip to the World Series. With most of their roster returning, it was not an unreasonable expectation. The defending champions, however, got off to an inconsistent start to the season. By the time the division-leading Chicago White Sox arrived in town for a four-game series on May 26, the Royals were only two games over .500 with a record of 24-22.

Kansas City was without the services of two key players. On the previous Sunday (May 22) in Chicago against the same White Sox, All-Star left fielder Alex Gordon and All-Star third baseman Mike Moustakas had collided chasing a foul ball. Gordon suffered a broken right wrist and would be out of the line up for a month, while Moustakas ended up missing the rest of the season with a torn ACL in his right knee.

The opening game of the series was rained out on Thursday, but in Friday's game, the Royals staged a four-run rally in the seventh inning to pull out a 7-5 win. As a result, the Royals found themselves in third place, only a half-game behind the second-place Cleveland Indians, and one game behind the first-place White Sox in the American League Central Division.

For the afternoon game of Saturday, May 28, Kansas City sent right-hander Yordano Ventura (4-3, 4.81 ERA) to the mound, while Chicago countered with left-hander Carlos Rodon (2-4, 4.47 ERA). After a scoreless first inning for both teams, the Royals quickly got two outs on the White Sox in the top of the second inning, but three straight singles by Brett Lawrie, Alex Avila, and Avisail Garcia led to the first run of the game. A three-run home run by White Sox shortstop Tyler Saladino followed, to give Chicago a 4-0 lead. The Royals responded by loading the bases in their half of the inning, but they stranded all three men on base. They got a run back in the bottom of the third when rookie left fielder Whit Merrifield, filling in for the injured Alex Gordon, led off with a double, stole third base, and scored on a single by first baseman Eric Hosmer. The White Sox answered back in the next inning with a two-run homer by Avisail Garcia, Chicago's designated hitter, to go up 6-1.

The White Sox added their seventh run of the game in the fifth inning when center fielder Austin Jackson led off with a single, advanced to second on a wild pitch by Ventura, and scored on an error by Royals second baseman Omar Infante.

With a comfortable 7-1 lead, Carlos Rodon handed over pitching duties to Zach Putnam in the sixth inning. Putnam put the Royals down in order, and neither team scored in the seventh or eighth inning. In the top of the ninth, the Royals survived a leadoff single by Saladino, but not without cost. While successfully chasing down an infield popup for the first out of the inning, All-Star catcher Salvador Perez collided with his third baseman, Cheslor Cuthbert, and left the game with a leg injury.

Having lost a three-run lead late in the previous evening's game, White Sox manager Robin Ventura was taking no chances, even with a six-run lead. He sent in his closer, David Robertson, to shut down the Royals in the bottom of the ninth inning. Robertson entered the game with a minuscule 0.96 ERA, and had already saved 12 games for the White Sox. He struck out the Royals' leadoff batter, Paulo Orlando, but a single by Cuthbert, a double by Brett Eibner, and a walk to Omar Infante loaded the bases. Alcides Escobar then drew a bases-loaded walk to bring in Cuthbert. A single up the middle by Whit Merrifield scored Eibner and Infante, and Escobar went to third. Lorenzo Cain hit into a fielder's choice, forcing Merrifield out at second, but scoring Escobar to make the score 7-5. With the Royals down to their final out, Eric Hosmer, their cleanup hitter, doubled to center field, scoring Cain.

With the tying run on second, the struggling Robertson was replaced by Tommy Kahnle. Drew Butera, batting for the injured Salvador Perez, hit a double to left field, scoring Hosmer and tying the game. A wild pitch from Kahnle allowed Butera to advance to third. Paulo Orlando was intentionally walked, and advanced to second on defensive indifference. Jarrod Dyson, pinch-hitting for Cuthbert, was given an intentional walk. With the bases loaded, rookie Eibner, playing in only his second major-league game, stepped to the plate. Eibner battled Kahnle to a full count and fouled off four pitches before hitting a single to right field on the 10th pitch of his at-bat to deliver the winning run from third.[1] Eibner's RBI, his second hit of the inning, capped off the largest ninth-inning come-from-behind victory in Royals history. The Royals, coming into the inning down 7-1, had sent 12 batters to the plate, collecting six hits (three of them doubles) and four walks, leading to the seven-run outburst. Chien-Ming Wang, pitching in relief of Yordano Ventura, tossed two scoreless innings to pick up his third win of the season.

Having been unable to hold a late-inning lead for a second game in a row, Chicago's understandably frustrated manager, Ventura, observed: "There's no shot clock, there's no time clock. If you can't close it out, that's what happens. Today we couldn't close it out."[2]

Unfortunately for the White Sox, the Royals were not done with their late-inning heroics. On the next day, they came from behind for the third game in a row, scoring three runs in the bottom of the eighth inning to overcome a two-run deficit on the way to a 5-4 win. In completing the three-game sweep of the White Sox, the Royals took over first place in the Central Division with a 27-22 record.

Their record-setting victory on May 28 turned out to be one of the few bright spots in what was ultimately a disappointing season for Kansas City. Plagued by additional injuries, the Royals fell well short in their bid for a third straight World Series appearance. They struggled to an 81-81 record and a third-place finish in the Central Division, 13½ games behind the division-winning Cleveland Indians.

Sources

In addition to the sources cited in the Notes, the author also relied on Baseball-Reference.com and Retrosheet.org for box scores, play-by-play information, and other data.

Notes

1 Dayn Perry, "Miracle in KC: Royals Overcome 1,000-to-1 Odds with Historic Ninth Inning," cbssports.com, May 28, 2016, accessed November 7, 2018, cbssports.com/mlb/news/miracle-in-kc-royals-overcome-1000-to-1-odds-with-historic-ninth-inning/.

2 "Royals Mount a Seven-Run Rally in the Ninth," New York Times, May 29, 2016.

DUFFY'S SWEET SIXTEEN AT ROYAL MASTERPIECE AUGUST 1, 2016: KANSAS CITY ROYALS 3, TAMPA BAY RAYS 0, AT TROPICANA FIELD, TAMPA

BY RICHARD CUICCHI

Two situations that can usually spin a crowd into a frenzy at a baseball game are when a starting pitcher goes deep into a game without yielding a hit or when he approaches a strikeout total in the double digits by midgame. Kansas City's Danny Duffy had both factors going for him when he faced the Tampa Bay Rays on August 1, 2016. But this particular crowd didn't get overly excited about Duffy's performance, since his pitching gem occurred in front of a small crowd of Rays fans at Tropicana Field.

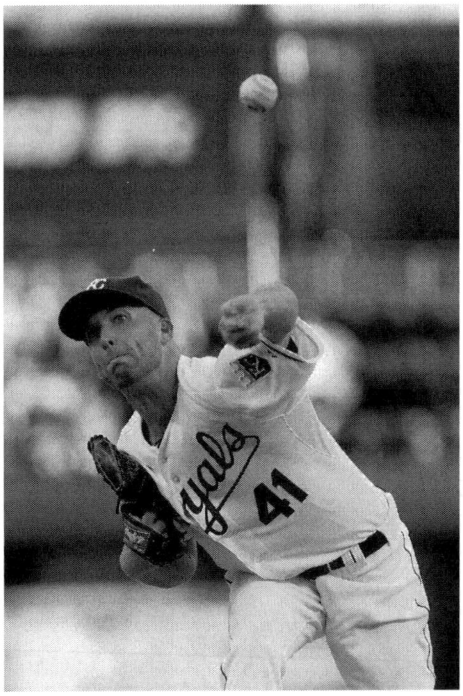

The 27-year-old Duffy turned in a masterpiece performance; he struck out a Royals record 16 batters and took a no-hitter into the eighth inning. Based on his five-year major-league record up to the 2016 season, Duffy wouldn't have been high on the list of pitchers who would be expected to turn in such a sterling performance. His career stats were average at best, a 24-30 record, 3.80 ERA, 1.360 WHIP, and 7.1 strikeouts per nine innings.

However, the 2016 season was developing into a breakout season for Duffy. He started the season in the Royals' bullpen and didn't get his first start until May 15. In his 14 starts since then, his record was 6-1, with a 3.27 ERA, 1.052 WHIP, and 9.69 K's per nine innings.

The defending World Series champion Royals had been hot and cold during the first half of 2016. They were in first place (35-30 record) as late as June 15, but by the end of July had sunk to fourth place, 12 games behind the Cleveland Indians in the American League Central Division.

The Rays were bringing up the rear of the American League East Division, 16½ games behind the first-place Baltimore Orioles. They were competing in a tough division; all four teams ahead of them were playing .500 ball or better. Even the fourth-place New York Yankees were only seven games behind the Orioles at the end of July.

The night game at Tropicana Field drew 13,976 fans, which was typical for games there.[1] It was the beginning of a four-game series that wouldn't have much bearing on either team's standing.

Tampa Bay manager Kevin Cash gave the starting nod to ace Chris Archer. Archer was having a terrible season with a 5-14 record and 4.42 ERA, after having finished fifth in the Cy Young Award voting in 2015.

An old-fashioned pitching duel ensued for the first six innings.

Right-hander Archer and left-hander Duffy were both perfect in the first two innings, with Duffy coming out of the gate strong with five strikeouts.

Paulo Orlando got a double with one out for the first Royals hit in the top of the third inning. After he was sacrificed to third, Archer got out of the inning on a grounder. Duffy struck out two more as he retired the side in order in the bottom of the inning.

In the top of the fourth inning, Archer gave up a single to Cheslor Cuthbert, but faced only three batters that inning with the aid of a double play. In the bottom half, Duffy allowed his first baserunner of the game when he walked Logan Forsythe. Forsythe advanced to third on an errant throw by Duffy in a pickoff move. But Duffy eliminated the threat of a Rays score by striking out two more batters.

Kendrys Morales got the Royals' third hit in the top of the fifth, but again Archer shut them down without any runs. Duffy countered with his 10th and 11th punchouts in the bottom of the inning.

Both pitchers threw scoreless innings in the sixth inning, as Duffy added another strikeout. Royals manager Ned Yost commented after the game, "Quite frankly, I wasn't even paying attention until about the fifth or sixth inning. I looked up and saw no hit. And I thought: 'Whoa.'"[2]

Through six innings, Archer had been almost as tough on the hill as Duffy. But the Royals broke the scoreless tie in the top of the seventh on a solo home run by Morales, a towering shot over the center-field wall, his 17th homer of the season. By now, the entire ballpark was well aware of Duffy's possibility for a no-hitter. He continued his no-hit bid in the bottom of the inning by striking out two more (13th and 14th), including Evan Longoria and Steven Souza for the third time each.

Yost started to think about Duffy's pitch count, which eventually reached 110 pitches, as a factor in the outing, but he concluded that Duffy wasn't coming out until he gave up a hit. Yost said after the game, "If he got through the eighth, he was going back out."[3]

The Royals added two more runs in the top of the eighth inning. Orlando singled and was sacrificed to second. Alcides Escobar then hit a line-drive single to left that scored Orlando. Kevin Jepsen relieved Archer and threw a wild pitch that advanced Escobar to second. Cuthbert singled and Lorenzo Cain hit a fly ball that scored Escobar to increase the Royals' lead to 3-0.

Duffy had been escaping into the clubhouse between innings to relax.[4] Perhaps he was seeking seclusion to avoid the long-standing superstition of being jinxed by someone in the dugout mentioning his no-hit bid.

Desmond Jennings, who was playing his first game since June 30, led off the bottom of the eighth inning. He disrupted Duffy's date with immortality when he broke up the no-hitter with a double to deep left field. Undeterred, Duffy got Kevin Kiermaier to line out to deep center and struck out his 15th and 16th victims to leave Jennings stranded.

With Duffy having given up the hit in the eighth, Yost didn't have to make a tough pitching decision in the bottom of the ninth. Kelvin Herrera relieved Duffy and retired the side in order for the save.

The last no-hitter by a Royals pitcher was on April 26, 1991, by Bret Saberhagen. Duffy's 16 strikeouts eclipsed the franchise record of 15 by Zack Greinke on August 25, 2009. "It's an honor to have a game like those guys," Duffy said, "But I understand they had a lot more of those consistently than I did. Here's to trying to do it more consistently myself."[5] Duffy's highest previous strikeout total for an outing was 10.

Jennings hit a 95-mph fastball off Duffy for the lone Rays hit. Royals catcher Salvador Perez blamed himself for calling the pitch after previously getting Desmond out on a changeup and slider in his two prior at-bats. But Duffy took Perez off the hook by offering, "I was perfectly content with the pitch and how it turned out. It was a fastball up and you have to tip your hat to (Jennings)."[6]

An indicator that Duffy was indeed at the top of his game was that Rays batters made contact on just 26 of their 60 swings against him. Reportedly, his swing-and-miss rate set a record for any starting pitcher over the past 15 years.[7] Fifteen of the 16 batters Duffy struck out went down swinging.

While Duffy was pitching the game of his life, Archer was hurling a credible game himself. He gave up three earned runs in 7⅓ innings. He yielded six hits and one walk while striking out six. Archer kept the Rays in the game into the eighth inning. He took the loss and wound up leading the American League with 19 losses for the season.

Duffy continued to pitch well in August, recording four more victories, including his 10th consecutive win. He finished the season with a 12-3 record and 3.51 ERA and wound up as the best performer among the Royals' starting pitchers.

Sources

In addition to the sources cited in the Notes, the author consulted Baseball-Reference.com and the 2017 Kansas City Royals Media Guide.

Notes

1 The average attendance for 2016 Tampa Bay home games was 15,879.

2 Rustin Dodd. "Sweet Sixteen," *Kansas City Star*, August 2, 2016: 1B.

3 Dodd.

4 Ibid.

5 Ibid.

6 Bill Chastain and Jeffrey Flanagan. "Duffy Flirts with No-No, Logs 16 K's in Beating Rays," MLB.com. August 2, 2016. mlb.com/news/danny-duffy-logs-16-strikeouts-in-royals-win/c-193030780. Retrieved July 31, 2018.

7 "Duffy Misses Bats, Sets Strikeout Record for Royals," ESPN.com, August 1, 2016. espn.com/blog/statsinfo/post/_/id/122251/undefined. Retrieved July 31, 2018. Baseball-Reference.com shows the total as 26.

CONTRIBUTOR BIOS

Mark Armour writes baseball from his home in Oregon, which he shares with Jane, Maya, and Drew.

Jeff Barto teaches two different baseball courses at UNC Charlotte, the History of Baseball and Baseball Through Critical Thinking. He resides in Huntersville, North Carolina with wife Jayne and two daughters. As a kid, he watched Freddie Patek play at Forbes Field, one of his favorite players. He was saddened when the Pirates dealt him to Kansas City. It pleased him to interview one of his boyhood heroes and to write his bio for this project.

Russell Bergtold is originally from the southside of Chicago. An avid Cubs fan, Russ joined SABR in 2015 when he submitted his first BioProject on the late Ray Poat. He later wrote a biography on Don Newcombe which was published in SABR's *From Spring Training to Screen Test: Baseball Players Turned Actors*, (2018). A member of the International Brotherhood of Electrical Workers (IBEW), Russ recently earned his M.A. in Communication from Governors State University. He currently resides in northwest Indiana with his spouse.

Richard Bogovich is the author of *Kid Nichols: A Biography of the Hall of Fame Pitcher,* about a longtime Kansas City resident and ballplayer. He has contributed to various SABR books, including *Bittersweet Goodbye: The Black Barons, the Grays, and the 1948 Negro League World Series* and biographies of Freddie Sanchez and Dewon Brazelton for *Overcoming Adversity: Baseball's Tony Conigliaro Award.* He works for the Wendland Utz law firm in Rochester, Minnesota.

Thomas J. Brown Jr. is a lifelong Mets fan who became a Durham Bulls fan after moving to North Carolina in the early 1980s. He was a national board-certified high school science teacher for 34 years before retiring in 2016. Tom still volunteers with the ELL students at his former high school, serving as a mentor to those students and the teachers who are now working with them. He also provides support and guidance for his former ELL students when they embark on different career paths after graduation. Tom has been a member of SABR since 1995 when he learned about the organization during a visit to Cooperstown on his honeymoon. He has become active in the organization since his retirement and has written numerous biographies and game stories, mostly about the NY Mets. Tom also enjoys traveling as much as possible with his wife and has visited major-league and minor-league baseball parks across the country on his many trips. He also loves to cook and makes all the meals for at his house while writing about those meals on his blog, Cooking and My Family.

Frederick C. (Rick) Bush was happy to see the Royals rise from the ashes to make consecutive World Series in 2014-15, including a championship in the latter season. After admiring the fountains at Kauffman Stadium on TV for decades, he finally had the opportunity to attend a Royals game there in 2016 and the venue did not disappoint. Rick and Bill Nowlin co-edited the 2017 SABR book *Bittersweet Goodbye: The Black Barons, the Grays, and the 1948 Negro League World Series* and are currently co-editing another Negro Leagues book about the 1946 Newark Eagles. Rick lives with his wife Michelle and their three sons Michael, Andrew, and Daniel in the greater Houston area, where he teaches English at Wharton County Junior College.

Bill Carle lives in Lee's Summit, Missouri with his wife, Valerie. He joined SABR in 1977 and has served as SABR's Biographical Committee chairman since 1988. He won the Bob Davids Award in 1993, the Henry Chadwick Award in 2013, and has been a Kansas City Royals season ticket holder since 1993.

Surrounded by Cub fans in the northern suburbs of Chicago, **Ken Carrano** works as a chief financial officer for a large landscaping firm and as a soccer referee. Ken and his Brewers' fan wife Ann share two children, two golden retrievers, and a mutual distain for the blue side of Chicago.

Alan Cohen serves as Vice President-Treasurer of the Connecticut Smoky Joe Wood Chapter, and is datacaster for the Hartford Yard Goats, the Double-A affiliate of the Rockies. He also works as a volunteer with Children's Reading Partners, working with at-risk elementary school students. He has written more than 40 biographies for SABR's BioProject, and has expanded his research into the Hearst Sandlot Classic (1946-1965), which launched the careers of 88 major-league players. He has four children and six grandchildren and resides in Connecticut with wife Frances and their cat, Morty.

Richard Cuicchi joined SABR in 1983 and is an active member of the Schott-Pelican Chapter. Since his retirement as an information technology executive, Richard authored *Family Ties: A Comprehensive Collection of Facts and Trivia about Baseball's Relatives*. He has contributed to numerous SABR BioProject and Games publications. He does freelance writing and blogging about a variety of baseball topics on his website TheTenthInning.com. Richard lives in New Orleans with his wife, Mary.

John DiFonzo grew up in Somerville, Massachusetts where he was the sports editor for his high school newspaper, *The Radiator*. He is a lifelong Red Sox fan and season-ticket holder since 2004 currently living in Boston with his wife Gabriella. John graduated of Tufts University with a bachelor's degree in Electrical Engineering, holds a Master of Science in Global Financial Analysis from Bentley University and is a CFA charterholder.

Michael Engel has been a member of SABR since 2013 and a Royals fan since as long as he can remember. He currently lives in Lawrence, Kansas, working at his alma mater, the University of Kansas. He is a co-host of the Kansas City Baseball Vault podcast, and has contributed at Baseball Prospectus, Pine Tar Press, and began writing about baseball as editor of Kings of Kauffman from 2010 to 2013.

Charles F. Faber was a native of Iowa who lived in Lexington, Kentucky, until his passing in August 2016. He held degrees from Coe College, Columbia University, and the University of Chicago. A retired public school and university teacher and administrator, he contributed to numerous SABR projects, including editing *The 1934 St. Louis Cardinals: The World Champion Gas House Gang*. Among his publications are dozens of professional journal articles, encyclopedia entries, and research reports in fields such as school administration, education law, and country music. In addition to textbooks, he wrote 10 books (mostly on baseball) published by McFarland. His last book, co-authored with his grandson Zachariah Webb, was *The Hunt for a Reds October*, published by McFarland in 2015.

Adam Foldes resides in New York City. He works as an Archivist at the Eastern Diocese of the Armenian Church of America. In his free time he cheers for the Miami Marlins. He has been a SABR Member since 2017.

James Forr is past winner of the McFarland-SABR Baseball Research Award and co-author (along with David Proctor) of *Pie Traynor: A Baseball Biography,* which was a finalist for the 2010 CASEY Award. He lives in Columbia, Missouri.

Brian Frank is passionate about documenting the history of major- and minor-league baseball. He is the creator of the website The Herd Chronicles (www.herdchronicles.com), which is dedicated to preserving the history of the Buffalo Bisons. His articles can also be read on the official website of the Bisons. He is a frequent contributor to SABR publications. Brian and his wife Jenny enjoy traveling around the country in their camper to major- and minor-league ballparks and taking an annual trip to Europe. Brian was a history major at Canisius College where he earned a Bachelor of Arts. He also received a Juris Doctor from the University at Buffalo School of Law.

Steve Friedman has been a SABR member since 1990. He has recently contributed articles for SABR publications and the BioProject. He has resided in the Pacific Northwest since 1985 and has been a season ticket holder of the Seattle Mariners since 1995. His youth was spent in the San Francisco Bay Area where he followed his beloved Giants. Steve is currently retired after a career of over 35 years as an owner and operator of cable television systems.

Adrian Fung lives and works in Toronto. At age 7, he attended his first major-league baseball game at the now-demolished Canadian National Exhibition Stadium. Cal Ripken Jr., in game 706 of the streak, hit a three-run home run that day. Adrian joined SABR (Hanlan's Point Chapter - Toronto) in 2014 and has contributed several stories to SABR Games Project, mostly about memorable games in Blue Jays history, including one that made it into the SABR book *No-Hitters*. He also writes for the maverick hockey website, thePensblog.com under the *nom de guerre* "PenguinsMarch."

Gordon J. Gattie serves as a human-systems integration engineer for the U.S. Navy. His baseball research interests involve ballparks, historical records, and statistical analysis. A SABR member since 1998, Gordon earned his Ph.D. from the University at Buffalo, where he used baseball to investigate judgment/decision-making performance in complex dynamic environments. Originally from Buffalo, Gordon learned early the hardships associated with rooting for Buffalo sports teams. Ever the optimist, he also cheers for the Cleveland Indians and Washington Nationals. Lisa, his lovely bride who also enjoys baseball, continues to challenge him by supporting the Yankees. Gordon has contributed to multiple SABR publications.

Peter M. Gordon is a long-time member of SABR who's written articles in 16 of our published books, including the history of the Tampa Bay Rays' first year for 2018's *Time for Expansion Baseball*. He's an award-winning poet with more than 100 poems published. His collection of baseball poems, *Let's Play Two*, made the Amazon.com baseball book best seller list. He lives in Orlando, Florida where he teaches in Full Sail University's Film Production MFA program.

Paul Hofmann, a SABR member since 2002, is the Associate Vice President for International Affairs at Sacramento State University. Paul is a native of Detroit, Michigan and lifelong Detroit Tigers fan. He currently resides in Folsom, California.

Mike Huber is Professor of Mathematics at Muhlenberg College in Allentown, Pennsylvania. He joined SABR in 1996, shortly before moving to Kansas for a year. This allowed him to attend many Royals games. He enjoys writing for SABR's Games Project.

Stephen Katsoulis is in his rookie season with SABR. He resides in Indian Land, South Carolina with his wife Jill and two children. His passion and love for the game stems from his early childhood when he would run onto the field during his dad's semipro baseball games ready to play third base. That passion has led to over 20 years in sports television producing for teams such as the Braves, Twins, Angels, Dodgers and ultimately his favorite team, the Boston Red Sox. Along the way he's had the unique privilege of learning the game from some of the top analysts and writers in baseball and is fortunate enough to call them friends (or as his wife calls it, name-droppers).

Norm King lived in Ottawa Ontario. Before passing away in 2018, Norm's baseball research focused on his dear Montreal Expos. He was senior editor and main writer of the SABR book: *Au jeu/Play Ball: The 50 Greatest Games in the History of the Montreal Expos*, and wrote biographies for several other SABR books.

Tom Knosby is a member of Kansas City's Monarch's Chapter. He has been a Royals fan since 1971. He saw his first major league game in 1973 at Royals Stadium (the year it opened). His favorite Royal was and still is Amos Otis who happened to hit a home run in the first inning of that game.

A lifelong Tigers fan, **Steven Kuehl** was born in Michigan's Upper Peninsula, but now resides in Wisconsin with his wife, Kathleen, son, Connor, and labrador retrievers, Lola and Oliver. An Assistant Professor of Mathematics and Department Chair at Silver Lake College of the Holy Family in Manitowoc, Wisconsin, he has been published in the Baseball Research Journal, *The 20/30 Game Winner: An Endangered/Extinct Species* (2013). He has also worked on the SABR book projects, *Tigers by the Tale: Fifty Great Games at the Corner of Michigan and Trumbull* and *From the Braves to the Brewers: Great Games and Exciting History at Milwaukee's County Stadium.*

Bill Lamberty, Sports Information Director at Montana State University since 1990, joined SABR in 1983. He was a founding member of the Deadball Era Committee, and has researched and written about college baseball and baseball stadiums. Lamberty grew up in Fremont, Nebraska, graduated from the University of Wyoming with a BS in Journalism in 1981, and earned his Master's degree from Montana State in history in 2009. His son Nate was a four-year baseball letterman at Whitworth, where his daughter Ellie scored baseball games for the school's Sports Information operation, and he and his wife Lynn reside in Bozeman, Montana.

Kevin Larkin retired after 24 years as a police officer in his hometown of Great Barrington, Massachusetts. He has always been a baseball fan and has been going to minor-league and major-league baseball games since he was 5 years old. He has authored two books on baseball: *Baseball in the Bay State* (a history of baseball in the Commonwealth of Massachusetts) and *Gehrig: Game by Game* (an account of all of the major-league baseball games played by his hero, Lou Gehrig. He has also co-authored *Baseball in the Berkshires: A County's Common Bond* along with James Tom Daly, James Overmyer, and Larry Moore. The book details a history of baseball in Berkshire County where Larkin grew up. He has authored numerous articles for SABR and also recently had published Legends On Deck, a list of who Larkin thinks are the top 100 Black Baseball/ Negro League baseball players. He does fact-checking and hyperlinking for SABR and according to him, is living the dream of writing and researching about the great sport of baseball.

Ryan Lefebvre resides in Greenwood, Missour with his wife Sarah and their sons: Micah, Evan, and Lucas along with daughter, Callie. As the son of former big-league player and manager Jim Lefebvre, Ryan's love of baseball is genetic – in fact, he was a first team All-Big Ten Baseball selection in 1993 at the University of Minnesota. But it has been behind the microphone where he has made his big-league mark. After starting his career on the broadcast team of the Minnesota Twins for four seasons, he joined the Kansas City Royals in 1999. Two decades later he has called many great moments in Royals history while becoming a Kansas Citian through and through. Actively involved in a number of Kansas City community activities, Lefebvre is the founder of Gloves For Kids and the Footprints Foundation, which raise money for youth programs in Kansas and Missouri.

Bob LeMoine grew up in Maine and has been a Red Sox fan since the days when Carl Yastrzemski was taking his final swings. He works as a librarian and enjoys research and writing for any SABR project. He is a co-editor with Bill Nowlin on a forthcoming book on the Boston Beaneaters of the 1890s. Bob lives in New Hampshire.

Len Levin is a retired newspaper editor (*Providence Journal*). He works part-time editing the decisions of the Rhode Island Supreme Court, and also spends a lot of time copyediting SABR's books, including this one.

Daniel R. Levitt is the author of several baseball books and numerous essays. He is a longtime SABR member and a recipient of the Davids Award and the Chadwick Award. His books have won the Larry Ritter Book Award, the Sporting News-SABR Baseball Research Award, and have twice been finalists for the Seymour Medal.

Robert Nash is Special Collections & Rare Books Librarian and Professor at the University of Nebraska at Omaha. He has been a SABR member since 1993.

Curt Nelson resides in Kansas City, Missouri which makes perfect sense because it is there that he has been fortunate to carved out a career of knowing more than an ostensibly sane person should about the Kansas City Royals. He joined the organization in 1999 as a seasonal staffer and later served on the Royals marketing team helping start promotions such as T-Shirt Tuesday and special events including Royals FanFest. He is currently the Director of the Royals Hall of Fame and has represented the club on MLB Network's *Baseball IQ*, appeared in *MLB Network Presents: Royal in Kansas City, 30 Years Later* chronicling both Kansas City World Series Championship seasons, and helped tell the Bo Jackson story in ESPN's *You Don't Know Bo* 30 for 30 documentary. He is the author of *So You Think You're a Kansas City Royals Fan?: Stars, Stats, Records, and Memories for True Diehards.*

Bill Nowlin lives, writes, and edits from Cambridge, Massachusetts. A lifelong Red Sox fan, he respects partisan fandom in others (perhaps feeling more generous after waiting nearly 60 years and then experiencing four World Series wins.) He has edited a few dozen books for SABR during the current decade. A co-founder of Rounder Records, he's also written a few other books (and sets of liner notes) on music.

Larry Pauley resides in Ozark, Missouri, from where he enjoys almost equal cheering distance between the Kansas City Royals and the St. Louis Cardinals. A church pastor for more than four decades, he also maintains the Baseballia.com website and frequently deals in baseball cards and memorabilia.

Carl Riechers retired from United Parcel Service in 2012 after 35 years of service. With more free time, he became a SABR member that same year. Born and raised in the suburbs of St. Louis, he became a big fan of the Cardinals. He and his wife Janet have three children and is the proud grandpa of two.

Max Rieper is the editor of *Royals Review*, an SB Nation blog about the Royals, and works full-time as a legislative analyst. He resides in the Kansas City area with his wife and three kids.

Curt Smith's 17th book was released in 2018, *The Presidents and the Pastime: The History of Baseball and the White House*, from the University of Nebraska Press, the first book to chronicle in-depth the relationship between two American institutions—baseball and the Presidency. It was praised by MLB TV, BBC TV, *Parade* Magazine, *The Wall Street Journal, SI Now, FOX Nightly News*, and the Franklin D. Roosevelt Presidential Library and Museum. Smith's prior books include *Voices of The Game, The Voice,* and *Pull Up a Chair.* From 1989-93, he wrote more speeches than anyone else for President George H.W. Bush. Smith is a GateHouse Media columnist, Associated Press award-winning commentator, and senior lecturer at the University of Rochester. He has hosted or keynoted the Great Fenway Writers Series, numerous Smithsonian Institution series, and the Cooperstown Symposium on Baseball and American Culture. The former *The Saturday Evening Post* senior editor has written ESPN TV's *Voices of The Game* series, created the Franklin Roosevelt Award in Communication at the National Radio Hall of Fame, and been named to the Judson Welliver Society of former Presidential speechwriters.

Glen Sparks has contributed biographies to several SABR books and is writing a full-length book on Hall of Fame shortstop Pee Wee Reese. Sparks grew up in Santa Monica, California, and is a life-long Dodgers fan. He and his wife, Pam, live in Cardinals country with their cats, Teddy and Lucy.

When **John Stahl** and his wife are not busy chasing around their three small grandsons, he has been fortunate enough to contribute to over 20 SABR bios. He has been a baseball junkie since birth.

Mark S. Sternman ripped off a fellow youngster by trading a Kansas City Steve Mingori baseball card for Reggie Jackson. Sternman made the trade by saying that the augmented mustache someone had drawn on Mingori made his card more valuable. Sternman's father vetoed the transaction when he learned of it. On a happier note, Sternman named his goldfish Lemon during Bob Lemon's tenure as manager of the Royals. A Yankee fan, Sternman still thinks Lee MacPhail erred in his ruling overturning the original result of the Pine Tar Game.

Andrew Stockmann is a student at Wichita State University pursuing a degree in Sport Management. He is from Liberty, Missouri, and grew up an avid Royals fan. He attended the 2014 American League Wild Card Game at Kauffman Stadium and wept a year later when the Royals won the World Series. He fondly remembers his high school closing so students could attend the parade in downtown KC. This is his first contribution to a SABR publication.

Clayton Trutor is the chairman of Gardner-Waterman (Vermont) chapter. He writes about college football and basketball for SB Nation and holds a PhD in US History from Boston College. You can follow him on Twitter: @ClaytonTrutor.

Darin Watson lives in Hot Springs Village, Arkansas, with his wife Michelle and three pets, including a cat named after Alex Gordon. In 2018, he joined SABR and also relocated to Arkansas from the Kansas City area; it was a busy year. He grew up in Topeka, Kansas, learning to love the Royals and considers himself lucky he is old enough to remember the 1985 World Series. He works for a media company and also blogs about Royals history at ulstoothpick.com.

Gregory H. Wolf was born in Pittsburgh, but now resides in the Chicagoland area with his wife, Margaret, and daughter, Gabriela. A professor of German studies and holder of the Dennis and Jean Bauman Endowed Chair in the Humanities at North Central College in Naperville, Illinois, he has edited nine books for SABR. He is currently working on projects about Comiskey Park in Chicago, Shibe Park in Philadelphia, and the 1982 Milwaukee Brewers. As of January 2017, he serves as co-director of SABR's BioProject, which you can follow on Facebook and Twitter.

Steve Wulf is a senior writer for ESPN. When he began covering baseball for the *Fort Lauderdale News* in the spring of 1974, he asked then-Braves outfielder Hank Aaron if he had ever thought about the significance of being both the first alphabetical listing in the *Baseball Encyclopedia* and arguably the greatest player of all-time. The Hammer turned on his heel and walked away. But Wulf has kept at it, writing about the sport for *Sports Illustrated*, *Time*, and *ESPN*. Along the way, Dave Aardsma passed Aaron in the alphabet, and Wulf and his wife Bambi raised four pitchers. If he had to name a favorite player, it would be Dan Quisenberry.

Jack Zerby became acquainted with the Kansas City Royals when, as a new arrival in southwest Florida, he watched them in 1981 spring training at old Terry Park in Ft. Myers. Those Royals were at the pinnacle of their success and had George Brett; the future Hall of Famer had flirted with. 400 for the 1980 AL champions. Jack, a retired attorney and estates/trust administrator, has been a SABR member since 1994 and is active in the BioProject and Games Project. He and his wife Diana, a professional violinist, live in Brevard in western North Carolina.

SABR BioProject Team Books

In 2002, the Society for American Baseball Research launched an effort to write and publish biographies of every player, manager, and individual who has made a contribution to baseball. Over the past decade, the BioProject Committee has produced over 6,000 biographical articles. Many have been part of efforts to create theme- or team-oriented books, spearheaded by chapters or other committees of SABR.

The 1986 Boston Red Sox:
There Was More Than Game Six
One of a two-book series on the rivals that met in the 1986 World Series, the Boston Red Sox and the New York Mets, including biographies of every player, coach, broadcaster, and other important figures in the top organizations in baseball that year. .
Edited by Leslie Heaphy and Bill Nowlin
$19.95 paperback (ISBN 978-1-943816-19-4)
$9.99 ebook (ISBN 978-1-943816-18-7)
8.5"X11", 420 pages, over 200 photos

The 1986 New York Mets:
There Was More Than Game Six
The other book in the "rivalry" set from the 1986 World Series. This book re-tells the story of that year's classic World Series and this is the story of each of the players, coaches, managers, and broadcasters, their lives in baseball and the way the 1986 season fit into their lives.
Edited by Leslie Heaphy and Bill Nowlin
$19.95 paperback (ISBN 978-1-943816-13-2)
$9.99 ebook (ISBN 978-1-943816-12-5)
8.5"X11", 392 pages, over 100 photos

SCANDAL ON THE SOUTH SIDE:
The 1919 Chicago White Sox
The Black Sox Scandal isn't the only story worth telling about the 1919 Chicago White Sox. The team roster included three future Hall of Famers, a 20-year-old spitballer who would win 300 games in the minors, and even a batboy who later became a celebrity with the "Murderers' Row" New York Yankees. All of their stories are included in Scandal on the South Side with a timeline of the 1919 season.
Edited by Jacob Pomrenke
$19.95 paperback (ISBN 978-1-933599-95-3)
$9.99 ebook (ISBN 978-1-933599-94-6)
8.5"x11", 324 pages, 55 historic photos

WINNING ON THE NORTH SIDE
The 1929 Chicago Cubs
Celebrate the 1929 Chicago Cubs, one of the most exciting teams in baseball history. Future Hall of Famers Hack Wilson, '29 NL MVP Rogers Hornsby, and Kiki Cuyler, along with Riggs Stephenson formed one of the most potent quartets in baseball history. The magical season came to an ignominious end in the World Series and helped craft the future "lovable loser" image of the team.
Edited by Gregory H. Wolf
$19.95 paperback (ISBN 978-1-933599-89-2)
$9.99 ebook (ISBN 978-1-933599-88-5)
8.5"x11", 314 pages, 59 photos

DETROIT THE UNCONQUERABLE:
The 1935 World Champion Tigers
Biographies of every player, coach, and broadcaster involved with the 1935 World Champion Detroit Tigers baseball team, written by members of the Society for American Baseball Research. Also includes a season in review and other articles about the 1935 team. Hank Greenberg, Mickey Cochrane, Charlie Gehringer, Schoolboy Rowe, and more.
Edited by Scott Ferkovich
$19.95 paperback (ISBN 9978-1-933599-78-6)
$9.99 ebook (ISBN 978-1-933599-79-3)
8.5"X11", 230 pages, 52 photos

The Team That Time Won't Forget:
The 1951 New York Giants
Because of Bobby Thomson's dramatic "Shot Heard 'Round the World" in the bottom of the ninth of the decisive playoff game against the Brooklyn Dodgers, the team will forever be in baseball public's consciousness. Includes a foreword by Giants outfielder Monte Irvin.
Edited by Bill Nowlin and C. Paul Rogers III
$19.95 paperback (ISBN 978-1-933599-99-1)
$9.99 ebook (ISBN 978-1-933599-98-4)
8.5"X11", 282 pages, 47 photos

A PENNANT FOR THE TWIN CITIES:
The 1965 Minnesota Twins
This volume celebrates the 1965 Minnesota Twins, who captured the American League pennant in just their fifth season in the Twin Cities. Led by an All-Star cast, from Harmon Killebrew, Tony Oliva, Zoilo Versalles, and Mudcat Grant to Bob Allison, Jim Kaat, Earl Battey, and Jim Perry, the Twins won 102 games, but bowed to the Los Angeles Dodgers and Sandy Koufax in Game Seven
Edited by Gregory H. Wolf
$19.95 paperback (ISBN 978-1-943816-09-5)
$9.99 ebook (ISBN 978-1-943816-08-8)
8.5"X11", 405 pages, over 80 photos

MUSTACHES AND MAYHEM: CHARLIE O'S THREE TIME CHAMPIONS:
The Oakland Athletics: 1972-74
The Oakland Athletics captured major league baseball's crown each year from 1972 through 1974. Led by future Hall of Famers Reggie Jackson, Catfish Hunter and Rollie Fingers, the Athletics were a largely homegrown group who came of age together. Biographies of every player, coach, manager, and broadcaster (and mascot) from 1972 through 1974 are included, along with season recaps.
Edited by Chip Greene
$29.95 paperback (ISBN 978-1-943816-07-1)
$9.99 ebook (ISBN 978-1-943816-06-4)
8.5"X11", 600 pages, almost 100 photos

SABR Members can purchase each book at a significant discount (often 50% off) and receive the ebook edtions free as a member benefit. Each book is available in a trade paperback edition as well as ebooks suitable for reading on a home computer or Nook, Kindle, or iPad/tablet.
To learn more about becoming a member of SABR, visit the website: sabr.org/join

The SABR Digital Library

The Society for American Baseball Research, the top baseball research organization in the world, disseminates some of the best in baseball history, analysis, and biography through our publishing programs. The SABR Digital Library contains a mix of books old and new, and focuses on a tandem program of paperback and ebook publication, making these materials widely available for both on digital devices and as traditional printed books.

Greatest Games Books

TIGERS BY THE TALE:
GREAT GAMES AT MICHIGAN AND TRUMBULL
For over 100 years, Michigan and Trumbull was the scene of some of the most exciting baseball ever. This book portrays 50 classic games at the corner, spanning the earliest days of Bennett Park until Tiger Stadium's final closing act. From Ty Cobb to Mickey Cochrane, Hank Greenberg to Al Kaline, and Willie Horton to Alan Trammell.
Edited by Scott Ferkovich
$12.95 paperback (ISBN 978-1-943816-21-7)
$6.99 ebook (ISBN 978-1-943816-20-0)
8.5"x11", 160 pages, 22 photos

FROM THE BRAVES TO THE BREWERS: GREAT GAMES AND HISTORY AT MILWAUKEE'S COUNTY STADIUM
The National Pastime provides in-depth articles focused on the geographic region where the national SABR convention is taking place annually. The SABR 45 convention took place in Chicago, and here are 45 articles on baseball in and around the bat-and-ball crazed Windy City: 25 that appeared in the souvenir book of the convention plus another 20 articles available in ebook only.
Edited by Gregory H. Wolf
$19.95 paperback (ISBN 978-1-943816-23-1)
$9.99 ebook (ISBN 978-1-943816-22-4)
8.5"X11", 290 pages, 58 photos

BRAVES FIELD:
MEMORABLE MOMENTS AT BOSTON'S LOST DIAMOND
From its opening on August 18, 1915, to the sudden departure of the Boston Braves to Milwaukee before the 1953 baseball season, Braves Field was home to Boston's National League baseball club and also hosted many other events: from NFL football to championship boxing. The most memorable moments to occur in Braves Field history are portrayed here.
Edited by Bill Nowlin and Bob Brady
$19.95 paperback (ISBN 978-1-933599-93-9)
$9.99 ebook (ISBN 978-1-933599-92-2)
8.5"X11", 282 pages, 182 photos

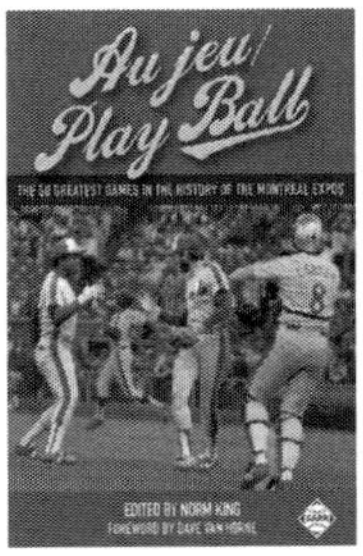

AU JEU/PLAY BALL: THE 50 GREATEST GAMES IN THE HISTORY OF THE MONTREAL EXPOS
The 50 greatest games in Montreal Expos history. The games described here recount the exploits of the many great players who wore Expos uniforms over the years—Bill Stoneman, Gary Carter, Andre Dawson, Steve Rogers, Pedro Martinez, from the earliest days of the franchise, to the glory years of 1979-1981, the what-might-have-been years of the early 1990s, and the sad, final days.and others.
Edited by Norm King
$12.95 paperback (ISBN 978-1-943816-15-6)
$5.99 ebook (ISBN978-1-943816-14-9)
8.5"x11", 162 pages, 50 photos

Original SABR Research

CALLING THE GAME:
BASEBALL BROADCASTING FROM 1920 TO THE PRESENT
An exhaustive, meticulously researched history of bringing the national pastime out of the ballparks and into living rooms via the airwaves. Every play-by-play announcer, color commentator, and ex-ballplayer, every broadcast deal, radio station, and TV network. Plus a foreword by "Voice of the Chicago Cubs" Pat Hughes, and an afterword by Jacques Doucet, the "Voice of the Montreal Expos" 1972-2004.
by Stuart Shea
$24.95 paperback (ISBN 978-1-933599-40-3)
$9.99 ebook (ISBN 978-1-933599-41-0)
7"X10", 712 pages, 40 photos

BioProject Books

WHO'S ON FIRST:
REPLACEMENT PLAYERS IN WORLD WAR II
During World War II, 533 players made the major league debuts. More than 60% of the players in the 1941 Opening Day lineups departed for the service and were replaced by first-times and oldsters. Hod Lisenbee was 46. POW Bert Shepard had an artificial leg, and Pete Gray had only one arm. The 1944 St. Louis Browns had 13 players classified 4-F. These are their stories.
Edited by Marc Z Aaron and Bill Nowlin
$19.95 paperback (ISBN 978-1-933599-91-5)
$9.99 ebook (ISBN 978-1-933599-90-8)
8.5"X11", 422 pages, 67 photos

VAN LINGLE MUNGO:
THE MAN, THE SONG, THE PLAYERS
40 baseball players with intriguing names have been named in renditions of Dave Frishberg's classic 1969 song, Van Lingle Mungo. This book presents biographies of all 40 players and additional information about one of the greatest baseball novelty songs of all time.
Edited by Bill Nowlin
$19.95 paperback (ISBN 978-1-933599-76-2)
$9.99 ebook (ISBN 978-1-933599-77-9)
8.5"X11", 278 pages, 46 photos

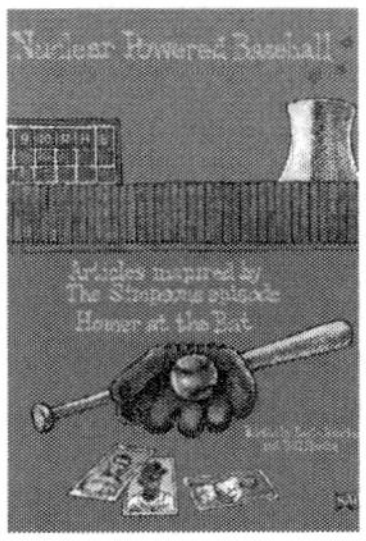

NUCLEAR POWERED BASEBALL
Nuclear Powered Baseball tells the stories of each player—past and present—featured in the classic Simpsons episode "Homer at the Bat." Wade Boggs, Ken Griffey Jr., Ozzie Smith, Nap Lajoie, Don Mattingly, and many more. We've also included a few very entertaining takes on the now-famous episode from prominent baseball writers Jonah Keri, Joe Posnanski, Erik Malinowski, and Bradley Woodrum
Edited by Emily Hawks and Bill Nowlin
$19.95 paperback (ISBN 978-1-943816-11-8)
$9.99 ebook (ISBN 978-1-943816-10-1)
8.5"X11", 250 pages

SABR Members can purchase each book at a significant discount (often 50% off) and receive the ebook edtions free as a member benefit. Each book is available in a trade paperback edition as well as ebooks suitable for reading on a home computer or Nook, Kindle, or iPad/tablet.
To learn more about becoming a member of SABR, visit the website: sabr.org/join

SABR BioProject Books

In 2002, the Society for American Baseball Research launched an effort to write and publish biographies of every player, manager, and individual who has made a contribution to baseball. Over the past decade, the BioProject Committee has produced over 2,200 biographical articles. Many have been part of efforts to create theme- or team-oriented books, spearheaded by chapters or other committees of SABR.

THE YEAR OF THE BLUE SNOW:
THE 1964 PHILADELPHIA PHILLIES
Catcher Gus Triandos dubbed the Philadelphia Phillies' 1964 season "the year of the blue snow," a rare thing that happens once in a great while. This book sheds light on lingering questions about the 1964 season—but any book about a team is really about the players. This work offers life stories of all the players and others (managers, coaches, owners, and broadcasters) associated with this star-crossed team, as well as essays of analysis and history.
Edited by Mel Marmer and Bill Nowlin
$19.95 paperback (ISBN 978-1-933599-51-9)
$9.99 ebook (ISBN 978-1-933599-52-6)
8.5"X11", 356 PAGES, over 70 photos

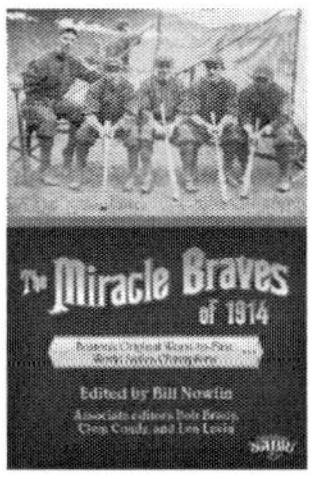

THE MIRACLE BRAVES OF 1914
BOSTON'S ORIGINAL WORST-TO-FIRST CHAMPIONS
Long before the Red Sox "Impossible Dream" season, Boston's now nearly forgotten "other" team, the 1914 Boston Braves, performed a baseball "miracle" that resounds to this very day. The "Miracle Braves" were Boston's first "worst-to-first" winners of the World Series. Refusing to throw in the towel at the midseason mark, George Stallings engineered a remarkable second-half climb in the standings all the way to first place.
Edited by Bill Nowlin
$19.95 paperback (ISBN 978-1-933599-69-4)
$9.99 ebook (ISBN 978-1-933599-70-0)
8.5"X11", 392 PAGES, over 100 photos

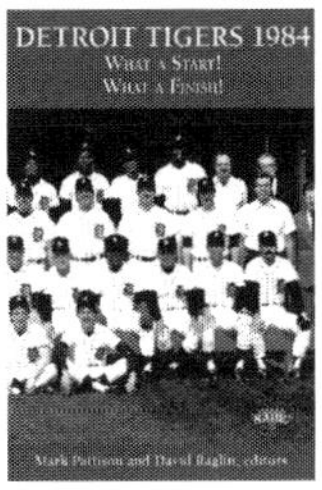

DETROIT TIGERS 1984:
WHAT A START! WHAT A FINISH!
The 1984 Detroit tigers roared out of the gate, winning their first nine games of the season and compiling an eye-popping 35-5 record after the campaign's first 40 games—still the best start ever for any team in major league history. This book brings together biographical profiles of every Tiger from that magical season, plus those of field management, top executives, the broadcasters—even venerable Tiger Stadium and the city itself.
Edited by Mark Pattison and David Raglin
$19.95 paperback (ISBN 978-1-933599-44-1)
$9.99 ebook (ISBN 978-1-933599-45-8)
8.5"x11", 250 pages (Over 230,000 words!)

THAR'S JOY IN BRAVELAND!
THE 1957 MILWAUKEE BRAVES
Few teams in baseball history have captured the hearts of their fans like the Milwaukee Braves of the 1950S. During the Braves' 13-year tenure in Milwaukee (1953-1965), they had a winning record every season, won two consecutive NL pennants (1957 and 1958), lost two more in the final week of the season (1956 and 1959), and set big-league attendance records along the way.
Edited by Gregory H. Wolf
$19.95 paperback (ISBN 978-1-933599-71-7)
$9.99 ebook (ISBN 978-1-933599-72-4)
8.5"x11", 330 pages, over 60 photos

SWEET '60: THE 1960 PITTSBURGH PIRATES
A portrait of the 1960 team which pulled off one of the biggest upsets of the last 60 years. When Bill Mazeroski's home run left the park to win in Game Seven of the World Series, beating the New York Yankees, David had toppled Goliath. It was a blow that awakened a generation, one that millions of people saw on television, one of TV's first iconic World Series moments.
Edited by Clifton Blue Parker and Bill Nowlin
$19.95 paperback (ISBN 978-1-933599-48-9)
$9.99 ebook (ISBN 978-1-933599-49-6)
8.5"X11", 340 pages, 75 photos

NEW CENTURY, NEW TEAM:
THE 1901 BOSTON AMERICANS
The team now known as the Boston Red Sox played its first season in 1901. Boston had a well-established National League team, but the American League went head-to-head with the N.L. in Chicago, Philadelphia, and Boston. Chicago won the American League pennant and Boston finished second, only four games behind.
Edited by Bill Nowlin
$19.95 paperback (ISBN 978-1-933599-58-8)
$9.99 ebook (ISBN 978-1-933599-59-5)
8.5"X11", 268 pages, over 125 photos

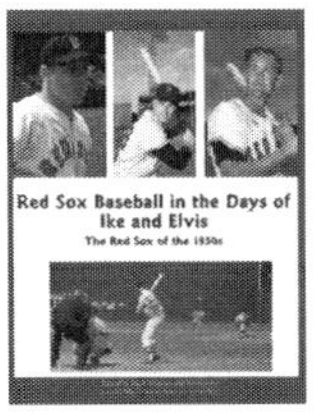

RED SOX BASEBALL IN THE DAYS OF IKE AND ELVIS: THE RED SOX OF THE 1950S
Although the Red Sox spent most of the 1950s far out of contention, the team was filled with fascinating players who captured the heart of their fans. In *Red Sox Baseball*, members of SABR present 46 biographies on players such as Ted Williams and Pumpsie Green as well as season-by-season recaps.
Edited by Mark Armour and Bill Nowlin
$19.95 paperback (ISBN 978-1-933599-24-3)
$9.99 ebook (ISBN 978-1-933599-34-2)
8.5"X11", 372 PAGES, over 100 photos

CAN HE PLAY?
A LOOK AT BASEBALL SCOUTS AND THEIR PROFESSION
They dig through tons of coal to find a single diamond. Here in the world of scouts, we meet the "King of Weeds," a Ph.D. we call "Baseball's Renaissance Man," a husband-and-wife team, pioneering Latin scouts, and a Japanese-American interned during World War II who became a successful scout—and many, many more.
Edited by Jim Sandoval and Bill Nowlin
$19.95 paperback (ISBN 978-1-933599-23-6)
$9.99 ebook (ISBN 978-1-933599-25-0)
8.5"X11", 200 PAGES, over 100 photos

SABR Members can purchase each book at a significant discount (often 50% off) and receive the ebook editions free as a member benefit. Each book is available in a trade paperback edition as well as ebooks suitable for reading on a home computer or Nook, Kindle, or iPad/tablet.
To learn more about becoming a member of SABR, visit the website: sabr.org/join

New Books from SABR

Part of the mission of the Society for American Baseball Research has always been to disseminate member research. In addition to the *Baseball Research Journal*, SABR publishes books that include player biographies, historical game recaps, and statistical analysis. All SABR books are available in print and ebook formats. SABR members can access the entire SABR Digital Library for free and purchase print copies at significant member discounts of 40 to 50% off cover price.

JEFF BAGWELL IN CONNECTICUT:
A Consistent Lad in the Land of Steady Habits
This volume of articles, interviews, and essays by members of the Connecticut chapter of SABR chronicles the life and career of Connecticut's favorite baseball son, Hall-of-Famer Jeff Bagwell, with special attention on his high school and college years.
Edited by Karl Cicitto, Bill Nowlin, & Len Levin
$19.95 paperback (ISBN 978-1-943816-97-2)
$9.99 ebook (ISBN 978-1-943816-96-5)
7"x10", 246 pages, 45 photos

1995 CLEVELAND INDIANS:
The Sleeping Giant Awakens
After almost 40 years of sub-.500 baseball, the Sleeping Giant woke in 1995, the first season the Indians spent in their new home of Jacob's Field. The biographies of all the players, coaches, and broadcasters from that year are here, sprinkled with personal perspectives, as well as game stories from key matchups during the 1995 season, information about Jacob's Field, and other essays.
Edited by Joseph Wancho
$19.95 paperback (ISBN 978-1-943816-95-8)
$9.99 ebook (ISBN 978-1-943816-94-1)
8.5"X11", 410 pages, 76 photos

TIME FOR EXPANSION BASEBALL
The LA Angels and "new" Washington Senators ushered in MLB's 1960 expansion, followed in 1961 by the Houston Colt .45s and New York Mets. By 1998, 10 additional teams had launched: the Kansas City Royals, Seattle Pilots, Toronto Blue Jays, and Tampa Bay Devil Rays in the AL, and the Montreal Expos, San Diego Padres, Colorado Rockies, Florida Marlins, and Arizona Diamondbacks in the NL. *Time for Expansion Baseball* tells each team's origin and includes biographies of key players.
Edited by Maxwell Kates and Bill Nowlin
$24.95 paperback (ISBN 978-1-933599-89-7)
$9.99 ebook (ISBN 978-1-933599-88-0)
8.5"X11", 430 pages, 150 photos

Base Ball's 19th Century "Winter" Meetings 1857-1900
A look at the business meetings of base ball's earliest days (not all of which were in the winter). As John Thorn writes in his Foreword, "This monumental volume traces the development of the game from its birth as an organized institution to its very near suicide at the dawn of the next century."
Edited by Jeremy K. Hodges and Bill Nowlin
$29.95 paperback (ISBN 978-1-943816-91-0)
$9.99 ebook (ISBN978-1-943816-90-3)
8.5"x11", 390 pages, 50 photos

MET-ROSPECTIVES:
A Collection of the Greatest Games in New York Mets History
This book's 57 game stories—coinciding with the number of Mets years through 2018—are strictly for the eternal optimist. They include the team's very first victory in April 1962 at Forbes Field, Tom Seaver's "Imperfect Game" in July '69, the unforgettable Game Sixes in October '86, the "Grand Slam Single" in the 1999 NLCS, and concludes with the extra-innings heroics in September 2016 at Citi Field that helped ensure a wild-card berth.
edited by Brian Wright and Bill Nowlin
$14.95 paperback (ISBN 978-1-943816-87-3)
$9.99 ebook (ISBN 978-1-943816-86-6)
8.5"X11", 148 pages, 44 photos

CINCINNATI'S CROSLEY FIELD:
A Gem in the Queen City
This book evokes memories of Crosley Field through detailed summaries of more than 85 historic and monumental games played there, and 10 insightful feature essays about the history of the ballpark. Former Reds players Johnny Edwards and Art Shamsky share their memories of the park in introductions.
Edited by Gregory H. Wolf
$19.95 paperback (ISBN 978-1-943816-75-0)
$9.99 ebook (ISBN 978-1-943816-74-3)
8.5"X11", 320 pages, 43 photos

MOMENTS OF JOY AND HEARTBREAK:
66 Significant Episodes in the History of the Pittsburgh Pirates
In this book we relive no-hitters, World Series-winning homers, and the last tripleheader ever played in major-league baseball. Famous Pirates like Honus Wagner and Roberto Clemente—and infamous ones like Dock Ellis—make their appearances, as well as recent stars like Andrew McCutcheon.
Edited by Jorge Iber and Bill Nowlin
$19.95 paperback (ISBN 978-1-943816-73-6)
$9.99 ebook (ISBN 978-1-943816-72-9)
8.5"X11", 208 pages, 36 photos

FROM SPRING TRAINING TO SCREEN TEST:
Baseball Players Turned Actors
SABR's book of baseball's "matinee stars," a selection of those who crossed the lines between professional sports and popular entertainment. Included are the famous (Gene Autry, Joe DiMaggio, Jim Thorpe, Bernie Williams) and the forgotten (Al Gettel, Lou Stringer, Wally Hebert, Wally Hood), essays on baseball in TV shows and Coca-Cola commercials, and Jim Bouton's casting as "Jim Barton" in the *Ball Four* TV series.
Edited by Rob Edelman and Bill Nowlin
$19.95 paperback (ISBN 978-1-943816-71-2)
$9.99 ebook (ISBN 978-1-943816-70-5)
8.5"X11", 410 pages, 89 photos

To learn more about how to receive these publications for free or at member discount as a member of SABR, visit the website: sabr.org/join

Made in the USA
Middletown, DE
04 January 2023

18494618R00201